George Kennan and the Dilemmas
of US Foreign Policy

GEORGE KENNAN
and the Dilemmas
of US Foreign Policy

DAVID MAYERS

OXFORD UNIVERSITY PRESS
New York   Oxford

Oxford University Press

Oxford   New York   Toronto
Delhi   Bombay   Calcutta   Madras   Karachi
Petaling Jaya   Singapore   Hong Kong   Tokyo
Nairobi   Dar es Salaam   Cape Town
Melbourne   Auckland

and associated companies in
Berlin   Ibadan

Library of Congress Cataloging-in-Publication Data
Mayers, David Allan, 1951–
p.   cm.
Bibliography: p.   Includes index.
ISBN 0-19-505139-4
ISBN 0-19-506318-X (pbk.)
1. Kennan, George Frost, 1904–   . 2. Ambassadors—United States—
Biography.   3. Historians—United States—Biography.
4. United States—Foreign relations—20th century.   I. Title.
E748.K374M39   1989   88-1418
327.2′092′4—dc19   CIP

The following journals have kindly granted permission to include in this book articles that were first published in their
pages in somewhat different form:

Copyright 1985 by the Biographical Research Center. "Young Kennan's Criticisms and Recommendations" originally
appeared in *Biography: an Interdisciplinary Quarterly*. Summer, 1985.

Journal of Contemporary History. "Soviet War Aims and the Grand Alliance: Goerge Kennan's Views, 1944–1946,"
Vol. 21 (January, 1986); 57–79.

The International History Review. "Nazi Germany and the Future of Europe," Vol. 8 (November 1986): 550–572;
"George Kennan and the Soviet Union," Vol. 5 (November 1983): 525–549.

International Security (Massachusetts Institute of Technology Press Journals). "Containment and the Primacy of
Diplomacy: George Kennan's Views, 1947–1948," Vol. 11, No. 1 (Summer 1986): 124–162.

10   9   8   7   6   5   4   3   2
Printed in the United States of America

To Elizabeth

PREFACE

By practically any standard of evaluation, the diplomatic and intellectual career of George Frost Kennan has been as important as it has been fascinating. Virtually every student of twentieth century US foreign policy tries to come to grips with Kennan's position and role in policymaking, especially during the early Cold War, and with his scholarly assessment of contemporary and historical American diplomacy. During the late 1920s and 1930s, he was one of a select group of Foreign Service officers who received specialized training about the Soviet Union and was called upon in World War II and soon thereafter to provide the American government with advice and guidance as it sought to order its relations with the USSR. Throughout the critical years of 1946–1950, when the Soviet Union and United States moved from being uneasy allies to major rivals, Kennan helped to define the problems and direction of US foreign policy. Henry Kissinger has recorded appreciatively that "George Kennan came as close to authoring the diplomatic doctrine of his era as any diplomat in our history."[1] He also served in 1952 as ambassador to Stalin's Russia and during John Kennedy's administration was accredited as American envoy to Belgrade. As a critic of US foreign policy, Kennan has always been lucid, often incisive, and widely followed, even though his views have never met with anything approaching universal agreement. Still, in the words of one young scholar, Barton Gellman: "Kennan would appear on any short list of influential thinkers on American foreign policy."[2] Whether in his capacity as participant in policymaking or as observer, he has been intellectually engaged for decades with the major international dilemmas confronting the United States.

Despite attention from a number of fine analysts, nobody has yet written a comprehensive, critical review of Kennan's service in government and subsequent political counsel. His own memoirs in two volumes are certainly useful; but they, like any such work, are partial and subjective and suggest that important material is still to be ferreted out. Studies to date by the distinguished historian John Gaddis and by Gellman are very good as far as they go, but neither has yet produced the sort of study undertaken herein. Gellman's excellent *Contending with Kennan: Toward a Philosophy of American Power* amounts to a distillation of Kennan's underlying assumptions and intellectual categories, but does not connect Kennan's ideas closely either to his more than twenty-five years in government service or to other critics of foreign policy and international relations. Kennan's thought is ably portrayed, but it is presented in an intellectual and historical vacuum. Gaddis's work thus far, especially his masterful *Strategies of Containment: A Critical Appraisal of Postwar American National Security Policy,* has concentrated almost exclusively on Kennan's career in the late 1940s, leaving more or less untouched both his earlier development and post-1940s career. In contrast to the existing published literature, exemplified by Gellman and Gaddis, I aim here to present a political and intellectual biography; and, although I have deep respect for my subject, this book does not constitute an apologia for Kennan.[3]

My study of him is not a full-scale biography, as that would necessarily draw upon all of his private papers, some of which still remain inaccessible. Instead, three sources, all of them in the public domain, have provided the basis of this book. First, scattered about in journals, various written reminiscences, and scholarly books on post-World War II US diplomacy, there exists—in addition to the contributions of Gellman and Gaddis—a useful literature dealing both with Kennan's ideas about international politics and his career in the Foreign Service. These works, especially those written by him, have been evaluated and incorporated. Second, the National Archives, the Mudd Manuscripts Library at Princeton University, the Truman Presidential Library, the Library of Congress, and the George Marshall Library in Lexington, Virginia have yielded a rich lode of oral histories, personal letters, memoranda, and various government documents. Minutes from meetings of the Policy Planning Staff, position papers, and official correspondence have proved especially helpful. Equally valuable have been the *Foreign Relations of the United States (FRUS)* series and *The State Department Policy Planning Staff Papers 1947–1949 (SDPPSP),* edited by Anna Kasten Nelson. Finally, some of Kennan's associates from the State Department and more recent colleagues have kindly answered various inquiries from the author, ventured opinions, and volunteered information.

The book, then, is not based on all the extant materials pertaining to George Kennan, nor does it attempt to examine him in his role as esteemed academic historian of European international relations and of Russian and Soviet affairs. Rather, the participation of Kennan in foreign policy—from fledgling diplomat in Moscow in 1933 to respected critic on the sidelines—and his commentary on US diplomacy form the core of this work.

In writing this book I have benefited from the assistance of a number of friends, colleagues, and institutions. Before making these acknowledgments, however, I want to express gratitude to Kennan for having patiently read and commented on most chapters. His careful reading and his correspondence with me have been of immeasurable help in my writing. In addition, Gaddis, who has been commissioned by Kennan to write his authorized biography, has been generous to me within the limits allowed by his project and privileged relationship with Kennan. Without

Gaddis's encouragement, I would not have gone forward in my research and writing. In some areas, our books will undoubtedly overlap, but, as their goals are differently defined and our critical opinions often at variance, I expect the results of our respective labors will represent two contrasting voices in a much larger discussion about George Kennan and US foreign policy.

Three institutions generously supported me in the course of writing this book. The Institute for the Study of World Politics, the Institute on Global Conflict and Cooperation, and the University of California at Santa Cruz provided several grants that enabled me to take academic leaves, travel to archives, and hire student assistants.

In addition to my two intelligent, hard-working student researchers, Gina Soos and Karen Johnson, I benefited greatly from the skilled typing of Judith Burton. She made sense out of an illegible hand and worked minor miracles with her trusty word processor.

It has been a pleasure to work with the first-rate staff at Oxford University Press. In particular I would like to mention three of its distinguished editors, Valerie Aubry and Susan Rabiner, and associate editor Catherine Clements.

Each of the following has provided me with some combination of constructive criticism, practical advice, or moral support. I am deeply grateful to: Susan Abel, Dane Archer, Jeremy Azrael, Deidre Bannon, Philip Bayer, Donald Brand, Vladimir Brovkin, L. Carl Brown, Charles Burdick, Richard Challener, John Dizikes, Anne and Dale Easley, Norman Graebner, Gregg Herken, Daniel Hirsch, Stephen Jones, Penelope Kenez, Jeffery Levi, Peter Loewenberg, Dean McHenry, Dennis McElrath, David S. McLellan, Eugene Mayers, Peter M. Mayers, Robert Meister, Richard Melanson, Charles Neider, Lucian Pye, Richard Sakwa, Paul Seabury, Joseph Silverman, Michael Joseph Smith, Page Smith, Karol Soltan, Kenneth Thompson, Richard Ullman, Stephen Van Evera, Laurence Veysey, Richard Wasserstrom, and Glenn Willson.

My very good friend and colleague Peter Kenez, who read all of this book with great care, saved me from factual errors and misinterpretations. No more than any of the aforementioned people is he responsible for the book's flaws, but whatever merit it possesses is in large part due to his constant assistance and wise advice.

Despite the heavy demands of her own professional career, my wife Elizabeth provided the most valuable assistance of anyone. She read every chapter and brought to it her keen editor's mind for organization, logic, and clear prose. And while our son Peter did not contribute directly to the writing of this book, his antics provided a happy diversion from it.

Santa Cruz, Calif.   D. M.
August 1987

PREFACE TO PAPERBACK

In the two years that have passed since the completion of my study, Kennan has continued to be the subject of considerable scholarly analysis and debate. Another biography of him has appeared (Anders Stephanson's impressive *Kennan and the Art of Foreign Policy*), and Kennan himself has published a third autobiographical volume, *Sketches From A Life*, drawn from his extensive diary.

Those interested in Kennan's intriguing inner life should read the *Sketches*. Far more than anything else written by him or about him (my book deals strictly with his public career), *Sketches* illuminates the personal passions and psychological drama of Kennan. In addition to his familiar yearning for what he imagines to have been Europe's and America's superior past, he reveals intense musings about his family and his earlier life and an almost mystical belief in the simultaneity of all events past and present.

Sketches also contains affecting passages about the Soviet Union and documents Kennan's admiration for that country's literary genius and his affection for its people—"a talented responsive people, capable of absorbing and enriching all forms of human experience." Their heroism in World War II, their suffering under a reckless Marxist regime, and their irrepressible powers of physical and moral rejuvenation are given their due. Anyone acquainted with the romance and poetry of Leningrad, Pavlovsk, and Peterhof will thrill at Kennan's wonderful renderings of them. And one can only be moved by his generous indulgence of those people, in Russia and elsewhere, who misidentified the 1917 revolution as the supreme ethical moment in history rather than just another expression—albeit a strenuous one—of the unchanging human condition. Contemporary entries in *Sketches* mark Kennan's appreciation for Gorbachev and his reforms as he tries to calm ethnic unrest, overcome the legacy of Stalin's totalitarianism—with its millions of victims—and revive a stalled economy. In this way the "author" of containment pays tribute to an innovative Soviet government that is striving to create a new Russia.

Taken as a whole, Kennan's new book does not change, but rather confirms, my view of him as a man guided by versions of Burkean conservatism and Protestant religiosity. From these have sprung both his occasional shortcomings as a political theorist and actor, and his wisdom.

Newton Mass.　　　　　　　　　　　　　　　　　　　　　　　　　　　　　D. M.
July 1989

CONTENTS

CHRONOLOGY OF GEORGE KENNAN

February 16, 1904—born in Milwaukee, Wisconsin
1917–1921—high school at St. John's Military Academy, Delafield, Wisconsin
1921–1925—BA, Princeton University
September 1, 1926—appointed Foreign Service officer
October 1926–April 1927—student in Foreign Service School, Washington, DC
May–August 1927—vice-consul in Geneva
August 1927–January 1928—vice-consul in Hamburg
April–July 1928—vice-consul in Berlin
July–December 1928—vice-consul in Tallinn
January–August 1929—vice-consul, third secretary in Tallinn and Riga
October 1929–August 1931—Russian language officer in the Oriental Seminary, University of Berlin
September 1931—married Annelise Soerensen
October 1931–September 1933—third secretary in Riga
October–November 1933—temporary assignment to the Division of Eastern European Affairs, State Department, Washington, DC
December 1933—aide and interpreter to Ambassador Bullitt in Moscow
January–February 1934—supervisor and secretary in Moscow
March 1934–January 1935—third secretary in Moscow
January–November 1935—consul, second secretary in Vienna
November 1935–August 1937—second secretary in Moscow
October 1937–August 1938—Soviet desk in State Department, Washington, DC
September 1938–September 1939—second secretary, consul in Prague
September 1939–December 1941—second secretary, first secretary in Berlin
December 1941–May 1942—interned at Bad Nauheim, Germany
June–August 1942—State Department, Washington, DC
September 1942–December 1943—counselor, chargé d'affaires in Lisbon
January–April 1944—counselor to European Advisory Commission in London
July 1944–April 1946—minister-counselor, chargé d'affaires in Moscow
1946–1947—deputy commandant for foreign affairs, National War College in Washington, DC

1947–1949—director of the State Department's Policy Planning Staff

1950—counselor, State Department

1950–1952—leave of absence to the Institute for Advanced Study (Princeton); Charles Walgreen Foundation Lecturer at the University of Chicago (1951)

1952—ambassador to the USSR

July 29, 1953—retired from the Foreign Service

1953–1955—member of the Institute for Advanced Study

1954—Stafford Little Lecturer, Princeton University

1956–1974—permanent professor in School of Historical Studies, Institute for Advanced Study

1957–1958—George Eastman Visiting Professor, Balliol College, Oxford University

1957—BBC Reith Lecturer

1961–1963—ambassador to Yugoslavia (leave of absence from the Institute for Advanced Study)

1965–1969—University Fellow, Harvard University

January–June 1969—visiting fellow in All Souls College, Oxford University

1974–1975—fellow in the Woodrow Wilson International Center for Scholars, Washington, DC

1975—helped found the Kennan Institute for Advanced Russian Studies, Washington, DC

1974–present—professor emeritus in the Institute for Advanced Study

George Kennan and the Dilemmas
of US Foreign Policy

Introduction

Since Walter Lippmann blasted the policy of containment as a "strategic monstrosity" in 1947, George Kennan has been a controversial public figure alternately heralded and damned by numerous critics, including liberals and conservatives, diplomats, journalists, and scholars. To the historian Louis Halle, Kennan's service during the Cold War was stunning and characterized by "Shakespearian insight and vision." John Paton Davies, a career diplomat and one of the original members of the State Department's Policy Planning Staff, has been especially impressed by Kennan's "intuitive and creative mind, richly stored with knowledge, eloquent in expression, and disciplined by a scholarly respect for precision." Though disappointed with some of his views, principally those regarding the Third World, the Harvard political scientist Stanley Hoffmann has likened Kennan's mind to the exact mechanism of a fine watch. The trustees of the Albert Einstein Peace Prize and the German Booksellers Association have accorded him special recognition in the early 1980s as an outspoken, articulate opponent of the nuclear arms race. Yet, in the pages of *The New Republic* in 1977, Henry Fairlie has attributed Kennan's advocacy of improved Soviet-US relations to advancing senility. And William Buckley and the social scientists Paul Hollander and Paul Seabury have all expressed dismay at one time or another for what they regard as Kennan's transformation from an unabashed opponent of the USSR and supporter of firm policies against it to a promoter of a rather abject species of appeasement.[1]

The reason why Kennan has been the object of intense conflicting feeling is that throughout his many years in government and later political counsel he has written or recommended strongly and eloquently on practically every important foreign policy dilemma that has confronted the United States from the period of Franklin Roosevelt to that of Ronald Reagan. These include not only the proper ordering of US relations with Soviet Russia and the avoidance of another, even more catastrophic world war, but also America's relations with Europe, the Far East, and the Third World. A study of Kennan, then, provides a ready lens through which to

3

examine the crucial issues of the past half century of American external policy. Consequently, the first task of this book is to reconstruct an accurate record and exegesis of Kennan's beliefs and recommendations to his government and compatriots. To understand the essence of his views, of course, we must also identify as closely as possible the various influences of historical events, political forces, personal experiences, ideas, and significant personalities in his life. In other words, we will seek to provide the international, domestic, and vocational context of Kennan's words and actions and to situate him in the ongoing debates since the 1930s about US foreign policy.

Broadly speaking, three lines of thought about international policy have competed for dominance during Kennan's career: isolationism, collective universalism, and unilateral universalism. In the 1930s, the majority of Americans accepted the notion that the United States should concentrate on correcting social and economic problems at home and avoid overinvolvement with Europe's quarrels and rivalries. Isolationism assumed its most obvious shape in America's refusal to join or cooperate closely with the League of Nations. After Pearl Harbor the new popular wisdom about international relations held that only in concert with the other great powers— first through the Grand Alliance and then the United Nations—could the United States assure its security and promote some semblance of stability and justice around the world. But with the onset of the Cold War, growing disillusionment with the UN, and a general recognition that the United States was not just one of several powers but the preeminent one in the West, a presumption developed that the US must act boldly around the globe—this was the gist of the Truman Doctrine and NSC 68—to protect its wide-ranging interests and safeguard the zone of liberty. To Kennan, none of these formulas has been compelling. Instead, he has advocated that the United States organize its foreign policy around a strict understanding of its vital interests and around the eternal, immutable verities of the balance of power. As we shall see, Kennan's conception of America's national interests and a sensible balance of power diplomacy has varied somewhat. Still, his insistence on the vocabulary of interest and balance of power and his determination that some rigorous version of them must stand as the common points of reference in any debate over international affairs have guaranteed his opposition to the three major patterns of thought (and action) in the United States about external policy.

The second task for this book is equally important as the first, but ultimately more elusive: to determine how politically influential and how representative of official American thinking Kennan's ideas have been in the past. It is not enough to explain his assessment, however incisive or otherwise arresting, of Soviet policy toward Eastern Europe, or political dynamics in the Middle East, or the permanent value of traditional diplomacy. It is also essential to examine Kennan's effectiveness as a purveyor of his own ideas. Apart from his fleeting successes, which have been mostly confined to his tenure as director of the State Department's Policy Planning Staff, Kennan has usually failed to persuade official Washington and the public at large of the soundness of his recommendations. Why? Has he, as he has often alleged, been misunderstood? The answers to these questions make possible an evaluation of Kennan and enhance our understanding of American policymaking and the variableness of its competing interests and outcomes. While Kennan served on the Policy Planning Staff, for example, his advice and that of his subordinates sometimes complemented, sometimes opposed, sometimes ignored the desires and causes of military planners, partisan politicians, and diverse American allies. What was the mix; what were the results for policy, intended or not? And what can we learn of a more general nature about the quality of making and executing foreign policy in the United States?

To Kennan the most thoughtful answer to this last question is very bleak. However confident and sound his judgment on some international issues, he has been vexed—indeed, it is the *leit-motiv* of his governmental career and is as prominent in his writings as in Lippmann's—by the dilemma of how a democratic society can sustain a sensible, consistent diplomacy that is not at the mercy of every vicissitude in the public mood. His long-standing concern for a foreign policy uninhibited by political interference and unsullied by amateurs betrays not just the impatience of a superior mind, but it also reveals Kennan's distrust about the possibility for lively public debate over external matters with steady, professional diplomacy. To him Alexis de Tocqueville's verdict in *Democracy in America* is indisputable:

> Foreign politics demand scarcely any of those qualities which are peculiar to a democracy; they require on the contrary the perfect use of almost all those in which it is deficient. . . . A democracy is unable to regulate the details of an important undertaking, to persevere in a design, and to work out its execution in the presence of serious obstacles. It cannot combine its measures with secrecy, and it will not await their consequences with patience. These are qualities which more especially belong to an individual or to an aristocracy; and they are precisely the means by which an individual people attains to a predominant position.[2]

Kennan has yearned for a diplomacy insulated from the habits of what he regards as an easygoing, sometimes arrogant mass democracy, and for an executive branch freed from pandering to public passions. This study thus directly raises the problem of how does and how should expertise in US foreign policy coexist with democratic constraints and commitments.

Incidentally, it should be stressed that what Kennan has in mind when he refers to expertise has nothing to do with narrow or technocratic specialization. Instead, he usually means by "expert" a student of a particular region of the world (e.g., the Soviet Union) who is literate in that region's primary language and who knows its history and culture as well as its political, sociological, and economic conditions. On other occasions—clear only from the context, as Kennan is short on definitions—he means by "expert" a policymaker who is not only well trained, but who is also above partisan ambitions and private interests and is devoted unceasingly to improving the public good. The fundamental difficulty, however, with Kennan's claims for the efficacy of expertise in foreign policymaking is that they require a readily identifiable, politically legitimate cadre of experts—in effect, philosopher-diplomats—who agree on all crucial matters about ends and means and are immune to the corruption and temptations of people not subject to public approval or censure.

The final task for this political biography is to assess Kennan's views about specific policy matters and to judge the overall worth of his intellectual contribution to US diplomacy. We will assess how realistic and imaginative Kennan's recommendations have been in the past and the pertinence and applicability of his more recent ideas. And finally, we will try to determine whether Kennan's concepts have any enduring value for the future conduct of American foreign policy. Kennan has often been perceptive on specific issues, such as when, immediately after World War II, he argued that the Soviet Union was militarily weak, but posed a political threat; therefore, economic and political measures, as well as moderate military ones, were appropriate against Moscow. As early as the late 1940s, he perceived that proclamations of international Marxist solidarity in Moscow, Warsaw, Bucharest, Budapest, and Prague, and in the Chinese communist party faintly concealed national diversity and tension. And he is among the more persuasive analysts in the 1980s when he argues for the urgency of arms control and contends that Soviet leaders are not working monomaniacally to subdue the West. Moreover, Kennan's basic ideas about the Soviet Union and how the United States should deal with it have not—as many have alleged—substantially altered over the years. Rather, it is the dominant perspective in the United States that has fluctuated—between friendship for and extreme hostility toward the USSR. Kennan has always maintained that the political and economic systems of the two countries are inherently incompatible, that the Soviets are opportunistic, and that Americans should stay alert and prepared to deflect any Soviet transgressions against their interests. At the same time, even during the bitterest periods of Cold War, Kennan has consistently and wisely upheld the virtues of diplomacy and *modus vivendi* as providing the only reasonable means by which to manage Soviet-US affairs. On other subjects, however, he has been astonishingly off the mark, such as in his condemnation of most American politics and in his biting remarks about North-South problems. How, then, do we explain the apparent contradiction of Kennan, who has been astute, indeed brilliant, in some spheres, but insensitive and myopic in others? A brief answer can be allowed here.

Within the framework of both those who have practiced and interpreted US foreign policy, Kennan has long been recognized, and correctly, as falling in line with the realist tradition, despite his private discomfort with the label. It represents a basically centrist position. On the one hand, it is at odds with a host of apologists for America's alleged international exceptionalism. Historians such as Dexter Perkins and Samuel Bemis and practitioners like Woodrow Wilson and Cordell Hull have maintained that the United States is unique among nations because it has pursued policies of humane inventiveness (e.g., the United Nations) and liberality (e.g., the Marshall Plan and aid to poor countries), and affirms regularly in its diplomacy the virtues of democracy and fairness. In Wilson's words, the United States is "the most unselfish nation in history."[3] On the other hand, the realist school has had to grapple with an economic interpretation of US foreign policy, represented by William Appleman Williams, Gabriel Kolko, and Walter LaFeber among others, who claim that the mainspring of America's international behavior is the multiple requirements of domestic capital. According to these scholars, in the service of capital the United States government has followed an increasingly aggressive imperial policy that mocks professed American idealism and over the decades has forced

Washington on more occasions than a democratic polity can afford to align itself with reaction and repression around the globe. To the realist, the United States has been neither spectacularly triumphant as a light to the nations and morally uplifting in its foreign policy nor singularly venal. The actual lineage of the realist tradition in the United States originates in Alexander Hamilton, who in surveying the cause of international disputes and wars concluded, "To presume a want of motives for such contests would be to forget that men are ambitious, vindictive and rapacious."[4] And, alas, Americans are no exception, but they, like the rest of humanity arbitrarily divided into states, must scrap for survival and take those measures necessary to safeguard security and prosperity. In the twentieth century, Reinhold Niebuhr, Hans Morgenthau, and Henry Kissinger have in their distinctive ways each shared with Kennan this orientation toward foreign politics that emphasizes a pessimistic notion of human nature, is deeply suspicious of utopian schemes, and relies on prudence and a strict respect for the shifting dictates of the balance of power.

As with any broad category of thinkers, there is among the American realists a wide spectrum stretching from orthodoxy to liberal to admixtures with other traditions, and it would be rash and misleading to minimize the differences, say, between Morgenthau the political scientist and Niebuhr the theologian. So, too, Kennan can be distinguished from the bloc of Kissinger, Morgenthau, and Niebuhr and their respective disciples. Far more than any of them, he is a conservative in the late eighteenth-century meaning of that word and sees in modern nationalism and mass democracy the sources of the twentieth century's political instability and its unprecedented disastrous wars. It is precisely this construction, really a variation on Edmund Burke, that is the source both of Kennan's intellectual weakness and his strength. His anti-popular bias and his aesthetic objection to modernity have led him to misread the character of the United States and of the Third World, and at one point even to be cautiously sympathetic toward the orderliness that he thought Nazi Germany would bring to central Europe. At the same time, he enjoys with such classic European conservatives as Otto von Bismarck and Klemens Metternich an unclouded view of the nature of international politics: it *is* a dreary game of high stakes in which power and the distribution of power are decisive; balance of power diplomacy and spheres of influence are more workable and therefore preferable ameliorations to the harsh realities of international life than are ideological crusades waged in the name of some presumed truth or such innovations as Wilsonian liberalism or other versions of internationalism and legality. Although many American realists would find much to agree with in this formula, its starkness—so convincing to Kennan, as well as Morgenthau—would repel some of them, notably Niebuhr, who warned that national "egotism" was not a cure for pretentious idealism and that it could easily degenerate into moral cynicism or blindness to the dangers of imperial purpose.[5] Kennan's eighteenth-century conservative *Anschauung* would make them all (Kissinger included) blanch. And it did cause difficulties for Kennan throughout his governmental career, especially during periods of crisis, because he has resisted fundamentally the necessity of policymakers in a democracy to cultivate carefully the goodwill and consent of the broad citizenry. His unyielding confidence in the efficacy and moral superiority of government by an intellectual elite, in which he has never hesitated to count himself, caused Kennan while in the

Foreign Service to ignore or often to underestimate the importance of domestic political factors with the consequence that his policy recommendations were frequently rejected or implemented in ways contrary to his intentions.

Kennan could easily endorse the bravado of Winston Churchill (a conservative very much in keeping with Kennan) in his statement to the House of Commons in 1941: "Nothing is more dangerous in wartime than to live in the temperamental atmosphere of a Gallup Poll, always feeling one's pulse and taking one's temperature. I see [it said that] leaders should keep their ears to the ground. All I can say is that the British nation will find it very hard to look up to the leaders who are detected in that somewhat ungainly posture."[6] Probably not even a Churchill, let alone Kennan, could have gotten too far with such an attitude in the political atmosphere of early Cold War America. The right wing of the Republican party demanded, in the crudest fashion, a continuous accounting of the government's diplomacy. In addition, Kennan's disdain for politics—in his case a temperamental affliction as much as a principled stand—meant that by the time he was highly placed in the government, he was reluctant to engage in the usual bureaucratic infighting, maneuvering for position, or temporary alignments with one group of people and agencies against others. He naively believed that the sheer validity of his ideas would be universally recognized and that they would therefore be adopted as the basis for policy. That these conditions seldom prevailed explains in part Kennan's desire in the early 1950s to quit public service. Still, by virtue of his intellectual position, Kennan has enjoyed advantages in understanding Soviet-US relations of the past fifty years because they are at heart a problem of traditional great power rivalry and power politics. Indeed, his views—whether in the 1930s, during and immediately after the Second World War, or in the detente phase of the early 1970s—have been sharp and sensitive to changes in the constantly evolving great power relationship. In reviewing Kennan's career, we encounter a traditionally conservative world view that is highly developed, notwithstanding whether or not one agrees with all of its elitist and programmatic implications. It provides a coherent framework in which to view US foreign policy, and seldom has any such framework been so fully drawn as by George Kennan.

*   *   *   *

Kennan's early career, the formation of his personality, and intellectual influences through the end of World War II are treated in the first section of the book. The object here is to identify, to the extent possible, the genesis of many of his ideas and thus set in clearer focus the opinions of the mature Kennan. The section begins with a synopsis of his family background, childhood, and youth, and then proceeds to his assignment of 1933–1937 in the Soviet Union.

He was not yet thirty when he was invited to join the first official delegation to represent American interests in Moscow. This tour in the Soviet Union, which coincided with the Great Purges and was dominated by them, was instrumental to the development of Kennan's early ideas about the Soviet Union, the nature of Russian-US relations, and American diplomacy. When later the Cold War began to erupt, these views of Kennan's found expression in his pronouncements and advice for Washington's policy. In fact, the underlying assumptions of his version of containment—the incompatibility of Soviet and American political commitments, the divergent nature of their security interests, the importance of patience and steady purpose in dealing with the Russians—can be traced to the 1930s.

Dating also to the 1930s is Kennan's abiding skepticism about prevailing American attitudes and mores in politics and diplomacy. We want to explain why it was that he came to adopt for his own a minority, elitist perspective at war with the dominant impulses in American life of greater democracy and social reform, which in one form or another have been immanent in Jeffersonian and Jacksonian politics, Populism, Progressivism, the New Deal, and the Great Society. Part of the answer resides in the irony that Kennan, though philosophically conservative, has always been a dissident by temperament. And one perfectly plausible form of dissidence in the Midwest of Kennan's youth, with its traditions of equality, populism, and plainness, was—as Kennan chose—to espouse or seek what one imagined to be more refined or aristocratic forms. We are here, obviously, near to the same genteel tradition of conservatism and protest that drove two New Englanders, Henry Adams and Henry James, to seek refuge abroad and in a civilization better formed and less gauche than the one that bore them. In any case, this predisposition of Kennan's was encouraged by what he found as an undergraduate at Princeton, in the Foreign Service, and in his first contacts with representatives from Europe's aristocracy and with the cultivated, and often personally charming, refugees of the Bolshevik Revolution. From such an angle—again congenial to an Adams or a James—the religious revival aspects of American political culture and the entire strain of populism that embraces in their different ways both Roosevelt and Reagan and millions of Democrats and Republicans have been anathema to Kennan and useful only as counterpoints to his own preferences. That he has stood apart, sometimes deliberately and with confidence, other times anxiously, is nowhere more evident than in his assessment of America's internal hardships during the Depression and in his suggestions for an improved Foreign Service and Foreign Service academy in 1942. His original ideas about both of these subjects persisted in one form or another in his later thinking when, as a prominent official and admired critic, he dealt with pressing domestic and international issues.

Between late 1938 and late 1941, Kennan served in German-occupied Prague and in the US embassy in Berlin. His observations about the actual workings of the Nazi government, combined with his earlier ones of Stalin's, function as a useful antidote to most of the standard wisdom about the operations and degree of control in totalitarian regimes. He discovered much that has been lost in the scholarly literature about totalitarianism (e.g., the works of Carl Friedrich or William Kornhauser), which often overlooks or inadequately portrays the disorderliness, confusion, and inefficiency that plagued the Stalinist and Nazi prototypes. Meanwhile, Kennan's exposure to the horrors of Nazi Germany did not blind him to the need for a revitalized, unified Germany after the Second World War. Kennan was actually among the first State Department officials to conceive of a reconstructed Germany able to assume a pivotal role in the postwar European balance of power. This understanding led him to oppose policies that he felt were vindictive, notably unconditional surrender and later the programs of denazification and the international tribunal at Nuremberg.

The second section of the book analyzes that part of Kennan's career for which he is best known. From 1946 to 1950, he was acknowledged as the American government's chief expert on Soviet affairs (with Charles Bohlen) and was engaged at a high level in the day-to-day formulation of foreign policy. His conception of containment, the way in which it departed from Dean Acheson's and Paul Nitze's implementation, and his influence on the character and goals of the Marshall Plan have little to do with the widespread image of Kennan as an unreconstructed hardliner in the late 1940s devoted to a military showdown with Russia. Regarding policy in the Far East, Kennan was also by-and-large a voice for moderation. He was practically alone in his opposition to American and United Nations troops crossing the thirty-eighth parallel; he advocated a policy of accommodation toward the People's Republic of China designed to discourage its exclusive reliance on the Soviet Union.

What was truly impressive about Kennan during the period of early Cold War, and set him apart from most ranking members of the Truman administration, was his sense—in the best conservative tradition of proportionality—of the limits of American power. He certainly perceived as well as anyone else that the United States in the aftermath of World War II was the world's economic and military colossus, but he also saw more clearly than most (i.e., the authors of NSC 68) that America's preeminent position was a temporary condition and bound to be diminished as the other traditional centers of international power recovered from the damage inflicted in 1939–1945. An indefinite policy of universal diplomatic and security commitments that could justify military intervention anywhere was not, Kennan rightly judged, possible or desirable for the United States. The overriding objective for him, therefore, was that the US should organize balances of power in Europe and Asia conducive to long-term American economic, political, and security desiderata.

The second part of the book also includes a chapter about Kennan's exceptionally unsuccessful ambassadorship to the Soviet Union in 1952 and his longer, happier stint as envoy to Yugoslavia during John Kennedy's administration. The major point here is to contrast in a dramatic way the differences between Kennan's philosophy of traditional diplomacy and the manner in which it often works, to the detriment of all parties, in the current age. A plethora of propaganda, a dearth of confidentiality, and the triumph of political sloganeering over questions of substance—all symptoms of mass politics—plagued both of his ambassadorships and made him doubt that the accumulated techniques of centuries of diplomatic art could claim any place in the modern world.

The final section of the book considers Kennan's record after his retirement from the diplomatic corps as a critic of America's external policy. In 1957, he alarmed Western audiences when he proposed in his famous BBC Reith Lectures that Soviet and Anglo-US forces withdraw from Europe; he wagered that such an arrangement could be realized without Soviet violations and that it would reduce the danger of war in the center of the continent. He was an early and penetrating opponent of US policy in Vietnam, though he severely attacked the student protest movement at the same time. He also has objected strenuously to what he terms as misplaced liberal guilt in the United States for the plight of impoverished Third

World countries. According to Kennan, the West is not equipped ethically or technically to lend much aid; he has preached that instead of meddling in the lives of faraway, "exotic" peoples, Americans should concentrate on solving their own problems of urban blight, environmental devastation, and the arms race. He thus defies most enlightened sentiment concerning international interdependence and the need for collective efforts to allay the suffering of the world's dispossessed. On the subject of South Africa, he has been reluctant to condemn the system of apartheid and has never endorsed the use of strong Western sanctions against the government in Pretoria. Yet his support of a policy of sensible detente toward the Soviet Union and of nuclear arms limitation as the only alternative to irreparable destruction has won him a following among liberals and self-styled progressives throughout the West. On the basis of his deepening religious convictions along the lines of Niebuhr's neo-orthodoxy, Kennan has railed against America's stockpiling of nuclear weapons and has condemned their use against tens of thousands of noncombatant Japanese in 1945.[7] In 1959, more than two decades before the American Catholic bishops issued their statement deploring the immorality of nuclear weapons, Kennan declared that in these things

> loom the truly apocalyptic dangers of our time, the ones that threaten to put an end to that very continuity of history to which we belong and outside which we would have no identity, no force, either in civilization, in culture, or in morals. These dangers represent for us not only political questions but stupendous moral problems. . . . And here our main concern . . . must be to see that man, whose own folly once drove him from the Garden of Eden, does not now commit the blasphemous act of destroying, whether in fear or in anger or in greed, the great and lovely world in which, even in his fallen state, he has been permitted by the grace of God to live.[8]

The book's last chapter assesses the merit of Kennan's "theories" on US foreign policy and international politics. We use "theory" here advisedly because Kennan has never deliberately set out to create one and has never claimed to be—like Morgenthau with his gothic conception of international relations, or even Niebuhr with his less imposing, more felicitous structure of thought and expression—a systematic thinker. Kennan has not produced any corpus of philosophical writings. Rather, he is a diplomat-turned-historian who most of his life has eschewed theorizing as too constricting or simply irrelevant to the affairs of state. Nevertheless, out of his personal experiences as a diplomat and his findings as an historian, he has produced since the 1950s a rich set of underlying assumptions and principles that in their aggregate amount to theory worthy of comment. The following words of Kenneth Thompson, a longtime student of politics and of diplomacy, apply directly in Kennan's case: "In the theory of international politics . . . the lasting contributions have come from men who resisted the fateful divorce of theory from practice. We note a fruitful relationship between their direct struggles with the intractable facts of political behavior and their evaluation of these facts."[9]

The cornerstone of Kennan's "theory" is, of course, that of realism, but it embraces more than the conventional formulas about fallen man, power politics, and the perils of utopian thought. True, as he has professed, Americans should not be ashamed to admit that balance of power politics persist and that spheres of influence are not inherently insidious. But he has also leavened these and other imperatives of international life by underscoring that the brutality of world politics is not beyond human ability to soften. Implicit in his identification of Niebuhr as intellectual guide and in his regret for the tragedy visited upon the peoples of Hiroshima and Nagasaki are a set of moral concerns normally not associated with conventional *realpolitik*. These concerns do, however, mesh with Kennan's conservatism, which has at its core the notion of custodianship. The elementary aim of the true conservative must be to preserve the world and pass it intact to the next generation; a nuclear war would be radically nihilistic, leaving in its wake the debris of all previous human achievement.[10] From such a standpoint, the maxim of Sidney Hook, a respected philosopher and a favorite of the American right, that it is better to be "dead than red" represents the purest nonsense and recklessness. In the end, Kennan's theoretical and fundamentally conservative musings point to a vision, at least for the Eastern and Western components of the industrialized world, of a more humane international political existence.

I

EARLY CAREER

1

Early Influences and Development

In his memoirs Kennan makes the claim in moving language that he has always remained aloof from his epoch and nation. Although professionally occupied with the weighty international issues of his era and for more than twenty-five years employed by his government to advance American interests, he has expressed a partiality for the eighteenth century and regret for not having been born into the life of a cultivated European. He has claimed that this preference for an earlier period and another place has endowed him with a subtle detachment from his own setting and has proved useful in his capacity as political observer and participant. But, in fact, Kennan was as self-deceived as anyone else would be when he referred to himself as a "guest of [his] time and not a member of its household."[1] His preferences for another, implicitly superior world notwithstanding, Kennan is like everyone mainly a product of his own social, regional, and temporal circumstances. Outside of them, it is impossible to make any sense of him. Kennan's pose as eternal outsider has functioned only as a flimsy disguise that cannot conceal his passionate involvement in his times or protect him from the blows suffered by a sensitive ego.

A brief review of Kennan's family background, formal and social education, and initial experiences in the Foreign Service foreshadows many of the themes of his diplomatic career and anticipates some of the strands of thought that have marked his political thinking. Son of a self-made man, Kennan became a self-made aristocrat. Distant cousin of a nineteenth-century critic of Russia and the Czarist autocracy, Kennan became his country's leading interpreter of the Soviet Union. Quietly ambitious as a young man, Kennan rose rapidly through the Foreign Service and enjoyed, however briefly, the chance to help formulate and direct external policy. Scholarly, sometimes sentimental, occasionally ruthless, the mature Kennan, citizen of the greatest world power, emerged from a simpler—and from the viewpoint of its adversaries, less menacing—United States.

Family and Education

Kennan's paternal forebears arrived in New England in the first half of the eighteenth century. These Scotch-Irish immigrants mostly farmed the rocky New England soil; a few became lawyers or clergymen. The pioneer Kennans were an unceremonious, dour lot and not very prosperous, though they never sank into abject poverty. Very likely they did not pity themselves or their lack of material success. Neither, according to Kennan, would it have occurred to them that the social system of their day was responsible for their plight: "They were poor enough at times, but they never became proletarianized. Because proletarianization is not an economic condition; it is an attitude toward yourself."[2] Industrious and determined to improve their fortunes, the Kennans did not habitually stay long in one place. Within a few generations, they had migrated from Connecticut to Vermont to upstate New York to northern Ohio. In 1850 Thomas Kennan, George's grandfather, settled in Wisconsin, and soon thereafter George's father, Kossuth, was born—named in honor of Lajos Kossuth, Hungarian freedom fighter who visited Milwaukee in 1851.

From these pioneer ancestors, certain Kennan family flaws sprang: most obviously, a lack of ironic detachment and a near total denial of levity. Not only were the Kennans traditionally cheerless, but they were neither intellectually nor artistically inventive. They uncritically accepted their received values and wisdom. These stern Presbyterians were, in Kennan's own words, too untutored "to learn to sin gracefully and with dignity, rather than to try unsuccessfully not to sin at all. [They] seem to have passed their neuroses along from generation to generation like the family Bible."[3] For them, all questions involving religious faith and Christian responsibility were resolved in favor of a complacent ratification of the existing social order. The difference between Kennan and his forebears on this score (in the direction of modern skepticism and less smugness) was one of gradation, not of kind. At the same time, these people were basically sturdy and admirably decent within the framework of their ethical understanding and frontier piety. And they were intelligent enough, albeit minimally literate.

The Kennan men married into families similar to themselves, and the maternal line included Smiths, Browns, Tullars, and Morses; typically, they could trace their lineage to seventeenth-century England. Kennan, who has always exhibited a sizable interest in his family genealogy, once proudly exclaimed: "You can comb the family records for three centuries back and you won't find a person who wasn't of straight Anglo-Saxon origin."[4] Kossuth's second wife, George's mother, was Florence James, daughter of an Anglo-Scottish family. Her father had been an itinerant adventurer, who had fled his Illinois home when he was thirteen, ridden draft horses along the Erie Canal, and whaled out of New Bedford. Before finally settling down to a successful business life (in insurance) in the Middle West, he had sailed as a hand around the horn of Africa, crossed the Indian Ocean, and reached the Sea of Okhotsk.

It appears that, as a rule, the Jameses were not especially compassionate toward people weaker and more distressed than themselves. Instead, to Kennan at least, they were impressive as high-spirited, natural aristocrats, both physically and tempermentally. They did not flinch or fail, nor were they sentimental—unlike the Kennans, who were depressingly prone that way. The ethical balance of the Jameses was apparently rooted in their sense of duty and *noblesse oblige*.[5]

The James family may have been prouder and more intrepid than the Kennans, but they had even less developed intellectual and aesthetic interests than the latter, on whom they tended to look down.[6] In a letter (1942) to his daughters, Kennan judged that the James family was "born to exercise power, and to exercise it well . . . they were unswerving individualists. If they had been great lords in feudal times, they would have run their own estates with dignity and distinction, and would have gone down fighting for their privileges in the face of the rising power of the kings. As it is, I fear for them and their male descendants if the coming order of society demands the subordination of the individual to the mass."[7] In these male descendants for whom Kennan feared, he undoubtedly numbered himself; he rarely wrote lines thereafter that were more revealing of his self-understanding.

His attitude toward his mother and relations with his father are not easy to reconstruct in the absence of earlier records. Regarding his mother, though, one thing is clear: he regretted not knowing her and felt acute deprivation. He once confessed, "There are so many times that I have wished I had known what she was like—that I could have had at least one conversation with her."[8] She died only two months after his birth. George's feelings toward his Michigan-born stepmother, Kossuth's third wife, were cool, never intimate. Kennan's sister Jeanette, two and a half years older than himself, virtually became his surrogate mother, but even she could not fill the emotional gap left by the missing parent.[9]

Kossuth Kennan had struggled most of his life to overcome the disadvantages of rural poverty; life on the Wisconsin frontier was harsh and unforgiving for his generation. His family was not spared any of those tragedies that plagued the Midwest during the second half of the nineteenth century and are so amply documented in Michael Lesy's psychological-historical *Wisconsin Death Trip*.[10] Suicide, dissolution and madness overcame a few of Kossuth's younger brothers and sisters. He, the eldest of his siblings, was fortunately made of tougher fibre, and although he began life as a ploughboy he ended as a cultured, if shy, gentleman.[11] He worked to pay for most of his elementary school education and also labored his way through Ripon College. After studying law he was admitted to the Wisconsin bar in 1878. Soon afterward he worked for a time in Europe, where he recruited Danish and Swiss families to settle in northern Wisconsin on lands then being developed by the Wisconsin Central Railway. He later served as an engineer on irrigation projects in the American West. Finally, he returned to Wisconsin— George was born in Milwaukee, February 16, 1904—and specialized in tax law, authored two books on the subject, and helped establish under the Progressive governor, Robert La Follette, America's first state income tax system. He produced several children—four by Florence, of whom George was the youngest and only boy.

Kossuth Kennan's experience amounted to a breakthrough from the traditions of physical toil, marginal education, and unaestheticism that had hitherto distinguished his line.[12] Not only did he develop a fine working knowledge of French, German, and Danish, but he also cultivated a taste for French literature and was able to

produce graceful, firm prose. The household of George Kennan's boyhood, however, did not revel in many things elegant or gay. Classical music and the visual
arts, both esteemed by him as an adult, were without place in the bare Milwaukee
home of his youth; not until college was he really exposed to the fine arts. Kossuth
Kennan was a man of considerable feeling, but nothing in his immediate background or in the family's unrelieved Calvinist tradition prepared him for an intensive encounter with forms beyond the written word or a church hymn. Still, that
severe Protestant could react violently, and once was overwhelmed. In a letter to his
mother, written from Europe, he reported on his attendance of the Passion Play at
Oberammergau, a unique experience for him. He was startled by what he saw and
could not bear it, and so fled the hall and ran down a road, weeping for the
unendurable beauty.[13]

Kossuth was probably the first Kennan to feel strongly the pain and release of
intensive, aesthetic beauty. He never felt comfortable with it, though; whatever
poetic aptitude he might have had, he deliberately repressed. Neither did he want to
instruct his children in the mysteries of a world so seemingly at odds with stark
Protestant virtues, so near to Calvinist fears of perdition. He actively discouraged
George's interests in music on the grounds that it was not a serious field.[14] Yet to
his credit, he did try to convey to his children something of his own marvel for
experiences and possibilities shunned by previous generations. These things,
largely intimated, played a delicate role in his children's development and accounts
partly for George's long daydreams that mixed beauty and menace and were so
satisfying that he could pass hours in "oblivion of immediate surroundings"—a
habit that persisted well into his adult years.

Kennan's childhood was physically comfortable, conventional, somewhat shel-
tered. His home on Cambridge Avenue in a respectable middle-class Milwaukee
neighborhood was three stories, built in a classical Victorian Connecticut style of
wood—indistinguishable from thousands of others in that day. In later years, he
liked to recall the provincial innocence and Booth Tarkington quality of his youth.
And he protested that problems involving race relations, ethnic disputes, and
religious rivalries did not impinge on his early awareness. Nor did the disturbances
of adolescence break with overpowering ferocity. Sex was, of course, a forbidden
topic of conversation, and like most boys, he was content to read intently "exciting
passages" from books.

Contrary to Kennan's recollections, Milwaukee was not everywhere safe and
prosperous in the first two decades of the twentieth century. In particular the city
was riven along ethnic lines that during the First World War resulted in German,
Austrian, and Irish demonstrations and clashes—sometimes violent—against their
Anglo-Saxon and Russian neighbors. Many of the non-German neighborhoods, as
was the case throughout the country, were swept by hysteria and vicious anti-
German propaganda after US entry (April 1917) into the war. In addition to being
"a polyglot ethnic hotbed," Milwaukee was a mosaic of religious communities that
bred the usual bigotry. Many Scandinavian Protestants inherited the standard
Anglo-Protestant fears about Polish, Irish, and German Catholics working in league
with the pope.[15] If Kennan really was oblivious as a youth to Milwaukee's ethnic
cleavages and related social problems, then that is, indeed, testimony to the protec-

tive environment of his home. It stretches credulity, however, to imagine that Kennan, a sensitive and intuitive adolescent, did not notice or was unmoved by the intensity and sometimes fever pitch of Milwaukee's ethnic life. Later, he developed as an adult the most pronounced distaste for ethnic and communal politics and saw in them an important source of political corruption and social instability.

To Kennan the boy, Milwaukee seemed as vital and bustling as any major city and more manageable than nearby Chicago. When he was eight, he made his first trip to Europe with Jeanette under the supervision of their stepmother; he visited various European cities and received some elementary education in Germany. Holidays, though, were usually spent nearer to home. During the summers he enjoyed outdoor activities—fishing, camping, swimming—at Lake Nagawicka in southeastern Wisconsin. But appreciation for these pleasures and for Milwaukee and its environs was gradually superseded in his adolescence by a realization that the local offerings were thin—at one point he likened Milwaukee's urban sprawl to Sinclair Lewis's Zenith and Milwaukee's denizens to George Babbit.[16] His father, for whom he always retained affection and sympathy, was too remote and forbidding for either intimacy or guidance. Kossuth was already in his fifties when Florence gave birth to their son. As with many an older father and son, relations between Kossuth and George were often marred by mutual incomprehension. The elder Kennan was also demanding of his son and taught him strictly to perform chores and chastised him quickly for any infraction of household rules.[17] According to one author, Kennan as a child longed vainly for the affection and approval of his parents, especially his father; this deep frustration led to Kennan's later "burning desire to succeed" and to be accepted by authority figures—in the State Department and throughout the executive branch—as a valued and competent counselor.[18] The explanatory power of such psychologizing is, though, doubtful and does not account for the fact that Kennan did form strong attachments of loyalty and respect for James Forrestal and George Marshall, but was fiercely at odds with other older, influential figures— notably Joseph Davies, Dean Acheson, and John Foster Dulles.

Kossuth's cousin, for whom his son was named, made a different and more obviously favorable impression upon the boy. George Frost Kennan, born 1845, was a renowned explorer and successful writer, who gained national attention in the early 1890s after making a harrowing trek through Siberia. His subsequent published account about the scandalous Czarist prisons and exile system won him worldwide notoriety; he was hailed by the Czar's disloyal opposition—by Bolsheviks too—for decades. His acclaimed *Siberia and the Exile System* (1891) chronicled the calamities that were visited by the Russian police on restless intellectuals, dissident liberals, and revolutionaries. The book's lively prose and stories of suffering helped make the resistance of Russian liberals and "nihilists" a *cause célèbre* in the United States and contributed to the general cooling of Russian-American relations around the turn of the century. George Kennan senior declared, "My sympathies are with the Russia of the people, not the Russia of the Czars."[19] Decades later, his distant relative expressed similar feelings distinguishing the Soviet peoples from their regime.

The elder George Kennan had no children, but discovered over the course of a single visit with his cousin's son a delightful substitute. In turn, the author became a great favorite with the boy who had thrilled to tales of Russian customs and society in Siberia. The old man, who had fired the boy's imagination, died when Kennan was nineteen. On several occasions since, he has paid tribute to his father's cousin and has been impressed by the curious ways in which their lives became entwined. (Incidentally, in 1922 George Kennan senior published a two-volume biography of Averell Harriman's father, the railway king, E. F. Harriman. Twenty years later the younger Kennan served under then-Ambassador Averell Harriman in Moscow during the fateful last years of the Grand Alliance.) When Kennan joined the Foreign Service and was given the choice of becoming a language officer in Arabic, Chinese, or Russian, he naturally chose Russian. By the account of Loy Henderson, who worked with Kennan in the late 1920s and 1930s, he was much taken by the elder George Kennan and manifested more interest in him than in Soviet political matters.[20] In his memoirs Kennan has admitted: "I feel that I was in some strange way destined to carry forward as best I could the work of my distinguished and respected namesake. What I have tried to do in life is, I suspect, just the sort of thing the latter would have liked a son of his to try to do, had he had one."[21]

Understandably, the romantic figure of his author-explorer relative was a more inspiring example to young Kennan than his own austere father, against whom George rebelled. At thirteen he was delivered to a military boarding school, St. John's Military Academy, in Delafield, Wisconsin. Any impulse threatening to push boys into criminality and delinquency was checked by the pundits of this stern, tightly regulated school. Its founder, Sidney Smythe, an Episcopalian minister, conferred on the academy its earnest motto: "Work hard, play hard, pray hard." The boys were also encouraged not to be mollycoddles and to "fight on to the last inning." Though Kennan disliked St. John's at the time of his attendance—he was lonely and not intellectually stimulated by what was a mediocre school—it taught him certain lessons that he valued as an adult and stood him in good stead in government service. The spartan atmosphere, strict discipline, and absence of pampering helped to counter his dreamy and otherwise self-indulgent proclivities.[22]

The physical education especially was designed to harden the cadets and decrease their nervous energy. They sometimes staged twelve-mile hikes, exercised in subzero weather, and improved their stamina through required, daily calisthenics. They were taught to obey, learned the rudiments of command, were marched in formations, were expected to respond snappily and dress sharply.[23] Kennan later praised the arduous instruction: "We learned what it meant to march in ranks, to merge one's effort with the efforts of other people, to bear a share of responsibility for the performance of an entire collective unit."[24]

The school taught other lessons. Once Kennan, acting as platoon leader, led his group out of wooded concealment a minute earlier than scheduled. Thereupon the field instructor halted the exercise, publicly reprimanded Kennan, and informed him that such misconduct in the regular army would have meant court-martial and execution. His overall performance, though, at St. John's was good. He reached the rank of lieutenant; earned excellent marks in Latin, French, and English; and participated successfully in football and track. General Roy Farrand, a teacher at St. John's during Kennan's period, remembered him as "decidedly of the quiet, manly, studious type. He stayed out of trouble and was well liked by everybody."[25]

Although he was not a malcontent, Kennan was far more complicated than Farrand knew. Whereas most cadets complained good-naturedly about unexceptional problems such as early reveille, formations, and mess assignments, Kennan was already brooding about larger issues, including "the universe." Usual cadet reading fare consisted of adventure books by the likes of Zane Grey, Jack London, and Rudyard Kipling, but Kennan by seventeen preferred the works of the iconoclast George Bernard Shaw. Meanwhile, he cultivated his poetic interests, wrote serviceable verse in school, and in his senior year was designated official poet for the graduating class. By the time of commencement his daydreaming still continued unabated, and he was prone to fantasy; his outwardly composed demeanor masked a vacillating, introverted personality.

His matriculation at Princeton University in autumn 1921 led to unhappy, unanticipated social trials. He had been urged to attend Princeton by the dean of St. John's, Henry Holt, a man whom Kennan trusted and has described as "a modest, shrewd, and dedicated pedagogue."[26] Also the lush, seductive depiction of Princeton in F. Scott Fitzgerald's *This Side of Paradise* fascinated seventeen-year-old Kennan. And he expected to find as Lewis had at Yale and Fitzgerald at Princeton—both fellow midwesterners—a world more charming, more sophisticated, more richly varied than Midwest America, damned by Fitzgerald as the "ragged edge of the universe."

In *Paradise* manicured gardens, mansions, and witty repartee provide the landscape against which are played the hero Amory Blaine's romantic escapades, his social triumphs and failures, and ultimately his coming of age. Princeton University is presented as ethereal, always alluring: "The night mist fell. From the moon it rolled, clustered about the spires and towers, and then settled below them, so that the dreamy peaks were still in lofty aspiration toward the sky. . . . The Gothic halls and cloisters were infinitely more mysterious as they loomed suddenly out of the darkness, outlined each by myriad faint squares of yellow light."[27] In this evocative setting, socially privileged young men meet, vie for honors, and prepare to assume their appointed roles in America's aristocracy.

To young Kennan, Fitzgerald's Princeton was irresistible, but his own experience was quite a different matter from the start. His scholastic preparation at St. John's was poor, and it was with difficulty—he failed two of the required entrance exams initially—and after a spell of special coaching by his sister Jeanette, that he gained admission. Worse still, he suffered greatly from and was appalled by the pervasive social snobbery, which effectively excluded him, and he spent an undistinguished four years as an undergraduate. He observed years later: "I was hopelessly and crudely Midwestern. I had no idea how to approach boys from the East. I could never find the casual tone."[28] Like Fitzgerald's Gatsby, Kennan found himself by reasons of regional deficiency to be unacceptable to eastern life.

These traits, combined with a certain knack for romanticized self-pity, caused him to seek his own at Princeton, to get along in an ordinary, inconspicuous way. Shortly after joining a selective eating club, he quit and thereafter dined among Princeton's inconsolable "social rejects." His few friends were mostly from the Midwest and by his estimate were as bewildered and insecure as himself. In addition, his limited financial resources were a constraint, and his career in the Key and

Seal Club was necessarily cut short. To meet the expenses of college and the cost of transport to and from Milwaukee, Kennan worked at various odd jobs. At Christmas time during his freshman year, he delivered holiday mail and nearly botched the job; as a result of overexposure to the cold, he was stricken by scarlet fever. He never fully recovered what had previously been a robust constitution, but was susceptible thereafter to various ailments. (At least one historian has suggested that because Kennan was subject during his diplomatic career to illnesses, including psycho-somatic ones and ulcers, that some of his memoranda and reports about the Soviet Union were peculiarly dyspeptic.[29] But this interpretation cannot explain anything significant about Kennan's views during the Cold War about the USSR, which were adduced from his understanding of geopolitics, Russian history, and contemporane-ous Soviet behavior.) Later at Princeton, he played banjo in a dance band, trimmed trees during the summer, and worked with crippled children at a Delaware River camp. The summer following his senior year, he hired on as a sailor to a ship that ferried passengers and freight between Boston and Savannah. Unfortunately, the popularly accepted notions at Princeton of what constituted proper gentlemanly pursuits did not include such exertions that were in Kennan's case required to afford an education at a private university. Princeton in the early 1920s was socially southern and intellectually eastern; Kennan was neither. Rather, he was high-strung, inward-looking, too poor to participate.

When commencement arrived, he avoided most of the festivities and cere-monies and held them beneath contempt: "As far as I could see, they were of no importance in themselves, and constituted only an attempt to telescope in a sym-bolic and over-simplified form, something which was of importance but which was much more complicated, more prolonged in time, more disorderly and inconclu-sive, and therefore not really susceptible to this sort of telescoping."[30] Despite his reservations, he did attend the baccalaureate ceremony. He had earned a BA with a major in history and emphasis on modern European diplomacy and international relations. Although he never faulted the university—indeed, felt the education available was sound and the professors able—he regretted in subsequent years that he had frittered his time at Princeton and had failed to develop an intellectual curiosity. His grades, as well as his social record, were undistinguished; even his marks in politics and history were lackluster and suggested nothing of his later achievements as an historian and political analyst. Still, the university did have its impact on Kennan's thinking, most importantly in the form of Professor Joseph Green, who taught about the effect of climate, geography, and resources on the formation of national character and human civilizations, which Kennan remem-bered for decades to come.[31] We shall see in following chapters both that Kennan has been inclined to rely on such determinants in assessing Russian, American, European, and other cultures and that this reliance has not always served him well; sometimes it has led him to commit unhelpful typecasting or make misanalyses, especially in relation to the Third World.

Kennan left college, like most young graduates, reasonably prepared in a few academic subjects, but not yet formed intellectually, and unsure about which career to pursue. He toyed with the idea of attending law school with an aim of pursuing an international legal career in the private sector; he also considered business and a career with General Electric. Only one thing was certain: Milwaukee did not attract him. Finally, on the basis of whim and for want of anything better, he decided after graduation to investigate the possibilities of a career in the Foreign Service. He guessed it might be worthwhile—he was at the time in his short-lived Wilsonian phase—and would prevent him from "falling into some sort of occupational rut." After a special course of preparation, Kennan took and just barely passed the Foreign Service examination.

The Foreign Service and Preparing for Russia

The Foreign Service that Kennan entered in September 1926 had recently under-gone a series of reforms that made it more open to merit than had previously been the case. Attempts to reform professional American diplomacy dated to the late 1800s when young career officers spearheaded a movement to promote expertise and social diversity at the expense of wealthier dilettantes who occupied most major positions in the diplomatic field. Joined later by prominent businessmen and politi-cal reformers of the Progressive type, they found satisfaction in the passage by Congress of the Rogers Act in 1924. It combined the old consular service, charged with promoting trade and protecting citizens abroad, with the more prestigious diplomatic corps into the new Foreign Service.

The Foreign Service was by 1926 just beginning to accept the concept of greater social heterogeneity and was increasingly serious about grooming a cadre of profes-sional, well-trained public servants, but it still retained much of the ethos of the previous diplomatic corps. With few exceptions the Foreign Service was staffed by white, native-born, Protestant men from upper-middle-class professional or wealthy business families. A majority of them had attended private colleges, and the largest percentage had been graduated from Ivy League universities. There were few Jews and Catholics, and a genteel anti-Semitism pervaded the ranks. Moreover, there was a general snobbery toward immigrant Americans from southern and eastern Europe and a skepticism that such people could accommodate themselves to politi-cal institutions and values in the United States.[32]

Because of his lack of private income, Kennan could not have made a career in the pre-1924 diplomatic corps. Even after the Rogers Act, an independent income was an advantage, and on more than one occasion he almost resigned from the Service for financial reasons. Still, he was able to make a career in the Foreign Service because of the expanded opportunities open to men from more modest backgrounds who in return for reliable, intelligent work could expect professional advancement and recognition. At the same time, he imbibed heavily from the aristocratic atmosphere that clung to the professional corps of American diplomats. Years after entering the Service Kennan recalled of himself and his young col-leagues that they believed a new era had begun in American diplomacy; the Foreign Service had a bright future, and they would be integral parts of that future.

Money, position, and the possibility of surrounding one's personal life with set-tings of dignity and distinction played a prominent role in [our] thoughts. There still existed, after all, an international society which was considered to have smartness and glamor. It was still assumed that that society was essentially a stable one, capable of providing security, comfort and a wide degree of popular respect for the successful individual. In short, there was still a faint gleam of the romanticism of the nineteenth century that fell on all of us like the beams of a setting sun, and we were preoccupied, like all romantics, with the shadows which our individual figures might cast in that mellow and seductive light.[33]

Kennan eventually embraced in himself both the traditional and innovative features of the Foreign Service. On the one hand, he was by the outbreak of the Second World War one of a small number of experts on Soviet Russia and fully dedicated to the principle of professionalism. On the other, his appreciation of professionalism came to coexist with that of elitism—both social, the superficial aspects of which he had found so repellent at Princeton, and intellectual. During his first overseas assignments (Hamburg, Berlin, Tallinn, Riga) he was drawn to the company of European aristocrats or Americans who had comparable self-possession and élan. Their pride and assurance inspired him to shed his residual clumsiness and shyness; he could not easily reproach the occasional rudeness or clannishness of such people whom he hoped to emulate.[34] The social discipline of the Foreign Service, meanwhile, and the responsibility of having to protect and care for Americans traveling or living abroad also helped to bolster Kennan's self-confidence: "Under this welcome mask [of the diplomat] I felt a hitherto unknown strength, a strength that was never entirely to fail me through a long Foreign Service career, at least not so long as I was in the office or appearing somewhere in the official role."[35] Russia, of course, provided the first important and most challenging test of Kennan's mettle as an American diplomat.

In anticipation of renewed Soviet-American relations, the government sponsored Kennan for two years (1929–1931) of language instruction and training in Russian historical studies at the University of Berlin. Four other Foreign Service officers, including Charles Bohlen, pursued similar courses in Paris. Later, most of them, as well as Kennan, were posted to Tallinn and Riga. These venerable cities were ideal for students of Russian history and politics. Located near Soviet territory, they were in the late 1920s and early 1930s still heavy with the influence and atmosphere of prerevolutionary Russia. They were also convenient posts from which to monitor current Soviet developments. In this respect, Riga was especially important. In the Latvian capital, between 1931 and 1933, Kennan and his colleagues closely followed the Soviet economy, interviewed emigrés, and analyzed Soviet journals, newspapers, and speeches. In fact, the Riga research division, which included an excellent library on Soviet subjects, was one of only four such centers outside of the USSR—the others being in Birmingham, England, in Prague, and in Koenigsberg's Osteuropa Institute—well versed on a broad range of Soviet economic and political issues. American Sovietology was, in effect, launched from this city on the Baltic littoral. There Kennan and the others poured over Soviet periodicals and books, plodded through Soviet economic statistics, and studied Moscow's propaganda. This group of Americans was, in Kennan's estimation, "among the first post-war students of international affairs to grasp and exploit systematically the fact that no propaganda is meaningless, that the prevarications of the propagandist can be as revealing to the thoughtful student as the evasive answers of the patient to the psychiatrist, that there is always some illuminating reason why just this particular lie, and not any other lie, was told."[36]

Daniel Yergin, in his *Shattered Peace,* contends that Soviet specialists in Riga became so immersed in the prerevolutionary atmosphere of the city, were so sympathetic to the colony of Russian exiles, and were anyway ideologically opposed to Bolshevism that they formed an identifiable, and increasingly influential, clique in the government opposed to decent relations with the USSR. Yergin contrasts the Riga mentality or "axioms" with the one that possessed Roosevelt at Yalta and had as its goal Soviet-US friendship and cooperation and lived on during the Cold War through the proponents of detente. Around this dichotomy of Riga and Yalta, Yergin organizes a very good book. But from the standpoint of historical accuracy, his framework based on conflicting Riga and Yalta "axioms" is overly schematic and distorts at least two important points. First, Roosevelt never had illusions about the USSR or the difficulty of maintaining cordial relations with it after the war against Germany ended. Second, and more important for our present purpose, Kennan, Bohlen, Loy Henderson, and other Americans in Riga were not as a result of experiences there implacably opposed to the Soviet Union. They certainly left Riga with a set of preconceptions about Soviet society, but they were on the order of intellectual categories and fascination, not of absolute hostility.[37]

Kennan himself fell more in love with the Russian language while in Riga and became fully absorbed in studying Russian history; moreover, his intellectual life quickened as never before when he debated, analyzed, and scrutinized with colleagues and emigrés alike the momentous unfolding of Stalin's first five-year plan and his humbling of the "right opposition." Though he was not immune to feelings of sympathy for the exiled survivors in Riga of the brutal Russian civil war and was moved by the human costs exacted by Stalin's collectivization of agriculture and rapid industrial drive, uppermost in Kennan's mind was curiosity and wonder. What sort of government, what kind of nation, what political vision were operating, pushing Russia from its obscure origins to an unknown destiny?[38] Riga had whetted his appetite; it had not formed him.

Despite the objections of some prominent Catholics such as Father Edmund Walsh of Georgetown University, the suspicions of leaders in the American Federation of Labor, and the opposition of Robert Kelley, chief of the State Department's Division of East European Affairs, President Roosevelt pressed throughout 1933 to establish formal Soviet-US relations. His talks in the late autumn with Maxim Litvinov, commissar of foreign relations, culminated in accords whereby the Soviets pledged to liquidate $75 million of their debt to the United States, agreed to respect the religious rights of Americans residing in Russia, and ingeniously promised not to support any international organization (e.g., the Comintern) whose aim was to topple American political institutions.

In the expectation of expanded Soviet-US economic relations, principally export trade and investments in Siberian development, the American business community was largely enthusiastic about Roosevelt's initiative. Although not oblivious to the benefits of improved relations with the USSR for a society gripped by economic depression and impressed by the anomaly of not having direct channels to a government ruling 160 million people, Roosevelt especially hoped—as did Stalin—that rapprochement between the two countries would have a salutary effect on Japanese aggressiveness in the northern Far East and on German alteration of the Versailles Treaty in Europe. After a brief period of "honeymoon" in 1934, however, Soviet-American relations deteriorated steadily and by the end of 1940 had reached such a nadir that Roosevelt himself occasionally doubted the desirability and feasibility of sustained regular relations with Moscow.[39]

Kennan, who had been much influenced by the scholarly and skeptical Kelley (he was known as one of Kelley's "bright boys"), shared the pessimism of most men in the Riga legation about immediate American advantages to be gained by recognition of Moscow. To them, the terms of recognition set an unfortunate precedent in which the United States jeopardized real interests—related to debts owed American creditors and Soviet meddling in US domestic affairs—in exchange for which the Soviets did nothing tangible except make vague promises. According to this line of reasoning, only a real *quid pro quo* would provide a solid basis for long-term, stable relations. Roosevelt, however, was not particularly concerned with the specific problems advanced by Kelley, Kennan, and the others, and was willing to soothe creditors by gestures and to pay rhetorical respect to the principles of sovereignty and noninterference. In fact, he rightly did not fear the influence of the Comintern in the United States, which was even more inept in the New World than in the Old; he also saw clearly that the question of debt repayment was minor in comparison with that of Soviet-US cooperation before the threat of Hitler and the Japanese militarists.

In late autumn 1933, Kennan, on leave from his post in Riga, was enjoying a temporary assignment in Washington, DC. In November, Henderson and Bohlen arranged for him to make the acquaintance of William C. Bullitt, recently appointed ambassador to Soviet Russia. Bullitt was exuberant about his forthcoming mission and confident that problems between Russia and America could be resolved and that relations between the two countries could once more be based on mutual concern and common interest. Bullitt, who had known Lenin personally and was familiar with other Bolshevik leaders, attacked his job, at least initially, with high hopes and infectious enthusiasm.

During his first meeting with Kennan, Bullitt quizzed him about Soviet economic conditions and policy. Upon receiving satisfactory answers and impressed by Kennan's fluency in Russian, the ambassador asked him to join the American delegation bound for Moscow just a few days hence. Kennan was thrilled by the offer, practically overcome: "The room rocked around me."[40] Despite his professional annoyance over what he viewed as Roosevelt's precipitance in opening relations with Moscow and his failure to safeguard US interests adequately, Kennan was eager to see the USSR personally, instead of filtered through the perceptions of emigrés and statistical and propaganda reports from Soviet authorities. His five years of postgraduate education, formal and otherwise, would be validated by duty in the Moscow embassy, and an assignment there would mean a direct encounter with the country whose language he admired, whose history, politics, and social progress filled his working hours. Without much difficulty he arranged for a hasty departure.[41]

*   *   *   *

On the eve of his going to Moscow, Kennan had already earned a reputation in the Foreign Service for being highly intelligent, a fine political reporter, very sensitive, and slightly imperious. His natural demeanor was dignified, though it could lapse into stiffness and awkwardness; his handsome face normally wore a faintly ascetic expression. The overall impression was of an elegant figure, an extremely able young diplomat. In contrast to many US diplomats of the late 1920s and 1930s, though, there was nothing of the patrician and little of the cosmopolitan in Kennan's background. He could make no claims for his family like those, for example, of his close friend and fellow student of Russia, Charles Bohlen, who was of a wealthy background, related to the aristocratic Bohlens of Prussia, and whose cousin directed Germany's immense Krupp arms industry.[42]

Though not the case at first—certainly not at Princeton—Kennan did eventually look upon his pioneer ancestors and his family's modest achievements as a source of permanence and steadiness. He, like them, remained puritanical and found through hard work, orderliness, and discipline an escape from aimlessness and misdirection. His oft-expressed love of beauty, palpable in the pains he has taken with his prose, does symbolize a departure from the provincialism and cultural coarseness of previous generations of Kennans. In any event, their pioneer experience has never struck him as being compatible with any of Marx's understanding or his broad categories. Rigid class division, class oppression, class struggle, and the grinding and brutal processes of capital have seemed irrelevant and were basis enough for him always to reject—unlike many distinguished intellectuals of his generation who at one time or another were at least titillated by "scientific socialism"—a Marxist diagnosis of and prescription for social ills. The Kennans, after all, did not exploit cheap labor, did not amass huge fortunes at the expense of others, and were not conscious of being abused by the powerful and rich. They valued their independence, and in difficult times they, like countless obscure pioneer families, simply moved away and thereby affirmed their basic understanding of freedom. Not until Wisconsin did the lot of the Kennans significantly improve. And, as we shall see, Kennan over the years has turned increasingly and nostalgically to Wisconsin as an exemplar of political and social virtues that has much to teach the world.

That Kennan was from early on something of an outsider temperamentally while outwardly conforming (as at St. John's) and as restless as his pioneer ancestors combined in his youth with one plain result: the desire to quit the prosaic Midwest as soon as adulthood would allow in search of some dimly imagined but infinitely more exciting life. The stimulation and glamor that he hoped to find at Princeton eluded him, however; instead he experienced the gall of feeling himself to be a pariah. "Yet cruel as it was," records Kennan in his memoirs, "there was something useful in the experience. It finally dawned on me, pondering this unhappy situation [at college], that to be fair to oneself one had to make one's own standards, one could not just accept those of other people; there was always the possibility that those others, in the very rejection of us, had been wrong."[43] This type of independence and self-confidence has, indeed, characterized much of Kennan's career in government and as a critic; at times he has seemed positively to revel in propounding a minority line.

It was not until his marriage in 1931 and his later friendship with Bohlen—a charming, socially relaxed, intellectually engaging individual—that intimacy began to displace loneliness, while the Foreign Service and living abroad satisfied some of Kennan's wanderlust and imagination. He believed that the profession of diplomacy was in the late 1920s something of "a refuge for escapists, for introverts, for romantics"—in other words suited to people like himself.[44] Within the Service his intellect was focused, friendships arose, life took on greater dimension. Always, though, there remained at the center of his personality vague yearning and reserve, traits not always understood or appreciated by his colleagues and superiors. (Some associates, like Acheson, would eventually conclude that he was supremely arrogant and self-righteous.)[45] And above all, there was Kennan's ambivalence. He was from the heartland of the United States, but confessed in his late twenties that he would like to be "de-Americanized"—something other than graceless, monolingual, and ignorant of history.[46] In later years, he has been simultaneously attracted to and repelled by the United States. Its commercialism, wastefulness, and wildly populist politics have dismayed him and partly explain his long attachment to Edward Gibbon's *Decline and Fall of the Roman Empire*. Still, Kennan has never wanted to expatriate permanently—he did think about it during the McCarthy period—and has brought his considerable intellectual talents to bear as diplomat, policymaker, and publicist for the precise benefit of the United States.[47] Nowhere has Kennan's devotion to American interests been more evident than in his continuing attempts since the 1930s to help set Soviet-US relations on a predictable, less erratic course.

2

First Tour in
the Soviet Union

Kennan's tour of duty in the USSR during the 1930s can be divided for purposes of review into three categories.[1] First, there was his direct encounter, intellectual as well as personal, with the Soviet Union. His assessment of the relative importance of that country's official ideology and the influence of the prerevolutionary past on the communist experiment was perceptive. He understood more clearly than many Westerners of the day that the weight of Russian political traditions and practice foredoomed the Bolshevik experiment of creating a new, humane communist order; the method of Stalin's despotism and the unrestrained activity of the police organs were perfectly in keeping with the worst autocratic rulers and habits that governed Russia before 1917.

Second, in the 1930s Kennan was involved in evaluating the nature of Soviet-US relations and on that basis to project, as best he could, their likely future course. Geopolitical principles, historical conditioning, and qualities of national character were in their sum as important to Kennan as were the ideological differences separating Soviet Russia from the United States. Finally, on the strength of his assignment to Moscow in the service of two ambassadors, William Bullitt and Joseph E. Davies, Kennan drew general conclusions on how US diplomacy (and government) might properly be organized.

That Kennan was becoming an excellent political reporter on the USSR is fully apparent in his analyses of Soviet politics and economy. In particular his interpretations of the purge trials were vivid and amount to one of the most thoughtful firsthand accounts of Stalin's campaign against the old guard in the CPSU (Communist Party of the Soviet Union) anywhere available. Kennan's ruminations about Soviet-US relations and American diplomacy also contained insights and useful recommendations. At the same time, his writings on these subjects were suffused with a growing impatience with the popular mind in the West, a scorn for what he regarded as the incompetence and occasional buffoonery of American statesmanship, as well as a horror for the practices of modern tyranny. Against them and in response to his first experiences in Stalin's Russia, Kennan shaped his versions of conservatism and realism.

The Soviet Union

Kennan worked effectively as Bullitt's translator for the trip (late 1933) to Moscow and once there helped arrange the ambassador's presentation of credentials to the chief of state, Mikhail Kalinin. Kennan's first impressions upon entering Soviet territory were breathless, ineffable. The American diplomatic party reached the Soviet-Polish frontier early in the morning of December 10 and then transferred to new trains. Once installed on the Soviet train, Kennan could not sleep: "I sat through the night, scratching the frost off the windowpane, staring out at the crowds on the little platforms." To the young diplomat the country appeared both vast and desperately primitive. Soon he was astonished to watch the futile efforts by which local political and railroad authorities tried to hide or explain away Soviet backwardness. At Mezhaisk, for example, he watched as railway workers noisily, but under the cover of darkness, pumped hot water from a switch-engine on the next track into the delegation's sleeping-car. He was amused by the episode and surmised that orders had been issued that the Americans were to lack nothing. Later, he lyrically recalled the incident: "Russia, Russia—unwashed, backward, appealing Russia, so ashamed of your backwardness, so orientally determined to conceal it from us by clever deceit, so sensitive and so suspicious in the face of the wicked, civilized west. I shall always remember you—slyly, touchingly, but with great shouting and confusion—pumping hot water into our sleeping-car in the frosty darkness of a December morning, in order that we might not know, in order that we might never realize, to how primitive a land we had come."[2]

Shortly after presenting his credentials, Bullitt returned to the United States and left Kennan in charge of preparing living and working premises for the ambassador and his staff. Until their return in March 1934, Kennan was the sole representative of the American government in Moscow. During this period he dealt with impecunious compatriots, issued new passports, and did his best to rescue American adventurers who had fallen foul of Soviet law. He also supervised repairs and renovation of those buildings selected to serve as embassy office and residence, negotiated leases, pushed through innumerable bureaucratic problems and conceits tossed before him by the Soviet and American governments. And he discovered that the more insignificant the issue, the more entrenched the respective Soviet and American bureaucrats became behind their precedents and regulations.[3] The US government, making matters worse, was slow to ship office furniture; when Bullitt and the staff arrived, the embassy had been stocked with nothing more than wall clocks. Kennan's diary from the period reveals scores of tedious problems confronted and sometimes solved, and suggests not a little exasperation.[4]

No matter how trying and hectic they sometimes were, the first couple of months of duty in Moscow were exhilarating for Kennan and his wife. Soviet life was noisy, chaotic, vivacious. The Kennans lived and worked in a crowded hotel room that served as bedroom, dining room, kitchen, and the American chancery.

Years later, Kennan recollected that within this confined space, "food was cooked, toilets were made, friends were entertained, while the telephone buzzed erratically, and official visitors, all of them curious and many of them exacting . . . trooped in and out and settled their business. Russia, always partial to intimacy and confusion, had promptly claimed its own."[5] Hotel clerks and commissars alike regarded any occasion with the Kennans, no matter how casual or inconvenient, as appropriate for effusive ceremony, vodka, and celebration. Consequently, to accomplish his work, Kennan retreated rather quickly from public areas in which chance encounters might lead to spontaneous demonstrations of Soviet-American friendship and to more food and drink than could prudently be consumed by a busy diplomat. Naturally, when Bullitt returned, much of the attention that had been lavished on Kennan was shifted to the ambassador.

Despite basic good faith, most of 1934 was for the Americans in Moscow and the Soviet Foreign Office officials who dealt with them something of an ordeal. The return of Bullitt and his entourage marked the beginning of a comical but honest struggle on the part of the Americans to start functioning as an organization. The government in Washington was not prepared for the novel problems of representation in Russia, and the Soviets were equally baffled by the demands and vagaries of forty newly arrived Americans.[6] Gradually, though, routines were established, and a modicum of order was introduced to American embassy life in Moscow. Kennan and his wife also frequented, often in the company of Bohlen, performances of the Russian ballet and theater and energetically pursued their interests in Russian history and literature.

Still visible amidst the violent Soviet experiment stood Old Russia, and it was exquisitely charming to Kennan. Years later he declared that, given the choice, he should have preferred to live among the intelligentsia of pre-1914 Russia.[7] An admirer of the dramatist Anton Chekhov, Kennan early in 1934 successfully sought an audience with his widow. At the time, he was actually planning to compose a biography of the great writer. (To his chagrin, Kennan never had time enough to complete the work.) Mme. Chekhov was for the American "an incarnation of what had previously been a world of the imagination." He also visited Tolstoy's home, Yasnya Polyana. The journey, though, and visit to the site were unpleasant, in some ways oppressive. Not only were the remains of Tolstoy's home lifeless and drab, but Kennan was trailed throughout the tour by security officers from the People's Commissariat for Internal Affairs (NKVD).

In the months that followed, Kennan came to believe that what was emerging as distinctive Soviet culture was crushing traditional Russian sensibility, and its significant landmarks, such as Yasnya Polyana, were indifferently kept up, no longer cherished. Kennan and his companions found that even the much hailed Soviet theater was stiff and devoid of subtlety, nuance, or true feeling. And, indeed, the traditional theater wanted innovation and clung to dated technique, and exhausted materials. The new theater was even more deplorable. Limited by the injunctions of social realism, it was crude and had plunged to an unprecedented nadir in dramaturgic art. It was, Kennan rightly judged, a form of chauvinistic propaganda. Invariably the principal heroes were one-dimensional creatures—self-sacrificing workers, paternal NKVD officers, determined aviators, brave arctic explorers—

who produced socialist miracles and confounded foreign spies. The over-drawn actors and actresses, too taken with "panting and flexing" of muscles, were for Kennan an instructive if sorry lesson on the failings of Soviet society and on the banality of the touted new Soviet man. To Kennan the dominant cultural life in the workers' state was suffocating: "The intellectual discipline of Soviet reality was always cruel, always relentless; and only one who has lived in Russia can understand how powerful was the yearning for escape."[8] Relaxing diversions, such as expeditions to the countryside and to seaside resorts, could not always be depended upon to provide succor, however.

Once, in March 1936, Kennan traveled to Sochi, a well-known health spa on the Black Sea. At the spa he met a number of vacationing factory workers. They were apparently a depressing bunch; most were bored, and many seemed homesick. He thought them disoriented and listless; some stared blankly at the sea, others shuffled dully through hotel lobbies and billiard rooms. These proletarians apparently had not the faintest idea of what to do with their holiday. To Kennan the scene was desolate, absurd. He asked himself:

> Had the fathers of the Revolution really imagined that once the upper and middle classes had been kicked out of their watering-places, the members of the proletariat would move in and proceed to amuse themselves gracefully and with taste? Did they not realize that the enjoyment of leisure in a place like Sochi . . . would presuppose a certain cultural level considerably above that of the average Russian worker? Did they fail to foresee that such simple people, usually only one generation removed from the peasantry, would make pig-sties of these hotels and villas, would have no appreciation for sky and air and mountain scenery, would lack the aesthetic resources and the imagination to devise their own recreation, and would merely huddle passively together for company in the trampled court-yards and gardens of the hotels or would wander aimlessly up and down in throngs on the main street, waiting for something to happen?[9]

Had he been consulted, Kennan would have advised the revolution's leaders along different lines. Factory workers just barely removed from rural life, he thought, could best be served by a return to their family villages. There, a bit of gossip, change of scene, and perhaps some agricultural work would help restore the flagging spirits of urban-dazed peasants.

In the middle 1930s, certainly, there was no shortage of problems in Russia that any reasonable person might criticize. The peasantry was still reeling from the government-created famine—millions of people had perished—of Stalin's first five-year plan; industrial workers were exhorted to overfulfill unrealistic quotas; all semblance of Soviet legality was vanishing in the explosion of the purge trials. In this context the appearance of industrial workers at a formerly fashionable resort and their inability to entertain themselves as ably as previous patrons were not worthy of comment. That Kennan did object—at some length and in the way he did—to a group of people who deserved sympathy far more than condemnation reflected both his aesthetic opposition to the revolution and his reflexive conservative preferences. Unfortunately, this was not the last time that he let his ethical and political judgment be colored by his personal sense of refinement and decorum.

To be fair, it should be added that the spectacle of enervated workers at their leisure suggested to Kennan issues greater than just the organizing of recreation in Stalin's Russia. The aimlessness of workers in Sochi and elsewhere in Black Sea resorts was to him a symptom of impoverished spiritual life and an expression of the country's underlying political and economic difficulties, which made themselves felt in practically every sphere of life. The whole country was poorly integrated both socially and economically. Kennan reported that the collective farms near Moscow were in a shambles and that entire agricultural districts produced far below capacity. Distant regions of the empire, such as Stalin's Georgia, seemed to belong entirely to another world: "Kutaisi and Tiflis were filthy, oriental and corrupt. Their streets were filled with male loiterers, swarthy and shifty-eyed." By contrast, Moscow, though tattered and disquieting, was for Kennan a comparative haven of comfort and civility.

In the 1930s the Soviet Union was foremost a poor country, unevenly developed, generally embarrassed by its lack of modernity. Its material poverty was pervasive, and attempts by the authorities to camouflage the fact, while touching at first, became for Kennan—as indeed they were—another instance of official mendacity. The appearance and operation, for example, of a particular frontier train station, briefly visited by him, rivaled the legendary Potemkin villages in both duplicity and in the implied abuse of Russian citizens. The station was designed solely to receive tourists and worker delegations from Western Europe. As with other showcase stations, it had a handsome customs hall, large murals, post office, barber shop, an elegant restaurant with an orchestra. Yet the entire complex was strangely spacious and empty of Soviet travelers. After each set of international passengers and train departed, the whole compound vanished like a stage set. It was literally folded up, accessories were locked away, and the station's personnel slipped away home. Relatively nearby, along the same stretch of track, stood an inconspicuous, ramshackle building that functioned as the real Soviet station. In its smoky interior dozens of peasant families camped for days on the dirty floor. For most Russians living in rural areas, there were few habitations that were clean or properly maintained. Kennan brooded that the propaganda station mocked the peasant hovels and offended everything else for hundreds of miles around.[10]

During his assignment in Moscow Kennan developed an intellectual intimacy with some associates, principally Henderson and Bohlen, and with them began to refine and conceptualize various impressions of Soviet life.[11] Bohlen and Kennan were especially committed to taking a scholarly approach to Russia—in this they were encouraged by Bullitt, as earlier they had been by Kelley—and based on their understanding of the Russian past they came to believe that Soviet poverty and premodern conditions were manifestations of chronic ailments dating far back into the Czarist era and beyond. The essential truth for these diplomats, faintly perceived at first but eventually an article of conviction, was that Russia had substantially changed communism, not vice versa. An outworn economic theory, discarded in the West, had been forced to adapt to the needs of a country for which it was never intended and was wholly unsuited. Marxism never had a chance. Russia and its problems were eternal and, if not absolutely immutable, were open only to marginal alteration. The abiding influences of a harsh natural environment, the Byzantine

Church, and the Asiatic frontier had shaped Russia, and Marxism-Leninism, no matter how scientific and cleverly applied, could not transform in decades what had been in inexorable process over millennia. Kennan observed that "Bolshevism, with all its hullabaloo about revolution, was not a turning point in history, but only another name, another milepost along the road of Russia's wasteful, painful progress from an [uncertain] origin to an [unknown] destiny."[12]

Kennan and Bohlen also believed that Soviet leaders, despite periodic verbal obeisance to international proletarianism, were decidedly Russian and made sense only if one recognized the basic medieval character of Kremlin politics and intrigues. Indeed, Stalin was far removed from the intellectual cosmopolitan world of Marx and Engels; the dictator's policies bore far more resemblance to the sanguinary exploits of Ivan the Terrible. As Kennan dryly noted, the fate of the old Bolshevik guard was similar to that of the sixteenth-century boyars dispatched by Ivan. Stalin too, like Ivan, piously professed a teleological faith. Marxist dogma might have replaced Russian Orthodoxy in the twentieth century, but Kennan and Bohlen recognized that the traditional political reflexes to dominate and the intellectual pretensions to universal validity were unchanged in Russian leaders.

It was apparent to Kennan that in Stalin's Russia ethical barbarism had been wedded to modern techniques of tyranny. The dictator's statecraft amounted to little more than fanatical gangsterism, unrelieved by the modern moral concern of Marx. And stubborn adherence to an ultimate vision reinforced the worst tendencies in Soviet political culture. The party bosses, themselves, were a tough, ruthless lot. In Kennan's words: "They held their positions only by whipping the tired, cumbersome apparatus of government into its brief spurts of activity, and by constant vigilance against the jealousies and intrigues of their party comrades. Theirs was a ladder which many had ascended, rung by rung, pushing, and tripping, fighting for position." Safe descent from the pinnacles of power was virtually unknown, and retirement when it came was usually in the style meted out to Chicago mobsters: "So these men had no choice but to carry on, enjoying their power, stimulated by the constant proximity to danger. They had no chance to get paunchy and flabby, like their bourgeois counterparts abroad."[13] Stalin and his lieutenants, alien as types to most British or American statesmen, were of an ilk that had ruled in Russia for centuries and could not conceivably constitute a radical break from the past. Their crude dinner-table humor and their continuous playing along the abysses of political and physical disaster reminded Kennan of those Dnieper cossacks painted by I. Y. Repin in the nineteenth century.

The sometimes cruel, treacherous nature of the self-appointed guardians of Marxian socialism was never more clearly evident than after the murder of Sergei Kirov, whose assassination in December 1934 sparked a reign of terror and plunged Lenin's closest partners into a catastrophe that inflicted unprecedented ruin both upon themselves and the highest echelons of the army and police commands. The American embassy staff was appalled by the Great Purges, by the display of young party careerists who groveled before Stalin and played skillfully on his morbid suspicions, smashing the old guard and seizing for themselves all positions of state, military, and party power. The best men and the most imaginative minds of 1917 were destroyed by pitiless epigones. In this respect, concluded Kennan, the party paid penance for the revolution's past frivolities and injustices. The purges also suggested to him that Soviet communism was degenerating; before long it would become indistinguishable from the German or Italian tyrannies. The whole system of Soviet government, he predicted, would soon lie shattered, and the state would wind up governed by a small group of sycophants and police thugs. They would continue to pay lip service to a politics of universal redemption, but the real basis of their authority would rest on "police power on the one hand and 'bread and circuses' on the other: in short fascism."[14]

As Lenin's trusted colleagues disappeared in large numbers, or were banished or executed after being humiliated in fraudulent trials in which they confessed to outlandish crimes, the same question was repeatedly asked. Why did the co-authors of a momentous revolution admit to fantastic acts against the Soviet people and government? Kennan, who witnessed the trial of Grigori Pyatakov and Karl Radek, ventured that the defendants in the public trials were willing to say or do anything, so long as they hoped their cooperation might mollify their persecutors and lead to clemency. Kennan impatiently observed that it was remarkable how few Britons and Americans understood a fact which was known to experienced European police officers and to European laymen besides: "When a man is completely in the power of a police organization which is uninhibited by any legal or humane restraints and which is skilled in the process of the destruction of the human mind and spirit, there is normally very little that cannot be done with him."[15] By contrast Sidney and Beatrice Webb, George Bernard Shaw, Harold Laski, and Anna Louise Strong were prominent among those Westerners at the time who praised the Soviet judicial and penal system. Duped by what they had seen at model prisons, such as Bolshevo, and anyway favorably disposed toward Stalin's regime, they were convinced that the Soviets were practicing a humane form of rehabilitation and justice without antecedents in world history. Laski, for one, was "struck by the excellent relations between the prisoners and the wardens" in Soviet jails and Strong was delighted to learn that the Bolshevik method of "remaking human beings" was so wonderful that political and criminal offenders occasionally applied for admission to prison.[16]

While such nonsense prevailed in various enlightened and progressive circles in the West, G. Yagoda and later N. Yezhov's henchmen were committing crimes that were not condemned by Soviet officialdom until 1956. The methods employed to break a prisoner and prepare him for public trial relied on every form of terror, ranging from the subtlest intimidation to unrestrained violence. Aware that they were hardly unimpeachable morally and that they had committed deeds which by any conventional rule were objectionable, Kennan, nevertheless, had sympathy for Stalin's party victims:

> Let one picture to himself the loneliness, the terror and the hopelessness of a man incarcerated in Russia. . . . He has no legal rights. He cannot consult a lawyer. . . . He cannot insist on a trial or even a hearing. If his captors wish to, they can hold him indefinitely, without a word of explanation, in that complete unbroken solitary confinement which is itself, for a man of active mind, one of the cruelest and most horrible forms of torture.[17]

The police interrogators, moreover, were not accountable to anyone; their prisoner had not the slightest chance of intercession from the outside. He was alone with his tormenters and could expect no compassion or mercy. In such a situation, what could any person do? The issue, Kennan saw, was not even so simple as choosing between life and death.

> It is a more difficult question: one of relief from indefinite pain, loneliness, strain and uncertainty. And the decision often has to be made [whether or not to confess] when a man is unnerved by long solitary confinement, bewildered by a mixture of true and false accusations, exhausted by hours of constant questioning, by loss of sleep and worry, shocked and discouraged by denunciations purporting to come from his own friends, intimidated by threats against himself and his own family. Is it any wonder that a man in this situation, forsaken—as far as he knows—by God and man, can turn around eventually and do the one thing that holds out hope of anything at all other than indefinite horror and suffering: namely, place himself completely at the disposal of his captors and say to them, "For God's sake, do what you want with me! I am yours to command!"[18]

Kennan during the 1930s would certainly have found the anguished ruminations of Arthur Koestler's Rubashov and his strident intellectualism wide of the mark, as well as sterile.[19] Kennan believed that most defendants—except N. I. Muralov and Sergei Mrachkovsky, both "fanatical old Bolsheviks" who confessed to crimes because they felt they owed that much to the revolution—wanted merely to save their lives and protect their families. It was for this reason then they admitted to crimes for which convincing proof was unavailable and which defied common reason.

That the top Soviet leadership was not infested with Western terrorists, fascist spies, wrecking crews, or Trotskyist cells Kennan and Bohlen well knew. They were inclined to view these supposed dangers as primarily the hallucinations of Stalin, nourished by unscrupulous aides whose only concern was for their own personal advancement. In any case, the dramatic trials of Stalin's real and imagined enemies were only the visible tip of a giant process. Hundreds of thousands of other people were liquidated without the theatrics.[20] The numbers involved approximately 80 percent of all the people who were prominent in national affairs in Russia in the mid-1930s; they were either physically destroyed or met ignominious fates in exile or Siberia. Once the process of party and army destruction had begun, it was difficult to control or stop. Kennan suspected that many valuable people whom Stalin had not originally wished to harm were, in fact, ruined: "And many of the new favorites had to follow their own victims over the cliff at a fairly early date: because they knew too much, or else because they were too foul material to be of permanent use to anybody, or because the people behind them just failed to stop pushing."[21] Only after the horrid fracas had impaired the government's efficiency and serious international problems presented themselves was Stalin able to discipline and slow down the terror. Before then, however, many of Russia's best human assets, including skilled diplomats, had been lost.

Soviet-American Relations

The Soviet and American governments failed during the 1930s to reach an agreement on the debts owed by Moscow to Washington. As a consequence the Soviets were unable to obtain a credit loan at favorable rates which, if secured, could have been used to purchase American goods. No boom materialized in trade relations, and by 1937 the United States was exporting goods to Russia valued at a paltry $43 million. And as the immediate Japanese threat to Soviet positions in the Far East began to fade in 1935, the Russian government became noticeably less solicitous of the United States. (Soviet obstruction, for example, of American attempts to build a new embassy in Moscow led to misunderstanding and needlessly complicated matters between the two governments.) By the late 1930s when the dual danger of German and Japanese aggression against the USSR was painfully apparent to Stalin, it was equally plain to him that the Americans were in no mood to join with others in checking fascist expansion. He concluded that if the United States was not going to accept a more responsible role outside of the western hemisphere, then there was no reason to further humor or court Washington.[22] Not until 1941 would events force the Soviet Union and the United States to cooperate on a hitherto unknown scale.

From the standpoint of those working and living in the American embassy in Moscow, the reasons for the poor quality of Soviet-US relations in the 1930s lay closer to hand. At first, Kennan suspected that the French government, through its embassy in Moscow, helped sabotage the various efforts aimed at improving Soviet-American economic relations. He supposed that the French government, under pressure from holders of pre-Bolshevik Russian bonds, was opposed to Soviet payment of debts to anyone else unless it paid them off to France as well. As long as the French debt to the United States was outstanding, the government in Paris was opposed to any great power that threatened to settle its financial obligations to America. He speculated, therefore, that the French delegation in Moscow had sought to strengthen the hands of those Soviet officials who "opposed any debt agreement at all and scoffed at the ill-will that a failure to pay was bound to arise in the United States."[23] No substantial body of evidence exists to support this contention of Kennan's, and he also exaggerated the importance of Comintern meddling in American political and labor life as a factor helping to undermine Soviet-US relations and effectively blocking important agreements. Still, Kennan was perceptive in analyzing the impact of the purges and terror on Bullitt's disappointing mission to Moscow.

Kennan maintained that, before the purges were inaugurated, the Soviet Union had been cautiously progressing along liberal lines. Although hardly democratic, they presaged a rough decentralization of authority and a more open approach to the capitalist world. Kennan emphasized that both the army and NKVD had been moderately successful in separating themselves from party control and, before December 1934, in building parallel columns of state. Eventually, the army and NKVD leadership might have freed themselves entirely from party domination and contained the party's activity to its monotonous scholasticism and endless internal bickering. The army and NKVD could then have continued in their traditional roles as guardians of the Russian state. "They wished," in Kennan's view, "to attach their loyalty to the state as such, in the early tradition of the German Reichswehr, rather than to any group in any political party."[24] Furthermore, the army and NKVD, insofar as they hoped to distance themselves from the party, enjoyed the support of numerous intellectuals and some high state officials. To Kennan, Bullitt, and Bohlen, these people were accustomed to thinking pragmatically and conducted themselves in a dignified, businesslike manner. Periodic dictatorial interference and the restraints of the CPSU discouraged these civil servants, lowered their morale and self-esteem, and cast doubt on all their endeavors taken on behalf of Russia. Yet these people persevered as best they could, all the while yearned for personal independence and for the respect and support of Soviet citizens, and enjoyed travel abroad and association with foreigners. These cosmopolitans hoped that the USSR would benefit through sustained contact with the outside world; with them Americans could expect to build a solid Soviet-US relationship.[25]

Such commendable people, to whom the American diplomats were often personally drawn and on whom they felt much rested, were mostly swept away in the middle 1930s. Their successors were usually poorly educated provincials who had little understanding of or interest in the outside world. "They were," in Kennan's words, "probably unable to conceive of anything like mutually profitable relations between Russia and the unknown lands beyond the Russian border. Themselves, they rarely went near a foreign embassy; and being aware of Stalin's suspicions that foreign interests had encouraged opposition to him in Russia, these young careerists did not hesitate to exploit any foreign connections which their enemies might have had, in order to compromise them." Indeed, few Soviet officials by late 1935, including high-ranking Foreign Office personnel, risked association with foreigners or showed signs of friendliness. And the drawing rooms of the American Embassy, which once attracted numerous curious and friendly Russian guests, unavoidably became emptier.[26] Nearly every Soviet citizen who had a personal connection with one of the members of the American legation met an unhappy end at the hands of the secret police, including such notables as Radek, Nikolai Bukharin, and the enigmatic "Baron" Boris Steiger.[27] Even Soviet employees of the embassy such as chauffeurs, servants, and gardeners were arrested or mysteriously disappeared.[28] Some friendships between Soviets and Americans persisted, but they were necessarily conducted in a clandestine, furtive manner and at great risk to the individual Russian. As for the American diplomats, the psychic toll was great. It could not be otherwise, said Kennan, "in a land where you were officially billeted as a sort of representative of the devil, evil and dangerous, and to be shunned; where your personal friendship, like some powerful curse, could spell ruin for those to whom it attached itself."[29] This malevolent environment wreaked havoc on a number of individuals and destroyed some marriages; every American envoy was subject to espionage, eavesdropping, and various forms of harassment—there were reports that even little children decried the diplomats as spies.

Under circumstances loaded with uncertainty and suspicion, diplomacy could not go forward. Kennan felt that Russia, as during the reign of Peter the Great, had begun a move toward the West but lacked the confidence to reach full accords with outside powers. An intelligent foreign policy based on a sober assessment of Russia's national interest had been, once again, destroyed by the exigencies of unforgiving Kremlin politics. Bullitt, who left the embassy in Moscow in 1936 to take a new post as ambassador to France, had done his best in Kennan's assessment, but Soviet conditions were simply not conducive to normal relations with any country, let alone the United States. Incidentally, Bullitt had lost Russian friends to Stalin's purge and was so personally revolted by what he had witnessed and experienced in Moscow that he became thenceforth an obstinate—occasionally hysterical—opponent of the Soviet Union.[30]

With respect to the long-term course of Soviet-American relations, Kennan was not optimistic. He believed that fundamental factors, namely history and geography, would in the future as in the past govern Russian-American affairs.

The great distances between the two countries, he noted, had hindered the development of close economic and political cooperation. Similarities in pace of development and cultural progress had also reinforced the isolation of the two countries from one another. Traditionally, both countries were poor in capital and well endowed in natural resources; consequently, neither had provided much market to the other nor had been a source of raw materials. As both countries were by European standards young in their cultural development, they turned to the older nations of Europe for inspiration and guidance rather than to each other. The advanced sections of Russian and American society, especially, had typically looked to Britain and the great seafaring centers of Europe for ideas as well as commerce.[31]

In the Far East, also, assorted lands separated the two powers and, as Kennan believed, their historic interests were unrelated. Russian interests lay on the Asian mainland, while America's were on the sea; after the Russian naval debacle in the 1904–1905 Japanese war, there were virtually no points in the Pacific where close contact could be established. Kennan realized, of course, that technical advances in communications and transportation had by the 1930s modified the obstacles posed by geography; he also guessed that eventually the Soviet Union might become a Pacific maritime power. However, the great port of Vladivostok was for the time being in the heart of a basically antagonistic Japanese empire. Only if Japanese hostility subsided or its naval power were broken could the Soviets open direct sea routes to the rest of Asia or to the American mainland. Because it was unlikely that Japan would be dislodged from its dominant position in the east by Russia and because Japanese-Soviet rapprochement was remote, Kennan doubted that the USSR could become a critical factor in East Asian international relations for America or anyone else. On this score Kennan's reasoning was perfectly sound; not until after 1945, when Japanese military strength was defeated and the country's prestige temporarily tarnished, was the Soviet Union able to exercise substantial influence in places such as Korea or China. And not until the late 1960s was Soviet naval power significant enough in the Pacific to cause concern to the United States or its allies.

Regarding trade and economic cooperation, Kennan reckoned that in the future, as before, Russia and the United States would have little to offer each other. Their economies remained essentially competitive, not complementary. They both exported large quantities of grain, timber, and oil and were rivals for many of the same markets. Furthermore, the Soviets, who had periodically purchased some American goods, would no longer be quite such reliable customers. Kennan predicted that Moscow's attempts to industrialize the country, already impressive, would mean a drop in demand in the near future for both foreign machinery and manufactured products. Soviet efforts at modernization came at a high cost, both human and otherwise. But, Kennan affirmed, there was no reason to assume that modernization would not be completed in the course of time. And then Russia's need for American manufactured goods, machines, inventions, and technical skill would be ended. As for miscellaneous trade between the two countries, such as the export of American cotton to Russia, Kennan thought it would continue at a moderate level but could not be significant to the economic fortunes of either country. Finally, Soviet-American trade, to whatever small degree it prospered, would be hostage to Moscow's political aims and interference: "Commercial policy will continue to be subordinated to the political necessities of the Russian state, and American-Russian trade may be adversely affected at any time by world political factors which do not even concern the United States directly—much less the laws of supply and demand."[32] Kennan therefore had no confidence that Soviet-American economic relations could ever be exceptional: in the best of circumstances the amount of trade would be trifling and would depend on the vicissitudes of Soviet diplomacy and politics.

Viewed from the distance of five decades, Kennan's prognostications about the Soviet Union's modernizing to a point where American (and Western) technology and industrial products would no longer be sought were simply wrong. Like many other observers, both sympathetic and not, he overestimated Soviet advances: measured against previous Russian achievements industrial progress in the 1930s was impressive, but it did not close the gap between East and West.[33] A lasting motive of Soviet leaders, characterizing their periodic policies of peaceful coexistence and detente with Western countries, has been to obtain goods and skills for raising the level of Soviet economy and industry. In addition, contrary to Kennan's fears, the Soviet Union has been an historically reliable trading partner for the United States and has not let political considerations interfere with business. The United States, though, has not always been so fastidious and has permitted political concerns to intrude upon economic arrangements—consider Congress's denial of most favored nation status (MFN) and of financial credits to the Soviet Union, and President Carter's grain embargo in the 1970s.

Despite their economic incompatibility, Kennan was in the 1930s impressed by some of the similarities that he detected in Soviet and American political culture. Russian and American character, for example, was not unlike to him; both peoples had been conditioned by comparable frontier conditions, agricultural plains, and the continental nature of their territories and by a common sense of affinity to—and distinction from—mainstream European culture: "All these things have contributed to the development of certain common characteristics which enable the Russian and the American to overcome . . . quickly the differences of background and language which separate them and to understand each other readily, as human beings."[34] Kennan was further convinced that both peoples exhibited in their personality sincerity and openness, were—in contrast to the West Europeans—fundamentally generous and were equally irritated by received conventional wisdom and tired traditions. Whereas the typical West European tended to be intellectually narrow and petty, the Russian and the American were receptive to new ideas and methods. Kennan observed that Stalin himself encouraged his subjects to learn the secrets of American efficiency.

Similarities in experience and to a degree in culture did not translate directly into mutual political understanding or diplomatic benefit, however. For one thing, contacts between the two peoples would be, as in the past, at the mercy of the Russian government. Kennan believed that no Russian regime—past or present—had sufficient confidence in its popular support that it would expose the popular mind for very long to foreign influences. In the case of the United States particularly, Czars and Bolsheviks alike were wary of "the outlandishly democratic and liberal character of American culture."[35] Consequently, the US government could reckon that, excepting a few temporary lapses, the Soviets would inhibit through censorship, the police, and travel restrictions any strengthening of cultural ties. Kennan concluded that the Soviet government was too constricted by its primitive political conceptions and low self-confidence to cultivate the sort of exchange of ideas and methods that might lead to greater understanding and cooperation between the two countries.

As for international power politics, Kennan was extremely skeptical about future Soviet-American relations. He speculated that in the Far East the two countries might encounter each other as rivals with one or the other associated with Japan. Yet he also held out for the prospect that the two might join forces against Japan. Such shifts, though, in the Far Eastern balance of power were unlikely. The immediate practical problem between the two states hinged on one critical fact: Soviet support of international revolution. As long as Russian universalism was in the form of the Comintern, headquartered in Moscow, relations between the United States and the USSR would be more complicated than mere geopolitical considerations would warrant. Political antipathy, then, combined with contrary military and diplomatic traditions. Taken together, they worked to inhibit Soviet-American intimacy.

Kennan maintained that the United States had historically regarded foreign relations as a peaceful enterprise, designed principally to enhance commercial, social, and cultural bonds. For the most part the United States had been successful in promoting its international agenda and had enjoyed the privilege of knowing peace through most of its past. The contrast with unfortunate Russia could scarcely have been starker. Russian history was dominated by war, by the preparation for war, and by the continent's merciless balance of power diplomacy. Kennan observed: "The idea of permanently profitable, normal, peaceful relations between two countries which never expect to make war against each other or to join in war against anyone else: this idea has been little known in Russia, and would probably meet with less response there at the present time than ever before."[36] Whereas the Americans had dealt with weak neighbors in Mexico and Canada and had conquered the continent with relative ease, the Russians had endured centuries of border warfare and had been subject to European and Asian invasions. During times of peace the Russian governments had dealt with powerful continental rivals, all of whom maneuvered constantly for diplomatic advantage in anticipation of the next fight. The foreigner was thus more often than not an enemy to the Russian and was in any case, even when respected, held in suspicion. The divergence in attitude between Russian and American toward international politics was therefore significant. Kennan judged that Moscow's view of such matters meant that the United States should not—excepting for occasional contacts—expect stable or close relations with Russia; as long as the Americans cleaved to their policy of isolation and refused to participate in balance of power politics they were likely neither to understand, nor to be understood by, the Soviets.

Kennan counseled, and it would resonate through his dispatches, reports, and other recommendations for decades to come, that over the long term the United States should be restrained in its policy toward the Soviet Union. At the same time, Americans should expect relatively little to be forthcoming from Moscow.

> The primary quality of [US] foreign policy must be patience. We must neither expect too much nor despair of getting anything at all. We must be as steady in our attitude as Russia is fickle in hers. We must take what we can get when the atmosphere is favorable, and do our best to hold on to it when the wind blows the other way. We must remain as unperturbed in the face of expansive professions of friendliness or in the face of slights and underhand opposition. We must make the weight of our influence felt steadily, over a long period of time, in the directions which best suit our interests.[37]

However unpredictable, then, the Soviets might be, however doubtful their loyalty to regular relations with any outside power, Moscow had to be dealt with in a consistent manner, firm in purpose. Kennan also believed that so long as the United States remained true to its best self, relations with the Soviet Union could develop along a reasonable course: "Above all, we must guard the reputation of Americans for business-like efficiency, sincerity and straight-forwardness. The biggest assets and the biggest possibilities we have in Russia are cultural, and they are based on these qualities of American character. There is no weapon at once so disarming and so effective in relations with Russia as sheer honesty."[38] In the late 1940s, when he helped devise and implement the strategy of containment, Kennan insisted just as in the above that policy toward the Soviet Union should be resolute, yet flexible. And if America was to prevail in the Cold War, then its citizens should continue to cultivate assiduously both their unique political institutions and liberal way of life. He warned that no greater disaster could befall the Republic than if these values were lost or transformed because Americans lacked the will to sustain them during a period of prolonged trial.[39] Ironically Kennan himself—we shall explore this in the next chapter—has had grave doubts about much in the American political tradition.

American Diplomacy

During the middle and late 1930s the Soviet Union still enjoyed wide support among reformers and progressives in Europe and the United States. To such people as Theodore Dreiser, Louis Fisher, H. G. Wells, Julian Huxley, Vincent Sheean, and I. F. Stone the Soviet Union deserved praise because it alone among the nonfascist powers stood up to Italy and Germany during the Spanish Civil War. And as the West wallowed in economic depression and millions of people went without work, food, or shelter, the Soviet Union charged ahead with full employment and increased its industrial production. The country to its outside admirers was dynamic, vigilant, prepared to tackle boldly any problem, domestic or foreign.[40] Sympathetic American visitors to Moscow and Leningrad were usually impressed by the spectacle of a great backward country transforming itself. One such visitor, a woman from California, was incredulous that Kennan and his colleagues did not join in: "I just don't see how you young men can live over here in the midst of all this and not be infected by it, how you can see it all with your own eyes and not be thrilled at what a great experiment it all is, how you can fail to want to participate in it yourselves."[41]

Sometimes Kennan did chafe under the restrictions of life in the Moscow diplomatic corps and felt vaguely superfluous and restless as a generation of young Soviets set about to recast their economy and society. He feared that the compulsion of political inactivity, self-restraint, and objectivity might actually lead to his own mental and emotional atrophy. During one period of depression and poor health he was visibly upset by the contrast between the shallowness of diplomatic dinner parties and the collecting of carpets, icons, and samovars with the drama of strenuous Soviet life.[42] Still, he was never tempted—indeed it was impossible from an official American government perspective—to join in any aspect of the Stalinist enterprise. He did feel that Soviet attempts toward modernization were worthy and that the self-sacrifice required and exacted was heroic, but the harsh methods used and his firsthand witness of the show trials instilled in him a repugnance for Soviet politics. For Kennan, the Soviet Union possessed no exciting answers to the social and economic difficulties then plaguing Europe and America. Furthermore, he believed that those people in the West who viewed Russian socialism sympathetically did so on the basis of misinformation and casual and selective analyses of Soviet life. He deemed their judgments thin as well as ill-informed; they contrasted sharply with those then being developed by the American Foreign Service officers in Moscow who felt themselves on the threshold of understanding fundamental things about the USSR. They "measured their progress by their ability to disprove competently any generalization" about Russian matters and increasingly derived satisfaction as their knowledge of Soviet affairs and ability to provide thoughtful analysis grew; they were becoming experts and recognized as equals by learned people in the Soviet field. Such expertise as the American diplomats were cultivating was not always appreciated in Washington, however, particularly not when it fostered interpretations and approaches to the Soviet Union incompatible with Roosevelt's policies.

In late 1936 Joseph Davies, a prominent Democratic party booster and supporter of Roosevelt, was appointed as ambassador to Russia. Mindful of Bullitt's disappointments and of the scanty results of his tenure in Moscow, Davies and Roosevelt were determined to make progress at improving Soviet-US relations. To Kennan, though, Davies was eminently unsuited to the position of mission chief in the Soviet capital. In Bohlen's words, Davies was "sublimely ignorant of even the most elementary realities of the Soviet system and of its ideology."[43] At one point Davies actually predicted Stalin's government would have to apply capitalist principles of economy and eventually would transform itself into a Fabian socialist polity. Equally unfortunate, he and his socialite wife did not treat the professional diplomats respectfully, but regarded them as little more than "hired help" and rarely listened to their views about the Soviet Union or anything else. Not only did Davies seldom consult his staff of Foreign Service officers, or evince the least interest in learning from them, but he curried favor with local American journalists. By doing so, Davies apparently expected the journalists to report favorably back home about him and his valiant efforts to improve relations with Stalin. In the opinion of Kennan, Bohlen, and many of the others, Davies was both ignorant and insulting and, worst of all, used his post to enhance his political career in the United States. In short, he was to the embassy's officers a constant affront, a shabby politico, paid off for his services to FDR with a plum position in Moscow.

To advance Soviet-American relations and to bolster his position with those in Washington, Davies was also extremely cautious in his reports; it seemed to his critics that he was either dishonest or naive to the point of stupidity. Bohlen recorded in his memoirs, "He was incurably optimistic in his reports to Washington, thereby misleading our government. His dispatches . . . were almost always superficial and heavily slanted."[44] Certainly, Davies's fantastical accounts of the show trials that he witnessed corroborate Bohlen's indictment. The ambassador reported that the trials were fairly conducted, and the Soviet authorities were dutifully routing out spies, traitors, and potential fifth columnists. He passed most favorably upon Soviet legality. "All of these trials, purges and liquidations, which seemed so violent at the time and shocked the world, are now quite clearly a part of a . . . determined effort of the Stalin government to protect itself from not only revolution from within but from attack from without. They went to work thoroughly to clear up and clean out all treasonable elements within the country. All doubts were resolved in favor of the government."[45] Kennan was so upset by the ambassador's rudeness, poor education, and opportunistic use of a government position that he nearly resigned from the Foreign Service.[46] And he was surely not disappointed to leave Davies and Moscow in September 1937 for reassignment to Washington, DC.

During his year-long stay in Washington, where he headed the State Department's Soviet desk, Kennan pondered upon his experiences abroad and about the condition of American diplomacy. To him the amateur, exemplified by Davies, rendered the country a disservice. Kennan theorized that "one can, of course, fill the old black leather executives' chairs . . . of our embassies abroad with the same type of individual who successfully manages party conventions at home. These persons will rarely do anything catastrophic. They lack the patience and understanding to exert any far reaching influence on international affairs."[47] Yet their subordinates, the professional diplomats, were distracted and their steadying influence eroded whenever American missions were led by maladroit envoys. While the political-ambassador blundered his way through diplomatic receptions or wooed the American press, his underlings suffered embarrassment and frustration. They had

had to cover up his mistakes, soothe his vanity, and meanwhile satisfy the important demands of representing US interests abroad.

In Kennan's view, the chief diplomat in Moscow, to be a useful instrument for his country, needed modesty, sound wits, a background in diplomacy, and an ideologically uncluttered view of the USSR. Such people were more likely to be found in the Foreign Service than among the political hustlers in Washington, who sought glamorous jobs and publicity overseas. Given such a situation, Kennan thought the embassy in Moscow and all of its operations should be run exclusively by the professional officers who did most of the work anyway. The mission in Moscow, because of the critical nature of Soviet-American relations, should not be just another repository of political beneficiaries. When Davies vacated his post in 1938, Kennan urged the administration to allow Loy Henderson, the chargé d'affaires, to continue as chief of the legation. And he pleaded that the officers in Moscow must never again be saddled with a nonentity: "Did the White House not realize what a heart-breaking problem these people meant to a Mission such as that of Moscow? How hard it was merely to arrange for their physical comfort in that strange place? How embarrassing it was to face the natural questions of foreigners as to why they had ever been appointed?"[48] Kennan went on to protest that representation abroad would stagnate if the Foreign Service became nothing more than hired flunkeys assigned to babysit the patronage creditors of the party in power. He stressed that the Foreign Service was a way of life, and in Moscow or places of equal importance to the United States, only a first-rate group of trained men could accomplish important tasks.[49]

The need for expertise and a professional attitude toward political work was daily becoming more evident to Kennan. This was as true in American domestic life as it was in foreign relations. Based on his experiences of diplomacy abroad and on his assessment of international political dangers, Kennan drew broad conclusions about what should be the organizing principles of American political life. He wrote: "If we could afford to preserve an opera-bouffe political system, in which everything was taken in the spirit of Strauss' 'Fledermaus,' I should be the last person to oppose anything which could add so materially to the humor of it as our type of amateurism in government." Behind his sarcasm lay this grim realization about a world grown earnest:

> It speaks a bitter language of steel and explosives, it does not respect the ubiquitous American wise-crack. But if death, torture and misery are not laughing matters, then neither is political life in these times; for death, torture and misery have become the penalties of political failure. And whether, in a game for such high stakes, we can continue to be frivolous about our methods and retain inefficient institutions, just because we find them picturesque and amusing, is another question.[50]

He recommended, therefore, that high posts in the government should henceforth be the preserve of the specialist. The political appointee was a luxury, a remnant from a simpler period, but inappropriate to an era menaced by the ruthless and well-armed. He believed throughout the late 1930s and beyond that the habits of a lackadaisical democracy should be tempered, as national success and integrity were at odds with a system that regularly produced the likes of Davies. Kennan advised that secretaries of the army or navy might properly be selected from men with a background in and understanding of military matters. And the formulation and execution of diplomacy should be left entirely to those well versed in the intricacies of international politics.

*   *   *   *

On the basis of his tour of duty in the Soviet Union, Kennan concluded in the 1930s that the USSR could never be a fit long-term partner of the United States. Subsequently, during World War II, he expressed his doubts about the durability of the Soviet-American alliance and warned repeatedly that it probably would not last much beyond the cessation of hostilities. To him the *raison d'être* of the wartime alliance was based solely on the mutual desire to destroy Nazi Germany. Although he recognized as early as the 1930s that a certain natural affinity might be said to exist between Russians and Americans, he was most impressed by their lack of common political conceptions and values, by their dissimilar diplomatic traditions, and by the irreconcilability of their economies. Thus, according to Kennan, the sinews for lasting cooperation were absent, and the American government should prepare itself and its citizens for a cooling of relations with Moscow. He warned specifically that Stalin was unlikely to place much faith in the idealistic principles of world peace embodied by the American-inspired United Nations Charter, nor was Stalin going to be persuaded that the UN's provisions for collective security could guarantee Soviet safety. Instead, as we shall later discuss, Kennan predicted to his superiors, principally Averell Harriman and James Forrestal, that Stalin would quickly grow suspicious of the universally pretentious international organization and would view it as a mere tool of the United States. Kennan added that perceived Soviet security needs required specific regional arrangements and that the Soviets would force subservient regimes upon any central and east European state occupied by the Red Army. Therefore the United States should abandon the chimera of Soviet-US peacetime partnership and prepare to assume an active role in the European balance of power. That the United States did not respond promptly or with finesse to the decline of its alliance with the Soviets and did not realize earlier the fatefulness of Stalin's designs on Poland, Rumania, and Hungary was symptomatic to Kennan of a foreign policy based on illusion and led by men not wholly attentive to or properly schooled in international affairs. America's failure in Eastern Europe during the 1940s was of a piece with America's mismanaged, inexpert relationship to the world at large and to Russia in particular, originally perceived by Kennan in the 1930s.

Although his predictions about the disintegration of the Soviet-American alliance proved well founded, he never felt much satisfaction at their realization and, in any case, sorely disapproved of America's conduct of the Cold War. The Marshall Plan, with which he was closely associated, was to him the appropriate sort of policy with which to limit Soviet influence. However, the militarization of containment, exemplified by the adoption of NSC 68 and establishment of NATO, was anathema to Kennan and out of proportion to the danger he thought was posed by communist ideology or Soviet intentions. He recognized, based on his first experiences in Moscow, that Soviet ideology faintly concealed an ancient form of Russian politics, but was not a source of true inspiration either in domestic or foreign policies. Instead, Russia, as in the past, was willing to justify its concern with stable borders and internal security by invoking a doctrine of generous promise but of little real meaning either to Russians or most other people.

As for the USSR's alleged military threat to the West, Kennan remained skeptical. He recognized that the country was poor in comparison to most of Europe and unable—even if it desired—to conquer the continent in the aftermath of World War II. Although the United States could not sustain a partnership with the Soviet Union, he believed that limited agreements based on mutual interest were possible and could prove profitable in the late 1940s and early 1950s over such issues as Germany, arms control, and European settlement. That the United States did not explore these possibilities more deeply and displayed in its actions and rhetoric the same simplicity of political imagination as in the 1930s demonstrated to Kennan that a fundamental lack of understanding and of strategic concept still handicapped the thinking of Washington policymakers.

Finally, a word about those American liberals and idealists who were seduced by the illusion of Soviet justice and righteousness: Kennan continued well after his first tour in Russia to bear them an intellectual grudge. He knew that had they been Soviet citizens, they undoubtedly would have perished in Stalin's imposition of iron conformity and obedience. Still, it is somewhat surprising that Kennan did not muster any greater sympathy for these admittedly misled, but often decent and serious people. For many of them, their commitment to the USSR—sometimes only an infatuation that disappeared in the wake of the Molotov-Ribbentrop agreement—was a measure of their dissatisfaction with the multiple deficiencies of their own Western society. And many of these defects were recognized as such by Kennan, who, as we shall see in the next chapter, was profoundly disaffected from the United States of the 1930s. At least on the plane of their complaining about the United States and in their seeking of extravagant answers, Kennan and a number of the Soviet Union's admirers were not so far apart. Kennan's sensibility, though, and proposed solutions to America's political corruption, social decline, and low level of cultural attainment did not lean in anything like a liberal or leftist direction.

3

Criticisms and
Recommendations

Kennan's assignment to the State Department's Soviet desk in late 1937 ended a decade of work abroad that had taken him to Berlin, Tallinn, Riga, Vienna, and Moscow. One of the effects of his peripatetic career was that he, like many American diplomats posted abroad for years at a time, felt in various ways unrelated to his native country.[1]

His sense of domestic impermanency was heightened by his tour in Washington, DC, where he discovered that outside of the State Department he lived in "that peculiar loneliness of the returned exile who has not forgotten his own country but who has been pretty thoroughly forgotten by most of the people he ever knew in it."[2]

Moreover, his years abroad had isolated Kennan from political moods, cultural currents, and major events taking place in the United States. As he himself admitted, the "exile" was not only increasingly estranged from contemporary America, but also sought some dimly remembered past: "The dominant reaction on my part to that entire year in the United States was a growing understanding and nostalgia for America's past and an uneasiness about her future. I felt a powerful longing to identify myself more closely with everything America had once been; and a decided reluctance to identify myself with what it seemed to be becoming."[3]

His firsthand witness, 1937–1938, of the grimness and social deterioration of Depression-era America merely reinforced his melancholy forebodings. His residence in Alexandria, a Virginia suburb of Washington, was not particularly happy; he complained about dirt, rats, and decay. And Alexandria's waterfront, two blocks from his house, showed signs of neglect comparable to the worst ruin in Europe: its sunken boats, silted slips, and rotting wharves left Kennan morose. Although he admired the courage and optimism of his few acquaintances in the New Deal administration, he felt they were destined to fail and so did not support them. At his most enthusiastic, he was neutral about Roosevelt's series of domestic reforms and improvisations to stabilize the economy.[4]

Among his business friends in Milwaukee, Kennan discovered frustration and mounting indignation at the allegedly sordid, dangerous course set by the federal government. In 1938, they opposed Roosevelt's wage-hour bill and his proposal to reorganize the management of government agencies along lines of greater efficiency and executive control. This latter proposal provoked outrage across the country as New Deal opponents and long-standing haters of the president charged him (in the estimation of Senator David Walsh) with trying to plunge "a dagger into the very heart of democracy" and with creating a despotism similar to Hitler's or Stalin's. Indeed, 1938 was a year of crisis for the New Deal administration—polls indicated a dip in the president's popularity; defeat of his court packing scheme and administrative reorganization plans suggested that Roosevelt had lost his magic; millions were unemployed and walking the streets. The fundamental questions were: Could the United States survive as a functioning society and in what form? Would it sink again to the level of Herbert Hoover's final year in office? As James MacGregor Burns has reminded readers in his biography of Roosevelt, "It was a major failure of American democracy that it was not able in the late 1930s to show that a great nation could provide jobs for its workers and food, clothes, and houses for its people . . . millions were living in shanties and tenements, and some were not far from starvation."[5]

Irrespective of where Roosevelt's domestic adversaries and other citizens fell along the political spectrum, Kennan thought they did not appreciate the complexity of their problems and mindlessly accepted as sacrosanct institutions and political habits that no longer had legitimate reason for existence. He lamented that the country in 1938 was literally crumbling away, but its citizens, however well meaning most of them were, were not prepared to take decisive, emergency measures. In the wake of this perceived neglect and limited imagination, Kennan the diplomat began to formulate criticisms and recommendations for his own society.

The Prerequisites

To Kennan, only a highly centralized, powerful national government—far beyond anything envisioned by FDR—could save the country. He recognized, though, that such a political creation was anathema to most Americans, who he feared were practically anarchical in their habits and thoughts. And he despaired for the future strength and coherence of the federal government: "I felt that sooner or later it was bound to flounder hopelessly . . . in its own failures, and to break down completely, as it had threatened to do in 1933." Chaos, suffering, possibly bloodshed, would ensue. He predicted that the social and political disorders would inevitably produce new conceptions of political life and eventually form the basis of a new American regime.[6] Kennan had definite notions about the shape that the next national government should assume; consequently, he began writing a remarkable treatise, "The Prerequisites: Notes on Problems of the United States in 1938." It was, if nothing else, an arresting testimony to his disenchantment with American institutions and democracy.

His thinking along these lines dated to 1935, when, during recuperation from severe ulcers developed in Moscow, he was assigned temporarily to the US embassy in Vienna for a light detail tailored to encourage recovery of health and spirits. During this convalescence, Ambassador George Messersmith asked Kennan to study a recently promulgated Austrian social insurance law sponsored by the reactionary regime of Kurt von Schuschnigg. Kennan was impressed that the government had appointed a committee of experts to draft a comprehensive law that unified medical and financial procedures and placed the entire system on firm economic and fair social bases. Members of Parliament were not allowed to tinker with or trade on this issue of national importance; the entire process—in Kennan's view—had thus been freed from demagoguery, public wrangling, debate by laymen, and appeals to the public's emotion and greed. He concluded that this episode was a tribute to foresight and thoroughness and conveyed larger lessons: a benevolent dictatorship had great capacity for good, and rule by a minority of dedicated, selfless servants was more beneficial to society than rule by representatives captive to special interest groups and parochial-minded voters in small districts. He later recounted: "During the years to come—the uneasy years from 1936–1939, when our country rang with shrill debate about the issue of 'dictatorship versus democracy'—I was never able to forget these impressions. . . . Were not dictatorship and democracy only phrases? Was it not actually cruelty, stupidity, ignorance, violence and pretense which we hated? And could these not appear in any regime, no matter what it called itself?"[7]

Kennan's "Prerequisites" began by elucidating the fundamental problems afflicting the nation. He asserted that its chief political institutions, exemplified by the Constitution, were dated and inapplicable, after one hundred and fifty years, to current crises. Since the founding, enormous changes had occurred, and the just regulation of human relationships had become infinitely complicated. Furthermore, American industrial and agricultural production no longer functioned smoothly, and the government for all its tampering could not restore vigor and health to the economy. He also complained that the social effects of uncontrolled industrialization and hasty development were pernicious: the population had lost confidence in its ideals, and crime, corruption, and racial antagonisms were rampant. The solutions offered by the two major political parties failed to comprehend the magnitude of unprecedented social calamities. A paternalistic central government had not succeeded where the advocates of *laissez-faire* had failed.

The inspired authors of the Constitution were not culpable, however. Indeed, if they could return, they would shudder to discover that their heirs had been too dull for continuing political work bravely begun. Kennan blamed subsequent generations, including his own, "for distorting the pattern which the framers of the Constitution laid down, for perverting what was supposed to be a representative government into a boss ridden democracy, for admitting into this country millions of new elements incapable of understanding our conceptions of government and determined . . . to constitute the means for the abuse of these conceptions by unscrupulous demagogues, and—finally—for a general cowardliness and reluctance to take responsibility in questions of political authority."[8]

Kennan's "Prerequisites" also contained an attack against the Congress. He protested that the legislative branch was inadequate to meet the demands of a modern state for intelligent legislation. Congressmen were not individually or collectively responsible for this state of affairs as they had not created the miserable political system; they were, instead, creatures of it. The method of their selection assured that only mediocre and timid men would succeed to office. Aggravating matters further, they were beholden only to the most conspicuous elements in their little constituencies, yet were charged with legislating for the whole nation's welfare. The majority of congressmen were frightfully bound, narrow-minded: "Even freed of their bosses and constituents, they would have a hard time finding reasonable answers to the problems placed before them, due to their limitations of intelligence and character. Saddled as they are with the demands of sectional and special interests, they do not even try to keep national interests in mind in their legislative work."[9] The laws they passed amounted to compromises among diverse, self-seeking interest groups and bore little relation to central issues.

Kennan believed that a mischievous minority—special interest groups and their professional politicians—had corrupted the principle of universal suffrage. This small portion of the population unfairly wielded the power of government in support of selfish concerns; the notion of a larger good, it could not or would not understand. Even if Americans could miraculously eliminate such impediments to majority rule, Kennan still doubted the principle and wisdom of popular government; most citizens were too unenlightened and varied in their political commitments to participate in a responsible government: "It is obvious that there are millions of people in this country who haven't the faintest conception of the rights or wrongs of the complicated questions with which the federal government is faced."[10]

These people were not only ignorant, but were also duped by frauds, bought off, shrewdly manipulated by party machines, altogether helpless and bewildered. They were untrained to political traditions, often lacked national feeling, and, when given political responsibility, inevitably turned it over to the most determined self-seekers. As this condition was unjustifiable and dangerous for the United States, Kennan recommended that the category of citizens composing the unfit should, for the good of the country, henceforth no longer vote.

Naturalized citizens—and resident aliens who Kennan erroneously thought were allowed to vote—ought in any new order to be disenfranchised. Since at least 1930 he had held, as did many Foreign Service officers, that the millions of immigrants from southern and eastern Europe exercised disproportionate sway over traditional political participants, who in turn were fast becoming neglected in the land of their forebears.[11] A self-conscious descendant of eighteenth-century New England settlers, Kennan wrote with feeling that "anyone who has held a position of any responsibility in the federal government can confirm the fact that a newly arrived alien who happens to belong to one of the well organized nationality groups can get much more in the way of favorable action out of Washington than the average Tom, Dick or Harry whose ancestors have so far merged into the American picture that their foreign origin, if determinable at all, can no longer be recognized." The true American, by nature diffident, was at risk of becoming a second-class citizen. He was modest to a fault, too decent and content with his small lot to be easy prey for political hucksters. Consequently, his meager status as a resident of the country and his party allegiance was unknown to the local ward-heelers. "The member of one of the nationality groups" by contrast was "registered and catalogued and the group has its particular congressmen and senators to do its bidding in the national capital."[12]

Kennan admitted that his proposal would bar some mentally qualified voters, but their sacrifice was necessary and they would eventually appreciate the advantages of a sound government and high-minded politics. In the meantime, dishonest politicians would lose an important source of their misbegotten power. Foreign governments, too, would no longer have direct influence in domestic affairs, and millions of confused "semi-digested" new arrivals would no longer fall victim to "rent-sharks, ward-heelers and confidence men of the big cities." Kennan's prescription for dealing with first-generation Americans was thus in the tradition of militant nativism and equaled, in some ways surpassed, the objectives of the Know-Nothings, who in the mid-nineteenth century had advocated increasing the five-year period of naturalization by nine or fifteen years and reserving political office for American-born citizens.[13]

Kennan believed that American women also possessed too much power. Similar to the treatment accorded naturalized citizens, women's political privileges required drastic revision. Elimination of the nineteenth amendment might be difficult to accomplish, but it was necessary as the United States had become a ridiculous matriarchy:

> In no other great nation have women been given remotely the power in social, economic and political affairs that they have in this country. They control in large part the family. They control in still greater part the nation's purse. They dominate cultural life, as the greatest market for magazines, books, films, etc. They have their lobbies in Washington and the politicians tremble at their approach.

Regrettably, despite her privileges and power, the American woman had not generally lived up to her duties. Her social clubs had become symbols of mindless activity. She had unwisely delivered great power to lobbyists, charlatans, and racketeers. And she had, according to Kennan, squandered the delightful qualities of her own sex. In comparison with the women of other countries, she was "delicate, high-strung, unsatisfied, flat-chested and flat-voiced. The higher she is in the social and economic scale the more true these things are—and the greater the part she takes in politics."[14] (Very likely Kennan here had in mind Davies's wife.) This unfortunate trend had to be reversed, and Kennan exhorted that women revert to traditional roles and limit their civic participation to family picnics, children's parties, church socials—the last, incidentally, should proceed unencumbered by outside speakers. By retreating in this manner, the American woman would spare herself and her country a great deal of stress and discomfort; she would recover the strength and dignity that had been so lightly forsaken.

In Kennan's view, the American black, bereft of power (in the late 1930s, Congress was still unwilling to pass an anti-lynching law) represented the most glaring failure in the country's political history. His condition was a national disgrace, and seventy years of nominal enfranchisement had done nothing to ameliorate his plight. While over the decades he had become a pitiable ward of the government, his economic misery and "physical and nervous disintegration" progressed unabated. Emergency conditions called for emergency measures, but Kennan doubted that they would be forthcoming from the representatives regularly supported by black voters: "On the contrary, these people merely clutter up the processes of government and impede any sort of constructive progress. The lack of the franchise could make the Negro little more defenseless than he is." Repeal of black suffrage, reasoned Kennan, would force the white population to develop a deeper sense of responsibility for the black man's welfare. After all, he claimed, "It is a national characteristic that we are kinder to those who, like our children, are openly dependent on our kindness than to those who are (supposedly) able to look after themselves."[15]

White, American-born men apparently occupied the best social positions from which to lead the nation. Kennan expected that by introducing voting restrictions the basis of political power would revert to those people who by virtue of background and experience were best qualified to exercise authority.

Given the failings of the Constitution, the political parties, and the electorate, Kennan taught that the best solution to problems in the United States lay "along a road which very few Americans are willing to contemplate: along the road which leads through constitutional change to the authoritarian state." To deflect predictable criticisms, Kennan argued that neither pure democracy nor pure dictatorship had ever existed anywhere. The terms stood for ideal types of political regimes, but were too imprecise and emotive to be useful in discussions about practical politics. In the case of "democracy," he contended that most people uncritically accepted the view that it consisted of some unspecified mix of personal liberty and majority rule. "But," he objected, "personal liberty in a society which has taxes, police and unemployment, is a relative term itself. And majority rule is a dangerous measuring stick to apply in a country where a good percentage of local and state governments are in the hands of political machines and where the mainsprings of federal legislation are lobbies, patronage and local interest."[16] As for "dictatorship," it was an elusive term, not a scientifically rigorous concept. The centralization of power involved questions of degree, and even the most entrenched, absolute rulers consulted advisors, took into account the needs of prominent citizens, and were concerned enough with popular opinion to try influencing it through propaganda.

Kennan argued that regimes in most countries did not fit neatly into the categories of conventional political typology. China, for example, was led by an autocrat, Chiang Kai-shek, but most Americans did not hold him in contempt as a dictator. Japan, however, was widely dismissed as undemocratic, though few people could recognize any one identifiable dictator. Other countries usually held in esteem— some in eastern Europe and in Latin America—were not, in fact, paragons of democratic virtue. Semantic ambiguity and partisanship thus confounded intellectual clarity. And Kennan held that both terms were clichés, loosely applied by people for emotional reasons and convenience; in reality, the bogey-man of dictatorship and the angel of democracy were equally irrelevant—just too amorphous—for a serious appraisal of American political defects and prospects.[17]

As for the proper ends of national government, Kennan posited that it should raise the standards and quality of the citizen's housing, food, clothing, and recreation. Citizens, he also recommended, "must be taught to be more humane and more decent in their relations with one another. Finally, if they are to be happy, they should be given the feeling that they are participating individually in a common program . . . that their efforts are not purely individualistic and selfish, that they are contributing toward the general improvement of the society in which they live."[18] Beyond this sketchy program Kennan did not venture, but simply wanted to suggest the proper direction for future American government policies. He refused to describe a distant millennium, a fault he ascribed to Marxists, and was only casually concerned with the exact shape of future political institutions. Instead, he was engaged by the question of the sort of people who would bear responsibility for government and who would participate directly in the exercise of power.

Kennan suggested the deliberate cultivation of a new political elite, specially groomed, recruited from every region and class of society. Fitness for service would be determined by character, education, and aptitude, augmented by later training and experience. An organization above political bickering, outside of narrow partisan causes, and indifferent to its own popular image would choose, primarily from the nation's youth, those men destined for a superior political education and ultimate leadership.

Once enlisted into the new elite group, each man would dedicate himself to a life of public duty. The conventional joys of private life and work aimed at amassing wealth would have to be renounced; members of the organization "would have to subject themselves to discipline as they would if they entered a religious order. Many of them would doubtless have to face—at first—the opposition of parents and pedagogues and the scorn of less idealistic fellows."[19] Yet the intrinsic rewards of service to the nation and true comradeship would provide ample compensation.

Meanwhile, the future leaders would be spared the philistinism of American colleges and would be mercifully freed as adults from the shallowness of ordinary American suburban life. They would constitute, in other words, a disciplined vanguard of untrammeled young people. Power would be theirs once the progressive decline of American morale and life convinced citizens of the need to surrender authority to a competent group, endowed with the courage to accept fateful responsibility. Other organizations also—unnamed, unworthy ones—would be waiting to pick up the shreds of political life and lead the country, but they would have in Kennan's youthful men obstinate competitors imbued with decency and justice. Neither demagogic nor tied to the "fetish of democracy," this elite entity, given the chance to govern, would chart unexplored worlds and forever discard bankrupt institutions and practices of the past.

After making these observations and posing these recommendations, "The Prerequisites" abruptly broke off. It was abandoned and never again directly drew Kennan's attention.[20] He recognized how extraordinary his advice would strike most Americans and never hoped seriously that his ideas could be implemented. But "The Prerequisites," like Plato's *Republic* on which it was partially modeled, shows vividly the author's fears, as well as his ultimate preferences. At the same time, "Prerequisites" shares an affinity with much of the managerial-statist elitism and anti-democratic temperament that characterized elements in the Progressive Era, the 1920s, and the New Deal. Clearly the animus that drove an H. L. Mencken to write his diatribes against American culture and politics was the same as that exciting Kennan. In his *Notes on Democracy,* for example, Mencken savaged interest groups, representative government, and *"Homo vulgaris"* and took swipes at ethnic minorities and newly enfranchised women. Of democracy he wrote: "In place of a government with a fixed purpose and a visible goal, it sets up a government that is a mere function of the mob's vagaries, and that maintains itself by constantly bargaining with those vagaries. Its security depends wholly upon providing satisfactory bribes for the prehensile minorities that constitute the mob, or that have managed to deceive and inflame the mob."[21] Kennan was also an admirer of Theodore Roosevelt, and his ideas about political reforms and the responsibility of enlightened people to serve the nation—the mugwump impulse—are echoed in "Prerequisites." So, too, the concern of Brooks and Henry Adams about the impact of modernity on American women, and Walter Lippmann's indictment of American politics and the desirability of giving freer rein to a class of expert managers— "organized intelligence"—reverberate in Kennan's half-finished essay. In fact, it reads very much like a queer interpretation or eccentric amalgam of Lippmann's literary-theoretical corpus as it stood in the 1930s. Consciously or not, Kennan borrowed heavily from Lippmann's broadsides against slovenly thought in the United States, antiquated institutions, and fickle public opinion; Kennan's emphasis on the need for increased discipline in social and governmental action and for more imagination in politics and cultural life also recall Lippmann.[22]

In addition, "Prerequisites" reveals not only that young Kennan shared many of the popular reservations of his countrymen about blacks and immigrants, but mixed them with other intellectual traditions that are anomalous coming from an American. The proposition that the incompetence and muddle of democratic politics could be overcome by a vanguard elite was then the object of experiment in eastern Europe, but outside of some intellectual circles was not widely appreciated in America. Kennan himself was disgusted by the cruelty and distortion of the elite principle as it was exercised by communist party rule in Russia. Yet his Brahmin-like instincts, so similar to Mencken's, his confidence in what a strong government could do if properly led for just ends, and his respect for the political and intellectual tradition of Europe's old aristocracy were woven into "Prerequisites." Taken as a piece, it invites considerable, obvious criticism. More important, though, than taking issue with it is to determine how the themes developed therein have recurred or been developed in subsequent years by Kennan, in relation especially to his preoccupation with foreign affairs.

Since rising to national prominence in the late 1940s, he has polemicized against the untoward influence of ethnic and special interest groups on American foreign policy. He believes that Croat-Americans, for example, helped influence, through their representatives in Congress, the Kennedy administration to adopt an ill-advised policy toward Yugoslavia in which MFN status for Tito's regime was— recklessly from the standpoint of American interests in the Balkans—revoked. During a delicate period of the Korean War he was dismayed by the damage inflicted on US diplomacy by the irresponsible and blatant interference of the China lobby and its congressional allies.[23]

He also attributes the delay in his repatriation and that of his colleagues in the

American embassy in Berlin to the meddling of congressmen unduly concerned about European Jews. Kennan and the rest of the embassy staff were detained (in Bad Nauheim, near Frankfurt) for five months by Nazi authorities after the start of German-US hostilities in December 1941. During the term of their captivity, which was unpleasant and yet did not approach the terror of a concentration camp, the American embassy group learned disappointing news. As Kennan explains in his memoirs: "half of us were to be left behind, in German custody, in order to free space on [an] exchange vessel for Jewish refugees. Why? Because individual Congressmen, anxious to please individual constituents, were interested in bringing these refugees to the United States, and this—although the refugees were not citizens—was more important than what happened to us."[24] Eventually, the entire embassy staff returned safely to the United States. Nonetheless, Kennan was outraged and charged that the State Department was more concerned with relieving itself of congressional pressures than rescuing its own employees.

Later, during the Cold War, Kennan, as director of the State Department's Policy Planning Staff, was not entirely convinced about the resilience and reliability of some minority groups. He explained in a 1949 memorandum that communism exerted a relatively strong appeal "to maladjusted groups: in our country—Jews, Negroes, immigrants—all those who feel handicapped in the framework of a national society."[25] It was, incidentally, during this period that the government revived in modern guise the notorious Alien and Sedition Acts and resolved to deport all communist aliens. Kennan, who at one point thought it might be useful to monitor the activities of obviously, or potentially, subversive groups, was flabbergasted by the excesses and hysteria of the early Cold War era.

His worst original fears about Congress and political hacks were vindicated in a sense by the triumph of Senator Joseph McCarthy and the damage he wrought on the State Department, including many of Kennan's friends and colleagues, such as Charles Thayer, John Service, and John Paton Davies. Kennan responded by championing several men who were unfairly accused and defended the department and the Foreign Service from some of its most implacable congressional foes.

He has also worried for a long time since about the impact of misguided, uninformed, changeable congressional opinion and ineptness on the purpose and resolve of American diplomacy. He wrote in 1951 that democratic foreign policy is "limited at the outset by the level of enlightment, maturity, thoughtfulness, and moral courage that prevails in the ranks of the legislators. . . . Plainly anything that would operate to raise that level, to increase awareness of international implications of domestic problems, to enhance the dignity and maturity of legislative procedures, and to heighten the congressional consciousness of obligation to the public weal (as opposed to parochial electoral interests) in matters affecting foreign affairs, would be important."[26] He has tried through his frequent testimony before congressional committees and in his writings to educate those American legislators active in foreign policy. Nothing, however, has caused Kennan to cease worrying about the damage sound diplomacy has sustained because small-minded politicians have found it inconvenient, or inexpedient, to transcend their petty concerns.

In 1956, he wrote with conviction and obviously with his own experiences in mind that the diplomat generally views domestic politics "as a seething cauldron in which rises to the surface, by the law of averages, certain mutation of the human species." The diplomat—that is, Kennan—has always harbored a dislike and suspicion for the pompous members of the political fraternity: "for the bombast, the demagogue, the jingo, the poseur, the man touched with the intoxication of power, the man for whom the issues at stake in his country's relations with the outside world are means to a personal end. And too often it seems, looking at it from an embassy in a foreign capital, that such are the natures bound by the law of averages to be propelled most often to the surface in the uninhibited workings of political competition."[27]

As for the role of public opinion in foreign policy, Kennan has long maintained that it should be minor, not a heavy constraint on trained policymakers who alone know the details of international problems and can carefully calculate a reasonable diplomacy. As he told a Haverford College audience in 1955, he was unconvinced that foreign policy should be the product of popular and casual discussions and public opinion polls. Instead, long-term foreign policy planning can be usefully accomplished only "by a group of people very carefully selected from the standpoint of experience and training and ability, and in a position not only to have access to all the information at the government's disposal (which the public can never have) but also to devote to this task their full time, and to approach it not just with speculations off the top of their heads but with hard, intense work, probing . . . for the real facts, balancing the most complicated sort of political equations." He cautioned that any person who is not in such a position of knowledge, experience, and training and who does not have time enough to study foreign policy problems deeply should be careful about setting his judgment up against that of the government. Better this statist approach, Kennan advised, "than to regard ourselves as a collection of 160 million grandstand quarterbacks and scream our hasty injunctions to our players on the football field, whose knowledge of the real situation is better than ours and who are too pressed by the din of battle to heed our voices."[28] Citizens who choose to speak on international political issues should be cool in their tone, always circumspect.

The debatable merit of the above advice notwithstanding, Kennan has usually been faithful to his own injunctions even when discussing the most controversial issues. In the early 1980s, for example, he warned the government about its nuclear policy and the arms race; these comments appropriately were based on a background of five decades of involvement in Soviet-American relations. During the Vietnam War, long after he played an important policymaking role, Kennan argued against American actions in Southeast Asia. But his most important remarks on the subject were addressed to—and at the behest of—Senator J. William Fulbright and the Senate Foreign Relations Committee. Kennan never went near a war protest rally.

With respect to another great, divisive issue, civil rights, Kennan's attitude seems to have shifted somewhat since he wrote "The Prerequisites." From the 1950s on, he has been vexed by the adverse effects of civil rights violations and racial strife in the United States for American policy in the Third World and has admonished Americans not to become complacent about this "most terrible and serious of our national problems." Failure to deal with it squarely would have adverse repercussions "for our population in a world whose population is largely of color different from that of the majority of Americans."[29] However, his commitment to racial justice for its own sake in the United States has been peculiarly qualified. He wrote a friend in 1965 that he had an attachment for the concept of apartheid and though the South African practice of it was full of problems, a modified version of it might work in the United States: "I would rather see the Negroes advance to self-respect and self-realization as a racial community than to witness the agonizing and unsuccessful efforts now being made in this country to find a proper place for them in our society by pretending to ignore the factor of their color."[30]

About his frank attitude toward American women, nothing important is publicly available. As director of the Policy Planning Staff, he did recruit a woman of indisputable talent and experience. Dorothy Fosdick, PhD, was a specialist in international organizations and had helped represent American interests at Dumbarton Oaks. Although Kennan was never sanguine about the contribution that the United Nations and other international agencies could make to world politics, he respected Fosdick and obviously modified somewhat his most caustic, earlier views.

Finally, a word about Kennan's original proposals for amending the Constitution. He never revived them, although he has on more than one occasion made strong intimations. And only once since 1938 has he publicly, explicitly urged modifying government institutions at all and then with quite different aims. He testified to the Senate in 1960, shortly after Francis Gary Powers and the U-2 affair, that to coordinate the various agencies and branches of government for purposes of foreign policy, a new post—more elevated than the secretary of state—should be created. The State Department, Defense Department, CIA, and FBI would be led by one man who would exercise ultimate authority for foreign policy and national security; such a czar of international affairs would function as a type of first minister to the president. Kennan advised that this new apparatus for centralized control and discipline in the executive branch should help produce a well-coordinated foreign policy. But, he insisted, it was not an adequate substitute for good men. While his proposal provoked a minor stir, it attracted little support. Whereas he hoped to replace the compromises and hodge-podge policies of the government's foreign policy agencies, his congressional and journalistic critics warned against unwitting steps toward dictatorship.

The Foreign Service

Horrified by what he perceived to be the banality of American politicians and the disorderliness of American social and political affairs, Kennan found refuge in the Foreign Service, which, more than the United States, was for years his true home. He once declared in a revealing moment, "The central fact about me is that I'm a career foreign service officer and proud of it."[31] Until he found identity as a scholar and safety in the Institute for Advanced Study in Princeton, he derived his professional purpose and satisfactions within the context of the diplomatic corps. His country may have been oblivious to his warnings, indifferent to his suggestions. The Foreign Service, though, often in peril itself, was a more manageable community and better suited to Kennan's taste. For a period in the late 1940s he served as president of the American Foreign Service Association and in one way or another worked over the course of decades for the Service's integrity and prosperity.

In this connection, just four years after writing "The Prerequisites," Kennan turned to a favorite theme: the need for excellence of character and intellect in those men charged with handling national affairs. Certainly he never again so baldly stated his case as he had in "The Prerequisites." Still, the attraction of a well-endowed, specially educated elite, removed from the partisan fray, and committed to the common good, never lost its luster for Kennan. Some of the farfetched recommendations contained in "The Prerequisites" found modified and respectable form in his plan (written in 1942) for improved Foreign Service recruitment and education.

Kennan's twenty-page memorandum on future Foreign Service needs and training was premised on the assumption that America's postwar commitments abroad would be large. To meet them, the United States would need to have at its disposal hundreds more professional diplomats. He proposed, therefore, that the Foreign Service take measures to attract the best, most dedicated men possible. Whereas in "The Prerequisites" Kennan compared his elite members' sense of duty with that of individuals in religious orders, he now urged that new Foreign Service officers regard their careers "as a calling and a way of life, like service in the army or navy, with standards of honor, discipline, and responsibility, with sanctions of precedent and tradition, with opportunities for authority and distinction no less than those which are aimed at in the armed forces." The men who would compose the diplomatic corps would hereafter constitute "an elite of American culture and character, and must . . . [be] for our own Government an instrument of maximum reliability, competence and utility in the foreign field."[32] Such a goal necessitated training the entire personality of the Foreign Service officer, not just his mind.

Kennan recommended the founding of a Foreign Service academy, similar in respects to West Point and Annapolis. Operated at government expense, administered by the State Department, the academy would combine aspects of a liberal arts college—smaller and more select than the Princeton of Kennan's experience—with qualities of military and naval schools. It would train carefully screened men from the ground up. Reflecting "The Prerequisites," Kennan wrote, "Its graduates would be bound to special standards of efficiency in their work, would be expected to subordinate their private lives to their work in a considerable degree, but would in return receive special advantages in advancement and in opportunity for the exercise of responsibility."[33]

The academy would, as anticipated in "The Prerequisites," admit only the most promising individuals, irrespective of their class and region. Within limits they would be encouraged to develop their particular interests and tastes; however, the academy would aim at producing a recognizable type that was intellectually mature and possessed impeccable character. The academy would even try to inculcate in its students something of the manners and traditions of late eighteenth-century American diplomacy. In this way, Kennan believed, the shallowness of native breeding and uneven education that had handicapped the careers of too many American diplomats would be purged from the corps.

Not only would the academy be extremely selective in its admission policy, but the requirements for graduation were to be far tougher than those of any private college in the country. Kennan reckoned that half the students in each freshman class would be winnowed out before graduation on the basis of scholastic deficiency or other unsuitability. Only the most exceptional men would remain. Apparently, he did not worry about the effects on student morale of an unusually high attrition rate. Discipline, moreover, would be strict for underclassmen, equal to that of West Point or Annapolis. And throughout all four years, the principles of discipline and obedience would be inviolable. A stringent honor system, administered in part by the students, would also obtain.

Students would be furnished with uniforms, and thereby false distinctions and snobbery—of the sort Kennan had suffered from in college—would have little chance to infect the students: "I know of no better way to impress on men's minds that the artificial advantages and protections of home life are no longer operative and that they must reconcile themselves to submission and cooperation in an organization, than by the wearing of a uniform." Kennan, the St. John's graduate, also felt that close-order drill and basic military training would be useful adjuncts to the academic curriculum.[34]

The course of study would emphasize history, foreign languages, geography, law, and English. The first two years of instruction would be prescribed, and upon graduation every student would have a working knowledge—both written and oral—of French, German, and Spanish. Instructors at the academy would be men with experience of life abroad and would typify in themselves serious values. They would participate much more directly in student life than faculty at most colleges and would take a personal interest in all aspects of each student's development. Two hours of physical education a day for underclassmen would also be mandated as the men would not have time for a normal social life: "only an exacting and physically hard regime could maintain nervous and physical health at the necessary level."[35]

Finally, during summer recesses, students would spend time working on farms and in industry or travel overseas under the auspices of a responsible organization. In this way the young diplomatic elite would know something of common life at home and abroad and would be immunized against effete habits.

Upon graduation, a student would be eligible to enter the Foreign Service or any other branch of the government involved with international relations. Also, the Foreign Service would accept a few men who did not attend the academy, just as the army accepts officers who do not train at West Point. Clearly, though, the academy graduate would belong to a privileged fraternity and would enjoy attendant advantages.

Kennan's proposal, although submitted, was never acted upon. In part his timing was poor; the State Department in 1942 was too preoccupied with war to study Kennan's ideas. In subsequent years, he has periodically called for such an academy and—despite bitter moments during the McCarthy era when he advised that young men could not expect to pursue worthwhile careers in the Foreign

Service—has urged that promotion of a superior diplomatic corps be given government priority.

Kennan has argued that such an august body should not only enjoy broad responsibilities in the international field, but should also be prepared to play a role in domestic affairs. In this regard, Kennan's remarks to a group of fellow Foreign Service officers in 1944 are significant. He explained to them that men returning from military service after the war would be dismayed to find widespread evidence of decline in American society. Family life, according to Kennan, had suffered greatly, juvenile delinquency was rising, and many people had grown accustomed to easy jobs, high wages, and soft living. He predicted that men back from overseas would be singularly lacking in sympathy "for people who have been drawing two or three hundred dollars a month and blackmailing the public for more, in return—in many instances—for precious little real effort on their own part, while soldiers and sailors have faced death on the meager pay of the armed forces."[36]

Kennan feared that these problems, combined with increased racial strife, would lead to political disorders and violence. Thus he, along with some other analysts at the time, warned that economic and social tensions might strain postwar America beyond endurance. In language reminiscent of "The Prerequisites," he stated that the new crisis would call for reforms both in public life and in basic concepts of society, reforms that would not be easy for most Americans to accept. After all, Americans had serious blind spots, "and one of the worst of them is our stubborn and reactionary belief that we have a form of government so superior that it needs no further development or improvement, and that it will automatically remain the acme of all political genius, without any further cultivation on our part." Relentless forces of cruelty and intolerance were already prepared to assault the United States and administer a severe test to the nation's brittle institutions. But US professional diplomats luckily occupied a superior position in the forthcoming contest: "We have had exceptional opportunities for judging our own country because we have had to learn something about other countries as well, and we, therefore, have a standard of comparison. It may well be up to us to take a prominent part in finding solutions for some of the really crucial internal problems." He ended his remarks by saying that in the future combat against various domestic malefactors the Foreign Service would have a peculiarly responsible and lonely part to play.[37] Postwar America, of course, was not nearly so bleak or desperate as Kennan supposed. Yet, when timidity and intolerance were later loosed on the land, embodied by the phenomenon of McCarthyism, the Foreign Service proved to be not a leader in the resistance, but a major victim.

Young Kennan believed that the Foreign Service officer, if properly encouraged, trained, and supported by his government, could confidently pursue the worthy objectives of his art: securing peaceful commerce and relations between his country and others. Establishment of a Foreign Service academy would constitute (as the outstanding Ecole Nationale d'Administration today produces France's civil servants) both a practical and symbolic commitment by the government and by the nation to expertise in diplomacy. Instead, Kennan has complained for years, in a case of classic projection, the American diplomat is isolated from his society, usually held suspect, and his special contributions to the country's domestic life and foreign policy have been rejected.

Despite the shock of McCarthyism and other instances of public abuse or neglect of the Foreign Service, the diplomat, Kennan has always stressed, cannot afford to indulge morbid doubt about his critical tasks. He must be willing to forego public approval and appreciation for the sake of his solemn obligation, at the heart of which is everything that people care about. Kennan wrote in 1957 that a diplomatic agency of "quality and excellence . . . could render signal service not only to [the government] but to our anxious, war-torn and atom-menaced world at large."[38] Unfortunately, according to him, such an institution has not been founded for want of public understanding.

*   *   *   *

Both "The Prerequisites" and his scheme for a Foreign Service academy reveal the degree to which young Kennan, son of a rather ordinary, middle-class, midwestern family, cherished—in an idiosyncratic way to be sure—the ideal of an unassailable aristocracy of character and mind. His presumption that foreign affairs occupied a position of primacy in the life of America and his own functioning as a diplomat led him to emphasize the needs for excellence in the Foreign Service. Besides, his real convictions, never mind his professed yearning for original, pristine American principles, were so alien to the United States in the late 1930s and early 1940s that he did not dare hope for the realization of his fondest political preferences on a national scale. They were then, as they would be today, simply astonishing.

There is no evidence available to indicate that Kennan showed "The Prerequisites" to anyone. Probably, however, he did share it or its main ideas with one or two close friends—Bohlen and Bernard Gufler would have been the best candidates—as he was not in the habit of writing only for himself.[39] Bohlen, in any case, since the 1930s was fully aware of Kennan's reservations about American democracy. Along with other of Kennan's colleagues over the years such as Carleton Savage (Policy Planning) and Llewelyn Thompson (Soviet expert), Bohlen recognized that Kennan's contempt for the workings of American politics led him on numerous occasions to advocate positions that neither the president nor Congress—both entirely sensible to public opinion—would endorse.[40]

Not until 1968, when he wrote "Rebels Without a Program," did Kennan record anything about his misgivings of American democracy comparable to "The Prerequisites." In "Rebels" he damned the student protest movement and declared that he was skeptical of whether civil disobedience had a place in American society.[41] This statement, indeed the whole tenor of the essay, disturbed many of Kennan's admirers, including W. H. Auden. In fact, although he later qualified some of its harshest language, the essay amounted to unvarnished Kennan and indicated the extent to which he has always stayed out of sympathy with political life in the United States.

So, too, he has been at odds with most of American foreign policy and has been distressed by what he has regarded as the oversimplified and inconsistent views emanating from Washington. He has credited this problem to a distaste within the

US political establishment for professionalism in diplomacy; consequently the foreign policy of the United States has been hobbled.[42] Inattentive to and distrustful of the requirements for genuine statesmanship, democratic America—for George Kennan—has cleaved to an external policy without ballast, easily subject to shifts in the public mood, and at the mercy of novices. Just as in his thirties, Kennan over the decades has attributed these facts to the persistence of bad political habits and dubious popular assumptions; the expert must languish, the amateur prevails.

4

Nazi Germany and the
Future of Europe

Kennan's despair in the late 1930s over what he viewed as the deplorable condition of American society and politics was moderated by a newfound higher regard in which he held his native Wisconsin. The disdain that he felt for it in his youth and at Princeton had been displaced during his years abroad by sentimental affection. His periodic visits to Wisconsin, particularly in 1938, affirmed in him an appreciation for the land and its inhabitants: he found them kindly, interested, and open-minded. He also entertained fanciful ideas about the political virtues Wisconsin embodied and the lessons it could teach the rest of the country. More than any other in the union, he believed his home state possessed

> the prerequisites for political development far in advance of the federal govern-
> ment. Could not the questions of the industrial era be more easily solved in this
> compact commonwealth, with its healthy political life, its admirable balance
> between industry and agriculture, its relatively sturdy population, and its tradition
> of humaneness and good nature? Could it not become, as some of the small neutral
> countries of Europe had become, a reservoir of human decency and common
> sense?[1]

He was tempted in the summer of 1938 to resign from the Foreign Service—which failed to meet adequately the financial needs of his family—and to pursue in Wisconsin, like previous generations of Kennans, a life in farming or some other "small job." After a period of close appraisal and doubt he chose instead to accept the government's next assignment: to serve as second secretary to the legation in Prague.

The Czechoslovak crisis had been simmering throughout that summer, and Kennan could not resist the chance of playing a role, however small. After all, he reasoned, he had watched the storm brew for ten years and did not wish to miss the climax.[2] He arrived in the beautiful baroque Czech capital at exactly the time when

Neville Chamberlain, Edouard Daladier, and Adolf Hitler reached agreement on Czechoslovakia's fate in Munich.

During the six years of war that soon afterward followed, Kennan served not only in Prague but in other European posts, all of which provided him with broad exposure to the conflict in its political and diplomatic dimensions. The first issue that dominated his thinking, coinciding with his tenure in Prague and Berlin, had to do with the nature of Nazi-German politics and Hitler's organization of economy and empire. After US entry into the war, while in London as counselor on the American delegation to the European Advisory Commission, Kennan was principally concerned with the conduct of hostilities and planning for postwar Europe. Then, in 1944 and 1945, when stationed back in Moscow under Ambassador Averell Harriman, he considered the prospects for Soviet-US relations after Germany's defeat.

Hitler's European Empire

By Kennan's standard of evaluation, Czechoslovakia did not qualify in late 1938 as one of the compact, well-balanced, neutral states of Europe that contained sufficient resources of social cohesion and venerable traditions. An artificial creation of the Versailles agreement, Czechoslovakia was young, polyglot, multireligious, unevenly developed economically, and riven by ethnic rivalries; moreover, the "historic provinces" of Bohemia and Moravia were surrounded on three sides by territory of the Third Reich. And in the Sudeten fringe lived a majority of the country's 3.5 million Germans, many of whom were disaffected and on whose behalf Hitler professed outrage against alleged Czech abuses.

As a result of Munich, the Sudetenland was incorporated into the German Reich, and a rump Czechoslovakia—deprived of its strategic fortifications, subject to Hungarian and Polish territorial demands, challenged by independence movements in Slovakia and Ruthenia, and deserted by the democratic powers—foundered pathetically. The denouement came in mid-March 1939, when units of the German army, contrary to promises made by Hitler, occupied Prague and established the Protectorate of Bohemia and Moravia. The property and lives of more than 390,000 Jews were instantly placed in jeopardy; backward Ruthenia was seized by Hungary; Poland acquired Teschen; and Slovakia declared independence, which it maintained against Hungary only on the basis of German sufferance.

However ignominious their own behavior at Munich and however startled they were by Hitler's cynical disregard of the Munich accords, neither the British nor the French were prepared to risk another war with Germany for the sake of Czech security or territorial integrity in 1939. Despite Churchill's repeated warnings, Britain had neglected the production of combat planes so that its air force was inferior to Germany's; the situation in available modern tanks and artillery pieces was little better. The government was also haunted by the specter of slaughter comparable to 1914–1918 and determined to avoid similar disaster. Compounding matters, the prime minister's attitude toward problems on the continent was

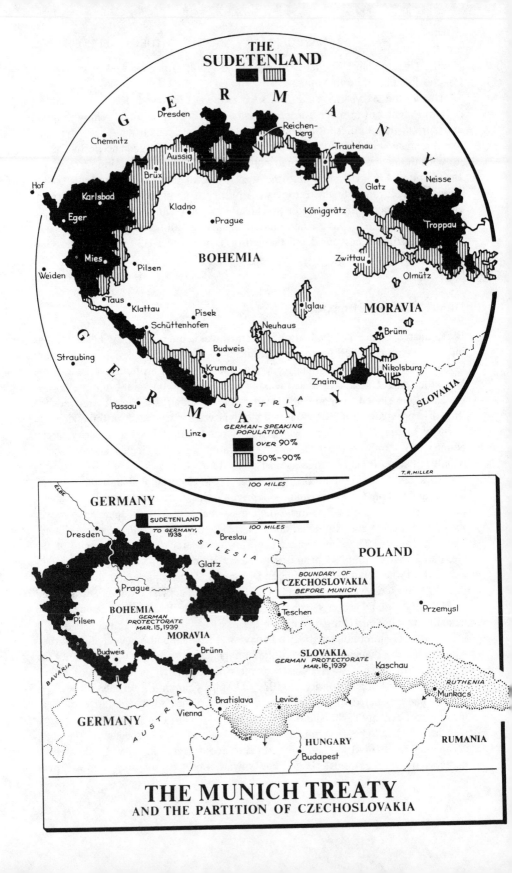

THE SUDETENLAND

GERMANY

Dresden

Chemnitz

Reichen-berg

Trautenau

Aussig

Brüx

Glatz

Neisse

Hof

Karlsbad

Kladno

Königgrätz

Troppau

Eger

Prague

BOHEMIA

Zwittau

Mies

Pilsen

Olmütz

Weiden

MORAVIA

Taus

Klattau

Pisek

Iglau

Straubing

Schüttenhofen

Neuhaus

Brünn

Budweis

Krumau

Nikolsburg

Passau

Znaim

SLOVAKIA

AUSTRIA

GERMANY

Linz

GERMAN-SPEAKING POPULATION

OVER 90%

50%-90%

T.R.MILLER

100 MILES

GERMANY

ELBE

SUDETENLAND

TO GERMANY, 1938

Dresden

Breslau

100 MILES

SILESIA

POLAND

Glatz

Prague

BOHEMIA

GERMAN PROTECTORATE MAR.15,1939

BOUNDARY OF CZECHOSLOVAKIA BEFORE MUNICH

Teschen

Przemysl

Pilsen

MORAVIA

Budweis

Brünn

SLOVAKIA

GERMAN PROTECTORATE MAR.16,1939

Kaschau

RUTHENIA

Munkacs

BAVARIA

AUSTRIA

Bratislava

Levice

GERMANY

Vienna

DANUBE

HUNGARY

RUMANIA

Budapest

THE MUNICH TREATY
AND THE PARTITION OF CZECHOSLOVAKIA

positively insular. During the period of war scare in 1938, Chamberlain exclaimed, "How horrible, fantastic, incredible it is, that we should be digging trenches and trying on gas-masks here because of a quarrel in a far-away country between people of whom we know nothing."[3]

The Czechs had never been lightly dismissed by the French; since Georges Clemenceau's day they had been regarded as worthwhile allies against a potential, revived German threat. Daladier's government, though, was not prepared to oppose German aggrandizement without British assistance. As for the USSR, the French had little confidence in the Red Army, the highest ranks of which were being decimated by the purges, and deemed Stalin's government as too unreliable to permit close cooperation.

The Soviets were bound by treaty to help protect Czechoslovakia, but only if France also acted. Daladier's capitulation along with Chamberlain's allowed the USSR to refrain from hostilities against Germany while not violating the letter of its pledge to Prague.[4] Not having been invited to send representatives to Munich, Stalin was never implicated by the Czech populace in the betrayal of their interests, a fact that explains the goodwill felt by many Czechs toward the Soviet Union during the war and in its aftermath until 1948. In any case, shortly after Munich the most industrially developed areas of Czechoslovakia became the first non-German territorial conquests of Hitler, and the only democratic regime in inter-war central Europe ceased to exist.[5]

The State Department viewed the German occupation and administration of Czech lands as a critical test case, the results of which would provide a fair indication of the ability of Hitler's regime in the future to rule over other non-German subjects. Consequently, after the US legation in Prague was abolished, Kennan was ordered to remain there and report events; until his assignment to Berlin in the autumn of 1939, he was the principal official American representative in Prague.

The demands of political reporting and analysis in German-occupied Prague were considerable, and Kennan recalled in later years that the experience was intellectually and emotionally invigorating. Although he subsequently complained that no more than five people in the State Department bothered to read his dispatches from Prague, they were in his assessment among his finest literary-political efforts. He felt that he was well equipped to follow Czech events in the wake of Munich as he was fluent in German, knew Slavic languages, and appreciated the main currents of European history: "Everything that I encountered, not only in Prague but in Bohemia and Moravia in general, was strangely understandable. . . . It all fitted into a picture . . . the story I had to tell almost wrote itself under my hand, . . . I had reached the peak of my usefulness as a political observer."[6] At the same time he was moved by the spectacle of a weak nation abandoned by erstwhile allies and subdued by powerful enemies.

Yet Kennan's attitude toward Czech democracy and its political viability was decidedly skeptical. At first, he mistakenly thought the new German-Czech

From *A History of Modern Germany*, 1840–1945, Vol. III by Hajo Holborn. Copyright © 1969 by Hajo Holborn. Reprinted by permission of Alfred A. Knopf, Inc.

arrangement might prove stable and improve overall the morale and material condition of the Czechs. Even though he respected many of the republic's achievements and correctly credited its civilian administration with a tolerance and decency notably lacking in its neighbors, Kennan was convinced that Czechoslovakia had grave weaknesses which no impartial observer could ignore, and which explained its final disappearance. He was signally impressed by Czechoslovakia's supposedly weak political institutions, which he related to his own misgivings about democratic politics, and found himself "unable to share that enthusiasm for democracy in Czechoslovakia that seemed almost an obsession to so many Anglo-Saxon liberals."[7]

Kennan maintained that any small European democracy based on the peasant and bourgeois classes would encounter severe problems, and one without an aristocratic ballast was bound to end badly; in the case of Czechoslovakia the absence of an aristocratic element amounted to a fatal handicap. Most politically active Czechs he dismissed as "little people," who derived primarily from the peasants and petty bourgeoisie involved in handicraft trades or retail merchandizing. And he regretted that many of the legislators and officials of the regime were jealous of the prestige and wealth of the Czech nobles, enjoyed exercising power over them, and took pleasure in deliberately exposing them to ridicule and humiliation. As a result, few aristocrats with a tradition of participation in the Austro-Hungarian empire or with the local authority and independence of judgment that comes from inherited wealth could be found in Prague's higher councils: "the new government apparatus came to be staffed largely with officials who [enjoyed] no great political prestige among their neighbors. As a ruling class, they suffered from the short-comings generic to social democracy. . . . They lacked courage, they lacked imagination, and they lacked self-confidence."[8]

Parallel to his diagnosis of social and political issues in the United States, Kennan believed that the competition of parties and partisan causes in Czechoslovakia prevented that country from dealing effectively with its bewildering domestic and international dilemmas. He predicted in August 1939, five months after the German invasion, that most Czechs would not welcome a return of the squabbling parties, middle-class timidity, and small-mindedness that had dominated life in the late republic.[9]

The defects that plagued democracies everywhere were aggravated, Kennan feared, by the density of population in Bohemia and Moravia. In such small territories as embraced by the two provinces, people were jammed together, and the distribution of goods and services was a cause of anxiety and dispute. Kennan pronounced:

> People who grew up in this atmosphere, whose education is confined to the. . . valleys between the Bohemian hills, do not enjoy the wide horizons of adventure and imagination which they might have acquired in the scope of youthful experience and if the vistas of mature accomplishment had been greater, and their behavior as officials is not generally characterized by any peculiar boldness or generosity.[10]

Kennan initially expected that association with broader, more varied Germany would provide future generations of Czech youths with the advantages of expanded social and intellectual education.

Kennan did speculate at one point that, if the Czechoslovaks were left to their own devices, they might evolve over one or two generations a governing class possessed of dignity and confidence, and internal dissension and jealousies could be contained at tolerable levels. But the very external conditions that had allowed the formation of Czechoslovakia in the first place were destined to cause its demise. First, the destruction of the Austro-Hungarian empire at the end of World War I created a political vacuum in the Danubian basin that inevitably would be filled by a new hegemonic power; the weak successor states to the Habsburg empire—Poland, Hungary, Czechoslovakia—could not guarantee stability in the heart of Europe and could not successfully oppose intervention by a strong, outside state.[11] Second, protested Kennan, Prague's inheritance from Vienna of the dismal problem of governing a multinational country damaged the entire Czechoslovak enterprise from the outset.

He believed that national feelings and antipathies, especially between German and Czech, ran too deep to allow resolution. The linguistic differences, conflicting values, and incompatible habits of the region's peoples had burdened the Austrian empire into collapse, and it was ludicrous to suppose that the unsophisticated provincials who composed Czech officialdom could better bind the wounds caused by centuries of ethnic conflict. In the twentieth century, German would never submit to Slav; the Slovaks were accustomed to being ruled by the dashing, essentially aristocratic Hungarians beside whom the Czech politicians seemed colorless and pedantic; the Ruthenians were pathologically opposed to Prague's attempts at improving their lot and besides were geographically and economically part of Hungary. The Czechs, whatever else they were and whatever good qualities they embodied, were not a natural *Herrenvolk*, and in their own interests should never have been charged with the thankless task of trying to organize their unruly neighbors under one government. "All in all," recorded Kennan, "I am inclined to question the conception of a Czechoslovak state entirely independent of any other large political unit in Central Europe and [composed of] a large proportion of non-Czech inhabitants. . . the Czechs are not equipped by tradition or by political development to bear such heavy responsibilities as an independent Czechoslovakia places upon them."[12]

Kennan, who had not the slightest sympathy for the fragmentation of Habsburg power, asserted—as had various central Europeans in the 1920s and 1930s, such as the Hungarian Oscar Jaszi—that establishment of a new, larger sovereign unit in the Danubian region was eminently desirable. The ideal solution to Kennan would entail the renunciation by local Germans and Czechs of their narrow national allegiances; in setting aside their particular pretensions they should also pay homage to transcendent symbols and authorities. If somehow the mischief inflicted by eighteenth- and nineteenth-century liberalism and democratic humanism could be undone, then Czech and German could return to the relatively harmonious relations of a previous epoch when both nations gratefully acknowledged the unifying, paternal, protective legitimacy of the Holy Roman empire.

Few other examples, he reasoned, in unconscious imitation of Henry Adams, better illustrated the wisdom of the past over the present than "the late Middle Ages, when Church and Emperor incorporated conceptions of divine and temporal power so vast and imposing that local rivalries paled before them like candles before the sunshine." Only with the recovery of the Church's sense of universal mission in Bohemia and Moravia and with the reenthronement of a monarch, identifiably neither German nor Czech, could social possibilities conducive to mutual forbearance and strength arise; the alternative was endless prejudice and suffering: "Until the Germans and Czechs of Bohemia are united in respect for a common symbol [which] is anchored firmly in the original Bohemian traditions of the Middle Ages, there will be no peace in this storm-tossed part of Europe, bitterness and revenge will remain the real rulers . . . to the detriment of all real peace and prosperity."[13]

Kennan did not expect that forms of political order rooted in the Middle Ages could be resuscitated in 1939. Nevertheless, his remarks on the subject are important because they reveal the depths of his conservatism and anticipate his later ideas about the need for a federation of European countries in which national feelings and separate state sovereignties would be subordinated to intra-European institutions and political symbols. In 1939, he hoped that the Czech nation could become a healthy component of the new comprehensive political unit then exerting itself in central Europe. Relieved of the burden of governing ungrateful subject peoples, no longer hostage to ineffective political parties, the industrious Czechs were sure to prosper in the new order; therefore, Kennan was cautiously predisposed toward the orderliness that German government in the "historic provinces" seemed to portend.

In retrospect, Kennan's specific charges against the Czech republic were as unduly harsh as his predictions about the virtues of Germany's protectorate were wrong. Czechoslovakia had within two brief decades established a robust, dependable parliamentary system that had sustained two statesmen of international stature, Tomás Masaryk and Edvard Benes. Although the landowning nobility's refusal to cooperate deprived the new regime from the start of one of the few elements that could lend prestige and stability of structure, Czechoslovakia enjoyed a remarkable degree of resilience and solidity. In this respect, in fact, the Czech state far surpassed that of its political model, the Third Republic of France.[14] It is fair to conclude that Kennan's bias against representative government distorted his analysis of Czech political problems, led him to magnify the country's social defects out of reasonable proportion, and enabled him to accept for a while the fantastical proposition that the German agenda for Czechoslovakia offered something sound.

At first it seemed to Kennan that his hopes would be confirmed and the successor to earlier Danubian federations would prove itself politically enlightened and benefit the Protectorate's culture and economy. The German army officers that he met in the Sudetenland and in Prague were correct, in his view, and hard-working, and they gave no obvious cause for alarm; they received "long lines of Czech, German and Jewish supplicants," all of whom they treated with "commendable impartiality." His conversations with army officers and enlisted soldiers in Prague suggested that the men of the *Wehrmacht* felt themselves entrusted with an elevated mission: wherever they went, they were carrying reason and enlightenment to deluded, sinking peoples. In the case of the Sudetenland they brought peace to German and Czech alike; into the Protectorate they introduced higher civilization and disciplined life.

It is not corroborated by other witnesses, but Kennan claimed that German policy was mild at first and aimed at placating the Czechs. In a private letter written two weeks after the Nazi occupation of Prague, he reported that, as gestures of goodwill, German officials had placed wreaths at the tomb of the unknown soldier, avoided baiting Jewish citizens, and did not molest prominent Czech figures. Though arrests quickly ran into the thousands, he explained that they were restricted mostly to communists, social democrats, political and Jewish refugees from the Reich, and others who in recent years worked against German interests. The rest of the population was encouraged to resume life as normal: "I am [hopeful] that the German attitude toward the mass of the Czechs may turn out to be a more reasonable one than many had anticipated."[15]

Kennan also expressed admiration for Czech "realism" in not vainly resisting the German armed forces. Any match would not have been remotely even, and neither the great Czech cities nor a large number of the younger generation would have survived. He argued that, having been spared the horror of war and the shock of defeats on the battlefield, the Czechs could adjust themselves to the power-political reality of the Danubian basin and cheerfully align themselves with the single most dynamic movement in Europe. The imperatives of the new order were not so bad; even in autumn 1940, Kennan believed, in what must be regarded as an idiosyncratic reading of history, that the Czechs enjoyed privileges and satisfaction in excess of anything they "dared to dream of in the Austrian days."[16]

Yet Kennan was obliged to report that the Czechs were far from appreciating the benefits of Nazi rule. Early on, he had perceived that Czech national feeling, in fact, was seething; German conciliatory acts did not compensate for the loss of political independence or injury done to Czech pride. He noted in April 1939 that there were no people anywhere who longed for a general European war more than the Czechs, who saw in such a conflagration their only hope of liberation from the German yoke. And in May he foresaw vividly the conditions of life as they evolved under the brutal Reinhard Heydrich, Reich Protector, 1941–1942. Czech resistance, already ranging from noncooperation to sporadic sabotage, might grow into guerrilla war that could never be wholly controlled by the Germans; in their attempt to preserve their gains, the Germans would resort increasingly to "imprisonments, shootings, deportations, intimidation and bribery."[17]

As Hitler's political policies in Bohemia and Moravia became more draconian and formal economic measures turned out to be little more than veils for plunder and expropriations, Kennan lost all his previous confidence in German order. He conveyed to his superiors in Washington a picture of greedy German looting: heavy orders were levied on Czech industries while no question of price was raised; large amounts of foodstuffs were directly seized from Prague, which led to shortages of dairy and meat products; Czech banking and industry were virtually annexed and administered by German masters; Nazi officials were invariably corrupt and displayed no sense of duty or responsibility for their Czech wards. The country, Kennan sadly realized, was falling into economic and administrative chaos. And by

June 1939, he was convinced that the German effort to govern Bohemia and Moravia would end in failure for all concerned parties: "Inflation, impoverishment, economic disruption, lack of confidence, and the moral disintegration of public administration can reap no good harvest either for victors or vanquished."[18]

Such conditions, Kennan understood, would constitute a long-term liability for the Reich and lead to an endless cycle of resistance and repression in the Czech zone of Hitler's empire. No empire, and certainly not one expecting to exercise authority for a thousand years, could afford a permanent slum, inhabited by people whose material lot steadily worsened and lived without hope for a better future. And he predicted that if Czech-German fortunes should ever be reversed, then "Czech retaliation" would be "fearful to contemplate."

After his transfer to the US embassy in Berlin, Kennan visited various parts of the expanding German empire in Europe—Poland, Denmark, Holland, Norway, Belgium, and France—and more than once returned to Bohemia and Moravia. He realized that, as in the "historic provinces," all indigenous social development was paralyzed in the newly acquired lands; the only acceptable political expression allowed by the authorities was a rehash of fascist principles holding little if any meaning to the conquered peoples.

The record of German occupation policies is now, of course, well documented and seldom disputed. Just as with Bohemia and Moravia, the Germans indulged in larceny on a grand scale. Shortly after the city of Danzig was taken, all of the property owned by Poles was seized without compensation; in France, Belgium, and elsewhere all airports, merchant fleets, dockyards, military bases, armaments, factories, fortifications, and real estate passed into the possession of the Reich; the "Aryanization" of Jewish property produced billions of marks. And as commerce between the occupied territories and the outside world was prohibited, they were forced to trade with Germany at exchange rates extremely favorable to Berlin. In addition, Germany profited by the import of cheap labor that included a million POWs by the spring of 1941. German profits through exactions equaled billions of US dollars for the same period, and the economic losses inflicted upon the conquered countries defied reasonable calculation. On all of these matters Kennan's estimates and reports to Washington were perfectly sound.

He suspected for reasons that he never divulged—there was an element of wishful thinking—that over the long-term the various national economies could adapt themselves to that of Germany's, and there would follow in them a slight increase in production and recovered earning power. During wartime such possibilities were slim, however; moreover, in any future period of peace he was certain that the Germans—assuming they won the war—would retain control of all "highly developed economic processes and force the populations of the acquired territories into occupations of a more modest, if not entirely menial, character." He predicted that as banks and finance in the new areas became German, as companies became German, as enterprise, initiative, and ultimate profits accumulated in Berlin, the outlying regions would become economically provincial. A Nazi continental economic system would cause a decline in production and industry and result in a permanent depression in the standard of material life throughout non-German Europe.[19]

The foreseeable political future of German-led Europe also appeared grim. Nazi efforts to enlist cooperation and enthusiasm from the defeated nations were meeting with little success, Kennan wrote in 1941, and the Reich officials in the new territories demonstrated unusual clumsiness and cruelty: student leaders were killed and thousands of others were arrested; intellectuals of every description were harassed; in Norway and Holland the royal families were abused; German police activity and mistreatment of Jews seemed pervasive.

However miserable much of Europe would be under German direction after the war, Kennan recognized that the Nazi Reich would be able to maintain its will indefinitely and realize the profits. As long as Germany retained its monopolistic power over military equipment, there was no practical limit to its powers of coercion: "entire nations or classes of people can be checked and policed with an efficiency which could never have been dreamed of one hundred years ago."[20]

Yet German power could be reduced, according to Kennan, and its worse aspects softened. No matter how ineffective from a purely military point of view, economic deterioration of the conquered states would one day cause disruption at the center. Kennan reported in November 1941 that a black market economy over which German authorities exercised little leverage and from which they could not benefit was already beginning to flourish.[21]

Kennan also believed that European resistance would eventually diminish German prestige. Nazi dogma would never satisfy Europeans as a whole, and he wondered how, for example, the French, Dutch, or Scandinavians, with their prewar high standards of living and their enviable records of political and cultural accomplishments, could ever reconcile themselves to an eternity of German domination. National Socialism was strictly a pan-German movement, and unlike the Catholic Church of the Middle Ages or the French Revolution or the Third International, it contained no basis for universal appeal. Kennan predicted that throughout the Nazi reign in Europe the national aspirations of non-Germans would be continually choked and that unmitigated envy and hatred would be directed against the Germans for years to come. Only in the east might the Nazis someday be well received: "In Eastern Europe, particularly in Poland, where the standard of living is very low and memories of political independence perhaps less glamorous than elsewhere, the hope of improved material conditions and of an efficient, orderly administration of public affairs may be sufficient to exhaust the aspirations of a people whose political education has always been primitive."[22]

Somehow or another the vast extent of Polish suffering under the German occupation—evident from the outset—was lost upon Kennan. In part, he misunderstood because he held the Poles in low regard and his residual Germanophilia, the Nazis notwithstanding, got the better of his judgment. Perhaps he also, like the naive Western visitors to various Soviet showcase sites in the 1930s, was fooled by the local administrating authorities.

According to Kennan, the chief threats to a victorious Germany in 1941 were twofold: either violent dissension within the Nazi hierarchy or the overextension of German power to the point where its success or failure depended on the loyalty of others could bring down the empire. And even if National Socialism did not "wander too far afield in its conquests" and did not "consume its own substance through internecine squabbles," Kennan speculated that the brutality of German rule in Europe would be temporary: Germany's political failure was of a moral nature that eventually would cause its power to mellow, its political influence to recede. The Nazis would inevitably be forced to "become more modest in their aims and to allow more scope for the spontaneous national aspirations of other peoples." Otherwise, German rule, although materially effective for the Reich, would fail as measured by Nazi standards of order and cooptation.[23]

Nazi Germany

In 1940 and 1941, Kennan thought not only that Hitler's empire was destined to confront administrative difficulties in its European provinces, but also that the heart of the empire, Germany, was riddled with problems. Its politics were inherently disorderly, it repelled many able men from government, and long-term popular support could not be counted upon.

In the tradition of other conservatives, Kennan saw in the Nazi triumph in Germany the ultimate victory of mass democracy: the peasant and shopkeeper had finally vanquished the aristocrat. The Junker estate owners, along with the cultural and political standards rooted in traditional Christian civilization, had been broken in the name of the people: "The basis of National Socialism was the petty bourgeoisie. . . . The Nazi movement was a common man's movement."[24] Unrestrained license had been mistaken for freedom and led to the semi-deification of a tyrant who in turn had reduced all social and intellectual life to the level of the lowest common denominator. Kennan believed that the democratic nationalism kindled in the French Revolution had achieved its ultimate political expression in Hitler; what Napoleon had failed to achieve in the early nineteenth century, the western powers had advanced under Napoleon III and later in the punitive Versailles dictate: "Western liberalism, ignorant and indecisive, has succeeded in conjuring up against itself—out of the nether regions where they were confined by centuries of successful French diplomacy prior to 1789—the evil spirits of German unity and German imperialism."[25]

In blaming the Nazis on European liberalism and Germany's lower middle classes, Kennan erred by underestimating the role played by industrial magnates and finance capitalists, the military caste, the professional element, and some intellectuals and aristocrats in Hitler's coming to power and continuous enjoyment of it. A large percentage of members in these groups maintained that Hitler was useful: he and his party were a bulwark against communism at home and abroad; Germans went back to work; the country's military power and international standing were rehabilitated under the Nazi regime; investment opportunities improved. Indeed, the true genius of Hitler and the Nazis was their ability to rally support across class, regional, and social lines. Thus Hitler's party was above all else a collective party and its broad appeal embraced more than just the "common man."[26] Still, Kennan was essentially correct in recognizing that Nazi rule in Germany represented a fundamental break with the past and was revolutionary. In a sense his observations from the early 1940s anticipate the later analysis of Ralf Dahrendorf, an incisive student of modern Germany, who has written that "the break with tradition and thus a strong push toward modernity was the substantive characteristic of the social revolution of National Socialism." Except for the Nazis, postwar Germany would resemble pre-World War I imperial, autocratic Germany rather than the liberal, open Federal Republic of today. From a patently bad cause, Dahrendorf contends, has sprung an unintended good, for odious as the Nazi episode was, it prepared the way for modernization in Germany—a condition characterized by "the autonomous equality of opportunity for all men."[27]

In 1940, Kennan did not expect that contemporary Germany, frantically trying to snap all bonds with the past and presuming in its recklessness to fashion a new world order, was going to last forever in its radical form. The Third Reich probably would not survive one or two generations after Hitler because the regime contained the seeds of its own disintegration: "Systems of government under which the ruler names his successor have never been long-enduring as compared with those which observe the dynastic principle."[28] After the flight of Rudolf Hess—Hitler's heir apparent after Hermann Goring—the pronounced jockeying of pretenders to the Fuhrer's position persuaded Kennan that any struggle for succession would be marked by extreme violence. The political education of Hitler's lieutenants was based on force and they knew of no other means by which to reconcile differences or achieve consensus. In the event of Hitler's death Kennan guessed that his henchmen would scramble for his mantle and make the Night of the Long Knives "look like child's play." Perhaps the state would be convulsed by civil war.

Standard scholarly literature about the totalitarian state stresses that it is marked by a high degree of political centralization, coordination of public and private life, strict discipline, and a widely accepted official ideology.[29] In contrast both to this literature and to the efficiency, coordination, and purposiveness that the Nazis boasted of, *Gleichschaltung,* Kennan perceived a crude form of interest-group politics which operated without benefit of clear direction or authority. A sort of chaos prevailed in Berlin. He noted that regular cabinet meetings were not held, and the leaders of great organizations—the army, labor front, foreign ministry, Gestapo, SS, propaganda, industries—often worked independently of each other; when their jurisdictions or interests overlapped, they quarreled fiercely until one or the other relented or the Fuhrer himself settled the issue.

Jealous of their own prerogatives and eager to expand the limits of their fiefs, Hitler's closest followers were engaged in a continuous war against one another in which the goals were to win the tyrant's favor and ultimately succeed him. Kennan reported that in Berlin, as in the Moscow of the 1930s, "only the least discriminating, the most thick-skinned, ignorant, and morally obtuse natures can tolerate without revulsion or at least a certain malaise this sordid free-for-all of lawlessness, corruption, fanaticism and mutual destruction."[30] Fastidious Germans, who in usual times might have assumed responsible positions in government, tended to shy away from both Berlin and the fracas of Nazi party politics, avoided the public limelight, and sought to fulfill their duties elsewhere.

Many of these people, Kennan reported, obtained acceptable positions in the army because service in it was safer, morally unobjectionable, and not entirely overcome by Nazi doctrines and functionaries: "Soldiers may die on the field of battle but they will not become the objects of internal political revenge. In the army, you can live unnoticed."[31] To Kennan, the army's gain was the regime's loss, for it was becoming progressively deprived of moderate men while succumbing to militant ones. In particular, the eradication of traditional elements, especially the aristocratic and religious, was a mistake, as the regime was denying to its future those sources of conservative strength that might be usefully mobilized in case of emergency—Hitler's death or military reverses.

The crucial question to Kennan was whether or not a regime that looked increasingly to radicals of the Heydrich ilk, employed every instrument of terror and compulsion, and discouraged contributions from prudent people could endure. Kennan concluded that the process of radicalization would increase general dissatisfaction in Germany and finally impair the war effort too; the attitude of typical Germans was already tending toward skepticism. If the Nazis won the war, according to Kennan, they could expect passive approval, but if they lost, popular retribution would be terrible and swift. In November 1941, he wrote that Hitler's political position in Germany might end abruptly by virtue of the Reich's own extremism: "It is a case of the Gods making mad a man whom they would destroy." If, however, Hitler's government should be spared during the war, then, Kennan conceded, the future of Germany and the rest of Europe would be inconceivably gruesome.[32]

While competition and constant maneuvering dominated existence among the political elites, the lives of ordinary German civilians proceeded without benefit of orderly and integrated domestic policies. Kennan realized that with the exception of the war machine, which was smoothly run by the army, other spheres of German life were confused. In effect, there was no civilian administration worth the name: "In cultural questions, in propaganda questions, in minor property questions, and in police questions there is an incredible *Durcheinander*. In these fields, there seems to be no unified leadership or authority."[33] Taking their cues from the top, the local political bosses and petty officials not only operated without guidance or restriction, but also spied upon and fought each other, all the while keeping the population terrorized and oppressed.

Kennan's assessment of the German people, especially the Berliners, contained regret for their suffering and sympathy for their predicament. They were subjects of a vicious regime against which resistance was both futile and which required a martyr's attitude toward life. He observed that many Berliners refused to give the Nazi salute and often found a conventional substitute for the official "Heil Hitler." He also doubted that most Berliners were enthusiastic about the war: crowds did not demonstrate much approval as Polish prisoners were paraded through city streets; the fall of Paris did not elicit popular elation. Instead, he believed, many people indulged their private thoughts and let the weight of minor concerns and daily routine block out the significance of momentous events:

> What struck one most about wartime Berlin was the undemonstrative but unmistakable inner detachment of the people from the pretentious purposes of the regime, and the way in which ordinary life went on, as best it could, under the growing difficulties of wartime discipline. The war dominated the public prints; but it was, so far as concerned the Berliners and to a large extent common people in other great cities as well, the regime's war not theirs.[34]

Widespread indifference, rooted in a deeper anxiety about the effects of protracted war, and "internal emigration" did not constitute active resistance to the regime, of course. The most potentially effective opposition came from the higher army ranks in 1944, when it was evident that Germany was losing the war and would pay a horrific price for waging it. Kennan's own attitude toward the army was certainly respectful and yet ultimately disappointed. On the one hand, he was aware that many of the older officers were critical of the regime, resented party interference in military matters, and disliked the arrogance and privileged positions of the SS and Gestapo. And he guessed—correctly in retrospect—that disagreement over military strategy aggravated problems between the general staff and Hitler's inner circle. Nevertheless, Kennan recognized that the differences, often based on dissimilar class backgrounds and generational cleavage, were not decisive and that army and government shared the same goal: establishment of a powerful Germany leading a captive Europe. He never believed that the Allies could negotiate peace with Germany by circumventing the party and dealing directly with the army; the army like every institution in Germany was too compromised, too corrupted. It had, in his words, a stern conscience "for the correctness of its own behavior toward those who [had] submitted to its authority, [but] then once its military work [was] done [turned] over its helpless charges without a quiver to the mercies of the National Socialist Party and the SS and the Gestapo."[35]

Kennan's contact with the German resistance was limited to its defeated but valorous aristocratic component. After the war he paid written tribute to those members of the Prussian aristocracy who had supplied enlightened and stubborn internal opposition to Hitler.[36] Gottfried Bismarck, grandson of the great chancellor, openly befriended Kennan in defiance of Nazi officials. And Count Helmuth von Moltke of the Kreisauer Kreis was greatly esteemed by Kennan: "There was no one I knew during the war, for whom I had a deeper admiration."[37] Kennan met him in late 1940 and after some initial suspicion of his motives came to comprehend the depth of Moltke's Christian-based opposition to Hitler and the genuineness of his idealism. Moltke hoped in the postwar period not only to help rebuild a physically destroyed continent—along the lines of European federation, the "majesty of the law," and a mixed socialist-capitalist economy—but also to repair in Germany the spiritual destruction inflicted by the Nazis. They had released the "beast in man," and the paramount task for the future was to restore "the picture of man. . . in the hearts of our fellow citizens."[38] To these ends Moltke studied Biblical scripture and a variety of other works, including the *Federalist Papers*. The impression made upon Kennan was considerable and quickened somewhat his own appreciation for the intellectual strengths of the American regime.

Kennan did not inform Washington closely of his talks with Moltke because in his view neither President Roosevelt nor Secretary of State Cordell Hull had the wisdom or insight to encourage discussions between the US embassy and Hitler's conservative opponents. Unfortunately, in fact, as did most Americans, Roosevelt and Hull assumed all German aristocrats and conservatives supported the Nazis. This misperception largely explains why the United States was hesitant and ineffective in dealing with or supporting anti-regime elements in the German army high command or elsewhere in the upper reaches of German society. In any case, from

Kennan's vantage point, the entire US government apparatus was too incompetent to achieve anything positive and so clumsy it might endanger a brave man's life. Two decades after the war, he wrote:

> I had little confidence, at that time, in our ability to conduct any secret negotiations with due discretion, and I was afraid that if I divulged what I knew about [Moltke] to anyone at all, the information might in some way get back to the Gestapo and lead to his undoing. . . . When I later learned of his arrest and death, I was very glad I had observed this discretion; for at least I had not in any way contributed to this disaster.[39]

Overall, Kennan was immune to propaganda of the US government that depicted the German people as bloodthirsty, barely human, barbarous, and so forth. One critic, Ronald Steel, charges Kennan with selective sympathy toward the victims of World War II and faults him for analytical dispassion in the face of Nazi horror. Steel accurately notes that Kennan's memoirs are disconcertingly reticent on the subject of Jewish suffering, and Wilson McWilliams discerns a fatal line of similar reasoning between Kennan's attitude and that of Adolf Eichmann in Jerusalem. This second charge is most exaggerated and unfair. Still, it is apparent from Kennan's conduct in Prague, when he had at least two opportunities to assist Jewish refugees, that he was disinclined—on the basis presumably of being a foreign diplomat and therefore not supposed to meddle in the internal affairs of his hosts—to help them escape from the Nazi authorities.[40] In effect, he let his official office and neutral standing in Czech politics stand as the basis for doing little to help endangered, innocent people. Indeed, Kennan was chillingly passive and correctly bureaucratic at a moment when something bolder was required—in the direction of Sweden's Raul Wallenberg, who did not hesitate to employ deceit and otherwise, from a strictly technical standpoint, misused his diplomatic position (in Nazi-occupied Hungary) to rescue thousands of Jews. Still, Kennan's critics (i.e., Steel) go too far when they accuse him of preferring Nazi Germany to Soviet Russia.[41] Kennan abhorred both the regimes of Hitler and Stalin. The difference for him was that Germany and most of Europe, unlike Stalin's USSR, could still be salvaged for civilized politics after the war: the social conditions that produced a Moltke had not been entirely obliterated in the West.

The Future of Europe

According to Richard Barnet, Kennan belonged to the school of State Department "traditionalists," who after World War II were skeptical of promoting regional cooperation in Europe and preferred to defend the legitimacy of the nation-state and the sanctity of international political borders.[42] In fact, practically the exact opposite was true of Kennan. Only a few days after the Allied landings at Normandy, he declared, "I see no resolution to the problems of Germany and the continent in terms of the sovereign state as we have known it in the past."[43] He was actually inspired by a conception of international relations in Europe that was outside of the modern framework agreed upon at Westphalia and reinforced by subsequent popular revolutions; his suggestions for a future peaceful Europe were based on an admiration for Europe as it existed before the spread of nationalism and the destruction of universal empires. The modern world, exemplified by aggressive nation-states competing in an anarchical international system, left Kennan appalled: "There is hardly a stone on the continent of Europe which does not speak of the superiority of the past."[44]

As we have seen, Kennan gave some expression to such ideas in his ruminations about the proper ordering of Czech-German relations. But not until February 1940, against the uncertain prospects of "phoney war," did he try to imagine the political forms that a Europe returned to its senses should assume if peace and prosperity were to be guaranteed for future generations.

To him the rise of Germany and Italy coinciding with the collapse of the Habsburg empire had destroyed the essential value of particularism that traditionally had supported a healthy cultural life and balance of power in Europe. During the halcyon period of Habsburg rule, Austrian officials had maintained order through indirect management and had not crushed all local aspirations or those monuments of intellect and imagination produced by subject peoples. Kennan, as mentioned previously, believed that Vienna's successors, the Nazi Germans, should emulate this example for both practical and humane reasons. And he felt that the standardization of cultural life and politics promised by the Germans—perhaps not so awful in the case of Poland—would prove disastrous for Western Europe. In place of German uniformity and coercion, Europeans should be allowed to reconfirm the political validity of cultural variety and national autonomy within sovereign units larger than the nation-state: "One must have the courage to recognize the value of diversity, of irregularity, of seeming irrationalism in so complex a continent. One must not shrink at the restoration of the Mozart court and the chocolate soldier. It is the real soldiers that are dangerous, the chocolate ones that are necessary to Europe."[45]

Europe ideally should repent for those mistakes committed in 1789 and in subsequent decades that had culminated in mass politics and finally established fascist regimes; nowhere was the failure of popular movements more evident to Kennan than in the hysteria of the Nazi party and the bombed-out cities of Europe. Only the remnants of a bygone era could make Europe again livable. The aristocracy with its record of comparative tolerance, its ties to the past, and its cosmopolitan character was still intact and, as always, available for service: "It is almost a miracle, and for the western world an undeserved one, that European aristocracy has survived to this day, for it is the only institution pliable enough, irrational enough, and at the same time stable enough, to bridge all the contradictions of the continent and to hold together the [diverse] parts with its implausible but effective web of common cultural standards and common traditions."[46] An admirer and friend of some of Europe's distinguished aristocracy, Kennan urged that "no one be frightened by the persons of its members: they are relatively unimportant. It is the symbolism, the continuity, the tradition, that count."[47] As for Germany, it should revert to its pre-1871 condition. And the many states and little kingdoms should resurrect those bonds of dynasty that had once connected them to the welfare and fate of Europe.

Kennan doubted that the United States could assist the Europeans much if and when they attempted to restore order and equilibrium along the lines he advocated. American political institutions and notions of government ran counter to the admirable traditions necessary to Europe's recovery; any projection of US conceptions on to Europe's problems would be invidious. The major tasks were for the Europeans: to devise a moderate armistice that did not duplicate the errors of Versailles and construct a political order based on sound principles of the past. The United States, meanwhile, should not be overly eager to involve itself in European issues, but should keep its economic strength as a force in reserve to be proffered when peace in Europe prevailed and progress had been made toward political reconstruction.

How these goals might be achieved Kennan gave no hint; his vague words on the subject cannot possibly be read as practical suggestions for serious action. Yet his later ideas about postwar reconstruction, US economic aid to Europe, and the desirability of European states to organize themselves in order to receive financial assistance—the Marshall Plan in other words—are traceable to these conservative and romantic musings in 1940.

Not until his appointment in December 1943 to the American delegation to the European Advisory Commission (EAC), led by Ambassador John Winant, was Kennan anywhere near a position from which to influence postwar planning. This assignment, however, ended in nearly complete frustration for Winant and Kennan because the commission, composed of British, Soviet, and US representatives, was invested with little authority by their respective governments. Roosevelt's government was adamant that the commission not "arrogate to itself the general field of postwar organization" by studying the entire range of political, economic, and military problems that would be encountered in Europe after Germany's defeat.[48] Following a testy correspondence with Secretary Hull, Winant—a weak, slightly incoherent, shy man—resigned himself and the EAC to a narrower task of arranging Germany's surrender and determining the exact zones of Allied occupation.[49] In this mission the American delegation received no leeway to negotiate, but was ordered to follow precise instructions from the State Department.

Given that the delegation had no scope for independent decisions or initiative, Kennan regarded his position of political advisor as superfluous. He also did not respect Winant and was at odds with the substance of tripartite action planned for Germany, most of which made little sense to him and was inadequate: Washington's instructions were "shallow and unrealistic—I did not feel they represented the best efforts of the government at large."[50] In these dark thoughts Kennan recognized himself to be essentially alone, however.

Neither solicited nor reviewed, Kennan's views about Germany and the postwar world diverged widely from those then being entertained by Roosevelt and his advisors, such as Secretary of the Treasury Henry Morgenthau. Their plans calling for the "pastoralization" of Germany, unconditional surrender, denazification, and a war crimes tribunal conjured up for Kennan the worst, punitive aspects of 1919.

Although he was convinced that the Allies had to impress upon the Germans the full extent of their wartime defeat to discredit Hitler's regime and prevent any resurgence of "stab in the back" theories, Kennan warned that severe punishment after hostilities ended would embitter the Germans permanently and make them again susceptible to the sort of blandishments offered by the Nazis. Apart from alienating the energies of the "strongest people in Europe" from common European purposes, a harsh settlement would result in the long-term economic weakening of the continent's center and wreak havoc. And the United States would have to acknowledge for its part "the collapse of the unity and the significance of western Europe in civilization."[51]

A punitive treaty, he warned Winant, could only please Kremlin leaders, who themselves had not the least interest in rehabilitating Europe economically or seeing it recover anything of its cultural preeminence and political vitality. The Soviets had shed all commitment to European civilization some twenty-five years earlier. Their only concern was to see Europe militarily weakened, hence their insistence on breaking Germany. And if Germany were demolished as a central player in the continent's balance of power, then the USSR would enjoy absolute advantage in future European diplomacy.

The declared policy of unconditional surrender raised additional doubts for Kennan: without even minimal assurances of humane treatment, the Germans were being ordered to surrender to the Russians as well as to the British and Americans. He argued that virtually no German leaders who possessed prestige among their people could accept the responsibility of placing their country at the mercy of the Soviets and retain authority afterward. Thus the unconditional surrender policy would only discourage opposition to Hitler and, once victorious, Allied governments in Germany would have to proceed without the advantages of cooperative German leadership. Kennan worried especially that difficulties posed by the housing and feeding of millions of homeless, idle Germans—their ranks swollen by the arrival of newcomers from Poland and Czechoslovakia and the demobilization of the armed forces—and the reestablishment of financial stability would prove overwhelming if the German population and officials failed to collaborate with the Allied Control Commission.

Another undesirable consequence of an unconditional surrender policy, according to Kennan, was to reduce the effectiveness of psychological warfare for the remainder of the war and to inspire German propagandists to greater exertions in depicting in lurid terms the disasters that would befall civilians and soldiers alike as Cossacks and backward Americans overran the Fatherland. Every German would realize the necessity of continued resistance and gladly do his share, thereby prolonging the combat even though the war's outcome was plain to see.

The planned prosecution of Nazi leaders and the denazification program also disturbed Kennan; if implemented, they would ensnare some basically useful people—scientists, experienced managers of industry, intellectuals—while others guilty of horrendous acts would inevitably escape. And those state officials and party members who were tried and then imprisoned or executed would acquire the aura of martyrdom and inspire future generations of extreme nationalists. By the time of Potsdam, Kennan advocated immediate execution of the highest-ranking Nazis by local Allied field commanders rather than indulging in lengthy publicized trials; their convocation anyway would be compromised in advance by the inclusion of jurists from another terrible tyranny.

The long history of Soviet atrocities, most recently palpable in aggression against Poland and Finland, the absorption of the Baltic states, and the massacre of Polish officers at Katyn forest, dismayed Kennan and justified in his view the exclusion of Soviet judges and lawyers at Nuremberg. As far as he was concerned, the international tribunal as later convened forfeited all claims to being an exercise in justice and was merely another example of the victors trying the vanquished and finding them guilty of moral turpitude.[52]

In contrast to elaborate plans aimed at revenge, Kennan maintained that British and American interests would be advanced by a swift, gracious restoration of Germany to Western civilization. Europe could not survive without Germany's contributions of economic might, cultural influence, and international weight, and the welfare of the two Atlantic powers required a vigorous continental system. Although such an approach to Germany would be difficult for Frenchmen, Poles, Belgians, and Scandinavians to accept, the Anglo-Americans occupied the leadership position and could dictate the terms of Germany's treatment: "We ourselves [must be] sufficiently mature and realistic to forego whatever emotional satisfaction we might obtain from the continued gratuitous infliction of suffering."[53] Kennan went on to argue that the impact of a failed revolution, military catastrophe, and subjugation by foreign enemies on the German consciousness did not require additional indignities; the ignominy of the defeated could never rebound to Nazi favor. Moral and prudential considerations thus combined in the logic of a lenient peace.

Kennan urged in 1945 that the post-Nazi German polity should not be forced to adopt democratic institutions of the American or British variety as they would lack organic connection to German political traditions and could not realistically last long. Attempts by outside powers to impose such institutions and values could only help discredit liberal concepts further; as it was, most Germans disliked democracy and identified it with the inefficiency, embarrassments, and failure of the Weimar regime.[54] Kennan predicted that a democratic system designed by the Western allies and implemented by Germans would degenerate into a "dictatorship of the left" and would appropriate to itself the attributes of National Socialism. The solution instead lay with German institutions of the premodern period: "The only reasonable respectable tradition of orderly and humane government in Germany is that of a strong monarchical government limited by an efficient bureaucracy and a powerful upper class."[55]

A united Germany was out of the question, but Kennan hoped that future aristocratic-led states (of Bavaria, Prussia, Hesse, etc.) could be integrated into a new European federation that was devoted to common security and prosperity; this federation should include all the nations situated between the Pyrenees and the western frontier (before 1939) of the USSR. A united states of Europe, which was not handicapped by association with the politically tainted regimes of the Iberian peninsula and which was confident and economically strong enough to resist falling into a Soviet orbit, could also safely embrace German dynamism and harness it for the benefit of everyone.[56] Kennan recommended that such a federation should grow gradually and its beginnings would be modest; but the Europeans should organize as soon as possible their fiscal, transportation, and postal services along uniform lines, coordinate economic policies, and prepare for eventual political integration. By this singular means of association he hoped the peoples of Europe could escape their historical "labyrinth of conflict."[57]

Kennan also held, in a reversal of his earlier ideas of 1940, that the United States, whether or not it welcomed or sought such a part, had a vital role to play in Europe, namely as guide and consultant on federation: "We must be prepared to give our sympathetic attention and help to this project for an indefinite period to come. The unity and prosperity of the continent of Europe is not something which will grow by itself from the planting of a single seed. It will require careful attention and cultivation on the part of extra-Europeans for at least two generations."[58]

Once Kennan realized that the Soviet Union was not about to relinquish its grip over eastern Europe or its zone in Germany, he suggested that the United States promote the goal of a federated Europe on a smaller scale: it would combine as separate entities the Rhineland, Baden-Wurttenberg, Bavaria, and Lower Saxony with Denmark, Holland, Italy, France, and Switzerland. The new European unit would also be encouraged to develop its economic and political ties to the Atlantic community of North America and Great Britain.[59]

In effect, Kennan wanted to rescue a potentially dismembered Germany from the likes of Secretary Morgenthau and to insert it into a larger scheme intended to salvage Germany and strengthen Europe. "Dismemberment," he advised Winant, "is unthinkable except within some framework of European federation."[60] And sovereign states in Western Europe would for their own good have to devise and then submit to a radically altered political framework. Kennan, of course, did not occupy in 1944 or 1945 any position within government from which to influence in a significant way the postwar picture of Europe. Nevertheless, he was during the war very close to the spirit and later policies of Jean Monnet, Robert Schuman, and Konrad Adenauer.

*　　*　　*　　*

Kennan's proposals for dealing with a defeated Germany anticipated some of the problems encountered during the occupation. Denazification, which he felt should have been scrapped, was unevenly applied to roughly 10 percent of the German population and yielded ambiguous results at best. The Soviets used it in their zone to liquidate so-called class enemies; the British were lackluster about the whole operation and conducted far fewer investigations and trials than the Americans (22,296 versus 169,282). And, as Kennan had foreseen, though General Lucius Clay's military government removed practically half a million Germans from their offices—which did complicate administration of the US zone and caused widespread bitterness during a period of economic misery—both valuable German scientists and Nazi officials with extensive knowledge about the Soviet Union were protected by the United States regardless of their past records: this included Klaus Barbie, who headed the Gestapo in Lyons, and Franz Kushel, who directed the execution of 40,000 Jews.[61]

As for the policy of unconditional surrender, it did not contribute to Germany's prosecution of the war or heighten people's commitment to the regime.[62] Contrary to conservative Kennan, moreover, democracy in Germany could indeed flourish: witness the Federal Republic. Yet, as he hoped, the bulk of Germany was preserved for the West, and once the Cold War started, rehabilitation rather than punishment was understood as a necessity in Washington; West Germany became pivotal to American military and diplomatic strategy in Europe. The German "miracle" was certainly compatible with American interests and, as Kennan viewed it, instrumental to the recovery of European civilization.

Kennan's advocacy, however, of the outright execution of top Nazi officials without trial was not in keeping with the restoration of elevated life that he sought. Incidentally, the only Allied leader whose thought coincided with Kennan's on this subject was Stalin. At Tehran, he suggested to Roosevelt, who took it as a joke, and to Churchill, who was appropriately horrified, that after the war ended the victors should summarily shoot 50,000 German officers and the entire General Staff.[63] In any case, Kennan's objections—later echoed by Senator Robert Taft—that justice applied unevenly was no justice at all and that a regime with a lamentable record of misdeeds was represented on the bench at Nuremberg were less important than the symbolic significance of convening an international court trial. Admittedly, it would have been fairer and less open to criticism if, as Moltke once suggested, the International Court of Justice at The Hague had been given the authority to judge German leaders. Still, after the carnage of total war precipitated by aggressive states, after the German policies of genocide, and after the deliberate mistreatment and enslavement of millions of POWs and civilians by Nazi authorities, it was necessary to reaffirm, however imperfect the procedure, the meaningfulness of civilized standards of international conduct. In addition, the spectacle of high-ranking government and military officials of the Reich brought to task for their inhumane misconduct and then punished focused public attention on the chief culprits and helped deflect charges (as after World War I) that the entire German people were guilty of crimes. Organized retribution of this sort also helped prevent sporadic, random acts of revenge against German nationals—of the kind that has soured Armenian-Turkish relations for decades—and paved the way for Germany's reentry into a peaceful Europe.

As for Kennan himself, his experiences in Germany and the Nazi empire reinforced his views, originally developed in the USSR during the 1930s, about the weaknesses of totalitarian states. Despite Hitler's attempted mobilization of the German population, the use of unchecked coercion and police terror, the smashing of traditional institutions, and the widespread acceptance of Nazi values and ideology, the Reich was rent with political fissures, could not fully overcome its domestic opposition, and was inefficient in regulating those spheres of life normally assumed by governments. Kennan concluded that totalitarian incompetence, whether Soviet or German, far outstripped democratic disorderliness; apparent totalitarian vitality not only failed to mask intellectual sham and waywardness, but was bound to change drastically in a moderate direction. Kennan's version of "containing" the Soviet Union in 1947 rested partly on this premise.

He also understood early on that the German empire could never hold together except through the sheer force of arms and appreciated the difficulty any state—totalitarian or otherwise—confronted in trying to dictate to advanced European nations; no matter who governed the peoples of eastern and central Europe, the strength of local feeling and nationalism would weaken and perhaps eventually debilitate any pretentious empire. Consequently, since the late 1940s, he has doubted that the Soviet center can indefinitely prevent its East European periphery from slipping away. The defection of Yugoslavia, the defiance of Albania, festering problems in Poland, independent initiatives by Rumania, and cultural liberalism in Hungary have confirmed Kennan in his approval of Gibbon's observation: "There is nothing more contrary to nature than the attempt to hold in obedience distant provinces."[64]

5

Soviet War Aims and
the Grand Alliance

During most of his tenure in Moscow, 1944–1946, Kennan was a disaffected diplomat who lived temperamentally outside of the passions of war and was on the verge of resigning from the Foreign Service. Although respected by his professional colleagues, he was otherwise unknown to officialdom in Washington. The president knew nothing of Kennan's analyses of Soviet policy during the war and probably would have discounted them in any event because they varied sharply with the administration's line about continued Allied collaboration and postwar universalism and collective security (i.e., the United Nations). In contrast to these means of assuring future international stability, Kennan preferred the traditional *realpolitik* devices of balance of power and spheres of influence. Their successful implementation, however, would have required a political framework other than the democratic one in which American diplomacy had to operate and for this reason, too, Roosevelt would have rejected Kennan's recommendations.

Not until late 1945–early 1946, when after Roosevelt's death and the emergence of problems related to the spoils of war and the organization of posthostilities Europe, did Kennan's views find a receptive audience in Washington, DC. By the spring of 1946, thanks to the interest shown by Secretary of the Navy James Forrestal, Kennan had become widely recognized in the Truman government as an expert on the Soviet Union and had authored a work, the "Long Telegram," destined to become a seminal document of the Cold War.

Soviet-US Wartime Relations

Kennan accurately described World War II in 1944 as a conflict of punishment and revenge.[1] By the end of the war the Soviet Union alone had absorbed dreadful casualties, including 20 million dead, upwards of 10 percent of its prewar population. Material damage inflicted upon Soviet cities, factories, and agriculture appeared practically beyond repair by war's end. Fully 1,700 cities and towns were devastated and 70 percent of the country's industrial installations demolished. The regime itself barely escaped destruction when, in the latter half of 1941, German armies were hailed by hundreds of thousands of Balts, Ukrainians, and Russians as liberators from Stalin's tyranny.

From the perspective of the Soviet leadership, its allies were as unreliable as some of its subjects. Stalin suspected in the late 1930s that Great Britain was not only reluctant to check Hitler's expansion, but seemed intent—this was the essence of Munich—on deflecting his ambitions eastward toward the USSR. Once general hostilities were under way, Stalin was exasperated by successive British-American delays before establishing a second front in France. Until June 1944, the Soviets bore the brunt of land fighting against Germany while Anglo-US armies dabbled in secondary theaters—North Africa, the Middle East, Italy. Earlier statements by such prominent Americans as Senator Harry Truman that it would be quite satisfactory to let Germans and Russians bleed each other white added to the discomfiture of Kremlin officials.[2] Anglo-American development of the atomic bomb and its eventual deployment without Soviet knowledge or meaningful consultation must subsequently have struck Stalin as indicative of Western bad faith. Such unilateral conduct was contrary to the most elementary rule of diplomacy: allies, if they are to remain allies, confer with each other over significant issues of mutual concern. The abrupt cancellation of American lend-lease aid shortly after V-E Day was further proof to Stalin of the US penchant for presenting the USSR with *faits accomplis*.

British and American leaders also had ample reason to be less than delighted with their Soviet partner. The rigors of war and requirements of allied cooperation did not erase the fact that V. M. Molotov and J. von Ribbentrop had signed the nonaggression pact in 1939, thereby precipitating Germany's invasion of Poland. Soviet connivance paid handsome dividends as the eastern portion of Poland was allotted to Moscow and quickly overrun by the Red Army. After the defeat of France, Soviet trade continued to flourish with Germany while Great Britain stood alone against the Luftwaffe and the U-boats exacted a heavy toll against British shipping. Soviet annexation of Estonia, Latvia, and Lithuania, meanwhile, and aggressive war against Finland were anathema to Britons and Americans alike. Neither did dissolution of the Comintern in 1943 compensate for two decades of virulent Soviet rhetoric and conspiracy against the West. Finally, Churchill and Roosevelt were chilled by the discoveries made at Katyn forest, dismayed by Soviet abuse of representatives from the Polish government-in-exile, and discouraged by Soviet refusal to rescue or even aid General Bor-Komorowski's underground army in Warsaw during the closing months of 1944; Soviet troops under Marshall Rokossovsky that had been within striking distance did not enter Warsaw until after the Germans razed virtually the entire city and killed most of the resistance fighters.

Despite Moscow's defects as an ally, Roosevelt and Churchill recognized that without Stalin's vast armies Europe would be dominated by Germany, and Britain and the United States would live in permanent peril. Consequently, in June 1941, following the start of Germany's offensive against the USSR, Churchill warmly welcomed the USSR into the war against fascism: "I see the Russian soldiers standing on the threshold of their native land, guarding the fields which their fathers have tilled from time immemorial. I see them guarding their homes where mothers and wives pray . . . for the safety of their loved ones, the return of their breadwinner, of their champion, of their protector." And he intoned heroically that Britons and Russians together in common cause would halt and then destroy the "hideous" Nazi war machine.[3]

Throughout the war Western leaders were eager to accommodate the Soviets. American lend-lease provided enormous amounts of foodstuffs, weaponry, and machinery crucial to the maintenance of the Red Army's effort. Roosevelt's insistence on Germany's unconditional surrender, moreover, was largely designed to impress Stalin with America's commitment and stiffen him against any temptation of entering into a separate peace along the lines of Brest-Litovsk. As for Polish grievances, the price of their just resolution was not considered in London or Washington to be worth jeopardizing Anglo-US wartime alliance with the Soviet Union. Western leaders anyway expected to satisfy Poland when, in compensation for moving the Soviet-Polish frontier westward, they assigned great parcels of Prussian territory to Warsaw.

By the time the Yalta conference convened in early February 1945, British and American leaders were increasingly concerned with the proposed impending conquest of the Japanese home islands, which was predicted to cause high casualties and perhaps involve one and a half more years of combat. General George Marshall's estimates of American casualties varied between a low of a quarter million to a high at one point of nearly a million; Churchill apparently believed half a million British soldiers and sailors would be sacrificed. To decrease their losses and shorten the war, Roosevelt and Churchill were determined that the Soviets join the campaign against Japan as early as possible and for this reason traded with Stalin at the expense of China and Poland. (The atomic bomb was simply an unknown quantity until it was tested in New Mexico in July 1945. Even then nobody was entirely confident about its usefulness as a weapon or its impact on Japan's will to fight.) During the Yalta meetings Roosevelt was especially solicitous of Stalin and in a period of delicate negotiating wrote soothingly to the Generalissimo: "I am determined that there shall be no breach between ourselves and the Soviet Union. Surely there is a way to reconcile our differences." To Churchill's chagrin, Roosevelt also tried to charm Stalin and convince the dictator that he and the president had much in common, including a distaste for the British empire.[4]

Practical issues of a most urgent sort thus impelled the Western governments to a degree of collaboration with Soviet Russia that had no precedent and obscured temporarily mutual distrust and fundamental rivalry. This situation allowed Roosevelt to entertain hopes for Soviet-US-British cooperation after the war, despite his appreciation of Soviet failings as a society and ally. Roosevelt anticipated that the three great powers, along with a revitalized France and strengthened China, could work together as global policemen to correct economic and political injustices wherever they threatened to erupt into violence, bomb any proven aggressor into submission, and lead the United Nations. Inspired by Woodrow Wilson, Roosevelt hoped to invest the UN with sufficient prestige and power so that it could play the decisive role for global stability and harmony. Spheres of influence, balance of power diplomacy, military alliances, and other allegedly obsolete, discredited devices of international politics could then safely be discarded. As mentioned in Chapter 2, neither Stalin nor Churchill had much confidence in the efficacy of such a grandiose collective security system, however. Stalin preferred local arrangements in Eastern Europe compatible with Soviet security and defense-in-depth strategy, while Churchill sought to revive a balance of power on the continent that would prevent Soviet hegemony. Although Roosevelt was not blind to these concerns, he chose to emphasize the virtues of a United Nations organization and was thoroughly gratified at Yalta when Stalin agreed to the American formula for the UN, an institution that, theoretically at least, could set to rights any problem of injustice in Eastern Europe or elsewhere.

Kennan's Dissent

Kennan understood better than most Westerners the impact of the war on Russia, the damage it caused, and the magnitude of Soviet effort. He wrote admiringly in the late summer of 1944 that "by their own extraordinary capacity for heroism and endurance, the Russian people have repelled the invader and regained their territories in a series of military operations second in drama and grandeur to nothing else that the history of warfare can show."[5] Yet he harbored misgivings about the political consequences for Europe of a simultaneously ruined Germany and a victorious, unchecked Soviet Union.

Kennan's views of Soviet conduct during a general European war were first formulated while he was in Moscow in 1935. He held then, as he did for years afterward, that Soviet foreign policy was based on the premise that relations between Moscow and the Western capitals were primarily adversarial. In large measure this attitude reflected the tension that had always existed between Russian universalism and the desire of neighboring nations to preserve their political independence and cultural identity. He maintained that contemporary rulers in Moscow should be regarded as the natural heirs to Kievian Russia, itself closely associated with a universally ambitious religion and not confined by distinct geographical boundaries. During their two centuries in Russia, the Tartars had also imposed an order that aimed at dominating the world, Kennan reported. And later, under the Czars, Russian pretensions included establishment of a "Third Rome." From a mid-nineteenth-century US ambassador to St. Petersburg, Kennan cited the following remarks: "A strange superstition prevails among the Russians that they are destined to conquer the world, and the prayers of the priests in the churches are mingled with requests to hasten and consummate this divine mission."[6] Kennan thus insisted that the traditional principle of Russian political universality, now in Marxist guise, was rooted in the limitlessness of the Eurasian plain and in the historical experience and aspirations of its Russian inhabitants; as with their pre-1917 predecessors, the reigning ideology encouraged Soviet rulers to look abroad.

Stalin and his colleagues, as acknowledged leaders of international proletarianism, were involved in the class struggle of every country and could not in good conscience ignore foreign workers or fail to assist them if asked. Soviet enmity toward Western governments in particular was the logical extension of Bolshevik opposition to the bourgeoisie everywhere. Naturally, Soviet leaders did not hesitate to express their "satisfaction at every defeat which [capitalists] may suffer, their bitterness at every success which they gain, their determination at some future date to overthrow them and—as members of the proletariat—to take their places. In theory, their political aims are not national but [global], and have nothing what-soever to do with friendly sentiments or with the principle of live-and-let-live."[7]

Such attitudes were typical of a state at war, and Kennan warned that Western countries could not afford to ignore the obvious inference. According to him, and his colleagues in the embassy were in agreement, Stalin viewed peace in 1935 simply as part of an armistice between socialism and capitalism that one day would collapse and lead to full-scale struggle. To the Soviets and their communist adherents abroad, diplomacy, trade relations, cooperation with so-called fellow travelers, temporary alliances, and nonaggression pacts were useful in prolonging the breathing spell during which Moscow prepared for the final showdown. In the words of Kennan's friend and colleague, Loy Henderson, Moscow was motivated by the imperatives of revolution and therefore pursued a more "progressively aggressive foreign policy than do most powers which are endeavoring by peaceful means to satisfy their international ambitions."[8]

Kennan was concerned that the theory of inevitable conflict and the "lessons" of allied intervention in the Russian civil war were incessantly preached to the younger generation, which was told to expect attack again by one or more foreign powers. Militarization of Soviet industry and society, meanwhile, proceeded at a tremen-dous pace: "The energies of the people have been harnessed for the execution of an enormous program of military industrialization, masked as a five-year period of ordinary economic planning . . . the country has undergone a moral militarization of almost inconceivable scope."[9] An entire generation was being prepared for war; in light of Hitler's professed aims to acquire German *Lebensrauum* in the east, Kennan might have allowed that Soviet anxiety was not entirely baseless.

Kennan believed in 1935 that Stalin's united front policy toward Germany was really intended to keep Western Europe divided and dissuade the British and French from composing their differences with Germany and making common cause against Russia. The Soviets were unalterably opposed to true peace in Europe and at every opportunity would stir up trouble amongst the Western powers; another war, pitting Germany against France and Britain, would probably be the outcome of this policy. As for the USSR's existing diverse treaty commitments and pledges to France and Czechoslovakia in time of conflict, Kennan doubted that they would be honored if Soviet security was seriously risked thereby. The Soviets were content to enjoy whatever safety such arrangements provided, but could be depended upon to resist the fetters of responsibility.

Kennan predicted that if and when war did commence in the west, Soviet Russia would stay aloof from hostilities. However, once the belligerents had exhausted their material substance, dislocated their economies, and were weakened by declin-ing morale, then Russia would swoop into the fray like a giant creature of prey. Social unrest in Europe subsequent to a major war might also spark Soviet interven-tion, for the prospect of advancing Marxist revolution should be too great a temptation.

To an impressive degree, Kennan's comments in 1935 about Soviet attitudes and policy in event of a European war proved prescient. After the start of war in 1939, the Soviet Union spared itself any effort on behalf of France and enjoyed the privileges of peace for nearly two years. During the period of nonaggression pact, the Soviets used their time to prepare for what Stalin realized—his mental paralysis in June 1941 notwithstanding—would be a difficult, protracted war against Germany. And the Soviets did, of course, promote their brand of Marxist revolution in territories controlled by the Red Army following the war. Still, Kennan never anticipated the Soviet-German nonaggression pact. Though apparently based on nothing more than a lucky guess, Joseph Davies did, and as a result, his standing as expert on Soviet affairs was enhanced in Roosevelt's estimation. Official neglect of his interpretations while someone like Davies influenced policy must account in part for Kennan's later querulousness when writing on the subject of Soviet-US wartime relations.

Throughout the war, Kennan was perturbed by the extent to which Roosevelt allowed the prestige of the United States to be identified with the objectives of the Soviet government. He believed that the extension of material assistance to the Soviets ought to be strictly commensurate with American security requirements and was concerned from the outset of German-Soviet fighting that America not be implicated in the Soviet destruction of the Baltic states, the conquest of eastern Poland, or Stalin's claims against Finland. While serving in Berlin in 1941, he wrote to Henderson (by then deputy chief of the Division of European Affairs in the State Department) that the Soviet Union was more feared in Europe than Nazi Germany. He was also adamant that the United States refrain from "anything which might [connect it] politically or ideologically with the Russian war effort. In short, it seems to me that Soviet Russia could more soundly be regarded as a 'fellow traveler' in the accepted Moscow sense, rather than as a political associate."[10] If the United States endorsed every strategic-diplomatic move of Moscow's, the Europeans would surely blame the Americans later for the social and political disasters following in the wake of Soviet expansion.

After the Japanese attack at Pearl Harbor, the German capture of Kiev, the occupation of the Donets Basin, and the beginning of the siege at Leningrad, Kennan's attitude softened somewhat. In June 1942, he stated that the Soviets required massive American aid if they were to withstand the German onslaught: "Maximum military support of the Russians is inexorably dictated by circumstance and cannot be questioned." Yet the cheerful attitude of the US government toward Stalin continued to rankle Kennan, and he was disenchanted by widespread American propaganda that portrayed the USSR as a basically democratic country and its leader as a kindly father-figure in whom one could repose confidence and affection. In the judgment of Davies, for example, the Soviet dictator was benevolent and had an exceedingly kind and gentle manner that appealed to the hearts of children and dogs.[11]

Walter Lippmann, with whom Kennan later had a complicated intellectual relationship, was one of the prominent commentators to popularize the image of a cooperative Soviet Union and promoted the government's view that postwar friendship with Moscow would be axiomatic for world prosperity and peace. Kennan was discouraged to read shortly after his release from Bad Nauheim a newspaper column (June 6, 1942) in which Lippmann declared: "No international order can be imagined without Russia as one of its supports. . . . If there is to be peace in the world, that peace has to be made in full partnership between the English-speaking sea and air powers and the massive land power of Russia."[12]

Kennan believed that the Soviets' international role in the postwar world, particularly in Europe, could be legitimately evaluated only through a tough-minded understanding of US interests: "Our interest, as I take it, is in the creation of the broadest and most stable possible foundations for reconstruction in Europe: in arrangements which give the maximum play to the natural and permanent creative forces of the continent and provide the least possible sources of national frustration and friction."[13] He had in mind, as we have seen in the previous chapter, the establishment of a European federation that would embrace safeguards designed to thwart any future German attempt at domination and would exclude the USSR.

Like Elbridge Durbrow, Loy Henderson, and other Foreign Service officers familiar with Stalin's regime, Kennan suspected in 1942 that after the Soviets rolled the German army westward they would make a bid for extensive influence in eastern Europe and would be uninhibited about using police and various internal security organs to consolidate their political control. This prospect raised the question for Kennan and the others of how far such an expansion of Soviet influence could be reconciled with Anglo-American demands for the future peace and balance of the European continent.

Kennan warned that Soviet control of lands occupied by non-Russians typically meant catastrophe. In newly occupied areas most of the intelligentsia, as well as anyone who enjoyed respect and prestige within the local population, would face deportation or execution. The indigenous peoples eventually would disappear into the giant Soviet melting pot, their cultures would vanish, and their standard of living would plummet: an established Soviet presence was bound to be "no less baneful for the people concerned than a permanent German occupation."[14]

Even if the Soviets imposed peace on their own terms in eastern Europe— thereby acquiring between 50 million and 100 million new subjects—that actually led to stability on the continent, Kennan doubted the morality of such a solution. Irrespective of professed ideology, there were plenty of harsh men in politically primitive eastern Europe who would gladly cooperate with any dictatorship, who would justify any method to achieve political ends: "There is a type of person in those territories who inclines to extreme and violent actions; it will lend itself to any ruthless [dynamic] leadership which gives the opportunity for petty power and emotionalism."[15] In view of Lippmann's misguided recommendations and the administration's misplaced optimism, Kennan wondered what the United States could possibly gain from its sacrifices during the war.

By September 1944, after returning to Moscow as Ambassador Harriman's chief lieutenant, Kennan was fully persuaded that Russia's major war aims included the establishment of permanent areas of influence in central and eastern Europe: "The Soviet government since the time of Munich has never relaxed its determination to have a fairly extensive sphere of influence in certain neighboring areas of Europe . . . in which its power would be unchallenged."[16] By extending their might westward, the Soviets meant to increase their military security. Nevertheless, Kennan perceived—in a reversal of his analysis of Soviet foreign aims in 1935—that commitments to revolutionary Marxism and expanding the zone of proletarian liberty were no longer animating the Kremlin. Would-be proponents of such ends had perished in the Great Purges, and Soviet policy under Stalin conformed simply to traditional power politics. Lenin's ideology that had once been employed to guide humanity's salvation and the radical restructuring of international politics was now in the service of a state preoccupied with conventional diplomatic-military concerns. Marxism merely justified state actions: "Russian efforts [in Eastern Europe and elsewhere] are directed to only one goal: power. It is a matter of indifference to Moscow whether a given area is 'communistic' or not."[17]

Kennan mused that, during the period of military dependence upon the United States, Soviet leaders had been careful to avoid offending opinion in Britain and America and had concealed their long-term goals of territorial aggrandizement. Once it became evident that Germany would be crushed and Russia would share in the spoils, Stalin and his colleagues were not so delicate—witness their bullying of Polish leaders trying to discover the fate of military officers captured by the Red Army. As neither threat nor allurement could cause the Soviets to abandon their project of creating a generous zone of influence for themselves, Kennan urged that the US government regard the European situation realistically and without false hope: "We must determine in conjunction with the British the limit of our common vital interest on the continent, i.e., the line beyond which we cannot afford to permit the Russians to exercise unchallenged power or to take purely unilateral action. We must make it plain to the Russians in practical ways and in a friendly but firm manner where the line lies."[18]

Although Kennan expected that such a clear understanding with Moscow would help preserve US-Soviet military coordination and increase the chances for cordial postwar relations, he dismissed all notions that the Soviets would ever act in accordance with far-reaching arrangements as envisaged by Roosevelt's United Nations. He advised Harriman that the administration lower its expectations: "We must remember that broad generalities such as 'collaboration' or 'democracy' have different meaning for the Russians than for us. We must not expect them to enter into forms of detailed collaboration which run counter to their traditional conceptions of Russian state security."[19]

Churchill, like Kennan, was dubious about long-term Soviet cooperation with Britain and America and wanted to delineate separate Western and Soviet zones on the continent. For this purpose he journeyed to Moscow in October 1944 and presented his famous formula to Stalin whereby the Soviets would retain dominant influence in Bulgaria and Rumania, Greece would be preserved for the West, and Hungary and Yugoslavia would be subject equally to Anglo-US and Soviet requirements. The American government, though, was not party to these negotiations, and when Harriman learned of the summary fashion by which the Balkans had been divided, he urged Churchill to drop the scheme altogether. President Roosevelt, after all, disagreed fundamentally with Churchill's underlying assumptions, and the prime minister never directly raised the subject again.

As mere deputy to Harriman, Kennan's frustrations in trying to influence the character and thrust of US foreign policy were certainly far greater than Churchill's. Still, through the ambassador, Kennan encouraged the government to explain immediately to US citizens the likely future of Eastern Europe and the quality of Soviet geopolitical advantage. "It would be futile," he wrote in 1944, "and would only lead to further trouble for us to attempt to conceal the Russian position from our people or to attempt to interpret it to them in any way that would mask or distort its significance."[20] Without such an adjustment, he feared that his compatriots would later grow impatient with the Soviets and consider themselves ill-used; domestic opponents of the administration would reap multiple benefits at the expense of reasonable diplomacy and destroy what chances did exist for postwar cooperation with Moscow.

By the time of the Yalta conference, the Red Army occupied Bulgaria, Rumania, the Baltic regions, much of Poland and Yugoslavia, most of Hungary, parts of Czechoslovakia; was about to enter Austria; and already controlled some of eastern Prussia. Although the Anglo-Americans had by then reclaimed France, the Low Countries, and most of Italy from the Germans, there was not a single Western combat unit in the east. Given this military situation, Kennan realized that Churchill and Roosevelt would only be able to extract promises from Stalin that he would abide by the high-minded principles of the Atlantic Charter and Declaration on Liberated Europe with their provisions for free elections and self-determination in Poland, Hungary, and Rumania.

Just a few days before the Yalta meetings commenced, Kennan dispatched an impassioned epistle to Charles Bohlen, who was then serving as Roosevelt's Russian translator and occasional advisor on Soviet affairs. During the war Bohlen and Kennan had agreed on various issues—such as the desirability of not forcing Germany to capitulate unconditionally and the inadvisability of creating a power vacuum on the continent that would invite Soviet interest—and were generally wary of Stalin's regime. However, throughout the war Bohlen was less critical of Roosevelt's diplomacy and believed that if Kennan were more fully apprised of the details and strategy of the administration, he would be less glum about Europe's future. One specific issue that divided the two men arose when the Soviets failed to rescue the Polish underground army and hampered Anglo-US attempts to aid it. Kennan felt the United States should have responded by suspending all further military assistance and supplies to Moscow. But Bohlen accepted Roosevelt's reasoning that such drastic action would not alter the outcome in Warsaw while it would undoubtedly impair US-Soviet relations and raise a concatenation of problems about Soviet collaboration in the Far East and the viability of the UN. Kennan and Bohlen also differed over their evaluations of Yalta.

Kennan argued to Bohlen that Soviet preferences absolutely excluded the economic and political rehabilitation of Europe: "They view with suspicion any source of unity or moral integrity in Europe that they cannot themselves control . . . Russia's security, in their view, means absence of cohesion, and of balance, of harmony, in the rest of Europe."[21] And it followed that to whatever degree they could, the Soviets would work to undermine recovery in Europe, thereby advancing their own future safety.

Kennan realized that the Red Army's "masterful and effective" war effort would find its reward to some extent at the cost of the eastern and central European states, but he still hoped that the United States would do nothing to dignify Soviet intrusion there. Apart from the human suffering the Russians were bound to inflict in their areas, a permanent Soviet presence in the east conflicted with the security interests of Britain and the United States. As maritime powers of the Atlantic, the Anglo-Americans had a large stake in the welfare of those European states lying along the north Atlantic littoral. They and the English-speaking powers formed a community of political and commercial interests any disruption of which would diminish America's strategic and political position. In turn the West European states of the Atlantic depended for their security and economic well-being upon an adjusted, confident central Europe. In language, though not in substance, reminiscent of Lippmann, Kennan warned: "A basic conflict is . . . arising over Europe between the interests of Atlantic sea-power, which demand the preservation of vigorous and independent political life on the European peninsula, and the interests of the jealous Eurasian land power, which must always seek to extend itself to the west and will never find a place, short of the Atlantic Ocean, where it can from its own standpoint safely stop."[22]

He also expressed regret that the Soviet Union on the one hand and Britain and the United States on the other had not earlier decided to separate Europe into spheres of influence with each side pledging not to meddle in the zone of the other: "That would have been the best thing we could do for ourselves and for our friends in Europe, and the most honest approach we could have made for the Russians." Instead of agreeing to such a tidy division and marking clearly the points of demarcation, the Americans had been vague about their goals in Europe and had failed to use mechanisms like the EAC effectively, while the Soviets purposefully carved out for themselves an enormous chunk of Europe that would include Poland and much of Germany: "In short, the sum total of our wisdom for the peace settlement in eastern and southeastern Europe has been to deliver the territory up without a murmur to the mercies of an uncertain and mistrustful Russia and to offer our sponsorship, in the form of a blank check, for whatever catastrophe might ensue."[23] The US government, meanwhile, unwisely justified its irresoluteness and imprecise goals by holding out for some hazily defined postwar partnership with Stalin.

Kennan suggested to Bohlen that as alternative to a settlement based on illusions, the Americans should quietly abandon all plans for a United Nations organization. As with the ill-fated League of Nations, the UN could not possibly restrain in the future strong states (i.e., the USSR) that were intent on aggression. In addition, Roosevelt's government should prepare the American population for broad peacetime responsibilities in the international arena and make plain that attachment to an international organization could not substitute for thoughtful foreign policy and adroit diplomatic action.[24]

Kennan also recommended that European territories occupied or about to be occupied by the Red Army should no longer claim the attention of Western statesmen; the British and Americans had not the slightest leverage in the east and should stop participating in the control commissions for Bulgaria, Rumania, and Hungary. Those countries could not be retrieved, and it would prove bitter and humiliating for their inhabitants to be teased by Western sloganeering about future guaranteed freedoms and democratic elections. "Where the Russians hold power, there our world stops; beyond that line we should not try to lift our voices unless we mean business."[25] All that was left for the United States and Great Britain to do was to begin organizing their remnant of Europe.

Kennan finished by admitting that his proposals amounted to a partition of Europe, precluded future close cooperation with Stalin, and resigned parts of Europe to another world impervious to Western values, influence, or needs. He argued, however, that adoption of such a program would conform to power realities and that in itself was an important virtue. The alternative held no promise:

> If we insist at this moment in our history in wandering about with our heads in the clouds of Wilsonian idealism and universalistic conceptions of world collaboration . . . if we insist on staking the whole future of Europe on the assumption of a community of aims with Russia for which there is no real evidence except in our own wishful thinking, then we run the risk of losing even that bare minimum of security which would be assured to us by the maintenance of humane, stable and cooperative forms of human society on the immediate European shores of the Atlantic.[26]

Bohlen replied to Kennan by agreeing that Roosevelt was indeed pursuing a policy involving risks, but countered that Kennan's ideas were neither constructive nor realistic and made sense only in the abstract: in view of America's publicly proclaimed commitments and the President's long-held policies, Kennan's suggestions were impossible and irrelevant. And, very telling, Bohlen admonished, "Foreign policy of [your] kind cannot be made in a democracy. Only totalitarian states can make and carry out such policies."[27] As for US-British association with the USSR, Bohlen reminded Kennan that it had been necessary to overcome Germany and that there had never been an alternative to the Red Army invading eastern Europe.

Bohlen also protested that by letting the UN die the administration would commit a colossal blunder. He did have doubts about the ability of any international organization to prevent aggression, but he agreed with Roosevelt that America should join, indeed lead, the UN and thereby save itself from the hazards of renewed isolationism.

Finally, Kennan's advocacy of dividing Europe into two distinct zones struck Bohlen as irresponsible and creating complications of the worst sort: "To me, acceptance of a Soviet sphere, instead of relieving us of responsibility, would compound the felony. Any formal, or even an informal, attempt to give the Soviet Union a sphere of influence in Eastern Europe would, as soon as the agreement became known, have brought a loud and effective outcry from our own Poles and Czechs."[28] He trusted before then that Roosevelt and Harry Hopkins would find the means by which to advance great power cooperation. After fighting a long war the American people deserved that a serious attempt be made to create a better world.

Kennan's worst fears about the direction of US foreign policy and the fate of Europe were confirmed by what he read in the public communiqué issued by the Allied leaders from Yalta in February. The announcement on reparations and the planned severe treatment and joint occupation of Germany left him stunned. Germany's immense potential strength was being left to the Soviets: "Since we ourselves have no constructive ideas for the future of Germany, our influence can only be negative. And without our support the British can do nothing. The result is that the Russians will do as they please, first within their own zone and then, in increasing measure, in ours."[29] From their position of advantage in Germany, Kennan predicted the Soviets would later apply pressure against neighboring France, Holland, Belgium, and Luxembourg.

He predicted that, under such conditions, the countries of Western Europe bordering on Soviet-controlled Germany could not safely revert to their prewar democratic habits and institutions: "If they are to have any hope for national existence they must seek protection in a fierce nationalist totalitarianism which will differ from Fascism only in that it is defensive and not aggressive." Britain itself could no longer expect to exercise any influence in Europe and would of necessity undergo extreme change; the instability and insecurity of continental politics would force the British to remain permanently militarized. The great sacrifices of the war seemed to have been in vain while the future of Europe could scarcely have appeared drearier. "It is questionable," wrote a despondent Kennan, "whether this solution will be appreciably better, from our standpoint, than that which would have prevailed had a compromise peace been made compelling Germany to evacuate Scandinavia and the western countries."[30]

The Long Telegram

Kennan informed Bohlen at the time of Yalta of his intention to resign from diplomatic service as soon as the war ended and an adequate replacement could be found for him in Moscow. And on August 20, 1945, less than a week after Japan's surrender, he submitted a letter of resignation to the secretary of state. To his colleague H. Freeman Mathews, Kennan mentioned various private reasons for wanting to leave the government: the trials of living abroad for many years, especially difficult in Moscow, had taken their toll, and he wanted his children to enjoy the benefits of life in the United States. His major reason, however, was rooted in a "frustration over our squandering of the political assets won at such cost by our recent war effort, over our failure to follow up our victories politically, and over the obvious helplessness of our career diplomacy to exert any . . . constructive influence on American policy at this juncture."[31]

In September, while in Washington for consultations at the State Department, Kennan was dissuaded from his course of resignation by Mathews and Bohlen, who appealed to his sense of duty and asserted that in the war's aftermath the government could not afford to lose capable, senior Foreign Service officers. Consequently, he returned to his post in Moscow but regarded it as the last leg of his last mission, as something of short duration and minor significance. He continued to brood that the congenital deficiencies of US foreign policy left no room for someone like himself: great modern democracies were incapable of dealing with the subtleties and contradictions of power relationships and lacked patience for anyone who did. Kennan explained to his friend Elbridge Durbrow in January 1946 that his anxiety about our treatment of Russian matters . . . lies less in any individual personalities than in [an absence] of understanding of the realities on the part of our public and in certain general [defects] of our governmental system in the conduct of foreign affairs. This being the case, it seems to me useless to look for remedies by continuing to try to make my views felt among persons responsible for promulgation of our policies. I feel that before we can successfully face the problem of dealing with Russia, we will have to have an entirely different approach, perhaps not to this problem alone but to the wider problems and techniques of our foreign policy in general.[32]

However frustrated Kennan felt about his small influence on Washington policymakers, he did enjoy growing success and prestige with his ambassador in Moscow, Averell Harriman. And although not fully appreciated by Kennan at the time, Harriman, whose voice carried weight in Washington, effectively presented his views there. The ambassador had originally gone to Russia in the spirit of Joseph Davies and was determined to keep Soviet-US relations on a firm basis during the war. By early April 1945, however, Harriman, like Roosevelt himself, was becoming disturbed and irritated about the Soviet government's attitude toward Poland and Eastern Europe generally: "We now have ample proof that the Soviet Government views all matters from the standpoint of their own selfish interests."[33] He feared, moreover, that the Soviets expected to erect dictatorial regimes where they could, "ending personal liberty and democracy as we know and respect it," and through the communist parties of Europe would try to influence the domestic politics and international relations of Western governments. Not until after the war, though, did Kennan—through Harriman—begin to have an appreciable influence on policymakers as they tried to assess Soviet intentions and the prospects for peace.

By the time Kennan returned to Moscow from Washington in late 1945, relations between Stalin and the US were starting to deteriorate rapidly. Despite Secretary of State James Byrnes's efforts at conciliation, a broad set of problems was tearing the wartime alliance apart: to their annoyance the Soviets had not been invited to share in the occupation of Japan; at the same time they were not budging from their sector in northern Iran, were exerting pressure on Turkey for easy access through the Black Sea Straits, and were initiating that process in Eastern Europe that resulted in Soviet-aligned, communist regimes. In China the Chiang-Mao war flared anew, and conventional wisdom in Washington placed much of the responsibility with Moscow. On February 9, 1946, Stalin delivered a major speech in which he emphasized the long-term incompatibility of communism and capitalism. One week later, the Canadian government made the shocking announcement that twenty-two people had been arrested for spying on behalf of the Soviet Union to obtain information on the atomic bomb.

Still, for all of these problems, there was not a consensus in official Washington either about Soviet foreign policy aims or the best method for managing relations with Moscow. To Secretary of Commerce Henry Wallace, it was crucial to devise a *modus vivendi* with the Soviets and treat with sensitivity their need for secure borders and reasonably friendly governments in Eastern Europe. By contrast, James Forrestal, secretary of the navy and a close personal friend of Harriman's, had long been critical of the USSR, and doubted the wisdom of Roosevelt's Soviet policy.

He thought that William Bullitt, who by 1944 was a devout anti-communist and relentless critic of Russia, and himself were the only people near the president who knew the Soviet leaders for what they were.[34] After Roosevelt's death, Forrestal was among Truman's most insistent advisors urging a hard line toward the USSR. In the person of the navy secretary, Kennan had a potentially most receptive and important audience.

In February 1946, the Treasury Department, itself a bastion for the advancement of Soviet-US relations, cabled the embassy in Moscow for information and analysis of Soviet reasons for recently refusing to join the International Monetary Fund and the World Bank. Against the gloomy events just mentioned, Kennan felt that Soviet reluctance to join global economic institutions was trivial. Yet he recognized, too, that Treasury's inquiry was the opportunity he needed to make one final attempt at influencing the government's Soviet policy:

> For eighteen long months I had done little else but pluck people's sleeves, trying to make them understand the nature of the phenomenon . . . [that] our government and people had . . . to understand if they were to have any chance of coping successfully with the problems of the post-war world. So far as official Washington was concerned, it had been . . . like talking to a stone. . . . Here was a case where nothing but the whole truth would do. They had asked for it. Now, by God they would have it.[35]

Kennan's famous message, the so-called Long Telegram (8,000 words) of February 22, 1946, described both Soviet attitudes toward the outside world and Stalin's foreign policy objectives. Essentially a reiteration of ideas that he had been expressing for years, his telegram posited that behind the ideological pose and inflated rhetoric the Soviets viewed the world in a traditionally suspicious Russian fashion borne of an instinctive sense of insecurity and inferiority toward the West. For the Soviet rulers, Marxism was a "fig leaf of their moral and intellectual respectability" behind which they justified oppression at home and sought political—not necessarily military—expansion abroad. In Kennan's words, the findings of Marx combined with Lenin's innovations legitimated "that increase of military and police power of [the] Russian state, . . . that isolation of [the] Russian population from [the] outside world, and . . . that fluid and constant pressure to extend [the] limits of Russian police power which are together the natural . . . urges of Russian rulers. Basically this is only the steady advance of uneasy Russian nationalism, a centuries old movement in which conceptions of offense and defense are inextricably confused."[36]

Kennan also explained that the party, although a successful instrument of Stalin's despotism, was no longer a source of intellectual or emotional stimulation in the USSR. However, he recognized that this condition did not inhibit the Soviets from exploiting foreign communist parties in order to promote Russian interests; so, too, they would try to employ international labor organizations, pan-Slavism in eastern Europe, and even the Orthodox Church. Through these organs, and through whatever else became available, the Soviets would endeavor to weaken the West and hamstring its recovery. The United States should also brace for problems: "All persons with grievances, whether economic or racial, will be urged to seek redress not in mediation and compromise, but in defiant violent struggle for destruction of other elements of society . . . poor will be set against rich, black against white, young against old, newcomers against established residents, etc."[37]

Given the nature of the Soviet challenge, Kennan repeated his plea that the administration inform the public closely but dispassionately about the real situation of US-Russian relations: henceforth dealings with the Soviets should be placed on a realistic and matter-of-fact basis. And he expressed hope that the United States would not only show itself to be resilient, but would also mature and strengthen as a result of the contest with Russia.

> Every courageous and incisive measure to solve internal problems of our own society, to improve self-confidence, discipline, morale and community of spirit of our own people, is a diplomatic victory over Moscow worth a thousand diplomatic notes and joint communiqués. If we cannot abandon fatalism and indifference in face of deficiencies in our own society, Moscow will profit.[38]

Harriman, who was in Washington at the time, agreed with Kennan's analysis of the USSR and sent a copy of the telegram to Secretary Forrestal, who leapt upon its presentation of Kremlin leaders and their world view. The secretary was so impressed by what he read that he ordered copies of it distributed to members of Truman's cabinet and made it required reading for high-ranking officers in the armed forces. Forrestal also arranged for copies of the telegram to be disseminated to diplomatic missions and military posts abroad. With a few exceptions—such as General Lucius Clay, the American military governor in Germany who was enjoying satisfactory relations with his Soviet counterpart—the telegram was favorably reviewed. In effect, it filled a conceptual gap in that it was the first lucid, extensive analysis of why the Soviets were not entirely enamored of America's international agenda and were unlikely to cooperate with it. A Cold War consensus was not yet established in Truman's administration, but the telegram and Forrestal's enthusiastic endorsement of it contributed to the hardening of official attitude in Washington against Russia. By the end of 1946 the cumulative impact of Kennan's telegram, Churchill's warnings (e.g., the "iron curtain" speech of March 1946), and the George Elsey-Clark Clifford confidential report about an alleged Soviet military threat confirmed Truman in his instincts about the USSR and the need to treat firmly with it.

For Kennan the telegram was a professional triumph. Cables and letters of commendation poured in, and Byrnes characterized Kennan's analysis as splendid. Along with the unexpected success of his telegram, Kennan's fortunes abruptly changed from being a little-known, rather prickly diplomat about to leave the Foreign Service to an acknowledged expert on Soviet affairs. In Forrestal, Kennan also had a powerful sponsor whose friendly intervention resulted in Kennan's transfer (April 1946) to the National War College, where he served as deputy commandant in charge of instruction in foreign relations. This prestigious college, based in Washington and owing its existence primarily to Forrestal, was charged with teaching geopolitics and strategy to senior military and Foreign Service officers. Kennan's usually well-received lectures were occasionally attended by, among others,

Forrestal himself. In early 1947 he helped orchestrate Kennan's appointment to lead the State Department's newly organized Policy Planning Staff (PPS).

Despite Forrestal's professional solicitude, relations between himself and Kennan were never personally close. And after Forrestal's appointment as secretary of defense in 1947, the two men, as we shall see in subsequent chapters, began to drift apart over policy issues. Nonetheless, there was always mutual respect and Kennan remained devoted. In 1962 he expressed these sentiments about his late champion:

> I had the feeling that he cared very little about me—or for that matter, any of the rest of us—from the personal standpoint. He was interested in what we had to offer for the solution of governmental problems. He was prepared to back us if we were on the right track and brought results; otherwise, he simply wouldn't have had time for us. . . . Mr. Forrestal was not so much himself a man of reflective and refined intelligence as he was a man who appreciated those qualities on the part of others and was anxious to see them used.[39]

*   *   *   *

According to Daniel Yergin, Kennan believed that the Soviet occupation and political organization of eastern Europe in 1946 were motivated strictly by ideological fervor and revolutionary commitment to exporting Marxism. Yergin also criticizes Kennan for allegedly overlooking the degree to which understandable power-political concerns and the trauma of Nazi invasion influenced Stalin's diplomacy.[40] In fact, Kennan's view of Soviet aims was considerably more sophisticated than Yergin allows; he emphasized conventional power factors when ascribing motives to Stalin and situated the communist regime squarely within the greater context of Russian history. Soviet foreign policy for Kennan was the product of tradition and environment and was beyond the scope of easy moral judgment. Ideology simply was not a vital factor. In 1945, he declared, "The fire of revolutionary Marxism has definitely died out."[41] And indeed, Kennan was right. Since the late 1930s Marxism has provided the idiom through which Kremlin leaders present themselves, but it has not been an explicit guide to action. Instead, the official ideology has functioned like a language, its effect on Soviet leaders being more subtle and psychological than overt. Soviet Marxism has mediated their perceptions and thoughts, but has not directly inspired their actions either at home or abroad.[42] Moreover, as Kennan recognized, traditional Russian cultural-political wisdom has remained the essential element in Soviet thinking even while its form has been modern and Marxist.

As we have seen, Kennan never doubted the ferocity of Stalin's regime, and, though he respected the Soviet peoples, he believed their expansion westward would be more detrimental to the Anglo-Americans and to the development of civilization in Europe than if Germany (forced out of Western Europe) were permitted continued mastery of central and eastern lands. In part, Kennan failed to understand in 1944 and 1945—and this was true of most Americans and Britons at the time—the magnitude of Nazi atrocities in conquered countries. In part, too, he failed to grasp completely the consequences for Europe if the Nazis ruled part of it because his attention was riveted to the gruesomeness of Stalin.

As for Kennan's hard judgment on Roosevelt's policy toward the USSR, it rested upon two major assumptions. First, international organizations, no matter how lofty their inspiration and clever their procedures, could never replace traditional diplomacy, and to link the future of US security and interests in Europe to the vagaries of the UN would be a monumental mistake approaching criminal negligence.[43] Second, expectations that Soviet-US relations could continue smoothly into the postwar era were remarkable and uninformed by any sober assessment of the Soviet regime and Russian history. Kennan, however, did not appreciate— indeed, he had no way of knowing—the true dimension of Roosevelt's ambivalence toward Russia and failed to guess that behind his public rhetoric the President held deepest reservations. He once characterized Stalin's regime as perfidious and regarded it as "a dictatorship as absolute as any other dictatorship in the world."[44] And yet Roosevelt was perfectly realistic and readily acknowledged the usefulness of the Soviet Union as an ally against Germany; after the war in Europe ended, it made good sense that Russia should again be useful against Japan—something that Kennan seems not to have grasped at the time.

Underlying his specific criticism of Roosevelt's foreign policy was Kennan's overall skepticism about the ability of the United States to conduct its international affairs in a thoughtful manner. His own sudden rise to prominence in the government provided case in point; the sending of his Long Telegram and resultant notoriety were simply a question of fortuitous good timing. He wrote years later that his message would have appeared alarming and unwarranted had it been sent six months earlier; had it been delivered six months later, the message would have seemed redundant and an elaboration of the obvious. Yet the telegram described realities that had existed for a decade and would obtain until the death of Stalin:

> All this only goes to show that more important than the observable nature of external reality, when it comes to the determination of Washington's view of the world, is the subjective state of readiness on the part of Washington [officials] to recognize this or that feature of it. This is certainly natural; perhaps it is unavoidable. But it does raise the question . . . whether a government so constituted should deceive itself into believing that it is capable of conducting a mature, consistent, and discriminating foreign policy.[45]

Over the years, as we shall see in the next section, Kennan's disquietude grew apace with his governmental responsibilities, and he endured doubts and frustrations greater than any he had known hitherto about the ability of the United States to conduct an effective diplomacy.

II

MAKING FOREIGN POLICY

6

Containment and the
Primacy of Diplomacy

Kennan's professional advancement in 1946 and 1947 coincided with the crucial transition in postwar history when the Soviet Union and United States lurched from being erstwhile allies to major rivals. Beginning in the summer of 1946, Kennan assumed responsibilities in Washington as the first deputy commandant for foreign affairs at the National War College and one year later started to direct the work of the Policy Planning Staff. In this second capacity he was ensconced in the highest echelons of the foreign policy apparatus and enjoyed ready access to Secretary of State George Marshall.

During this period of promotion and growing responsibility in the government, Kennan emerged as a widely recognized public figure and authority on the Soviet Union and US policy toward it. His celebrity in these two fields owed much to the publication in July 1947 of his famous "X article" in *Foreign Affairs*. This essay helped to rally popular support behind the Truman administration's attitude and actions toward the USSR, just as Kennan intended; but the article amounted to a critically deficient representation of his overall views. Only by looking at the origins of the "X article" and by placing it in the context of his other writings and lectures of the time can Kennan's understanding of the Soviet problem, the ultimate significance of the Cold War, and his recommendations about diplomatic and military measures be fully grasped.

At first Kennan was gratified by the palpable impact his words (in *Foreign Affairs* and elsewhere) had in helping to shift opinion away from the naivete and wishful thinking that he had railed against in the era of Grand Alliance. Soon, however, he became distressed by both the growing hysteria among the public about communism and prevalent, exaggerated notions in branches of the government that sooner or later a costly war must be waged against the Soviets. Drastic swings in popular opinion and a reflexive tendency to rely heavily upon military correctives to international problems vexed Kennan and were contrary to his insistence on adroit diplomacy and patience. Still, the examination that follows casts Kennan in a somewhat more negative light than has been allowed by the historian John Gaddis. Contrary to the Kennan of Gaddis's *Strategies of Containment* and to the self-portrait in Kennan's memoirs (1967), he was more uncertain intellectually and more of a Cold Warrior in the late 1940s than he later wanted to admit. At the same time, it is important to emphasize that Kennan's conception of "containment" *was* more subtle and varied than many other analysts have recognized. He certainly did not, as Richard Pells has alleged, believe that the USSR was operating under a compulsion to conquer the world; nor did he advocate military measures as the most important means by which to cope with the USSR, as Eduard Mark has charged.[1] Instead Kennan never thought the Soviet Union desired or was capable of world conquest; he never eschewed diplomacy and was not tempted to resign himself (or his countrymen) to an inevitable global Soviet-US war.

Educating for Cold War

Shortly after World War II, many Americans in and out of high office began defining foreign policy choices according to a false framework: either Soviet Russia and the United States would continue to collaborate and thereby insure the peace or their security interests would diverge radically and lead to another disastrous war. As unconvinced of the necessity for vast violence as he was doubtful of a harmonious Soviet-US future, Kennan emphasized the need for revitalizing diplomacy. He believed that the only desirable, realistic course open to Soviet and American leaders was to enter into negotiations when a fair possibility of compromise solution presented itself; otherwise both sides should frankly acknowledge the depth of their security and political differences and refrain from indulging in a war of rhetorical fulminations. Quiet waiting alone would hasten the day of thawing. Kennan was anxious that the United States, meanwhile, not lose sight of its interests abroad, as after previous wars, by retreating into sulky isolation or cleaving to a utopian international agenda.

Early on, he sought to convert other officials to his view that, if the Truman administration employed a few straightforward methods, then the integrity and prosperity of America and its allies could be maintained and expanded: economic and diplomatic instruments should be used without ceasing while US military might was held in reserve—understated and never provocative, but plainly apparent. The government should also act to protect and strengthen the moral fabric of the United States and educate the public about the nature and complexity of the Soviet problem.

In this last connection, Kennan agreed to undertake a speaking tour on behalf of the State Department of midwestern and Pacific coast cities in late July and August of 1946. Apart from explaining the Soviet Union to his audiences, he expected to generate support among businessmen, civic leaders, academics, and other prominent citizens for the emergent tougher line against Moscow. The critical national task, he told assemblies in Chicago, Milwaukee, Seattle, and San Francisco, was for the United States to confront the USSR with such superior political and military strength that it could not erode the Anglo-American position or encroach further upon the independence of Western Europe. By denying the Soviets new territory for annexation, by frustrating their attempts at political subversion, by confronting them with a bloc of vital, disciplined, abundant societies, the United States could expect to have decent, normal relations with the Soviet Union in roughly a decade.[2]

Kennan counted his lecture tour a success and believed that he had imparted to his listeners a sober view of Soviet-US relations, one that did not alarm unduly or raise unrealistic expectations about reconciliation. He found that all-male gatherings of businessmen were exceptionally responsive and appreciative. The men were in his estimation knowledgeable about human nature, judicious in their evaluations of political personalities and events, and refreshingly free of preconceived ideas. Academic audiences and study circles constituted around foreign policy issues were less impressive, however: "The women's clubs and organizations devoted to the study of international problems have a large percentage of members for whom 'foreign affairs' are apparently a form of escape from the boredom, frustration and faintly guilty conscience which seem to afflict many well-to-do and insufficiently occupied people in this country."[3] He was bothered by what he considered to be the sophomoric quality and tone of discussion in such gatherings and doubted that, however much some fashionable liberals or professional dabblers were titillated by serious talk about high policy, these people could not really be edified.

Kennan was especially repelled by the predominantly academic audiences at Stanford and Berkeley in which he detected numerous odious traits: "There hung over them something of the intellectual snobbery and pretense, the jealousies and inhibitions, and the cautious herd-instinct which have a habit of creeping into college faculties, whether liberal or conservative, unless there are enough honest and courageous people to combat them." He also perceived that these California intellectuals suffered from a regional inferiority complex and envied those people in Washington who occupied influential positions within the government: "Nowhere else did I encounter anything like the distrust and disparagement of the Department [of State] that I found in the academic world of the San Francisco region . . . it stemmed partly from the fact that many of the professors there had an understandable yearning to be closer to the actual operations of diplomacy and a sneaking suspicion that if they were in on it, they could do it all much better."[4] He was annoyed, too, by the apparent lack of political sophistication exhibited by the scientists he encountered and was disgruntled that the university groups contained a number of obvious leftists and Soviet sympathizers. Although the presence of Marxists and others did not inhibit him in what he said, he urged that on future occasions the department screen or monitor such people when topics of a confidential nature were discussed by government officials. And for some long period afterward he wondered what might be done by the government to gain the understanding, even trust or allegiance, of academic and liberal minds—they were, irrespective of their shortcomings, too significant to be alienated from the international purposes of the United States.

Commencing in autumn 1946, Kennan's teaching at the National War College exposed him to a distinctly different quality of student and faculty than he had met on the West Coast, and marked an opportunity for close, sustained work with officers of the armed forces. Charged with examining aspects of national policy—

diplomatic, military, and economic—and how they should be conceptually and practically related to each other, the college was a center for development of American thought about international strategy. Kennan later traced his own mature thinking about the need to limit warfare and forswear first use of nuclear weapons to the discussions and study he pursued during his tenure as deputy commandant.

He judged the students, mostly of senior field and junior general grades, to be excellent, and he enjoyed association with the admiral (Harry Hill) and two generals (Alfred Gruenther and Truman Landon) who administered the college. The four civilians on the faculty, including the strategic theorist Bernard Brodie, himself on the brink of a distinguished career, and Arnold Wolfers, one of the most respected students of international politics of his day, provided Kennan with a type of intellectual companionship that had usually eluded him in the Foreign Service. "Purely from the standpoint of my own education," he assured a friend, "I have found the work here something I would not have missed for anything."[5] In the first term alone, the college sponsored nearly ninety lectures on world affairs by prominent scholars and policymakers; several discussion groups flourished, and Kennan lectured extensively both at the college and in various army and navy installations around the country.

Even more important than the stimulation he discovered in this unusual academic setting and the satisfaction he derived from new personal attachments was Kennan's conviction at the time that he was helping to bridge the gulf of misunderstanding that had separated the Pentagon from the State Department ever since the hapless days of Cordell Hull. It was imperative, he felt, to instill in military figures and their civilian superiors an appreciation for the complexity of international issues, a respect for the usefulness of diplomacy, and a more generous view of the department and its accumulated expertise. Unless something was done to restore the reputation of the State Department, he feared that it would continue to languish as it had since Pearl Harbor and that future foreign policy would bear little or no impress of men privileged with years of international experience and practical wisdom: "Many of the catastrophes that befell the Foreign Service and also American foreign policy itself during the past war resulted from the fact that there were simply no men high up in the Service who had both the prestige and the guts to talk up successfully to the military leaders."[6] Kennan was convinced that his year at the National War College had provided him and the few Foreign Service officers in the student body with a wider acquaintance with top and future army and navy commanders than any other State Department officials; this would benefit the secretary of state when called upon to supply representatives to high-level policy groups, such as the recently created National Security Council (NSC).

Most of Kennan's teaching and research at the National War College naturally dealt with the Soviet Union and with examining the reasons for the progressively miserable condition of Soviet-US relations. And he took considerable pride in being able to articulate a political and diplomatic interpretation to military officers: "The work I have been able to do in the straightening out of military thought on this subject has been many times worth the effort and probably of much greater importance than anything else I have ever done or will do in the Foreign Service . . . our Government is pitifully poor in people who can give this sort of guidance."[7]

Numberless men under arms and a bountiful supply of the tools of war, he told his students, were sufficient neither to guarantee peace with Russia nor to overcome its political influence.

Throughout his stay at the college, Kennan still basked in the high regard of James Forrestal and on occasion was called upon to consult with the navy secretary and his office about defense-related subjects. In autumn 1946, Forrestal had a report, "Dialectical Materialism and Russian Objectives," circulated to a number of leading academics and policy analysts in the Soviet field. Written by Edward Willett, a Smith College professor temporarily assigned to Forrestal's staff, the essay purported to analyze the relationship between Marxism and the domestic and international behavior of the USSR. Along with such men as Professors Philip Mosely and John Hazard of Columbia University, Kennan was asked, as a matter of routine, to comment upon Willett's paper.

Handicapped by leaden prose and a sluggish, convoluted argument, Willett's essay began by trying to define and explain the historical evolution of dialectical materialism. He discussed its origins in ancient Greece, its refinement by Hegel and Marx, and its application and theoretical development in the Soviet Union. Willett dismissed Marx and his disciples as morally and intellectually bankrupt, and his essay was peppered with the usual invidious comparisons between Marx's predictions and the actual unfolding of events and society in advanced capitalist countries.

Willett placed strong emphasis on the centrality of Marxism-Leninism to contemporary Soviet leaders and claimed that their belief in inevitable conflict between capitalism and socialism inclined Stalin toward military aggression against the United States: "If Soviet Russia is motivated by principles of Communism, if Communism regards it a duty to take steps to [hurry] the proletarian revolution as a means of attaining a true Communist society, if the proletarian revolution must be global in scope in order to be successful, and if it can be achieved only by violence, then violence between Soviet Russia and the United States would seem to be [unavoidable]."[8] He concluded his report by affirming that the Soviet Union was a dangerous power animated by fanatical devotion to a revolutionary, albeit historically discredited, ideology and that the United States could assure its future safety only by building its military services anew and greatly restocking their equipment.

Kennan agreed in his written critique of Willett that most Soviet and US interests were at odds, but he strenuously objected that lavish military measures were necessary to guarantee peace and security. Indeed, there was no reason for overexcitement or a feverish replenishing of the nation's arsenals: "I personally have no fear about our being able to contain the Russians for the foreseeable future, if we handle ourselves reasonably well."[9] For one thing, Kennan argued, the USSR was in no condition or mood to promote a militarily expansionist policy after its exertions against Nazi Germany. Because reconstruction of Soviet farms, factories, and cities was urgent and heavily drained what remained of capital and human assets, far-flung adventures aimed at conquering additional lands were not plausible Soviet options:

> I think it unrealistic to assume that there could be a real possibility of a communist sphere of influence embracing a substantial part of the rest of the world and grouped around Russia. Russia's resources are already severely taxed to maintain

the sphere of influence which the Soviet Government has already acquired around the borders of the Soviet Union. There is no indication that Russia has the manpower or the skill to go much further in the line of dominion over other people.[10]

He believed, too, given the great disparity between Soviet and US economic capabilities and total military prowess, that Stalin at no time in the predictable future would dare directly threaten the United States or its friends.

In responding to Willett, Kennan cautiously avoided the larger issue of ideological conflict—a subject of near obsession to Forrestal—and was content to acknowledge that close relations with capitalist governments had never been a Soviet priority, but then neither had Stalin's government sought intimacy with any foreign party or regime. As for Moscow's relations with non-Soviet Marxists or others on the left, obedience, not ideological purity, mattered most: "I daresay that even if there were to be a violent overthrow of capitalistic democracy by an internal [communist] revolution in the United States, unless it were to be led by people who accept the authority of Moscow, the only reaction of men in the Kremlin would be to stamp it a form of fascism and to oppose it even more violently than they now oppose the purposes of the present government of the United States."[11] In Eastern Europe, also, the Soviet leaders were less interested in spreading proletarian revolution and inaugurating a new human epoch than they were with consolidating control over areas of western approach to Russia. Soviet power, prestige, and influence mattered to Stalin and his lieutenants; Marxist orthodoxy and revolution were questions of ritualistic form: "The main thing is that these [East European] governments should follow Moscow's leadership."[12]

In contrast to Willett and to much of the prevailing wisdom of the time, Kennan also warned that there was no obvious correlation between material standards of life in a given society and the degree of its immunity to communism. Referring to the strong communist parties in economically advanced France and Czechoslovakia and the virtual absence of one in Salazar's Portugal, Kennan generalized that communism reflected deeper causes than material maladjustment: the Soviets would try to manipulate these profounder causes (disenchantment in elements of the intelligentsia with their political impotence; the impulse of war-weary, disoriented people to forsake their responsibilities and surrender power to those who promise redemption), but they could never control them.

Despite its many problems, Kennan never doubted that the Soviet Union was a formidable contender for power and that it would be folly for the United States to revert to some version of fortress America or view its vital interests as being restricted to the western hemisphere. Such a geopolitical perspective, which he apparently thought was implied in Willett's paper, ought to be disregarded as narrow and unsound. Not until a couple of years hence, though, did Kennan begin to clarify in his own mind and specify for others what he thought should be the range and nature of US geopolitical interests.

Forrestal's office thanked Kennan in October for his comments about Willett's essay and asked him to produce an analysis of his own that would be more "academically sound." After some hesitation—he pleaded being too busy—Kennan complied and began writing a composition, "Psychological Background of Soviet

Foreign Policy." He did not respond point by point to Willett and was not confined by his language or the conceptual boundaries of his argument, but it was clearly Willett's essay that Kennan had in mind as he wrote his report. An initial rejection by Forrestal forced Kennan to rewrite portions of it, and he did not submit a final, and tougher sounding, draft until late January 1947.

Following Willett's example, Kennan began his paper with a lengthy discourse about Marxian ideas, but departed from him by illustrating how the ideological pretensions of the Soviet regime meshed with historically conditioned Russian attitudes and fears about the outside world: "Again, these [ideological] precepts are fortified by the lessons of Russian history: of centuries of obscure battles between nomadic forces over the stretches of a vast unfortified plain." Kennan was economical in his language and, regardless of whether one agrees with him or not, more incisive than Willett. Just as Willett did, Kennan next examined the Soviet Union's foreign objectives. And he emphasized that, because of economic difficulties and the disruption caused by war and the regime's domestic practices, there were tight restraints on Soviet foreign policy. He italicized the following, and in his view important, passage:

> It is difficult to see how these deficiencies can be corrected at any early date by a tired and dispirited population working largely under the shadow of fear and compulsion. And as long as they are not overcome, Russia will remain economically a vulnerable, and in a certain sense an impotent, nation, capable of exporting its enthusiasms and of radiating the strange charm of its primitive political vitality but unable to back up those articles of export by the real evidences of material power and prosperity.[13]

Finally, whereas Willett chose to portray grandiloquently democracy's heroic struggle against communism in his conclusions, Kennan closed by briefly and vaguely stating the type of policy the United States should adopt. In the first version of his essay, he wrote that *diplomatic* "counter-pressure" and the example of America's own dignified behavior in international affairs were the best means by which to thwart Soviet mischief. In the final draft, he discussed the need for a policy "designed to confront the Russians with unalterable counter-force at every point where they show signs of encroaching upon the interests of a peaceful and stable world."[14]

Partly a recapitulation of ideas that he had been expressing for years, Kennan's essay was an oddly ambiguous piece by virtue of its being inspired and subtly restricted by Willett, having been tailored to fit Forrestal's requirement for a study about communism, and being subject to the secretary's personal intervention. Even if not deliberately calculated, nothing could have more easily won Forrestal's approval than Kennan's invoking of God and history at the end of the essay as the just and final arbiters of the Soviet-US contest.[15] The secretary's amateurish interests in philosophy and history ran in the direction of grand theorizing, and he had a preference for flowery prose which he sometimes mistook for profundity. Kennan indulged, as Willett had on previous occasions, Forrestal's intellectual predilections—a type of small favor and easy to perform for one who was materially fostering Kennan's own career. (In January 1947, Forrestal was recommending to

Marshall that, when the time came to organize the Policy Planning Staff, he should hire Kennan as its chief.) The memorandum, in any case, was meant simply as an internal government document, and neither Kennan nor his original readers in the Navy Department considered the paper as anything like an official declaration of US foreign objectives or policy against Russia. In fact, little of the essay addressed such issues. Yet, ironically, the paper, later published as "The Sources of Soviet Conduct" in *Foreign Affairs* (July 1947), has occupied a singular position in postwar political literature and has often been interpreted as the most concise and definitive statement of US aims in its competition with the Soviet Union.

Most of the Cold War historiography that examines what Kennan really meant in the article hinges on his conception of containment and the degree to which it embraced military, or political-diplomatic, or economic policies against the USSR. The debate was actually sparked in the 1960s by Kennan's repudiation of containment as popularly understood. To many commentators, it seemed that he wanted to escape responsibility for helping to shape US diplomacy and relieve himself, in particular, of any culpability for decisions leading to the Vietnam War. Nevertheless, the question remains: why did Kennan submit his memorandum to Forrestal for publication in a widely read, influential journal in 1947?

In early January of that year, Kennan delivered an enthusiastically received lecture to the Russian Study Group of the prestigious Council on Foreign Relations in New York. As in forums the previous summer, he discussed the origins of Soviet habits, traditions, and ideology, and the quality of Soviet domestic politics. He warned against a "get-tough policy" and insisted in his usual manner that US policy should impress foreign capitals, particularly Moscow, as cool and confident: "As long as we show that our purposes are decent and that we have the courage to follow them through, the Russians will never challenge us." He opposed quick answers and liberal solutions and pronounced solemnly that the United States would have to gird itself for a long period of twilight when neither comfortable peace nor open war would prevail. Ancient Russia, in any event, could not be goaded into friendship: "The Russians cannot be approached, as Mr. Wallace would have us do, on a personal basis, by the glad hand and the winning smile. We do not have to deal with individual whims and personalities but with deep-seated habits of thought, with the driving force of a great idea and a method of looking at the world which is anchored in the experience of centuries."[16]

He explained that, ever since the nomadic period in its history, Russian diplomacy had been characterized by tremendous flexibility in which room was always preserved for retreat and regrouping. The Russians were also traditionally cautious, careful not to let their ambitions outstrip their capabilities, and strangely susceptible to superior intellectual and ethical strength: "When they do find themselves up against force, especially moral force, they acknowledge it with a grin and they do not hold it against you." The United States, therefore, should be correct in its dealings with Moscow, scrupulously satisfy its own international obligations, and be willing always to negotiate while never appearing false or weak: "Nothing is to be gained by . . . fatuous concessions without receiving a *quid pro quo*. They balance their books every night and start over every morning. . . . They expect you to proceed in a hard-boiled way and not to give them things without getting something for them."[17] Kennan advised, too, that US leaders not treat their Soviet counterparts with arrogance and refrain from boasting about American accomplishments and condemning Soviet defects, many of them centuries old and not specifically attributable to the communists.

Finally, as to the ominous day when the United States would lose its nuclear monopoly and the Soviets would be able to launch atomic bombs against West European and North American cities, Kennan counseled calm. He doubted that possession of these devices would transform military thinking in Moscow or that the Soviets could ever convince themselves of the weapons' political utility: "They know that [using atomic bombs] would defeat their aims and that no one wins in an atomic war. They are wiser than we are in that sense."[18]

Hamilton Fish Armstrong, editor of the Council's *Foreign Affairs,* had missed Kennan's lecture. Upon learning that it had been informative and having been urged to do so by those who did attend, Armstrong asked Kennan for an article based on his talk. Kennan felt too harassed by the demands of lecturing at the National War College and elsewhere and consulting with the State Department to write an essay suitable for publication; the notes on which he based his lecture were very rough. The course of least resistance was to send an existing paper, and closest at hand was the just finished memorandum to Forrestal, mercifully free of classified information. After obtaining permission from the State Department, which insisted that he conceal his identity as author—hence "X"—Kennan forwarded the document, without changes, to *Foreign Affairs* in May.

Nobody within the administration, least of all Secretary Marshall who had never seen the article, expected or wanted Kennan's essay to be interpreted as a doctrine or setting forth of operational principles underlying US foreign policy. In fact, the decision to let Kennan submit his article to *Foreign Affairs* was made by a middle-level office in the State Department, the Committee on Unofficial Publications, and was cleared as a matter of bureaucratic routine. Armstrong, himself, viewed the paper *solely* as a lucid assessment of the Soviet Union.[19]

Shortly before the article's publication, and just before his joining the Policy Planning Staff, Kennan conveyed to Armstrong how pleased he was that *Foreign Affairs* was serving as his vehicle for reaching an important segment of the population. He recognized that in the future, as an active policymaker, he would have to be circumspect in stating his private views, however: "With the new job I am now undertaking in the Department of State I shall have to be more careful about what I say and write personally."[20] Thus, in an important sense, Kennan regarded his contribution to the journal as a final exercise, at least for the duration of his duty under Marshall, in affecting public discussion about the Soviet Union.

The article's appearance in a periodical commonly (but incorrectly) regarded as a semi-official government mouthpiece and following close upon the proclamations of the Truman Doctrine (March 12, 1947) and the Marshall Plan (June 5, 1947) caused a sensation.[21] Once it was discovered that a high-ranking functionary—no less than the recently named director of policy planning at the State Department—had authored the essay, there rapidly grew a consensus among prominent journalists that the article represented the administration's true understanding of the Soviet Union and how best to defeat the foreign danger. Walter Lippmann, for one, judged that the essay was not just another report in a series of government studies about Soviet Russia. It was "an event." In effect, the Truman administration "had made up its mind, and was prepared to disclose to the American people, to the world at large, and of course to the Kremlin the estimates, the calculations, and the conclusions on which the [State] Department was basing its plans."[22] And the *New York Times* columnist Arthur Krock, who was responsible for identifying Kennan as the mysterious "Mr. X," later expressed the opinion of many people when he linked early Cold War policies to the strategic framework of containment, as publicly revealed in the pages of *Foreign Affairs*.[23]

The Lippmann Critique and Kennan's Response

Although hailed by commentators in America and abroad, the "X article" did not meet with universal approval and became for liberal and conservative critics of US policy, both at the time and for years afterward, a target for their criticisms. Many of the liberals whom Kennan most wanted to persuade attacked his essay as an apology for misguided, confrontationist policies that failed to account for the legitimacy of Soviet security interests in Europe, and foreclosed any possibility of negotiations aimed at achieving broad settlement; the analysis was flawed, its prescriptions dangerous.

To Walter Lippmann, occupying a decidedly more conservative position on the political spectrum than most of Kennan's critics, containment was a "strategic monstrosity." It could not be implemented well, and any attempt to do so would be wasteful, lead to the demoralization of the United States, and lower its international prestige. He charged in a dozen elegant articles published in autumn 1947 that foreign policy, as enunciated by Kennan and embodied in the Truman Doctrine, was handicapped by a host of conceptual and tactical mistakes. The United States was failing to distinguish vital interests from peripheral ones and demonstrated no sense of gradations. The government, for example, was unwisely placing secondary regions, such as Asia, on a par with areas like Europe that were vital to America's continued economic and political health.

The central problem with Kennan's analysis, according to Lippmann, was that he exaggerated the importance of ideology in ascribing motives to Soviet diplomacy and failed to realize that communist Russia, like Czarist Russia, pursued objectives based primarily on concerns about defense and suppositions regarding the balance of power: "For reasons which I do not understand, Mr. X decided not to consider the men in the Kremlin as the rulers of the Russian State and Empire." Consequently, his recommendations were worthless: his picture of Soviet conduct had no pattern, but was amorphous. His conclusions about how to deal with the Soviets had no pattern, and were also nebulous. And what was not vague was just wrongheaded.[24]

Containment would soon overextend US military resources by stretching them everywhere around the world in the impractical hope of checking communist incursions wherever they occurred: "There is . . . no rational ground for confidence that the United States could muster 'unalterable counterforce' at all the individual sectors." Lippmann stressed that US military advantage lay with its naval and air superiority and that the country would lose any war of attrition fought on the Eurasian land mass. He predicted that the Americans would grow frustrated and fatigued by a policy of containment long before the resolute Soviets ever dreamed of capitulating. Finally, Lippmann blasted containment for being a purely passive, defensive strategy—John Foster Dulles sounded this same theme during the 1952 presidential campaign—that surrendered all initiative to the Soviet Union: "For ten or fifteen years Moscow, not Washington, would define the issues, would make the challenges, would select the ground where the conflict was to be waged, and would choose the weapons."[25]

Lippmann advised that the United States immediately write off the liabilities of Kennan's formulation and not waste its substance by intervening in every civil war or international conflict on behalf of just anyone who hurled the epithet "communist" against his adversary. Nobody should expect to enlist aid so easily from America, and the country should reject the temptation of leading an ideological crusade. Policymakers would be wise "not to make Jeffersonian democrats out of the peasants of eastern Europe, the tribal chieftains, the feudal lords, the pashas, and the warlords of the Middle East and Asia, but to settle the war and to restore the independence of the nations of Europe by removing the alien armies—all of them, our own included." He recommended that the government explore every means of coaxing the Soviets into withdrawing the Red Army from its emplacements, in return for reciprocal action by the Anglo-American forces, and thereby hasten the reemergence of a single European economy that one day might evolve into a federated political entity. Similar to Kennan's hopes during World War II, Lippmann advocated an integrated Europe that would embrace a Germany devoluted into its major state components—Bavaria, Saxony, Hesse, Prussia, and so on. "Not German unity but European unity, not German self-sufficiency but European self-sufficiency, not a Germany to contain Russia but a Germany neutralized as between Russia and the west . . . should be the aims of our . . . policy."[26] Containment bluntly meant, by contrast, the indefinite partition of Europe, uninterrupted preparations for war, and constant danger.

Lippmann concluded his public criticisms of "Mr. X" and the Truman Doctrine by telling his readers that the international approach he supported was being promoted by Secretary Marshall, but it was still far from being designated the primary policy. The competition between the two lines constituted "the central drama within the State Department, within the Administration, within the government as a whole." Lippmann applauded the secretary for taking seriously the limits of American power and for not trying to dictate the outcome of every complicated international problem. When the United States could realistically advance its own interests and be of assistance to others, as in Europe, then Marshall pushed for aid, but under any other conditions he urged caution and, often, waiting. In the case of the Chinese civil war, reported Lippmann, the secretary prudently opposed underwriting Chiang Kai-shek's weak government and tried to apply the venerable American tenet that the country avoid entanglement in distant disputes beyond its means to understand or control; such a sensible precept was, unfortunately, lost on the likes of "Mr. X."

A longtime admirer of Lippmann's, with whom he sometimes discussed international politics, Kennan was simultaneously stung by the writer's faultfinding and exhilarated by his attention, by his challenge. As he wrote Armstrong, "I have never doubted that in the end the paths of Mr. Lippmann and myself would meet. History will tell which was the more tortuous."[27] Kennan's eagerness to defend himself, however, faded after some early discouragement, and he wound up not explaining himself—at least not until the publication of his first volume of memoirs in 1967.

He felt that Lippmann had attacked him for insisting on precisely those features of Truman's policy with which he most strongly disagreed, while those aspects of policy that he had helped promote were being held up to him as an intellectual reproach and a model of the type of diplomacy the United States should pursue. In April 1948, while in the Bethesda Naval Hospital stricken with another spell of ulcers, Kennan took time to write a considered reply to Lippmann.

He began his letter by protesting that, although he had supported the decision to assist the Greek and Turkish governments, he had violently disagreed with the extravagant rhetoric of the Truman Doctrine.[28] And, in fact, Kennan had drafted and submitted alternative language to the president's advisors that was less sweeping and dramatic, but it had been rejected on the basis that it lacked the inspirational appeal necessary to rally congressional support. On the other hand, contrary to Lippmann, Kennan properly reported that he had been involved with both the formulation of Marshall's Harvard address and with the development of plans for European recovery. As for Lippmann's criticism that he had overemphasized military factors, Kennan was more puzzled than anything else: "You have chosen to interpret 'containment' . . . in a military sense, and have talked of it as though it implied readiness on our part to hold the Red Army at any point where it touches the free world. I do not know what grounds I could have given for such an interpretation."[29]

Kennan admitted that the military strength of both sides played a role in European continental politics, but it was hardly decisive and the Red Army did not pose the principal problem for most West Europeans. And never would he have suggested so foolish an idea as that the United States try to be equally strong everywhere in a military sense; anyway, most existing American military commitments—in Japan, Germany, and Italy—were the result of previous war problems, which originally had nothing to do with checking the USSR. America's continued, and small, military presence in Europe was meager as a sanction against Russia, but useful as a symbol of US interests.

The Soviet campaign against the West was essentially political, according to Kennan. In Western Europe native communists, with the aid of concealed Soviet help, were busily working to exploit the dislocations caused by war. He worried that, if communists succeeded in forming governments, they would immediately align their foreign policies with the Soviet Union, thereby diminishing the Anglo-American world. He stressed that the Soviets' spearheads were the local communists, and the counter-weapon that could beat them was the vigor and soundness of political life in the intended victim countries. But, alas, the Europeans were afflicted with weak nerves; and, while their attention was diverted by a phantom invading army, they dealt inadequately with more imminent dangers: they "could do away with two-thirds of their own danger if they would face up to the problem of their own communists." Domestic violence in various countries, stirred by local communists, might suit Soviet leaders, but one of their major goals was to avoid every kind of large-scale fighting. "The Russians don't want to invade anyone."[30] The chances of war in the near future were, therefore, remote.

Yet Kennan had discerned in 1946 that many liberals and intellectuals despaired that a Soviet-US conflict was fast approaching; his article in *Foreign Affairs,* he claimed, was intended to overcome this ignorance and defeatism. He wanted to educate reasonable people in, and fortify them for, a period of difficult diplomacy when political arts and skills would dominate. They had to understand that military solutions would be used only as an absolutely last resort:

> I wanted to get across to those people . . . that war was inevitable only if they let all of Europe go by default to the political onslaught which the Kremlin was conducting. They were prepared to leave off at the point where real diplomacy should have begun. They assumed that a firm policy on our part would provoke the Russians to military conquest. It was my task to persuade them that only a firm policy on our part had a chance of preventing a deterioration of the world situation which would eventually be bound to engage our military interests.[31]

Kennan's evaluation of foreign policy as it had actually evolved, 1946–1948, was mainly favorable, and he took sharp issue with Lippmann. In particular, he chided Lippmann for saying that the United States would fail by squandering its resources in trying to hold the line. Instead, US aid to European countries had been well within the nation's means, and it had been directed toward political and economic reconstruction, not toward some preposterous military scheme against Russia. Containment deserved credit: "Has Iran gone? Or Turkey? Or Greece? I can assure you that not one of them would have been an independent country today if we had not done what we did. Has Trieste fallen? Or Austria? Has not new hope and spirit been infused into western Europe?" In France, notably, the democrats had weakened the communist position and a new optimism was replacing postwar fatalism. As for communist successes in Czechoslovakia and China, Kennan professed not to be overly anxious: "I never said we would—or should—be able to hold equally everywhere. But I felt there was a good sporting chance that we would be able to hold in enough places, and in sufficiently strategic places, to accomplish our general purpose."[32] Europe's steady recovery and America's continued economic and political unassailability were in themselves vindication of State Department policy.

Lippmann's further suggestions that the United States would grow weary of containment before the Soviets and that a series of reverses would follow galled Kennan. He countered that America and its allies could far more easily maintain their positions along the east-west partition than the Soviets, who really were overcommitted and were as short on moral values as they were economically disadvantaged. And he exclaimed, once again, that it was not merely a question of comparative physical resources—the Soviet political system, itself, would undermine Russia's external policies. In the *lingua franca* of the Cold War, Kennan declared, "It is the Russians, not we, who cannot afford a world half slave and half free. The contrasts implicit in such a world are intolerable to the fictions on which their power rests. . . . If only one ray of light of individual dignity or human inquiry is permitted to exist, the [Soviet] effort must eventually fail."[33] Soviet Russia, with its panoply of autocrats, police organs, and pompous ideology, was like other bloated bullies: inherently frail and bound to lose in any comparison or political contest against the West.

This line of reasoning led Kennan back to the subject always dear to him, namely that the United States must carefully guard its own political vitality and social balance. And he readily admitted that ideological crusades and extreme posturing were as repellent to him as to anyone, including Lippmann: "Let us find health and vigor and hope, and the diseased portion of the earth will fall behind of its own doing. For that we need no aggressive strategic plans, no provocation of military hostilities, no show-downs . . . and no pat slogans with a false pretense to international validity."[34] The Americans only had to bide their time peaceably and with patience while helping to educate the Soviets in the virtues of diplomacy.

He insisted to Lippmann, as he had with others, that the Russians would eventually find it necessary and helpful to talk; perhaps negotiations were not too far in the future. He denied, however, that limited understanding and compromise agreements could ever lead to a comprehensive resolution of fundamental problems. Soviet-US rivalry ran too deep and its chief impetus sprang from the moral defects of Soviet philosophy and practice: as with their precommunist predecessors, Soviet leaders justified repression at home because of alleged hatred and danger emanating from abroad.

Kennan confessed that he, and probably others within the government, were willing to excuse or forget for purposes of diplomacy past Soviet misdeeds and injuries inflicted upon Europe and the United States. In the best of all possible worlds, the two countries could achieve a *modus vivendi:* "I would be willing to let Russia go ahead with the development of its own political tradition in its own cruel and wasteful way. I would not refuse to give it help in economic development if it ceased to threaten us." Given the fate, though, of Poland, Hungary, Rumania, Bulgaria, Czechoslovakia, East Germany, and the Baltic states, one had to acknowledge the moral and political limits of accommodating the Kremlin's ruthless men: "Today I am afraid that they have staked their political fortunes, for better or for worse, on the . . . destruction of the soul of the western world."[35]

Kennan did agree with Lippmann that the Soviets should be eased out of Europe, but he doubted that they could be persuaded to do so by promises of reciprocity or even by the example of unilateral Anglo-American withdrawal. Besides, the Soviets were congenitally unable to leave any non-Russian territory with good grace and order, and their cruelties in Eastern Europe guaranteed complications for any future day when Soviet power did recede: "whether anyone can really help them to escape the consequences of the enormous injustices and follies they have perpetrated is questionable." War in central Europe might even explode in the wake of the political confusion and social disorder that would follow a Soviet retreat and the collapse of Marxist governments in Bucharest, Budapest, Prague, and Warsaw. At a minimum, the Soviets would then have to contend with a wall of hostile East European states, even more antipathetic to Soviet interests than in the

1930s, and willing to cooperate with any distant protector, including Germany. Did Lippmann not realize how unacceptable such a situation would be from the Soviet standpoint?

In summing up, Kennan wrote that the status quo was not so bad; at least it would do for the time being. Recovery in Europe was progressing at a satisfactory rate, the principal countries there were cooperating nicely with the United States, and the future held promise for negotiations with Moscow. Yet Kennan was nagged by doubts concerning how long the United States could sustain an effective European policy. The government, he complained, employed few individuals who knew much about the USSR or Europe, and these existing experts were endlessly checked by a jealous Congress and prohibited from representing the US abroad in a single, coherent voice. Even when the State Department was successful, few people— including, Kennan must have brooded, the Walter Lippmanns of the world— perceived or appreciated it: "To me the saddest part of this year's experience with the high affairs of state is not the realization of how hard it is for a democracy to conduct a successful foreign policy—although that *is* sad. It is the realization that if it did conduct a successful foreign policy, so few people would recognize it for what it was."[36]

After finishing his letter, Kennan expected, or at least hoped, to make it public by having the *Foreign Service Journal* print it. Because the journal's editor, Henry Villard, objected to the "personal angle" from which Kennan mounted his defense, its publication was refused; and for reasons still murky Kennan never mailed the missive to Lippmann either. That he was extremely exasperated, though, is clear. From his hospital bed he fretted, "I don't know what the hell to do with it, and if Chip [Bohlen] would like to show it to Lippmann he can."[37] Bohlen declined, however, to act as intermediary; and, as a result, a chorus of scholars have doubted Kennan's interpretation in 1967 of what he wrote in 1947 for *Foreign Affairs*. After all, they reason, when he could have disavowed the military interpretation of containment that Lippmann and others gave the article, Kennan remained silent. But, in fact, the truth lay elsewhere: for reasons of their own neither Villard nor Bohlen was helpful, and, for the duration of his official duties, Kennan was inhibited by Marshall's stern command that "planners don't talk." In the secretary's view, his subordinate had made the mistake once—writing for *Foreign Affairs*— and he must not repeat the offense.[38]

Principles of Cold War Policy

Defining the Threats to US Security

It was within the strict confines of the National War College and the State Department, not in the public prints, that Kennan developed and stated most clearly his views on how to manage the USSR. Although he refined a number of principles, they did not in their aggregate amount to a formal strategy or policy formula. Indeed, he has never been drawn to abstract thinking and has a visceral dislike for any all-encompassing doctrine—invariably it will become rigid, distort changing realities, and hopelessly reduce policy choices. In his mind, containment should not have been elevated to resemble anything like a strategy: "It was merely another of those semantic vulgarizations to which our mass media are prone when they lack the patience and inclination to look at things carefully."[39]

Kennan's most important premise in the late 1940s—one that he had wanted to impress upon Lippmann—was that Soviet Russia had suffered immense damage during the recent war and occupied an even weaker position than in 1939 from which to challenge the United States. He reported in summer 1946 that Soviet iron and steel production was less than half of its prewar level; untold cities, towns, and bridges were destroyed; the entire transportation system was in shambles, and only a single track of railway connected Moscow to Leningrad. Moreover, Stalin and his colleagues were cautious in their foreign policy for domestic political reasons. They feared that their support at home was slender and that a major international conflict would trigger mutinies—large-scale defections to the invading Germans in 1941 surely haunted Stalin's imagination. Kennan also believed that Soviet leaders, like their nineteenth-century predecessors, worried that leading elements in the army would be debilitated, or worse, by overexposure to the cultural superiority and technical achievements of the West should they ever come to occupy extensive portions of it. As it was, the Soviets were encountering problems aplenty in trying to organize tens of millions of subjugated aliens in Eastern Europe and were not eager to add new responsibilities. In view of these circumstances, Russia could not be regarded as a power that had solved all its internal problems, was armed to the teeth, and stood ready to instigate a third world war. Even in periods of relative strength and affluence, there was nothing to encourage Soviet leaders into believing that Russia could suddenly and victoriously wage an aggressive war. In tiny Finland, for example, they had "got their fingers burned."[40]

Kennan, nevertheless, remained convinced during the Cold War that, however unsuited it was for enlarging influence by military means, Stalin's government was incurably "power-minded" and wanted to make its weight felt as far as possible— especially if that could be done without acquiring burdensome new obligations. In the case of Soviet pressure against Turkey in 1947, for example, preferred Soviet tactics were evident: "Their expansion has to go through the channels of subterranean penetration, and they have to make it look as though it were a spontaneous rise of Communism, or what they call progressive feeling in other areas."[41] Everywhere in the zones of the Middle East, Mediterranean, and Europe, the Soviets were seeking to establish a hegemony basically no less hostile to Anglo-American interests than that proposed by Hitler's Reich. Only the method of expansion and the means of control would differ.

Given the Soviet Union's proclivities to subvert, outflank, and disrupt US concerns, Kennan urged, contrary though it was to American sensibilities and traditions, that the government explicitly identify its foreign interests and fashion a policy in which means and ends were closely coordinated. If the government was too intellectually indolent to do this and was content with only the most inchoate notions, then it would quickly lose the political advantages that its arms had won, 1941–1945. In dealing with the Soviets the United States had to be firm and clear about where it stood.

As some scholars have already noted, Kennan determined America's foreign interests according to geopolitical criteria. It was not, however, until one year after Lippmann had leveled his charges against containment that Kennan began to specify the nature of these criteria. Very likely, Lippmann's severe criticisms had the effect, and Kennan gives some evidence for this in his memoirs, of forcing him to face squarely the problem of defining vital interests and distinguishing them from secondary ones.[42] Yet he seems never to have fully resolved the issues.

He declared in August 1948, four months after writing his long response to Lippmann, that the administration should identify those areas of the world that were primary to US security in the sense that they could not be permitted to fall into hostile hands. The United States had to "put forward as the first specific objective of . . . policy and as an irreducible minimum of national security the maintenance of political regimes in those areas . . . favorable to the continued power and independence of our nation." Many of the states he deemed crucial bordered on the Atlantic and included such obvious ones as Canada, Great Britain, and Mexico. But that was just a beginning. He also included Greenland and Iceland, the rest of Scandinavia, the Iberian peninsula, the continental states along the English Channel, "Morocco and the west coast of Africa down to the bulge, and the countries of South America from the bulge north."[43] He mentioned, further, all the countries of the Mediterranean and the Middle East as far as and including Iran. In East Asia and the Pacific, he was emphatic that the United States retain the cooperation and friendship of Japan and the Philippines. This enormous area, historically diverse, culturally varied, and economically uneven, represented as wide a sphere of influence as any entertained by the most zealous advocate of Manifest Destiny and was only too compatible with the intent of the questionable Truman Doctrine. Kennan soon recognized this and, consequently, tried to produce something more reasonable.

In a lecture at the Naval War College (October 1948), he drew another sketch of geopolitics and how Soviet-US rivalry might be viewed. It, too, was tentative, however, and did not constitute a universally recognized axiom in the administration: "It is nothing that has been thrashed out and approved by the government . . . in Washington. It's something which I am thinking out here personally and before you."[44]

In his reevaluation of geopolitical interests, he stated that most of the lands in what later was called the Third World were strategically unimportant to the United States. He justified this exclusion of the Asian mainland, Africa, and most of Latin America from US concerns on the basis of a rather crude theory of climate determinism. Kennan explained that only in temperate climates had people been able to produce vigorous civilizations "capable of developing the resources of the earth in a formidable way. Perhaps you may find someday," he hypothesized, "that it is only the challenge of having to house and clothe themselves before the demands of winter and of the cold . . . that have really brought things out of men, things that have enabled them to develop industry. I think we may as well recognize that in most of the tropical areas of the earth there is no great likelihood of a vigorous civilization springing up within our time."[45] He did speculate that eventually the problems of high birthrate, political underdevelopment, poor public health, and poverty might be solved in such parts of the world and that they would advance toward the "spiritual and physical vigor" that existed in the temperate zones. Until then, the US should concentrate its energies on the northern hemisphere.

He argued that there were only four centers of power outside of the United States that by reason of their natural resources, industrial capacity, and talent of population could produce significant military and naval power. And they all lay within or near the Eurasian land mass. Two of them, Great Britain and Japan, presented no difficulties for the United States in 1948. The other two, however, Western Europe (primarily Germany) and the Soviet Union raised fundamental issues: "Our problem lies in the relationship between these two power centers and in the question of who controls them."

The only conceivable threat to US security would be an immense concentration of power in Eurasia. To date, the US had been successful in averting Soviet political seizure of Western Europe; the remaining tasks were to keep Russia weak and ultimately maneuver it back to its former boundaries by means short of war, and to prevent the reemergence of radical nationalists—like the Nazis—in Germany. But above all else, a balance of power had to be reinstituted on the continent between Germany and the Soviet Union. "Because as long as that balance exists, as long as each of them has to look over his shoulder at the other . . . neither will be able to risk the diversionary effort of an attack on the North Atlantic community, with which we stand or fall." The United States, then, had to cultivate this balance of forces while abstaining from a dissipation of its national resources on secondary objectives which were of marginal significance.[46]

According to Kennan, and this was similar to Churchill's ideas at the time, the best way for the US to organize its international policy was in close cooperation with the other two English-speaking powers of the Atlantic, Canada, and Great Britain. On the continent it would be desirable for France and the western portion of Germany to break with their centuries-old, tragic tradition and cooperate, too. These two great centers of power, the Anglo-Saxon and the Franco-German, could through their combined efforts and common policies guarantee both Europe's future vitality and international stability. In the Middle East, to assure direct and secure access to petroleum sources, they had to maintain political order and buttress allies, making them impervious to Soviet influence.

The Instruments of American Policy

Kennan's attitude toward the purposes and correct uses of military force in the late 1940s is more complicated than most commentators have realized. On the one hand, he had a sheer horror of it and believed that its use again on a scale comparable to World War II would mean the end of everything worthwhile in civilization. Yet, on the other, he believed that the United States had to maintain its military power and on occasions use it in small theaters and for periods of limited duration. And under extreme provocation, the Americans should even be willing to wage total war.

Though an enormous military establishment was unnecessary, Kennan believed that it was important that the nation sustain a military posture sufficient to inflict prohibitive costs on any state that might tangle with the United States or one of its allies. He was also, in the jargon of a later era, a proponent of flexible response and never hesitated to state that the Americans retain enough strength and enough varied means to use different calibrations of military force in at least two theaters of operation simultaneously. In any event, the underlying lesson should be manifest: "that everyone know we can pack a mean punch in a short time."[47]

Kennan was inclined to view past wars and nonnuclear wars of the twentieth century according to Karl von Clausewitz's classic dictum: war is a continuation of national policy by other means. And though he expected that political and diplomatic measures against Russia would succeed in mitigating the worst aspects of Moscow's anti-Western policy, he did not shrink from contemplating the worst case and urged that the United States be prepared. If the Soviets should prevail by "means of civil wars and violent actions on the part of communist factions in intimidating and seizing power basically throughout the continent—then there is no question but that we should be up against a situation in which military force would be the deciding factor. . . . Then we would have to regard our military force as the leading component of our policy." But whether peace endured or war erupted, the United States had to improve on its record of separating political and military means to achieve international goals. As he told officers at the National War College, US policy against Moscow should inextricably mix military and political methods: "It is you in the armed forces who must help us today in the battle of political containment. If this battle is not won, it is we [diplomats] who will have to help you . . . to give political effect to the utilization of armed force."[48]

Fairly confident that a Soviet-US war would not occur, Kennan concentrated on the importance of using military assets in a diplomatically skillful fashion during peacetime. Temperamentally and by principle opposed to anything impetuous, he felt strongly that they not be used casually or in a threatening manner; such behavior was gratuitous and silly, usually forced the other side to adopt a more intransigent stance than was warranted, and introduced a jarring tone to diplomatic negotiations. It was better, instead, to regard one's military might along the lines preached by Kennan's political hero, Theodore Roosevelt: "All we really have to do is be strong and ready to use that strength. We don't have to broadcast it."[49] Not only did US military power act as the ultimate sanction, but it lent seriousness and authority to the statements of the government as it operated in world affairs. In Europe, for example, US military forces cast a shadow out of all proportion to their actual size that encouraged allies and worried those parties beholden to the Soviet Union. During the Trieste crisis, when Tito's Yugoslavia pressed for Italy's surrender of the city, Kennan urged that Anglo-American forces be promptly reinforced throughout the eastern Mediterranean and Adriatic. This should be done discreetly, "without any further comment [while we] act in the [UN] council sessions as though we never even thought for a moment that anyone would be capable of an act of armed force." Yugoslavia would get the message, the issue could quickly be resolved. "You have no idea," he philosophized, of "how much it contributes to the general politeness and pleasantness of diplomacy when you have a little quiet force in the background. People who are otherwise very insulting and very violent become just as pleasant—why, they couldn't be nicer if they belonged to the same golf club and played golf together every Sunday morning."[50]

While he hoped that military instruments would be kept in perspective as only one category of tools in foreign policy, and subordinate to diplomacy, Kennan recommended that the attitudes of American leftists and pacifists be altogether isolated from policy formulation. He evidently had lost all sympathy with those he encountered in 1946: "A lot of them have it firmly ingrained in their psychology that if you maintain your strength and keep it in the immediate background of your diplomatic action you are courting further trouble and provoking hostilities." Years later, Kennan the historian—in his research and writing about the origins of World War I—did conclude that the maintenance of armaments, navies, and armies leads to their use, but in the late 1940s he had no qualms about the proposition that peace is best preserved through strength. "What our pacifists are incapable of understanding," he lectured students at the National War College, "is that maintenance of strength in the democratic nations is actually the most peaceful of all the measures we can take short of war because the greater your strength, the less likelihood you are ever going to use it. . . ."[51]

Not only did liberals of the Henry Wallace ilk carp about the hazards of war, while never proposing serious suggestions for managing dangerous situations, and grossly underestimate the degree of Soviet antipathy for the West, but they also lacked in Kennan's view an appreciation—and this was their major fault—for the volatility and violence of the American people. Once their wrath had been aroused, they were likely to charge off in any number of directions: the use of atomic bombs and a policy of unconditional surrender were examples of their most recent and unrestrained passion. Timely and limited use of armed force in the service of clearly defined, obtainable aims had much to recommend by contrast: "I think the thing you have to ask the American liberals who want to go easy on the Russians at the moment is 'Where do you expect us to draw the line?' and, 'Is it not better that it be drawn at a point where American emotions and the feelings of the American people are not too [deeply] engaged rather than at a point nearer home where you are going to get a more violent reaction on the part of our people which nobody can control?' "[52]

Wherever they exerted political influence, the Soviets were likely to push to the limit of America's danger zone of patience. Therefore, the United States must be prepared for any type or size of war: "For great nations as for individuals today, there is no real security and there is no alternative to living dangerously. And when people say, 'My God, we might get into a war!' the only thing I know to say is 'Exactly so.' The price of peace has become the willingness to sacrifice it to a good cause and that is all there is to it."[53] Yet Kennan believed through the late 1940s, even during the bleakest days when Russia denied the West access to Berlin, that measures short of war would suffice to safeguard US interests. Luckily, as the airlift vividly demonstrated, the Anglo-Americans were capable of inventive policy that matched means—superior Western air power—with the desirable, obtainable ends of keeping peace and holding a vulnerable salient.

Generally, the United States would not have to improvise so spectacularly in Europe, but should continue supporting the Marshall Plan until such time as the major countries were politically rehabilitated and secure against the boring in of Soviet puppets and sympathizers. And the use of armed force in Europe should not only be considered as a last resort; rather, Kennan held, it should be viewed as a tool normally of little usefulness, as something clumsy. Soviet subversion and support of local communists were simply not susceptible to correction by armed force: a failure on America's part to recognize this fact would cause more harm than good.

In dealing with the Soviet government, Kennan hoped that US officials would understand that its perceptions of the world were not monolithic and that they would bear in mind that the United States had potential friends as well as enemies in the Kremlin.[54] Those well-placed people favorably disposed toward America wished for peace; thought the United States did, too; wanted future collaboration; and believed that genuine Soviet security did not require political suppression, widespread police activity, and arrogance throughout Eastern Europe and Soviet Asia. For the moment, however, the worst chauvinistic elements within the Soviet leadership were ascendant and the moderates on the defensive. That they were a pathetic, helpless minority was partly due to US policies: "We have [compromised them] with our unceasing appeasement," Kennan stated in 1946, "which has tended time and time again to cut the ground out from under their feet and to make it look as though they were wrong, as though it paid to push us around, as though there were no necessity of heeding our views."[55] It was important, then, in order to encourage Soviet moderates, that the United States make its diplomacy as worthy of respect as its science, technology, and industry.

Kennan doubted, though, and never mind the indiscriminate language—mainly for Forrestal—in the "X article" about the breaking up of Soviet power, that the United States could ever do anything that would abruptly or significantly alter Stalin's regime. A sensible balance of power policy was about the best America and its allies could expect from the Soviet Union. It was useful to realize at the same time that the communist government, like any government, was sensitive to domestic popular opinion, and it, in turn, was subject to outside influences—totalitarian constraints notwithstanding. Kennan was optimistic, in particular, about the impact that propaganda aimed against the civilian population would have on Soviet international behavior. Western radio broadcasts and journals, books, and newspapers smuggled into the country were certain to have a psychological effect over time: "Anything we can do . . . to keep on bringing it home to the Soviet people that the propaganda of their own government is false, that the outside world is not hostile to them, that it is only their own leaders who stand in the way . . . that all just increases the strain on the system, and it is all to the good in the end."[56]

Kennan was also hopeful that the United States could translate its economic power into an effective Cold War weapon; this idea eventually became an article of faith in the Policy Planning Staff. He did doubt that Russia itself was vulnerable to economic warfare, but he knew that America's dazzling, intact economy fascinated the impoverished East Europeans, especially the East Germans and Czechs who were used to high standards of material life. Perhaps the entire satellite area could be lured from the Soviet sphere; at the very least its exclusive and economically artificial dependency on Russia could be weakened. Although the Soviets had nothing of economic value to offer to their assorted European clients, they could be relied upon to resist the economic penetration—even under the guise of rehabilitation—of Eastern Europe by outside powers. And therein lay the basis for sowing discord between Soviet masters and their so-called junior partners: "As long as the democratic powers continue to possess by far the greater part of the world productive capacity they ought really to . . . make it highly uncomfortable . . . for any smaller power to be outside their economic orbit. To the extent that they exercise economic pressure against such smaller powers they ought to be able to produce discontent, trouble and dissension within the totalitarian orbit."[57] This principle of Kennan's was given tangible expression when the administration, expecting that the Soviets would block it, decided to offer Marshall aid to Eastern Europe. In the case of Yugoslavia, the results were dramatic, as one of the chief reasons for Tito's defection from the Soviet fold was Stalin's veto of US assistance to the Balkans.

Finally, according to Kennan, there were a variety of diplomatic techniques that the United States should employ against Moscow. Although he was disinclined to take the United Nations seriously, he hoped its diverse forums could be used to embarrass the Soviets. There were already occasions in the late 1940s, and undoubtedly there would be more in the future, when power issues involving US strategic interests coincided with the moral feelings of many people abroad. It was worthwhile, in other words, for the United States to cultivate support for its policies within the UN; the welfare of the international organization did not matter beyond the point where it could be used for American advantage, however. And the US government should be equally unabashed in dealing with Soviet officialdom. If necessary, the government should not hesitate to withdraw its chief of mission in Moscow or otherwise reduce representation to Russia; threatening or actually severing relations with the Soviets could be useful in the face of extreme discourtesy to American diplomats. He also advised that the administration limit private business between Soviet and American nationals and, through whatever means available, discourage collaboration in cultural and technical tasks until such time when the Soviets started acting politely and in good faith. It was with obvious feeling and on the basis of his personal experiences in Moscow that Kennan averred that he would like to see the United States turn such controls on and off like a faucet, exactly in proportion to the treatment Americans themselves received abroad.[58]

Domestic Considerations

At the heart of Kennan's concern about the Cold War's outcome was his long-standing preoccupation with the resilience of American society. As he told Forrestal, and later the readers of *Foreign Affairs,* "the issue of Soviet-American relations is in essence a test of the over-all worth of the United States as a nation among nations."

When the first flushes of what was later labeled McCarthyism began to appear, Kennan feared that internal disharmony, intolerance, and dogmaticism might break—as they had threatened to do in the 1930s—the moral and political structure of the United States. Why else except for the persistence of defects that he had analyzed in "The Prerequisites" did the Soviet Union, an economically weak and politically backward country, come so near to disrupting American confidence and morale? The Soviets could never be a menace to the US except as Americans were a menace to their own society. Old failings were beginning to catch up in the late

1940s: "The real threat to our society, the threat which has lain behind the Soviet armies, behind the *Daily Worker,* and behind the aberrations of confused American left-wingers, will not be overcome until we learn to view ourselves realistically and purge ourselves of some of our prejudices, our hypocrisies, and our lack of discipline."[59]

Kennan wanted the government to take the leading role in stiffening the public against hysteria while helping it to understand that, although problems existed between Russia and the United States, they were manageable. The executive branch in these circumstances also had a responsibility not to whip popular feeling into such a frenzy that it antagonized the Soviet peoples or ruled out future negotiations—the rhetoric of the Truman Doctrine must be dropped. Americans had to see plainly that the Soviet Union was a great power, worthy of respect; the Russians were an energetic, creative people to whom conventional courtesy was appropriate: "I do not want intelligent and realistic people to lose patience with [them] too soon." Ideally, their expansionist tendencies could be rebuffed in so unprovocative a manner that basic American purposes would not be subject to misinterpretation.[60]

Instead, the public and the government (and at times to his everlasting chagrin Kennan himself) indulged throughout the late 1940s and beyond in an exaggerated type of self-congratulation, excessive condemnation of others, and intellectual fantasy. The United States in Cold War was slightly ridiculous. As Kennan phrased it to the respected diplomatic historian Norman Graebner: "We Americans like our adversaries wholly inhuman: all-powerful, omniscient, monstrously efficient, unhampered by any serious problems of their own. . . . It is the reflection of a philosophic weakness—of an inability to recognize any relativity in matters of friendship and enmity."[61]

Kennan was well satisfied by the promulgation of the National Security Act in 1947 because he hoped it would have the effect of insulating foreign policy experts from the scrutiny and, as he saw it, gross ignorance and emotionalism of the public. It also created machinery, notably the CIA and NSC, that would enable the government to develop practical policies unencumbered by fashionable slogans and high-minded generalities popular with elected representatives. Marshall's creation of the Policy Planning Staff was itself part of the State Department's reorganization for Cold War. Absolved of any operational responsibilities, the PPS was charged with advising the secretary in the long-term crafting of foreign policy objectives, in studying political-military problems, and in evaluating the quality of current policies. It examined these issues from the standpoint only of the secretary of state and did not try to reflect the broader views of the whole government apparatus or shifting public opinion.

Marshall himself embodied for Kennan—as he did for others, including Dean Acheson and Churchill—the perfect public servant and American gentleman: honorable, orderly, devoted unswervingly to the national interest, and disdainful of narrow partisan causes. He did not seek popularity or the limelight, but meant only to do his duty as he conceived it: "He valued the considered judgment of history; but for the day-to-day applause of contemporaries he had as little concern as for their criticisms." With the Policy Planning Staff he was also correct and guarded his dignity; he called Kennan only by his surname—a useful antidote, the latter agreed in retrospect, for "a Government addicted to the point of absurdity to the outward show of informal good-fellowship."[62] Kennan was, in any case, intensely proud of his association with Marshall and appreciated his injunction to "avoid trivia." At the same time, Marshall was respectful of his subordinates and did not intrude himself rudely upon the operations of his sensitive bureaucracy which possessed procedures and traditions quite foreign to his own army career.[63]

Kennan and Marshall were eager to involve the most able people available in the activities of the Policy Planning Staff. By early June 1947, they had formed the nucleus of a young—average age was forty-two—and spirited group, aptly dubbed by an attentive press as Marshall's "brain trust." Carleton Savage was a twenty-year veteran of the State Department and held an MA in History. Joseph Johnson, PhD Harvard, was a former university professor and during the war had been chief of the department's Division of International Security Affairs. Ware Adams was a career diplomat, expert on Europe, and recently stationed in Vienna. Thirty-five-year-old Jacques Reinstein was an economist by training and had helped negotiate the peace treaty with Italy. And John Paton Davies, a first-rate student of Chinese politics and society who had personal experiences of Russia as well as the Far East, returned from overseas at Kennan's request. Although the membership roster changed during the late 1940s with the addition and departure of individuals, it was a constant source of thoughtful advice to Marshall and later Secretary Acheson, and represented for Kennan the government's best effort at analyzing the world and America's place in it: "For us in the Planning Staff, the world was our oyster."[64]

For Kennan, his appointment to the Staff's directorship was a triumph and a recognition by the State Department of his intellectual merit and achievements. (Marshall had held Kennan in good regard ever since their first meetings during World War II.) He was responsible for a collection of talented men and answerable only to one of the few people that he truly admired. At last and under promising conditions, Kennan must have reflected, he had a chance to help shape in most compelling ways the direction of foreign policy. Yet it was at precisely this time when the "red scare" began to exact its toll on diplomacy and foreign policy-makers. To cite one example, Truman's nomination of John Carter Vincent to the position of career minister stalled throughout the first half of 1947 because of extraordinary allegations by Senator Styles Bridges and publisher William Loeb that Vincent had attempted to sabotage America's China policy, had deliberately misled his superiors, and was conspiring to deliver China to the communists. In response to these charges, Acting Secretary of State Acheson championed Vincent, whom he described as "a gentleman and a disinterested and loyal servant of our republic."[65] Acheson's impressive count-by-count refutation of the groundless charges cleared his subordinate.

Kennan's own first encounter with the domestic reaction could hardly have been less pleasant or more discomforting. While assembling the Policy Planning Staff he had become interested in recruiting Professor Emile Despres, a Williams College economist, as a consultant for the summer of 1947, when the most difficult planning and execution of the Marshall Plan would occur. During the war he had served with the State Department and later toured overseas as an assistant to William Clayton, undersecretary of state for economic affairs. Despres was as eminently qualified to serve as any member of the permanent PPS, and Kennan gladly made him an offer. But, because of suspicions about Despres's integrity and loyalty raised by Karl Mundt of the House Un-American Activities Committee, matters soon became delicate. The problem was compounded by the fact that Mundt was helping at the time to sponsor legislation supporting European recovery, and for this reason the State Department was being careful not to antagonize him. Consequently, although the evidence and charges against Despres were scanty, Kennan retracted his offer of appointment in mid-June on the grounds that Despres's association with the PPS would become a subject of unfavorable comment and probably of altercation with Congress. He told the professor candidly: "I think this would not be in your interest, and I am sure that it would not be in the interest of the planning work, which is only in its infancy and which has already received more publicity than is good for it."[66]

Both Despres and James Baxter, president of Williams College, were enraged by the shabbiness of the affair and protested that a courageous man would have fought for a patently just cause against the irresponsible charges of a bigoted congressman. Responding hotly to Baxter, Kennan said that he was now burdened with grave responsibilities more important than Despres or even his own sense of fair play: "They involve the interests of the country in the most immediate sense, and I do not think that those interests would be served by having this relatively minor matter made a *cause celebre.*"[67] In a telling counterpoint to Kennan's earlier condemnation of the academic fraternity, Baxter rejoined that the episode was just another illustration of why men of the highest character and distinction often chose university careers over government service.[68]

Kennan was embarrassed and pained by the episode and, although a fair case can be made for his wanting to protect his fledgling staff, the Despres incident indicated that, by Kennan's own standard, the United States was beginning to lose the most important battle of the Cold War. The Despres case was, of course, like that of Vincent's only a modest foreshadowing of disasters to come that eventually ruined the careers of many of Kennan's friends—including Davies, whom he defended unstintingly—and in the end helped him decide to leave the Foreign Service.

*   *   *   *

Kennan's debut as a nationally prominent figure in 1947 was ambiguous, his performance uneven. On the one hand, he assumed the role of educating the public with characteristic earnestness. Although his "X article" and lectures around the country were clearly in line with the government's larger campaign to garner public support and understanding for policies against Russia, his own conception of intellectual responsibility and teaching was multifaceted. He felt that he had worthy instruction and insights about Soviet Russia and US policy to impart to military figures (at the National War College), to ranking civilian authorities (such as Forrestal), and to articulate political observers and intellectuals (academic liberals, Lippmann) who themselves had a part to play in shaping American opinion. Unfortunately, with the publication of the "X article," he came a cropper on that problem that has always plagued pedagogues: how to keep distinct and separate one's diverse students and audiences. Originally meant for Forrestal, the article was interpreted by Lippmann as supporting many of the ideas that Kennan had been arguing against to military figures. An imperfect representation of his total views, it also was later used to justify actions, exemplified by NSC 68 and the establishment of NATO, that he opposed. Finally, its flamboyant language did nothing to counter—indeed, just the contrary—the increasingly strident tone of public discussion that so incensed Kennan and handicapped policymakers such as himself, who were trying to fashion diplomacy according to rational calculations about the balance of power. The conclusion, then, is inescapable: in a fundamental sense, he failed as an educator.

Quite apart from Lippmann's criticisms at the time, Kennan's views in 1947 about America's place in the world were unclear and unfinished. Although he had long agreed with Halford Mackinder, whom he studied, that geography was an aid to statecraft, it was not until Lippmann prodded him that Kennan began really to grapple with the questions of what constituted power and how foreign centers of power related to US security. One result of Lippmann's having offered little that was positive in his critique was that Kennan's defining of concepts was awkward at first. He did agree that vital and peripheral interests had to be distinguished; but, because he rejected formulas as being too rigid and simple, his designations of what formed vital US interests varied. This will become more evident in the next two chapters as we analyze Kennan's specific recommendations for US policy in Europe and Asia. Only his essential indifference to Third World politics, oil notwithstanding, can be clearly traced to his theorizing in 1947.

As for dealing with the Soviet Union, Kennan's recommendations have been subject to much scholarly debate. Whereas John Gaddis, for example, has stressed the political and economic aspects of his thought, Eduard Mark has focused on the military and interventionist components. Neither view is wholly incorrect, but both are incomplete. Kennan believed in the late 1940s that all possible means should be employed to prevent Soviet expansion. He disagreed with those people who emphasized military methods to the exclusion of political ones, and so he expended a great effort in informing military men and their civilian superiors about the importance of political methods and concepts. He was equally opposed to prevailing liberal opinion and tried to overcome its reservations about US policy and to persuade it that military instruments were perfectly appropriate to diplomacy and that without them even the most moderate foreign policy was impossible: "There are situations in this world where not even worthy and necessary ends can be achieved without the application of force."[69] Early in 1949 he reiterated these apposite points to the newly named secretary of state, Dean Acheson: "The thesis of the X article . . . was that our main problem was a political one and that we had a good chance of coping with it by political means (at least means short of a full-scale shooting war) if we would stop moping, face up to the situation cheerfully and realistically, and conduct ourselves rationally, in terms of our epoch. I still feel that way."[70]

Kennan would surely have bridled at the idea, but his major principles in the late 1940s could probably be boiled down to this: during times of war the government should not lose sight of specific, concrete political objectives; during peacetime, it must not forget that military measures can be effectively and subtly used to advance foreign policy goals. The methods of war and politics, then, were absolutely intertwined in Kennan's thought. During the Cold War, the United States should cease having "separate patterns of measures—one pattern for peace and one pattern for war. We must select them according to the purpose we are pursuing . . . [and] what is indicated by the circumstances."[71] Diplomatic thinking and strategy for the duration of contest with the Soviet Union had to enjoy primacy over the less ambiguous, but less applicable, practices of simple war or peace.

Finally, Kennan expected that the quality of cultural and political life in the US would determine the ultimate success or failure of the country's diplomacy. The extremism that emerged in domestic society in the late 1940s startled him and caused him to retreat hastily from Despres. During the height of McCarthyism, Kennan despaired for a foreign policy at the mercy of demagogues and the most mean-spirited, parochial elements in society. He declaimed to the Century Club (May 7, 1953):

> I do not see how you can have a satisfactory situation as long as an atmosphere exists in which shibboleths are allowed to be established and to prevail, to the detriment of normal discussion—an atmosphere in which simple alternatives of foreign policy cannot even be discussed without leading to charges of subversion and treason—an atmosphere in which namecalling and insinuation take the place of calm and free debate.

The necessary first conditions for a thoughtful diplomacy were thus being superseded in Kennan's view by unchecked domestic political forces. Whatever residues of faith he still possessed in a democracy's ability to conduct steady, coherent foreign policy were irrevocably swept away in the late 1940s.

7

Cold War in Europe

Kennan's ideas of 1947–1949 about waging the Cold War in Europe met with mixed results. He did succeed in helping to shape the Marshall Plan in three distinctive ways: the West Europeans assumed the major responsibility for devising a program of economic relief; the Soviets bore the embarrassment of refusing an offer of apparent American generosity and had to accept much of the onus for the partitioning of Europe; West Germany's economic and political rehabilitation was achieved within a framework of general European recovery. In Kennan's view, the Marshall Plan was, overall, the single most important step taken by the United States to promote a stable balance of power in posthostilities Europe. It prevented the Soviets from exploiting a power vacuum and for a while, at least, promised to lighten the American burden in a bipolar world. He declared in the autumn of 1947: "It should be a cardinal point of our policy to see to it that the elements of independent power are developed on the Eurasian land mass as rapidly as possible, in order to [create a multipolar international order]. To my mind, the chief beauty of the Marshall Plan [is] that it [has] outstandingly this effect."[1]

Kennan's work on behalf of West European political and economic integration and German reunification was frustrated by a variety of factors, however. And he had expected that a skillfully manipulated US policy in Eastern Europe—cutting along the region's traditional national rivalries and playing to the fact that Soviet domination there lacked all claims to economic sense and political legitimacy—would greatly damage the links between the USSR and its satellite states. Their eventual independence would deprive Soviet Russia of substantial manpower pools, natural resources, and agricultural and industrial products. But with the exception of Yugoslavia, none of the countries in the eastern zone managed to break from Moscow. Part of the reason for this disappointing outcome, according to Kennan, lay with America's overmilitarization of the Cold War, which effectively deepened Europe's division and rendered unalterable Russia's grip on the East.

In directing the research, writing most of the recommendations, and supervising other operations of the Policy Planning Staff, Kennan was heavily taxed both emotionally and physically. Moreover, he was not an administrator by talent or training and, at first, the problems confronting US policy seemed almost to overwhelm him. After one unusually gruelling night session of the Policy Planning Staff, in which issues related to European recovery were analyzed and debated, Kennan became overwrought and tearful and so abruptly left the meeting; only after completing a long saunter through the deserted corridors of the State Department building did he return self-possessed.[2] As he once tried to explain to officers at the National War College, the endlessness and complexity of policymaking were bound to depress anyone, no matter how conscientious or intellectually nimble:

> [An] . . . astute person, working furiously against time, may indeed succeed in getting himself to a point where he thinks that with respect to one [problem], he is some three or four months ahead of events in his planning. But by the time he has gotten his ideas down on paper, the three or four months have mysteriously shrunk to that many weeks. By the time he has gotten his ideas accepted by others, they have become days. And by the time others have translated those ideas into action, it develops that the thing you were planning for took place day before yesterday, and everyone wants to know why in the hell you didn't foresee it a long time ago. Meanwhile, other things are occurring with maddening persistency [everywhere], and throngs of people are constantly plucking at your sleeve, looking knowingly in a certain direction. . . . And when you sit down to explore the problems of one particular area of this harried globe, then begins a babble of tongues and opinions which would shake the mental equilibrium of an oracle.[3]

Despite the continuous pressures bred by postwar crises, Kennan acquitted himself well as director of Policy Planning and won the admiration, if not always agreement, of his subordinates. Carleton Savage, John Paton Davies, Ware Adams, Robert Tufts, and others recalled in later years that Kennan was loyal in friendship, always articulate, intelligent, and dutiful in conducting the Staff's affairs. Typically, after a period of informal discussion with PPS colleagues about a given subject and consultation with experts from the department and universities, he would draft a position paper; before submitting a final paper to the secretary of state, Kennan would subject the original version to additional Staff discussion and criticism. With few exceptions the PPS reports and recommendations of 1947–1949 were basically his creations.[4]

The initial success of the Marshall Plan seemed to auger well for Kennan's career in policymaking circles. Yet the Truman government's mounting impatience with Stalin and a concomitant reliance upon military means to check the USSR led to an eclipse in Kennan's influence. When he resigned (December 1949) from the directorship of Policy Planning, ostensibly to devote full-time to his new job as counselor of the State Department, he was essentially isolated from the major thrust of US foreign policy. This isolation was symbolized by new procedures (inaugurated September 1949) in the State Department, whereby Kennan would have to submit for review by diverse interested agencies any PPS paper bound for the secretary. The effect was to dilute the Staff's recommendations and diminish its direct influence on the secretary and NSC.

Kennan's growing estrangement was confirmed by Acheson's choice of Paul

Nitze to succeed as the next chief of Policy Planning. Before joining the PPS in 1949 and serving as Kennan's deputy, Nitze had enjoyed a varied, successful career and had won wide recognition for this work on the Strategic Bombing Survey. He tended to be somewhat fatalistic about the future use of atomic weapons in wartime and in 1950 was the chief architect for NSC 68, the underlying assumptions of which were profoundly contrary to Kennan's views. It briefly mentioned national differences among communist states, but stressed the fundamental compatibility of Marxist regimes everywhere and their common policy purposes. It presented American-communist rivalry as a total contest in which highly coordinated Soviet-directed policies endangered all US interests abroad: "In the context of the present polarization of power a defeat of free institutions anywhere is a defeat everywhere."[5] Finally, whereas Kennan believed the USSR was a formidable adversary, but neither able nor eager to wage aggressive war, NSC 68 underscored an alleged imminent military threat posed by the Soviet Union and international communism. The implementation of NSC 68 in fiscal 1951 (and the Korean War) increased American military manpower by one million, quintupled aircraft production, and drove the defense budget to a level dizzying for those days: just below $50 billion. This measure and the thinking behind it offended Kennan and reinforced his decision, readily approved by Acheson, to take a leave of absence from the Foreign Service. He expected in June 1950 to assume residence in Princeton and begin diplomatic historical studies at the Institute for Advanced Study—a form of protest against contemporary foreign policy and a move toward permanent retirement.

West European Economic Recovery

In the immediate aftermath of World War II, Europe lay in a condition of unprecedented human and material ruin: in addition to the millions of people who had perished in the war, millions more were homeless, hungry, and unemployed; many of the great cities from Leningrad to Rotterdam had been severely damaged, and entire neighborhoods were obliterated; by the beginning of 1946, European industrial and agricultural production was less than half of its prewar level. Throughout France and the Low Countries harbors were clogged, bridges destroyed, and railway systems unusable. Indeed, the elaborate infrastructure of communications and transportation in the western portion of the continent appeared to have disintegrated. And the area's production of pig iron, steel, and coal had plummeted by a half to one third of 1939 levels.

Albeit technically victorious in the war, Great Britain went reeling in the immediate posthostilities period and quickly consumed for purposes of economic maintenance a multimillion-dollar US-Canada credit, originally intended for capital improvements. During the unusually harsh winter of 1946–1947, Clement Attlee's government reduced coal allocations to industry by 50 percent; factories were forced to curtail or close their operations, and 5 million workers lost their jobs. In February 1947 half of British industry lay idle. Food was strictly rationed in this period, even more so after blizzards destroyed the winter wheat. Electricity for domestic use, as well as for commercial consumers, was also cut. Consequently, instead of ushering in a new period of generous redistribution and social progress, the Labour government was forced to compromise its agenda and supervise a program of national austerity. At the same time, Britain began to liquidate its overseas empire—in 1947 India was granted independence—and retreated from various other international obligations that in their sum were straining the country beyond the limits of its diminished resources. This latter category of expendable commitments included Greece and Turkey.

In the first two years after the war, Britain had provided economic and military sustenance to the Greek government as it tried to establish order and suppress a communist insurgency. The British had also been helping to finance Turkey's economic and military modernization as a means of buttressing that country against Soviet pressures to revise the border (Kars, Ardahan) and provisions governing use of the Straits. British ambassador Lord Inverchapel—one of the more eccentric, colorful figures of the day—informed the American government in late February 1947 that within six weeks Britain would, of economic necessity, discontinue further assistance to Greece and Turkey. The financial and technical needs of Greece and Turkey (approximately $280 million and $120 million, respectively) would have to be met by some other country. This news, actually long anticipated by State Department insiders, caused the administration to respond with the required aid—and a new statement of international intentions, the Truman Doctrine—and thereby helped preserve the eastern Mediterranean for the West. In taking these actions the United States departed from its tradition of aloofness from the political life of peacetime Europe, and a *pax Americana* emerged.[6]

Kennan agreed with Marshall, Forrestal, and Undersecretary of State Acheson that the Greek government needed outside help and that such assistance coincided with American interests. Kennan feared that, if the United States failed to be forthcoming, a Marxist tyranny similar to those already established elsewhere in the Balkans would take hold in Athens. And he predicted that, once the Soviets recovered from the war and commanded revitalized naval and air units, they could develop in cooperation with a sympathetic government the Greek mainland and archipelago into a formidable strategic position, which would be unbreechable to all but the most determined military assault. Over the short term, he worried that Greece's collapse would have a depressing impact on the confidence and morale of nearby non-Marxist states (i.e., Turkey) and would embolden indigenous communists to undermine established authority. If both Greece and Turkey succumbed, the effect of this twin disaster would radiate throughout the Middle East and then to Europe. In a line of argument congruent with Acheson's and anticipating the exaggerations of a later day "domino theory," Kennan held that the actual or imagined success of Soviet-dominated elements in the Middle East (Iran, Iraq, Palestine) "might well be sufficient to push both Italy and France across the . . . line which divides the integrity and independence of national life from the catastrophe of communist dictatorship."[7] From thence the Iberian peninsula and Western strong points in North Africa would be jeopardized. Under these conditions, might not Britain sue for a precarious neutrality in the expectation that future years would produce hopeful changes?

Kennan recognized from the outset that measures needed to fortify Turkey's will to resist and enhance stability in Greece were within America's technical competence and financial means. And the prospective favorable results should carry far beyond those two countries. "It seems to me," he told a class at the National War College, "that there is a very fair possibility that with the expenditures in Greece and Turkey of a relatively small amount of American funds and American personnel . . . we might turn a critical tide and set in motion counter-currents which could change the entire atmosphere of Europe to our advantage."[8]

Congress and the public at large debated the merits of aid to Athens and Ankara between mid-March and mid-May 1947, when the House and Senate passed the proposed legislation by comfortable margins.[9] During the weeks of uncertainty, when a combination of midwestern isolationists, fiscal conservatives, and political liberals raised hard questions about the aid package, Kennan's doubts soared anew about the collective wisdom of elected officials and professional pundits. This diverse group included Henry Wallace, Senators Claude Pepper and Robert Taft, Representatives Everett Dirksen and Harold Knutson, and the editorial writers of the *Nation* and *New Republic*. Many of these did finally endorse assistance for Greece and Turkey, but it seemed possible for a time that Wallace's declamations against a "reckless adventure" and "military subsidy" to the reactionary government in Athens and Taft's warning that the US economy was not rich enough to underwrite every self-improvement program adopted by foreign governments would defeat Truman's legislation.[10] To Bohlen, Kennan confided that most congressmen and members of the press lacked even an elementary knowledge of Western interests in the Mediterranean and "bleated" questions that any child could answer.[11]

The administration waged a brisk campaign to overcome the combined opposition of economic conservatives, reflexive isolationists, and residual sympathies for the Soviet Union and by doing so won exceptionally broad popular and congressional support for its aid policy. In Acheson's assessment, this campaign required the administration to portray Greek and Turkish issues as urgent and unambiguous. As he argued in a somewhat different (but applicable) context: "The task of a public officer seeking to explain and gain support for a major policy is not that of the writer of a doctoral thesis. Qualification must give way to simplicity of statement, nicety and nuance to bluntness, almost brutality, in carrying home a point. . . . If we made our points clearer than truth, we did not differ from most other educators and could hardly do otherwise."[12] Certainly, the president's address to Congress (subsequently famous as the Truman Doctrine) requesting authorization for the assistance program fitted this approach. He exclaimed that the world was dividing into two camps, one despotic, the other democratic, and it was incumbent upon the United States to help liberty-loving peoples everywhere in their struggle against communist totalitarianism: "The free peoples of the world look to us for support in maintaining their freedoms." If the United States failed them, it would betray its better self and endanger the peace and welfare of the world.[13]

Truman's speech and similar official statements that followed alarmed some State Department officers, notably Marshall, Bohlen, and Kennan. None of them had delusions about the purported democratic nature of the Greek or Turkish regimes. More important, they doubted the wisdom of justifying a practical economic-political policy by placing it in a Manichaean framework that relied on emotional, universalistic language. After reading a predelivery version of the President's talk, Kennan told Acheson and other drafters of the speech that its ideological content was overblown and its commitment to rescue anti-communists so openended that the Soviets would probably view it as a deliberate step toward war. He said that it was surely possible to persuade a majority of congressmen of the propriety and prudence of determined US action in the eastern Mediterranean without resorting to overstatement. After composing an alternative moderate text, which was immediately rejected, Kennan warned Acheson that the administration's decision not to discriminate explicitly among international dilemmas and American choices, and its lapsing into hyperbole, would exact a high cost in public and congressional confusion about foreign affairs.[14]

Kennan's concerns soon proved warranted. After Truman's speech, it fell upon Acheson to present the administration's case before various congressional committees. He was plagued by questions about whether the government, in keeping with Truman's declaration, would want to lend help to people everywhere in the world who claimed to be fighting Soviet-supported enemies. "How about more aid to Chiang Kai-shek?" queried the Generalissimo's Senate allies. Others raised questions about the desirability of assisting assorted European states lying along the Soviet periphery, for example, Finland and Hungary. Before long, Acheson was compelled to admit the obvious: circumstances varied around the globe and US interests in providing aid were not everywhere the same. In other words, Truman's language should not be interpreted literally.[15]

Because the chief executive is the main educator in the United States about international policy, Truman's public analysis and idiom became the standard reference by which success and failure were evaluated in the early Cold War years. And unforeseen by either him or Acheson, the right wing of the Republican party soon appropriated the administration's rhetoric to scourge Truman, his cabinet, and the Democratic party for not doing enough to champion freedom in its battle against the Soviet-Marxist menace. McCarthyism was, in an important sense, intellectually rooted in the emotionalism of the Truman Doctrine text. As for Kennan, this so-called doctrine exemplified that most harmful tendency in American life: to mix ephemeral, limited interests abroad with grand formulas. The result has been to blur political vision in the United States, hence the country's difficulty in conducting a sensible diplomacy in the twentieth century.[16]

Irrespective of the Truman Doctrine's conceptual defects and the domestic political problems it helped to spawn, Western interests in Greece were secured by the summer of 1949. America's financial and technical assistance, together with Stalin's and Tito's withholding of further support from the rebels, enabled authorities in Athens to impose order throughout Greece. Yet, had the government crumbled in 1947–1948, Kennan and the PPS were prepared to urge that the United States increase its naval, air, and army presence in the Mediterranean. If necessary and if requested by the Greek government, US forces should occupy any noncommunist territories that might remain after a cessation of civil conflict. This or similar strong actions, Kennan predicted, would cause the Soviets and their confederates abroad to pause before embarking on additional campaigns of intervention or subversion in Italy, Turkey, and the Arab Middle East.[17] In contrast with Loy Henderson (head of State's Middle East desk), however, Kennan never favored sending US forces to support the Athenian government *during* the civil war. In this position, he was backed by the NSC.[18] The final triumph of the Greek government, of course, spared American policymakers from making additional calculations about the benefits and hazards of deploying large combat units in the southern Balkans. In Turkey, where the danger to Western interests had always been less immediate, the national government made progress in improving the resilience of the economy and the quality of the armed services. And though the wisdom of admitting to NATO two countries harboring ancient enmity for each other was doubtful from the standpoint of that organization's welfare, the security of Greece and Turkey against the USSR was later bolstered when they joined the alliance in 1952.

Although not so obvious to contemporaries, the Truman Doctrine and policy toward Greece and Turkey smoothed the way for that much more ambitious program of US assistance to Europe: the Marshall Plan. Evaluations of its motives and achievements were at the time, and are today, diverse. On one side, Churchill called the injection into Western Europe of American capital—$13.3 billion over a four-year span—the most unsordid act in history. Another Briton, Alastair Buchan, claimed that without massive aid, sustained by American idealism, Western Europe could not have recovered from the war. To Louis Halle, the Marshall Plan was one of those rare expressions of grace that reveals itself in human affairs and indicates that the honor of mankind is still redeemable. Yet the sociologist Franz Schurmann has charged that the goal of the Marshall Plan was base: to defend capitalism in Europe as a means of preserving the world market system and America's privileged position in it. The launching of the program marked the United States as the world's new *imperium*. As for Soviet analysts, they agree with V. M. Molotov's 1947 indictment that Marshall aid was a vehicle through which the United States attempted to destroy national sovereignty in Europe, gain political and economic control of the continent, and rebuild West Germany for sinister purposes.[19] A more objective appraisal of the Marshall Plan—one that does not view it as part of an international morality play—must give credit to the Europeans for their rapid economic recovery while recognizing that American assistance was, indeed, helpful. It made a sizable financial, and major psychological, contribution to transforming Western Europe from a poor dependency to a mighty capital unit that in recent decades has helped erode postwar US economic hegemony.[20] But more important for our purposes than any of these interpretations is that the Marshall Plan constituted a new point of departure, and here Kennan's role is significant, in international relations: the use of direct and massive economic aid by great nations in the service of power-political and diplomatic goals.

Like most large-scale, long-term government policies, the Marshall Plan was not the product of a single intensive study by one individual or group of people. Rather, it evolved, and some of its political and intellectual origins are traceable to Europeans and Americans who, during the war, tried to anticipate the future needs of a world at peace.[21] Even in 1940 (see Chapter 4), Kennan was concerned with defining the economic and political means by which the United States might best encourage postwar European stability. Seven years later, when Marshall ordered him to assemble a planning staff and quickly construct a reasonable design for

European renewal, Kennan was able to draw upon a large fund of other ideas, partial plans, and models of past and current *ad hoc* aid programs. Acheson and Assistant Secretary of Economic Affairs Will Clayton, for example, had advised Secretary Byrnes in 1946 that it would be useful for the United States to grant financial assistance to Europe and to integrate such aid into a final peace settlement. Clark Clifford had advocated to Truman a similar program that would embrace not only Europe but possibly the Soviet Union, too: "Economic aid may . . . be given to the Soviet Government and private trade with the USSR permitted provided the results are beneficial to our interests and do not simply strengthen the Soviet program."[22] Jean Monnet, meanwhile, was helping to shape a recovery scheme that allowed France to incorporate into its economy the coal and steel resources of the Ruhr, Rhineland, and Saar. In response to Acheson's request (March 1947), the State-War-Navy Coordinating Committee began a systematic study of European problems. Some weeks later, and with Truman's approval, Acheson delivered an address to the Delta Council in Mississippi in which he announced that the United States would have to sponsor an extensive recovery plan so that the war-devastated countries could rebuild and maintain balanced economies. Otherwise, the cause of human dignity abroad would be defeated and American security and democratic institutions endangered.[23]

The chief virtue of Kennan's advice and reports to Marshall in 1947 was not their originality, but that they drew wisely from the aforementioned ideas and gathered them into a coherent plan of action. Into them Kennan was also able to weave his particular concerns with geographical and psychological factors.

He denied that communist activities or Soviet support of them were the root evil of Europe's difficulties. They sprang, instead, from the war's destructive impact on the continent's established patterns of economic, social, and political life: both physical plant and spiritual vigor had been exhausted. These maladies were, in turn, aggravated by the division of Europe into Anglo-US and Soviet spheres of influence, and the activities of communist parties in the West were hindering the restoration of economic and political order. As long as confusion and uncertainty reigned, the European communists would exploit the situation to their and Moscow's advantage; eventually, they might seize local governments, and through them Soviet influence and prestige would expand. The Anglo-US community would then be forced on the defensive as it faced a superior Soviet-European aggregation of economic and military power. To preempt this eventuality, Kennan argued that the United States had to subdue the social disorders in Europe upon which the USSR and its adherents thrived. In sum, the difficulties confronting the United States in Europe were far more pressing and subtle than any posed by the Red Army.

He recommended to Marshall that as soon as practicable the administration should proffer a quantity of capital sufficient to explode the most impacted economic bottlenecks (for example, the production and distribution of coal and steel) in Europe. In addition to providing some temporary economic relief, the main effect of this action would be psychological. It would signal that the United States was abandoning its political passivity for a policy that was confident and assertive. Kennan reasoned that Europeans of every ideological stripe would be impressed by an early show of American decisiveness, and the hitherto sagging morale of non-communists would rise appreciably; they would be willing to hold on for a while longer. Thus swift action—this coincided exactly with Marshall's own view—could purchase the time required for fashioning a long-term solution.

Kennan advised Marshall that the crafting of a comprehensive program for European revitalization should not be the exclusive or even the primary duty of the United States. Rather, the participating European governments must understand that the responsibility was theirs for organizing a relief plan and they should submit at an appropriate moment requests for American assistance. Designated officers of the US government could help in drafting a European program, but they had to keep a discreet distance from its formal creation and presentation. If this ceremony was not observed, Kennan warned, the United States would be vulnerable to the charge that its offer of economic and technical help was a cover for compromising Europe's independence and annexing its economic life. Another merit of this approach was that if major problems arose preventing the United States from assisting Europe (an uncooperative Congress or communist victories in Rome and Paris), the administration could disavow the program with little loss of face. For the sake of European self-respect and American diplomatic maneuverability, Kennan cautioned: "With the best of will, the American people cannot really help those who are not willing to help themselves. And if the requested initiative and readiness to bear public responsibility are not forthcoming from the European governments, then that will mean that *rigor mortis* has already set in on the body politic of Europe as we have known it and that it may be already too late for us to change the course of events."[24] On the positive side, by constructing a joint economic project, the Europeans would foster among themselves a sense of collective identity conducive to some form of future political union.

Kennan was principally concerned with aid to Western Europe as he believed the eastern zone was beyond the reach of perceptible American influence for the time being. Nonetheless, he insisted that a direct and generously phrased offer of help be made to the regimes under Soviet sway. If these governments did cooperate in an American-inspired European recovery, they would perforce revise the exclusive orientation of their economies away from the USSR, and a very thick wedge would be driven between Moscow and its clients in Warsaw, Budapest, Belgrade, Sofia. If Stalin blocked interested East Europeans from receiving American aid, then their resentment toward the Soviets would deepen, and they would have to bear most of the opprobrium for the continuing division of Europe. Either way, Soviet development of a unified, cohesive zone of its own would be disrupted or, at the minimum, delayed.

During discussions in late May with Marshall and the chiefs of various State Department offices, Kennan and Bohlen argued that aid should also be offered to the Soviets, but should be tied to conditions that Stalin would have to reject for the sake of Russia and all countries enjoying its "protection." When the secretary expressed apprehension that the Soviets might accept an invitation to join the recovery program, thereby assuring Congress's opposition to it, Kennan and Bohlen expostulated that a cooperative venture with the West, in which the United States played the leading role as donor *and* monitor of aid programs, would be anathema to

Soviet leaders. Therefore, the United States could seize the moral high ground by making an offer to the Soviets and remain confident that they would refuse.[25]

These ideas of Kennan's, along with an impassioned report filed by Clayton about Europe's economic plight, were the major sources used by Bohlen in composing Marshall's Harvard address of June 1947. It portrayed a Europe that was politically dazed and in economic chaos. Drastic measures were required to correct the problems, for if allowed to fester, they would eventually threaten the security of the New World. In contrast to the Truman Doctrine speech, Marshall's excluded strident anti-communist or anti-Soviet flourishes: "Our policy is directed not against any country or doctrine but against hunger, poverty, desperation and chaos." Still, the address implicitly associated the Soviet Union with one set of disagreeable forces operating in the world while making clear where America stood: "Governments, political parties, or groups which seek to perpetuate human misery in order to profit therefrom politically or otherwise will encounter the opposition of the United States."[26] The Americans were willing to help revive a workable international economy and a world political environment compatible with democratic institutions. For their part, *per* Kennan, the Europeans must act in concert to draft a feasible program for recovery with which to approach the United States.

Not until nine months after the secretary's speech did Congress pass (March 1948) legislation embodying the Marshall Plan, formally titled the European Recovery Program (ERP). To move it forward, Kennan argued within the government apparatus—in person and through the medium of Policy Planning reports—for the administration's project. He repeatedly emphasized that if economic and social deterioration continued unabated in Europe, the entire area would be lost as an important supplier of products and services needed by the world. And if, through a series of civil conflicts and political disorders all of Europe fell to communist parties, America's margin of international safety would be severely reduced. Therefore, a comprehensive plan was necessary, not just continued *ad hoc* responses to Europe's pauperization.[27] Kennan was also instrumental in the State Department's effort to steer the West Europeans toward the conclusions and formulas preferred by Truman's government. To cite an important example, both he and Bohlen impressed upon Inverchapel that the British must help make certain that the Soviets declined to participate in the Marshall Plan. Perhaps, the British would convey to Molotov that not only was all of Eastern Europe eligible for infusions of American capital, but the Soviets also should contribute to overall continental reconstruction.[28]

The British did not have to do much to ease the Soviets out of ERP. As Bohlen and Kennan had anticipated, they were unwilling to reveal to the West the extent of their economic problems or involve themselves in a detailed program that for an indeterminate number of years would render their economy partially dependent upon the United States. After meeting with Britain's Ernest Bevin and France's Georges Bidault in Paris, Molotov declared that the USSR discerned the treacherous nature of the Marshall Plan and warned that it was a device for American capitalism to ensnare and forever dominate European life. In early July, he and the large Soviet delegation that had assembled in France returned to Moscow.

Although pleased with the Soviet withdrawal from European discussions of ERP, Kennan became steadily depressed through the summer weeks of 1947 by the inability of the West Europeans to coordinate their purposes and prepare a collective request for US aid. In control of his irritation but with considerable force, he instructed (late August) European and American representatives meeting in Paris on how the continent's "economic machine" might be reprimed: currencies must be stabilized, economic order restored, trade barriers eliminated, and steps taken to establish a customs union; an administrative unit to oversee and manage the distribution of US aid should be organized. Finally, the Europeans could expect the Americans to be generous, but the sometimes-quoted figure of $29.2 billion was "much too large" and exceeded anything Congress would ever grant. By September the Europeans had lowered their estimates for aid to $17 billion.[29]

Still, Kennan was not reassured. He told Marshall that political leadership in Western Europe would continue to stumble and was too disoriented after the war to produce realistic plans for the future; the ongoing Paris meetings, mixing representatives from sixteen European states, manifested all the weakness and escapism of a region ravaged by conflict and unable to adjust creatively to its reduced international standing.[30] The British in particular, according to Kennan, were unable to understand or manage their situation realistically as evidenced by the Labour government's dogged commitment to social policies that made no sense in conditions of scarcity. And economic processes in France were unraveling with "terrifying rapidity." He pronounced grimly: "If nothing is done for [the French and British] within two or three months, they both face genuine hunger by winter, and other complications of unpredictable dimensions, with unforeseeable effects in other areas of the world."[31] To stave off disaster, the United States should immediately send interim aid that could tide Western Europe over until a full-scale assistance regime had been accepted by all relevant parties. Numerous congressmen and senators who conducted "fact finding" tours to Europe in autumn 1947 agreed with Kennan—an especially important one was led by Representative Christian Herter, chairman of the Select Committee on Foreign Aid. In December a $600-million aid package for Europe was approved by Congress.

Not only were the complicated, protracted talks in Paris of concern to high-ranking State Department officials, but so, too, were Congress's lengthy deliberations. The actual "selling" of the Marshall Plan is a fascinating subject ranging beyond the scope of this book.[32] Suffice it to note that the liberal wing of the Democratic party was generally predisposed to support a constructive approach to Europe's political and economic problems, but the isolationist faction of the Republican party, led by Senator Taft, was skeptical about peacetime involvement in European affairs and opposed to investing billions of dollars in struggling economies overseas; undoubtedly there would be little, if any, return on such an investment. With some exceptions, the majority of American businessmen were also unenthusiastic about shipping a large sum of capital, generated by US free enterprise, to governments in which socialists and communists held important portfolios. In response to these and similar expressions of reluctance, Truman courted, as assiduously as ever, Senator Arthur Vandenberg and other internationally minded members of the Republican party. On the strength of the president's support, Harriman rallied a number of prominent business leaders—including Paul Hoffman, president of Studebaker Corporation and later director of the Economic Cooperation Administration—behind the Marshall Plan. Meanwhile, Truman championed the cause in numerous public speeches (some of which were prepared by Kennan and his staff), as did Acheson, Secretary of the Treasury Clinton Anderson, and Robert Patterson, formerly the secretary of war.[33] And the State Department helped initiate "grass roots" organizations, such as the Citizens Committee for the Marshall Plan, while Bohlen, a great favorite of Marshall's and respected by senators and congressmen alike, served as the department's liaison with Congress. He proved especially adept in deflecting charges that ERP was just another example of outlandish American charity or that it should be condemned as unseemly interference in Europe.

Whereas Bohlen cheerfully soldiered on through tedious and sometimes punishing congressional questioning and testimony, Kennan brooded that he was a professional diplomat charged with representing his government's position abroad, but he had neither expected nor desired to justify US external policy to his own countrymen.[34] Nevertheless, he *did* deliver speeches on behalf of the Marshall Plan to civic organizations and groups of businessmen and hit upon a variety of familiar themes: a demoralized Europe required the assistance that ERP would provide in order to alleviate the political paralysis caused by fear and insecurity; the inroads of the Soviets and their communist allies into Europe would be blunted only if they encountered a balanced, resilient Western community; US economic and, most important, security interests depended on the Marshall Plan's success. To one audience after another he declared:

> The countries of Western and Central Europe represent . . . [together] the only single [unit] of industrial and technical skill capable of equalling that of this country and of far outshadowing—thanks be to God—that of the Soviet Union. With it they can continue to dream their dreams of the smashing of our society and the domination of the world. Without it, they are going to remain basically just Russia, and they know it. If we fail to seize this chance to keep the area out of their hands, we will suffer the single greatest deterioration in our international position that our history has ever known.[35]

Invariably, Kennan would end his forensic exercises with an exhortation to his listeners to support the Marshall Plan and a statement of confidence that an informed, fair-minded Congress and public would accept the responsibilities of world leadership.[36]

Whatever impact his brave words had on his listeners, they did not dispel his private doubts. By the end of 1947, Kennan was aghast at Congress's inability or unwillingness to act, even while the communist parties helped spread economic and political disorder in France and Italy. And he wondered whether the American government was inherently able to check the USSR through means short of war. Was it too much to wish that the United States could operate politically in the foreign field? As the best hope for containing Russia in Europe seemed to wither away under Congress's mishandling, Kennan mused bitterly: "The very method of decision, as to whether or not to extend aid, is so wearisome, so encumbered with uncertainties and hesitations, that half the psychological benefit is dissipated while Congress debates. And even if Congress passes the aid bill, its administration will be cumbersome, inflexible, and unpolitical."[37] By February 1948, the entire situation had become a nightmare to Kennan, and he was convinced that any more congressional dilatoriness would nullify the recovery plan's desired effect.[38]

Ironically, it was the Soviet Union that saved Kennan from further torments, as in 1948 it inadvertently took measures, and was widely seen as colluding in other actions, that caused popular opinion in the US and congressional sentiment to coalesce in support of the Marshall Plan. The Czech Communist party came to power in Prague through *coup d'etat* in February, and Jan Masaryk, foreign minister and son of the country's first president, died under mysterious circumstances; he was probably killed by Soviet or Czech communist agents. During this same period, the Finns were pressed to align themselves with Russia against the West. The US embassy in Rome was cabling continuous warnings to Washington of impending Italian communist electoral victory. And from Germany, General Lucius Clay relayed that, based on little more than his own intuition, he felt a war in Europe might soon erupt "with dramatic suddenness." The combined impact of these events, coinciding with a worsening situation in China for the anti-Marxist Kuomintang, was enough to convert agnostics and most nonbelievers to the Marshall Plan. It became both the symbol and substance of US determination to resist Soviet and communist expansion. The enabling legislation was overwhelmingly approved by Congress in late March, with a Senate vote of 69 to 17 and the House voting 329 to 74.

Kennan did not believe that any of the events that frightened his compatriots into supporting the Marshall Plan *en masse* (save the activities of the Italian communists) were closely related to the real merits of ERP. He had earlier concluded that Czechoslovakia sadly, but logically, fell into the Soviet zone of control and that the communist takeover meant the Soviets were consolidating their position, not pursuing new and dangerous initiatives. He was also disinclined to lump Soviet and Chinese communist interests into the same category, and was unimpressed by Clay's jitteriness.[39] Yet, regardless of the reasons for its passage, Kennan was immensely satisfied when Congress finally acted to adopt ERP.

In his capacities as director of the PPS and chief of an auxiliary group attached to the advisory committee of ERP, Kennan had ample opportunity in 1948–1949 to monitor the progress of the Marshall Plan. He was pleased with its course and later recounted: "It was more successful and produced its results within a shorter time, than we had ever dared to hope. Within eighteen months after [Marshall's Harvard address], all of western Europe was on the way to recovery that actually surpassed our most optimistic expectations, and it was clear that any immediate danger of a communist seizure of western Europe had passed."[40] Indeed, not only did economic life on the continent revive sooner than most experts believed possible at the time, but communist parties in the West were forced onto the defensive; communist ministers functioning in West European governments were, in important instances, compelled to surrender their cabinet positions. And meanwhile, modest, but seemingly irreversible, steps were taken toward West European political and economic integration. Despite Kennan's pessimism, delays, and in the end rather explicit

American guidance, West European leaders had combined in 1947–1948 to devise some plans for the continent's recovery.

Germany and European Integration

One of the most bedeviling questions confronting advocates of postwar European integration concerned the question of Germany. How should it be fitted into a peaceful world? This issue was of utmost importance as Germany occupied the economic center of Europe and was the state most likely to cause, depending on its disposition, either mischief or—if properly domesticated—international stability.

Kennan realized by 1948 that the prolonged Anglo-US occupation in Germany was increasingly expensive and politically disadvantageous to the West. He also believed that the Soviets preferred a divided Germany over which they exercised some control to one that was united and able to withstand communist penetration. In the best of all possible worlds, the country should be allowed to reunite. But a united Germany would not be easily countenanced by the French, Belgians, Dutch, Danes, and others. The issue was therefore how to accommodate these fears *and* advance American interests.[41]

Against the background of the Berlin blockade and airlift and in anticipation of a foreign ministers' conference about Germany, Kennan formulated a plan for reunification. He suggested that the four occupying powers withdraw their armed forces from the major sections of Germany and garrison them in peripheral territories—along the Rhine or in Silesia, for example. They would remain there as unobtrusively as possible and discontinue their administration of civilian political affairs. These would be assumed by an independent German government endowed with real political authority.

The West would reap considerable benefits from such an arrangement, according to Kennan. First, the partition of Germany, and by extension all of Europe, would not be allowed to congeal, thereby preserving the possibility that at some future date the satellite states could gravitate toward a larger European unit. The alternative was to acquiesce to a permanent political and military division of the continent: "If we carry on along present lines, Germany must divide into eastern and western governments and western Europe must move toward a tight military alliance with this country which can only complicate the eventual integration of the satellites into a European community. From such a trend of developments, it would be hard—harder than it is now—to find 'the road back' to a united and free Europe."[42]

Even if a united Europe should never materialize, Kennan's German plan would have its virtues. The Red Army could not conduct additional military maneuvers on German soil. For such purposes, the Soviets would be forced to use Polish territories or those within Russian frontiers, and these activities thus would thenceforth "be less satisfactory to [the USSR] and less menacing to the western European countries than the present situation."[43] Kennan also believed that his proposal would help solve the Berlin dilemma. With their credibility and moral integrity intact, the Anglo-Americans could, simultaneously with the Soviets, withdraw from the city—

in effect, abandon a geographically untenable position over which the Soviets enjoyed every conceivable logistical advantage. The presumably grateful citizens of Berlin, at long last delivered from Soviet custody, could also be counted upon in the postoccupation era to prevent local communists from capturing power and help erect a reliable, non-Marxist government in Germany's traditional capital. Finally, Kennan contended, adoption of his plan would minimize the cost of maintaining an American military establishment in Germany as its mission and size were therein slated for reduction. Apart from any economic concern, he was determined about this matter because of his revulsion for the way in which some US occupation troops, of all ranks, comported themselves among the defeated Germans. Never one to waste sympathy on his compatriots abroad, Kennan maintained that what the vanquished Germans required was intellectual and spiritual nourishment, but what the Americans provided were only models of cultural poverty, arrogance, and material self-indulgence.[44]

Kennan was not oblivious to the potential drawbacks of his own plan and worried that a national German regime might tilt—or worse—toward Moscow. Even if nothing so unfortunate should occur, he feared that the inclusion of Russia's German zone in an expanded Germany would add to the strain on ERP's funds and political-administrative organization. Over the long term and in the absence of a sturdy European federation, the reestablishment of a single German entity could mean a return to the European status quo of the 1920s and invite the sorts of disasters that later had ensued. He even conceded the possibility that, under the right circumstances, a unified German nation might renew its effort to dominate the continent and thereby nullify the war's decision and America's contribution to it. Such a prospect seemed farfetched in 1948, but Kennan was still reluctant to see Germany returned to a more powerful condition and at an earlier period than most North Americans or Europeans were prepared for psychologically. As it was, even a gradual implementation of his ideas would cause difficulties. The French would be alarmed at the retirement of most British and US forces from Germany; the Soviets would enjoy increased opportunities for covert political actions throughout central Europe.

Notwithstanding the risks, Kennan thought his German plan possessed enough potential benefits to push it forward. Besides, the moment for German unification, and for first steps toward European integration, was as good in 1948 as it was ever likely to be. "It is my feeling," he told Marshall, "that if the division of Europe cannot be overcome peacefully at this juncture, when the lines of cleavage have not yet hardened completely across the continent, when the Soviet Union . . . is not yet ready for another war, when the anti-communist sentiment in Germany is momentarily stronger than usual, and when the Soviet satellite area is troubled with serious dissension . . . then it is not likely that [chances] for a peaceful resolution of Europe's problems will be better after a further period of waiting."[45] If the opportunity was lost, Europe would continue to be divided, Germany would remain hostage to the Cold War, and the European balance of power would rest indefinitely and precariously on extra-European states.

Kennan submitted his German plan not only to members of the PPS and specialists in the State Department, but also to a number of outside consultants, among whom the most prominent were Dean Acheson (temporarily returned to private life), Hamilton Fish Armstrong, Sarah Blanding (president of Vassar College), James Conant (Harvard), and Edmund Walsh (Georgetown University).[46] The result of these consultations was a more detailed, slightly revised version of Kennan's original scheme—labeled Program A—which was delivered to Marshall in November 1948. In accordance with Kennan's ideas, the final text included an explicit provision against extensive German rearmament and called for an end to Germany's payment of reparations. A reunified Germany would thus be more palatable to its neighbors while no longer the object of punishment incompatible with Europe's economic rehabilitation.

Kennan did not expect the Soviets to accept every point in Program A, but thought the administration should present the plan as a starting point in negotiations.[47] Unfortunately for Kennan's future Germany, Program A was diametrically opposed to that plan agreed upon earlier (in London) by representatives of France, Britain, the US, and Low Countries, and continuously reconfirmed. According to it, a West German regime should be established that would be closely linked to the emergent coalition of American-led states. In compliance with this scheme, the Western allies had introduced currency reforms into their section of Germany—the catalyst, incidentally, for the Soviet blockade of Berlin—well before November 1948 as an important measure in creating a West German entity.

To its critics, Program A appeared too late and possessed far more flaws than virtues anyway. John Hickerson, director of the State Department's European Affairs Division, warned that the Soviets could not be trusted to abide by any agreements envisioned in Program A and would act to violate its provisions at the first opportunity. Western Europe, moreover, should be militarily and economically stronger before Germany was allowed to reintegrate and pursue a neutralist course. In the meantime, if the administration adopted or even appeared to endorse partially Kennan's proposal, all manner of mayhem would result: the united Western front toward Germany might crack, and policies already operating successfully in Germany could be fatally disrupted. Jacques Reinstein, then serving with the assistant secretary for economic affairs, maintained that democratic institutions should be firmly implanted in Germany before the country was permitted to determine its own domestic and diplomatic policies. This goal could be achieved only after a longer period of democratic apprenticeship under the supervision and protection of the Western allies. Also with the State Department, Charles Saltzman added that the eventual removal of Anglo-US forces would encourage the Soviets to exert all types of pressure against a demilitarized Germany and that the West would possess no leverage to enforce agreements. Similarly, Bohlen, Clay, and Robert Murphy, the US political advisor for Germany, opposed a large-scale removal of Western troops from Germany at any time in the near future. To station troops on Germany's periphery was, in Clay's phrase, "totally impracticable." Did Kennan not understand that the presence of the American army was all that kept Europe stable? Its retirement would be tantamount to "turning the show over to Russia and the Communists without a struggle." Finally, Defense Secretary Forrestal advised that any policy contemplating withdrawal from Germany meant retreat from Europe that would culminate one day in a third world war.[48] The cumulative impact of these objections was to put the quietus on Program A for the remainder of Marshall's tenure. As Undersecretary of State Robert Lovett let Kennan understand, "A" required further work and discussion before anyone else in the administration reexamined it.

Kennan was tenacious on the subject of Germany, however. After a tour of the country in March 1949, he was all the more eager that the US military occupation be terminated and a four-power agreement adopted. And he tried hard to press his program with Dean Acheson, who in January 1949 replaced Marshall as secretary of state. But again, Kennan's ideas were resisted by Hickerson, Murphy, and others on the grounds that the United States was now enmeshed with France and Britain in building a new West Germany. Certainly, by the time when he met (late March) with Robert Schuman and Bevin, Acheson seems to have been persuaded that West Germany should be snugly fitted into a Western framework. This view, in turn, accorded with that of the French and British foreign ministers and together they agreed to theoretical and precise forms by which to establish a German Federal Republic. Kennan did not concede, though, and Acheson was evidently still willing to listen about Program A in late spring 1949. In part, this was so because Kennan had managed to recruit to his cause Phillip Jessup, who at the time was charged by Acheson with canvassing opinion in the government bureaucracies about the German issue.

When "A" was refloated among Defense Department officials in 1949, it met with criticism even more blistering than when originally submitted. Clay protested that "we have won the battle but under [Kennan's] proposal are writing an armistice as if we had lost the battle." He feared that the Soviets could easily seize an abandoned Germany and, one day, an exposed Europe if Kennan's plan was implemented. The idea was implausible, simply "suicidal." Newly appointed Defense Secretary Louis Johnson and JCS chief General Omar Bradley reiterated that "A" compromised the entire Western position by surrendering initiative and geographical advantage to the Red Army. And then on the eve of additional foreign ministers' meetings scheduled in Paris for late May, details about Program A were leaked through the *New York Times* column of James Reston. Undoubtedly traceable to Defense Department officials, Reston's revelations administered, as Kennan phrased it, a "spectacular *coup de grace*" to his German solution.[49]

Both the French and British governments roundly and publicly condemned it. Underlying the French protests was a vehement hatred for any notion of a united Germany from which Anglo-US troops had been evacuated. As to the British, they were resolved to bolster Western defenses in Europe and believed the Soviets could not yet be coaxed or maneuvered back to their own frontiers. In the end, as a result of the criticisms leveled by army and Defense officials and of the reactions by Bevin and Schuman to the Reston article, Acheson dropped any lingering ideas he might have had about broaching "A" to the French and British representatives. Instead, all three ministers paid lip service to the idea of German unification, but they were unprepared to consider the matter seriously, let alone present it as a Western proposal to Soviet minister Andrei Vishinsky. Consequently, there was nothing to hinder the rise of a West German state tied to Anglo-US-French economic, political, and strategic interests. The Bundestag convened for the first time in September 1949, and Konrad Adenauer was elected chancellor of a new, increasingly powerful state, though one destined to exist for decades along the political fault line of a divided Europe.[50]

Not only did Kennan's ideas about the desirability of reuniting Germany fall victim to American security planners, Anglo-French fears, and general disinterest, but his ambitions for European integration were equally unsuccessful—despite the fact that, throughout the late 1940s, Truman's administration repeatedly broadcast its support for some version of West European economic and political unity. For example, in November 1947 Marshall told an audience in Chicago: "Europe is a natural grouping of states designed by geography and history to function as a community if it is to function well. . . . The logic of history would appear to dictate the necessity of this community drawing closer together not only for its survival but for the stability, prosperity, and peace of the entire world."[51] Acheson, as secretary of state, expressed similar views, as did the Republican spokesman on foreign affairs, John Foster Dulles. All of these pronouncements were vague, however, because the government did not want, lest it appear meddlesome, to sponsor any particular program for European federation.

This official American delicacy and uncertainty about just exactly what to recommend partly explain why the PPS did not directly address itself to the peculiar problems of European integration until summer 1949. In any case, while still head of Policy Planning, Kennan solicited the views of a broad range of academic and government experts, business leaders, and even the theologian Reinhold Niebuhr on the subject of Europe. The basic questions for the PPS and its consultants were: What geographic areas should be embraced by the European unification movement? What would be the political criteria for membership in a European community? How, if at all, should the United States encourage European integration?[52] These queries had been raised originally by the British through the Foreign Office's Sir Gladwyn Jebb. In effect, the Labour government was wondering to what extent Britain should implicate itself in a pan-European political enterprise. And what, specifically, was the American attitude toward a possibly unprecedented British involvement in the life of the continent?

As Kennan conveyed to Acheson, some form of European unity was mandatory if the industrially advanced nations there were to withstand Soviet political intrigues and diplomatic pressures over the coming decades. And by including the larger, more economically important western sector of Germany, that nation's dynamism could be harnessed for a grander good and its pathologies held in check.[53] Thus, while Kennan tacitly admitted that an independent neutral Germany was no longer in the offing, he continued to hold that Western Europe's problems were still centered on Germany (and Russia) and that they were manageable. In contrast to overriding political issues, the economic ones were of secondary importance. Kennan was unsure, in fact, whether European union would lead to a healthier continental economy or whether the weight of a federal bureaucracy might burden or otherwise inhibit economic growth and productivity.

Kennan explained to Acheson that he had no illusions about the difficulties related to national sovereignty and was uncertain if the continent's fragmentation into independent states could ever be overcome. He posited that owing to their fundamentally more successful and longer periods of independent national life, the Atlantic seaboard countries were less likely to desire real union than the states of central and eastern Europe. The British especially were unenthusiastic as they retained extensive overseas commitments and unhappy memories about past entanglements on the continent. He wagered that only if the United States and Canada were also willing to join would Britain attach itself politically to Europe. In the absence of such an unlikely move, the British would surely maintain their traditional distance from peacetime Europe. Meanwhile, the fact remained that none of the standing regional arrangements, such as the Council of Europe, Brussels Pact, or Organization for European Economic Cooperation, was fostering anything like genuine European unity.

Despite the inevitable problems of economic and political adjustment for all parties, Kennan's ultimate preference, as previously mentioned (Chapter 6), was for Britain, Canada, and the United Sates to move toward a closer political association. Concurrent with the emergence of an English-speaking Atlantic union, the Western continental states should create a new all-embracing framework that, among other things, would be pliable enough to incorporate Soviet satellite states when, and if, they broke from their Moscow orbits. Kennan allowed that for such a union to flourish on the continent, France and other countries must be reassured about continuing US military commitment to their security against Russia. Indeed, he was emphatic that without such an American guarantee the Western continental states could not progress toward unity: "As long as division of Europe continues, US must maintain firm military engagement to entire Atlantic Pact group, plus Germany and Austria, and we should encourage no development, domestic or foreign, which would weaken or obscure that engagement."[54]

Shortly after presenting his ideas about Europe to Acheson, Kennan visited Paris and London, where he probed French and British attitudes about integration. His findings were more discouraging than anything for which he was prepared. Henri Bonnet expressed the French concern that the British and Americans were developing an exclusive, special relationship while leaving France alone on the continent to deal with Germany's economic might and whatever political agenda it might concoct in the future. The French attitude of suspicion and contempt toward Germany depressed Kennan as it promised to help perpetuate West European weakness: the French seemed determined on keeping Germany economically handicapped and divided. Under these conditions, a robust and confident Western Europe could not emerge. To Bohlen, Kennan wrote: "[The] . . . reaction on the part of the French [is] worlds apart from the concept of European unity which will have to be established on the continent fairly soon if there is to be any hope at all of the psychological integration of the Germans into the community of western Europe. And I do not need to point out that without such a psychological integration western Europe is destined to remain a divided entity, dangerously vulnerable to Russian pressures . . . and with us, as usual, on the side of the weaker, more timid, and less imaginative parties."[55] Kennan concluded that, so long as Germany was excluded from a continental framework, Western Europe's capacity to resist a

Soviet military attack would become an empty pretense or else, even worse from a French standpoint, by its own efforts Germany would revive its military strength for purely national purposes.

Kennan's talks with Jebb and various British officials revealed that they were unprepared to take into account future East European developments that *might* produce truant satellite states ready to join a larger Western bloc. In fact, concluded Kennan, the British did not expect or particularly wish to see Soviet power loosened in Eastern Europe and saw no reason to plan for the hypothetical defection of Poland, East Germany, Czechoslovakia, or Hungary. Instead, Britain felt committed, within the limits imposed by Commonwealth and other overseas obligations, to cultivating those qualities and undertaking those duties that would enable the Western continent to repulse every form of diplomatic and military danger emanating from the East. By adopting any of Kennan's idea, Attlee's government would jeopardize a budding security arrangement in Europe while having nothing tangible with which to replace it.[56] And besides, Britain could not approve of any plan that encouraged the buildup of an *independent,* giant conglomeration—in this case Franco-German—of continental power and thereby depart from a centuries-old policy.

Kennan also failed to persuade official American opinion of the soundness of his European program. Acheson remained uncommitted while State Department officials with European responsibilities were overtly cool. This category included Bohlen, then serving as minister-counselor under Ambassador David Bruce in Paris. Bohlen emphasized that, to retain any allies on the continent, the United States must be unequivocal about its devotion to the intactness of the Atlantic community as both a military and a political unit. And the United States must give no cause for continental Europe to suspect that Britain enjoyed a favored relationship with North America. To act otherwise would leave the US eventually bereft of allies on the European mainland; these states would then follow neutralist policies and increasingly accommodate themselves to the USSR. "I can only tell you," Bohlen informed Kennan, "that if it becomes evident that we are creating an Anglo-American-Canadian bloc as a political reality in our European policy we will not be able to hold on to the nations of Western Europe very long." Such an English-speaking grouping, along with the psychological repercussions of Russia's recent explosion of an atom bomb, would strengthen those elements in Europe that already preferred a neutral course. As it was, too many Europeans had "sought to take refuge in the illusion that this is essentially a struggle between the US and the USSR and that France and the smaller continent countries are . . . innocent bystanders."[57] Regarding Britain, Bohlen insisted that, for an integrated Western Europe to work well and to harness German energy safely, the British would have to be intimately involved with the continent's diplomatic, military, and economic affairs. He frankly doubted that France, absent Britain, would take the leadership in forming any kind of European union.[58]

Ultimately, Kennan's ideas about Europe did not provide the basis for an American policy initiative and never found sympathy in the Paris or London of 1949. Yet the idea of a closely coordinated British-Canadian-US relationship remained for decades his "fondest dream."[59] And in the years subsequent to 1949, he took satisfaction in those European efforts (principally by Adenauer, Charles De Gaulle, and Schuman) that helped put to rest Franco-German enmity and built a recogniz- able West European bloc manifest in the communities of European Coal and Steel, Common Market, and Euratom.[60]

European Security

Kennan never objected in principle to the deployment of US military assets to safeguard West European security, but he cautioned that their employment be selective and in proportion to the problem; an excessive display of force could only rebound to America's political disadvantage. The major value of maintaining some forces in Europe was that they could be concentrated or exhibited in such a way as to influence any local political struggle. In 1947, for instance, when there was a distinct possibility that communists in northern Italy would seize power, Kennan recommended that the United States expand its military and air facilities in Italy following an outbreak of civil disorders. If necessary, American forces might join local noncommunist authorities in suppressing pro-Soviet rebels. He offered similar advice in 1948 as the Italian communist party flexed its national electoral strength. The expansion and possible use of American force might also be appropriate in Iceland if it succumbed to a communist *coup d'etat*. As for the Soviets, they should understand that a reduction of communist activity in a given European area would meet with a corresponding contraction of US military power in the same neighbor- hood, while increased communist pressures would invite a greater show of Ameri- can arms. Kennan assumed, and correctly when viewed historically, that the Soviets would usually discourage foreign communist parties from pursuing policies that might set them on a collision course with the United States. If not, the Soviets would be placed in the awkward position of either disavowing the Marxist-Leninist cause somewhere or testing the resolve and strength of the militarily superior Americans.[61]

For the most part, Kennan expected that West European police and intelligence operations in cooperation with their American counterparts could monitor and coun- ter Soviet-supported communist activities in Italy, France, Greece, and elsewhere. To be helpful, of course, the Americans would have to further refine and expand their psychological warfare and covert techniques, which could range from the cultivation and practical use (propaganda, education) of intellectual refugees from Soviet bloc countries to development of a guerrilla warfare corps.[62] A veteran in the supervision of intelligence work (including espionage and counterespionage) con- ducted from wartime Lisbon, Kennan was persuaded that the United States needed a greatly improved covert operations capability for the waging of Cold War. On the basis of recommendations from him and the PPS, the government established the Office of Special Projects that developed programs in propaganda, sabotage, sub- version, and guerrilla warfare. Kennan would have preferred that Special Projects be placed under the direction of the secretary of state, so that close supervision by the diplomatic establishment would prevent the initiation of programs in Europe embarrassing to the United States. The NSC decided to house Special Projects within the CIA, however. Still, Kennan did not doubt the wisdom or potential efficacy of skillfully conducted covert operations in Europe, and in 1948–1949 he served on a board with the director of Central Intelligence to clarify the policy and oversee the operations of Special Projects. "The need was real," he recalled in 1972, "and many things done were constructive and effective actions."[63] Only many years later—after a series of public revelations about CIA misdeeds and bungling—did Kennan conclude that the United States should suspend covert operations as the government could not control or direct them wisely.[64]

Even though Kennan believed that the occasional display and use of American force, in concert with covert guerrilla actions, were enough to secure Western Europe's physical safety, British and French leaders wanted assurances that the United States would remain committed to their security and not—as after World War I—embrace a version of isolationism. To Ernest Bevin, the ideal solution would involve the United States in a formal multilateral treaty of alliance, pledged to resisting Soviet military pressure or outright aggression. That he succeeded in achieving this was, according to his biographer, the peak of Bevin's achievement as British foreign secretary.[65] Even as the Brussels Treaty (March 17, 1948), joining Great Britain and France in common cause with the Low Countries, was moving toward completion, Inverchapel was promoting Bevin's case to Marshall: the United States must somehow invest itself unequivocally in halting the Soviet Union in Europe.[66]

Against the ominous background of communist coup in Czechoslovakia and Soviet military rumblings—related, as it turned out, to preparations for the Berlin blockade—the Truman government began investigating the means by which the United States might best support the Brussels coalition. Public opinion, as measured in the Gallup polls, was growing in favor of a permanent American alliance with the principal states of Western Europe, but Kennan was unimpressed, and he told Marshall that a formal US-West European military connection was incidental to thwarting the type of threat really posed by the Soviets.[67] Despite their attempt to disrupt Western access to Berlin, the basic Soviet aim was still "the conquest of western Europe by political means."[68] Kennan did admit that a transatlantic security pact would probably boost the confidence of Frenchmen, Britons, and others, but he worried that a heightened concentration on military matters would divert attention from the urgent problem of completing Europe's economic recovery and would prejudice all efforts to find diplomatic answers to the East-West conflict. As it was, he lamented, too many people on both sides of the Atlantic were preoccupied with a military balance of power on the continent. Of course, a healthy balance was essential, but Western Europe's ultimate success and safety depended on the outcome of its struggle for internal political stability. In other words, a US-centered military alliance would "address itself to what is not the main danger."[69]

Once it did become certain that the United States would join some variety of European security pact, Kennan hoped to limit its geographic scope to those states bordering (plus Luxembourg) on the north Atlantic. If this geographic criterion were removed, it would mean that virtually any noncommunist state might be eligible for pact membership and theoretically, at least, would justify a global anti-Soviet alliance system: "To get carried into any such wide system of alliances could only lead to one of two results; either all these alliances become meaningless declarations . . . or this country becomes still further over-extended politically and militarily."[70] Either way, such an American-based collective security arrangement would inevitably collapse. By contrast, the north Atlantic region was a tidy unit, an identifiable community based on historical, cultural, commercial, and security interests.

Kennan also worried that, if a US-West European military organization were established to include states east of the Atlantic zone (e.g., Italy, Greece, West Germany), the political division of Europe would deepen and chances of its future eradication would be slight. None of the satellite regimes could thereafter contemplate a slow reorientation away from the Soviet Union: "Any move in that direction would take on the aspect of a provocative military move."[71] An eventual Soviet-US withdrawal from the center of Europe would be foreclosed; no third force assuring a more stable balance of global power would issue from the continent. To avoid such an acutely strained international division, the North American and European Atlantic powers should assure West Germany, Italy, the Scandinavians, Greece, and other affected nations of their lively concern for the security and interests of non-communist Europe. In case of emergency, the Atlantic states would take appropriate measures in consultation with the inland governments, but an enormous, tightly formed Western military alliance ran counter to winning political victory in the Cold War.

Bohlen was Kennan's only significant ally on this matter (in the State Department) and agreed that the administration should proceed cautiously before tying the United States to a solemn security arrangement in Europe.[72] To his dismay, Kennan's own Policy Planning Staff voiced contrary views and during his absence (to the Far East) in March 1948 produced a set of recommendations going beyond what even Bevin thought necessary. These proposed that the Brussels Treaty states expand their membership to include all of Scandinavia, Portugal, Italy, and eventually Ireland, Switzerland, Germany, Spain, and Austria. And it would be understood that a military attack against any one of them would constitute an attack against the United States.[73] In mid-April, the NSC adopted most of this advice over Kennan's protests.

His failure to carry the PPS on the vital question of US-West European military relations was partly attributable to Hickerson, once again, and to his assistant in the Office of European Affairs, Theodore Achilles. They were early believers in formalized collective security and campaigned very effectively for it within the State Department. In contrast to Kennan's inability to persuade his staff, Hickerson had formed his office into a "bastion" of support for a broadly conceived transatlantic pact. He was also a keen "bureaucratic infighter," who unabashedly wooed the PPS to his side while Kennan was abroad and finally prevailed upon Lovett, Marshall, and Acheson.[74] In the end, Kennan resigned himself to the concept of a North American-West European defense pact; ironically, in late 1948 he was assigned to help devise NATO's specific provisions and institutions. He nevertheless remained skeptical about Italy's admission and later was adamant in his opposition to the entrance of Greece, Turkey, and (in 1954) West Germany.[75] His desire remained for a looser arrangement relying on a US-Canada alliance that would cooperate with a European military coalition centered in Britain, France, and Benelux as circumstances warranted.

The establishment of NATO in 1949 indicated as nothing else probably could that, in the face of all his recommendations, the US would nevertheless pursue a course of Cold War involving conspicuous military rivalry and blocs. Although he did believe a Soviet-US war might occur through inadvertence or blunder in the late 1940s, Kennan consistently emphasized means short of war for checking Soviet expansion in Europe. In the event of war, he hoped the United States would seek to neutralize Soviet power rather than to eliminate it along the lines of World War II's "unconditional surrender" doctrine. In any event, he held that the US should aim to establish a workable arrangement with Stalin's Russia, not to act as though a European war was inevitable.[76] In these thoughts, Kennan was increasingly in a minority, and once the Soviets exploded an atom bomb (August 1949), majority opinion in Washington ran heavily against him and found expression in widespread support of NATO.

The success of NATO has, of course, precluded Western Europe from developing into the "third force" in international politics preferred by Kennan. Still, NATO's establishment and with it the American guarantee provided a supportive psychological environment for Britons, Scandinavians, Frenchmen, etc. in 1949 and the early 1950s. And the pervasive sense of security endowed upon the West Europeans by NATO has enabled them to produce a set of superior social and material conditions that have provided—as Kennan hoped they would—a "constant contrast with those prevailing behind the iron curtain," and over the decades has complicated Soviet domination of Eastern Europe.

Eastern Europe

Long before the Marshall Plan was enacted by Congress and its impact felt in Europe, Kennan had predicted that the Soviet Union would have difficulty in managing its zone east of the Leubeck-Trieste line: Soviet police methods might allow them to maintain an imperial prerogative for years to come, but the Soviets would also be in the unenviable position of disciplining "millions of Europeans with a higher cultural level and with long experience in resistance to foreign rule."[77] Russia could not be expected to hold them in permanent subjugation. Still, Kennan, along with most observers in the West, was surprised by the swiftness and completeness with which Yugoslavia broke from the USSR in the summer of 1948. Until then, Joseph Broz Tito had been the most dogmatic, militant Stalinist in Europe and had demonstrated utter hostility toward the United States on recent occasions. In apparent recognition of and confidence in Yugoslavia's ideological orthodoxy, the Soviets had allowed Belgrade to serve as headquarters for the recently organized Cominform.[78]

Behind mutual protestations of fraternal feeling and Yugoslav paeans to the Fatherland of Socialism, though, problems had long been accumulating between the Yugoslav and Soviet communist parties. During the Second World War, Moscow had unwisely urged Tito's partisans to cooperate with Draja Mikhailovich's royalist resistance. The Soviets also had been slow to establish liaison with Tito's headquarters and sent a military mission to it two years after the British already had. Then, following hostilities, the Soviets were mild in their support of Tito during the Trieste crisis and may have chastised him after Yugoslavia downed an American plane. And after initially supporting the project, Stalin decided in early 1948 that Tito's proposed Balkan federation—in which Bulgaria and Albania would merge with, and be subordinate to, Yugoslavia—was inconsistent with the principle of supreme Soviet leadership in communist southeastern Europe and should be canceled. Finally, as Kennan was later to underscore, Stalin had discouraged Belgrade's considerable interest in ERP.[79] By March 1948, for the first time in history, the CPSU's relationship with a foreign communist party lay in tatters, and authorities in Belgrade arrested local people thought to be serving Soviet interests. Three months later, delegates to the Cominform conference—meeting in more hospitable Bucharest—pilloried Tito and his colleagues for "national deviationism" and called upon true Marxist-Leninists in Yugoslavia to abolish the disreputable leadership. Having failed to display appropriate contrition, the Yugoslav party was then excommunicated and damned for its apostasy.[80]

The US embassy in Belgrade immediately urged Washington to lend Tito some type of support, lest Soviet assassins or elements of the Red Army stationed in neighboring countries squelch him and his heresy. The naval and military attachés cabled: "Believe Tito cannot long withstand Soviets alone. Believe that if he really wants to try and is given full support from the West he would have good prospect of a success which would lead to the solution of our major problems in Europe."[81] Kennan's own reaction to the Yugoslav-Soviet dispute was almost as enthusiastic as that of American diplomats in Belgrade, and he presented ideas to Marshall and the NSC that served as the foundation for policy.[82] He noted with scarcely concealed delight that Yugoslavia's defiance of Stalin might foreshadow a time when other communist states would escape Soviet bonds. The US response to Yugoslavia's defection would surely set an important precedent and influence whether other satellite states would be tempted to follow suit or else more closely weld themselves to Kremlin purposes.

Kennan recommended that the United States adopt an attitude of modest restraint. He cautioned that Tito's regime was still avowedly communist, hostile to the bourgeois camp, and publicly committed to reconciling its differences with Stalin. And yet a new immutable fact of international life had arisen. Tito's actions meant that the once monolithic communist movement was damaged beyond repair: "By [Yugoslavia's] act, the aura of mystical omnipotence and infallibility which has surrounded the Kremlin power has been broken. The possibility of defection from Moscow, which has heretofore been unthinkable for foreign communist leaders, will from now on be present in one form or another in the mind of every one of them."[83]

Kennan hoped the United States would not fawn on Tito or do anything to arouse revulsion for him among earnest Yugoslav communists. At the same time, the Americans should not regard him with frosty reserve. If Yugoslavia was treated as an enemy or pariah by the West, then Moscow could legitimately contend that any communist state deserting Russia would be subject to international isolation and have to live at the tender mercy of capitalist wolves. The United States and its allies, said Kennan, should therefore make clear their interest in entering into regular economic and diplomatic intercourse with Yugoslavia for so long as that country was not subservient to the USSR.

Although some doubts persisted among British and US officials about Tito's likely physical and political longevity and about the real severity of the Soviet-Yugoslav division, Belgrade and Washington improved their relationship through the summer months of 1948.[84] In July the two governments signed agreements covering compensation for US property nationalized in Yugoslavia and settled their lend-lease accounts. The American treasury also lifted its freeze on Yugoslav assets ($47 million in gold) in the United States. By 1949 the United States was granting tens of millions of dollars to Yugoslavia, and two-way trade increased. All of this economic activity was satisfactory to, indeed encouraged by, Kennan and the PPS, which counseled the administration to relax its export license controls in favor of Yugoslavia; through these and similar means Tito's resistance to Stalin might be strengthened. And perhaps the Yugoslavs would be considerate enough to halt *their* assistance to Greece's communist guerrillas.[85] No matter what, however, the Truman government must do everything possible to keep Tito's Yugoslavia afloat; its continuing success represented a wonderful setback to "Kremlin control of international communism as an instrument of Russian expansion."[86] In the event of war between Yugoslavia and the Soviet Union, Kennan advised that Britain and the US furnish Belgrade with necessary military equipment and economic help. The NSC agreed; by 1951 the United States was supplementing its economic aid with military, and meetings were convened among British, US, and Yugoslav army officers to coordinate joint action should Russia, or some combination of its satellites, invade Yugoslavia.

Tito's challenge to Stalin's authority reinforced Kennan's conviction that non-military strategies could be used to weaken Soviet hegemony in Eastern Europe. Contrary to the interpretation promoted by historians, such as Barton Bernstein and Gabriel Kolko, that Eastern Europe represented an economic prize to American policy planners, Kennan viewed it strictly from the standpoint of power politics. The states there were "in themselves of secondary importance on the European scene." But in a bipolar universe they were significant to the degree to which they functioned as "politico-military adjuncts of Soviet power and extend[ed] that power into the heart of Europe." As Kennan conceived it, they were part of the Soviet monolith; the American task was to crack it.[87] This meant the United States should do what it could to encourage communist heresy in Soviet-occupied Europe and foment the growth of non-Stalinist communist regimes that eventually might yield democratic leaderships. To these ends, the US should exert maximum pressure "on the structure of relationships by which Soviet domination . . . is maintained." And Kennan judged the economic weapon to be especially capable of disrupting, or at least delaying, international communist coordination. As in the case of ERP, Stalin would be forced either to permit a fair degree of economic collaboration between the satellites and the West, thereby contributing to a loosening of their orientation toward Moscow, or, at a high political cost to the USSR, to prevent their receiving succor from the Marshall Plan. "Everything," said Kennan, "which operates to tear off the veil with which Moscow likes to screen its power, and which forces the Russians to reveal the crude and ugly outlines of their hold over the governments of the satellite countries, serves to discredit the satellite governments with their own peoples and to heighten the discontent of those peoples and their desire for free association with other nations."[88] Kennan was an equally enthusiastic advocate of waging intensive propaganda campaigns against the Soviet bloc, which, in tandem with US economic policy, might one day break open the subterranean national fissures that laced Eastern Europe. As Ambassador Walter Bedell Smith assured him and the PPS, the Soviets feared "Titoism" more than anything else, as it could destroy their *cordon sanitaire*.[89]

By the late summer of 1949 Kennan urged that the moment had arrived for the United States to move rapidly to reduce or even eliminate Soviet influence in Albania, Bulgaria, Czechoslovakia, Poland, and Rumania. The westward advance of Soviet power had been checked; non-Marxist Europe was making rapid progress toward becoming a weighty political counter-force. These defensive tasks achieved, it was time to seize the offensive and force Soviet power to recede to a geographical area compatible with enhanced Western security. Accepted by Acheson and approved by Truman and the NSC, these ideas (as well as Kennan's advice about economic and propaganda instruments), were expressed in diverse forms. They included a barrage of Voice of America broadcasts to East European audiences that stressed their vassalage to an economically exploitive, politically brutal, culturally backward USSR. Covert activities were also employed, as were different combinations of economic inducement, pressure, and threat.[90] The results were not immediately impressive, however.

There were several reasons for the failure of satellite states other than Yugoslavia to bolt from the Soviet fold during the Stalinist era. Unlike Tito and the Yugoslav communist party, other East European regimes—in Warsaw, Budapest, Sofia—enjoyed scant popular support. Without widespread backing, it is doubtful that Tito could have sustained his independence from the USSR. The veteran core of the Yugoslav army, moreover, was accomplished in guerrilla warfare and could be depended upon to give a good account of itself had the Soviets attacked. Stalin must have reasoned that a Soviet-Yugoslav war would be more costly and protracted than he could afford and, besides, Yugoslavia was of secondary geostrategic importance. In contrast to Poland, for example, Yugoslavia could not serve as a corridor for invasion from the west; Soviet control of East Germany was not logistically connected to Yugoslavia. In addition, Tito's internal security apparatus was efficient, loyal to him, and ruthless enough to destroy all Soviet-leaning Yugoslav communists. Similar conditions simply did not obtain in the other East European states, which were occupied by the Red Army and policed by Soviet agents. Consequently, Stalin was able to impose "reliable" people and arrange for the purging of real and imagined "Titoist" elements, such as Laszlo Rajk in Hungary and Wladyslaw Gomulka in Poland. Meanwhile, as Kennan later emphasized, the United States squandered what little leverage it did have to coax East European leaders away from Moscow. American thinking about European matters became overly militarized in 1949–1950 and created a psychological climate conducive only to political and military rigidity. In particular, the establishment of a military bloc, NATO, meant that a Western community was arising that provided no plausible framework for accommodating potential defector regimes. Rather, the division of Europe was made more final and the official American line became one demanding nothing less than total communist capitulation in Eastern Europe—a mock heroic posture in Kennan's view unrelated to reality or to any genuine desire to erase Europe's division.[91]

*   *   *   *

A close sifting through the evidence related to the mostly familiar story of Kennan and the Cold War in Europe supports two broad conclusions. First, he clearly believed that a policy blending—in descending order of proportion—political-economic, covert, and military means was most likely to succeed in checking Soviet international ambitions. Second, an examination of PPS and NSC records from the late 1940s shows that—*contra* the familiar revisionist and new corporatist historiography—neither of these two critically important policymaking institutions was especially concerned with, let alone driven by, a desire to strengthen America's economic hegemony in Western Europe or extend it to the East. For Kennan, who served with both of these governmental bodies, the principal issue was the balance of power, not the energetic expansion of capitalism or increased corporate profits.

His advocacy of a revitalized balance of power in Europe led him in a couple of directions. Regarding the Soviet zone, he advocated a policy that conformed to classical diplomacy's *modus operandi:* the United States should try to divide its enemy's alliance system by drawing the weaker party (the satellite states) away from the USSR. To this end, Kennan saw NATO as an impediment, whereas covert and economic policies could be most useful. As to Western Europe, he recognized that US military force should be readily available and, if necessary, used without hesitation. At the same time, he was concerned lest the United States and its allies relied too heavily on military instruments and security pacts for the resolution of international questions. He complained to Acheson in 1951: "We have over-emphasized the military problem" and the US was spending too much on NATO.[92] By contrast, ERP had more to recommend it.

It did not particularly matter to Kennan that Churchill and others praised the Marshall Plan as an example of unalloyed American altruism or that the shrillest anti-communists endorsed it as a method for stemming the Red Tide. And it did not matter that Stalin denounced ERP as a diabolical scheme proferred by the premier capitalist state to capture new markets and territories for the investment of surplus capital—as opposed to the "generous" Molotov plan for Eastern Europe. For Kennan, and those people associated with him in framing it, the Marshall Plan was an economic instrument to advance America's security interests in Europe. As such, it was meant to keep French, Italian, and other communist parties off balance and out of power; to embarrass the Soviet Union and increase strains between it and the satellite states; and to fortify the morale and outlook of those West Europeans who feared the United States would return to its venerable isolationist policy in a period when elements of the Russian army stood farther west than any time since the defeat of Napoleon. And ERP would help restore and retain West Germany for peaceful purposes. A skillfully implemented ERP would thus help thwart the Soviets from filling any temporary vacuum in Europe, and a new balance of power would emerge favorable to long-term North Atlantic and North American safety. For these reasons, Kennan also supported a continental union grouped around a French-German core, which eventually would dispense with American aid and patronage and stand as an independent, effective third force in the power balance of the West. In other words, America's "best chance of avoiding war with the Soviet Union lay in the opening up of a wide area in central Europe which was neither 'ours' nor 'theirs' and therefore not too much of a source of concern to either side."[93] Hence Kennan's advocacy, too, in 1948 of withdrawing occupation troops from Germany and permitting the country to reunite.

After some hesitation, Acheson by late 1949 opposed any concept of a "third force" in Europe and was committed to the proposition that Western Europe pool its economic and military resources with those of the United States. His disagreement with Kennan over European policy, in turn, highlighted the philosophical differences between the two men: Kennan still thought in 1949 that American diplomacy could discover some common ground with Stalin which would lead to limited agreements, while Acheson insisted that only Western military strength would inhibit Soviet aggression. And as negotiated compromises would be undermined by Stalin, they should command no attention by the Truman government.[94]

Despite their divergent views on these and a host of issues (including America's development of the hydrogen bomb, to be discussed in Chapter 13), Kennan and Acheson remained on decent personal terms. Even in 1959, after having been castigated by Acheson for ideas expressed in his Reith Lectures, Kennan was able to write: "In many respects I think Mr. Acheson was an excellent Secretary of State . . . I shudder to think what the government would have done without him at that time; for he was surrounded, in the Truman administration, by such incompetence and mediocrity, and there were times when I think he alone held things together."[95] Still, Kennan faulted Acheson for being a poor organizer and for failing to cope better with the McCarthy phenomenon. This second charge was closely connected in Kennan's mind with the damage sustained by the Foreign Service during Acheson's incumbency. It might also have rested on some idea of Acheson's irresponsibility in the sphere of public political education, for irrespective of its foreign policy consequences, the Truman Doctrine helped lead to the era of domestic bitterness associated with Joseph McCarthy. Kennan had warned Acheson in vain against the doctrine's inflated rhetoric and decried a policy publicly justified on indiscriminate anti-communism and the bugaboo of universal Marxist danger. Yet Kennan's recommendations about how to portray problems in Greece and Turkey seemed inept to Acheson and Truman as they struggled to conduct a mass democracy's foreign policy. Slowly at first, but then with shattering anxiety by late 1949, Kennan realized that he and his advice to Acheson—like the age of cabinet diplomacy that he revered—were irrelevant and unwelcome.[96]

8

Far Eastern Dilemmas

By most any standard of evaluation, US policy toward Europe in the late 1940s was a triumph; after 1948 the Soviet Union was unable to expand its zone of influence west of the German Democratic Republic; thanks to the Marshall Plan the West European economies were reviving, and the French, British, German, and Italian societies were beginning to recover their cohesion and political confidence. However, unlike the Truman administration's European policy—preventing communist expansion and providing the resources and incentives for recovery—the Far Eastern record was ambiguous and eminently open to criticism. On the one hand, the government did preserve Japan for the West and kept a privileged position for the United States in the councils of Tokyo. But, on the other, the Korean War was a costly, inconclusive affair, and the communist conquest of China was a momentous event and suggested to many people around the world that the Far Eastern balance of power had drastically altered to Soviet advantage. In fact, few American misadventures have caused greater popular apprehension and debate than the "loss of China." Many intemperate critics—Joseph McCarthy, William Knowland, Herman Welker, Patrick McCarren, among others—blamed China's subjugation by "international communism" on the State Department's general "leftist orientation." By selling out China, "red" Dean Acheson and his presidential dupe had jeopardized American security and global peace.

Kennan's views about Cold War problems in East Asia were organized around two major principles and two corresponding goals for US diplomacy. His first principle was that, as in Europe, the expansion of Soviet influence in Asia depended primarily on the cooperation of various local communist parties whose sense of national identity and cause was at least as great as their commitment to "international proletarianism" and the Soviet Union. Despite their ideological solidarity with Moscow, despite their willingness to collaborate with Stalin in reducing through all available means—including military ones—the overall position of the United States, and despite their eagerness to obtain assorted kinds of Soviet assistance, most Asian Marxist parties could be expected to possess some important aims independent of, and not necessarily congenial with, those of the CPSU. By exploiting apparent and potential differences between the Asian parties and the senior one in Moscow, the United States could check Soviet influence in Asia, help debase Russia's international prestige, and promote a Far Eastern balance of power conducive to Western interests.

Kennan also recognized that America's standing as the preponderant power in Asia was a temporary condition and bound to be eroded as the regional states recovered from the war. In anticipation of the Soviet Union's future ability to project naval and air power, as well as political influence, from numerous points along the Asian mainland, the United States must distinguish among the diverse centers of authority in the East and concentrate on retaining in some form, for Western purposes, only the most vital: whatever else happened in Asia, Japan must not be allowed to slip into a Soviet orbit. If Japanese industrial strength and with it Japan's war-making capability became aligned with Soviet foreign policy, the United States would face difficulties aplenty in the Pacific and of a magnitude comparable to 1941.[1]

Kennan's respect for Japan's potential power was so great that in 1949, as the country lay in ruins and under an American army of occupation, he referred to the Japanese as the only truly dynamic and inventive people in East Asia.[2] The narrowness of such a judgment notwithstanding, it was Kennan's belief in it that led him to play a creditable role in the US effort to rehabilitate Japan in the immediate postwar period. He recorded years later that his contribution to the restoration of Japanese economy and politics constituted his second most significant service in government, surpassed only by his work on the Marshall Plan.[3]

The ambitious task of transforming Japan from a war-devastated enemy into a prosperous American ally, while advancing in 1948–1950, was, of course, overshadowed in the public mind by the more obviously dramatic events of the Chinese civil war and Mao's coming to power and the frustrating, sanguinary struggle in Korea. Kennan managed to keep these two crises in perspective for the most part, but his advice was not always heeded and explains in part his continued dissatisfaction in government and departure (late August 1950) for an extended leave of absence from the Foreign Service.

Japanese Rehabilitation

General Douglas MacArthur, who in his capacity as military governor of Japan exercised practically unlimited power, liked to preach that the American occupation was unique in the annals of modern history and far transcended the traditional purposes of nations victorious in war; the Americans were engaged in a noble, epoch-transforming mission, namely the recasting of ancient Japan from a warlike, feudal society into one modern, peaceful, democratic, and increasingly Christian. MacArthur assured his superiors (1947) that the reformation of the Japanese soul and mind was evolving satisfactorily: "Japan is now already governed by the form of democratic rule and the people are absorbing its substance. . . . Having repudiated war and renounced all rights of belligerency, [the Japanese] have placed their full reliance for future protection on the good faith and justice of mankind, and are proceeding through legislated reform to develop a state dedicated, in full reality, to the welfare of the people." He also estimated that two million Japanese had accepted the tenets of Christianity and millions more might be converted as they realized that their lives hitherto had been dominated by "mythical teachings and legendary ritualism," which blinded people to the benefits of peace and seduced them into glorifying and seeking war.[4]

By late 1947, MacArthur had reviewed at least three drafts of a proposed treaty ending the state of war between Japan and the Allies. Although he had reservations about some of the specific suggested provisions, he was looking forward to the ratification of such a document by all concerned governments and ending American occupation of the Japanese mainland.

When consulted by the administration about the impending peace treaty and evacuation of US servicemen from Japan, Kennan and his Asian specialist, John Paton Davies, scoffed that such action by the United States, though desirable and ultimately inevitable, was premature in 1947. They reminded Secretary Marshall that US interests demanded a stable Japanese society and polity integrated into the Pacific economy and that Japanese regard for and cooperation with the United States should be as securely based as possible before MacArthur relinquished control in Tokyo; yet the ideas thus far advanced in the draft versions of peace treaty failed to harmonize with these fundamental objectives. Continued international supervision, for example, of disarmament and of "democratization" in Japan, however well intentioned, were in fact paving the way for communist subversion and the coming to power of a pro-Soviet government. To Kennan and Davies the treaty writers—mostly middle-level figures in the State Department's Far Eastern Division, led by the Japanese specialist Hugh Borton—were not adequately concerned about relating Japan's future to the long-range interests of the United States in the Pacific. Until the Policy Planning Staff had a chance to review the entire pattern of Eastern problems might the process involving international negotiations, treaty articles, and final settlement be delayed? On the basis of this advice, the secretary limited further work on the treaty until the PPS had completed a thorough study.[5]

After conferring with Davies, as well as with Joseph Grew, former ambassador to Japan, and a number of specialists in the Far Eastern office, Kennan submitted to Marshall a tentative position (October 1947) about the shape a peace treaty should assume. He emphasized his and Davies's objection that Japan's early or abrupt return to independence would run counter to US interests because—irrespective of MacArthur's efforts—the country was vulnerable to political capture by elements hostile to the West. Only when Japan was economically stronger and more resilient internally should the United States remove its stabilizing influence; otherwise, Japan would founder and fall prey to any determined, ruthless party (probably communists, but possibly fascists) that cared not a whit for the United States and would challenge its Eastern security arrangements at the first opportunity.

At the same time Kennan realized as well as anyone else that the American occupation could not continue indefinitely, as the cost was beginning to wear on the

United States and Japanese forbearance toward their overlords was slowly evaporating. (Between September 1945 and June 1948 the United States spent nearly a billion dollars to provide Japan with such items as food, fuel, and medicine. In 1949 occupation costs for that one year totaled $900 million and there seemed no end in sight.)[6] He recommended, therefore, that negotiations for a multilateral treaty go forward to placate Tokyo's impatience and congressional eagerness to "get the boys home." But the Japanese-US-British-Soviet (and other Allies) talks should not be so hurried that US interests in Japan and the Pacific were jeopardized; a peace treaty should not be in place before June 1948, by which time the Pentagon and State Department could determine exactly which Japanese possessions were of strategic value and should be kept for use by the US army and navy. Might the United States want to keep or lease military facilities scattered among the Japanese home islands and the Ryukyu archipelago? What about Okinawa?

Kennan was ambivalent from the start about the ongoing program of demilitarization, but felt that whatever its outcome Japan must be allowed, indeed assisted, in building and maintaining a national police force with paramilitary training and equipment and a serviceable coast guard. He expected that these forces would be sufficient to uphold domestic order and safety, but, given Japan's constitutionally mandated prohibition of regular armed forces, the United States would have to guarantee Japanese security against overt aggression: "In the coming period Japan's military security must rest primarily on the proximity (or, in extreme event, the presence in Japan) of adequate US forces, and . . . it should be accepted as a principle of American defense policy to retain in the Pacific areas [enough] armed strength to make plain our will and determination to prevent any other military power from establishing itself in [Japan]."[7] While the United States accepted responsibility for Japan's external security, Kennan hoped the country's leaders and citizenry would increase the imperviousness of their society against both Moscow-directed communists and the remnants of the *ancien regime* which, given the chance, would return Japan to a militant, aggressive course. For the sake of the West, then, the majority of Japanese had to gain confidence in using the political institutions bequeathed by the occupation—about which Kennan was pessimistic. More important, the national economy must be allowed to flourish.

Kennan worried that Japan's economic recovery would be patchy and incomplete because much of the national wealth had been consumed by the war effort; extensive markets and raw materials on the Asian mainland were lost to Soviet domination; conditions in China, Indonesia, India, Indochina, and other zones of traditional Japanese investment and export were chaotic. And the feasibility of future Japanese exports to the dollar area was in doubt: "As things stand today, the information we have does not satisfy us that Japanese society, if turned loose on its own now or in the near future, would be able to survive successfully the resultant strain on its political structure."[8] He advised that, if the State Department finally concluded that Japan was unable to stand on its own economically and politically for the foreseeable future, the whole project of designing a peace settlement should be postponed. In any event, not until there was reasonable certainty in Washington that Japan could survive in the hostile environment of Cold War should the United States occupation cease.

As of late 1947 neither Kennan nor other State Department policymakers really knew whether MacArthur's administration was contributing to Japan's economic and political revitalization. (Given the policies of reparations, decartelization, limited industrial production, purges, and war crimes tribunal, Kennan harbored private doubts.) To obtain more reliable information about the occupation and how it could fit into a peace treaty and a renewed Japan, General Marshall dispatched (February 1948) Kennan to Tokyo for meetings with MacArthur and a tour of the major islands. At the time the State Department's relations with MacArthur and with SCAP (Supreme Commander, Allied Powers) headquarters were in disrepair. Even though the administration allowed MacArthur wide scope in handling Japanese matters, far surpassing the leeway granted Clay in Germany, personal relations between Marshall and MacArthur were cool. MacArthur also had little liking for professional diplomats, and the department's representative in Japan, William Sebald, played a decidedly inferior role in the making of SCAP policy. He was rarely consulted about major issues by MacArthur and was thus unable to provide Marshall or the Policy Planning Staff with detailed analysis and information about the occupation. An important part of Kennan's mission was therefore to improve the liaison between SCAP and the State Department, and led to his later recommendation that a full-fledged envoy, not the least dependent upon MacArthur, be posted to Tokyo. Presumably, a regular ambassador would be excellently situated to compile complete reports for the secretary and enter into relations with the Japanese government and other diplomatic missions in a way in which MacArthur, as SCAP chief, was unsuited. This idea was unfortunately not strongly pushed by Kennan nor endorsed by Marshall. Despite their reservations about MacArthur, they deferred to his conceit that an effective US occupation required the United States to speak with only one voice in Tokyo—his own.[9] This delicacy of avoiding arrangements disagreeable to MacArthur probably reinforced his inclination to pursue his own line in vital questions and so indirectly contributed to his fateful confrontation with the Truman administration in 1951.

Kennan's encounter with MacArthur began poorly. At their first meeting MacArthur showed his disdain for the State Department by ostentatiously ignoring Kennan and directing all remarks and attention to his military escort, Brigadier General C. V. R. Schuyler. For reasons still unclear, MacArthur did later warm toward Kennan and before long he was allowed to enjoy a couple of private interviews that covered the whole range of occupation, peace treaty, and Asia's future.[10] Following Marshall's suggestion, Kennan let MacArthur hold forth in their conversations for as long as he wanted—which he did at length—and was cautious in making criticisms about SCAP or the occupation.[11]

During their meetings MacArthur worked some of his favorite themes: Not since Julius Caesar had left his mark on Gaul and Albion had any occupying military power the opportunity, as the United States now possessed in Japan, of imprinting its culture and values on a vanquished enemy. The spiritually disoriented Japanese were embracing democracy and Christianity as their own. Through the Japanese, the United States had a unique opportunity of transmitting to all Asians the blessings of higher religion and superior political culture. Unhappy memories of totalitarianism were helping to fortify all Japan from succumbing to communist domination and propaganda. And even if some of the Japanese communists were impressive as individual personalities, their movement was weak and their strength diminished since SCAP had preempted a threatened, communist-inspired strike. In summation, the United States and its beneficence were propelling Japan on an irreversible, enlightened course.[12]

Under Kennan's prodding (and flattery) MacArthur descended from the lofty heights of grand historical interpretation to wrestle with more immediate practical questions of treaty and Japanese political and economic policies. On this more mundane level the two men found areas of common ground and agreement. They both affirmed that the US must promote a security policy in northeast Asia whose fundamental objective would be protecting Japanese sovereignty. The United States must also oversee an intensive program of economic recovery in Japan and steadily relax the coercive controls—already substantially eased according to MacArthur—of the occupation. Through these policies the United States would be exercising the best means to assure the integrity of its western flank, which in MacArthur's view now ran along the eastern shore of the Asian continent and depended on US strategic control of the Aleutians, Midway, the former Japanese-mandated islands, Okinawa, and air and naval bases in the Philippines. As for Japan proper, MacArthur and Kennan decided that the Americans should not retain permanent bases anywhere in the post-treaty period as that would legitimate the claim of other states (i.e., the USSR) to do likewise.[13]

Despite the broad areas of their agreement, Kennan did not go along with all of MacArthur's reasoning. He was certainly not convinced that, because most Japanese abhorred totalitarianism, their country was immune to communist intrigue and conspiracy: "To the communists, the problem of capturing Japan is not a problem of winning over the majority of the Japanese people. It is a problem of penetrating Japanese society and seizing its key positions. At present, it looks to me as though Japanese society were vulnerable to such attacks."[14] Also contrary to MacArthur, Kennan doubted Soviet good faith in observing an Allied-Japanese treaty premised on Japan's total demilitarization; only if Russia were far weaker than at present could it be expected to observe restraint toward a disarmed Japan. Kennan was willing, in fact, to entertain the idea of stationing US troops in Japan for a long time—notwithstanding his uneasiness about the dire effects on the morale of servicemen and host population—until Moscow showed itself willing to drop all hostile aims against Tokyo. If a peace treaty were eventually signed, the United States should encourage Japanese rearmament to the point needed to deter any open military aggression. In effect, Kennan concluded that disarmament had gone too far and questioned the wisdom of article nine of the American-imposed Japanese constitution, which forbade Japan from maintaining "land, sea, and air forces, as well as other war potential."

On the basis of his visit to Japan and MacArthur, Kennan was confident enough to recommend (March 1948) to Marshall a plan for the proper handling of Japanese-US issues. In essence, the peace should be lenient and every US initiative made to bend in one direction: Japan must be made to fit comfortably and contentedly into a US-designed pattern of Eastern international relationships. The administration must consequently do nothing to hasten the day when a multilateral peace treaty was signed and insist that when finally drafted it was nonpunitive. For the remainder of occupation, the numbers and role of American forces in Japan should be reduced sufficiently to minimize their cost to Japan's psychological well-being. (Incidentally, Kennan was repelled by the sycophants that surrounded MacArthur and dismayed by the spectacle of Americans living abroad in comfortable surroundings while the native population suffered their insults and insensitivity and lived in poverty. How, he wondered, could the Japanese with their ancient culture and traditions bear to have the bad tastes and inane habits of American suburbia imposed upon them?)[15] The complete withdrawal of US troops, of course, and the advisability of limited Japanese rearmament would depend over time on Japan's internal stability and on whether or not the Soviets demonstrated unprecedentedly peaceful intentions toward their old Asian adversary. Kennan also stressed the importance to the United States of Okinawa as a base from which American naval and air power could be projected simultaneously along the northern and southern perimeter of the Asian continent and, if necessary, west to the heartland.

Kennan was even more adamant than before his trip that the State-Army-Navy-Air Force Coordinating Committee (SANACC) and SCAP quickly join Japanese authorities in building a well-trained, adequately staffed national police force and coast guard. To boost Japanese self-confidence, SCAP's authority should be gradually slackened to the point where it would merely observe the activities of Japan's government and occasionally confer with it about national issues. SCAP should also curtail its various reform programs of Japanese society and under no circumstances cajole the defeated country into adopting new liberal measures. The purges, too, of people associated with the wartime government and military organizations should be halted, and in some cases categories of minor offenders barred from business, news media, and government should be made reeligible.

To energize Japan's economic recovery, Kennan suggested that the government in Tokyo henceforth be freed from paying the expenses associated with Mac-Arthur's occupation. Direct financial aid should be introduced to buttress the faltering Japanese economy, and the pertinent agencies of the American government should explore means of restoring Japan's foreign trade and stimulating the development of products for export. The unworkable, nonsensical policy of forcing Japan to pay further reparations should also be restricted and entirely phased out by July 1, 1949. And, thanks partly to Kennan's direct intervention, the more radical American plans for the decartelization of Japan's great commercial conglomerations, *zaibatsu,* were shelved and the reparations program was terminated.[16]

Finally, to help rejuvenate Japan and repair the emotional wounds of a lost war, Kennan argued that the trials of high-ranking military and civilian leaders for alleged war crimes be discontinued. Just as with Nuremberg, he maintained that they had precious little to do with justice and functioned only to confuse and inflame popular feeling against the United States: "The Japanese public has long since ceased to feel any reactions toward the trials other than ones of sympathy for . . . fellow Japanese who are forced to sit through these endless and humiliating ordeals which have so little to do with anything that anyone in Japan can understand."[17] Along with scrapping the war crimes trials, the United States should lift existing censorship programs in Japan, with the proviso that SCAP still be allowed to conduct counter-intelligence such as spot-checking of the mails. In this same vein of magnanimity, Kennan hoped that Washington would disseminate American books, magazines, and radio programs in Japan and establish cultural exchanges for Japanese and US nationals—principally scholars, scientists, teachers, and students.[18]

After being reviewed by various State and Defense Department officials, Kennan's suggestions, with minor revisions, were accepted by the NSC as the basis for policy in mid-spring 1948.[19] All did not go smoothly in practice, however. Walton Butterworth, Director of State's Far Eastern Affairs, complained (May 1949) that widespread restlessness in Japan over the occupation was strengthening the mass appeal of the communist party, which charged the Americans with pursuing crude imperialism under the guise of administering order and reform. And how ominous that during a recent election the communists had polled strongly and increased their representation from five to thirty-five in the Diet. Butterworth also noted that the revival of Japanese trade and production was lackluster, the latter standing at 65 percent of 1930–1934 levels. Meanwhile, US financial assistance to Japan was increasing, and Butterworth predicted that not until 1954 or 1955 would Japan approach self-sufficiency again. He particularly regretted that Kennan's agenda of the previous year, intended to lighten the onerousness of occupation for the Japanese and create political conditions favorable to a return of self-rule, had only been only partially implemented. Butterworth insisted that, if absolutely nothing else was accomplished, steps must be taken to accelerate the repair of Japan's industry before the departure of US troops; the establishment of strong, disciplinary police organs required urgent attention, too.[20]

MacArthur's vanity brooked little criticism, and he grew irritable with most anyone—including Kennan and Butterworth—in Washington who complained about the occupation. He informed Acheson tartly that many of the criticisms generated in the State Department were unfair and unfounded, and insinuated they were the work of left-wingers and congenital malcontents. The Japanese themselves, by contrast, were not whining. The general boasted:

> The United States has emerged through three and a half years of a predominantly American Occupation to occupy a unique position in the hearts of the Japanese people. It is a position of respect bordering on reverence and veneration . . . the great masses of the Japanese people [have] a sense of confidence and faith and a feeling of complete security in the American effort and purpose. This is the strong spiritual front which has been erected here in Japan against the Communist advance in Asia.[21]

Kennan was still not persuaded that Japanese affection for the United States went deep or that demonstrations of it were sincere; MacArthur's bragging about Japan's conversion to Christianity and democracy was hollow. He hoped the US government would concentrate on real possibilities—not pious rhetoric—and recognize that no "Japanese political system, capable of standing permanently on its own feet, will be recognizable as 'democracy' from the US viewpoint . . . what is necessary in Japan . . . is the development of a stable and independent political system which will be strongly resistant to communism if not sympathetic to western ideas or trustful of western governments."[22] A resuscitated Japan, he reiterated, was necessary for the correct functioning of a balance of power in the Far East, but it was ridiculous to imagine Japan as a distant outpost of American civilization. Kennan speculated that one day, well in the future, Japan might cleanly cut all its connections with the United States; however, as long as such a Japan remained anti-Soviet, the Americans and their allies should rest content. A restored, socially conservative Japan that retained traditional mores and political structure—absent the aggressive martial element—was not in Kennan's mind ever going to align itself with the USSR.[23]

In the final analysis the Korean War was more instrumental in rehabilitating Japan's international prestige and economy than either MacArthur's rule in Tokyo or Kennan's ideas about reconstruction and peace settlement. With the advent of Korean hostilities, every question about reparations, the breakup of industrial combines, and trade and production policies was resolved in Japan's favor. During the war Japanese manufacturers helped produce some of the military equipment used by American and other United Nations forces, and the country's international balance of payments in 1950 ended in the black—by $40 million—for the first time since World War II. The economy's growth was further spurred by the spending of dollars by US troops in Japan, and by the end of 1952 it enjoyed an excess of receipts on all account transactions to the tune of $150 million. Unemployment plummeted, too, and Japan began its steady ascent out of economic depression.[24]

During the period of Korean fighting, strong measures were taken by Shigeru Yoshida's government and SCAP to undermine the Japanese communists. In 1950 a police reserve of 75,000 men was authorized, thousands of leftists and suspected communist sympathizers were fired from government and business positions, and most leading members of Japan's communist party were expelled from public life. As many as 22,000 people were directly affected by the "red purge." The Korean War thus dealt a hammer blow to communism in Japan.[25]

In view of Japan's growing stability and recovery and of the desirability of finding a Korean solution short of world war, Kennan proposed to Acheson in late August 1950 a US-Soviet *quid pro quo*: For its part the US would agree to the neutralization and demilitarization of Japan—the paramilitary police forces would stay—and would withdraw all American soldiers and air and naval units. The Soviets in exchange would end their proxy aggression in Korea, oversee the withdrawal of North Korean forces to north of the thirty-eighth parallel, and permit the UN to exercise political control in the country for a year or two. To counter the objection, which he himself would have raised only two years earlier, that the removal of US troops from Japan would amount to a colossal self-denial for the US of military infrastructure, forward bases, and relatively protected positions, Kennan recommended the creation of a compact, mobile US military unit—a conceptual forerunner of Jimmy Carter's rapid deployment force: "We would maintain in being and in a state of readiness at all times a mixed combat force, commanded and operated as a unit, capable of dealing a sharp blow on a limited front almost anywhere in the world on short notice." If the Soviets reneged on their part of the Korean-Japanese agreement or took naval or air action against Japan (hardly within Soviet capability in 1950) the United States could respond swiftly and masterfully in the threatened theater.[26]

On balance, Kennan's idea of a Korean-Japanese exchange was not a bad one, but to his chagrin nobody in the administration examined it closely. Had such an arrangement been organized, the United States could have spared itself further sacrifices of men and materiel in Korea and could have ended earlier what was becoming an increasingly expensive and unnecessary occupation of Japan. Acheson, though, was convinced that the Soviets would never honor such an agreement, and, after the US had left northeast Asia, they would come storming back into Korea and be all the more emboldened against Japan.[27] The United States would then have to choose between accepting a humiliating Soviet *fait accompli* or militarily challenging the Russians in the Far East and risking the disasters of World War III. Not only was Kennan's suggestion unworkable on its own terms, in Acheson's view, but it opposed the secretary's desire (and that of most policy-makers in Washington) that Japan be fully committed to the United States and to its strategy of checking Soviet ambitions in the East.

In September 1951 the United States and Japan entered into a security pact, which dashed any possibility of the latter's becoming just another independent actor in the balance of power. The pact allowed the stationing of US armed forces in Japan; forbade the introduction of any third country's land, air, or naval units without Washington's consent; and anticipated the need for Japan to establish defense forces of its own able to deter thrusts by external "irresponsible militarism."[28]

This turn of events left Kennan dejected and with a sense of foreboding about America's Asia policy. It had forsaken a reasonable balance of power diplomacy toward Japan in favor of an indefinite military commitment to that country and in the process had lost a plausible opportunity for ending the Korean War: "I consider the Korean problem soluble only in the framework of a real agreement with the Russians on Japan, which would in turn imply a readiness on our part to neutralize the Japanese archipelago." Indeed, from Kennan's melancholy perspective in 1951, US policy seemed to be stumbling everywhere in the Far East and nowhere was this fact more evident than in US relations with China.[29]

Chinese Turmoil

In devising the Policy Planning Staff's attitude toward China, Kennan relied heavily upon the knowledge and expertise of John Paton Davies. He enjoyed the rare distinction of being one of the people in government for whom Kennan had unequivocal respect. Their friendship, dating to service together in Moscow 1945–1946, rested on an uncommon degree of intellectual and temperamental affinity. Both self-consciously tried to muster emotional detachment from their chosen fields of study while being passionate about analytic rigor and academic tools. Both viewed the current politics and social conditions of a given country within the larger context of its history and were wont to emphasize the psychological dimensions and presumed national characteristics of its inhabitants.[30] Equal to their preference for a scholarly approach to diplomacy, both were disgusted by anyone who smacked of the unprofessional. They especially resented amateur ambassadors, such as Joseph Davies and Roosevelt's envoy to Chiang Kai-shek, Patrick Hurley, who were political liabilities to the United States and personal catastrophes for their younger subordinates. Kennan and John Davies also viewed the recent world war with misgivings. They had shared anxiety about Yalta, opposed the punitiveness and extravagance of unconditional surrender as war aims against Germany and Japan, and advocated the concept of balance of power in Asia and Europe as the best means of safeguarding US security. As they understood it, Roosevelt's postwar planning amounted to the most utopian internationalism.[31]

To Kennan, the China-born Davies was an astute teacher of Far Eastern affairs, the one man most responsible for guiding him through the intricacies of modern Chinese history.[32] It was in discussions with Davies that Kennan first developed his convictions that historically the United States had been sentimental, vacillating, and unrealistic in both its official and popular treatment of China. How else to explain that since the nineteenth-century thousands of American Christian missionaries— including Davies's parents—had been trying to save China from its heathen ways and yet by the middle of World War II the US President was trumpeting China as one of the great powers that in future years would help police the world's peace? Where was the realism in such a bundle of contradictions? Perhaps Kennan's notion that the Chinese, for all of their cultural achievement, are peculiarly without the capacity for pity and lack a sense of sin derived from Davies, too; certainly the two men were not far apart in their casual prejudices about China.[33] In any case, Davies was the member of the Policy Planning Staff indispensable to Kennan in coming to terms with China and the civil war. In subsequent, sadder years it was entirely understandable that he helped defend Davies against the scurrilous charge—first raised by Hurley—that he had connived to deliver China to Mao Tse-tung and the communists: "[Davies] was a man of broad, sophisticated, and skeptical political understanding, without an ounce of pro-Communist sympathies, and second to none in his devotion to the interests of our government."[34]

Davies's perceptive assessment of the Chinese civil war held that the conflict between the Nationalist government and communist insurgents was rooted in the giant upheaval of social and political forces accompanying China's emergence from a feudal past into the modern world. As General Marshall's earlier attempt at mediation had shown, China's domestic division and violence were beyond the ability of the United States, or any other country, to tame. Short of an American military occupation of China, which would exact an exorbitant cost in men and materiel, there was little the US could do to influence the civil war's outcome. No matter how generous the supply of outside military equipment and financial and technical assistance, Chiang's ultimate victory or defeat depended on the skill of his leadership, the morale of his soldiers, and the social cohesion of cities and territories under his authority. As for the American people, said Davies, they should hope for the best and support their former wartime ally within the limited resources of US power and the extent to which Chiang's regime could efficiently use the aid proffered by Washington. Most important, the American government should labor under no illusions about Chiang's prospects, but prepare to deal with a wholly communist—or communist-dominated—China.

Davies was certain that the Soviets had shed whatever illusions they might once have entertained about China and were as impressed as he by the mixed record of CPSU-Chinese Communist Party (CCP) relations. Mao and his colleagues were avowed Marxists to be sure and naturally susceptible to Moscow's guidance. Since at least 1943, however, Davies was alert to the nationalist values and *esprit* animating most of the People's Liberation Army (PLA) and realized that a schism might erupt along the line between those advocating close relations with Moscow and those favoring a more independent foreign policy.[35] Davies was aware, too, of the resentment engendered among many CCP cadres by the past clumsiness and sometimes sheer stupidity of Comintern directives. The CCP, for example, had entered (1926) into a near fatal alliance with the Kuomintang as a result of Stalin's order that the Chinese comrades cooperate with Chiang's government against assorted warlords and imperialistic schemers. In 1927 the Kuomintang had turned furiously on its erstwhile communist partner and killed, captured, or scattered the CCP's leaders and adherents.[36] Davies believed further that since World War II the Chinese communists were largely self-sufficient from a military standpoint, did not request much Soviet aid, and were not inclined to follow any and all Soviet dictates.[37] Finally, Davies understood that Soviet encroachments (1945–1949) on peripheral parts of China adjacent to the Soviet frontier—Sinkiang, Inner Mongolia, and industrialized Manchuria—conflicted with the nationalistic sensibility of all Chinese, communists included.

Davies and other "China hands" such as Edmund Clubb and John Service expected that, in view of these facts, relations between the Soviet Union and mainland territory ruled by the CCP would not automatically be intimate and easy. If the United States acted correctly toward the Chinese communists and was careful to avoid becoming their enemy or treading hard on their overwrought nationalistic imaginations, then American diplomacy would be in a decent position to salvage something of Western prestige in Asia and to deflect whatever political advantage the Soviets might obtain during the first period of communist triumph in China.

Davies's analysis persuaded Kennan, and through him influenced Marshall and later (albeit somewhat less) Acheson. Kennan was clearly echoing Davies when in June 1947 he asserted that simultaneous with their victories the Chinese communists were likely to decrease their already modest dependence on Moscow and to distance themselves from Soviet policy in Asia. And Kennan suggested that the United States try to split the Chinese communist movement between the core of Moscow-indoctrinated cadres and the explicitly nationalist elements in the CCP. Regarding US aid for Chiang's regime, it should be confined to specific *ad hoc* projects that had a fair chance of adding to the social-economic vitality of Republican China.[38] But like it or not, Kennan warned, the United States had few options in China: "There is not much we can do, in present circumstances, but to sweat it out and to try to prevent the military situation from changing too drastically to the advantage of communist forces."[39] At the same time, he hoped the administration would not exaggerate Soviet influence in China or overrate the security threat to the United

States and its allies if all of China became aligned with the Soviet Union. As he later explained: "We need neither covet the favor, nor fear the enmity, of any Chinese regime. China is *not* the great power of the Orient."[40]

When in early 1948 Chiang's fortunes started to wane precipitously because of battlefield defeats and troop defections, Kennan resigned himself to the communist conquest of virtually all of China. He told Navy Secretary John Sullivan that unlike Europe, however, the situation in China was still too fluid to permit the United States to make clear-cut policy choices and bemoaned that most Chinese were like emotionally volatile children and disposed to believe communist propaganda. Kennan also regretted that, in contrast to Chiang's entourage of corrupt, incompetent nepotists, the CCP leadership contained some of the ablest, most determined individuals in China. In light of these stubborn facts, the United States should continue to hold back from directly intervening and, better yet, adopt a "grimly neutral" attitude toward the civil war, for soon enough the administration would have to treat with a unified Red China. At best the United States might derive satisfaction in knowing that the Soviets were unenthusiastic about CCP victory: "A united communist China would be much more dangerous to Russia than the present sort of China and might threaten Russian security and Russian control of the communist movement."[41] The Soviets would probably prefer a China fragmented into two or three separate political entities, all vulnerable to being played off against one another, and all subject to Moscow's influence.[42]

Kennan submitted his most comprehensive views about China to Secretary Marshall in September 1948. Although they reflected Kennan's continuing consultations with Davies, with various academic experts (for example, John King Fairbank), and with members of the Far Eastern Affairs Division, the underlying premises that China was hopeless and of secondary strategic importance were pure Kennan. He emphasized that China's "classically Malthusian" demographic problems, weak industrial base, scarce natural resources, primitive agricultural economy, administrative confusion, and a century of political instability would prevent China's becoming a military power any time soon:

> The effectiveness of Chinese armies is seriously restricted by poor training and leadership, deriving from the very nature of Chinese society. This places limitations on the role which Chinese armies could play in a US-USSR war, no matter on which side they were fighting. And at least until China develops a modern transportation network in its vast hinterland it will, excepting for its coastal fringe, more closely resemble a strategic morass than a strategic springboard.[43]

As for the ongoing Chinese civil war, the United States should bide its time and face up to the unpleasant fact that Chiang's practically uninterrupted defeats had much to do with his political deficiencies and poor generalship while the PLA enjoyed high morale, growing and widespread support, and dynamism. Why should the United States indulge Chiang in a program of "all-out aid"—as advised by some in Congress—that could easily be misidentified as overt intervention? Such a course would fly headlong against the onslaught of China's new nationalism and traditional xenophobia and rebound to CCP favor; already the communists had successfully portrayed themselves to most ordinary Chinese as being violently anti-imperialist. At a minimum, the Americans must be careful to conduct themselves in such a way as not to raise more doubts about the national government's independence from Washington. Besides, any deeper military and financial responsibility for Chiang's discredited regime would prove burdensome to the United States: "All-out aid to the National Government is . . . a [form] of action of huge, indefinite and hazardous proportions. The American Government cannot rightly gamble thus with American prestige and resources."[44] Instead, urged Kennan, the United States must brace itself for the defeat of Chiang and begin to anticipate the problems involved in establishing working relations with a communist China.

Kennan expected that following their victory ("liberation") the Chinese Marxists would confront problems aplenty, many of which would be novel and lacking obvious solutions. The CCP's administrative technique, such as it was, would be heavily taxed by the responsibilities of governing China's cities and endless countryside. Blindly obedient to their own ideology, the communists would probably rush to undertake the daunting task of socializing China's economy at a time when its factories and farms had still not recovered from war and when no large investment could be expected from abroad; the Soviets were too poor and parsimonious to furnish the amounts of capital necessary for renovating Chinese industry and agriculture. Coinciding with the appearance of these dilemmas, the contradiction between the CCP's nationalist commitments and its ideological links to Moscow would become more manifest, and the Soviets could be counted upon to aggravate the CCP's problem of retaining popular standing in China as champion against foreign trespassers. "It is a nice piece of irony," Kennan reflected, "that at precisely the time the Chinese Communist leadership is most likely to wish to conceal its ties with Moscow, the Kremlin is most likely to be exerting utmost pressure to bring the Chinese Communists under complete control. The possibilities which such a situation would present us, provided we have regained freedom of action, need scarcely to be spelled out."[45]

Turning to the question of Moscow's perspective, he guessed that Stalin perceived the bulk of China as a giant poverty pocket for which responsibility should be shunned. True, the Soviets might try to exercise leverage over Manchuria and Sinkiang, thereby closing the gaps in Siberia's defensive buffer zone and enjoying ready access to China's few existing industrial centers and mineral resources. If Soviet appetite for Chinese buffer, minerals, and factories were thwarted, Stalin still had no reason to complain: China's ingrained weaknesses rendered it a potentially cooperative ally at best, a relatively harmless enemy at worst for the USSR. Nonetheless, Kennan knew that Soviet leaders were calculating shrewdly that in the competition against the West, the allegiance of China's millions was worth having: "Capture of it would represent an impressive political victory and, more practically, acquisition of a broad human glacis from which to mount a political offensive against the rest of East Asia."[46]

Kennan predicted that through Stalin loyalists, such as Li Li-san, the Soviets would try to gain control of the CCP and work to eradicate any Tito-like heresy. Because the Soviets had not fully infiltrated the CCP apparatus with their own creatures, had no secret police force in place, and lacked command over the PLA, they had every reason to worry about Chinese communist truancy: "Moscow faces a considerable task in seeking to bring the Chinese communists under its control, if for no other reason than that Mao Tse-tung has been entrenched in power [in Yenan] for nearly ten times the length of time that Tito has."[47] Accordingly, a communist victory in China might be prelude for a new violent political struggle, pitting exuberant indigenous Marxists against the suspicious, control-minded Soviet leaders and their henchmen in the CCP.

It was of overriding importance that the United States do whatever possible to prevent China's becoming an adjunct of Soviet politico-military power. To accomplish this goal, said Kennan, the administration had to recognize that continued entanglement with the losing faction in China would hinder US diplomatic maneuverability in the post-civil war period. And, besides, US military strength could not be brought to bear effectively on Chiang's behalf and would be largely irrelevant in coping with the political and diplomatic problems posed by China's becoming Marxist. Kennan argued that "in the battle for the mind of China" the most efficacious application of US power would be through political, cultural, and economic means. In particular the administration's skillful handling of economic and trade issues in the post-Chiang period could draw the Chinese in a direction favorable to the United States.

In late February 1949, when it was evident that Mao would shortly organize a new Chinese regime, Kennan and Davies elaborated for Acheson—Marshall's successor as of January—their familiar views about events and prospects in China: Mao's crew would have enormous difficulty in trying to build a new centralized state apparatus from the ground up; the violent and unpredictable force of Chinese nationalism might cause the Soviets inestimable problems; already there were several points of friction between new China and the USSR. To regain initiative and a position of flexibility toward China, the United States should discontinue all economic and military aid to Chiang. Current programs were ineffectual, indirectly enhanced the PLA's strength, and worst of all perpetuated the "delusion" that China's safety and integrity could best be preserved by the CCP and its link to Moscow.

Kennan and Davies urged Acheson that assistance be granted to the noncommunist resistance *only* when it started to demonstrate uncharacteristic vigor. If and when an anti-communist grass-roots movement emerged over the next twenty-five years, it should be eligible for US aid. Until then, the United States ought to maintain contact with all political elements in China, retain and if possible intensify informational programs in Mao's new state, and cultivate conditions favorable for indigenous communists to resist Soviet entreaties and dictates. This last aim was the most crucial, as the United States had to drive a wedge into, or otherwise disrupt, any alliance between Russia and a communist China: "While scrupulously avoiding the appearance of intervention, we should be alert to exploit through political and economic means any rifts between the Chinese Communists and the USSR and between the Stalinist and other elements in China both within and outside of the communist structure."[48]

On Chiang, who removed himself and the remnants of his government and armed forces to Taiwan in 1949, Kennan wasted no sympathy. He felt bitterly that despite generous US assistance to the Nationalists—far greater in quantity and quality than anything obtained by the PLA from abroad—Chiang and his followers had lost the civil war through bungling, decadence, and cowardice. Chiang had thoroughly disgraced himself and deserved not an iota more of American solicitude. He was also a liability as his continued control of Taiwan and the Pescadores islands posed direct problems to US Pacific security. Kennan simply disbelieved that, with the momentum of PLA victories on the mainland, Chiang's Taiwan could withstand external communist assault or internal subversion for very long. An extension of Chinese communist power to Taiwan would then mean that America's long-term privileged position on Okinawa and the Philippines would be compromised. At some future date the Soviets and Chinese communists might use an improved, fortified version of Taiwan as a naval and air base from which to launch all manner of mischief.

Kennan preferred that such an eventuality be preempted by the United States, which should—the sooner the better—unilaterally assume authority over Taiwan and administer its politics, economics, and defense. Concommitant with this seizure, the 300,000 Republican troops on the island and most of the Chinese refugees would have to be returned, "by force if necessary," to the mainland.[49] According to this plan provision would be made to let Chiang remain on Taiwan and be accorded political refugee status, however.[50] Kennan also advised that US allies be coaxed into cooperating with the scheme to rescue Taiwan for the West: in such a potentially controversial operation the leading role of the United States should be as inconspicuous as possible. Eventually a plebiscite might be allowed whereby the island's native inhabitants—at the time seething under Chiang's dictatorial rule and the influx of Chinese fleeing Mao—could choose their type of political organization, that is, UN trusteeship, renewed association with Chiang, or sovereignty. In any case, every effort should be made to deny Soviet and Chinese communist access to Taiwan and later to guarantee US influence over the island through more indirect means.[51]

Kennan had no doubts about the legal, moral, political, or logistical obstacles to such an audacious, and one must judge grandiose and unattractive, venture but neither did he have qualms. The alternative, he contended, was for the Unites States to stand by idly and watch as communists first captured Taiwan and later deployed it as a forward base to intersect America's western line of island security. Still, he recognized that there was little danger of the US government's taking action; the executive branch, military leaders, and legislators would balk at adopting anything so imaginative or risky. In fact, Kennan's own PPS resisted his recommendations and he delivered them to Acheson in a private memorandum representing no one's views but his own. Nevertheless, he could not be dissuaded from his project, which he claimed if "adopted . . . and carried through with sufficient resolution, speed, ruthlessness, and self-assurance, the way Theodore Roosevelt might have done it, would be not only successful but would have an electrifying effect on this country and throughout the Far East. I have nothing to support this view but my own instinct."[52]

Very likely had Kennan's recommendations been acted upon, they would have led to bloodshed between US armed forces and those of Chiang, dismayed all onlookers as the United States destroyed what was left of a once honored ally, and caused a furor in America as the administration confronted the wrath of Chiang's congressional and other allies. Kennan's scheme for Taiwan was also contrary to the logic of wooing communist China away from Soviet influence: Mao claimed— as did the Nationalists—Taiwan as an integral part of Chinese territory and as such not available to American occupation, American dispensation, or anything else that partook of the traditional white, imperial order. Acheson's political and diplomatic instincts were better honed than Kennan's on the Taiwan issue, and he let the plan succumb to a quiet and deserved death.

Neither Marshall nor Acheson had any more esteem for Chiang than did Kennan or Davies and, like them, attributed his defeat in the civil war to Nationalist misrule and popular disaffection. On the basis of his own disappointing experiences in China and on what he personally had determined about Chiang's government and pathetic military capabilities, Marshall was predisposed to accept the Policy Planning Staff's views. Before the Staff was even assembled, Marshall had warned the Senate Foreign Relations Committee that the United States should not provide the Nationalists with more aid than they could properly handle. Why pour money down a rat hole? Marshall also taught, along the reasoning later advanced by Kennan and Davies, that the CCP, however Marxist and sympathetic to Moscow, was unlikely to fall strictly subservient to Stalin.[53] Marshall subsequently accepted without reservation Kennan's broad advice: the United States should separate itself from the losing Chiang, thereby recovering detachment and flexibility toward China, and Washington must develop a strategy for preventing or spoiling any Sino-Soviet combination.[54] Marshall's resignation for reasons of health spared him the disagreeable and complicated tasks of implementing these plans. Their execution went to Acheson, whose misfortune was to assume office when PLA victory was imminent and yet many people in Congress and elsewhere still thought Chiang's cause could be redeemed if enough timely US assistance was forthcoming.

Acheson did manage to recruit Truman to the Kennan-Davies line, though with some difficulty.[55] The secretary also campaigned in the government's security bureaucracy and in Congress for a policy to loosen ties with the Nationalists and prepare the groundwork for a realistic diplomacy toward China. With the support of Kennan and Davies—who helped write speeches, produced up-to-date and background information, and gave testimony of their own—Acheson's efforts had an effect. In early 1949, military aid programs for Chiang were reduced; "informational" programs in China warning against Soviet imperialism in Manchuria and Sinkiang were inaugurated; the lure of economic assistance and trade relations with the United States was dangled before the CCP in the expectation of discouraging new China from relying exclusively on Russia. In February 1950, Acheson had State's Far Eastern Affairs Division explore the possibility of America's breaking diplomatic relations with Chiang's government in Taipei.[56] Yet the dual policy of wooing communist China from the Soviet Union and disengaging from further sponsorship of Chiang was undercut by a series of international events and impediments in the United States.

Ranking military officers and civilians in the Pentagon, notably Defense Secretary Forrestal, were not persuaded by the wisdom of State Department policy. In March 1948, for instance, Forrestal and other Defense representatives on the NSC urged the administration to transfer substantial amounts of military supplies and technical aid to Chiang's beleaguered army. Forrestal also argued that, contrary to the PPS's analysis, the "loss" of China would constitute a severe reversal for Western strategic standing in the East.[57] And he chastised the State Department for having "no policy" toward China—a silly charge that aroused Kennan's ire.[58] In 1949 Admiral William Leahy and the rest of the Joint Chiefs of Staff, plus Mac-Arthur, hoped the US would help Chiang establish himself on Taiwan and through him the West could keep its influence on the island. They suggested that American soldiers be stationed on Taiwan and naval ships assigned to protect the island's sea lanes.[59]

The objections and suggestions generated by Defense officials did not, in the end, divert the State Department from its purposes: the president's confidence in Acheson was nearly absolute and enabled him to stand his ground within the government apparatus and in interagency meetings. The combined weight, however, of extra-governmental bodies—the China lobby, the China bloc in Congress, partisan politicians eager to embarrass the Truman administration—and the vagaries of public opinion did much to hinder a sound balance of power diplomacy toward China. Kennan himself was dumbfounded by the spectacle of a moderate policy assaulted by people in the employ of a foreign government, denounced by the leaders of the party out of power, and damaged by opinion polls and editorial commentaries that in their sum indicated that most Americans lacked even the faintest insight into China's epic revolution and knew practically nothing about the nature of US interests in Asia. He blamed the interference of the China lobby and its friends in government for forcing the administration to oppose the seating of People's China in the United Nations.[60] And he watched in vain as the State Department's *China White Paper*, whose compilation and issuance had originated with him and Davies, caused a veritable explosion in the nation's political life.

Kennan had hoped in 1949 that the monumental, documented history of Sino-American relations would go far toward justifying US policy toward China and quiet most of the administration's critics.[61] In essence the *White Paper* explained how the United States had endeavored to foster a stable, democratic China sympathetic to the West, but had run afoul on the realities of Chiang's defects and Mao's ruthlessness. But instead of helping to cool public passions, the *White Paper* aggravated misunderstanding and fanned domestic debate. Normally dispassionate, Walter Lippmann "marveled" at Chiang's "stranglehold on American foreign policy." The publisher, William Loeb, by contrast, charged the State Department with whitewashing its abject failure in China. Senator William Knowland pronounced that the *Paper* illustrated the democratic virtues of Chiang and revealed how misguided the Truman government was to neglect sterner measures against the worldwide communist conspiracy.[62]

Kennan must have concluded that, once again, the public was showing its unwillingness to learn about or grapple with international issues. But, in fact, he was not always fair on this score, and his difficulty in taking seriously the concerns expressed by various elected officials—who included perfectly respectable people such as Senator Robert Taft, Governor Thomas Dewey—and public commentators resided in the fact that his theoretical outlook on politics and international relations diverged fundamentally from that of most of his compatriots. Their usual preference was to support abroad the political values and institutions regularly affirmed at home: political freedom, fairness, economic opportunity. As case in point, through-out 1948 various congressional leaders believed that as prerequisite to additional aid for his regime, Chiang should adopt domestic reforms aimed at eradicating corruption, justly distributing land, and promoting democracy, thereby expanding the base of his popular support against the communists. Kennan dismissed such congressional deliberations and sporadic attempts to force reforms upon the Nationalist government as being superfluous. Instead, the United States must base its foreign policy according to the unyielding truths of power and power politics. In what must be the most vigorous statement favoring a *realpolitik* ever delivered by an American policymaker, Kennan declared:

> We should stop putting ourselves in the position of being our brother's keeper and refrain from offering moral and ideological advice. We should cease to talk about vague and—for the Far East—unreal objectives such as human rights, the raising of the living standards, and democratization. The day is not far off when we are going to have to deal in straight power concepts. The less we are then hampered by idealistic slogans the better.[63]

However sound such an interpretation was and however convinced Marshall and Acheson were by it, it could not soothe Congress or the nation at large for the passing of China into the communist camp. Over the reservations of both secretaries and Kennan, Congress passed appropriations in 1948 and 1949 to buttress the economic and military position of Chiang. American financial aid for his regime 1945–1949 was valued at almost $2 billion and military help at over $1 billion. Obviously, under such circumstances the administration could not gracefully disengage the United States from Chiang. Finally, the advent of Korean fighting marked the denouement of the Kennan-Davies line toward the Nationalists. Almost literally overnight, Truman and Acheson's appreciation for Taiwan's strategic value and the island's political status quo quickened: Chiang must be protected for the duration of Korean hostilities as his island was crucial to the success of US naval and air operations.[64]

Although it is appropriate to underscore the domestic political reasons for the defeat of Policy Planning's strategy, it would be a mistake to minimize the responsibility that Mao and his colleagues also bore for the failure of China and the United States to reach a *modus vivendi* in 1949–1950. Despite the covert contacts and cautious signals inspired by leaders such as Chou En-lai who sought an accommodation with the West, the Chinese communists persistently pursued policies that blunted the Kennan-Davies approach in Washington. Mao's statement on July 1, 1949, that China would "lean to the side of the Soviet Union," the mistreatment and incarceration of American diplomats by CCP authorities, the destruction and seizure of American property—notably the invasion of the US diplomatic compound in Peking—and vitriolic propaganda against the West, all served to weaken the argument of anyone who held that Mao was a potential Asian Tito and a clever policy could induce China into playing the role of a Far Eastern Yugoslavia. Then, in late October 1950, contingents of the PLA ("volunteers") engaged US forces in

North Korea. China's intervention in the Korean War not only was the most palpable expression of Peking's distrust and fear of the United States, but it consummated America's failure to draw China away from the USSR. Even though a number of policymakers, including John Foster Dulles, were aware in subsequent years of the tensions between Russia and China, more than twenty years elapsed before the United States again sought an arrangement with China intended to encourage its sustaining an independent position in the Far Eastern balance of power.

The Korean War

Kennan's scheduled leave of absence from the State Department, to begin late June 1950, was delayed because of the North Korean invasion of the South. Kennan stayed on at Acheson's request to advise him and other administration officials about Soviet capabilities and motives as they related to Korea. At first pleased to be of continuing service, Kennan soon discovered that he was not to enjoy a policymaking role in the Korean crisis and felt his usual frustration with Acheson at being neglected, overridden, or otherwise unsuccessful.[65] Undoubtedly Acheson, for his part, realized that he needed all the friendly help he could get and was glad to keep Kennan around a bit longer.

Kennan was as startled as most people in Washington by the breakout of full-scale fighting in Korea, June 25, 1950. He and a number of PPS colleagues a few weeks earlier had seen evidence suggesting that one or another of the Soviet satellite states was preparing to take military action against an exposed Western salient. Based on what they learned from Pentagon intelligence, though, they dropped Korea from their list of suspected trouble spots.[66] They had been told that the local communist armed forces were no match for the better trained, US-equipped South Koreans and were persuaded by the assessment of General W. E. Todd (director of the JCS Joint Intelligence Group) from the previous year: "If the Soviets attach any priority to areas in which they would like to move by means of armed aggression, Korea would be at the bottom of that list of priorities."[67]

Since the 1970s some Western scholarship has raised questions about whether or not Stalin ordered the North Korean attack. Robert Simmons, for one, has hypothesized that the communist Korean invasion was prematurely and probably accidentally launched by an overly anxious Kim Il-song, catching both Moscow and Peking unprepared.[68] In any event, Kennan accepted the standard interpretation in Washington that the Soviets were testing the outer limits of Western resolve through the use of proxy military forces. Moreover, despite his regret for the many defects afflicting the South Korean polity and his earlier endorsement (1947) of US withdrawal from Korea because it lacked strategic value, Kennan agreed with Acheson that for the sake of American prestige in the East and to validate Washington's claim as guarantor of Japan the United States had to counter the North Koreans and restore the *status quo ante*.[69] Yet Kennan did not go along with every aspect of US government policy.

First, he opposed Truman's use of the United Nations, its resolutions, and its prestige as a means of justifying US actions in Korea. As the occupying power in

Japan and responsible for the preservation of order in South Korea in the absence of a Japanese peace treaty—not signed until September 1951—the United States had every right to intervene. Why confuse the issue of America's legitimate sphere of responsibility with the machinery and encumbrances of the United Nations? Neither the well-being of that organization nor the interests of the United States could be advanced by overly close US-UN coordination in Korea.[70] In addition, Kennan— unlike Acheson, Nitze, and many in the Defense Department—never viewed events in Korea as preliminary to generalized Soviet military incursions either in Europe or the Far East. Contrary to the majority view, he also maintained that the underlying assumptions in NSC 68 were not confirmed by Korea and that the Soviets were merely taking advantage of a specific target of opportunity; they still lacked the basic desire and materiel wherewithal to expand the scope of Korean hostilities into anything approximating a third world war.[71]

On the day following the North Korean crossing of the thirty-eighth parallel, Kennan expressed skepticism that communists anywhere in the world would take *military* initiatives in the near future, not even if the communist armies won in Korea. He did assert that the nature of future non-Soviet communist moves would be influenced by how quickly and effectively the United States responded in Korea, however. The political and psychological repercussions of an ignominious rout in South Korea would reverberate around the world: "There will scarcely be any theater of the East-West conflict which will not be adversely affected thereby, from our standpoint. Such a turn of events might . . . produce a number of new reverses to the noncommunist forces in the world which would not be the results of any orders received from Moscow but would stem from the encouragement which the communist elements had received and from the corresponding discouragement of their opponents."[72]

Kennan thought, as did Davies, that Taiwan was the territory most likely to be affected by a Korean debacle. Given that Korean fighting had focused Western attention in northeast Asia, there was a good possibility that the Chinese and Soviets, in cooperation with communists on Taiwan, would take political action to forestall the consolidation of Western power on the island. He predicted that the Nationalist regime would crumble under such an assault, or even the threat of one, and Taiwan would drop into communist captivity "without military action launched from the mainland." If, however, the United States and South Koreans managed to repulse the northern invaders, then the conquest of Taiwan by political or military means would be a more formidable task for the communists, and they would have to postpone the entire project.

Kennan feared, too, that Iran and Berlin would be more vulnerable to Soviet pressure—possibly they would be absorbed into the Russian empire outright—if the United States were dislodged from South Korea. With sufficient Soviet moral and political backing, the Tudeh Party in Iran could mount a viable offensive in Tehran as uncertainty spread about American guarantees and determination to oppose Russia. In Berlin, where the East German authorities already occupied a splendid position from which to make life hard in the Western zone, the local communists could deny electricity or renew the blockade as a means of eroding the morale and robustness of Western soldiers and civilians. Soviet prestige and troops need not be involved in either Berlin or Iran, and Moscow's influence could expand almost silently.[73] Eventually, the Soviets might exert pressure on Turkey and Yugoslavia to intimidate those states and cause a political softening.

Except for these specific areas, Kennan could not imagine the Soviets taking any steps against positions important to the West. Rather, the Soviets wanted to acquire strategic control over the Korean peninsula and confront the United States with some tough choices. By becoming involved in a costly war against a Soviet client, the US and allied countries could be weakened, and popular feeling in Asia was bound to run high against white soldiers intruding in what was yet another civil war in the East. Under these circumstances the Americans might be well advised to withdraw from Korea and letting the nation's rival factions determine their country's fate. Any hasty US departure, however, with the attendant inevitable capitulation of the regime in Seoul would amount to a "tremendous prestige defeat" and loss of respect everywhere for American arms and steadiness: "In either case, [US departure or continued involvement] the Kremlin hoped that the ultimate outcome would be our complete and disgraceful retirement from the Asiatic scene."[74] To this end the Soviets would probably stir up Asian communist parties and armed partisans to do what they could to embarrass the United States.

In August, after the Pusan perimeter had been secured but before the US landing and victory at Inchon, Kennan submitted a particularly thoughtful analysis of Soviet intentions to Acheson. He reemphasized his earlier point that the Soviets had not instigated the Korean adventure as first step toward East-West Armageddon or even as one of a series of smaller provocations designed to drain US strength in various secondary theaters. He also surmised that the Soviets had been surprised by the spiritedness of US intervention, and, although they had not originally wanted a broad confrontation, the Soviet leadership might have concluded that war in Korea would soon embrace areas farther afield. Meanwhile, the Soviets must be alarmed that a large portion of North Korean military strength, transportation, and communication was being destroyed in the maw of US land, aerial, and naval firepower: "The Kremlin leaders are . . . well aware that the military fortunes might easily soon be altered to their disfavor."[75] He guessed that once the tide of battle in Korea had clearly shifted to US advantage, a new and more dangerous phase of the campaign would begin. The Soviet Red Army might occupy North Korea; Chinese soldiers might enter the fray.[76]

After the defeat of North Korean armies in the south, the question immediately arose in Washington of whether or not to pursue the enemy forces north beyond the thirty-eighth parallel and then unite the Korean halves under a Western-leaning government; all of this would be dignified by the formal blessings of the United Nations and the continued service of token UN forces under MacArthur's command. To Kennan such an operation conducted far from American centers of strength and supply and perilously near the Soviet and Chinese borders was rash in the extreme—it should not be launched. A full six weeks before MacArthur's multinational army crossed the parallel (October 1950), Kennan warned that from a Soviet perspective the introduction of American soldiers along the North Korean-Soviet border would be a notch away from a *casus belli*: the naval and population center of Vladivostok and its environs would be subject to constant Western surveillance and exist in permanent jeopardy. Perhaps the Soviets would respond by sending troops to North Korea and directing North Korean air strikes against US installations in Japan.[77]

Not only was Kennan concerned that the United States not annoy Stalin's government in an area about which it was pathologically sensitive, but he saw no good reason to reunify Korea under an anti-Soviet regime. As he explained to Acheson, the United States had been perfectly correct to deflect the North Korean invasion, but from the standpoint of geopolitics, a brazenly anti-Soviet Korea did not make sense.[78] Surely the US could tolerate a future setup that allowed for a Korea nominally independent but in reality amenable to Soviet manipulation. He readily admitted that such an arrangement would require a secure, internally confident Japan able to withstand falling into a Soviet orbit. As for the United States, Kennan doubted its capacity over the long run to keep Korea permanently free of Russian political domination—historically that duty had been Japan's. Invoking Theodore Roosevelt again as authority, Kennan claimed that Korea could not exist independently in face of Russian and/or Japanese pressures. Though obviously a Korea aligned with Japan was better than one associated with the USSR, in 1950 and for the foreseeable future, Japan was too debilitated to compete for Korea: "We must hope that with the revival of her normal strength and prestige, Japan will regain her influence there."[79]

Kennan believed that during the long interval between Japanese weakness and recovery, the United States would have to relinquish its responsibilities in Korea; the peninsula was not of major importance, and finite American resources had to be allotted elsewhere. The Soviets then should be allowed to exercise primary influence in Korea provided that they exerted it gradually and without resort to massive violence. Although not perfect, such a solution had its merit:

> A period of Russian domination [of Korea] while undesirable, is preferable to continued U.S. involvement in that unhappy area, as long as the means chosen to assert Soviet influence are not, as was the case with those resorted to in June [1950], ones calculated to throw panic and terror into other Asian peoples and thus to achieve for the Kremlin important successes going far beyond the Korean area. But it is important that the nominal independence of Korea be preserved, for it provides a flexible vehicle through which Japanese influence may someday gradually replace Soviet influence without creating undue international repercussions.[80]

One can only imagine the incredulity with which Acheson received Kennan's advice. The United States, after all, had fought a lengthy war against Japan to curb its self-aggrandizement on the mainland and was now in the midst of combat to prevent Soviet expansion in Asia, but here was a proposal anticipating US evacuation from northeast Asia and advocating a policy of aloofness as the Soviets carved out more territory for themselves. To Acheson, Kennan's idea was flatly unrealistic and irrelevant to the crisis at hand; a detached balance of power approach could not win in an America racked by the emotionalism of Joseph McCarthy and, even in its better moments, prone to filter international politics through the distorting lenses of moralistic sloganeering. Years later Acheson wrote that Kennan's notions about Japan and Korea were "typical of [their] gifted author, beautifully expressed, sometimes contradictory, in which were mingled flashes of prophetic insight and suggestions . . . of total impracticality."[81]

When the decision was made in Washington (and in the UN) to send MacArthur's forces north of the thirty-eighth parallel—with all due caution—Kennan was virtually alone with Bohlen in opposition. Kennan protested that such a course of action would pose explosive questions for the Soviets and Chinese and might entangle the United States in a war against one or both of these states in a theater immensely undesirable from the standpoint of US logistics and ultimate security interests.[82]

Prior to China's intervention, Kennan ascribed a secondary role to Mao's regime in the promulgation of communist policy in Korea and doubted that China possessed any concrete aims in the conflict. He also figured that the CCP and most Chinese citizens would shortly view their identification with a Soviet-backed aggressive war as a blunder and that US diplomacy might later take advantage of this general feeling to help loosen the ties between the CCP and its subjects and between the People's Republic of China and Russia. Still, Kennan realized that for the time being China was committed against the United States and shared with the USSR a longing to witness the eradication of American power in Asia and the Pacific.[83] And he agreed as of late June 1950 with most military strategists that the United States would have to enlist severe measures if Chinese troops joined the North Koreans and marched south of the thirty-eighth parallel. Similar to MacArthur's later suggestions to Truman, Kennan remarked: "If [the Chinese] became engaged in the theater we would have adequate grounds for air and sea attacks on targets in Communist China directly related to the enemy effort in Korea." Kennan did hedge, however, by adding that unpredictable future circumstances might argue against spreading the war to China.[84] By August, he was persuaded that Mao had no wish to send any units of the PLA to fight in Korea and that Soviet pressures on China to do so would prove futile.[85]

When Chinese "volunteers" entered Korea in force (late autumn 1950) and began to inflict defeats and high casualties on US and UN forces, Kennan's initial impulse was to inquire about getting a commission in one of the armed services.[86] He did not want to be accused, as were many Foreign Service officers during World War II, of shirking military obligation in a national emergency. In any case, just as most of official Washington, he was gripped by the crisis, a situation of such desperate proportions that Truman intimated on November 30 that the United States might use atomic weapons against the Chinese in Korea. Once it became evident that China's armies were forcing MacArthur's troops to retreat hastily south, Kennan counseled the administration to prepare itself and the American people for a military catastrophe:

> If we accept it with candor, with dignity, with a resolve to absorb its lessons and to make it good by redoubled and determined effort—starting all over again, if necessary, along the pattern of Pearl Harbor—we need lose neither our self-confidence nor our allies nor our power for bargaining, eventually, with the Russians. But if we try to conceal from our own people or from our allies the full measure of our misfortune, or permit ourselves to seek relief in any reactions or bluster or petulance or hysteria, we can easily find this crisis resolving itself into an

irreparable deterioration of our world position—and of our confidence in ourselves.[87]

In subsequent meetings with Acheson, Nitze, and Harriman, Kennan argued just as eloquently as the above that UN forces must not retire from Korea in disarray. And he maintained that action against Chinese forces in Korea and general harassment of the People's Republic—trade embargo, freezing Chinese assets in the US—would not cause the Soviets to take military recourse against the West; mercifully the Sino-Soviet alliance, ratified only in February 1950, was soft.[88]

On the home front, Kennan was nervous that the public might crack under the strain and reverses of the Korean war. He was extremely upset by widespread sentiment on Capitol Hill in December that condemned the Korean venture as a mistake and insisted that US forces be rapidly withdrawn. By contrast, Marshall, by then secretary of defense, was less concerned and averred that fluctuation in congressional opinion was nothing new and that the mood of defeat—like the euphoria after Inchon—was unlikely to last long.[89] Later on, Kennan became irate with those in Congress who urged the administration to wage an "all out war in Korea." How, he wondered, could anyone be so oblivious to the danger of a Korean conflict spreading to include the Soviet Union? And he helped prepare public statements for Acheson to use in damping down any enthusiasm for another world war.[90] In this task, Kennan and Acheson were largely successful, but the hysteria whipped up by McCarthy and those of his ilk was reaching a crescendo in 1950–1951 and contributed to the political atmosphere in which a MacArthur could question the wisdom of his civilian superiors. As Kennan later wrote, it took great courage on Truman's part to sack (April 10, 1951) the popular general and thereby restore a single direction and voice to US policy in Asia.[91] Once this was accomplished, prospects that the United States could successfully enter into diplomatic negotiations and achieve a Korean peace settlement markedly improved.

As early as March 1951, Kennan (on leave from the Foreign Service, in Princeton) circulated a number of ideas to Acheson and Nitze on how the US might proceed toward a Korean cease-fire agreement. First, the relative stabilization of the UN line in Korea meant that the United States—now in a position of comparative strength—and its partners should find means of directly negotiating an armistice with Moscow. The Soviet Union, of course, was the great land power in northeast Asia, and it made no sense to deal only with its Chinese junior colleagues and Korean puppets: "By leaving [the Soviets] out . . . one would leave them without obligation and free to do whatever they pleased, which is in many ways just what they wish. To build an arrangement which does not include them would be building on sand."[92] He recommended that through informal and private channels the US government might reach Soviet officialdom. No publicity should be directed to such an enterprise because the Russians would instantly view it as part of a larger US propaganda stunt signifying that the Americans were not really serious about Korean negotiations. In any preliminary talks with the Soviets, the government should use as its chief instrument a discreet person who would explain that the United States had intervened in Korea for legitimate reasons of self-interest: to protect US positions in Japan and the Philippines. In the US view, naturally Korea was not worth starting another world war. Could an armistice agreeable to all parties not be established? Kennan also urged that the American intermediary play on Soviet anxieties about China and stress how gratifying it was to talk with self-possessed Soviet representatives rather than those immature, overzealous Chinese.[93]

By May, the administration was ready to act. At Davies's suggestion Acheson chose Kennan to approach the Soviet ambassador to the UN, Jacob Malik, about Korean talks. Malik reportedly regarded Kennan, whom he had never previously met, as a person whose malevolent influence in Washington had helped kill US confidence in the Soviet Union. Still, Malik acknowledged Kennan as America's leading expert on Russia and as a person whose voice carried weight with Truman and Acheson.[94] In accordance with instructions from the Kremlin, Malik met twice with Kennan in late May and early June. The talks were cordial and covered numerous problems: the Far East as a whole, China, and Korea. Who would the Soviets like to see participate in cease-fire discussions, asked Kennan. At what level of diplomatic status should the armistice talks go forward? If a control commission were established to oversee a cease-fire, which countries should furnish personnel to supervise compliance? In turn, Malik replied that the Soviets very much wanted peace in Korea and, of course, the feelings of the North Koreans and Chinese must be taken into account. The Americans should get in touch with them, too.[95]

Kennan told Acheson that Malik underscored Soviet desires for a cessation of hostilities in Korea at the earliest possible moment. Kennan guessed that a prolongation of the war ran contrary to Soviet interests, and he had the distinct impression that the Soviets were pressing the Chinese and North Koreans to show themselves willing to cooperate in finding a peaceful political settlement. In view of these considerations and the dangerousness of the situation in the Far East—"I have a feeling we are moving much closer to the edge of the precipice than most of us are aware"—Kennan beseeched Acheson to seize upon the first signal from the Soviets indicating *their* willingness to begin formal talks about Korea.[96]

On June 23 the Soviet government declared—through Malik—that it was receptive, indeed eager, to begin negotiations: "As a first step discussions should be started between the belligerents for a cease-fire and an armistice providing for the mutual withdrawal of forces from the thirty-eighth parallel."[97] Beginning in July the first fruits of Kennan's demarche sprang forth: armistice talks began and, though they were protracted and plagued by asperity, did lead finally to a truce which has survived in Korea since 1953 despite periodic violations and continuous strain.

Years after his role in helping to usher in Korean negotiations, Kennan professed to see in it an important lesson for American diplomacy: The Wilsonian ideal of open agreements, open negotiations—open diplomacy in short—is often inferior to old-fashioned diplomacy conducted between representatives of rival countries. Private confidential talks between adversaries can produce solutions of enduring worth. A valuable weapon in the diplomatic arsenal of any country, therefore, and something that no democracy should self-righteously eschew is that "of wholly secret, informal and exploratory contacts . . . as adjuncts to the overt and formal processes of international diplomacy." In this, as in other aspects to be explored in the next chapter, Kennan has regretted the neglect by many US statesmen of traditional diplomatic methods and technique.[98]

*   *   *   *

To Kennan, US problems in the Far East were mostly of America's own making and stemmed from Franklin Roosevelt's wish during the war to destroy every vestige of Japanese power; the president had failed to imagine the sort of international difficulties likely to emerge when a pillar of the Eastern balance of power system was eliminated. Kennan was convinced that the Soviets had been tempted in the case of Korea because the Japanese were no longer able to check them. In any event, the important task for the United States in the Cold War was to restore Japan to a position of prestige and of political (and partial military) strength. For these reasons, Kennan, and most others in the Truman administration, were willing to ride roughshod over the concerns of the Chinese Nationalists, British, Filipinos, French, and so on, all of whom expected that reparations, disarmament, and humiliation would prevent the resurgence of an aggressive, revengeful Japan. Kennan was not greatly bothered by the fears expressed by the victims of Japanese imperialism that unilateral American leniency in the occupation was paving the way for unrepentant expansionists in Tokyo to husband their power and push again for Japanese hegemony in the East. Instead, Kennan clung to the idea in 1947–1950 that Japan be allowed another chance to play a responsible role in Far Eastern politics; in more recent years he has called Japan *the* cornerstone of US policy in the East upon which the success or failure of the United States in all of Asia may well depend.[99] Overall, his record on Japan was sound. Only his extremely conservative preferences for established forms and his skepticism about democracy misled him; fortunately his opposition to Japan's democratization (for which MacArthur of all people deserves some credit) represented a minority view in Washington and did not prevent Japan's establishing one of the more successful democracies in the postwar world.

As for the People's Republic of China, Kennan was among the most discerning in Washington when he argued that relations between the CCP and the Soviet Union were ambiguous in the late 1940s and early 1950s. Besides, how could the Soviets in the aftermath of World War II really be of much material help to China in its rebuilding drives? Might the Chinese comrades, like the ungrateful Yugoslavs, one day turn on their old retainer? "I would be willing to bet," he said in 1953, "that in strange ways the Chinese are putting the Russians before some of the most excruciating alternatives they have ever faced."[100] Unfortunately, Kennan's preference for a subtle policy to weaken ties between Moscow and Mao was difficult to implement. Prevailing opinion in the United States did not easily allow for a policy that discriminated among communist states. Any gesture toward China intended to reduce its reliance on Russia was likely to be condemned as appeasement of Chinese tyranny, itself just an Asian variant of monolithic international communism directed from Moscow.

Acheson for one was astonished by Kennan's inability to appreciate the nature of internal constraints operating on US foreign policy. His proposal for swapping a neutralized Japan for a communist retreat from Korea constituted proof to the secretary that Kennan lacked good political instinct.[101] Indeed, Kennan was by temperament and principle unable to compromise with the necessity of tailoring foreign policy in a fashion to avoid domestic political turmoil and garner popular support. Still, Kennan did realize that the entire complex of US problems in the Far East required governmental freedom to take actions and to maneuver with finesse. That the government was inhibited by the continuous criticism, hostile scrutiny, and accusations of betrayal leveled by the right wing of the Republican party indicated to him that the time had arrived for a final reckoning, especially in regard to China: "The tie to the Chiang regime I hold to be . . . discreditable, and I feel it should be severed at once, at the cost, if need be, of a real domestic showdown."[102] That, of domestic political necessity, Acheson pursued a more cautious policy toward the problems of China and Taiwan explains in part Kennan's terse observation that his and the secretary's "minds had never really worked the same way."[103]

Despite their mutual respect and because of their growing impatience with each other, it undoubtedly was a source of mutual relief to Kennan and Acheson when the former departed for his long-awaited leave to the Institute for Advanced Study in Princeton. Robert Oppenheimer, director of the Institute and responsible for Kennan's coming to it, assured him that he was welcome to stay for however long he needed to complete his program of reading and research. Although Kennan liked Oppenheimer and was grateful for the opportunity to conduct academic study, he was anxious from the outset about his post-sabbatical life. An invitation then came to him during the autumn of 1950 asking whether he would like to join the Ford Foundation as a senior staff associate. Would a professorial position at Columbia University appeal to him, asked the school's president, General Dwight Eisenhower. If it could be arranged, would he like to stay on at the Institute for Advanced Study for several years? Harvard, Yale, and University of Chicago also indicated interest in Kennan's plans. Yet he decided, in spite of his frustrations with government work and notwithstanding the attractiveness of a new career in academic or foundation life, that he wanted definitely to return to the Foreign Service. In the meantime he was set to enjoy a period of intellectual exercise and respite from the buffeting received by his nerves and ego in Washington. As Bohlen had told Robert Lovett somewhat earlier, he had had "for some time a feeling that a breathing spell for a year or so would not be at all a bad thing in [Kennan's] case."[104]

In November 1950 Kennan informed Acheson—who must have been delighted to learn it—that he had no desire to return to making foreign policy, but would prefer a diplomatic posting overseas: "It is my feeling that I have been long enough around Washington for a single spell and that for a whole series of reasons . . . I ought to go abroad [after Princeton], rather than return to any policy-advisory function in Washington."[105] Subsequently, he was pleased to accept, though not without sensible trepidation, the government's next assignment: to serve as US ambassador in Moscow.

9

Two Ambassadorships

Kennan's leave of absence from the Foreign Service beginning in autumn 1950 lasted through the spring of 1952, when he succeeded Alan Kirk as ambassador to the Soviet Union. During the interim Kennan conducted research on what he termed the utopian tendencies in US foreign policy, wrote articles about current political issues, and delivered lectures to civic and university groups on a variety of historical and international topics. It was a productive period for Kennan and foreshadowed the prolific and distinguished scholarly career that awaited him. He was regularly in touch with such intellectual luminaries as Robert Hutchins, Walter Lippmann, Hans Morgenthau, Arnold Toynbee, and, of course, Oppenheimer, all of whom encouraged him in his academic endeavors and praised his literary accomplishments. During this period he published his first book, *American Diplomacy, 1900–1950*. Based on a series of lectures he delivered at the University of Chicago, it was widely admired from the outset as a succinct statement of the realist position and became a primer for college students interested in foreign affairs.

Kennan's brief tenure as envoy to Moscow ended abruptly and embarrassingly in October 1952, when the Soviet government pronounced him *persona non grata*. After it became clear in subsequent months that the new Republican administration of Dwight Eisenhower and John Foster Dulles had no permanent need for his services, Kennan returned to Princeton and the Institute for Advanced Study and resumed in earnest his second career as professional historian of Russia, European diplomacy, and Soviet-US relations. He rapidly gained distinction in these fields, authored numerous books, won academic awards and honors—including the Pulitzer Prize—and eventually became president of the American Academy of Arts and Letters. This phase of his life was interrupted only once, 1961–1963, when he served as President John Kennedy's ambassador to Yugoslavia.

Although Kennan's second ambassadorship proved to be personally more rewarding than his earlier stint in Moscow, it, too, was ultimately disappointing and must be counted a failure as complete as the first. His mission to Belgrade illus-

189

trated vividly the hazards of democratic diplomacy which he, one of the most lucid proponents of the classical form, could not redeem. On the other hand, Kennan's conduct in the Soviet instance plainly revealed that even the most knowledgeable and well-trained diplomat is not automatically immune to *faux pas* and blunder; for a momentary lapse in forbearance he paid the price of being an object of astonishment in the State Department and of official reproach and ridicule in the USSR.

Stalin's Soviet Union, 1952

A review of Kennan's tour in Moscow in 1952 is important not only because it raises significant questions about the proper handling of diplomacy in a difficult foreign environment, but also because his reporting from the Soviet capital about social, political, and economic conditions constitutes one of the few revealing, firsthand accounts by an informed Westerner of Russia during the waning days of Stalin. In the continuing absence of many or very good scholarly monographs about Stalin's Russia in the early 1950s, Kennan's impressions from that period are all the more valuable.[1] His accounts about the Soviet Union in 1952 are also noteworthy for the student of comparative politics as they cast doubt on some of the assumptions and intellectual constructions valued in the 1950s by observers of the totalitarian state. In contrast, say, to the totalitarian syndrome of Carl Friedrich and Zbigniew Brzezinski—with its emphases on an official chiliastic doctrine that gives purpose to citizens, and rule by a dedicated, small political party led by a charismatic leader—or William Kornhauser's proposition that the totalitarian regime exercises continuous control over every feature of human activity, Kennan found in Soviet Russia a withered ideology, an uncertain and stagnating communist party, and a population increasingly indifferent to and distant from the government.[2]

If any set of imperatives may be said to have dominated Soviet life in the years immediately following World War II, they were to repair the war damage and to surpass the economic might of the United States. The first task was feasible, though costly and not finally achieved until after Stalin's reign; the second was ludicrous when viewed against America's unscathed, super-productive economy and the Soviet Union's accumulated losses. Reconstruction had to be shouldered by a population that had been devastated by millions of war dead, and by millions more who had been maimed, left shelterless and impoverished, and had not been properly nourished for years. Disproportionately high numbers (compared to pre-1941) of old men, women, and adolescents were drafted into the agricultural and industrial rebuilding drives; sufficient numbers of able-bodied men in their prime were simply unavailable. One shattering demographic impact of the war was that by 1946 there were only 31 million men of arms-bearing age versus 52 million women in the same cohort.[3] The better part of a generation of males, the backbone of the labor force, potential husbands and fathers, had perished. And one can only imagine how this imbalance in the population affected the psychological and social well-being of the nation.[4]

The pervasiveness of poverty in postwar Russia and the plight of ordinary citizens were underscored by the great Ukrainian drought and famine of 1946–

1947, which before it ended forced some starving people into cannibalism.[5] While the majority of the population in Belorussia and the Ukraine lived in crudely thatched pits in the ground during the immediate postwar years, the denizens of Moscow, Leningrad, and Kiev packed themselves into small unhygienic hovels and apartments; typically three, four, or five families inhabited a double-room residence. Yet it was this same Soviet population, through means of effort no less herculean than their humbling of the *Wehrmacht,* that rebuilt Russia's cities, salvaged its farms, recovered its coal and steel processing, and reestablished its industrial production by the middle 1950s. To these ends, Stalin cajoled, terrorized, inspired, and exhorted his subjects.

Kennan was appropriately impressed by the Soviet Union's powers of rejuvenation and commented favorably in 1952 about the spectacle of a great nation repairing its wounds. During his stay in Moscow, construction of nine new skyscrapers was advanced, and the city everywhere seemed alive with the activity of other ambitious projects: "Merely to see the edifice of the new university building on the drive from the Moscow airport is tremendous."[6] Trees were planted along the city's major streets; various forms of public transportation were intact and running smoothly; private garden plots flourished; and the number of privately owned automobiles was increasing. Although the off-streets were dominated by dilapidated log cabins and outdoor plumbing and the number of recreational facilities had not increased since the 1930s, Kennan noticed a tangible improvement in the average Muscovite's food, clothing, and overall appearance since the war.[7] Industrial progress was also much in evidence. And in Leningrad repairs, albeit occurring more slowly, were making a visible difference, too.

In the outlying rural districts conditions were not so promising, however. Kennan was struck both by the lack of material progress in the seven years since the war ended and by the sharp contrast between the state-run farms and private agriculture. Along with many Western commentators, he had always doubted the wisdom of Soviet experiments in socialized land reclamation, crop management, and animal husbandry; presumably the peasant's interest in his own private cow and litter of pigs would outstrip his concern and care for the entire collective's corresponding herds. Kennan's skepticism was deepened further by what he learned as ambassador. An avid gardener and amateur farmer, he condemned the Bolsheviks in 1952 for having disregarded fundamental laws of nature: "The collective farm system was drawn-up in ignorance of the basic delicacy of the essential relationship between man and earth, man and plant, man and animal in the agricultural process . . . the early communists who conceived and imposed it were city people."[8] While the private lots prospered and consumed most of the physical energy and enthusiasm of the farmers, the collective enterprises languished. In distant provinces, for example Stalin's own Georgia, the state farms were in disrepair and a private economy hummed, which in turn spawned corruption as officials indulged themselves.

This type of unabashed corruption, something new since Kennan's first posting, was only one aspect of a fundamental problem that was afflicting Soviet society in 1952: the rapidly widening social and economic breach between rulers and ruled. The ownership by the bureaucratic caste of private cars and private cottages on the outskirts of Moscow was an outward display of wealth and power accessible only to

a few. The absence of extensive purges and a concomitant increase in social stability meant that class stratification, not really a salient feature of the 1930s, was
becoming fixed, upward mobility was more difficult, and the younger generation
more conscious of class distinctions. None of this was lost upon Kennan:

> Influence and position have now been retained by the same people for a relatively
> long time. . . . Older people are beginning to complain of "snobbishness" among
> the young. The behavior of different groups of people . . . begins to reflect not in
> just the jobs they happen to hold at the minute but their general estimate of
> themselves and of their place in the hierarchy of Soviet society.[9]

In effect, Kennan was testifying to the emergence of a Soviet ruling class variously
described and deplored by such Marxist critics as Leon Trotsky and Milovan Djilas.
Kennan, by contrast, viewed the consolidation of such a class with some approval
and hoped that its attachment to a higher standard of living and rising expectations
would incline it toward predictable politics and toward an improvement of relations
with the West.

Despite strides made since 1945 in their material lot, it seemed to Kennan that
the majority of Soviet citizens had withdrawn emotionally—in a manner not apparent, or perhaps possible, in the 1930s—from the explicit purposes of the regime.
Although the legitimacy of the state was beyond question, most of its institutions
were accepted by the population in a lukewarm, almost apathetic fashion: "They
were seen," said Kennan, "as a natural condition of life, not always agreeable or
pleasant, sometimes even dangerous, but nevertheless something that is simply
'there,' like the weather or the soil, and not to be removed by anything the individual could possibly do."[10] To their subjects, the rulers were inscrutable and unap-
proachable behind the Kremlin's parapets; their names, Kennan believed, possessed
a mythical quality for most people, but they seemed hardly real or part of daily
concern.

Those Russians who were internally detached from Soviet politics led relatively
normal lives and found satisfaction in family life, friendships, and to a certain
degree in religious observance. (Roughly one quarter to one third of Muscovites
were religious in the early 1950s and had their children baptized and their dead
buried according to Christian Orthodox rites.) Although a sentiment not shared by
the typical Soviet man, Kennan, his ascetic side getting the better of his judgment,
believed "the fact that there are narrow limits to the field in which his [the citizen's]
ambitions can roam, with respect both to wealth and position, is perhaps rather a
source of spiritual health than otherwise."[11] At the same time, he was sensibly
aware of the frequency of drunkenness and delinquency among younger people,
especially men. Such behavior, however self-destructive, was in his view another
reflection of the primacy of private life, and he concluded that the regime was losing
the battle for the spiritual loyalty of its subjects: "There are two lives being led in
the Soviet Union today—a life of the people and a life of the regime, and there is no
intimacy between the two, only the relationship between master and slave."[12]

Regime-inspired terror helped keep the broad population in order. On Stalin's
orders Siberian prison camps were filled during the late 1940s with hundreds of
thousands of returning POWs who had failed to obey his original command that no

part of the Red Army should surrender to the German invaders. Anyone who dared to raise the question or intimated that the Generalissimo and Genius Leader of Progressive Mankind might bear some responsibility for Soviet military disasters in 1941 and appalling casualties was also incarcerated. This second category included Alexander Solzhenitsyn, a committed Leninist and army officer at the time of his arrest in 1945. As a technique of governmental rule, terror had actually reached its postwar peak in 1949 and 1950 when Stalin's internal security forces routed and then executed a nest of alleged Titoist-Zionist-US "spies" and "wreckers" who had supposedly infiltrated the Leningrad party organization; in Eastern Europe similar "vile" elements were purged from the people's democracies. Very likely in 1952, the official apparatus of terror was being readied for a new campaign against enemies of the state.[13] Albeit too late for a couple of their victims, A. Zhdanov and A. Shchrebakov, a "conspiracy" by Jewish doctors to poison top Soviet military and civilian leaders was "uncovered" early in 1953. This last, much-publicized, discovery was a prelude to new party purges along the lines of 1935–1940 and may have been intended to pave the way for a series of government-sponsored pogroms. Certainly, as Kennan realized, the expulsion of the entire Israeli delegation and its ambassador in January 1953 was perfectly in line with Stalin's own anti-Semitism. Only after his death (March 1953) did the government concede that the Jewish doctors were innocent and not acting on behalf of foreign or domestic enemies.

The Russian intelligentsia, a segment of society that had always fascinated and attracted Kennan—in 1952 he made another pilgrimage to Yasnaya Polyana—was, as a consequence of the terror and the *Zhdanovshchina,* more timid and afraid than any time in recent history. Though Kennan recognized that most artists and literati had not suffered arrest or anything worse than semi-exile in the late 1940s or early 1950s, the majority of talented ones had been barred from work in their chosen fields, denied association with their colleagues at home and abroad, and officially shunned.[14] Meanwhile, the career artists and court musicians who retained official favor were periodically trotted out for public performances or put on exhibition when it suited the government's purpose to impress the world public with the freedom of expression permitted to Soviet artists and intellectuals. In fact, though, they could never bring credit upon themselves or the authorities, but were in Kennan's characterization

> people whose real profession and source of strength lies in their political collaboration with the regime but do have just sufficient talent, or did have it when they were younger, to pass plausibly as artists, authors, or what you will. Only a handful of writers of any real prestige remain, and those—instead of producing anything of great literary value—vie with each other on the overt level, in blood-thirsty propaganda speeches about bacteriological warfare and, behind the walls of the Writers' Union in waspish personal duels with one another, conducted in guise of comradely literary criticism and counter-criticism, but against a background of the most savage party and police intrigue.[15]

Even research in the natural sciences was damaged by the triumph of frauds such as Trofim Lysenko. And members of the intelligentsia that Kennan encountered appeared to wear taut, anxious faces—much in contrast to the reasonably contented expressions of the popular visage—and bore other physical marks of a life entirely dependent on the shifts of favor and disfavor in the higher echelons of Stalin's Kremlin.

Officialdom in the USSR was also under strain in 1952, its vigor was in doubt, its loyalty under constant scrutiny. Although Stalin did convene a party congress in October, rearranged the Politburo, and seemed to increase his physical activity, these demonstrations were empty and suggested to Kennan that Stalin was losing his grip on events and retained only enough power to make his last days as wretched as possible for his junior colleagues. While he played them off against each other, Stalin tried to enhance his own personal safety and intellectual prestige: hence the cult of personality, his pronouncements on linguistics, and his stimulation of research on the extension of human life. Small wonder, then, that members of the Soviet upper class seemed unhappy and subdued; Kennan reported, "There is a deadness about them that is almost frightening." At the 1952 party congress, Stalin demoted those in his official entourage who seemed overly eager for his mantle or otherwise diluted their influence; the Politburo, rechristened the "Presidium" in October, was expanded to include Stalin's new favorites, while the positions of old retainers, such as A. Andreyev, L. Beria, V. Molotov, and G. Malenkov, were drastically weakened.

To Kennan the mysterious circumstances surrounding Zhdanov's death (1948) ran parallel to Kirov's and would provide a pretext whenever Stalin needed one for inaugurating purges encompassing far more than just the Leningrad party apparatus. The whole party organization seemed smothered in an atmosphere as "sultry and explosive as the Deuce." And while Malenkov, Molotov, Beria, and the others maneuvered for political advantage, every pretense of mutuality and trust fell away among the elite. "We can be absolutely sure," Kennan wrote, "that there cannot be bonds of personal confidence among these men at the top, neither as between Stalin and any one of them or between any two of them. In the first place, Stalin has ruled for many years by preserving suspicions among his [lieutenants] and secondly because he himself has betrayed a staggering number of his close associates that no one . . . can think that he has any security in the immediate neighborhood of Stalin. . . . [He] has in his makeup a most incredible and morbid streak, particularly preoccupied with ways death can occur."[16] What, Kennan must have wondered, would it mean for a government so strangely constituted to assess itself against the heroic, and more humane, standards of 1917?

In lieu of the vital ideology that still animated Russia when Kennan knew it as a young man, there stood in 1952 only Stalin, the sole object of legitimate veneration, the one living Soviet leader who along with Lenin was worshipped as a species of deity. Indeed, the disciple had outgrown his master; his greatness had, said Kennan, "merged into divinity, and [his] magic, unerring truth caused problem after problem to dissolve into the gold of 'the right solution' by the peculiar alchemy of genius and infallibility." This glorification of the leader, combined with official dwelling on past successes—electrification, improved literacy, industrialization, the victorious Fatherland War—indicated as nothing else could the fact that Marxist ideology was dead and that intellectual and spiritual decay had overcome the soul of the regime. According to Kennan, a tremendous crisis lay in store for the Soviet leaders when their collective imagination would be called upon to deal with urgent issues. Being worn out, they would fail to match the standard of previous mythological achievements: "Into every nook and cranny of Soviet life flows the insidious paralyzing influence of this dilemma—the dilemma of a group of men who have officially portrayed themselves as just one bit too successful and too [ingenious]."[17]

As during the 1930s, the genuine deficiencies of Soviet society and the existence of social problems were depicted by the government as related to the machinations of anti-Soviet external forces. This time the United States specifically was made into the chief scapegoat for all that was awry. The official interpretation apparently had little persuasive explanatory power, however. Kennan noted that most people were too perceptive to accept a thesis which told them that they lived in the best of all possible worlds and the worst possible world lay immediately beyond Soviet borders. Instead of an Orwellian perfection in which ruler and subject were perfectly synchronized, there was only stagnation in Russia; and the future, Kennan guessed, was fraught with dangers for the Stalinist state. Because the glamor and appeal of a revolution promising a better world had been exhausted and because the aftermath of a colossal war meant still greater exertions rather than a deserved respite, the regime had lost most of the popular goodwill it once enjoyed. "What is coming in this immediately approaching period," Kennan predicted in July 1952 to superiors in Washington, "may well be a crisis of Soviet power quite comparable in scope and seriousness to the original civil war or the death of Lenin or the purges of the 1930s—but entirely different in form."[18]

These were prescient observations. Half a year later the Soviet Union was rocked by the Jewish doctors' scandal; three and a half years later the entire communist world was shaken to its core by Khrushchev's denunciation of Stalin and revelations about his crimes which, in turn, accelerated the process of communist polycentrism and ushered in a new era of reform in the USSR. Until then, however, the extreme tension and fear that pervaded the state apparatus and party organization made normal relations between the Soviet Union and most other governments problematic.

Diplomacy Thwarted

Kennan's misfortune was not simply that his ambassadorship fell during the final year of Stalin's life, when the infirmities of old age, combined with the moral corrosiveness of absolute power and an acute sense of his country's vulnerability, made him and his government more fearsome and suspicious than any time before or since in Soviet history. The outstanding issues between Russia and the United States—Korea, nuclear weaponry, Germany's future, Eastern Europe—also remained unresolved. Consequently, there was no reason for Kennan, or any other conceivable American representative to Moscow, to feel optimistic about his chances for substantially improving US relations with the Soviet government. And yet when Truman announced in December 1951 that Kennan would proceed to Moscow in May, considerable speculation arose in the press and elsewhere about whether his appointment might occasion a shaking-up of the Cold War and shift it in the direction of detente. Among the many commentators who contributed to this expectation was Arnold Toynbee who, somewhat pedantically and rather misleadingly, told a BBC audience: "In the present state of international affairs, it is no exaggeration to say that the American ambassador in Moscow is one of a half dozen men in the world on whose wisdom, ability, and good will the fate of mankind may depend."[19]

Kennan never entertained any illusions about his assignment and was sobered by the Soviet Union's seeming intractability on substantive issues and the violence of its war of words against the United States. He expected under these circumstances to reside in Moscow with as much cheerfulness and patience as he could muster and lend himself to whatever negotiations might occur. He reckoned that, for the remainder, he would have to steel himself and his staff against the disorientation and demoralization that occasionally overcame foreign diplomats working in Moscow. The capital in 1952 was even heavier than in the late 1930s with an atmosphere noxious to Americans. In Kennan's words, they had to function coolly despite "hostility and insults . . . suspicion and misinterpretation of their every action . . . attempts to belittle their world and their beliefs . . . [to live where] the very essence is the unceasing effort to induce people to abandon the evidence of their senses and of all objective criteria and to accept as valid a version of reality artificially created, unconnected with objective fact, and calculated to reduce them to a state in which no reactions are operative but those of fear and respect for . . . Soviet power."[20]

Shortly before his departure for Moscow, Kennan tried to sound a less pessimistic note for the sake of American newspaper reporters and their readers. He told them that the Soviet Union would prefer a reduction of international tensions and a return to more hopeful relations with the United States; he expected to achieve some small success and emphasized that he was sanguine about his prospects for helping revive cultural exchanges between the two countries as existed during the 1930s. And for the convenience of Soviet analysts trying to decipher his intentions, Kennan told the reporters that his deportment as ambassador would be perfectly correct and that he was unsympathetic to anyone who urged that the embassy in Moscow be used for damaging or toppling the Soviet regime. In opposition to Dulles, who was already employing provocative Republican rhetoric about "liberation" and "rollback," Kennan averred reassuringly that he had misgivings about any form of radical interference by one power in the internal affairs of another:

> If you go in . . . to unseat a government you place yourself under the moral obligation to have in your pocket something with which to replace it, if you succeed. And I don't think that is a responsibility that I would like to see any of us Americans have for Russia. . . . I have great sympathy . . . for the Russian people and great respect for many qualities that they have in them. And I think we have reason to hope that things will not always be as difficult as they are today.[21]

Neither this statement nor others like it that Kennan issued at the time allayed Stalin's fears about Western embassies being centers of espionage, sabotage, and subversion, and about their ambassadors being hell-bent on the destruction of Soviet security and prestige.

Apart from maintaining a modicum of decorum and seeing after the needs of his professional staff in Moscow, Kennan was uncertain about how best to proceed: both Truman and Acheson had failed to advise him of any policy agenda and had not recommended a set of goals that he might pursue. He did decide early on not to appear unduly eager to arrange a meeting with Stalin, unlike the British ambassador, Sir Alvary Douglas Frederick Gascoigne, who had been kept waiting unceremoniously for months before his request for an audience was granted. Unfortunately for Kennan, this departure from standard protocol—politely asking to see the resident potentate—may have been his first mistake as ambassador. "God knows," he wrote two decades later, "what impression was produced by it on the aging and semi-mad dictator."[22] Very likely, however, any Soviet leader, not just Stalin, would have been piqued by the discourtesy and implied assertion of American superiority when the president's personal representative studiously did not extend himself.

Kennan was determined that, if he should meet with Stalin or another ranking member of the Politburo, their discussion would be private and serious and not used by Soviet spokesmen to score propaganda points against the United States or made into an event for widespread, unrealistic theorizing about the future course of Soviet-American rivalry.[23] Kennan made it known that he would be willing, if called upon, to confer with any high Soviet official, but no such meeting was ever held, and the American ambassador was confined to dealing with middle-level functionaries of the Foreign Office.

Kennan's presentation of credentials in May to Nikolai Shvérnik, titular head of the Soviet state, was stiffly delivered and glumly received, and probably served as a reminder to all in attendance of the multiple disappointments that had plagued Soviet-US relations since the effervescent days of 1933. Kennan did refer hopefully in his prepared remarks to Stalin's latest endorsement of peaceful coexistence and stressed that the United States had been acting on this premise since the first administration of Franklin Roosevelt. He also mentioned, though it smacked of *pro forma*, that he hoped tolerable, mutually beneficial political arrangements would be forthcoming. Beyond this Kennan did not venture. He was without clear instructions from his own government and, besides, the immediate Soviet reaction to his appointment and purpose in Moscow was impossible for him to read. To H. Freeman Mathews, the undersecretary of state, he reported: "My reception here has been what you would call one hundred percent 'deadpan.' If it reflected any special orders or directives from the top, they could only have been a rigid injunction to avoid anything that might give me a clue to the feelings of the Kremlin about my . . . presence in this city." Shvernik's formal statement was certainly unexceptional, and his private words with Kennan were also trivial and protocolaire; the same held for A. Vishinsky, the foreign minister, and for other deputy ministers upon whom Kennan called. In turn, he, too, was laconic and guarded: "I think I may say . . . that if they have kept me guessing, I have kept them guessing in equal measure, which is so far about the only enjoyment I have from this job."[24]

Irrespective of the satisfaction he apparently derived from being cagey, Kennan tried from the beginning to place himself and his embassy on an irreproachable footing with his Soviet hosts. For this reason he wanted to discourage the American naval, air, and military attachés from conducting their easily detectable intelligence operations, Soviet knowledge of which would embarrass the United States and confirm Stalin's fears about the true nature of Western diplomacy. At one point, these attachés mounted a telescopic camera on the roof of the chancery to photograph Soviet war planes as they flew over Red Square during holiday celebrations. From a nearby building, Soviet counter-intelligence agents photographed the Americans in the middle of their spying, which caused them to retaliate by photographing the Soviet agents. "It had all become," Kennan later wrote, "a silly and discreditable game, merely fortifying the Russians in their cynicism about the purpose of our embassy in Moscow and about the inspirations of our policies generally."[25] Powerless to prevent this sort of activity emanating from the embassy—the attachés were working independently, under orders from the Pentagon—Kennan demanded later, after Moscow, that all chiefs of mission retain complete control over, and be informed in advance of, every type of US government activity in lands to which they were assigned.[26] Responsibility without authority in the Moscow mission was a recipe for disaster.

Kennan was perturbed during his months in the Soviet Union by the adverse effect that sensationalist American propaganda was having on diplomacy. He had long maintained that carefully phrased informational programs aimed against politically literate Soviet citizens could help overcome their doubts and fears about the West and encourage them in a moderate direction (see Chapter 6), but he objected to name-calling, indictments of Russian backwardness, and harping upon Soviet misbehavior in the past; extreme propaganda would preclude any opportunity for diplomatic breakthrough and might cause the scuttling of existing negotiations in Korea. He warned Truman and other members of the government about the vices of stridency, the virtues of circumspection: "With respect to those things which represent by-products of the internal struggles of the Russian people, which would have been bound to be present in some degree in whatever regime had existed in Russia, and which people have the honesty to overcome by manful and courageous self-criticism, let us observe the discreet silence of the outsider who cannot know all and cannot be expected fully to understand." Ever mindful of America's social and political shortcomings, he cautioned that there would be things in the national life of his own country which would require a similar indulgence. Kennan recommended that US propagandists concentrate instead on those features of Soviet activity and attitudes—continuous lying, morbid and self-destructive politics, unwarranted hostility toward the outside world—against which the West had legitimate grievances.[27]

Not only should hyperbole be avoided, but, when in August 1952 the House Select Committee on the Katyn Forest Massacre completed its investigation, Kennan urged that its findings be consigned to the government's archives and not deployed as another weapon in the propaganda war. Despite his certainty about Soviet culpability for Katyn, he feared that public dissemination of the committee's report more than a decade after the event would be perceived by the Soviets as an unprovoked escalation of the propaganda war and as a singular affront. From a diplomatic standpoint nothing would be gained; overall Soviet-US relations would sink to a lower nadir.

If . . . we are prepared to accept the fact of Soviet ruthlessness as one of the regrettable but basic [facts] of the Bolshevik system, and if our concern is less to establish in the eyes of the world our ethical superiority over this system than to find means of living in the same world with it and defending the cause of freedom generally without having to fight a costly and pointless war against it in the coming period, then I think we would do well to try to persuade the interested Congressional figures to [shelve] this report . . . [and regard it] as an interesting study of a revealing historical occurrence and as further evidence of a feature of Soviet political personality which has constituted a constant element in our problem of dealing with Soviet power ever since the institution of the terror by Lenin in 1919.[28]

Alas, Kennan was overruled—actually ignored—and the committee released its findings to the press with much fanfare, which caused an outpouring of Soviet vituperation.

Soviet publications and spokesmen blasted the United States for using chemical and germ warfare in Korea, torturing POWs, committing one atrocity after another around the world, and scheming to conquer and kill all peace-loving peoples. This relentless condemnation inflicted something of a psychic cost on the American embassy staff and its ambassador in Moscow. Kennan was really speaking for all of them when he admitted to a friend in August, "I do not particularly mind the life here, but I find it impossible to adjust comfortably to the incredible volume and hatefulness of lies these people manage to put out about us."[29] By September, he was filled with revulsion for the anti-American tirades. Nonetheless, in what was probably a futile exercise anyway, he tried to evaluate them analytically and argued that the Soviet attacks were aimed at rallying sagging popular morale and stiffening it against the day when dangerous encounters would occur with the United States. From today's perspective, it is entirely plausible that underlying the cacophony of the hate campaign was a note of real concern about the apathy and latent disaffection of large numbers of people in the USSR. Kennan, in any case, did not think, as was widely held in Washington, that Soviet fulminations were designed to stir popular support in the USSR for an aggressive war against Europe or an expansion of the one in Asia; other measures needed to prepare for such a conflict were not evident elsewhere in Stalin's empire.[30]

While Kennan tried to counter the alarm in Washington about the imminence of great power war, he worried about anti-American propaganda for other reasons. First, it would erode what little gratitude remained among Russians for American lend-lease aid and collaboration during World War II; over the long term, it would probably have a detrimental impact on popular attitudes toward the United States. In a letter addressed to the editors of *Trud,* official mouthpiece of the Soviet labor unions, he fired: "You must realize that such deficiencies [defamations of the US and its armed forces in a recent article] in knowledge and understanding place serious limitations on the ability of people to make a positive contribution to the discussion of international subjects. The responsibility for such ignorance on your part must rest with those to whom you are accustomed to look for enlightenment and instruction about world events."[31] To nobody's surprise, least of all Kennan's, his letter was not reprinted nor were any of his other protests conveyed to Soviet followers of the press or radio.

The acerbity of Russia's anti-US propaganda, coinciding as it did with shabby treatment meted to the noncommunist diplomatic corps in Moscow, indicated to Kennan that the regime was contemptuous of the values and safeguards inherent in the maintenance of regular diplomatic channels. By recklessly disregarding the basic amenities of international life, the Soviets were virtually cutting themselves off even more deeply from the Western world. This barrier they were erecting of bravado and imperiousness was something unprecedented and disturbing:

> I can say on the basis of personal experience in the 1930s and again during the war that there was visible in the behavior of these people a certain ultimate caution about their overt relations with the capitalist West—a certain solicitude for the intactness and state of good repair of the normal and polite channel—a certain recognition that there might be times when this channel would prove useful and necessary to them—indeed perhaps the only thing they might have to fall back upon. Today, that caution seems to be gone.[32]

Although the embassy staff was large, it did not enjoy any means for a direct exchange of views with leading Soviet officials. Instead, the Americans were surrounded by restrictions and otherwise ignored by the Soviets as if formal US-USSR relations did not exist. Unless Stalin ordered his subordinates to adopt a snappier, more respectful manner toward the Americans, Kennan felt all chance for improved relations was nil.[33] Furthermore, in Kennan's view, the Soviets not only lacked confidence in diplomacy, but also many of them harbored an antipathy against him personally and were content for the moment with intermittent conversations between Soviet spokesmen (including Stalin) and representatives of the Western press. Government-to-government relations no longer mattered, and, in the case of the United States, the Soviets had abandoned all efforts to cultivate popular opinion. "They have ceased to care what we think or how we react," Kennan surmised, because, "they don't care how much the Americans hate them . . . their own calculations tell them it will be folly [for the US or the USSR] to make war."[34]

Until the Soviet leadership reversed its attitude on the value of diplomacy and decided to break the country's self-imposed isolation, life in the American embassy was going to remain unpleasant and tense. Kennan was trailed closely by plainclothed officers of the police armed forces whenever he sojourned outside of the embassy compound grounds; his living and working quarters were bugged; his every attempt to make social contact with Soviet citizens, no matter how casual, was monitored or else forbidden outright. The Soviet government even tried to entice him into aligning himself with a fabricated and grotesque conspiracy to assassinate Soviet leaders. Under such circumstances Kennan decided that the United States was wasting time and expense by maintaining an ambassador in Moscow. Better to reduce the staff, withdraw the ambassador, and let the chargé d'affaires direct a minimal American operation in Moscow. Kennan wrote to his old friend, Bernard Gufler, in August:

> I am not sorry that I have returned here for this period of service. It is impossible, living outside of the Soviet Union, to retain a comprehension of the ugliness and

dangerousness of this whole business. I find that unless I am brought face to face with it from time to time I tend to become smug and complacent about it. So I regard service here as good for my soul. . . . Why the Government wants an ambassador here . . . is difficult for me to fathom.[35]

Less than two months later, because of Kennan's own actions, Truman's administration had no ambassadorial representation in Moscow.

Not only did Kennan despair of the Soviet political environment as an impediment to improved US-Russian relations, but he was also unhappy with his embassy staff. He complained that it was needlessly encumbered by more people than could be usefully employed. At least fifty of his subordinates, including many Foreign Service officers, had no productive functions to fill; they cluttered the embassy and made for endless administrative headaches. But worse than this redundancy, in Kennan's view, was the unwillingness of his junior colleagues (who included Malcom Toon, later ambassador to Moscow) to attempt to establish rapport with their chief. To Bohlen, Kennan confided, "I have been puzzled by the Russian language officers here and their attitude. I cannot for the life of me tell from my contacts with them whether they hate me, despise me, or fear me. I rarely see them unless I specifically summon them, and they rarely comment of their own accord about anything that goes on." He lamented further that the good old days of intellectual intensity—when he, Bohlen, Loy Henderson, and others would discuss, analyze, debate, and theorize into the late night about the Soviet universe—were gone. That spontaneity of interest which bound together in former days all of those who cared about the interpretation of Soviet affairs seemed missing. And where, he wondered, was the respect due to a man who had been personally involved with Soviet-US relations since the inception of diplomatic exchanges in 1933: "When I look at the men we have here now and note their deadpan faces and utter lack of readiness to commit themselves, I wonder sometimes whether they do not consider themselves a hundred times wiser than us, their elders, and are not treating me with the same weary correctness which we reserved in our youth for chiefs whom we thought were hopelessly behind in their mental processes." Perhaps, despite his obtuseness, Ambassador Joseph Davies had felt a similar type of contempt emanating from Kennan and some of the others in 1937. However, in 1952, apart from Kennan's complaints to Bohlen, there is no evidence supporting the notion that embassy officials bore a grudge or disrespect toward their boss. In point of fact, according to Frank Rounds, Jr., an American journalist stationed in Moscow in 1952, morale among the US embassy staff increased considerably when it was learned that Kennan would be serving as ambassador.[36] Very likely he was feeling overwrought for reasons connected to living in Stalin's Moscow, not being fully appreciated by Acheson and other ranking members of the administration, and having to supervise the practical and ceremonial affairs, many of them tedious and time-consuming, of a large legation. By temperament, Kennan was suited for scholarship or research and analysis of political affairs. Practical matters and executive responsibility had never been his forte. His views about his subordinates' perception of himself, in any case, were groundless and imagined.

Still, Kennan's feelings were deeply held, and with the exception of one officer,

John McSweeney, Kennan believed that his staff ignored him and were insulting in not evincing interest in the quality of cables and messages he regularly sent to Washington: "None has even offered any word of comment or given me any indication that [the dispatches] were of any interest. . . . The result is that I feel very lonely in this work and . . . it would not make the faintest difference to me if the mission were reduced from nearly one hundred to fifteen or twenty."[37] For years afterward, Kennan's pet peeve was that the Foreign Service was becoming too large, wasteful, and full of overweening bureaucrats: a small, select number of students of international relations was preferable in overseas missions to ones staffed by faceless careerists.

Kennan's attention to duties in Moscow was also diverted and his discontent aggravated by the plight of various colleagues in the United States whose patriotism and integrity were under suspicion. In particular, he was upset by the misfortunes of John Paton Davies, who had become an object of right-wing hounding. During the summer of 1951, Kennan had testified on Davies's behalf before Senator Patrick McCarren's subcommittee on internal security. Upon learning later, July 1952, that the issues involving Davies had still not been satisfactorily resolved in his favor, Kennan prepared to resign in protest from his ambassadorship and from the Foreign Service. As he explained to Acheson, his long-standing admiration for Davies was based on the latter's intelligence and sense of duty; it was absurd to suppose that he had ever done or would contemplate doing anything against US interests. If Davies should be undermined as a result of McCarren's continuing investigation, Kennan warned that he would feel that his own judgment, dating to his directorship of Policy Planning, was open to question and therefore his current position, and usefulness generally to the government, could not remain unaffected. He made the point, too, that both the attorney general and McCarren should understand that the handling of Davies's case could have repercussions reaching beyond Davies alone.[38]

Kennan was also angry at the State Department for not doing more to protect those employees—such as Davies and Edmund Clubb—who after years of honorable service fell suddenly afoul of hysterical loyalty boards and investigating committees: "It is to me a nightmarish thought that this sort of thing can happen to a man by no fault on his part and only by virtue of his effort to do his job as he saw it, and I cannot believe that there is not something grievously and terribly wrong with the procedures of a government in which such a thing is possible."[39]

It was against this background—of Soviet hostility and shrillness, spying and counter-spying, isolation from his staff, and growing personal anguish about the fate of men he admired and had led—that Kennan made his notorious slip. While at the Tempelhof airport in Berlin (September 19, 1952), on his way to a conference in London devoted to NATO issues, he told a Western reporter that American diplomats in Moscow were treated shamefully, no differently than Americans at Bad Nauheim were by Nazi officials: "Had the Nazis permitted us to walk the streets [under guard] without having the right to talk to any Germans, that would be exactly how we have to live in Moscow today."[40] This public equating of the Soviet Union with Nazi Germany was bound to cause a fury; possibly, given his feelings about the futility of keeping an ambassador in Russia, combined with his state of overall dissatisfaction, he hoped subconsciously to provoke the Soviets into responding the way they did. At any rate, after lambasting him in *Pravda, Izvestia,* and elsewhere, the Soviet government declared him *persona non grata* and forbade him to return to Moscow: "[His] crude anti-Soviet sally leaves no doubt that such a statement could only be made by a person unable to restrain his malevolent hostility to the Soviet Union, who not only desires no improvement in American-Soviet relations, but uses every opportunity to make them worse. Kennan long ago acquired the reputation of an enemy of peace and hence of the Soviet Union."[41]

Some evidence gathered by Charles Bohlen in 1955 suggests that Stalin had a high regard for Kennan, was amazed by his undiplomatic outburst, and regretted that there was no alternative to demanding his removal.[42] But such an interpretation is overly charitable to Stalin, who along with most of the leadership at the time had little need for an American envoy who assiduously followed their politics, studied their history, and knew the Russian language almost as well as any native speaker. They were probably glad to be rid of him in 1952 and grateful for his inadvertently providing them with a pretext for dismissal. Yet it would be a mistake to overlook the quality of Kennan's insolence in Soviet eyes, and the fact that he had been standing on German territory when he lumped the Soviet Union into the same category as Hitler's regime must have cut deeply into Soviet (popular and official) sensibilities. A. I. Mikoyan later explained to Bohlen, "That we should be insulted precisely from Berlin was intolerable."[43]

In subsequent years Kennan had numerous occasions to reflect on the ignominious way in which his first ambassadorship ended. He reveals in his memoirs that the episode caused him much self-doubt and to question whether he possessed the intellectual and temperamental wherewithal to acquit himself credibly as America's chief representative to Russia; he was also pained by Acheson's sharp barbs about his lack of self-control and inability to marshal appropriate sangfroid.[44] Still, Kennan's initial response to the Soviet action was aimed at exonerating himself and attributing the reason for his expulsion to "Soviet hardliners"; his remorse was not obviously great and, again, suggests that he was glad to be out of the American embassy.

It is clear from Kennan's post-Moscow debriefings that the personnel of the Soviet Foreign Office had dealt with him pleasantly in 1952 and seemed satisfied to treat with someone who knew their country well. Interestingly enough, Kennan did not ascribe hard feeling or blame to Stalin, but thought that the Generalissimo had been misinformed for years by his police-security organs about the nature of the outside world and about Kennan's diplomatic mission and record of activities. In retrospect, the accuracy of such an assessment seems farfetched. Stalin kept his own counsel and was not easily led astray by his police henchmen: more often than not they turned out to be *his* dupes and pawns. Nonetheless, Kennan placed the locus of Soviet hostility to himself and other Western residents in Moscow squarely in the security organizations. "I could not help," he professed in 1953, "but be aware that in the police apparatus there were people animated by the most violent feelings about me."[45] To the degree that this is correct, the police doubtless believed along the lines already mentioned that it was undesirable to have an informed American ambassador around when questions of leadership succession and Politburo division were daily becoming more manifest. Kennan later claimed that his expulsion was partly based on the fact that in one way or another he appeared to be trying to touch the sensitive nerves of this political division.

Shortly after his ouster from Moscow, Kennan, back in Washington, tried to overcome his embarrassment and deflect some of the private criticism that was pouring in from Western governments by emphasizing the humorous side of the episode. "I came out of Moscow and blew my top," he confessed to colleagues in the State Department. Yet he contended that nobody had cause for regret, certainly not the Soviets who had wanted to get rid of him from the outset. As for himself: "I desperately wanted to leave, and succeeded in doing so. The American public was pleased, because its concepts of diplomacy incline generally to the dramatic and defiant rather than to the epic and conciliatory."[46] And probably, he thought, the Soviet public enjoyed watching its government's explosion of indignation on an issue that everyone knew was true. He allowed that the Truman government was upset because of the jolt administered to its diplomatic arrangements; but the administration could not afford to upbraid anyone for making an anti-Soviet crack just weeks before the presidential election. Outwardly, at least, most people should have been amused.[47]

However unfair he thought Acheson had been to him in the past, the secretary of state had reason to be extremely displeased with Kennan in October 1952. At a time when Acheson was engaged in finding a diplomatic solution to the protracted Korean fighting and expected to involve the Soviets in producing an armistice, the ambassador to Moscow had precipitated an unnecessary and easily avoidable crisis. To compound problems, Senator William Knowland, supported by assorted congressmen and journalists, demanded that the United States break relations with Russia and send its envoy packing in reprisal for Soviet actions against Kennan. While Acheson was able to squelch this unhelpful proposal and, for the sake of attending to more urgent matters, ignored the subject of the feckless ambassador in conversations with Vishinsky, the Kennan episode and Acheson's handling of it fitted conveniently into the Republican brief that the Democrats were spineless and soft on communism.[48] Thus Kennan's misstep in Berlin led to yet another occasion for Truman's—and now Adlai Stevenson's—domestic adversaries to heap abuse upon the administration and on the hapless secretary of state in particular. The McCarthy wing of the Republican party must have been gleeful at the secretary's most recent discomfort and Kennan's accidental contribution to their cause.

For the period of political hiatus between Eisenhower's electoral victory in November 1952 and his inauguration in January, Kennan remained America's officially designated ambassador to the Soviet Union. During most of this period, he actually resided on his farm in East Berlin, Pennsylvania, awaiting his next assignment. But he did make one important trip to Washington. Late in December 1952 Kennan was subpoenaed by the Subcommittee for Internal Security of the Senate Judicial Committee and, in his phrase, "brutally" interrogated for two hours about his former subordinates in the Policy Planning Staff and his own actions as director. The experience left him incensed and dumbfounded: "I am not aware of having done anything to warrant this lack of confidence and am at a loss to know what sort of evidence could have given rise to it."[49] He insisted to Acheson as a consequence that the FBI be ordered to make a complete reexamination of his fitness for governmental responsibility and that the executive branch as well as the Senate be fully apprised of all findings. Unless such clarification was brought to bear on his record and accomplishments, he had no desire to stay on under any government.[50]

By early spring 1953, it became evident that Kennan was not to occupy any niche in government under the new administration. Bluntly put, he was too much of a political liability. Kennan was to John Foster Dulles not merely a conspicuous remnant from the previous administration's foreign policy—which the secretary pronounced "immoral"—but by including him Dulles also ran the risk of antagonizing right-wing elements in the Senate and House, to whom the new administration was politically beholden and would need for support in both domestic and foreign affairs. To certain key Republican senators, Kennan was stigmatized by his association with John Paton Davies. And even though Dulles respected Kennan intellectually, he was not prepared to court trouble for his sake, especially not at the start of a new Republican period. In a sense, Kennan was Dulles's Despres: a valuable man to have around, but not worth fighting for. As for the Davies case, it continued to burn all through 1953. In September Kennan paid a visit to Attorney General Herbert Brownell in the hope of helping to clear Davies; in this, as with so much else in 1953, Kennan was disappointed, as his pleading was rejected and Davies's career in the State Department ruined.

In the meantime, Kennan had further damaged his standing with Dulles when on January 16, 1953—just days before the secretary-designate assumed official responsibilities—he told the Pennsylvania Bar Association that he had grave doubts about the advisability of encouraging East Europeans to think that the United States would pursue a policy of "liberation" and "rollback." The next day the *Washington Post* featured a major article ("Dulles Policy 'Dangerous', Kennan Says") elaborating the crucial differences, real and imagined, between Dulles and the ambassador to Moscow. Despite Kennan's hasty attempt to patch things up with Dulles and explain how his remarks had been misinterpreted by the press, the damage had been done. Kennan's meetings with the secretary in March and April were frosty and Dulles's manipulations to dispense with Kennan obvious. Although both John Foster Dulles and Allen Dulles raised the possibility of Kennan's joining the CIA, he rejected it and was content to leave government altogether, "at a time when so much viciousness and falsehood and lack of discrimination seems to mark our public counsels."[51]

At the age of forty-nine Kennan thus left the Foreign Service for good. In September, he and his family resettled in Princeton, where he had secured a grant for another year of study at the Institute for Advanced Study. He and his wife also toyed with the idea of moving to Vienna or Munich in the near future. Indeed, the life of an expatriate seemed enormously appealing: "The mass of our countrymen," Kennan told his friend Charles Thayer, "still find nothing wrong with the state of the country or the trends of the times. As long as this is the prevailing sentiment, there is nothing much that any of us can do to oppose the McCarthyite trend or to escape it. And in these circumstances I can imagine that life might well be pleasanter and more productive somewhere else."[52]

Kennan did decide eventually to stay on in the United States and earned a permanent position at the Institute which provided him, as well as Oppenheimer, some refuge from the bristling anti-communist hysteria. Nevertheless, he was afraid that the country as a whole might embrace many features of totalitarianism in its domestic life while trying to protect itself and its allies from the radiations of totalitarianism abroad. Extravagant internal security arrangements and flamboyant rhetoric about the need to expose and purge communists in the government, schools, and elsewhere represented to Kennan the continued failure of Americans, both high and low, to grasp the essence of the Cold War. He was pessimistic in 1952 about whether or not his compatriots would ever understand: "America's problem of coping with the Soviet threat is still predominantly the problem of coping with the crises of our civilization here at home. The road to success in a foreign policy still lies over those strong and forbidding heights marked by the achievement of real national self-discipline and morale and gaining their dominance through the neglected factor—the power of example."[53] A full decade later most Americans had still not learned this lesson. Kennan's second ambassadorship was an instructive exercise in the pernicious influence of residual McCarthyism in Congress and the congenital inability of the United States to pursue and maintain reasonable policies abroad.

Kennedy's Ambassador

Except for a brief flirtation with the idea of running for Congress and active support for Adlai Stevenson in 1956, Kennan remained aloof from government and politics throughout the 1950s. He concentrated on his academic career and contented himself with occasional critical writing and lectures about international relations. When called upon, he also proferred his advice on policy matters to diverse people and institutions, including Eisenhower (the Solarium project), congressional committees, and individual legislators such as Senator John Kennedy.

Kennan's encounters with Kennedy during the 1950s were few and minor.[54] They once shared a platform at Brandeis University during commencement ceremonies and met once or twice at parties in Washington: Kennan's only strong early impressions were of Mrs. Kennedy's beauty and the senator's youthfulness. The first noteworthy exchange between the two men occurred when the senator sent a letter to Kennan expressing admiration for his 1957 Reith Lectures. The ensuing correspondence between them revealed significant differences of views, with Kennedy cleaving to the mainstream position about the need to cultivate support in the Third World for US purposes and the desirability of retaining the first-use option of nuclear weapons in case of European war. Kennan, in contrast, opined that it would be better to let some Third World states "go communist" than to submit to their "blackmail" about cozying up to the Soviets if the United States failed to be forthcoming enough with foreign aid.[55] Concerning nuclear weapons, he believed the United States had developed an unhealthy reliance upon them and in 1959 called for improved, expanded conventional forces that would allow the US to respond credibly and with an appropriate level of force to various forms of Soviet or Chinese assertiveness. Regarding the nuclear-conventional weapons problem, he did strike a sympathetic chord with Kennedy and, according to Kennan, might have influenced his actions as president. "It does seem important," Kennan recalled in 1965, "that [Kennedy] should have concentrated on this question of the atomic bomb. It is important from the standpoint of the fact that during his subsequent administration he did move both to the limitation of testing and, also, to the strengthening of conventional weapons as a means of getting away from an exclusive dependence on the atomic ones. Both of these things began to appear in [the early Kennedy-Kennan correspondence]."[56]

Sensing the senator's receptiveness to his ideas and possibly hoping to enjoy a high position in government (since 1956 some journalists had speculated that a Democratic president would appoint Kennan to lead the State Department), Kennan wrote a lengthy letter to Kennedy during the 1960 election campaign, in which he reviewed the condition of Soviet-US relations and ways in which a new administration should seize the international initiative. He warned that, in light of the U-2 incident and subsequent cancellation of the Eisenhower-Khrushchev conference, the Soviets were more willing than before to play close to the edge of military conflict and were increasingly susceptible to Chinese blandishments that the communist camp adopt a bolder policy. And he prophesied darkly, wrongly as it turned out, that the international situation prevailing at the time a new administration took office might be as calamitous and menacing as was the internal situation of the United States when FDR was first inaugurated.

Kennan told Kennedy that the Soviets and Chinese were resolved to erode America's prestige, military might, and the Western system of alliances and that, given the complacency and paralysis of Eisenhower's administration, a new government would have to act quickly before irreversible and disastrous events overwhelmed the international standing of the United States. Careful planning and adroit execution of policy were urgently required: "What is needed is a succession of . . . calculated steps, timed in such a way as not only to throw the adversary off balance but to keep him off it, and prepared with sufficient privacy so that the advantage of surprise can be retained."[57] (Although such a line of reasoning seemingly would be compatible with a successful Bay of Pigs invasion, neither Kennan nor Bohlen was ever enthusiastic about such an operation; both of them were concerned with the disagreeable effects on American morale and honor if such an operation failed.)

Kennan also urged that the overextended United States reappraise its existing foreign commitments and eliminate those that were strategically unsound or overly expensive. In the case of Quemoy and Matsu, for example, he recommended that the US depart from the scene while taking propaganda credit for unilateral moves designed to increase stability in a volatile region. In the meantime, the government should organize greater political and material support for its *important* allies in Europe and Asia. Finally, Kennan lay particular attention, as he had ever since Policy Planning days, on the desirability of weakening the existing bonds among communist parties and states. The emerging Sino-Soviet split should be played for all it was worth: "Nothing is more important to us, in this coming period, than to assure a divergence of outlook and policy between the Russians and Chinese." The best method to achieve this was for the Americans to improve relations with both the Soviet Union and Khrushchev, who Kennan rightly recognized was eager to distance himself from the Chinese communists and avoid World War III. A political opportunist, as well as one of the last true believers, Khrushchev could be wooed: "We should . . . without deceiving ourselves about Khrushchev's political personality and without nurturing any unreal hopes, be concerned to keep him politically in the running and to encourage the survival in Moscow of the tendencies he personifies." At the same time, the US ought to work toward undermining Soviet power and authority in Eastern Europe and foster the independent proclivities of various satellite governments. Indeed, the main goal of American diplomacy should be to heighten the divisive tendencies within the Soviet bloc.[58]

Between election day and inauguration, Kennan and Kennedy were again in touch with the former volunteering advice about the sort of people who might be selected as policy advisors. Kennan did not put his own name forward, and Kennedy's inner circle, in which Acheson was respected as the éminence grise, never considered Kennan for an important position. Nevertheless, despite his previous association with Stevenson, Kennedy wanted Kennan and his wealth of experience and knowledge to be used somehow and for this reason offered him the choice of ambassadorship to Poland or Yugoslavia. His long-standing interest in the latter inclined him naturally toward Belgrade. Although both Kennedy and McGeorge Bundy, the president's national security advisor, took a personal interest in Kennan's telegrams from Belgrade and made time to see him during his leaves to Washington, these singular signs of esteem were not widely appreciated within the larger administration.

Kennan arrived in Yugoslavia in early May 1961 and served through July 1963, by which time he was no longer a useful instrument in promoting US interests in Yugoslavia. In addition to assuring mutually profitable and cordial US-Yugoslav relations, his goals as ambassador were to help fortify Yugoslavia's position of independence against the Soviets and thereby embolden other Eastern bloc states in the direction of autonomy from Moscow.

On the face of it, there were several reasons why Kennan might have succeeded in achieving these goals. Unlike in Moscow, and despite what he feared about the "curtain of deference" that hangs between most subordinates and their boss, Kennan liked his staff in Belgrade and was relieved to discover a mutuality of respect. Neither did he think the embassy was too large, although it—including the library, US Information Service, and sixty-four official vehicles—was far more elaborate and the staff more numerous than the equivalent Moscow establishment in 1952: "I was favored in being surrounded with a group of exceptionally able and loyal assistants, whose abilities I myself admired, whose judgment I valued, and whose attitude toward myself was at all times . . . enthusiastically cooperative. . . . Who was I to complain?"[59] After Belgrade, he dropped his carping about the Foreign Service being bloated, its people timid, colorless. And he admitted in 1964 that the United States had a Foreign Service second to none, and better than it had a right to expect, given the lack of respect exhibited by the public for its tasks and achievements.[60]

Kennan was also invigorated by immersing himself in the history and culture of a country so varied as Yugoslavia. He studied the Serbo-Croatian language, undertook scholarly research about medieval Serbia, and mastered much about the country's complicated linguistic, religious, and ethnic mix. Unlike his view of Czechoslovakia in 1938, he did not regard Yugoslavia's incomparably greater diversity as a fatal flaw, but merely as a problem well within the managerial capacity of a basically decent government. In his second volume of memoirs, he includes several vignettes attesting to his affection for the Yugoslav children, peasants, clergy, and others who showed him kindness and were hospitable. To Max Beloff, he cheerfully wrote that the people and country were wonderful—and life was full of interest.[61] The Yugoslav government, too, in another departure from Stalin's, treated Kennan and the other American diplomats politely, at times warmly. Kennan enjoyed access to Joseph Broz Tito, with whom he met on different occasions, and found him a gracious host: "He has treated me and my predecessor in this post with courtesy and kindness. He is an entirely different sort of person than any of the communist leaders I ever met in Moscow."[62] In his memoirs, Kennan's assessment of the Yugoslav leader goes far in the direction of praise and softens some harsh realities, such as Tito's continuing persecution and jailing of Djilas in 1962. In any case, it seemed to Kennan that most Yugoslav officials—this did not, interestingly, include Tito at first—were glad that he had been assigned to Belgrade. He was, after all, something of a known quantity, had earlier made Tito's acquaintance, and his famous Reith Lectures and career in the Washington foreign policy establishment had been followed in Yugoslavia: "They considered me, rightly or wrongly, a distinguished person in the US, and they were pleased that someone whose name they had heard before was being sent to Belgrade."[63]

Contrary to these auguries of a successful mission, there was simultaneous with their appearance a series of portents indicating trouble ahead. For one, Tito and Koca Popovic, Yugoslavia's foreign minister, viewed Kennedy with reservation on account of his Roman Catholicism. They were aware that Catholic Croatian exiles in the US had been lobbying the American Catholic hierarchy against Yugoslavia for years; the net effect of this might incline Kennedy to embrace a stiff anti-Yugoslav line. These fears of Tito's and Popovic's were intensified when in June 1961 Kennedy reversed his earlier decision not to observe Captive Nations Week. Instead, the president honored the week and by implication all that it stood for, including the overthrow ("liberation") of the communist government in Yugoslavia. By declaring Captive Nations Week, Kennedy was acting in accordance with Eisenhower, namely throwing a sop to that part of public opinion that derived satisfaction from official anti-communist posturing and that, if left unappeased, could make trouble by casting aspersions about the democratic integrity of those people entrusted with running foreign policy. Kennan, however, was unimpressed by such political expediency, really contemptuous of it, and felt compromised in Belgrade because his government, at least formally, was dedicated to destroying the very regime to which he was accredited as ambassador.[64]

Tito apparently feared that the CIA and Pentagon set the true direction and tone for US foreign policy. Kennan worked to dispel this illusion, but his case was not helped when on the day of his departure to Yugoslavia the Bay of Pigs invasion began. As Kennan was informed by Tito, that fiasco was just another demonstration—along with the U-2 affair and later the Captive Nations incident— of what he regarded as America's unusually inept, militarily oriented foreign policy.[65] Tito also disliked NATO; believed the Americans were responsible for overly militarizing the Cold War; and was angry with the United States for mistakenly supporting reactionary regimes—Taiwan, South Korea, Iran—and, worst of all, rearming the German Federal Republic, thereby encouraging dreams of reunification and revanche.

Despite Kennan's efforts in the opposite direction, US-Yugoslav relations began to unravel soon after his arrival in Belgrade. In early September, Tito's government played host to the conference of nonaligned nations, of which twenty-five sent representatives, including many heads of state. From a US standpoint, Tito's speeches to the assembly were troubling because they slanted heavily toward the USSR and reflected practically no pretense of neutrality. Tito declared, for example, that he understood perfectly well why the Soviets had to resume testing huge H-bombs—beginning on September 1, the very day the conference convened—in violation of their tacit agreement with the Americans to uphold a testing moratorium. Undoubtedly had the United States taken a similar action, it would have been loudly condemned by Tito and the Yugoslav press. And many observers in the US, both congressmen and newspaper editors, wondered aloud if the Soviet Union was starting to reestablish direction over Yugoslav foreign policy and politics.

Kennan's interpretation of Tito's expressions of solidarity with Moscow showed greater acumen. He argued that Tito's pro-Soviet stance during the conference was motivated from a desire to buttress Khrushchev's position within the Politburo against hardliners opposed to improving relations with the West and against China, which was pushing for a major Soviet-US showdown. By supporting Khrushchev on the H-bomb testing, Tito was also earning credit in the Kremlin to be drawn upon against future Chinese attacks on his communist credentials. And most important, he was helping to strengthen the position of *the* Politburo member most disposed toward better relations with Yugoslavia. Nonetheless, while Tito was willing to make such verbal concessions to the Soviets, he had no intention of surrendering his independence.[66]

Kennan was compelled at the time of the Belgrade conference to register with the Yugoslav government his and Kennedy's displeasure with Tito's public statements. This along with some choleric articles and editorials in American newspapers caused Yugoslav spokesmen to protest that the Americans were overreacting as usual. Yet it appeared to Kennan that for all the commotion no real wounds were inflicted and some good for the cause of Yugoslav-US relations would result. "The experience," he informed Hamilton Fish Armstrong shortly afterward, "has been painful to us all; but it was necessary that the Yugoslavs should come to understand at some point, that the US, too, can be sensitive to political values and that there are limits to American patience with positions which . . . support the Soviet Union."[67] And, in fact, the political atmosphere was cleared somewhat, and the Yugoslav press adopted a more restrained line toward the United States than it had for a couple of years hitherto.

The Yugoslav news media did not abandon all of their traditional imprecations against the West, however; and, as he had tried vainly to do in Moscow, Kennan did not hesitate to take responsible communist editors to task. On more than one occasion he accused them of applying a double standard, whereby the major Western powers were criticized for every real or imagined injustice, but little was leveled against the Soviets for their sway in Eastern Europe, police practices, or censorship. Yugoslav moral support for all and sundry liberation movements in the Third World, as long as they were anti-Western, also annoyed Kennan: "What is really important to you is not the internal social and economic system but rather the extent to which countries participate in the general world revolt against the older countries of Europe and North America."[68] Why else, he asked rhetorically, were the Yugoslavs so little concerned with social democracy in the West and with countries that had evolved some genuinely socialist institutions, such as Norway, Denmark, or Britain, while being attentive to and demonstrative in supporting states without traces of socialism—at the time, Cyprus, India, Tunisia, Brazil. And whereas the editors of *Borba* attacked the United States for pursuing an imperialist policy in Vietnam, Kennan countered that the US was protecting the zone of liberty against totalitarianism.

Kennan's vexation with Yugoslav leaders and journalists for their periodic condemnations of the West was pointed enough, and his stout defense of the US on such occasions was appropriate. He was not, though, greatly worried by the long-term consequences of Yugoslavia's verbal excesses as Belgrade helped lead the nonaligned countries. Nor was he especially bothered by the fitful Soviet-Yugoslav detente that occurred in the early 1960s. It seemed to him that the Soviets were acknowledging, if belatedly, that Yugoslavia was an independent state and their outward show of deference guaranteed that Tito would never wish to subordinate himself again to Moscow. Under no foreseeable circumstances would the Yugoslavs be tempted to join the Warsaw Pact or link their economy to COMECON.[69]

Tito's support for the Soviets over Berlin and warmly received visit to Moscow (December 1962) indicated that the quality of Marxist sentiment and conscience was still powerful in parts of the Yugoslav leadership. Tito in particular was rooted in the emotions of Lenin's Russia, and it was understandable that he should want a reconciliation with people who had banished him from the political movement to which he had devoted his life. According to Kennan, Tito's assumed role in the nonaligned cause was motivated with a view to negotiating his revalidation as a proper Marxist with Russia: "He would do everything to rally around him the unaligned and uncommitted nations, so that when the decisive moment came in relations with Moscow, he would have something, namely the political support of a large unaligned bloc, which he could deliver, or deny, as the case might be."[70]

Though Tito naturally sought a type of emotional and intellectual intimacy with the Fatherland of Socialism, this did not translate into any desire of the Yugoslavs to duplicate Soviet domestic policy or identify too closely with Soviet diplomatic aims. Reconciliation did not mean resubordination. As Kennan told Lippmann, Tito perceived that a new situation had arisen by late 1960 which presented prospects for a final composition of differences with Moscow on terms favorable to him.[71] The Sino-Soviet rift and East-West tensions over Berlin had the effect of leaving Russia more isolated and vulnerable than it could afford. Khrushchev's acceptance of Tito as a good Marxist and leader of a people's Yugoslavia might win the Soviets a needed friend; at the minimum it would lead to rapprochement with an old adversary. Tito, meanwhile, could be expected to play his cards shrewdly. Hence, according to Kennan, his violently anti-colonial and anti-Western utterances in 1961 were directly linked to his relations with Moscow and had little to do with the "intrinsic value" of nonalignment in the Cold War as a solution to Yugoslavia's problems. This strategy, however, did not necessarily enjoy much support from many senior Yugoslav officials, who generally wanted stronger ties with the West and were discouraged that Tito's behavior at the Belgrade Conference had been so obviously tailored to make a good impression upon Khrushchev. To reduce American anxieties, Veljko Micunovic, the Yugoslav undersecretary of state, implored Kennan: "Don't let yourselves be overly influenced by the ideological views of a single aging individual. All this will pass."[72]

Unfortunately, the cumulative effect of Tito's rhetorical identification with some Soviet goals and with figures like Gamal Nasser grated on opinion in the United States and caused numerous people—notably in Congress—to reach erroneous conclusions about Yugoslavia and its relationship with the Soviet bloc. Kennan, to his credit and despite Tito's provocation, never lost sight of Yugoslavia's anomalous position in the Cold War that objectively suited US purposes. It was a communist country that not only lacked economic bonds with the Soviet Union, but traded mainly with the West; its well-equipped, well-trained army was not at Soviet disposal; its coastline was not available to Soviet navy ships or air bases that, if they existed, would have presented a potential threat for two NATO members—Greece and Italy—and would have been a source of continuous instability in the Adriatic and eastern Mediterranean; the Yugoslav population was free to travel abroad and enjoyed a more liberal culture and better standard of living than were possible elsewhere in Eastern Europe; most important, Yugoslavia's independence stood as an impressive example to other Eastern states of the benefits that awaited them should they defect from the Soviet fold.

Although Kennan did not use the term, the "Yugoslaviazation" of the Soviet bloc clearly held for him, just as it did in 1948, the most realistically favorable outcome to the problem of Soviet hegemony in Eastern Europe. He believed that in 1961 the full force of Yugoslavia's example was starting to work and that its economic and political successes were beginning to penetrate the consciousness of the other satellite regimes: the Yugoslavs were doing better competitively than they themselves. Kennan estimated that within the next three or four years the leaders of these states would, citing Belgrade's progress, demand greater leniency from the Soviet Union in organizing certain aspects of their social and economic life: "Now this, I think, will be a very useful thing because if Moscow lets them do it Moscow already weakens to some extent its moral authority over them, and if Moscow refuses to let them do it an additional strain is imposed on the relations between Moscow and the satellite governments."[73] In light of these considerations, Kennan hoped that the United States and its allies would not take too much umbrage at Tito's periodic outbursts against them and instead continue those policies that demonstrated that fruitful collaboration was possible between communist and capitalist countries. He hoped, too, that continued liberalization in Yugoslavia would help turn Third World states away from their infatuation with Soviet-style socialism.

Despite Kennan's efforts, Tito's apparent demarche to the Soviets resulted in a number of congressmen reviving the sterile, punitive concept that the United States should work to overthrow, or damage as much as possible, any communist state. Blithely ignorant of the advantages of trying to maintain good relations with Yugoslavia, Senator William Proxmire and Representatives Paul Findley, Wilbur Mills, and Charles Halleck managed in 1962 to steer legislation through Congress that denied future grants of financial aid to Yugoslavia, revoked its most favored nation (MFN) status, and interdicted the sale of spare parts for some antiquated warplanes previously purchased by the Yugoslavs.

Ironically, during the early period of Kennan's ambassadorship, the United States—on the basis of prior agreement with the Yugoslavs—had already dismantled the small American aid programs that had existed in Yugoslavia; they had served their function, and nobody sought to renew them. And Kennan, never a champion of financial assistance to countries outside of Western Europe and Japan, had been pleased to help supervise in the liquidation of these US programs. But he objected vehemently that Congress was committing a mistake in 1962 by pledging to deny aid in the future: such a denial effectively diminished future Yugoslav connections to US industry, hamstrung the chief executive who was prevented from granting aid under all circumstances, and served to insult the Yugoslavs who at the time were not even requesting outside help. As for the warplanes, they had never been part of any aid package, but had been purchased outright in dollars. Kennan protested that by denying the Yugoslavs the needed extra parts—electronic components necessary to fly the planes—the United States was reneging on a pure and simple business agreement.

The revoking of MFN was the most gratuitous and deepest injury from a Yugoslav perspective. At the time, Yugoslav exports to America totaled a mere $50 million per annum; trade going the other way was valued at $400 million. Even during the height of US-Yugoslav antagonism, 1946–1948, the Americans had not rescinded their trading arrangements with Belgrade—first stipulated in a US-Serbian commercial treaty in 1881. This repeal of MFN and the other congressional actions left the Yugoslav leadership bewildered and uncertain how to regain American favor. Kennan himself was unable to provide a satisfactory explanation or give guidance, but he did return to Washington in the summer of 1962 to lobby against these measures.

Unfortunately, Kennedy, though sympathetic to Kennan and his ideas about Yugoslavia, did not speak publicly on his behalf. The president was unwilling to risk his narrow margin of goodwill in Congress on a "fuzzy, unsatisfactory issue" that could easily develop into a major conflict with the majority of congressmen. His entire legislative agenda, including civil rights, would be jeopardized if it appeared that he appeased communism and was unwilling to defend freedom everywhere, including in the southern Balkans. Kennedy only expressed his support of Kennan in private and suggested that he write letters to the *Washington Post* and *New York Times,* try personally to persuade the relevant legislators of the folly of their thinking, and ask Eisenhower to exert whatever influence he could among the Republicans. All of these things Kennan dutifully did, but to no avail: Eisenhower got in touch only with Representative Walter Judd; Kennan's letters stirred no popular support; his attempt to intervene among the congressmen was ineffectual to the point of embarrassment.

Kennan was devastated by Congress's anti-Yugoslav actions. He felt personally rebuffed, and therefore obliged to leave his post in Belgrade after a decent interval of time had passed.[74] How, he wondered in the meantime, could Congress have persisted in its obstinate course against the advice of one who had been involved with the affairs of Eastern Europe for years and served personally in Yugoslavia?[75] As for Kennedy, Kennan was sore with the president for failing to support him publicly, but at the same time sympathized with his problems in dealing with Congress. In Kennan's retrospective judgment, the president's chief fault throughout his short term in office was his unwillingness to teach the American public basic facts about world politics.[76]

For a long period afterward, Kennan remained livid about those individual congressmen who had meddled so mindlessly in diplomacy. He ascribed to their actions two sets of disreputable, mutually reinforcing concerns. On the one hand, they had succumbed to the lobbying efforts of organized Croat-Americans, one of whom was the infamous Andrija Artukovic. A resident of southern California, he had been the interior minister of the Nazi-sponsored Croatian government of Pavelic during the time when it murdered hundreds of thousands of people.[77] In the early 1960s, his group's anti-Yugoslav lobbying in Congress was couched in anti-communist terms that found a receptive hearing among congressmen anxious to prove their mettle to constituencies back home. Indeed, Yugoslavia was valuable for those congressmen who wanted to pose tough against tyranny, but wanted to avoid reputations for recklessness. It served these elected officials, in Kennan's words,

> as a sort of target against which to demonstrate the depth of their own anti-communism . . . as something that they could use as a target for hostile sentiments with a view, then, to going back and confronting their electorate and beating their breasts and saying: "Boys, you see how anti-communist I was, I told them where to head in." It was harder to do this in the case of the Soviet Union because you are always apt to be asked: "Well, what is it you want? A war?" But in the case of Yugoslavia, everybody knew that Yugoslavia was not going to make war on us. And you could use this as a sort of symbol of communism and draw a certain political advantage . . . from it.[78]

By summer 1963, when Kennan tendered his resignation, US-Yugoslav relations had deteriorated to such a low point that some American merchants publicly burned items produced in Yugoslavia and canceled other orders. Stevedores on the east and west coasts refused to service ships bound to and coming in from Yugoslavia, and there emerged an informal, spontaneous boycott of Yugoslavia. In the autumn when Tito, his wife, and official party toured the eastern seabord, they were harassed by hostile demonstrators, some of whom wore Nazi uniforms. The demonstrations in Washington and New York resulted in the physical beating of three Yugoslav officials; some of the women were subjected to spitting, obscenities, and lewd gestures.

Kennan, called upon by Kennedy to act as part-time host and escort for Tito, was embarrassed by the treatment of the Yugoslav delegation, and his misgivings about his countrymen's lack of discipline and decorum seemed proven. This, combined with his experiences as ambassador in Belgrade, underscored for him how much at odds his public philosophy was with the one still dominant in Congress and in the broader population: only an inefficient and incoherent polity would permit small-minded politicians and some members of a specific ethnic minority to shape national policy in a fashion contrary to the larger American interest. Congress itself was a millstone, a disgrace, *the* institutional reason why US foreign policy could never be deft. "I am so shocked," Kennan declared, "at the evidence of the state of mind of our Congress at the present time that I am more than ever inclined to doubt that we should accept to play a role in foreign affairs against the background of all this provinciality and Philistinism."[79]

The corollary to this proposition was that the executive branch should enjoy sole responsibility for the formulation and execution of foreign policy. The nation, in turn, should be willing to exempt diplomacy from the alternating fortunes of political party and partisan cause: "The external affairs of the country should be given precedence over the internal ones, and . . . foreign policy should not be permitted to become a function of domestic-political convenience."[80] Kennan actually spoke these words in defense of the priority of foreign policy in 1964, the same year when Congress granted the president virtual exclusive prerogative in a critically important area of international policy: the Gulf of Tonkin resolution led to a monumental defeat in Vietnam that neither Kennan nor most other foreign policy experts could have imagined.

*   *   *   *

Kennan has been throughout his career an insistent advocate of diplomacy, which in its essence strives for compromise and common ground between governments and requires the steady application of tact and intelligence. Ironically, when assigned as his country's chief diplomat to two decidedly distinctive postings, Kennan failed. Admittedly, in the Soviet case, his official host was defiant and menacing, and overall Soviet-US relations were so deplorable that the likelihood was remote that any American ambassador could move relations forward. Still, it was Kennan who was unable to command the internal calm necessary to all successful missions. Disaster struck only when he departed from Talleyrand's sage advice: "Et surtout pas trop de zéle."[81]

Irrespective of his irritability and disgust for conditions in Moscow, Kennan never eschewed the principle of diplomacy as holding out the best alternative to the violent settlement of Soviet-US problems. Even in late 1952, he was able to rise above the circumstances of his personal calamity in Russia and affirm:

> We should be concerned to hold out at all times a real and plausible possibility of negotiation with respect to our major differences with the Soviet government. . . .

You can negotiate with enemies, as well as with friends. . . . If a possibility arose of easing [dangerous] situations by arriving at new arrangements to replace those already in effect, I would not hesitate to seize it, and I would negotiate with Soviet representatives coldly and brutally and in full acceptance of the fact that their ultimate aim is to ruin us and that they believe our ultimate aim is to ruin them.[82]

In the meantime, Kennan remained convinced that the United States, to prevail in the Cold War, had to overcome its social-political problems, of which McCarthyism was the most scandalous manifestation, and organize its domestic life along orderly lines.

A continuing lack of national political discipline combined with Congress's intellectual shallowness not only led to the undermining of Kennan's second ambassadorship and his resigning from Belgrade, but also confirmed him in his regret for the passing of an era when international negotiations were conducted beyond public surveillance; when the ambassadorial function was not regularly eclipsed by sensational summit conferences or usurped by parliaments; when reticence and civility were not superseded by public posturing and overblown ideological pretensions. In short, he yearned for the golden age of diplomacy which existed in the eighteenth century when the aristocratic few presumed to understand the national interest and agreed across state lines about the nature and necessity of the balance of power.

Whether or not Kennan would have performed especially well in the age of the great ambassadors, when transportation, communications, and the exigencies of international politics made the sovereign's personal envoy perforce a policymaker, must obviously remain an idle—if intriguing—question.[83] The Moscow episode does suggest a negative answer, however, and indicates contrary to Kennan's bias that the professional diplomat is not necessarily endowed on the basis of his accumulated experience abroad and specialized training with the requisite technique to pursue the diplomatic art successfully. Indeed, people from other walks of life can be, and have proven themselves to be, useful instruments for advancing American interests in distant capitals. Kennan himself has admitted that two political appointees under whom he served—Averell Harriman and Bedell Smith—were competent and compiled enviable ambassadorial records while in Moscow.[84] In fact, a perfectly reasonable case can be made that it was their broad executive experience in other demanding fields, their personal ties to the president, and their autonomy from the contraints and ingrained caution of the career Foreign Service that quickened their imagination, initiative, and overall effectiveness. Kennan, of course, has never accepted the central thrust of such an argument and has regarded Harriman and Smith as exceptions to the rule that professional diplomats should fill the top posts abroad.[85] As it was, in 1963 ethnic group politics in America and Congress's large influence over foreign policy were as repellent as ever to Kennan, were fatal to his Yugoslav ambassadorship, and drove him back to the academy and the safer realm of the scholar and critic.

III

ON THE SIDELINES

10

Cold War Critic

Kennan's major contribution to scholarship during the 1950s was his two-volume study of Soviet-American relations, 1917–1920, which remains to this day the definitive and most elegant treatment of its kind.[1] By the end of 1960, he had also published three volumes of lectures about past and current Soviet-US problems and a short, useful documentary history of Russian diplomacy from the Decree on Peace to the nonaggression pact with Nazi Germany.[2] In his career as historian and master of *belles-lettres* Kennan won acclaim abroad as well as in the United States. He was elected to the prestigious Eastman Visiting Professorship (1957–1958) at Balliol College, Oxford, and delivered the BBC Reith Lectures, which in previous years had been given by such notables as Oppenheimer, Toynbee, and Bertrand Russell. In the years subsequent to Balliol, Kennan studied and occasionally taught at Princeton and briefly at Harvard, returned for another sabbatical to Oxford, helped found the Kennan Institute for Advanced Russian Studies—named after his distant cousin and namesake—in Washington, DC, and continued his prodigious outpouring of articles and books. The latter included his memoirs, commentary on contemporary affairs, and an exhaustive diplomatic history about the origins of the First World War.[3]

Notwithstanding the meticulousness of his research and the measuredness of his judgments, Kennan's labors in the academic subjects of European diplomacy and the history of Soviet-US relations have been intended to serve more than conventional scholarly ends. His histories are also exercises in political edification and resonate with lessons for American readers. That Kennan has never let his attention stray far from the current scene of political and diplomatic events, even when preoccupied with exacting historical research and writing, is a fact readily apparent to partisan observers of both the left and right. In 1956, William Appleman Williams, one of the original proponents of Cold War revisionist historiography in the United States, attacked Kennan's first book about early Soviet-American relations as a mere requisitioning of facts and episodes designed to justify containment and gain the author's appointment—should Adlai Stevenson win the upcoming election—to secretary of state. Williams concluded that Kennan's study was not only an example of mediocre, self-serving history, but it also failed to exonerate him as a hawkish policymaker in the late 1940s. Another historian, Christopher Lasch, was more generous and more astute when he recognized (1962) in Kennan's same account of Russian-US affairs an extended plea for a restoration of the traditional techniques of professional diplomacy unencumbered by amateurs and parochial-minded politicians. In 1986, the neo-conservative political scientist Paul Seabury has criticized with some justification, though the tone was overly harsh, Kennan's chronicle of events leading to World War I as a barely disguised allegory of the political and military problems afflicting superpower relations in the late twentieth century.[4]

Kennan's *The Decision to Intervene* offers an excellent illustration of his approach to historical scholarship, as a warning from the past and implied rebuke of present trends. Following a detailed exposition of the motives for US intervention in the Russian civil war, a critical evaluation of the major protagonists, and an assessment of the long-term consequences on Soviet perceptions of a poorly advised, misconducted American policy, Kennan passed severe verdict:

> The reasons for this failure [intervention] of American statesmanship lay . . . in such things as the deficiencies of the American political system from the standpoint of the conduct of foreign relations; the grievous distortion of vision brought to the democratic society by any self-abandonment—as in World War I—to the hysteria of militancy; the congenital shallowness, philosophical and intellectual, of the approach to world problems that bubbled up from the fermentations of official Washington; and the pervasive dilettantism in the execution of American policy.[5]

These lines published in 1958 carried for Kennan enduring truths about the United States, and their pertinence could not be relegated to "dead situations" or the illusory aura of quaintness that inevitably envelopes the struggles and peoples of previous eras.[6] In fact, this passage could be applied directly to the conditions of political administration and foreign policy in Eisenhower's and Dulles's America.

Despite his success in commanding respect as an historian in the 1950s (against which Williams represented a distinct minority), Kennan's critique of and recommendations for US external policy were not everywhere well received. His proposed method, for example, of easing the strain of Cold War, as enunciated in his Reith Lectures, caused a storm of criticism to be visited upon him. Democrats and Republicans, West Europeans and Americans, friends and rivals took him to task for advancing ideas widely held to be unrealistic, dangerous, or impolitic. Upset by the abrasiveness and sometimes *ad hominem* arguments of those who disputed his advice (Acheson was especially cutting), Kennan nevertheless adapted well to his role as Cold War critic and at times seemed to welcome controversy. In contemplating what he might say over the BBC, Kennan admitted early in 1957 to Anna Kallin that practically everything he had written to date about contemporary issues had been in the nature of a polemic against what he regarded as erroneous views prevailing in the United States: "My stock and trade . . . has been the demolition of the prejudices and superficialities of my own countrymen, in their approach to international affairs generally and the Russian problem in particular. I fear I am a person who rouses himself to intellectual activity only when he is stung. The more outraged I become at the preposterousness of the things other people say, the better I do."[7]

Certainly it was with flair and enthusiasm that he cudgeled the bombast of the Eisenhower administration's "rollback," "liberation," "new look," and "massive retaliation." Still, Kennan's proposed alternative to the Republicans' conduct of Cold War, exemplified by his support of Adlai Stevenson in 1956 and embodied in his Reith talks, failed to commend itself either to the majority of his compatriots or the most influential segment of official opinion.

Eisenhower, Dulles, and Foreign Policy

Since the late 1960s, the foreign policy and overall quality of Dwight Eisenhower's presidential leadership have been subjects of renewed examination by a number of historians and political scientists, who have often been kinder in their evaluations than were their counterparts in the 1950s. Kennan's own view of Eisenhower as chief executive has been ambivalent and with the passage of time more sympathetic, but it has never accorded with the standard liberal notion that he was inept, bumbling, or extraordinarily maladroit in managing the affairs of state.[8] From early on, Kennan was impressed by Eisenhower's essential clarity of mind and expression. "He was a good talker," Kennan recalled in 1965, "and much more intelligent than he was given credit for being." To Kennan, the president was easily superior to every member of his cabinet in understanding international politics, except for Dulles with whom he was on a par. Also, Kennan, always susceptible to marks of civility, was charmed by Eisenhower's relaxed and gracious manner which he likened to European aristocracy: a conversation with the president "was just like talking to Queen Elizabeth. I mean, you came in and were well treated; he said interesting things."[9]

Yet, in Kennan's estimation, Eisenhower for all of his intelligence, practical experience, personal prestige, and political power could have made more of his high office than he did. One of his major faults was to indulge in a florid policy rhetoric that misled and confused the popular mind at home about the real substance of US international aims, sounded provocative to adversaries abroad, raised false expectations in Eastern Europe about future intervention by the West, and alarmed allies. Kennan knew that Eisenhower realized that a direct American challenge to the Soviet sphere of influence in Europe or attempt to rescue the subject peoples—for example, the Hungarians in 1956—would invite the catastrophe of a third world war. Instead, the Republican administration would have to follow the example of its Democratic predecessor and rely on a combination of political, economic, and limited defense measures to check the Soviet empire. Why not, therefore, drop the cant about "rollback" and "liberation"? Another of Eisenhower's faults, according to Kennan, was his unwillingness to condemn publicly Senator Joseph McCarthy and the entire phenomenon of fanatical anti-communism with which his name is associated. This failure, too, Kennan attributed to an unwarranted modesty or mysterious inability on the president's part to exercise the full power of his office and not, as some commentators have charged, to his being captive to reactionary businessmen and politicians supportive of McCarthy.[10]

In certain respects, Kennan also admired John Foster Dulles, as he was a well-informed secretary of state who combined his excellent formal training with unique experience.[11] Beneath their differences of style and temperament, Kennan suspected that he and Dulles shared "a great intimacy of thought" about foreign policy. He meant by this expression that Dulles understood that he must follow in practice—his public utterances about the immorality of containment and the need to replace it with "forward" and "positive" strategy aside—the line laid down by Kennan during his years on the Policy Planning Staff.[12] Still, his resentment of Dulles ran deep, and he held him responsible for much of the damage and demoralization suffered by the Foreign Service during Eisenhower's administration; the secretary was too craven and intimidated by right-wing elements within the Republican party to defend his department against the onslaught of McCarthy.

Horrified by Acheson's ineffectiveness in retaining bipartisan support and by the savageness of attacks against him and his policies, Dulles did embrace some unseemly measures to guarantee the support of reactionaries in Congress and elsewhere. His solicitude of such people indicated to Kennan that the secretary was opportunistic and lacked both principle and genuine idealism. Dulles never expressed any of "the discomfort and disgust that I think I would have experienced in playing up to these people," complained Kennan in 1967. "He was perfectly willing to do it and do anything that would really please them."[13]

The two men first clashed in 1950, when Truman, in a belated effort to save bipartisan diplomacy, appointed Dulles to devise the final version of the Japanese peace treaty. Contrary to Kennan, he advocated the indefinite retention of US troops in Japan, that country's rearmament, and its integration into the anti-Soviet coalition of Pacific states. Worse still was Dulles's reaction in 1950 to Kennan's suggestion that, if the majority of member states in the UN General Assembly favored China's admission to the international body, the United States should not block it. Dulles actually misrepresented Kennan's ideas on this matter in a leak to the press and charged that he was a dangerous person for *urging* the seating of the People's Republic of China and Taiwan's expulsion. This distortion of his views that had been confidentially expressed in a meeting with Acheson and other high-ranking State Department officials was a revelation to Kennan and raised for him "serious problems about the privacy of discussion among top [governmental leaders] in the presence of the policy advisor from the Republican Party."[14] Thus began Dulles's shabby treatment of Kennan, which culminated with Dulles's easing him out of the Foreign Service. As if designed to assure insult, neither Eisenhower nor Dulles notified Kennan in 1953 that his appointment as ambassador to the USSR was officially ended. In fact, it was through the news media that Kennan learned Bohlen would replace him as chief of mission in Moscow—though not until after a difficult confirmation hearing and an embarrassing performance by Dulles before the self-appointed congressional keepers of patriotism and conjugal propriety.[15] Only the friendly intervention of White House staffer Emmet Hughes resulted in

Eisenhower's sending Kennan a polite, albeit unexceptional, letter of commendation for his quarter-century of public service.[16]

Dulles's personal distaste for what he ridiculed as Kennan's "philosophizing" about international relations and his connection to the previous administration's foreign policy inclined the secretary—a naturally cold man, indifferent to the anxieties of most people—to be needlessly rude toward the preeminent expert on Soviet affairs in the government's employ. But despite Dulles's coarseness and mishandling of his personnel case, Kennan hoped and half expected for a number of years after his premature retirement to be recalled for service in either the diplomatic corps or State Department. Notwithstanding the satisfactions he discovered in academic life, he was saddened, and many administration critics were outraged, that he was not asked to return in any capacity. And in the meantime, he was infuriated by Dulles's management of the State Department, which included the bizarre use of loyalty boards and internal investigations of people who had accumulated records of honorable service.[17] It seemed to Kennan that Dulles, a fellow Presbyterian, lacked all trace of Christian sentiment or virtue: "Foster Dulles, in my deep conviction . . . did not have an ounce of real piety in his system; the hypocrisy was pure, as was the ambition. Both were unadulterated by any tinge of genuine Christian charity or obligation."[18]

Although the strain in their relations with Kennan grew steadily worse and their mistreatment of him became a scandal of sorts, Dulles and Eisenhower did not hesitate to seek his advice on matters related to the Soviet Union. At the same meeting (March 14, 1953) in which Dulles told him that there was no "niche" for him in the new Republican government, the secretary asked Kennan about the circumstances and possible consequences of Stalin's recent death. While unhappy and in a state of some bewilderment over his dismissal, Kennan replied well: the post-Stalin leadership was uncertain, but already seemed desirous of solving basic problems such as the final dispositions of Korea, Germany, and Austria; in any case, the Soviets were sensitive about the painful question—for them—of succession and might be more flexible than before in diplomatic negotiations.[19] Kennan must have felt somewhat vindicated a few months later when the Chinese, under Soviet pressure, signed a Korean armistice; and in 1955, while the "spirit of Geneva" was still palpable, the Soviet and Western governments agreed to withdraw their military forces from Austria and pledged to guarantee the country's neutrality.[20]

At the behest of the president, Kennan also participated in Operation Solarium, which ran through the summer months of 1953. The purpose of this secret exercise was to study the range of options available to the Eisenhower administration in its policy toward the USSR. Three teams consisting of Department of State, CIA, and military officers, and a smattering of academics, were created to examine and then advocate as forcefully as possible one of three strategies. Major General James McCormack, an air force expert on nuclear weaponry, led a group (Task Force B) that was instructed to promote the case for drawing a line between the Soviet Union and its clients on the one side and the United States and its allies on the other. According to this scheme, the Soviets would be warned that, if their armed forces or those of a country aligned with Moscow crossed over the line of global partition at any point, then the United States would respond with the full vigor of its might and at a time and place of its own choosing—in effect, the massive retaliation doctrine. Admiral R. L. Conolly directed another group (Task Force C) that argued for a "dynamic" policy aimed at "liberation" in Eastern Europe through a blend of psychological, political, economic, military, and paramilitary techniques. Conolly's team, then, took seriously Republican campaign rhetoric and sought means of implementing it. Presumably, a policy of unrelenting pressure against the Soviet bloc in Europe and against China would weaken the cohesion of international communism and eventually, perhaps in a decade, substantially diminish Soviet prestige and power.

Kennan led Task Force A, the mission of which was to make a case for the continuance of Truman-Acheson policy: maintaining current levels of US military strength, fortifying America's allies, discouraging the Soviets and Chinese from taking aggressive actions against Western positions, exploiting vulnerabilities as they appeared in the Soviet Union and its bloc, and avoiding the hazards of direct confrontation or war between the major powers. The underlying assumption here too was that these measures over time would force a retraction of the Soviet system abroad and reduce its power.[21] In the wake of Stalin's death and Georgi Malenkov's public endorsement of "peaceful coexistence," Kennan's group was especially confident in emphasizing traditional diplomatic prudence: patience and resolve were required to deflect Soviet ambitions; mass violence and other extreme measures should be discarded as unnecessary. In a reaffirmation of Kennan's long-held views, Task Force A declared:

> We must try to weaken Soviet power and bring about its withdrawal within tradi-
> tional Russian boundaries . . . rather than press for the destruction of the Soviet
> state, we should wait for an evolution in Soviet life and patterns of behavior which
> might follow from such a withdrawal. There is [a] possibility that the Soviet Union
> will change. There are signs of evolution, particularly in recent events.[22]

Kennan and his team also contended that, to avoid provoking Soviet suspicions or strengthening the position of hardliners in the Kremlin, West Germany should not be integrated into NATO or plans for the European Defense Community. Rather, the Republican administration should try to organize a final peace settlement that would provide for a unified, neutral Germany. And the question of German rearmament ought to be decided by the Germans alone and subsequent to a final peace treaty; any rearmament that might occur should be monitored by the United Nations, which should also be responsible for enforcing a set of regulations and restrictions designed to insure German moderation. Until the ratification of a formal peace, the current level of American troop and logistical commitments to West Germany should be maintained. As always, Kennan was fast to assert that Germany was the key to rehabilitating the vitality and sturdiness of society in Western Europe, notwithstanding the fears and wartime memories of French, British, and other NATO allies.[23]

In contrast to what he records in his memoirs, Kennan's team did not win the president's unqualified approval in the Solarium exercise. Eisenhower, with his instinct for compromise and consensus, was initially more impressed by the similarities than the differences among the three positions and stated that they should and could be made reconcilable—a most unlikely goal, thought Kennan and Conolly. Yet the president was obviously echoing Kennan when he exclaimed that the only outcome worse than losing a global war would be winning one and that, following a victory over Russia, the United States would not possess the faintest idea of how to reorganize or govern the Soviets.[24] Discussions from the Solarium project later influenced the writing of NSC 162 (September 30, 1953) which outlined basic policy toward Russia and did manage to incorporate some of the diverse ideas presented by McCormack, Conolly, and Kennan. It determined that the United States should retain its level of military power and work to weaken the political solidarity and security cooperation among communist states, but under no circumstances should it initiate military actions against the Sino-Soviet bloc. With the NSC's eschewing of provocative types of "liberation" Kennan did prevail over Dulles in the area of formal policy formulation.[25] But West Germany soon became a member of NATO (1954), an event that obliged the Soviets to create their own security organization, the Warsaw Pact, thereby making more intractable the division of Europe into two armed camps.

Dulles and Eisenhower never diverged in practice from Truman's course in Europe and were not tempted to risk a war by invading the Soviet zone of influence. When cracks appeared in the Soviet European empire in 1953 (East Germany) and in 1956 (Poland and Hungary), the United States merely registered ineffectual protests in the United Nations, and abstained from intervention—a wise move, but one that implicitly acknowledged the legitimacy of the European status quo. Although the Republicans continued to talk a tough line, they thus proved unwilling to match their rhetoric with action and forsook "forward" steps on behalf of the "captive nations." As for Kennan, he viewed Polish and Hungarian events in 1956 as the beginning of a prolonged process that would end in the collapse of Soviet hegemony in Eastern Europe. Sooner or later, he believed, the social pressures that triggered quasi-revolution in Warsaw and rebellion in Budapest would make themselves felt throughout Soviet-controlled Europe and cause immense, fundamentally insoluble difficulties for Moscow. And he predicted that the Soviet Union could never recover its position of undisputed leadership in international communism or again act as the sole interpreter of Marxism-Leninism.[26] Kennan did not go so far as such optimistic observers as Joseph Alsop or Walter Burnham, who reported in 1956 that full-fledged, Western-style democracies would shortly displace the communist regimes in Prague, Warsaw, and Budapest. Instead, he clung to his old interpretation that—as long as the Red Army occupied their lands—these East European capitals and their subjects would have to pass through a political limbo, featuring neither total Soviet domination nor meaningful freedom. This intermediate stage, moreover, could be hurried only with the direst results. "I am inclined to think," Kennan wrote in late October 1956, as events in Budapest approached their fateful climax, "that Titoism is a necessary [phase] in liberation and fear that the Hungarians are running tremendous risks in trying to force so many issues at once."[27]

That US policy during the most dramatic days of Hungarian resistance to the

Soviets was hamstrung by the Suez crisis struck Kennan as a double calamity. Not only did the United States fail to present the Soviet Union and Warsaw Pact with a solid Western front leading an international chorus of condemnation, but it fell to bickering with and taking actions against its two chief allies, Britain and France. Kennan wondered how the Eisenhower administration could have allowed relations among NATO's pillars to degenerate to such an extent that the alliance's entire design threatened to crumble. Why align the United States in the UN with the USSR and Arab nations? Why join their protests?[28] All likely answers to these questions confirmed for Kennan that the leadership in Washington was bankrupt.

He disagreed with Eisenhower and Dulles even more than he had with Truman and Acheson over the broad thrust of US foreign policy in the 1950s. The Republicans did not abate in the militarization of policy toward Russia, and their dependence upon nuclear weapons amounted in Kennan's view to an intensification of the most dangerous trends in American thinking about security. The Republicans were no more imaginative than Truman and Acheson in finding a workable solution to Europe's east-west division and repeatedly showed themselves unreceptive to proposals that might lead to a relaxation of Cold War tensions; the government seemed oblivious to post-Stalin changes in Soviet society that were transforming it from a totalitarian polity to a traditional, oligarchically run authoritarian state with which one could more easily negotiate.[29] Kennan also objected to Eisenhower's Far Eastern policy that continued the Democrats' practice of thwarting Japan from playing an independent role in the region and failed to take advantage of existing and potential problems between Russia and the People's Republic of China. The administration seemed sometimes lackadaisical, sometimes adventurous in its international policies, and Kennan puzzled over how long the United States could survive such erraticism during the Cold War.

Alternative Approaches to Cold War

Adlai Stevenson

To millions of American liberals in the 1950s, Adlai Stevenson commanded an abundance of respect and affection previously reserved only for Franklin Roosevelt. Against the garbled syntax of Eisenhower and the ponderousness of Dulles, against the ferocity of McCarthy and the rampant anti-intellectualism of the era, and against the unprecedented dangers of nuclear arms race stood Stevenson. Patrician by birth and intellectual by choice, he was eloquent and witty. And to his followers he seemed moved by an uncommon decency that promised a compassionate and worthy American future.[30] He became for his votaries the personification of liberal idealism and practically a cause in himself. Archibald MacLeish once credited the twice-defeated Democratic nominee for president with improving "the tone and temper of political life in the United States for a generation. [He] humanized the quality of international exchanges throughout a great part of the world. [He] enlightened a dark time."[31] Even Kennan, despite his visceral dislike of American politics and politicians, was drawn to Stevenson, campaigned for him in 1956, and served as co-chairman (a largely honorary position) of Stevenson's New Jersey election committee.

Kennan's participation in party politics before 1956 had been slight, as he recognized no real difference between the two major parties. Until the Eisenhower-Dulles years, he had consistently registered as a Republican; but, as he quipped to a journalist in 1956, Foster Dulles had made him into a Democrat.[32] Still, the point stands that the choice of party allegiance never mattered much to Kennan, and when there was talk and even a little action by the Democrats to run him for office—for Congress in the early 1950s, for the Senate in 1966—he made it plain that he could as easily have been approached by the Republicans. In any case, he preferred to spend his time as a professional historian rather than as an elected representative in Washington; besides, the tribulations and financial expenses of a political campaign seemed too daunting.

In essence, Kennan's peculiar brand of conservatism and academic tempera-ment inhibited him from playing a substantial role in practical American politics. Nevertheless, the intellectual and moral appeal radiated by Stevenson in 1956 and the possibility of his assuming the foreign policy portfolio in a Stevenson cabinet overcame, at least temporarily, Kennan's dislike for and traditional aloofness from partisan affairs.[33] He declined to join Stevenson's circle of excellent tutors, known collectively as the Finletter Group (which included Averell Harriman, John Kenneth Galbraith, George Ball, Arthur Schlesinger, Jr., Richard Musgrave, and Thomas Finletter), but performed important service as occasional consultant on foreign policy.[34] In this capacity, Kennan was also able to campaign against Eisenhower's and Dulles's approach to the Cold War and affirm an alternative strategy.

Kennan first exchanged ideas with Stevenson in 1954, by which time it was clear that he would make another bid for the presidency. They were of one mind about important policy issues: Dulles's ritualistic sacrificing of Foreign Service officers and State Department officials to the right wing of the Republican party; the unwise dependence of US defense policy upon the arsenal of nuclear bombs; the absurdity of the government's pledge to retaliate with strategic weapons against communist centers if Marxists somewhere in the world seized local power. Should this last possibility come to pass, the United States would lose the support of every ally, forfeit the regard of every neutral, and incur irredeemable moral odium. Kennan's words on the subject attained a level of conviction and lucidity that later made Stevenson exclaim that he wished he were as eloquent. In a letter to the former governor, Kennan warned:

> If we were to attempt to use the atomic bomb because—let us say—Italy might go communist in an election, we would be taking upon ourselves a most hideous moral responsibility for the sake of an extremely questionable issue. I cannot believe that our allies would bear with us in such an act of petulance. At best, the upshot could only be that we had earned for ourselves the horror and distrust of the world, had blasted the last foundations out from under our own system of alliances and interna-tional associations, and had inflicted limitless suffering on masses of people who had absolutely no sense of guilt and would have no means of knowing why this was done to them.[35]

By 1956, Stevenson was regularly seeking Kennan's advice—as he did that of Dean Rusk, Paul Nitze, Ben Cohen, and Robert Tufts—on international and security affairs.[36] He urged Stevenson to attack the Republican administration for being smug and boastful, and for behaving in a manner that frightened allies and encouraged enemies of the West to be impudent; particularly galling was Dulles's complacency as the US position in Asia weakened and the Atlantic pact exhibited signs of disintegration. Kennan also recommended, with personal feeling no doubt, that criticisms be redoubled against Dulles's inability to attract people of intelligence and character to the inner sanctum of foreign policymaking and his forsaking of the Foreign Service. To distinguish himself and his proposed government from the mediocrity of the Republicans, Stevenson should commit himself to reenlisting the best people for policy work: "If these people are not being used at present, it is not really for partisan reasons but because the security investigations were permitted to run wild and because the administration is temperamentally uncomfortable in the presence of people who like to use their minds."[37] Stevenson should also limit to a moderate degree the secretary of state's foreign travel (Dulles's excesses in this regard were legend and often lampooned by political cartoonists as well as by the Democratic opposition) and curtail the government's resort to Madison Avenue techniques of self-glamorization. In short, a Stevenson administration must restore dignity to the procedures of government and diplomacy. And a Democratic president should make evident from the outset that he would consult with people from beyond the California-Texas nexus—a region that in Kennan's demonology was synonymous with intellectual shallowness and cultural poverty. For public purposes Stevenson should attribute the defects of external policy under Eisenhower to the failure of his administration to understand the concerns of other nations and an undue emphasis on pleasing a domestic constituency imagined to consist mainly of individuals with the limited knowledge of a Senator William Knowland. The Democrats would replace amateurism and clumsiness with statecraft.

As for specific issues in foreign policy, Kennan was not very forthcoming because he recognized how quickly international circumstances could change and render irrelevant a candidate's most sober recent pronouncements. Kennan also felt diffident in advancing his views because he was removed from the daily study of current world affairs; he read the newspapers, but since his departure from government, he lacked detailed information and other means for making really helpful suggestions: "I think it dangerous to [volunteer] constructive answers to the many [diplomatic] problems unless one has been fortified by adequate staff work and complete information."[38] Yet he *was* willing to advise broadly on substantive matters. He said that Stevenson ought to attack the militarization of Eisenhower's rhetoric and Dulles's thought and that the Democrats should endorse with fullest enthusiasm a mutual Soviet-US moratorium on the testing of nuclear weapons. The administration must also be forced to defend the premise of its policy toward the neutral states: namely, that unless they were wholeheartedly with the West and against communism, then they were unsuitable for any kind of association with the United States. Regarding the Middle East, Kennan hoped that Stevenson would discontinue the Republican practice of unqualified support of Israel, a country that could easily become a stupendous political and military liability for the United States.[39]

Most of Kennan's recommendations, including some of his language, were incorporated into Stevenson's speeches on foreign policy. Yet however gladly he received Kennan's advice and made use of it, Stevenson did depart from it in two important respects. First, he went much further than the bilateral arms control favored by Kennan when he proposed (April 1956) in public that the United States take the moral lead and unilaterally desist from the further testing of nuclear weapons. Second, Stevenson took a strong stand on behalf of Israel, partly in order to insure the confidence and contributions of that mainstay of the Roosevelt coalition—Jewish voters.[40] The Stevenson-Kennan relationship was certainly strong enough to withstand differences over the arms race and the Middle East; Kennan had more than a grudging respect for Stevenson's attitude toward nuclear weapons and in subsequent years moved near it. But by the late spring of 1956, matters between the two men became very much more complicated due largely—from Kennan's perspective—to yet another instance of intrusion by mischievous ethnic concerns upon the American political process.

In May 1956, Congressman Thaddeus Machrowicz (Democrat-Illinois) complained to Stevenson that Kennan's position on a number of international issues was unacceptable to Polish-Americans of both political parties. Kennan was alleged to be resigned to the permanency of Soviet occupation in Eastern Europe. Instead of encouraging the satellite nations into thinking that they could revert in the near future to their interwar status of sovereign entities, Kennan lamely advocated waiting in the hope that the communist governments in Moscow, Warsaw, Prague, and elsewhere would evolve in the direction of greater liberalism. Thus Machrowicz misunderstood Kennan's rather subtle ideas about Eastern Europe and portrayed them as something equivalent to surrender. The congressman was so indignant by what he took to be Kennan's position that he declared himself unable to campaign for Stevenson until the candidate provided a satisfactory clarification of his views and of his relationship to the appeaser Kennan. The congressman warned Stevenson: "I can assure you that any implication that [Kennan's opinions] have your approval, tacit or expressed, would lose for you the vast majority of votes of Americans of Polish descent and of all others who have roots of forefathers in any country behind the Iron Curtain."[41]

Stevenson's response was pusillanimous. He told Machrowicz privately that Kennan was not a member of his staff and that he had not talked to him during the campaign. From a technical standpoint, both statements were true, but they were also misleading. Kennan was never among those most intimate with Stevenson and was not a member of the headquarters staff, but he was certainly part of Stevenson's official circle—in New Jersey—and although he had not recently talked in person with Stevenson, they had corresponded at length about foreign policy matters, and Kennan sometimes did speak with Stevenson staffers, for example with Finletter.[42] Stevenson also tried to disassociate himself (in a letter to Machrowicz and in public statements) from Kennan by emphasizing that he was fully cognizant of and moved by "the tragedy of Eastern Europe" and that he rejected the status quo on the continent as constituting anything like a final arrangement. Furthermore, Stevenson protested, he was not responsible for Kennan's ideas, especially not those incompatible with his own.[43]

Kennan was angered and insulted by Stevenson's disavowal of him, and thereafter relations between the two men, though respectful, became noticeably more reserved. Kennan did continue to support Stevenson through 1956, and offered ideas for statements about foreign policy and for his acceptance speech at the Democratic convention.[44] Following the November elections, Stevenson and Kennan were occasionally in touch. Stevenson congratulated him on his Reith Lectures, and he expressed doubts in 1960 to Stevenson about John Kennedy; but they were not close and it was only the passage of years (after Stevenson's death, 1965) that soothed Kennan's disappointment over the Machrowicz episode.[45]

The Reith Lectures

Stevenson's defeat in November 1956 meant that Kennan had not the slightest chance to serve in any government capacity for at least four more years. And he would, therefore, have to express his ideas about foreign policy and alternatives to the Cold War from unofficial forums. His most far-reaching advice was contained in his six Reith talks, which he delivered over the air-waves of the BBC in the late autumn of 1957. Only his "X article" has attracted greater attention over the years; and, like that essay, his Reith Lectures have remained a topic of debate among critics.

Kennan's delivery of the Reith broadcasts coincided with a crucial meeting in Paris of NATO representatives who were deliberating on whether or not to deploy tactical and theater nuclear weapons on the European continent. This question had acquired urgency for Western security planners because in August 1957 the Soviets had successfully launched a rocket into outer space: Sputnik raised the likelihood that the Soviets could soon equip similar rockets with nuclear warheads capable of striking North American and West European targets. To many people in the United States (and Kennedy made it a prominent theme in his 1960 presidential campaign) Sputnik indicated that the strategic balance had shifted to Soviet advantage and the United States had fallen behind in the "missile race."

What was to be done? Kennan's radio talks—all of them widely reprinted and appearing in publications such as the *Daily Telegraph, Washington Post,* and *Neue Zürcher Zeitung*—touched on some of the implications of this question and were followed by politically literate audiences in Britain, France, West Germany, the United States, and the Soviet Union. By contrast, Dulles, Konrad Adenauer, Harold Macmillan, and other leaders of the Western alliance seemed strangely mute on Sputnik and its possible consequences. And for a time, news coverage of Kennan's Reith remarks dwarfed all public reports about NATO talks in Paris. In the words of one close observer in 1957, Robert McKenzie of the London School of Economics, "At the Palais de Chaillot, where the NATO conference was being held, it was literally true that the nineteen-hundred journalists seemed to be spending more time discussing the arguments advanced in this year's Reith Lectures, than in discussing any of the public speeches . . . of the leading statesmen present."[46] In a short period of days Kennan's talks caused a debate that Lippmann labeled "historic" in its dimensions.[47]

In fact, it was only the third and fourth of Kennan's Reith Lectures that aroused controversy. His first two, dealing with Russian economic developments and the world view of Soviet leaders, were perfectly sound, but basically innocuous and politely received. He explained that the USSR's economic recovery from the war surpassed anything that he had thought conceivable a decade earlier. The Soviet achievement, however, should not be a cause for alarm in the West where the rate of economic production and earned spending power was also impressive. Above all, and contrary to popular depictions and to the assumptions underlying US foreign policy, the Cold War was not really a zero-sum contest between East and West. Kennan called for "greater detachment and reservation on our part toward internal happenings in Russia. Their world is not our world; their future need not always be the diametrical opposite of our own; we have neither reason to quake before the spectacle of Soviet economic progress, nor to crow over the fact that the Soviet Government faces political dilemmas at home."[48] Regarding recent political events in Moscow, he noted that Khrushchev's position within the party was stronger following Georgi Zhukov's expulsion from the Politburo, but not absolutely secure, as relations in the top leadership were still unsettled. The relationship between leaders and led in Russia was also ambiguous and under stress as a result of new sanctions against political and cultural liberty—in 1958, the Soviet government would make it impossible for Boris Pasternak to accept the Nobel Prize. Kennan mentioned the Kremlin's congenital suspicion of outside influences and its unyielding opposition to the Western world. And he pressed his pet themes: old-fashioned diplomacy and Western anti-propaganda and informational programs were apt to produce desirable outcomes in the Soviet-US field. Any reliance, though, on the United Nations, summit meetings—Kennan was probably thinking of Geneva 1955—or sensational sounding accords would prove futile.

He delivered another lecture (number five) concerned with Soviet-US rivalry in the Third World and expressed his conviction that the West could afford a more relaxed attitude than hitherto exhibited toward Soviet meddling in Asia and Africa. The Cold War would not be decided in territories characterized by marginal industrial development and political immaturity. In his sixth talk, he urged the NATO nations to remember that the military balance was only one aspect of the Cold War for the Soviet Union and its adherents abroad. If the West was to prevail, it must cultivate its political institutions, strengthen its social cohesion, and otherwise improve the moral and material quality of its internal life. Local communists, Soviet operatives, and Soviet propaganda would exploit any failure of the West to satisfy its own standards of conscience and culture. If, however, the member states of NATO were resilient and confident they should not block the path to a future settlement between East and West.

Only those two talks that related directly to European security sparked criticism of Kennan. In one, "The Problem of Eastern and Central Europe," he made public his ideas—first expressed in 1948–1949 to senior State Department officials—on how to remove the lines of partition cutting through Germany and Europe. He had argued, it will be recalled, with Acheson and others that the continent's division would deepen if Britain and the United States failed to advance proposals for a withdrawal of Soviet and Western forces from Germany. And the countries falling within the Soviet zone would continue indefinitely in their nebulous status as part captives and part wards of Moscow. Radio listeners in 1957 heard Kennan explain that the existing division of Europe between the Soviet Union and Anglo-US power was both abnormal and dangerous. Abiding popular resentment in Eastern Europe of Soviet power constituted an important source of instability that surely would lead to new crises—of the 1956 Hungarian variety. These might then entangle the United States and its European allies. At the minimum, another mass revolt in the East (or a new crisis over Berlin) would present the West with the dilemma of either intervening, thereby risking a third world war with all of its unprecedented horrors, or standing by again as a helpless observer. Kennan feared that one more instance of Western passivity would result in East European despondency over the unshakability of Soviet domination, stagnation of their cultural and political life, and permanent forfeiture of their potential contributions to civilization. The West's only solution was to organize a total Soviet military evacuation of the satellite states and of East Germany. But how to orchestrate the Red Army's departure?

Kennan proposed, as he had years earlier, that Anglo-US and Soviet forces be retired simultaneously from the center of Europe. The West should seize the initiative by publicly suggesting this solution to Moscow. If the Soviets balked at the *quid pro quo* then they would bear the onus of destroying a European settlement. Not only would a Soviet veto of the plan generate protests among Western publics, it would also further antagonize the peoples in the satellite states, practically all of whom looked forward to the Red Army's withdrawal from their territories. Thus additional strains would be placed within and among Warsaw Pact countries that would help undermine the alliance's solidity. If the Soviets could be persuaded that a mutual East-West retreat from Europe was compatible with Soviet security and political interests, then Europe proper might, at last, be allowed to evolve new institutions and interconnections leading to federation. Europe might eventually return to an important position in global political life. As for the German problem, whose resolution would have to be concomitant with a European settlement, Kennan expected that a reasonable expedient could be devised.

Following Soviet and Anglo-US evacuations from Europe, Kennan held that Germany could be allowed to reunite along political lines acceptable to the German majority. But instead of aligning itself with either Warsaw or NATO—an obviously odious prospect for the alliance deprived of German strength and resources—Germany would accept restraints on its freedom to shape its military and diplomatic policies. In other words, it would adopt, and the great powers would respect and help guarantee, a neutral position in the Cold War. As to a NATO deprived of West Germany's military forces and a united Germany forbidden from attaching itself to a Western system of defense—contrary to what most Germans would prefer—Kennan offered that the alliance depended for its success on a community of spiritual and cultural values, from which Germany would never be alienated. Western Europe, in any case, was not threatened by an imminent Soviet invasion, and those people who were fixated on a security threat emanating from the East should appreciate that the

West's geo-strategic position would enjoy new advantages after the Red Army had left its emplacements west of the Oder-Neisse and, later, west of the Bug.

Kennan hoped that the recomposition of a united, independent Germany would not frighten people. He argued that contemporary Germany was in a period of transition and one could make a safe wager that the younger generation of Germans, if accorded guidance and respect by the West, would assume a responsible, peaceful international role. Once more, then, he asserted that the memories and emotions of the recent past should not deny to Germany an honorable return to Europe.

Kennan's other controversial Reith talk, "The Military Problem," dealt with problems connected to the nuclear arms race and contained an unorthodox suggestion for enhancing West European security. He began by repeating his oft-expressed view that nuclear weapons represented a radical danger to humanity and that their use in wartime would not serve worthwhile political ends for any belligerent, including the USSR. He went on to say that widespread belief in the inevitability of a Soviet-US war and brisk preparation for it by Moscow and Washington meant that authentic steps must be taken to avert a nuclear disaster. And in the event of large-scale international violence, measures must be in place beforehand that would limit hostilities to a level commensurate with the integrity of the gene pool and natural environment. In the absence of such measures, the chance that future generations could enjoy physical health or contribute to civilization would be negligible.

Although Kennan believed that Britain and the United States ought to retain their levels of nuclear force as a deterrent until diplomacy and agreements with the USSR had insured other protection, he opposed all increases in the numbers, variety, delivery speed, and destructive power of Western strategic weaponry. And he opposed as in vain the different schemes then being discussed that sought to protect Western societies from nuclear attack. "Are we to flee," he asked, "like haunted creatures from one defensive device to another, each more costly and humiliating than the one before, cowering underground one day, breaking up our cities the next, attempting to surround ourselves with elaborate electronic shields on the third, concerned only to prolong the length of our lives while sacrificing all the values for which it might be worthwhile to live at all?"[49] He denounced as especially objectionable the notion then entertained by NATO governments that the deployment of nuclear weapons in Europe would add depth and flexibility to Western defense.

Animating NATO discussions in Paris, the overriding desire of Western states was to be freed from their heavy reliance on long-range strategic defense and the multimegaton hydrogen bomb; the wisdom behind smaller, discriminating weapons was that they could limit the physical scope of any war and enable NATO to use a variety of graduated responses to Soviet aggression in Europe. But to Kennan the premises justifying tactical and theater nuclear weapons were illusory: any pre-hostilities understanding between NATO and Warsaw about the destructiveness of weapons to be used and the sort of sites to be struck was bound to disappear in the extremity of war. The cultivation, meanwhile, of smaller weapons would have the effect of lowering the psychological inhibitions of military planners, and populations generally, against ever using nuclear weapons and increased the prospect that some Western policymakers would deceive themselves into believing that another

European war would not prove disastrous, but could yield positive results. Kennan condemned any European conflict fought with nuclear arms of any size as something sickening to the imagination:

> Can we really suppose that poor old Europe, so deeply and insidiously weakened by the ulterior effects of the two previous wars of this century, could stand another and even more horrible ordeal of this nature? Let us by all means think for once not just in the mathematics of destruction—not just in these grisly equations of probable military casualties—let us rather think of people as they are; of the limits of their strength, their hope, their capacity for suffering, their capacity for believing in the future. And let us ask ourselves in all seriousness how much worth saving is going to be saved if war now rages for the third time in a half-century over the face of Europe, and this time in a form vastly more destructive than anything ever known before.[50]

Kennan also warned that, even if East-West violence never occurred in Europe, Anglo-US deployment of nuclear weapons on the continent (presumably followed later by the French and West Germans) would produce consequences contrary to a negotiated settlement to the problems of Germany and European partition. Russia would be more intent than ever on preserving its East European buffer and would probably increase its conventional military and nuclear presence therein. In addition, predicted Kennan, with the proliferation of nuclear arsenals in Europe any minor international difficulty on the continent would immediately, almost automatically, attain crisis proportions.

In the event that NATO did drop its plans to introduce tactical and theater weapons and Anglo-US and Soviet armies left the continent's center, Kennan confessed that the West Europeans would have to accept increased responsibility for their security while continuing formal links of alliance to the English-speaking powers of the Atlantic. He also urged the Europeans to forswear development of atomic weapons and strengthen their nonnuclear forces. On this last point, he was not thinking primarily of large conventional forces of the World War II variety, designed to resist an outright Soviet invasion. He repeated that such an invasion was extremely unlikely, as the Soviets did not want to risk actions that might jeopardize their post-1945 achievements in rebuilding and salvaging. And by concentrating too much on an alleged Soviet military threat, the West Europeans were neglecting the more urgent political danger posed by the USSR. The fundamental security problem in France, Italy, West Germany, and the Low Countries, said Kennan, was intertwined with "the internal health and discipline of the national societies, and of the manner in which they [are] organized to prevent the conquest and subjugation of their national life by unscrupulous and foreign-inspired minorities in their midst."[51] To counter this threat, he recommended that the Europeans maintain some standing formations of conventional military might, but shift their security emphasis to developing paramilitary or territorial militias of the Swiss type. Though their primary mission would be of an internal police nature—as it was within the domestic sphere that Soviet communism was most likely to make inroads against Western societies—these paramilitary forces would also be prepared to resist, at a rather low level, overt Soviet aggression and, in case of occupation by the Red Army, would form the nucleus of an organized civil resistance movement. Indeed, the training of the paramilitary forces would emphasize their function as the core of a civilian-based defense. Even if British and American forces remained in Europe, Kennan suggested that serious thought be given to adopting this feature of Swiss defense policy.

It had much to recommend, according to him. First, it was inexpensive. The cost of maintaining small-scale, lightly equipped military units would come at a fraction of expenditures for current military establishments. Second, the deterrent value of such an organization should not be underestimated. Would the Soviets really want to pay the costs in blood and treasure of ruling a prickly Western Europe in which the occupation of each village, bridge, and country crossroad meant another Red Army casualty? Kennan claimed that every nation could confront the USSR with a defiance that combined elements of guerrilla warfare and uninterrupted political-civilian resistance. In effect, Western societies could say:

> Look here, you may be able to overrun us, if you are unwise enough to attempt it, but you will have a small profit from it; we are in a position to assure that not a single Communist or other person [inclined] to perform your political business will be available to you for this purpose; you will find here no adequate nucleus of a puppet regime; on the contrary, you will be faced with the united and organized hostility of an entire nation; your stay among us will not be a happy one; we will make you pay bitterly for every day of it; and it will be without favorable long-term political prospects.[52]

In Kennan's opinion, any NATO country in Europe militarily and politically organized to give meaning to the passage just quoted would no longer need British or American garrisons or nuclear weapons to deter a Soviet invasion. An essentially ungovernable zone in Europe, countless miles from Moscow and requiring constant policing, was repellent to Soviet appetite.

Senator Kennedy told Kennan that, although there were portions of his Reith Lectures with which he disagreed, they were wonderfully lucid and pervaded by thoughtful judgments. Stevenson was not entirely convinced by the disengagement proposal, but was persuaded Kennan's talks had been significant. Oppenheimer was most enthusiastic and "deeply moved" by the insights conveyed in "The Military Problem." Kennan was naturally encouraged by these and other communications of support.[53] But they constituted a small minority view.

A broad range of political leaders, academics, journalists, and some of his personal friends—Bohlen for one—disagreed in the strongest terms with his recommendations about mutual withdrawal, Germany, and the militias defense. Led by Acheson, Kennan's most influential critics included Dulles, Selwyn Lloyd (the British foreign secretary), Heinrich von Bretano (the West German foreign minister), Donald Tyerman (editor of *The Economist*), Dennis Healey, Sidney Hook, Carl Friedrich, Arnold Wolfers, Richard Lowenthal, Joseph Alsop, Raymond Aron, and Walter Lippmann. In newspapers, television and radio interviews, numerous public forums, and scholarly journals, Kennan's ideas were subjected to review and found wanting: the Soviets could not be trusted to abide by a solemn pledge of mutual withdrawal and sooner or later following joint East-West evacuation, the Red Army would return to its previous encampments in Germany and from there exert greatly increased power against the rest of Germany and Western Europe. The paramilitary idea, even if by Kennan's admission not yet fully developed, was foolish and did not warrant further investigation. The Swiss case was unique and could not be used to generalize about the more complicated problems involving NATO's security. The fact was that Warsaw Pact forces enjoyed a numerical and logistical advantage over their NATO counterparts, which therefore needed buttressing by acquisition of theater weapons, not weakening by a shift to territorial militias and quixotic civil resistance strategies. That Kennan even entertained such notions was conclusive evidence to Acheson that the former director of Policy Planning had "never grasped the realities of power relationships," but took "a rather mystical attitude toward them." "Disengagement" was just a euphemism for isolationism, that most dangerous and discredited of past US policies.[54]

Protests were also raised—and here the Europeans were conspicuous, especially the French intellectual eminence Aron—that Germany united, independent, and neutral presented an uncertain future. Not only would NATO be deprived of West Germany's military contribution, which was already considerable and expected to grow within the next few years, but from a general European standpoint an integrated, resurrected Germany provoked fear. Kennan's reassurances about the younger generation of Germans, the physical and moral demolition of the Nazis, and the undisputed legitimacy of the Bonn regime were insufficient to reassure millions of Frenchmen, Belgians, Dutch, Scandinavians, Poles, Russians, and others harboring vivid memories of German invasion and occupation. A divided Germany, with its larger and more important part embedded within a Western framework, was preferable to most Europeans on either side of the East-West partition than the imponderables inherent in a single German entity. Might it one day press irredentist claims against Poland, Czechoslovakia, or France, or in other ways become a center of jealousy, rivalry, and unrest as in the past? The international system in 1957 was working reasonably well with a divided Germany and the existence of a clear line demarking the Soviet and Anglo-US spheres of influence; German energies were confined at a tolerable level, and the European balance of power enjoyed a geographical clarity conducive to international stability. And, despite the cost to human values and the spectacle of Hungary crushed in 1956, a Soviet-imposed peace in Eastern Europe was better than throwing open a Pandora's box stuffed with the resentments, ambitions, and illusions of grandeur that still excited the imaginations of people living in the area encompassed by the Warsaw Pact. In summation, Europe as a whole was stable under the international regime organized by the two extra-European powers, and that was preferable to the politically fluid—potentially explosive—condition that would arise if Kennan's proposals were adopted. As Aron pronounced, "The partition of Germany [and Europe] is unnatural but it leaves no room for ambiguity."[55]

Only the Soviet leadership seemed to endorse Kennan's viewpoint. In early December 1957, Nikolai Bulganin offered Chancellor Adenauer a deal whereby, in exchange for withdrawing Soviet troops from East Germany and the other states of Warsaw, British and American forces would leave the continent. The government in Bonn promptly rejected the Soviet demarche and did not, unlike Kennan, see it as a signal that the Russians were prepared to enter into negotiations aimed at achieving significant agreements.[56]

Kennan was taken aback both by the high level of interest in his lectures and by the intensity of attacks against them. His initial response was one of nervous exhaustion and he was overcome by sinus infection and a resurgence of duodenal ulcers, all of which required a period of hospital convalescence. While recovering from his physical maladies, he also nursed hurt feelings and reflected upon his critics in a spirit and idiom worthy of Henry Adams:

> Seldom can a speaker ever have made himself the beneficiary of a more impressive volume of instruction than did the one who ventured in the autumn of 1957 to share with the listening public of the BBC . . . some of his ruminations and misgivings about the present state of world affairs. From quarters too numerous to recount . . . reproof, correction and wise instruction have been heaped upon his head; his nose has been sternly rubbed in his errors; the nature of the true light, as seen . . . by each of his critics, has been laboriously expanded for his benefit. In the ranks of this anxious chorus his friends, alarmed and indignant, have stood in first place. . . . Only a person with the self-confidence and insensitivity of the true fanatic could fail to emerge the wiser from so intensive and elevated a course in world affairs.[57]

In a defense reminiscent of his explanation of the "X article," Kennan was soon claiming that had he had more time and flexibility than allowed by six short lectures delivered over the radio medium, he would have better refined his ideas and preempted many of the critics. He did concede, somewhat disdainfully, that his lectures had underestimated the insecurity felt by most West Europeans who in recent years had allowed themselves to become addicted to the American military presence on the continent. He had passed too lightly over the widely perceived hazards of a united Germany, but was nevertheless disappointed to realize that the European idea and Germany's future were still hostage to 1939–1945. Yet Kennan held to the core of his ideas and in the years since the Reith broadcasts has periodically tried to advance them publicly. In 1959, as a new crisis in Berlin worsened, he told readers in *Foreign Affairs* that elements of a decent compromise in Europe and Germany still existed: American statesmen should push for mutual East-West withdrawal and devise a strong conventional supplement to NATO's nuclear weapons. In the 1960s, he warned that the continued divisions of Germany and Europe were bound to bear unforeseen, ominous consequences. And in the mid-1980s, he endorsed the similar, if more refined, ideas of the scholar/activist Gene Sharp about civilian resistance in Europe as a means of discouraging Soviet aggression. In the meantime, he has never hesitated to express his displeasure with those people (in 1957–1958) who either misunderstood or deliberately distorted his views and has sought to reassure friendlier critics—for example, Louis Halle and Hans Morgenthau—that nothing in the Reith talks should be interpreted to mean that he advocated unilateral Anglo-US withdrawal, desired a disarmed NATO, or thought the West alone should abandon its nuclear deterrent.[58]

On balance, Kennan's ideas about West European security and Germany's future were uneven. On the one hand, he was persuasive—as were numerous

American analysts of the day, such as Acheson, Henry Kissinger, and Albert Wohlstetter—in pointing to the dangers inherent in the massive retaliation doctrine and in stressing the need for promoting varied and discriminating means of responding to Soviet actions. He was also perfectly correct to challenge as erroneous a putative large-scale Soviet offensive against NATO. Despite their success with Sputnik, the Soviets had neither the military capability nor the political will to seize Western Europe in the late 1950s. Khrushchev's government was having difficulties aplenty in administering Soviet control in Eastern Europe and could not possibly be enthusiastic about annexing additional millions more troublesome Europeans. Besides, any such Soviet effort would trigger a violent Anglo-American response, regardless of whether or not British and US troops were stationed in Europe, which would cause damage to the USSR far beyond anything experienced in World War II, in excess of any sacrifice acceptable to the Kremlin leadership. Even if fighting should break out in Europe but did not escalate to the nuclear level—the worst situation from the standpoint of Western military planners who feared that in a conventional war their positions would be overwhelmed by enormous armies from the East—there was no reason to assume that Warsaw forces would necessarily defeat NATO. True, the Soviet-led Warsaw Pact possessed, as it does today, more soldiers, more guns, more planes, and more tanks than NATO. But Warsaw did not enjoy a three to one numerical superiority in these categories, that ratio of offense to defense usually needed to assure a successful attack against technologically advanced, well-entrenched forces.[59] In addition, the leading element of the Warsaw Pact, the Red Army, was burdened by a dual mission. Soviet forces were not just aimed against the West. Then, as today, the regimes of most East European nations depended for their survival on the presence of the Soviet army. In effect, the Red Army prevented Moscow's East European empire from disintegrating and to a large extent Soviet soldiers (consider Hungary) functioned as occupation troops charged with maintaining order and Soviet preeminence. Finally, if full-scale fighting erupted in central Europe between NATO and Warsaw, questions remained about the reliability of Russia's so-called East European allies. Would they risk their destruction for the Soviet Union? Would they obey a Soviet high command? Might they declare neutrality? Might they even rebel? Nobody, of course, could answer these questions with certainty in the 1950s, but they were troubling for the Soviets and were undoubtedly taken into account by strategists in Moscow and inclined them to caution.

On the other hand, not all of Kennan's ideas were soundly based. His militia concept, no matter how preliminary or tentative his thoughts on the subject, was unrealistic and deserved rejection. It required a level of social discipline and political coordination in and among West European states that was extreme and impossible to achieve in any mass democracy. It also did not rest on any record of experience, the recent European war having provided much counter-evidence to its feasibility or probable success. The entire spectrum of resistance activities in Nazi-occupied lands, from nonviolent disobedience to partisan warfare, contributed little to the defeat of German arms and ambitions and typically led to fearful reprisals by the *Wehrmacht* and other Nazi organs against local civilian populations. Whether a

Soviet army of occupation would have conducted itself with more self-restraint in the bitter environment of a hostile population and various forms of low-level combat was certainly open to debate. The Red Army's war record of conduct, though, in mistreating Polish POWs (Katyn) and, later, German civilians was not reassuring; from the perspective of the late 1980s and the war in Afghanistan, there is no doubt that the Soviet army is capable of acting cruelly in policing foreign peoples. Kennan himself had observed during World War II that civil societies could not muster effective resistance against the organized might of a modern army (see Chapter 4). And that Switzerland was not overrun by the Germans during the war had nothing to do with the organization or deterrent power of Swiss defense forces. Rather, German diplomatic and espionage purposes were served by preserving Swiss neutrality and freedom. Ultimately, the success of Swiss independence from Germany depended on the great victories won by the Red Army and later the Anglo-US air and land forces. Had Germany prevailed in 1939–1945, nothing would have prevented Switzerland's eventual surrender and incorporation—the civilian militias aside—into the Third Reich's empire.[60]

The bulk of informed opinion in the West rejected Kennan and agreed with Dulles and Acheson when they urged that NATO equip itself in Europe with nuclear weaponry adequate to deter Soviet attack or coercion, thereby maintaining the balance of power; at the same time, NATO's conventional forces should be strengthened as a way of decreasing its dependence on weapons of mass destruction. From its position of comparative strength with the Soviet Union, the United States could later initiate negotiations aimed at establishing a nonnuclear zone in Europe. The success of the Dulles-Acheson line and the introduction of tactical and theater nuclear weapons to NATO in Europe did, of course, leave unresolved the problems of Germany and a divided continent. But here, too, Kennan was unrealistic to imagine that many European nations would view Germany's reunification with composure a mere dozen years after the defeat of Hitler. Only the gradual disappearance of the wartime generation and a collective fading of memory in Europe permitted (in the 1980s) the question of Germany's future as a single political entity to become an acceptable subject of political debate in the Federal Republic—and even then there was hesitation and embarrassment. As for Kennan's concern that the peoples of Eastern Europe would become demoralized in the face of indefinite Soviet domination, it was highly exaggerated. Instead, a type of Titoism, deeper than any envisioned by Kennan in the 1940s or early 1950s, has taken root—cultural and consumer in Hungary, diplomatic in Romania, spiritual in Poland—which is not easily susceptible to Soviet dictate. Indeed, one can only be impressed that the states of Eastern Europe today, which perforce are communist and call themselves allies of the USSR, enjoy varying degrees of independence from Soviet foreign and domestic policies. Greater variation, not abject uniformity, has been the rule in post-Stalinist Eastern Europe. Like Dulles's touted "liberation" policy, Kennan's proposed mutual withdrawal, lacking, by the way, any provision for a gradual phasing out of Soviet and Anglo-US forces from Europe, was too impatient and premised on a logic contrary to the longer time required for fundamental, nonviolent changes in Europe's international power relationships.

Anti-Communism in America

In his opening Reith talk, Kennan reiterated his conviction that the real rivalry between the United States and Russia was not military or diplomatic in nature. Rather, the contest would be decided by the country that first solved its social and economic problems and best fulfilled its professed ideals. If the United States could cure its racial, urban, educational, and environmental woes, and otherwise advance its version of morality at home, then the American polity would be immune to communist nefariousness and able to check the Soviets abroad: "Whether we win against the Russians is primarily a question of whether we win against ourselves."[61]

Unfortunately, America's method of waging Cold War in the 1950s along the domestic front threatened to damage US security and confidence in ways more immediate and more disruptive than anything accomplished by the Red Army in Europe. Congressional committees to expose anti-American activities, zealous loyalty boards in government agencies, self-appointed protectors of public welfare who ransacked municipal libraries for seditious and pro-Marxist literature, investigations of Hollywood actors and screenwriters, professors hounded for alleged communist sympathies, and the purging of the State Department and Foreign Service amounted to a Soviet victory. Kennan himself has conceded that the leadership in Moscow must have rejoiced at the discomfort caused to established government bureaucracies in Washington and at the disorientation aroused in the American public by "revelations" and accusations produced by Joseph McCarthy, Patrick McCarran, Styles Bridges, William Jenner, Karl Mundt et al. The Soviets know, Kennan told a convention of lawyers in 1953, "that for the mass as for the individual the preoccupation with possible conspiracy can easily become an escape from a realistic facing up to responsibility, and the beginning of irrational behavior."[62] As it was, the United States lost the contribution of thousands of able government officials in the 1950s while suspicion and innuendo took the place of free debate about public issues. To some Europeans, displays of outlandish anti-communism in the United States smacked of neo-fascism and raised doubts about American society and Washington's fitness to lead the Western alliance.[63]

Kennan was directly involved in the loyalty cases of three Foreign Service officers, on whose behalf he testified, but in vain. He was especially upset by his failure to redress the injustices done to Davies and suffered from feelings of guilt. Almost certainly, he would have resigned in 1953 over the Davies case had he not first been dropped from the State Department. Kennan was also called in 1950 as an expert witness for John Service in his effort to clear himself of charges that he had helped mastermind Mao's victory in China and sought to mislead the State Department into believing that the CCP represented the democratic impulse in China.[64] In a similar capacity, Kennan lent his authority to Edmund Clubb's defense. Kennan was also concerned with, but not directly involved in, the fate of Philip Jessup and Charles Thayer, both of whose careers were cut short; few criticisms ever stung Kennan more sharply than Bohlen's insinuation that he had betrayed Thayer by not supporting him in his fight against right-wing congressmen.[65]

People whom Kennan valued and who pursued careers outside of the State Department were also injured by the anti-communist hysteria. The most famous of these was Oppenheimer, who, despite his crucial role in the Manhattan Project, was declared in 1954 by a specially commissioned personnel security board to be unfit (by reason of his objecting to the hydrogen bomb project and exercising "poor judgment" in matters related to security) for government service and was barred from acting as a consultant to the Atomic Energy Commission. In Kennan's life, few men—perhaps Bohlen at one time or, in another quite different way, Marshall—touched him so deeply as Oppenheimer, in whom he doubtless perceived a fellow high mandarin. They had first met in 1946 at the National War College and by the mid-1950s were devoted friends. "It is hard to overstate how much I miss you," Oppenheimer (in Princeton) told Kennan (in Oxford) during the first weeks of commotion and unhappiness following his Reith Lectures.[66] Years earlier, Oppenheimer had become something like an intellectual conscience to Kennan and had sharpened his opposition to America's developing the hydrogen bomb.[67] Kennan also felt indebted to Oppenheimer for helping launch his scholarly career and for shaping the Institute for Advanced Study into an intellectual oasis, where the life of the mind could proceed gracefully and with utmost scrupulousness.[68]

In the spring of 1954, when the issue of Oppenheimer's loyalty was examined, Kennan gladly took his side in sworn testimony before the Atomic Energy Commission's investigating body, chaired by Dr. Gordon Gray. Kennan's statements about Oppenheimer's superior intellect and devotion to the United States were eloquent and complemented the evidence provided by other friendly witnesses such as James Conant, Enrico Fermi, David Lilienthal, and Isadore Rabi. For his efforts, Kennan had to endure a homily about the importance of telling the truth and was warned about the penalties for perjury. He was asked if Oppenheimer was a dissembler. Were most intellectuals "screwballs?"[69] The hearings and the outcome left Kennan both exhausted and depressed. Years later he wrote: "For . . . the formal levying of . . . charges against [Oppenheimer] in the 1950s, I can conceive of no motive other than personal vindictiveness and shameless, heartless political expediency. The United States government, if it is to realize America's possibilities as a great power, will have to learn that even our country is not so rich in talent that it can afford to proceed thus brutally and recklessly with that which it has."[70]

Not only did Kennan testify for specific persecuted individuals, he also spoke against anti-communist excesses from university lecterns—notably Notre Dame and Radcliffe; campaigned against Eisenhower in part because of his reluctance to confront McCarthy directly; wrote letters to various newspapers and journals in which he defended friends and attacked McCarthy; and protested in articles published by *Look, The Atlantic,* and *The New York Times Magazine.*[71] He counseled that while the United States would be morally justified in outlawing the American communist party, such a course was neither wise nor expedient. It was infinitely preferable to avoid making martyrs out of party members or inadvertently to dignify their cause by paying them undue attention. By allowing American communists to operate in the open, the government could also better monitor their activities, and citizens at large could see how remote from their ideals and aspirations was the US communist party, itself entirely beholden to Soviet masters. Yet in contrast to this liberal reasoning, Kennan also averred that communists ought to be denied any place in the national educational system; they lacked the requisite tolerance and open-mindedness necessary for sound teaching or serious research. Academic free-dom should thus be subordinated to the broadly perceived national interest. As for fellow travelers and those people temporarily infatuated by Marxist interpretations or Soviet purposes, Kennan believed that they required tolerance and should not be subjected to public humiliation. Eventually, most of them could be counted upon to render useful service to the nation. What a pity to make them embittered outcasts before they reached their intellectual maturity and shed their illusions about Moscow, communism, and the Cominform.

Kennan was at his most emphatic and best when he declared that the chief danger to the United States was not posed by the infinitesimally small communist party or its sympathizers; but that, in its eagerness to eliminate these elements from sensitive positions in society, the American polity might indulge in witch hunts, censorship, and other forms of internal repression on such a scale that a dictatorship little better than Stalin's would result.[72] At the minimum, public life in the United States was being debauched. In the summer of 1954, after verdict had been passed on Oppenheimer, Kennan declared:

> We have seen . . . the faith of our people in great and distinguished fellow citizens systematically undermined; useful and deserving men hounded thanklessly out of honorable careers of public service; the most subtle sort of damage done to our intellectual life: our scholars encouraged to be cautious and unimaginative in order to escape being "controversial," a pall of anxiety and discouragement thrown over our entire scientific community, our libraries and forums of knowledge placed on the defense before the inroads of self-appointed snoopers and censors, a portion of our youth encouraged to fear ideas on the pretext of being defended from them.[73]

Why should such fearfulness and cynicism grip the United States in the early 1950s? Kennan answered that Americans, and here their nineteenth-century experi-ence figured large, were accustomed to believing that total immunity from both domestic malefactors and foreign enemies was not merely possible, but normal. The absence of absolute security in the postwar years indicated to the popular mind that some public authorities charged with assuring national safety were either derelict in their duties or guilty of treason. Kennan urged his compatriots to understand that total security, like any other form of perfectionism, was opposed to all reasonable solutions. Citizens had to realize that multiple dangers exist and learn to live with partial solutions and accommodations. By balancing peril against peril, a tolerable situation combining security, order, and calm could be induced: "The first criterion of a healthy spirit [individual or collective] is the ability to walk cheerfully and sensibly amid the congenital uncertainties of existence, to recognize as natural the inevitable precariousness of the human condition, to accept this without being disoriented by it, and to live effectively and usefully in its shadow."[74]

The inability of large sections of the public to maintain this degree of equa-nimity in the face of real but not overwhelming danger in the 1950s, and their predisposition toward extremism, reinforced Kennan in his belief that the American experiment in orderly liberty was a "tragic failure." McCarthyism might have been a passing episode, but it was also a manifestation of deep currents in American political culture: distrust of serious thought, suspicion of foreign ideas and contact, provincialism, conformity, cheap chauvinism. Against them, the voice of no Cold War critic or proponent of justice for public servants could prevail.[75]

*   *   *   *

Already begun in the late Truman years, Kennan's career as a dissident from and critic of most US foreign policy acquired an unmistakable urgency in the 1950s as he became convinced that America's choices between war and peace and its range of military and diplomatic maneuverability were narrowing dangerously. No longer constrained by the discipline of official discretion, Kennan was able to campaign openly in the 1950s for positions that he had long held about Germany, Europe, international security, and the scope of Soviet intentions and capabilities. Given the public setting and debates into which his words were cast, Kennan's advice also acquired a different coloration than it possessed during the 1940s. In opposing "rollback," "massive retaliation," and "brinkmanship," he was obviously at odds with the Republican administration and therefore, concluded many Democrats, available for the liberal cause. But, in fact, he was anything but a liberal, and his endorsement of Stevenson must be understood as an extension of his disenchantment with American diplomacy generally as it was comprehended and promoted by a majority of Democrats and Republicans.

Kennan's opposition to McCarthy and his ilk also had nothing to do with conventional party concerns, but was based on a revulsion for the damage inflicted on the deeper processes and values of the American government. It should be underscored that, during his diplomatic postings in the 1930s, Kennan had been alive to alleged Marxist and Soviet influences in the American government apparatus and had not hesitated in some instances to alert higher officials. He also endorsed the FBI's surveillance of "obviously subversive" groups and individuals in the United States. Still, what he regarded as proper security precautions in peacetime against betrayal and espionage were unrelated to what passed for prudential measures of public safety in the McCarthy era. It was a time when W. B. Yeats would have observed, "the best lack all conviction, while the worst are full of passionate intensity." Kennan did try to champion some victims and in so doing was bruised, and a little suspicion even came to rest on his loyalty and political preferences. Was he a Marxist? Did he secretly approve of the USSR?[76]

To him, the fundamental danger to the United States in the 1950s, in both domestic and external affairs, was rooted in intellectual rigidity and a sterility of political imagination at the top. For a while, Kennan entertained hopes for Stevenson, but his capitulation to Machrowicz boded ill, and, in any event, the electorate's repudiation of Stevenson was massive. In the meantime, at least to Kennan, the Eisenhower administration showed itself unable to improvise in the wake of changing international realities. The Republicans did not appreciate, for example, that the evolution of post-Stalinist Russia and Europe's recovery from the war might mean that the United States could usefully explore with Moscow the possibility of ending the continent's division. Neither did the Republicans seem to understand that the extreme bipolarity of the late 1940s was breaking apart under the weight of "desatellitization" and Third World neutrality.[77] Oblivious to these and other complexities, the administration followed only those policies that placed military above diplomatic means and employed exaggerated rhetoric over refined strategy. Perhaps nowhere more than in its handling of problems related to the demise of Europe's overseas empires was the United States, according to Kennan, so seriously handicapped by its failure to understand the fundamental facts of international life.[78]

11

America and
the Third World

On the subject of the Third World, Kennan has been at his least generous and most skeptical. His views, moreover, have remained basically unchanged ever since the late 1940s and 1950s when the United States first deployed various economic and political inducements to gain support, or at least benign neutrality, among the emergent states of Asia and Africa. He has worried that Washington's newfound interest in regions traditionally of secondary or tertiary importance to the United States would distract from vital matters—concerning Europe and Japan—and drain precisely those limited resources required for the successful waging of Cold War.

In particular, he has been unconvinced about the presumed wisdom of supplying capital and technical assistance to developing countries attempting to diversify and modernize their economies. To Kennan, American aid programs—no matter how lavish or useful to the recipients—were (and are now) unlikely to purchase the thanks or friendship of foreigners anywhere and, consequently, are of dubious value to the United States: "Such sentiments [of gratitude], if they appear at all, are not apt to be enduring ones, and by permitting other peoples to [habituate] themselves to various sorts of one-sided assistance from us we will be creating situations that cannot be easily terminated except at the cost of new misunderstanding and resentment."[1] As case in point, Kennan might have cited the bitter feelings aroused in Moscow by the abrupt cancellation of lend-lease aid in May 1945. In any case, he has countenanced large-scale assistance only in instances where the United States has had clearly defined interests: for example, in Europe with the Marshall Plan. Otherwise, he has taught that the United States should be most circumspect about granting financial favors.

He has also been critical of the value that many Third World governments attach to rapid economic and industrial development. In effect, he has questioned the veracity of those teleological theories of progress positing that all human societies are moving along the same path and will eventually realize a similar degree of economic, political, and technological uniformity. Such theories, which enjoyed a respectable following among social scientists in the 1950s and 1960s, neglect the distinct possibility that a multiplicity of starting points, paths, and outcomes exist for different human societies around the world; value-laden comparisons usually fail to recognize that equally valid, though varied, forms of development take place. For Kennan certainly neither normative nor scientific reasons are apparent for supposing that European and North American models of modernization would or ought to provide *the* patterns for Third World development. Therefore, he has asked, why should the United States try to help countries along a direction for which they are unsuited and ultimately not even bound? Under these circumstances, irrespective of how lofty its motives, the United States would be causing more harm than good by diverting assorted societies off their singular courses and trying to remake them in the image of the democratic-capitalist West.

He has also recognized that the cultural and sociological structures in many Third World states are more vulnerable than those of industrialized countries to the disruption caused by dramatic changes in modes of technology and production, and that the social continuity indispensable for any healthy society might be annihilated in settings unaccustomed to the incidental, but necessary, regimentation of modern life. Patterns of extended family, traditional hierarchy, and society based on sea-sonal rhythm would no longer make sense. In their place, unfamiliar and fearful habits and institutions would arise and squelch—as they had in Kennan's once-pristine Wisconsin—the wholesomeness of agrarian society. Kennan has feared that in countries experiencing unrestrained population growth, the mix of demographic and sociological change will overwhelm and destroy the most well organized of regimes. "I think it would be possible," he wrote in 1955, "to name a number of peoples in other parts of the world whose political adjustment has not been aided by the destruction of their customs and ways of life, and the replacement of these by a new industrial civilization to which their whole spiritual outlook was inadequate. I do not mean to say that they should remain forever 'undeveloped'; but I think great danger can be brought to them if technology is permitted to revolutionize their lives too rapidly, too dramatically and in a manner calculated to disrupt their traditions, . . . and their faith."[2]

And Kennan, long infuriated by environmental damage in the United States and by urban problems of sprawl and congestion, has wondered if advocates of Third World industrialization really know what they are proposing. He has argued that what passes for modernity in the West is at best a mixed blessing: "Our pioneer forefathers in this country, while they lived in primitive conditions, were certainly happier and better adjusted people than we ourselves."[3] The Third World is thus in a splendid position to learn by the negative example of Western mistakes, should not rush madly into adopting new ways, and should choose so-called appropriate technologies.

As for the Americans, Kennan has held that they are severely limited in their means of alleviating poverty abroad or promoting political stability in the Third World. By 1977, when discussion of a new international economic order had gained some currency, he was willing to entertain the possibility that the United States should adopt a set of tariff reforms designed to encourage Third World exports and that Washington should increase financial contributions to international organizations charged with dispensing aid. However, he has doubted that America's abundance of food surplus can be transported in adequate quantities and in time to make a difference to the drought- and famine-stricken regions of the Third World. Nor has he believed that America enjoys enough influence in such places to assure that its aid is fairly distributed among the needy: "We in the United States did not create this problem (it is fundamentally an unavoidable result of overpopulation), and it is far beyond our powers to solve it. Such surpluses as we are capable of producing . . . would scarcely scratch the surface of the difficulty, even if we were to do all in our power to increase a surplus and to decrease our share in the consumption of it."[4] At most, the United States should continue to provide what it can through multilateral organizations, and Americans might try to moderate their extravagant eating habits and consume less rich foods. Although not materially benefiting starving people overseas, these actions would place the United States on a higher moral ground in relation to the problem of global want and deflect some of the envy and enmity of poorer peoples.[5]

Kennan has been aghast for years at the hatred for the United States and Western Europe that he has perceived in Third World nations. He has surely exaggerated its intensity, but is right to attribute such feelings to the emotional legacy of imperialism and the ever-expanding disparity between Western wealth and Third World privation. The potential consequences of such antipathy have especially troubled him as the United States and its allies have become dependent upon natural resources in distant lands inhabited by people who, under the best circumstances, harbor no affection for the West. "We are faced," he declaimed in one of his Reith Lectures, "with the task of defending a high standard of living and all the luxuries of a permissive society against the jealousies . . . of countless millions who are just awakening to an awareness of world affairs, and who would witness without pity or regret the disappearance of much that we value . . . we are becoming increasingly dependent on the resources of this jealous outside world for the maintenance of our life."[6] He therefore urged that, to preserve their privileges and superior position, the United States and its allies should stockpile those natural resources—oil, especially—necessary to run industrial economies, cultivate alternative sources, and limit the domestic use of such materials. And, though fully aware of alleged Third World desires to see the West humbled, Kennan has insisted that producers of raw materials be made to respect the needs of the West for their natural products. As early as 1954, in light of the previous year's Iranian crisis, he urged that the exporters of resources make guarantees about supply and accessibility: "They must not permit our great and in many cases delicate economy to become dependent on them . . . unless they are prepared to acknowledge a clear obligation to guard the durability and reliability of the respective [existing business] arrangements."[7] In a sense, then, Kennan has maintained that need constitutes the basis of legitimate control over and claim to a resource; moreover (as will be seen later), this need can sometimes be used by the West as a rationale for suspending traditional observance of another state's sovereignty.

Whereas Kennan has argued that the West must of necessity enjoy certain prerogatives in the Third World, he has been incensed with any Third World leader or apologist who contends that the former European colonial powers and the United

States bear any responsibility for the uneven economic development and poverty afflicting large sections of Asia, Africa, and Latin America. Periodic calls for compensation or reparations have struck him as irrelevant in the case of the United States and as a symptom of political immaturity among Third World leaders. He has insisted that their problems are their own; and, in view of their cheerful and heedless contribution to the destruction of overseas European empires, they should acknowledge their responsibilities and shoulder them bravely. Guilt, in any event, should not play a part in America's attitude toward the Third World; Europe, too, should not permit itself to be psychologically handicapped in such a fashion: "I . . . reject the suggestion that our generation in the West has some sort of cosmic guilt or obligation vis-a-vis the underdeveloped parts of the world. . . . We will do no good by scratching around to discover whose descendants owe the most to the descendants of the other."[8]

History itself, he believes, is mostly the record of humanity's mistakes, and no doubt the West has committed plenty of them in dealing with other peoples. "But mistakes," he has ventured, "have also been made on the other side; and the American people . . . are not encumbered with any sense of guilt vis-a-vis Asia and Africa commensurate with the bitterness that seems to prevail there against us."[9] Along with Reinhold Niebuhr, he holds that virtue and moral right do not reside exclusively with the poor and disenfranchised any more than greed and depravity can be said to be the monopoly of the rich and powerful. For Kennan, good and evil are too interwoven to allow any discussion of North-South relations to sink to the didactism of a morality play or, as he would characterize it, the shallow categories of Marxist historical understanding. In this connection, he has hoped that his compatriots will overcome their embarrassment for America's great power status and put aside their sentimental preferences for new and small states. By divesting themselves of their self-consciousness and faintly shameful feelings in dealing with poorer countries, Americans can better face the realities of the world and their position and duties in it. As this notion applies to the Third World, the United States should maintain a correct, essentially reserved attitude, and not concern itself unduly when one or other Third World states adopt domestic practices that conflict with democratic ideals.

Kennan has doubted that American political values are easily exportable and has never possessed an evangelical fervor about democracy or its universal applicability. By 1960, he was convinced that the United States should resist all future temptations of converting the world. He believed, although he did not actually use the expression, that the Americans had suffered too long from the white man's hubris: "to see one's self as the noble big brother and protector, the object of admiration, appreciation, and gratitude on the part of people weaker and darker than ourselves, uninitiated, as yet, into the sacred mysteries of the American outlook."[10] Most of the world outside of North America and Western Europe was simply unprepared for or unreceptive to experiments in democracy. For this reason alone, nobody should expect many Third World nations to embrace institutions and procedures that had evolved in an alien culture over centuries. Neither has Kennan gotten excited, as did many of his contemporaries, about the prospect of some Third World states succumbing to communism and replacing their former European masters with new ones in Soviet guise. Rather, he has rightly recognized, as early as the 1950s, that most Soviet attempts to curry favor among Third World peoples would fail; yet their elites would eagerly and sometimes skillfully play the two rival powers off against each other and reap economic contributions from each. Consequently, Kennan has advocated not only that the United States limit its aid to Third World states, but also that it not involve itself deeply with their security affairs. The proliferation of diverse military arrangements between the West and various Third World countries has struck him as one of the most perplexing phenomena of the postwar era.[11] In his view, SEATO, CENTO, and all the others never had any substantial justification.

Kennan's general concepts for the proper ordering of US-Third World relations have allowed for some variation in assessing specific issues. This is evident in his ideas about the four areas of the Third World that he has directly addressed during his career: the Middle East, Latin America, South Africa, and Indochina.

Middle East Dilemmas

The only part of the Third World that significantly involved Kennan in an official capacity was the Middle East. During the period when he directed Policy Planning, he and his staff had to reckon with the Israeli-Arab conflict and its implications for US diplomacy. His and his colleagues' irreducible goal was that nothing occur in Palestine that allowed or encouraged the Soviets to gain advantage in the Middle East. Their greatest anxiety was that, as Britain's traditional hegemonic position eroded, the Soviets would move quickly to acquire political influence over various postmandate areas, thereby jeopardizing Western access to oil supplies and compromising overall the eastern flank of the Mediterranean. Italy, Greece, Turkey, and Iran might then be despoiled through a combination of intensified communist insurgency and Soviet pressure and ultimately lost to Anglo-American purposes.

After consulting closely with Loy Henderson, director of the State Department's Middle Eastern Office, and discussing the matter with Dean Rusk, head of the department's Division of UN Affairs, Kennan committed himself and the PPS to the following in January 1948 (four months before the state of Israel was proclaimed in Tel Aviv). He affirmed that Palestine occupied a strategic position, as it was useful for controlling the eastern Mediterranean and the Suez Canal, was an outlet for Middle Eastern oil, and was situated at the center of major political cross-currents that flowed in numerous directions. He understood that the UN's proposal for a Palestine divided between two sovereign states—one Jewish, the other Arab—was unlikely to satisfy either party. It was also clear to him that, despite support for partition from the Jewish Agency, other leading Jewish groups such as the Irgun and the Stern gang were vehemently opposed; in addition, the nearby Arab states and Arab Palestinians were uniformly against partition and seemed intent on boycotting the official transfer of authority from Britain to local Jewish and Arab officials. Meanwhile, the United States bore a moral and practical responsibility for having helped orchestrate, along with the USSR, the General Assembly's endorsement of the partition scheme.

There was no reason in Kennan's view to hope that the conflict between Jews and Arabs would soon subside. Since the UN's adoption of the partition plan (November 1947), the number of Jewish-Arab clashes in Palestine had soared; there had been attacks on Jewish quarters in some Arab states combined with anti-American demonstrations; and the declaration by several Moslem leaders of "jihad" against Jews in Palestine promised to unleash a full-scale war. At the same time, organized military units from Iraq, Syria, Egypt, Transjordan, and Saudi Arabia were being prepared for transfer to Palestine, where they would surely come into violent contact with the Haganah and other Jewish military organizations.[12]

Kennan doubted that the proposed Jewish state could survive by itself. Therefore, its representatives could be expected to seek arms, volunteers, and financial help in the United States, among other places, despite the fact that Washington had earlier suspended authorization for the export to Palestine of war materiel of any sort. He also believed that Zionist leaders might press for some type of UN-sponsored military intervention to include US and Soviet troops. Should the USSR accept such an arrangement and the Americans reject it, as they were almost certain to do, matters could get most awkward. Kennan predicted that an introduction of Red Army units into Palestine would instantly open new possibilities for Soviet infiltration and subversion in the Near East and lead to the establishment of peoples' governments among the Arabs.

If the Truman administration should decide to send American troops to Palestine on a rescue mission, then existing Arab disillusionment with the United States would be aggravated: on top of partition, the Americans would appear to be actively working athwart their much-touted principle of self-determination for the Arabs. In past decades, of course, American officials, missionaries, and educational institutions operating in the Middle East had benefited from the common belief that the United State possessed no aims in the region inimical to Arab security or prosperity. Following any American intervention, Kennan predicted the worst: US oil concessions and air base rights in Saudi Arabia would be forfeited if King Ibn Saud and Prince Faisal decided under Arab pressure or their own sense of grievance to sever ties with America; moderate leaders and intellectuals, such as Azzam Pasha, would probably be swept away in a violent fit of Arab anti-Zionism that would extend to all Westerners in proportion to their support for partition and Jewish armies; extremists such as the Grand Mufti of Jerusalem would then lead an Arab world, seething and revengeful because of America's betrayal. The United States should also brace for a curtailment of trade with Moslem countries and the possible cessation of all oil investments and exchange over the long term; very likely the US would permanently lose access to British air, naval, and military facilities in the Middle East. American universities in Beirut and Cairo might also be closed or abolished, and mob actions against US nationals could be expected for years to come. Obviously, any one or combination of these things would amount to a serious setback for the United States. Kennan's chief fear, however, was that American support of the Zionist project would jeopardize the Marshall Plan; Europe would never recover if Middle East oil bound for America and the West should be suddenly cut or radically diminished.

The Soviets, meanwhile, stood to gain something, even if they decided against sending in forces of their own. Kennan recognized they might prefer to let the United States bear the burden of enforcing the Palestine partition, thereby incurring the disapprobation of all Arabs and Moslems. Come what may, the Soviets were still free to continue shipping arms to Jews and Arabs alike, in the expectation of making the entire situation even more untenable for the Anglo-American powers. And while the British and Americans were preoccupied with containing civil and international violence in and around Palestine, the Soviets could enlist the precedent of partition as a pretext for "protecting" minorities elsewhere. This could lead to Soviet encouragement for partitioning areas in Iran, Turkey, and Greece and might yield a patchwork of Soviet-supported new states in, say, Macedonia or Azerbaijan. Thus US enforcement of partition carried a dear price, as did any American alignment, real or imagined, with the Zionist cause. The entire balance of power in a vital region could shift or else collapse amidst unholy confusion. In Kennan's words: "So numerous would be the ramifications of mounting Arab ill will, of opening the door to Soviet political or military penetration, and of generally chaotic conditions in Palestine and neighboring countries that the whole structure of peace and security in the Near East and Mediterranean would be directly or indirectly affected with results . . . injurious to US interests."[13]

He recommended that the United States not send any armed forces and resolve to dissuade, through all available means, any other country from sending its soldiers to Palestine. He guessed that the sending of US troops would actually hamper rather than help the cause of world Jewry. Although the Zionists would achieve a temporary victory, their kin in Moslem countries would probably be slaughtered *en masse,* and anti-Jewish agitation would quicken in other parts of the world, including the United States: "The position of [American] Jews would be gravely undermined as it becomes evident to the public that in supporting a Jewish state in Palestine we were in fact supporting the extreme objectives of political Zionism, to the detriment of overall US security interests."[14]

The United States should withhold ammunition, arms, and financial assistance to the Zionists and refrain from taking future initiatives on behalf of partition. To do anything less, Kennan warned, would amount in Arab minds to a US declaration of war against the whole Arab nation. As for specific, positive actions, the government must continue its embargo of arms to Palestine, try to spread international responsibility for a solution, and—after the inevitable failure of partition and the Zionists—refer the entire matter to the UN General Assembly. In that body the United States could work to encourage a peaceful settlement between Jews and Arabs in Palestine and investigate other formulas, such as federal state or trusteeship, that might be expected to work without reliance upon outside armed intervention. By such measures Kennan hoped the US could divest itself of the imputation of international leadership for a dilemma too complex and volatile for producing anything but evil for the West.

Rusk objected to Kennan's basic "hands-off" policy toward Palestine on the grounds that it proposed no alternative to a Jewish-Arab war which, in turn, would mean the extinction of the Jewish political entity. And neither Truman nor the overwhelming majority in Congress was inclined after the recent suffering and decimation of European Jewry to abandon Israel. To Rusk's concerns, Kennan countered that the United States had to recover an independent position on Palestine—he ignored the moral dimension of Israel's claim—and salvage something of American prestige and standing in the Arab and Moslem universes. The alternative, he argued, was an endless military and economic commitment to a status quo in Palestine fiercely resented by the bulk of the Arab world. As for the violence that would engulf Palestine, the US did bear partial responsibility, as did the British and Arabs; but the main responsibility would continue to rest with those Zionist leaders who had pushed energetically for goals which, by their nature, led to violence.[15] The best course, Kennan told Rusk, would be for the United States to reverse its support for partition and work to establish in Palestine a federal state with cantonization, as originally envisaged by the British. In February, he and the Policy Planning Staff predicted hopefully that such an arrangement would restore US prestige among the Arabs and enhance the country's strategic position in the Middle East: "Our national interests would . . . be served and our national security strengthened, notwithstanding the disfavor with which such a procedure would be viewed by Zionist elements."[16]

Kennan's worst fears were not realized during the ensuing summer of 1948 when Israel and its Arab antagonists—Egypt, Transjordan, Lebanon, and Syria—waged their first war. True, the issues of early recognition of Israel and its admission to the UN placed a burden on US-British cooperation, as Clement Attlee's government was reluctant to take measures contrary to its interest in decent Anglo-Arab relations. But the divergence between British and US policies in the Middle East was not great enough to damage the foundations of Anglo-American alliance. As for the UN, it did attempt to mediate Arab-Israeli fighting in June and July; however, neither American nor Soviet nor Soviet satellite troops were dispatched under UN auspices to quell the violence. And although US recognition and moral support of Israel hurt Washington's position in the Arab world, the USSR did not automatically gain bountiful diplomatic benefits. There was nothing like an Arab volte-face toward the Soviet Union, and most governments in the region still sought assistance, economic and otherwise, from the United States and its allies.

By 1949, Israel was an accomplished fact, though one destined to be at the vortex of international controversy and war for decades to come. The United States, which had immediately recognized the provisional government as the de facto authority in Israel (May 1948), extended full diplomatic recognition to the Jewish state in January 1949. The National Security Council was naturally determined that Israel be oriented toward the West and that Israeli facilities and military forces be available for campaigns against the Red Army and Navy in event of Soviet-US war.[17] To these ends the Truman administration supported Israel's application for a $100 million Export-Import Bank loan and its bid for UN entry. The NSC also hoped, naively as it turned out, to encourage Israel and its Arab foes toward reconciliation, at least to the point where they would act in concert against Soviet aggression or generalized communist incursions. In conjunction with Great Britain, the United States also tried to solve the Palestinian refugee problem and help develop key Middle Eastern states both economically and socially.[18]

Kennan's line about Palestine in 1948 was in keeping with that of most Foreign Service officers charged with responsibility for the Middle East (Henderson) and with State and Defense Department officials, notably Marshall and Forrestal. While on leave at the Institute for Advanced Study in the winter of 1952, however, he was willing to push much more independent, less patient views about the Arab states (and Iran) than were current in Washington's diplomatic and military circles. Against the background of political unrest in Egypt and agitation against British control of Suez, and British-Iranian quarreling over the oil refineries of Abadan, Kennan submitted to Acheson the most uncompromising notions. All of the understanding for Arab sensibilities that he had managed to muster in 1948 had vanished in an explosion of Kennanesque irritability and scorn for peoples who he thought were acting recklessly and irresponsibly against the venerable orderliness imposed by the West.

He explained to Acheson that one of the major reasons for America's ambiguous record of achievement and mainly failure in the Middle East was that the US government in its collective wisdom (especially its advisors in the State Department) failed to understand the depth of irrationality and erraticism of that region's inhabitants—particularly evident among its intellectuals—in responding to Western ideas and political purposes. Arab bitterness toward the United States was particularly unwarranted, despite the Israeli-American connection, and made sense only in the context of emotional instability: "To ascertain the reasons for the intensely anti-American attitudes manifested by these people would be to delve deeply into the psychological reactions and the origins of various forms of neurosis."[19]

Part of the problem, too, he believed, was that the US was spendthrift in doling out aid and thereby strengthening the most foolish attitudes among the recipients. They already felt inferior and jealous of American affluence and were wildly happy whenever the United States moved in a fashion that acknowledged something of their cherished dreams about occupying important international status: "The major psychological effect of our pressing various forms of aid on individual governments will be . . . to convince the peoples generally in that part of the world that in addition to being white and imperialistic we are stupid, uncertain, weak, and obviously on the skids of history, and that they are more important than anybody ever told them they were."[20] The chauvinisms of the Middle East, fanatical in Kennan's view, could not be tamed by the United States and converted into anything reliable from an American standpoint; they should be encouraged against the Soviet Union, but the United States would be deceiving itself if it ever reached the conclusion that such chauvinism and xenophobia would produce governments upon which the West could count. The extreme nationalist movements, being permeated by violence and immaturity, were bound to produce "bloodshed, horror, hatred, and political oppression" on a vast scale.

Kennan was glad that Arab and Iranian leaders had balked up to that point at entering their countries into American-sponsored military pacts. Why do anything to increase their inordinate self-regard? They should shift for themselves, and, if they cozied up to the Soviets, then so be it: "They—not we—would be the main sufferers if they placed their heads in the mouth of the Soviet lion." And what of the strategic assets of the area, such as Suez, various port facilities, and oil fields? Kennan answered that Western access to them did not depend upon political intimacy between the local regimes and the United States. Such intimacy or diplomatic understanding was anyway impossible. The Western positions could be secured on the ground through other, albeit indelicate, means: "To retain these facilities and positions we can use today only one thing: military strength, backed by the resolution and courage to employ it. There is nothing else that will avail us—least of all, attempts to incur the benevolent predisposition of these dreadful characters who in many instances bear the responsibility for local political leadership and on whose bizarre frames the trappings of statesmanship rest like an old dress suit on a wooden scarecrow." Kennan argued that the West should be unapologetic in retaining facilities and privileges that had been acquired by right of usage over long decades. Great Britain and the United States, as leaders of the Western alliance, bore special world responsibilities that transcended charity for "primitive" people:

> Such things as Abadan and Suez are important to the local peoples only in terms of their *amour propre*. . . . To us, some of these things are important in a much more serious sense, and for reasons that today are sounder and better and more defensible than they ever were in history. Let us then feel the dignity that goes with responsibility; let us call our national soul our own—and not be ashamed or uncertain if we have to say that we require certain things and mean to [keep] them. After all, we *do* also live in this world, and bear heavy [duties] in it, and we are fully entitled to insist that people show some respect for our interests, even when they neither understand nor sympathize with them.[21]

(Years later, after the 1973 Arab oil embargo, Professor Robert Tucker of Johns Hopkins University expressed similar views: he called for a Western military takeover and administration of oil fields in the Persian Gulf.)

Even if strong Western actions drove some local regimes to align themselves with the Soviet Union, it would hardly matter, according to Kennan, as long as key positions were safely in US-British keeping: "Our basic interests can best be guarded if we have quietly and firmly dug in, betimes, at those places that are really vital to us. Had the British occupied Abadan, I would personally have no great worry about what happened to the rest of the country." So, too, with Suez and Egypt. A consolidated Anglo-US position along the Canal, relying on no other country for assistance or approval, could withstand any challenge posed by the Egyptians. Only in case of general hostilities involving the Soviet Union would such a Suez arrangement be imperiled. In any event, said Kennan, the American government had to decide what in physical terms was essential for Britain and the US to keep in the Middle East and to take suitable measures—particularly military ones—if local, hostile populations jeopardized Western holdings. Except for issuing a flood of harsh words and threatening violence, the aggrieved peoples could not really do much to redress these defiant Anglo-American actions; obviously they could turn to the Soviets, but such a move was more likely to cause Egyptian or Iranian destruction than force a Western retreat.

Kennan urged that, short of such drastic policies, Truman's government strongly support the British in defending their holdings scattered throughout the Middle East and not succumb to the temptation of publicly chiding Britain when it took emergency measures to safeguard its—and America's—interests. He complained that too often the Americans, with perverse pleasure and contempt for how Britain was working for Western interests generally, had tweaked the British for their imperialism. This annoying habit, of course, had its origins in the late eighteenth century when the Americans first began championing the republican cause against monarchy and empire, and had been recently expressed in FDR's ill-timed cracks against British imperialism during the war. Kennan was perfectly right to opine that the British were either America's friends or they were not—one could not have it both ways. His other views, however, did not necessarily follow, namely that the British rightly knew—and the Americans should learn—that to appease Middle Eastern potentates, to indulge them with concessions and partial withdrawals, and to soothe their exercised imaginations was naivete and in the long run would tarnish Western prestige in a vital region. And his claim that only the "cold gleam of adequate and determined force" could save the Middle East for Western purposes showed not only how little he valued diplomacy in dealing with weak powers, but also how much he exaggerated the utility of methods belonging to a defunct era. The very Middle Eastern nationalisms that he deplored and sought to contain would have guaranteed that any Anglo-US seizing of specific areas would cause protracted, bloody imperial wars and amount to a considerable drain on Western Cold War resources. Kennan's recommendations were—and so, too, Tucker's in 1973—imprudent and unrealistic in the extreme. If nothing else, the Soviets would have harvested a political windfall in Arab and Iranian wrath against the West.

Kennan's unabashed apology for maintaining Western imperial prerogatives was roundly criticized by those State Department officials engaged with Middle Eastern affairs. Burton Berry's Near Eastern Office, in particular, disapproved of Kennan's analysis and recommendations: Kennan had underestimated the strategic value of the Middle East as an intercontinental highway and producer of petroleum. Middle Eastern nationalism was complicated and should not be dismissed as irrational, irresponsible, and anti-Western; for better or worse, it was similar to that in other parts of the world that had yielded nation-states. Denying Middle Easterners the rights of self-determination and sovereignty could eventually endanger Western investments and holdings. And why should the United States take actions that objectively forfeited much of the Middle East to Soviet Russia?

Berry also protested that Kennan defined strength, prestige, and influence too narrowly as they applied to American and British policies in the Middle East. By way of illustration, he argued that a British military occupation of Abadan would have produced inconceivably disastrous consequences in Iran and all of the surrounding region for America and Britain alike. Instead, the West should not hesitate to use normal diplomacy and emphasize its peaceful intentions toward and respect for distant peoples: "It is certainly true that the US and the rest of the free world have an interest . . . in such places as Abadan and Suez. But so do the peoples of the Middle East. We do not condone their recent practice of unilateral denunciation of international agreements, but when difficulties arise, we still believe that patient, intelligent, constructive statesmanship offers the best prospect of basic solutions." Berry added that, by continuing and expanding existing programs of technical and economic assistance in the Middle East, the United States was contributing materially to raising the standards of living and literacy there and thus was building the foundations for durable political stability. Even though these social programs could not be expected to work miracles, they were a better bet to help the Western cause in the Middle East than arrogance and the flaunting of raw military strength.[22]

Kennan was unimpressed by Berry's rebuttal and believed that, to whatever degree the government followed his advice in actual policy, the US was headed for trouble. He told Bohlen that Berry was mistaken to suppose that the mere trappings of self-determination would imbue Middle Easterners with qualities comparable to those of the advanced countries of Europe. Britain's decline in the region was already allowing the extreme nationalists to gain political ascendancy. Time was running out on the West; and, if it were to save anything of its vital interests, it must act with resolve. It was high time, indeed, that the Americans grow up and begin "discarding our fatuous desire to be 'liked' and make it clear that the Russians are not the only serious people in this world."[23]

Only a year after the Kennan-Berry exchange, the CIA helped engineer the overthrow of Muhammad Mossaddeq in Tehran. Although Kennan was a private citizen by then and not involved in the operation, he must have approved of it: the Anglo-Iranian Oil Company was retrieved for the West and with it the Anglo-US position was buttressed, at least temporarily.

Meanwhile, along Suez and in Egypt proper matters were taking another serious turn. The "Free Officers" coup in July 1952 resulted in some semblance of political stability in Cairo, but popular resentment against the British continued unabated and caused a spate of clashes near the Canal zone and elsewhere. Yet it was not until the summer of 1956, after Gamal Nasser had finally subdued his domestic enemies and was firmly established as strong man and prime minister, that a united Egypt was ready for vigorous action against the remnants of imperial order. In late July, in response to the discontinuation of promised Western aid, Nasser nationalized the Suez Canal—just previously evacuated by British forces. This action sparked a new crisis with Britain and France and led directly to the October–November Suez War.

Kennan was, once again, in complete sympathy with the British actions and disconsolate over Eisenhower's pressure on Britain, France, and Israel that forced their withdrawal and resulted ultimately in the retirement of Anthony Eden from government. Kennan did not agree with Eden's equating of Nasser with Hitler, but he was revolted at America's violent turning against its major European allies. He also thought that Dulles's actions and vacillation had helped create the conditions in which France and Britain were forced to take extreme measures; at a minimum, the Eisenhower administration should have mustered the good grace to maintain silence while France and Britain took steps to safeguard their security. And why criticize Israel when it was defending itself against a mortally dangerous encirclement?[24]

Kennan's assessment in 1956 of the long-term implications of the Suez imbroglio showed vividly how much at odds he was with the thrust of US policy and attitude toward the world's newly independent countries. First, he doubted that national self-determination was advisable in all cases. Ought the status of sovereignty, he asked an audience at Johns Hopkins University, really be granted to any group of people—large or small—just because they wanted it? America's traditional adherence to the principle that all peoples should shape their destinies had not caused serious problems in the nineteenth century or in the period following World War I. In the past, Americans had typically identified struggles for national independence with the battle for republican institutions and had, within the limits of national wealth and power, extended help as well as sympathy for groups trying to break an unwelcome political association with a grander, imperial body. However, in the contemporary world national independence and political liberty were not necessarily correlated and Kennan pointed out that on numerous occasions a dependent status had been replaced by a tyrant or local demagogue. The United States, then, had to realize that much of the spirit behind anti-colonialism was not animated by a desire to promote Western concepts of human rights and democratic government.

Kennan also questioned the tendency toward egalitarianism in international life and whether it and the application of universal law were adequate substitutes for the previous century's international organization along the lines of imperial hierarchy and empire. He admitted that the aristocratic and imperial character of the nineteenth century seemed irrational: "In the great colonial empires and in that mixed pattern of political forms and gradations of status that characterized the dynastic system of Europe, you had what looked like a veritable crazy-quilt of institutional arrangements, running all the way from the majesty of the great imperial courts to the more humble ambiguities of personal unions, principalities, vice-realms, sheik-doms, . . . tributary states, various forms of servitudes."[25] He believed that such arrangements offended American sensibility, based as it was on constitutionally guaranteed equality and law. Americans were also unacquainted with all forms of intermediate status and gradations between complete dependence and total sovereignty. Hence their insistence that all nations be tidily divided into separate, distinctive states. But, to Kennan, the previous order had much to recommend it, for it was generally attuned and better suited to the underlying disorder of human society than any uniform pattern of international status could be. The old order, he said, could more adequately embrace the variations of human experience and perspective, the accidents of geography, the results of history, and all the other vagaries of existence that shape a given people's ability to contribute to international life and politics: "In the old crazy quilt, under forms of international status that had grown up like topsy in response to the demands of a thousand varieties of historical experience, all the subtle national differences could be taken into account and given their due. Under the theory of complete equality of sovereign status, they could not."[26]

Kennan also decried the predominance and success of the theoretically sovereign state that had destroyed the old irregularities of international status and had triggered a proliferation of new states. While at the turn of the century 54 political entities enjoyed sovereignty, by 1956 there were 104 states with many more emerging from the overseas empires of Europe. He maintained that these young states, such as Egypt, were new to the responsibilities of self-government and that their political instincts were as shallow as their experience; unlike the older empires to which they had once belonged, these states were unpredictable and usually lacked a stake in the international status quo that in past ages had helped assure moderate diplomacy—witness the history of Britain.

In addition, the appearance of freshly minted states since 1900 and the fragmentation of power around the world had resulted in unexpected setbacks to American interests. Still bemoaning the passing of the Habsburg empire and Wilson's contribution to its demise, Kennan observed, "Today, outside of the tiny rump state of Austria itself, every one of the component portions of that empire . . . is a communist state; and all but Yugoslavia are arrayed against us in the Soviet orbit."[27] In China, where the US had worked for half a century to oust the European powers, the rise of a communist regime allied with the Soviet Union was also contrary to American expectations and desires. And in Korea, American pressures and war against Japan had produced ambiguous results. Now in the Middle East, American actions were effectively conferring unlimited sovereignty on flimsy Arab sheikdoms while undermining Britain and leaving it no option but to abandon positions vital to the West. Although necessary and desirable in some cases, the multiplication of national sovereignties around the world could thus hardly be considered an absolute good to Kennan.

Parallel to his optimistic thinking about Germany and Czechoslovakia, 1938–1939, and his hopes for postwar Europe, Kennan argued that larger political frameworks, transcending narrow national feeling and the barriers of provincialism and language, were worthier of promotion than the ordinary state. They inspired a broader focus of obligation and responsibility than was possible in a condition of political fragmentation; he wished that the old empires could have yielded their pride of place to something greater than themselves. Only the British Commonwealth approached his ideal. In most cases, he recognized, the process of political fragmentation was running far ahead of any European attempts to solidify or rebuild larger units of power.

The concept of sovereignty as conventionally understood in the United States, namely the right of any government to do practically anything it wants, was also open to serious question in Kennan's view. In particular, he was critical that the notion of sovereignty had been used earlier by Iran and now by Egypt as a pretext to nationalize foreign property. And more than the issue of compensation to the foreign owner was at stake, for the damage caused by such instances of expropriation affected entire foreign peoples and the world community generally. Indeed, drastic measures of nationalization by independent governments acting theoretically within their sovereign competence could cause others the worst sort of harm in a world that every day was becoming more interdependent. "The question," he stated, "is whether the Egyptians have a right to deny abruptly to the international community, without consultation or even forewarning, an arrangement on which a number of economies have been oriented, to one degree or another, over a period of several decades. In other words, when one permits other nations to develop a dependence on something that is under one's sovereign control, does one not thereby assume . . . an obligation to the world at large for the stability of such an arrangement?"[28] Again, for Kennan, habitual usage constituted over time a right to such usage—very like the right dignified in Anglo-American legal tradition.

Egypt's annexation of Canal property also meant that Cairo could monitor and deny or grant as it pleased right of passage to any foreign ship. According to Kennan, in previous years the entire world community was protected against every sort of arbitrariness on the part of any government in operating Suez. In fact, the record did not support him, as ever since 1948 Egypt had prevented Israeli ships and all ships bound to or returning from Israel from using Suez. Nonetheless, he insisted that a problem unprecedented in the history of Canal operations was about to cripple it: "The nationalization of the canal, if Nasser's initiative is successful, will mean that this assurance [of use and access to all] no longer exists and that the dependability of Suez, with all of its immense importance for international trade and for the economies of individual countries, will henceforth depend on the good graces not only of this particular ruler of Egypt but of all those who come after him."[29] A similar situation existed with respect to other former colonial countries that could easily restrict the exploitation of natural resources (important to the industrialized West) or otherwise monopolize and manipulate them for political ends.

Kennan was impressed that some Third World governments behaved responsibly (i.e., cooperatively toward the West), but he feared that most of them were too hostile, too consumed by the residual neuroses of colonialism for the United States to place much stock in them: "We would be lacking in sheer sobriety if we failed to take account of the many potential sources of future instability involved in a process so sudden, so violent, so wracked with passion and bitterness and excitement, as in the disintegration of the great colonial empires of our day."[30] The new countries as a rule were usually susceptible to outside pressure and penetration. And, although the United States should try modestly to help the emergent states, it had to realize that anti-white and anti-American feelings were widespread and not conducive to any real partnership between the West and Third World. To Kennan, Nasser provided the Western world with an example both of the demand by new countries for control of facilities and natural resources on their territories and of erraticism and irresponsibility by which their statesmanship was often marked.

From a somewhat different angle than he had before, the Suez crisis also caused Kennan to consider what America and its West European and Japanese allies should do about their steadily growing dependence upon foreign facilities and raw resources. He reaffirmed that increasing consumption of materials from abroad meant that the most advanced, technological economies belonged—when it came to reliance on the stability of international exchanges—to the most fragile portion of international society. This condition had to be corrected. He urged that Western governments and publics at large take cognizance of their new vulnerability and begin implementing measures to relieve their dependence on external parties. Never one to underestimate the latent violence and dark passions of his compatriots, Kennan warned that an America abruptly deprived of essential materiels, such as oil, would be a menacing thing: "If ever the flimsy fabric of this relationship between our growing demands on our world environment and the readiness or willingness of other countries to meet them is suddenly torn . . . if, in other words, we suddenly find ourselves, by virtue of our dependence on others, face to face with acute physical inconveniences or a real threat to our military security, as many English and French and Israeli people feel to their own situation today by virtue of the Suez incident, then I would not wish to vouch for our behavior." America's historical self-righteousness, he was convinced, was rooted in fortune and a type of physical luxury unavailable to most people; geographic and social conditions, not innate virtue, were the real sources of Americans' presumed moral superiority and attachment to the pacific resolution of international disputes. The impatience of Americans with European nations that felt compelled to use violence, he surmised, was predicated on a national experience in which few foreign problems directly involved the security and comfort of the broad citizenry. In any case, Americans should not take their own good conduct too much for granted.[31]

Kennan predicted that the Suez crisis might be repeated in different forms over the coming years if the supplier and consumer nations failed to understand the nature of mutual responsibilities and obligations that had developed and linked them all in an intricate web of delicate relationships. The best way for governments to ward off future problems was for them to revise their adherence to absolute sovereignty as a guiding principle and to accept a new paradigm: true freedom exists in international life only with the acceptance of obligation and responsibility. He even suggested—in a radical departure from his standard line about the primacy of diplomacy and the poverty of legalism in international affairs—that some sort of institutional and contractual arrangements could be established that would specify and codify the particular obligations states owed their neighbors in their handling of economic affairs. Consistency and a healthy regard for others would then characterize the whole global economic system and not be restricted to the formal arrangements of Benelux and the Iron and Steel Community in Europe.

In this improved world in which political symbiosis formed the core, the users of facilities and consumers of raw materials would have obligations toward the supplier nations, too. Just what they would be, Kennan did not say, though presumably they would involve something about fair fees and prices. This omission was just another indication of how little concerned he really was with the new producer states. Indeed, should they prove themselves to be uncooperative, the West he insisted would have to play rough and perhaps employ its financial and productive powers as weapons in the international game.

Kennan publicly suggested, as an alternative to Western-Third World economic warfare or an ambitious legalized world economic order that would guarantee Western dominance in perpetuity, that the United States and its allies drastically curtail the scale of their demands on the outside world through development of new sources, including synthetics, and by conservation. Public transportation should replace the privileged position of the wasteful, dangerous car. New fuels and technologies should be developed that cost less and provided more and cleaner energy. The Western governments, meanwhile, would not have to establish a general monopoly over foreign trade, as during wartime, but they should impose some limits on international commercial activity: the private sector with its blind faith in *laissez-faire* lacked the purposefulness to pursue policies in keeping with Western security. And Americans generally would have to unlearn their egregious habits of wastefulness, inefficiency, poor discipline: "The time for empty . . . prattling has passed; and the Suez crisis should be proof of this to any thoughtful person."[32]

The real lesson of Suez, contrary to Kennan, was that the imperial European order could not be resurrected in a pseudo-legal form—or any other—in 1956. His preferences on this score, on the order of Churchill's ideas about British rule in India, were so out of date as to be irrelevant to the United States as it tried to deal with the social forces and new political agendas being generated in territories previously under European tutelage. Eisenhower and Dulles can be criticized for their Middle Eastern foreign policy. The secretary of state *was* clumsy in his handling of Nasser and the Aswan Dam project; lack of diplomatic finesse *did* lead Eisenhower needlessly to humiliate American allies and align the United States with the Soviet Union in condemning them in the UN forum. Still, the administration was correct in attempting to salvage America's standing in the Middle East at a time when its chief NATO associates were creating a political and military situation inhospitable to long-term Western interests.[33] Then, as now, if the United States was to succeed at all in areas outside of Europe and Japan, the sensibility of a Berry had to prevail.

Kennan, nevertheless, has remained skeptical, and nothing that has occurred since Suez has inclined him to change his views about the Middle East or the larger issue of Third World-Western relations. He privately abhorred both the Bagdad Pact and the Eisenhower Doctrine and ridiculed them in 1958 as pure nonsense. Although he did publicly defend the dispatching of Marines to Lebanon that year as a means of shoring up a Western position, his heart was not in it. The public anger with which this action was met in some parts of the Arab world and elsewhere depressed him: "I am thoroughly sick of this anti-American hysteria on the part of a world which has no right, on the basis of experience, to expect any great power to act with half the decency in world affairs that we, in our bumbling way, have manifested." He sorely missed the old international order, and with respect to the Arabs felt himself "the most rabid of imperialists."[34] Two decades later, he was still warning against the dangers of Western dependence upon Arab oil and was advocating conservation and a concentrated search for alternative energy sources. As for Israel, Kennan viewed it (three decades after its birth) as important, but not really crucial to the United States, a country to be aided but not worth the sending of American troops. As with other countries in shaky areas of the world, such as Latin America, the US should maintain a certain detachment, a realism about the costs and benefits of political intimacy.[35]

Latin America

Citing Kennan's trip to Latin America, February-March 1950, and his address to local US ambassadors, the historian Walter LaFeber assigns Kennan with partial blame for the militarization of US policy toward the southern hemisphere during the early 1950s.[36] In fact, he had virtually nothing to do with policymaking during this period, and his general line anyway was in a contrary direction, toward a diminution of US involvement with that region.

During his Policy Planning years, Kennan had directed little attention toward the area and tended, like most North Americans, to take it for granted. For example, his and the Staff's resume of the world situation in 1947 (PPS 13, November 6) did not once allude to South America. This neglect was not really corrected in 1948, when the Staff decided a rather simple matter, namely the criteria by which the United States would extend or withhold recognition of Latin governments. In the case of Venezuela, where a military junta had come to power through violent means, the Staff recommended that recognition be granted as it was compatible with US economic and political interests; it was understood that recognition did not convey moral approval, however.[37] The PPS also paid some attention to the type of anti-communist measures that the United States could coordinate with its Latin neighbors, but the recommendations were unexceptionable and did not bear much impress of Kennan's ideas and personality.[38]

Only in 1949, after the establishment of the Organization of American States (1948), did Kennan and the PPS draw up a detailed position toward Latin America, and even it was restricted to assessing US military obligations as specified under OAS provisions. Contrary to the NSC, Kennan doubted that the grooming of Latin American military forces was terribly important. They were, after all, handicapped by the technical and economic conditions prevailing in their countries and would prove themselves of little value in a global war. He also cautioned that the injection of large quantities of military assistance into Latin America would reduce what little solidarity existed there by aggravating local fears and suspicions and perhaps rekindling old rivalries. A Latin America divided against itself and heavily armed was hardly an asset to the United States. Therefore, Kennan believed, the US should avoid committing itself to the southern sphere's military development. Real security for the Latin Americans from the threat of the Soviet Union and its minions in the New World lay chiefly in political, economic, and social rehabilitation.[39]

Kennan's visit to Latin America in early 1950 did nothing to alter his notions that the region's problems were the responsibility of its inhabitants and that US attitude and behavior should be ones of detachment. His trip's itinerary included most of the capitals of countries important to the United States: Mexico City, Caracas, Rio de Janeiro, Montevideo, Buenos Aires, Lima, Panama.

Instead of exciting Kennan with their ebullience or quickening his curiosity about them and their national histories and traditions, these cities dismayed him, jangled his nerves, and were antithetical to his aesthetic sense. He described Mexico City as "disturbed, sultry, and menacing." Caracas blared with "screaming, honking traffic jams," and its economy was "feverish" and "debauched." Rio was "noisy" and "repulsive." Glare, gleam, poverty, and self-indulgent luxury all seemed to bear down on Kennan. He could not rest in such settings and felt smothered by a type of claustrophobia. Adding to his discomfort, he was greeted in several cities with anti-US demonstrations and graffiti telling him to "go home." Communist students burned him in effigy, and to his consternation he was guarded by shotgun-toting Indians in Brazil. As for the indigenous government authorities and representatives, he found them to be banal, obsequious, and conceited.[40]

Soon after his return to Washington, Kennan submitted a long memorandum (thirty-five pages, single spaced) to Secretary Acheson in which he explained Latin America's place in US global concerns. Similar to his later attempt to enlighten his superiors about the Middle East, his assessment of Latin America and US relations with it were not sympathetically reviewed by the responsible regional office in the State Department. In fact, Edward Miller, the assistant secretary of state for Inter-American Affairs, found Kennan's report so replete with errors and misconceptions that he prevailed successfully upon Acheson to forbid its dissemination through the department.

Many aspects of the report were inoffensive to US government thinking at the time, however. For example, according to Kennan, a well-ordered US-Latin American relationship would serve as a useful illustration of why the United States was fit to lead the non-communist world and would encourage Latin Americans to function contentedly in the capitalist economic system. He added that, in time of war, raw materials necessary for the production of weapons and the maintenance of fleets, planes, and tanks would be available in a favorably predisposed Latin zone and that the goodwill of South Americans should prove valuable in influencing the larger world community to back the US.

It was only where Kennan delved into theory and history that Miller expressed disapproval. To begin with, Kennan once more exercised his ideas about climate and geography as chief determinants of civilization and progress: how unfortunate that Latin America was close to the equator, the region least conducive to vigorous human activity. Its human history, moreover, was almost unbelievably tragic. Kennan regretted that the Spaniards had arrived in Latin America when their cultural development was practically moribund and when they were left only with "religious fanaticism, a burning, frustrated energy, and an addiction to the most merciless cruelty." In this condition, they were in no mood to spare the native traditions or institutions of the New World. They imposed their rule with ferocity and heartlessness: "Human history, it seems to me, bears no record of anything more terrible ever having been done to entire peoples. The shock to the national consciousness was profound and irreparable." The legacy of a human society so broken that it could never be put to rights was a permanent social and psychological fragmentation that would hobble all future Latin attempts at political stability and general well-being: "Here is the true illustration of the crimes of the fathers being visited on their progeny; for, as the Spaniards intermarried with these native peoples the course of whose history had so ruthlessly been interrupted, they had to share the scars and weaknesses which they had themselves inflicted."[41] The later importation of slaves from Africa into other parts of Latin America and subsequent intermarriage made for another sad admixture and for inherent weakness of character among succeeding generations.

Kennan also posited that, in their subconscious desires to overcome the traumas of defeat and slavery, the modern Latin Americans sought compensation in gaudy and pretentious surroundings—hence the plush villas and posturing of the *nouveaux riches*. He pronounced that the Latins were, as a rule, exaggerated in their self-importance and egoism and that their shows of courage, intelligence, and virility were sorry expressions aimed at overcoming their heritage of bondage and mass murder. In such a neurotic part of the world, the staid and sober North American diplomat (i.e., Kennan) was at a disadvantage: the constructive virtues were not only seldom observed in the daily operations of Latin American officials, they were not appreciated. Consequently, most every northern diplomat was forced to indulge the stylized fictions and ceremonies dear to his preening hosts. Kennan judged that most non-Latin diplomats assigned to South American posts sought escape in various forms of cynicism, unhappiness, and inappropriate participation in the intimate affairs of national life.

From the standpoint of the Soviet Union, its major tools in Latin America— native communists—left much to be desired in Kennan's opinion. As products of their environment, they exhibited traits, such as indiscipline and excessive individualism, that made for volatile, undependable revolutionaries. They possessed too personalized an approach to communist tactics and goals and, unlike the more doctrinaire and obedient communists of Europe, were not aware of their roles as instruments of the USSR; indeed, Kennan was convinced that Moscow viewed the Marxist revolutionaries of Latin America with a combination of amusement and contempt. Still, the Latin communists, however farfetched they were in some respects, posed a danger to the US even if they failed to seize a single government. Their objective of converting South America into a region of hostility and trouble for the US was possible as their activities tied into the existing body of anti-American feeling present in every Latin state. Although the military dangers were not significant, Kennan hoped Washington would recognize that communist activities in Latin America even during peacetime could damage its place in US security policy and disturb US relations with other continents. In case of global Soviet-US war, he predicted that several South American states would be engulfed by civil violence or lost by communist *coup d'états*. These events would in turn spoil political confidence in the US on an international scale; and, to the detriment of long-term relations with Latin America, the US would probably have to seize by force raw materials and strategic facilities in the south.

To help safeguard the southern hemisphere, Kennan recommended that the US promote more and better informational programs about the hazards of communism; abstain from periodic military intervention and direct pressure which, if used, would produce the opposite intended effect; and employ "total diplomacy," whereby all government officials and agencies dealing with Latin America would accept and strictly adhere to the secretary of state's line. Such centralized control would have the double advantage of flexibility and greater policy coherence. Presumably, the flow of benefits and hardships for any country from relations with the United States could be manipulated and the overall temperature of the relationship easily lowered or raised as the situation required. At the same time, the US should preserve some detachment when engaged in multilateral conferences and negotiations and not allow itself to become ensnarled in contests for leadership in inter-American bodies. The United States was the undoubted preeminent power in the New World, and it was undignified for it to become involved in petty competitions about prestige with lesser states. The US-Argentine contest in the 1930s, for example, was perfectly meaningless. Indeed, the overall US approach and tone should be commensurate with the real distribution of power and international weight:

> It is important for us to keep before ourselves and the Latin American peoples at all times the reality of the thesis that we are a great power; that we are by and large much less in need of them than they are in need of us; that we are entirely prepared to leave to themselves those who evince no particular desire for the forms of collaboration that we have to offer; that the danger of a failure to exhaust the possibilities of our mutual relationship is always greater to them than to us; that we can afford to wait, patiently and good naturedly; and that we are more concerned to be respected than to be liked or understood.[42]

In countries where there was some tradition of self-government, Kennan thought the existence of a communist party and activity could be tolerated without danger to the United States or the Latin Americans. This sort of liberal approach was not always possible, though, and in some places other, sterner imperatives would have to operate. He explained that where the concepts and traditions of popular government were too weak to absorb successfully the fury of communist attack, then the United States must concede that harsh governmental measures of repression were the only answer; and that these measures would have to proceed from regimes whose origins and methods would not stand the test of American democratic procedures. He hoped that his compatriots would appreciate that the usual alternative to such policies would be successful communist incursions and the eventual triumph of regimes that would naturally seek alignment with Russia. If only the Americans could suspend their preaching about democracy for once, if they could refrain from their moralizing and quick judgments: "Of the degree to which Latin American statesmen may be said to have acquitted themselves of their responsibilities to their own peoples, to their own traditions, and to themselves—of their relations, in other words, with whatever answers to the name of 'conscience' in these confused and unhappy societies—of these things I feel . . . that we should prefer to remain ignorant."[43] The US ought to remain cool and composed in handling Latin political leaders. And there was no justification for Washington to continue its "haunted anxiety" and "cramped reactions" in facing the problems of complicated and largely unpleasant peoples: leave them to themselves.

Coinciding with Kennan's South American tour, concern was rising in Washington about the political direction Guatemala was taking. Kennan himself advised Acheson that Guatemala's labor movement was communist dominated and that from an American standpoint the situation was progressing badly. He urged the administration to express to Guatemalan authorities through diplomatic channels that continued anti-US activities on a large scale and the constant danger to which US commercial interests were exposed were bound to affect state-state relations adversely. If the Guatemalan government failed to take corrective steps, it should be forthrightly warned that henceforth no American official—in Washington or Guatemala City—would be of any further assistance in promoting Guatemalan interests. If this step also failed to remedy the condition, then the administration should launch a coordinated diplomatic assault, "Operation Freeze." For Kennan, this would amount to a type of diplomatic warfare:

> Each government agency having anything to do with matters affecting the interests of the Guatemalan Government would become extremely sticky in its handling of all such operations, and would be as unobliging in every form of its dealing with the Guatemalan Government or Guatemalan interests as it could possibly justify itself in being. . . . We will find . . . that there are few government agencies, if any, doing business with the Guatemalan Government which do not have grievances arising out of their particular business. Once this operation is launched, they should become as disagreeable as possible in their dealings with Guatemalan interests. [44]

And the Guatemalans, he predicted, should come around soon enough.

Kennan's proposal was opposed to the spirit of traditional US gunboat diplomacy in Latin America and equally at odds with the covert demolition of Jacobo Arbenz and his government conducted by the CIA in 1954.[45] Indeed, Kennan was unenthusiastic about the manner in which the position of the US and the United Fruit Company was rehabilitated; nothing that occurred in such a country could in any way diminish or damage the United States, but detectable US interference could lead to a chain reaction of emotions and events in the south opposed to Washington's political interests.

In the years since the defeat of Arbenz's reforms and quasi-revolution, Kennan has paid infrequent attention to Latin America; when he does he has always returned to the same themes. The United States should not fuss too much over Latin Americans, but "expect less of them and to try to get them to expect less of us, to give up the search for understanding or popularity, to wait for them to come to us."[46] Regarding the periodic flareups of violence and controversy about the Panama Canal during the 1960s and 1970s, Kennan thought the Latins generally and the Panamanians especially were outrageous in their demonstrations of resentment. By 1964 he had come to the tentative conclusion that the United States should unload its responsibilities for the expensive Canal: it was no longer of strategic importance; perhaps the OAS would like to run it as a cooperative project. By 1977, he was convinced that the US should turn control of the Canal directly over to Panama. Not only was it costly to maintain, but continued US operation of it would confirm most Latins in their views of US villainy and imperialism. If the Panamanians wanted the Canal, they could have it, and the United States would be well rid of the annoyance and burden.

Beyond Panama, only the peculiar problem of Cuba has caused Kennan much concern. He hoped during the 1970s that the United States could come to terms with Castro's regime and that Cuba would not have to exist permanently as a Soviet client. To his mind, this issue, along with the general problem of Central American security, was entirely manageable. Mercifully for the United States, there was nothing pressing about Latin America: "Let us be generous in small things, courteous in all circumstances, and helpful wherever we can be, but beyond that not greatly concerned for their opinion of us, and happy enough not to be active in their affairs."[47] The Latins should also be respectful of US interests and not take American forbearance for granted. In this connection, Keenan was puzzled and irritated when, after US overtures, Castro sent thousands of Cuban troops to southern Africa—Angola—to assist in a revolution and in the overthrow of one of the last European-ruled areas of the continent.

South Africa

While director of the Policy Planning Staff, Kennan's attention was drawn only twice (1948) to African problems. Both cases were related to the disposition of European imperial holdings—French North Africa and former Italian colonies in Libya, Eritrea, and Somaliland. The central concern of Kennan and the Staff was that nothing inimical to Western interests occur in any of these areas; in the French instance, everything should be done to preserve and enhance the metropole's status and legitimacy.[48] For the most part, Kennan regarded Africa as marginal to the global balance of power and saw no reason to draw it into the great powers' Cold War contest. The African continent itself never seems to have interested him personally very much.

Yet in 1967 he did conduct a lecture tour of the Republic of South Africa at the behest of the US-South Africa Leader Exchange Program. He was well received in that country, though upon his return to the United States was criticized by various civil rights groups, including the NAACP, for having lent his personal prestige to the apartheid government. For his part, Kennan was unapologetic and argued that affairs in South Africa were too complex and entrenched to allow for obvious liberal solutions, and, in any event, as a private citizen of a democratic country, he was free to travel where he chose and owed explanations to no one.

Despite its internal and foreign problems, South Africa impressed Kennan as something inspired and offering hope for the future. Like an American Tocqueville, he was exhilarated by what, at age sixty-three, he saw in the southern zone of a vast and mysterious continent: "This is one of the great developing areas of modern civilization—an area which, precisely because of its uniqueness in many respects, of its vitality, and of the lateness of its arrival among the ranks of the great industrial centers, is going to make its own important contribution, in the field of ideas as well as in science and technology, to the solution of the problems of this precarious late twentieth century world."[49]

In theory, apartheid did not strike him as especially reprehensible, but rather suited to the local situation. Judging by the practical effects of forced racial integration in the southeastern United States, he found no reason to condemn codified segregation elsewhere: "It seems to me that the attempt to force a general mingling of the races in all aspects of residence and education, where this does not rest on a general natural acceptance and preference by both parties, either leads to unnecessary conflict where it is physically successful or—more often and most ironically—produces . . . an unintended apartheid which is worse than an intended one."[50] For this doubtful judgment, he offered no evidence. Still, he maintained that in some spheres of life—education, residence and recreation—the case for separate and truly equal development was persuasive, so long as it was unaccompanied by coercion.

Under ideal conditions, separateness could be expected to correspond with the preferences, aesthetic and otherwise, of blacks and whites, and would produce less violence and hard feeling than state-backed integration. According to Kennan, the case for a humane apartheid was further strengthened because there was some question of whether or not the blacks indigenous to South Africa were intellectually limited and could participate as fully and responsibly in modern society as their kin in other parts of Africa. "I wonder," he told a friend, "whether there are not real differences in native aptitude between the Khoza and the other herdsman tribes of South Africa, on the one hand, and the obviously intelligent and adaptable peoples of the center of the continent, particularly West Africa. If there are, then it is incorrect to apply to South Africa all the same standards one would apply to peoples and situations further north."[51] Separate development at its best was not devoid of merit, he felt, at least not to anyone who was honest enough to view facts for what they really were.

He was willing to admit that apartheid as practiced by the South African government had led to many unhappy results, however. Not only did the racial policies offend the bulk of Western opinion, but they were unable to satisfy South Africa's own long-term needs and their ultimate failure would lead to untold suffering and hardship. The disparities in wages and services, the officially sanctioned abuse of the coloreds and educated blacks, the limits imposed on nonwhite participation in politics and in the higher echelons of business, separate universities, and segregated professions and work places could all be eliminated, in Kennan's estimation, without doing damage and would go a long way in preserving the real separateness essential to a harmonious South African society.

Left to themselves, white South Africans, led by the English-speakers, would exert themselves in the direction of greater humanity and political stability. Their cause, though, was not being helped by the behavior of foreign governments trying to hasten the day of black liberation; just the opposite in fact. Kennan recommended that enlightened internal South African forces be allowed to work their will in their own time and develop just and workable solutions in a manner tailored to local traditions and context; hope lay in the gradual realization by the European minority that the practical forms of apartheid were unrealistic and unjust, and failed as a basis for the future development of an advanced industrial country. Therefore, South African whites needed exposure to intelligent criticism from the outside, not sanctimonious lecturing or threats. In other words, for Kennan, the West should maintain maximum contact with the ruling elements so that their intellectual and political imaginations could be quickened; international pressures aimed at isolating the South African regime should be reduced because they narrowed Pretoria's opportunities to learn, forced it to be more insular, and encouraged its martyr complex.

Kennan believed that, if the West or others did precipitate an abrupt end of minority rule in South Africa, an uncontrollable disaster would engulf all South Africans, blacks as well as whites. The Republic's blacks were, for various reasons—Kennan thought the whites bore blame through neglect of their educational responsibilities—grievously unprepared to govern an industrial, intricate society. In any one of the agrarian countries found farther north, South African blacks would have fared well both economically and in their political self-management, but in South Africa black rule would lead directly to the collapse of politics, industry, and economy. Depression and chronic instability for the blacks and coloreds would make a mockery of "liberation."

Moreover, the whites could not be expected to accommodate themselves gracefully to any sudden establishment of black government and many would prefer to emigrate or "go down fighting." Kennan noted that some Europeans had found temporary niches for themselves in postcolonial Africa, but their positions were fragile, and the flourishing of white communities in a future dominated by blacks was pure chimera. Besides, there was no precedent of a secure place for white people in any African-ruled state. In South Africa—where the numerical proportion of whites to blacks was greater than elsewhere, where the energy of white areas had not been sapped through emigration and demoralization, where investment, profits, and industrialization were great, and where the white population could trace its origin of settlement to the seventeenth century—Kennan assumed that a quick transition to majority rule would be attended by devastating white violence.

Even if large-scale violence should prove technically successful for the blacks, there was no guarantee that majority rule in any meaningful sense would be forthcoming. Kennan suspected that, as elsewhere in Africa, the white ruling circle would be replaced by a black elite little acquainted with and interested in democracy. Although such an arrangement might amount to an improvement in the eyes of most people around the world, the white South Africans—in effect, disenfranchised—would leave the country *en masse* before teaching their successors how to operate the economic plant designed by Europeans: "What one is talking about, when one speaks of the introduction of 'majority rule' in South Africa as a result of external pressure, is a bloody and terrible business indeed, the results of which would probably be greatly different from what we picture."[52]

Thus, attempts by outside parties to enforce their standards of moral rectitude and political propriety in South Africa were unjustified in Kennan's view and would leave in their wake horrid results. Those in the West who advocated disinvestment, divestiture, assistance to dissidents or rebels, or armed intervention were incurring for themselves, however unwittingly and however good their intentions, a moral responsibility for the destruction of life and society in a part of the world in which they did not live and would not suffer direct consequences. Intervention of any kind—moral, political, economic, or military—was also unwarranted in the neighboring countries of Rhodesia, Mozambique, and Angola: "It is not our business, nor does it lie within our capabilities, to sit in judgement on the internal political institutions and practices of other countries and governments and to compel their alteration when they do not meet with our approval."[53] South Africa and the others were not the only places in the world where a visible minority of the population ruled and where the rest of the population was restricted in its civil and political rights; a selective moral policy amounted to political and intellectual nonsense and, according to Kennan, could only confuse the public mind about the principles which govern US foreign policy.

He hoped that the United States would make it quietly clear to the southern African governments that the West lacked ultimate confidence in them and that this placed limitations on the extent of future mutually profitable relations. Within the confines of this concept some bilateral US-South African practices might be curtailed. Visits by US naval ships to South African ports, for example, might be reduced or eventually eliminated. But even within this framework of mild rebuke and sanctions, Kennan reemphasized that South Africa should be basically left alone and that the Europeans there, who possessed the overwhelming majority of educational competence and experience, should devise means of their own for coping with the country's political dilemmas. He placed much confidence in South Africa's continued economic growth for possessing the social logic that would overwhelm apartheid. The United States should therefore not worry that its economic links to South Africa were strengthening an untenable situation: a complex economy was inconsistent with the continued stagnation of most of the population in a situation of ignorance and civil impotence; the most effective enemy of apartheid was the commercial interest that led whites to expand South Africa's economy at a "stormy pace." Thus, according to Kennan, the economic demands for greater efficiency, managerial competence, skilled labor, and domestic purchasing power would force upon South Africa irreversible social and political progress.

Kennan expressed sympathy to the white South Africans with whom he met in 1967 for the enormity of their racial problems and agreed with their government that solutions satisfying to all concerned parties would require a great deal (unspecified) more time. And he reaffirmed the wisdom of apartheid as it existed in theory. He had no qualms, however, about telling white South African audiences that he, a private citizen of another country, could not endorse Pretoria's practical racial policies. They were morally deficient, were out of accord with the temper and demands of the age, and harmed South Africa's position as a full and equal member of the Western world:

> I think you will have to move much faster, much more imaginatively and humanely, that communication between racial groups will have to be greatly improved . . . that you will have to give the various non-white racial elements prospects of political expression, of educational development, of employment, of remuneration, and better possibilities for the expression of their talents in every way, if you are going to meet even the minimum of their inevitable expectations and if you are going to make of them hopeful partners rather than alienated drones in the development of South African society. And unless you do make such partners of them, I do not see any hopeful answer to the problems of your relations with the rest of Africa or with world opinion.

In the end, by way of a parting shot, Kennan the Presbyterian moralist joined Kennan the pragmatic diplomat in issuing these words of warning and exhortation to change. "I cannot," he told his white listeners, "see any hopeful answer to your relations with yourselves; for you, too, will never be complete members of a human society which is itself tragically incomplete."[54]

During the decade between his visit to South Africa and the occasion when (1977) he again addressed the issue, nothing occurred to weaken him in his convictions that political change must be gradual in South Africa and that the West should refrain from applying undue pressure. To Kennan, the relinquishment of Portuguese power in nearby Mozambique and Angola had resulted in worsened conditions for the black populations and augured ill for the day when white rule ended in Rhodesia or South Africa. He also ascribed much of the blame for problems in Mozambique and Angola to liberals in the Western media who, in their haste to strike heroic poses and unimpeachable moral attitudes, had written reckless criticisms of Lisbon and wound up abetting the real enemies of progress: hunger, poverty, civil war. Turning to South Africa, he resisted all the more fervently those in the United States who called for disinvestment, divestiture, economic embargo, and assorted political sanctions. He denounced these proposals as preposterous and self-defeating and claimed that black South Africans opposed them.[55] Nothing, he urged once more, would be gained by the departure of Western industrial plants and capital and probably considerable injury would be inflicted upon the blacks as they were deprived of the moderating influence concomitant with American economic involvement: "The foreign firms operating branches in that country have stood in the forefront of the effort to achieve better treatment, both in wages and in responsibility of function, for black workers; and they have had some success."[56]

Kennan's proposition, that the South African situation would correct itself over time, and its corollaries, that outside pressures or even "constructive engagement" were inappropriate, undesirable, and unwanted, have thus far proved erroneous.[57] By 1987, the South African regime had fostered cosmetic changes—a new constitution, the creation of bantustans, separate parliaments for Asians and coloreds, repeal of the pass laws—designed to deflect Western criticisms, but in fact so transparently false that popular indignation in the West had grown appreciably. Nothing substantive had been done by Pretoria to improve the lot of black subjects: rather, the forced removal of black families to impoverished lands, killing of black leaders by state organs, harsh crackdowns on organized black labor, and shootings in townships reflected the reality of an increasingly intransigent regime. And the most articulate black representatives, including Steven Biko, Albert Luthuli, and Bishop Desmond Tutu, had insisted, contrary to Kennan, that the international community take economic measures—including disinvestment—against South Africa. They argued that the policies of Western corporations improved the condition of only a small number of black workers while leaving the remainder untouched; meanwhile the Western corporate presence added to South Africa's overall economy, which in turn supported a formidable apparatus of police and military control. Continued bloodshed in Soweto and elsewhere has not only upset consciences in the West and boded ill for any peaceful, evolutionary progress toward political change, but has belied Kennan's hope for emergent comity between the contestants and his expectation that the white minority could correct the folly of its political ways in a timely manner.

*   *   *   *

It is tempting, and not at all inaccurate, to accuse Kennan of obtuseness in his understanding and political recommendations about the Third World. Incidentally, the term "Third World" is objectionable to him. He could point out with justification that it stands for no clearly defined group of countries, but is a residual category that, while it excludes Western and most communist societies, embraces a broad range of countries as diverse as Argentina, India, Chad, New Guinea, and Gambia. He has never addressed this conceptual issue directly, however, but impatiently and ill-humoredly has registered his disapproval with quotation marks around the difficult term. Indeed, his frequent resort to quotation marks and use of such phrases as "so-called" are conspicuous in his writing about Third World topics: "so-called white-ruled" countries of Africa, "majority rule," "independence," "Namibian" people.[58] His use also of epithets and references to diseases, especially mental disorders, in referring to various Third World peoples reflects his tendency toward stereotyping and raises doubts about the quality of some of his intellectual and political judgments. As we have seen in previous chapters, he has used hard terms at one time or another in discussing communists, Soviet culture, McCarthyites, and other phenomena or people that draw his ire. But in referring to the Third World he has often surpassed himself: he has described the residents of Bagdad as "unhygienic" in their habits, fanatical and bigoted in their religious faith;[59] Mexicans as "neurotic, stubborn, violent" and their country atavistic;[60] and he has condemned the peoples of Southeast Asia for conducting "immature and impetuous policies."[61] In 1977, he asserted without qualification, through an invidious comparison between his Wisconsin forebears and Third World inhabitants, that inordinate laziness, violence, and improvidence largely account for the latter's misery.[62] Thus he has been inclined to compress into superficial and misleading categories those vast human experiences encompassing European imperialism and clashing civilizations that helped lead to economic and social dislocations in the Third World and the striking disparities in national wealth around the globe. Very likely, Kennan's commendation of "old fashioned American values"—thrift, honesty, hard work, civic pride—that he believes his pioneer ancestors embodied and that enabled them to overcome the hardships of nineteenth-century Wisconsin and develop it into a prosperous commonwealth are rooted in his own self-conscious Calvinist background: the elect flourish, the poor and outcast suffer because of their iniquities.

And yet, lest we go too far in the direction of psychologizing and reductionism, it is useful to recall that Kennan is hardly alone in his generation—or in others since—in attributing all manner of regrettable traits to various ethnic, racial, and religious groups. The State Department in his day was rife with type-casting of one sort or another. For example, Gordon Merriam, Middle East expert on the Policy Planning Staff (1948–1949), observed that Jews were deeply insecure and that this manifested itself in various "pathological" ways; they were also mentally sharp, exclusive, and selfish; and their conspiratorial techniques and influence in the United States decisively shaped early punitive postwar policy toward Germany.[63] That nonsense of this sort abounded does not excuse Kennan in his own careless characterizations of peoples unknown to him; but, to borrow from his Gibbon, Kennan's imperfections in this regard largely "flowed from the contagion of the times."

His concerns that the US is the object of immense hatred in Asia, Africa, and Latin America and that the country is handicapped in its Third World policies because of liberal guilt are certainly overdrawn. Anti-Americanism has varied considerably in intensity over time and place, and envy of US wealth has been alloyed with respect—and not always grudging as Kennan sees it—for US scientific and industrial achievement. Gains in racial equality have also done something to counter the image of a hypocritical polity. As for Kennan's contention about liberal guilt, it is unclear just how this phenomenon has helped shape foreign policy in the United States. In fact, its impact has been negligible. Periodic calls by Third World leaders and apologists for reparations, compensation, or generous aid have found little resonance with US governments, Jimmy Carter's rhetoric notwithstanding. Even the 1980 Brandt Commission Report, which detailed the problems of poverty in the Third World and suggested innovations by which to solve them, did not lead to any comprehensive joint North-South action, let alone US initiatives. Indeed, the United States has been skeptical historically about the efficacy of aid to poor countries and has concentrated its efforts on a select number of clients such as South

Korea, South Vietnam, Taiwan, and, more recently, Pakistan and Egypt. Of the seventeen donor countries in the Organization for Economic Cooperation and Development, the United States ranked thirteenth by 1980 in the percentage of GNP allotted to foreign assistance, behind every other Western industrial democracy, including little Norway and Belgium. By the standard of Kennan's advice, the US has not erred very much. Unfortunately, and contrary to him (and others such as Robert Tucker), America's failure to take a leading role in helping to alleviate conditions of poverty and social disintegration in regions of the Third World— through preferential trade agreements, debt renegotiations, technical and financial assistance—has meant increasing international instability, which over the long term can only jeopardize US (and Western) economic and political interests.[64] A policy of realism must aim at preempting the spread of hardship in the Third World, lest revolutions therein spawn anti-US regimes, lest wars therein ensnare the Soviets and the Americans and lead to superpower confrontation, lest economic chaos therein swamp entire areas, thereby disrupting the world's interdependent economic order upon which the prosperity and success of the United States depend.

Beneath Kennan's cantankerousness about the Third World and US relations to it is his conservative attitude toward change anywhere; he has always emphasized that continuity and tradition are necessary to any healthy society. Modernity as such is not an unqualified value to him; and, although he has never disavowed the benefits of advancement in medicine, transportation, and communication, he has been incorrigible in his romantic longing for the simpler, wholesome life that he imagines his pioneer ancestors to have enjoyed. He has been very eloquent on the subject of rapid and bewildering social change, as when he addressed the Congress for Cultural Freedom in Milan, 1955:

> Wherever change proceeds so swiftly that the experience of the father becomes irrelevant to the problems of the son, with the result that the family relationship— the natural and fundamental source of all social discipline—loses its validity and power, there one may expect a lessening of the structure of society by which personal freedom can scarcely fail to be endangered. This means that one must not make a fetish out of technological innovation, and must not permit to alter the conditions of existence too suddenly and violently, lest the true sources of self-discipline and good behavior be carried away, together with familiarity of environment, the power of habit, and the sense of inner security.[65]

Of Kennan's understanding of change, pace of change, and generational differences, we will have more to say in the next chapter.

Finally, as to Kennan's acceptance of cultural-political relativism: in an extreme form such relativism can be invoked to justify or exonerate all manner of foolish and repugnant practices abroad. In Kennan's case, a more moderate version has inclined him to support policies of aloofness, abstention, indifference. In addition, the fact that he has not always harbored a balanced regard for the customs of peoples outside the Western world has strengthened his skepticism about the universal applicability of US political institutions and mores. At the height of Cold War presumptuousness in the United States about American universalism, Kennan argued the opposite: "Our national experience is in most respects a unique one; and it is not only possible but something logically to be expected that the institutions flowing from that experience, and organically intertwined with it, should be largely irrelevant to the requirements of peoples whose national experience has been different."[66] Such a categorical statement is surely open to criticism, and, as we have discussed in previous chapters, Kennan was incorrect when he expressed doubts about the suitability of democracy in a German or Japanese cultural context. Nevertheless, his caution in this regard has had some foundation, especially when one considers that attempts by successive US governments to graft American economic and political principles onto societies outside the West have not been spectacularly successful. Consider Vietnam.

12

War and Protest

Kennan and the Policy Planning Staff urged Truman's administration in 1949 to press France in the direction of granting meaningful concessions to nationalism in Indochina and eventually to confer independence upon the area. As did virtually all of the Southeast Asian area specialists in the State Department, Kennan deemed French attempts to recover its Indochinese empire as futile—explainable only in terms of "Gallic mystique"—and that the so-called Bao Dai solution was a deception that could not possibly satisfy the demands of nationalists or capture any of the popular support then accruing to Ho Chi Minh and the communist insurgents; only by aligning itself unequivocally with the forces of noncommunist nationalism could the United States expect to retain Indochina over the long term for Western economic purposes (as a supplier of natural resources and foods) and political ends. Kennan warned that military measures, whether undertaken by the French or the Americans, would accelerate the shift of most national elements into overreliance upon the communists and—as turned out to be the case—would sap the wealth, strength, and especially the morale of any militarily engaged Western power.[1] Despite the soundness of this advice, the United States gradually, and without a clear or firm sense of purpose, became engaged in the 1950s in a campaign against Vietnamese communism.

The protracted, costly, and inconclusive Indochina war of the 1960s and the domestic divisiveness it caused in the United States saddened Kennan. In a spirit approaching resignation, he said at the very height of the war in 1968: "This is a tragic involvement for which no one has derived any particular profit."[2] He had been skeptical from the outset of heavy American intervention under President Lyndon Johnson about whether anything solid or enduring could be achieved in Southeast Asia from the standpoint of US interests. Yet it was only after a period of relative silence and growing discouragement that he openly dissented from the government's war policy and added his voice to those already advocating disengagement.

He was also filled with revulsion at the evidence, as he understood it, of progressive and rapid deterioration in the United States. Racial strife, urban decay, pollution of the natural environment, student protests, and experiments in sexual and social life suggested to Kennan that the anarchical strain in American sensibility had finally triumphed and the national fabric was unraveling forever. The sheer extravagance of American commercialism, culture, and democracy was as bankrupt for Kennan as US foreign policy was discredited by the hopeless war in Asia.

Vietnam

In early March 1965, Kennan allowed to a British friend, "I am dreadfully worried about what our people are doing in Southeast Asia. It seems to me that they have taken leave of their senses."[3] Only a week earlier, President Johnson had ordered the start of sustained, intensive bombing of North Vietnam (Operation Rolling Thunder). And in Saigon, Dr. Phan Huy Quat was trying to organize yet another South Vietnamese government. On March 8, two Marine battalions waded ashore to defend Danang airfield and thereby became the first officially designated US combat troops in Vietnam. By this action the American government signaled how serious it was about defending its Vietnamese client, though the fateful decision to wage a large-scale ground war was still in the offing. To his friends in Washington, notably McGeorge Bundy, Kennan urged that the United States proceed cautiously and keep in mind that, whatever the outcome of conflict in Southeast Asia, the world balance of power and American security would not be affected one way or the other.

Arguably, one of the critical early moments of American involvement in Vietnam occurred in April 1965, when Johnson unveiled a plan at Johns Hopkins University wherein, in exchange for peace, Ho Chi Minh's government could participate in an elaborate US-sponsored program for Southeast Asian renewal and economic development. This proposal was rejected immediately by the North Vietnamese, who insisted that a final peace settlement must conform to the Vietcong program. As with most close observers, Kennan was disappointed by the quick and unyielding communist response, and he wondered if the Chinese were exerting undue influence in Hanoi. He thought that if they should ever attain a position of leadership over the Vietnamese and if Southeast Asia should be delivered to the "fanatical, power-hungry and wholly intolerant" Marxists of the region, then there would never be a chance for the United States to play a constructive role there again.[4]

Yet, to reiterate, the ultimate political disposition of Vietnam and its neighbors in Indochina did not concern Kennan overly much; it was an area of marginal power or potential. The chief danger, he told Reverend Sloan Coffin of Yale in 1965, was that the United States in its preoccupation with Vietnam was being forced into a rigid international position from which it would be difficult to take advantage of existing and future divisions within the communist world. As long as the Americans continued to bomb the north, neither Moscow nor Peking could respond positively to any initiatives aimed at improving Soviet-US or Sino-US relations: "It is the tragedy of our present situation that our government has involved itself in Vietnam in such a way as to lose almost all flexibility of choice not only in that particular area but in our approach to the communist world generally." Responding to Coffin's query about whether he would speak forcefully in public against Johnson's war policy, Kennan demurred that his views were well known in government circles, and that, whether about Vietnam or anything else, they did not command much following. He complained, too, that his private words with officials, as well as his few public statements about Vietnam, had not only been overwhelmingly rejected by influential opinion, but had also come at the expense of scholarly research and writing for publication. He had done his bit and at personal cost: "I can do no more, it seems to me, than to fall silent."[5]

By the end of the year, though, with 200,000 US servicemen in Vietnam and the bombing only temporarily halted, Kennan issued his first unambiguous public warning in the *Washington Post*: a dangerous imbalance in American foreign policy was taking hold because of the Vietnam diversion. Equilibrium must be restored.[6] Still, he was disinclined by conviction and by the discipline of years in government service to break sharply with official Washington, especially the State Department, over an issue so tangled and grave as Vietnam.

By February 1966, American bombing had resumed, and Johnson and South Vietnamese leaders were determined to pacify the south. The new prime minister, Cao Ky, was also committed, at least rhetorically, to undertaking land reforms and other programs of social rehabilitation intended to strengthen the fragile Vietnamese democracy. In the United States popular patience was wearing thin, however. Opinion polls, to say nothing of college campus protests, showed growing discontent with the scale, behavior, and thrust of US policy in Southeast Asia. According to a Stanford-University of Chicago poll, 88 percent of Americans favored negotiating with the Vietcong, and 52 percent thought the Vietcong should be allowed some role in a South Vietnamese coalition government; the weight of opinion was in favor of deescalation.[7] Much more impressive to Kennan than opinion polls was the fact that many thoughtful figures, some of whom he counted as friends (such as Hans Morgenthau and Walter Lippmann), were publicly criticizing US efforts in Vietnam. And under the leadership of J. William Fulbright, an early war dissenter, the Senate Foreign Relations Committee had commenced a series of widely publicized hearings about American involvement in Vietnam. Kennan decided to accept an invitation in February to testify before the Arkansas senator and his colleagues.

To Fulbright's committee, Kennan explained that, by virtue of its lack of industrial economy and inability to produce the machinery and tools of war, Vietnam would ordinarily be of little consequence to the United States. "It is difficult to believe," he confessed in understatement, "that any decisive developments of the world situation would be determined in normal circumstances by what happens on that territory."[8] Even a South Vietnam ruled exclusively by the Vietcong could hardly present a security threat to the US or its main allies justifying direct military intervention. He testified further that, given the intensity of the Sino-Soviet conflict, a unified communist Vietnam would probably pursue an independent foreign policy and could not be regarded as anything like an extension of monolithic communism. In this connection he revised his earlier qualms about Chinese leverage in Hanoi and expressed doubt that a Vietnamese communist regime would be willing to assume a subordinate role as Peking's puppet. In view of these circumstances and of the soaring costs and injuries borne by the United States in Vietnam, he urged Johnson to liquidate American military activities as quickly as US prestige and the political resilience of Saigon would admit.

Kennan opposed any precipitate withdrawal, as it would damage the prospects for peace in the region and leave confusion and panic in its wake. Ideally, the Americans and their allies should fortify the positions they already held on the ground (along the coast and around cities, ports, and air fields), and, simultaneously with turning these "defensive enclosures" over to the South Vietnamese army, Washington could gradually evacuate its own soldiers and capital equipment. While Kennan maintained that a hasty and sudden American departure would tarnish US prestige and interests and undermine the region's stability, he was emphatic that the United States do nothing to expand the fighting. For one thing, the North Vietnamese and Vietcong could not be easily broken; they were politically adept and had the stamina to wage a bloody war of attrition. As for any total rooting out of the Vietcong and military defeat of the North, Kennan predicted that they would be prohibitively expensive and cause such extensive damage to Vietnamese civilian life that the United States would bear an awful moral, as well as economic, responsibility for years to come; in addition, as in Korea, a land campaign against North Vietnam would draw the Chinese into another war against the United States.

Kennan restated to Fulbright his earlier expressed view that, by concentrating on Vietnam, the United States was neglecting other and more important interests elsewhere and that soon enough Washington would lose all ability to exercise international initiative: relations with Russia were suffering, while problems of overriding mutual concern—Germany, arms race—were ignored and allowed to fester; popular support of the United States in Japan (the only vital and industrial power in the East) was eroding, and America's saturation bombing of an Asian people struck especially sensitive memories. And he emphasized that the spectacle of impoverished Vietnamese being pulverized by American bombs, artillery, helicopters, and infantrymen was producing reactions throughout the world detrimental to US standing. Though Kennan had no sympathy for the communist soldiers and guerrillas, their tactics, or their ultimate political purposes, he did believe that the image, however unfair or overly simple, of an American Goliath wreaking untold damage on the weak was depressingly salient internationally. Could the administration therefore not moderate its military operations and increase its efforts at finding a peaceful political solution? Even one less than perfect from a US perspective would be preferable to such a demoralizing and pointless war.

Kennan was unimpressed by those official arguments holding that a defensive military posture and a diplomatic attitude stressing withdrawal from Vietnam would damage US stature among Washington's allies or raise questions about credibility and commitment to their security. He countered that the world at large would look favorably upon the timely cessation of unproductive policies and that US prestige would thereby be enhanced rather than debased. Respecting the government in Saigon, in reality one of the two principals involved in civil war, the United States had never been formally committed to its internal security; that responsibility was

Saigon's and could not be interpreted as falling within US competence on the basis of an ordinary military alliance.[9]

Kennan concluded his remarks to the Foreign Relations Committee by praising the bravery of American combatants in Vietnam and condemning the communists for cruelty. But the virtues of the former and the viciousness of the latter did not justify US attempts to determine the "political realities" of a country whose history, culture, and land were so profoundly distant. America's political institutions and experience were just as inapplicable to Vietnam as to most other Third World countries: "This is not only not our business, but I don't think we can [win the war and transfer US values] successfully." He closed by quoting John Quincy Adams's famous statement of July 4, 1821, which provides as concise a summation as any of Kennan's thought about the inadvisability of US intervention abroad in service of anything loftier than a calibrated balance of power diplomacy:

> Wherever the standard of freedom and independence has been or shall be unfurled, there will be America's heart, her benedictions, and her prayers. But she goes not abroad in search of monsters to destroy. She is the well-wisher to the freedom and independence of all. She is the champion and vindicator only of her own. She will recommend the general cause by the countenance of her voice, and by the benignant sympathy of her example. She well knows that by once enlisting under other banners than her own, were they even the banners of foreign independence, she would involve herself beyond the power of extrication, in all the wars of interest and intrigue, of individual avarice, envy and ambition, which assume the colors and usurp the standards of freedom. The fundamental maxims of her policy would insensibly change from liberty to force. . . . She might become the dictatress of the world. She would no longer be the ruler of her own spirit.[10]

Although Johnson declared after Kennan's testimony that there was little difference between his position and the government's goals, Kennan had obviously been very critical, and his foreign policy reasoning was at variance with Johnson's. Unfortunately for the president, Kennan's voice carried intellectual and moral influence in academic circles and among the politically literate and, in combination with the protests of other eminent Americans, could not be easily dismissed. Johnson's weaknesses, of course, were precisely in the areas of Kennans strengths: he knew something about the political and intellectual cleavages that had rended international communism asunder; he also possessed a far more refined understanding of the limits of American power and of the complicated, usually unsatisfactory, relationship between using massive military means and achieving desirable political ends. But because Johnson and Secretary of State Dean Rusk intimated to Kennan, as well as to the public generally, that criticisms of America's Vietnam policy objectively aided Ho Chi Minh and the Vietcong, Kennan felt inhibited—a "reluctance deference" in his words—after the Senate hearings about speaking publicly against the war. Still, as the conflict wore on Kennan's disenchantment with it grew apace and became more intractable. In his private correspondence he said a great deal. To Klaus Knorr, for example, he declared that the victory and consolidation of Soviet-style communism or its Chinese variant in all Vietnam would not matter. And neither the Soviets nor the Chinese could make out of Vietnam anything more than what the country's population, resources, and traditions permitted. Vietnam, after all, was not Germany or Japan; the country's chronic backwardness could not be transformed into a military asset for anyone. How ironic that a country and region of slight potential power and correspondingly minor political weight had become the object of enormous American expenditure, a sponge sopping up endless resources. Nothing lay ahead for the United States in Vietnam except further difficulties and possible catastrophe. Why not cut US losses and start getting out?[11]

For these reasons Kennan labeled as repulsive the government's attempt to whip up popular feeling behind the war effort: "It is shocking to see the President and the Secretary of State doing all in their power to stimulate and enlist behind this hopeless [enterprise] the most violent sort of American patriotic emotionalism— conveying the impression that what we are now involved in is a great patriotic cause, that we have passed the point where any useful purpose could be served by discussion about the desirability of an action, that we must all stand together behind the boys on the battlefield, that we are full of 'determination,' etc."[12] He feared that an immoderate government and public might eventually involve the nation in a Southeast Asian war that would culminate in hostilities against China, currently in an extremely militant mood. The Cultural Revolution and the ever-expanding dimensions of suffering inflicted on the Vietnamese people through the war's prolongation argued in favor of a restrained US policy—beginning with a tapering off of the bombing and shading quickly into full moratorium—as containing the better part of wisdom. If nothing else, the good regard of mankind was at risk. In a letter to the *New York Times* (September 25, 1966), Kennan stressed that the bulk of world opinion, including UN General Secretary U Thant and Pope Paul VI, viewed the war with increasing anxiety and looked hopefully to its early discontinuation.

By the latter part of 1967, Kennan believed the best course of US action would be to stop the bombing unilaterally and without condition, desist from the search and destroy missions, and adopt the sort of defensive policy around key South Vietnamese locations that he had earlier urged upon Fulbright and his Senate colleagues. These measures would not only lessen hostilities and lead to a settlement, but they would allow the United States to evacuate from the scene both gracefully and with integrity intact. During the first stages of lull in the fighting, U Thant, acting alone or in cooperation with the pope, could use his influence to promote an armistice; but, until such a lull occurred, they and other world statesmen would be unable to negotiate a peaceful settlement or do much to help extricate the Americans from a bottomless quagmire.[13]

Probably Kennan's finest appraisal of America's troubles in Vietnam appeared in a letter he wrote (October 1967) to Arthur Schlesinger, Jr., by then a fellow war dissenter and critic of Johnson's. In it, Kennan neatly dissected the various elements of analytic confusion underlying the nation's war policy. First, both the president and Rusk erroneously equated communist guerrilla actions in South Vietnam with military aggression across internationally recognized borders. Much of Saigon's difficulty actually rested on the unpleasant fact that people indigenous to the south and aided by the local population were conducting an insurrection against the government; in a situation of civil war the traditional devices of alliance with other countries and external military assistance could not solve what was essentially a case of domestic political crisis and lack of popular confidence. By portraying

North Vietnam as a totally separate, sovereign country unrelated to South Vietnam, the administration was ignoring the complexity of the historical and current situation and compounding the general level of misunderstanding in American political debate.

Kennan complained further that the administration was demonstrating the limits of its own conceptual embrace whenever it depicted North Vietnamese and Vietcong "aggression" as an extension of Chinese "aggression" and subsumed them both under something larger and more ominous, "Asian communism." In fact, China's relation to the war and to Hanoi was ambiguous. Without question, Mao's China in the grip of xenophobia and Cultural Revolutionary zeal would be pleased by any defeat or setback sustained by the United States in Vietnam. And Kennan still believed, as did most people in official Washington, that China would send troops to North Vietnam if the United States threatened to invade and occupy it. In retrospect, such a judgment is open to question because, although China surely would have been displeased at the prospect of American and South Vietnamese troops stationed along a ("soft") portion of the Chinese frontier, the country's military forces were woefully unprepared, the political leadership distracted and uncertain, the economy in a shambles. Besides, in contrast to Korea, Vietnam did not border on any important industrial or population centers; as a springboard into China, it was fairly useless and not worth the sacrifices exacted to secure vulnerable and vital Manchuria during 1950–1953. Finally, as the Chinese discovered to their unhappiness in 1978, the logistical and materiel problems of fighting a well-equipped, veteran force in northern Vietnam were huge. In 1967, as in 1978, the People's Liberation Army was not adequate to displace a determined adversary, and the government in Peking probably would have avoided a set-piece battle or campaign against American fire-power. Of course, an American invasion of the north would not have been politically desirable or feasible. These observations merely suggest that Kennan, like many others (both "doves" and "hawks"), was at least as fixated on China as on Vietnam in proposing a way out for the United States.[14]

Still, Kennan's analysis of Vietnam and China was far more astute than that of most people (George Ball being an exception) near to and advising Johnson. Kennan pointed out that, despite Chinese rhetorical support of Hanoi, the People's Republic had not been particularly generous with materiel assistance—indeed, we now know that the USSR overwhelmed China in the contest of competitive aid to Ho's regime—and, if the North Vietnamese finally captured the south, there was no reason to suppose that Peking would reap much or even any political benefit. "On the contrary, just as in the Balkans," explained Kennan to Schlesinger, "a recalcitrant Communist Yugoslavia proved more resistant to Soviet Communist pressures than any non-Communist regime would have been likely to do, so a militarily successful Hanoi would prove a tougher nut to crack, from the Chinese standpoint, than would a similar Saigon."

Events a decade hence were to reveal that Kennan was mainly right about the nature of postwar Peking-Hanoi relations. Yet even he could not foresee the possibility of military conflict among Asian communist states. Instead, he predicted that China would refrain from ever attacking a communist Vietnam and would subvert its southern neighbor only by subtler forms of penetration and disruption; an armed attack on another Marxist country would presumably destroy China's prestige throughout the communist camp. As with every informed and responsible person in 1967, Kennan did not anticipate that intracommunist wars—Sino-Soviet border fighting; Chinese invasion of northern Vietnam; Vietnamese conquest of Cambodia—would become a standard feature of international relations by the late 1970s.

Nevertheless, his major assertion that no close links existed between Peking and Hanoi was well grounded and explains why he was so angered by the administration's misleading statements to the public about communist conspiracy, timetables, and unified purpose: "To allow the American public to infer that what we are confronted with here is something like an intimate Peking-Hanoi partnership—a partnership so intimate that the two regimes may safely be treated as one from the standpoint of our policy formulation—is simply to disorient public understanding on a [crucial] point of interpretation." Sad to say, Kennan should not have been surprised, especially in light of his ambassadorship to Belgrade and earlier experiences in the Policy Planning Staff: most American political leaders were either grotesquely uninformed about the most fundamental facts regarding communist polycentrism or chose not to educate the public and instead employed terms dating from the early Cold War. Such a political vocabulary provided some psychological comfort to diverse political constituents, as it was both constant over time and required no new mental exercise among rulers or citizens. Like most people elsewhere, the majority of Americans let their political fortunes and diplomacy be organized around shibboleths.

As for America's continuing assistance to Saigon, Kennan repeated his point to Schlesinger that no outside power could do more for the regime than it and its supporters were willing to do for themselves. The presence of nearly half a million US servicemen could not translate into the social and political reforms necessary to Saigon's rehabilitation. Worse still, the American military presence distorted and aggravated the overall political problems of Saigon by helping to shift the locus of authority elsewhere—namely, to the US high command and ultimately to the White House—and thereby cast the legitimacy and independence of the South Vietnamese government more deeply into doubt. Meanwhile, US soldiers, by virtue of their prowess, if not their numbers, had become the leading element in South Vietnamese security, but these forces were constrained by Saigon's lackluster morale, shaky determination, and weakness of leadership: "If the non-Communist South Vietnamese, as it seems to have been the case all along, were incapable of producing out of their midst a political vitality commensurate with that of the Vietcong, then we should have recognized at the start that this patient was beyond saving, either by us or any other outside party, and our concern should have been to soften the impact of his demise, not to try to keep him alive by crawling into his skin."[15]

Only an astronomical American expenditure going far beyond the half million troops dispatched and the billions of dollars dispensed could prevent South Vietnam's capitulation, according to Kennan. This quandary was the price for Washington's failure to grapple with the issues of Saigon's political feebleness, its lack of popular support, and Johnson's misplaced confidence in the efficacy of military means to decide an essentially political struggle. Better to adopt the "enclave" concept as put forth by Generals James Gavin and Matthew Ridgway (similar to Kennan's "defensive enclosure") and buy time for negotiations and a settlement that would permit the Americans to leave Vietnam while allowing for a decent interval before South Vietnam collapsed. The Americans, meanwhile, should immediately cease their bombing raids: "They obviously represent an extravagant and profoundly misconceived undertaking, in which the relationship of military result to the resources committed is absurdly uneconomical, and which suffers further from the fact that it flies in the face both of the sensibilities of the world public and of the moral conscience of our own."[16]

Although Kennan stressed to Schlesinger, Coffin, and others that his opposition to the war was based on pragmatic concerns about limited resources, lopsided policy and strategic misconceptions, it would be a mistake to claim that he was oblivious to larger moral issues. Heavy aerial bombardment of cities as both a concept and practice of modern warfare revolted him. He perceived in the bombing of North Vietnam the same Western impulse toward indiscriminate destruction that had laid waste the cities of Europe two decades earlier.[17] This conclusion led him in time to consider those issues of just-war theory clustered around the problem of legitimate and illegitimate methods of waging war: *jus in bello*. The actions required to "save" South Vietnamese villages horrified Kennan, as did the bombing, and he wished for these reasons alone that the US had avoided the whole encounter with the Vietcong: "The methods to which we have felt ourselves driven, in the effort to crush by purely military means an elusive and disguised adversary, have been so destructive of civilian life, even in the South Vietnamese region to the protection of which our efforts were ostensibly addressed, that no conceivable political outcome could justify the attendant suffering and destruction."[18] In effect, Kennan came to the position that the means necessary for the Americans to win the war were out of proportion to the ends sought and, therefore, in keeping with just-war theory, the American war effort was invalid. He did not actually use these precise terms or reasoning in an explicit manner. But he did say, and it amounts to roughly the same as above, that no matter how great US pressure against Ho—short of invading the north or using nuclear weapons—it was impossible to make Hanoi surrender. By the standards of just-war theory—fair means, obtainable and desirable ends, proportionality—American policy was indefensible.[19] Still, it should be underlined that Kennan had not the slightest sympathy for the "International War Crimes Tribunal" sponsored by Bertrand Russell's Peace Foundation, which judged (1967) US government leaders "guilty of genocide against the people in Vietnam"; nor was Kennan drawn to the similar conclusions of the international law expert and Princeton professor Richard Falk. Even Telford Taylor's agnostic appraisal of the applicability of Nuremberg principles to Vietnam struck Kennan as beside the point.[20]

Against the background of the Tet offensive and more than three years of campus protests and civil demonstrations, Kennan dropped altogether his relative silence and openly supported Eugene McCarthy in 1968 in his bid to replace Johnson as the Democratic nominee in the November presidential elections. Kennan did not think of himself as a zealous or vocal dove, but by 1968, "in considerable agony of spirit" and because the international situation was more fearful in his view than in any time since 1942, he felt there was no alternative to supporting the peace candidate openly and condemning the war. Although he supported McCarthy in New Jersey and appeared with him in public, Kennan did not know the senator personally very well and shared few of his views about domestic issues. But Kennan expected that, if McCarthy made a respectable political showing, this would have a sobering impact on Humphrey, Nixon, Reagan, Rockefeller, and all others— Democrats and Republicans—who believed the war could be continued despite deep divisions in popular opinion. Indeed, by 1968 Kennan was anxious about the possible consequences of an unprecedented national humiliation abroad on the morale and politics of the United States: the war's deplorable effect on youth, dislocations in the national budget, and the continuing neglect of urgent domestic problems were all signs that the war must be soon ended. As for the current group of Democratic leaders, Kennan criticized them for pushing on "stubbornly and heedlessly . . . like men in a dream, seemingly insensitive to outside opinion, seemingly unable to arrive at any realistic assessment of the effects of their own acts." Their miscalculations and errors were massive and rarely rivaled in US history; these charges were doubly serious and inexcusable because of the number and quality of the warning voices that have been raised against the war.[21]

Yet toward the majority of anti-war college protestors, Kennan had crushingly little sympathy. To him, they were mostly another species of opinionated, but not really knowledgeable, people whose solutions to complicated issues were as simple—albeit in the opposite direction—as Johnson's and his war policy advisors. Kennan was among the students in his opposition to the war, but was deliberately and disdainfully not of them.

Protests and Recommendations

Students and Revisionism

Kennan reacted with dismay to the demonstrations, riots, and other forms of overt political protest that the Vietnam war triggered in the United States, primarily on college and university campuses, and the more or less concurrent explosions in poor, mainly black inhabited urban centers. In 1968, the year of the Columbia University sit-in and the assassinations of Martin Luther King and Robert Kennedy, Kennan declared that the country was at its most dangerous impasse since the Civil War: "This is a time in our national life more serious, more menacing . . . than any I have ever experienced or ever hoped to experience."[22]

He despised in particular the behavior, both public and private, of liberal and leftist college students who combined, according to him, every manner of arrogance, self-righteousness, vindictiveness toward their parents, and absurd optimism about the allegedly just, humane intentions of the Vietcong and Hanoi. The slovenly appearance, unfortunate private habits, and obscene language of what he considered to be the typical student were also symptomatic of a national and younger generational malaise. It should be said that Kennan had never been an especially sympathetic observer of American university students and their collective life. In the 1950s, for example, he railed against beatniks and their influence on college mores. He urged students at Princeton to abstain from premarital sex and to avoid the pitfalls of Hollywood notions of love: "Take women, I beseech you, as an adjunct to achievement—not as a substitute for it."[23] The student unrest of the 1960s, however, was of such magnitude and scope that Kennan not only recoiled personally from some of its more exotic manifestations, but felt compelled to protest against it in the public prints. Hence his bristling rebuke in *Democracy and the Student Left* of every real and imagined foible of the student generation.

Kennan's anger at student protestors and at their "life styles" had an obvious visceral quality and reflected in part his estrangement at the time from his teenage son Christopher, who endured his own share of adolescent trials, which in turn were heightened by the turmoil of youth culture in the late 1960s. The problem of "generation gap" drew this intemperate pronouncement from Kennan: "There is a point when we [of the older generation] are . . . impelled to place the needs of children ahead of the dictates of a defiant idealism, and to devote ourselves, pusillanimously, if you will, to the support and rearing of these same children—precisely in order that at some future date they may have the privilege of turning upon us and despising us for the materialistic faint-heartedness that made their maturity possible."[24] Although Kennan did admit in a grudging fashion that many university students were genuinely concerned about questions of justice involving Vietnam and civil rights and had convictions about the preservation of the natural environment, he was inclined to look elsewhere for explanations of their discontent.

In part he blamed his own generation, including himself, for having failed to adhere to high standards of conduct and self-restraint and not having inculcated them as values into the lives of children: "People like myself can[not] view this [student unrest] from some sort of smug Olympian detachment, as though it were not our responsibility, as though it were not in part our own ugly and decadent face that we see in this distorted mirror."[25] These were harsh, self-revealing words from a man who tried all his life to cultivate an aura of one who lived politically, intellectually, and psychologically apart; not far below the surface of his outward civility and high-mindedness was a furious soul.

He also blamed American materialism and affluence for the nervous, agitated condition of youths. The country was swamped by a plethora of useless objects that passed under the guise of convenience, but actually threw into vivid relief the spiritual poverty and intellectual-aesthetic underdevelopment of the United States. He regretted that the pioneer discipline—Wisconsin again—that accompanied scarcity and struggle was gone, and nothing serious or purposeful had emerged to take its place. A generation of youth in trouble (drugs, disorderliness, easy sex) meant that the civilization that had borne and reared these youngsters was in crisis. Kennan remarked in August 1968:

> It is becoming increasingly evident that if people are to be freed from the old discipline of material need, some other form of discipline and purpose must be found for them. Unless this discipline and this purpose are present, it is only too easy for people to become soft, bored, self indulgent, given to passive and inane forms of recreation. And what is worst of all, it becomes difficult for them to exercise an adequate moral authority over their own children. One sees the effects of this in the student disorders that have . . . marred the life of a number of

advanced countries, including our own. Young people, it is clear, do not easily
accept the boredom of a secure and satiated society.[26]

He feared that brawling, chanting students—at heart existentially aimless—
would help create such national disorder and feuding that a reaction might set in
whereby right-wing demagogues would win political benefits; a Joseph McCarthy-
like dictatorship might even be established. As it was, Kennan recommended that
universities such as Columbia would be better off in closing themselves down than
to permit their educational functions to be further frustrated or destroyed by student
rebellion.[27]

More than just being spoiled by the excesses of a materialistic civilization, the
younger generation's disorientation and lack of appreciation for America's contributions were related to the historical problem of mass immigration and contemporary education, Kennan believed. Just as in the 1930s, he remained unpersuaded in
the 1960s about the wisdom of granting entry and citizenship to large numbers of
people far removed from Anglo-American concepts of politics and propriety: "We
have played fast and loose generally with our national tradition, taking little care to
see that its philosophic and ethical foundations were adequately communicated to
the millions of strangers admitted to our body politic."[28] The entire system of
education in easygoing America had not instilled in its younger citizens any
thoughtful or realistic view about human nature or the lessons of political history.
How, asked Kennan, were such Americans, who were fundamentally untutored and
without knowledge or wisdom, going to play a constructive role in the world?[29]

Matters were not helped in this sphere when, during the 1960s, a new school of
political and historical interpretation gained wide attention in challenging the
assumptions and evidence underlying conventional American historiography of the
Cold War. To Kennan the "revisionist" thesis was nonsense, and its scholarly
findings masked the partisan purposes of its authors. Their stress on the economic
forces at work in the US and America's alleged bad faith during World War II,
which caused the Soviets to respond defensively in Eastern Europe and elsewhere,
overlooked in Kennan's estimate the real complexities of 1941–1950 and the
treacherous nature of Stalin's regime and diplomacy. Kennan also had as little
patience for what he imagined to be the political preferences of most revisionists as
he did for their research and writing. Consider, for example, his response to a letter
from one such scholar, David Horowitz, in which the subject of the People's
Republic of China had appeared. For Kennan, nothing could be less appealing than
life in that country in 1966: "To be clothed in blue uniforms, taught to eschew such
things as love, sex, family feeling and humor in favor of proletarian enthusiasm, to
do . . . physical jerks every morning, to sing . . . little regimented chants of hatred,
and to espouse an indignant determination to see international questions settled by
war and violence rather than—as in the views of the Russian traitors—by peaceful
coexistence. In this, I gather, we disagree."[30]

Despite his distaste for the revisionist viewpoint, Kennan tried to deal fairly
with its individual representatives. After seeing a prepublication version of Gar
Alperovitz's manuscript of *Atomic Diplomacy: Hiroshima and Potsdam*, Kennan
warned him that if he should be required to comment publicly about the book, his

words might well be—despite Alperovitz's effort of research and pains at literary presentation—very critical.[31] Alperovitz's references in the book to Kennan were, incidentally, unexceptionable. Five years after the book was published, Kennan condemned it for being replete "not only with misleading language, but with most inaccurate use—sometimes careless, sometimes obviously unscrupulous—of reference material. So slippery and dishonest that its very publication is a disgrace."[32] To another revisionist historian, Theodore Sands, Kennan politely recommended that he discard his research project, which amounted to impugning the goodwill and judgment of Truman, Henry Stimson, and Harriman; Sands was going to imply that through intimidation and economic pressure these national leaders had tried to frustrate the reasonable aims of postwar Soviet statesmanship.

These and other familiar themes and works of revisionist scholarship offended Kennan, not only because he doubted the standards of its rigor and fairness, but because he felt that it was politically pernicious and harmed the judgment of college students on matters of great public concern. Books and articles by Horowitz, Alperovitz, et al. were "shaking the confidence of the present student generation not just in the historical personages concerned but in the integrity of American statesmanship generally."[33] By 1970, Kennan concluded that the entire school of revisionist interpretation was intellectually bankrupt and needed to be refuted before it sowed more misunderstanding and damage among the young.[34] Along with the orthodox, well-established diplomatic historian Herbert Feis, Kennan supported Robert James Maddox in his writing of extremely critical articles attacking the intellectual merit and political motives of the revisionists. Kennan also recommended to the editors of Princeton University Press that they publish a book by Maddox in which he examined and found wanting the works of seven well-known revisionist historians, including Gar Alperovitz, Gabriel Kolko, David Horowitz, and Lloyd Gardner. Maddox's controversial *The New Left and the Origins of the Cold War* (1973) caused a sensation among professional historians of the Cold War and prompted spirited rebuttals from its victims. Horowitz dismissed the book as an intellectual fraud; Kolko stated that Princeton's publishing of a book so disreputable might lead to a boycott of the Press by left and liberal scholars; Gardner circulated a long refutation within the membership of the American Historical Association. By contrast, Arthur Schlesinger, Jr. praised Maddox for having conducted a meticulous examination of the Cold War controversy and was impressed by the responsible manner in which serious questions were raised about revisionist scholarship. And Kennan believed that Maddox had provided a long overdue corrective: "The liberties taken with historical evidence in much recent literature about the origins of the Cold War are quite shocking; and Mr. Maddox has performed a needed service in bringing them to public attention. His examples are fairly chosen, and he is not exaggerated in his condemnation of them."[35]

In fact, *The New Left* did uncover a few examples of sloppy footnoting, factual mistakes, and incorrect, or at least questionable, scholarship in some areas, such as selective quoting from documents or misleading juxtapositions of evidence that led rather too easily to an author's conclusion. However, the tone of Maddox's book was so plainly partisan, quarrelsome, intemperate, and picayune that it could not stand either as solid, persuasive scholarship. And, though it might have indicated some inconsistencies and academic unevenness in the works of Alperovitz, Horowitz, and others, it was hardly adequate to demolish the revisionist thesis which in the years since Vietnam has established itself as a respectable, competitive school within Cold War historiography. In any event, the battle between Maddox's supporters and detractors continued for a while into the middle 1970s and was marked by unusual vituperativeness and *ad hominen* arguments on both sides.[36] In American intellectual life, as elsewhere in society, the Vietnam War was exacting its toll.

Urban Turmoil

As Kennan's strength—foreign relations—was Johnson's weakness, so was Kennan's weakness Johnson's strength: an understanding of the complexity of domestic politics in the United States and an empathy for the traditionally poor and disaffected. Even though Johnson's Great Society foundered and was sabotaged by Vietnam, it represented in its marshaling of numerous resources behind the war on poverty a serious effort at overcoming, among other things, the legacy of slavery: namely, the rage of black Americans at continuing white injustice and the burden of poverty that afflicted great segments of the black community. Alas, Kennan was mainly oblivious to the underlying social, economic, and psychological reasons that drove some urban youths as they rioted or conducted violent demonstrations. He was visibly impressed only by those instances of lawlessness that meant sections of US cities became off-limits to law-abiding citizens and ungovernable for the local forces of order and authority. Newark, for example, not terribly far from Kennan's Princeton, became a notable casualty of fire and violence, and the nation's capital required the deployment of National Guard troops to quell civil disturbances. "Surely, if there has been any excess to these disorders," Kennan declared in the wake of events following Martin Luther King's murder, "it has been an excess of tolerance toward such things as arson, looting, sniping and the malicious harassment of police and firemen endeavoring to perform their duty. Such things cannot be justified by any cause or grievance." Black lawlessness and violence very likely would provoke an even more unrestrained white reaction; might the country be convulsed by race war?[37]

As mentioned in previous chapters, Kennan believed that the conventional liberal line about racial integration of schools, neighborhoods, and places of recreation was unproven and weak. In 1968, he was inclined to agree with the recommendations of those black militants and separatists who urged construction of a physically distinct and politically autonomous black entity within the United States. He asked:

> Is it realistic to suppose that the American Negro is going to find his dignity and his comfort of body and mind by the effort to participate and to compete as an individual in a political and social system he neither understands nor respects and for which he is ill-prepared? Will it not be necessary to permit him first to have, as a number of his leaders are now demanding, a local political community of his own, through which he can express himself collectively and in which he can find his identity and gain the dignity of both authority and responsibility."[38]

Though drawn to the concept of a black-white cantonization scheme, Kennan did strongly support the government's attack against black poverty in the rural south. But he also believed that some thought should be given to curtailing the import of southern black misery into northern cities through imposing administrative restrictions barring the movement of poor people to urban centers. He was not at all convinced, however, that mainstream American opinion could ever be persuaded of the feasibility or advisability of such a measure.[39] It would have smacked of traditional South African practice.

The Environment

Kennan's interest in the condition of urban America was, in important part, an outgrowth of his long-standing concern about the natural environment, particularly the quality of water tables, topsoils, forests, wildlife refuges, and the overall balance of nature in the United States. Damage to them and the depletion of energy resources represented to him the symptoms of overurbanization, industrialization, and large population. Modern America was becoming unlivable. Only if it recovered something of its agrarian past could it expect to survive as a sane society: "This society bears the seeds of its own horrors—unbreathable air, undrinkable water, starvation—and until people realize that we have to get to a much simpler form of life, a much smaller population, a society in which the agrarian component is far greater in relation to the urban component—until these appreciations become widespread and effective—I can see no answer to the troubles of our time."[40] Indeed, by the late 1970s he was convinced that the dangers posed by pollution, urban decay, and an environmentally and culturally ravaged America were more imminent and menacing than the Soviet Union. He believed that a wildly expanding economy must reckon with the concept of limited healthy growth or otherwise be submerged by an avalanche of waste products, insecticides, and ugly environment.

Kennan was indignant that his own private world was being invaded and practically overrun by the internal combustion engine, real estate developers, and commercial debauchery. Downtown Princeton was every weekday clogged with commuter and truck traffic; the agricultural lands around his Pennsylvania farm were given over increasingly to suburban residences, new highways, and shopping centers; the tranquillity of his summer cottage on the southern coast of Norway was disturbed, as he phrased it, by local "dirty teen-agers, with their jeans, their sweaters, their indistinguishableness of sex, and their crackling motor bikes."[41] All of these unwelcome intrusions of the modern world—"impairment of the places I loved"—reinforced Kennan's congenital dissatisfaction with contemporary society, especially the United States, where the circumstance of man apart from nature had become advanced and where people were ensnared in a glittering but foolishly mechanized life. Despite his own misgivings about the efficacy of mass democratic politics, Kennan issued a public appeal in 1972 for the creation of a third major party in America that would base its agenda along the lines of the environmental movement. This notion attracted little support and Kennan soon afterward abandoned the idea, but it stands as a poignant reminder of the importance he—an enthusiastic sailor, gardener, and outdoorsman—has ascribed to nature, wilderness, and their continued existence in the late twentieth century.

Recommendations

In view of the violence perpetrated by some university students, racial tensions, labor strikes—strikes by public employees against community services astonished him—and environmental problems, Kennan hoped that the United States would at last be willing to accept a new discipline along the lines he had advocated ever since the Depression era. He realized that a radical change of popular attitudes toward political authority and a reorientation of public philosophy would be required: "To correct these conditions [of society, politics, and environment] will indeed require a revolution—a revolution in the social and intellectual and spiritual environment of American childhood and early youth—but a thoughtful and orderly and constructive revolution."[42] Notions of service to the greater collectivity, the intrinsic merit of group effort, and the value of affirming something higher and nobler than increasing personal financial wealth or the GNP had to be integrated into the American polity. As before, Kennan warned that the musty political institutions conceived in and appropriate for the late eighteenth century and the Democratic and Republican parties were insufficient either as guides or as vehicles of change. Rather, the establishment of an improved political life would "have to begin with people banding together, outside the existing political framework, initially—coordinating their own ideas and then seeking public support for them."[43]

Attainment of assorted desirable goals—expanded and more efficient public transportation, curtailed use of private automobiles, smaller cities, cleaner industries, racial peace—would eventually require broad acceptance of a larger and more energetic public leadership. "In general, changes of this nature are going to require a drastic stiffening," Kennan asserted in 1968, "of public authority—the imposition of some sort of public discipline in areas of our life to which such discipline has never before been applied and where the very idea of applying would be abhorrent to many of our people."[44] The alternative would be a continued, inexorable deterioration of the United States and a decline in its world standing. America simply must put its house in order as a prerequisite to coping successfully with the international political environment. And the place to start, as always for Kennan, was with the right sort of people—above narrow partisan causes, unswervingly devoted to the national interest, informed and well educated—and to insure that they were selected to lead the American polity.

By 1975, Kennan was willing to discuss in public some of the ways in which an aristocracy of character and intellect might take charge in the United States. Although, in the end, he did no more than intimate the political forms he would have preferred that the United States adopt, these hints taken together recall his original "Prerequisites" and suggest how the domestic crises of the 1960s and early 1970s evoked responses in an aging Kennan similar to his youthful criticisms and fanciful recommendations of the 1930s:

> I still think today, that we ought to create a panel, or pool of outstanding people that would comprise perhaps 500–1000 souls. Appointment to it would be by some detached and austere authority such as the Supreme Court, and membership in it would represent recognition of distinction in our national life achieved by a man's own efforts outside the field of political competition.[45]

From this august body, American voters could select their senators and return to the original intentions of the American founders: people occupying responsible offices of public trust should be chosen from the best, not from the vulgar and partially educated. Kennan insisted that such a political hierarchy based on the differentiated talents of men would be far superior to the random production of mediocre national leaders, only rarely alloyed by the accidental appearance of a worthy and dedicated public servant.[46]

*   *   *   *

To Kennan, America's Vietnam War was a monstrosity based on a fatuous theory of falling dominoes and lacking a coherent, realistic objective. And the war destroyed one of America's most important diplomatic assets, its image in the world as an exemplar of humanity and decency.[47] Yet the war did convey lessons about how the United States might more wisely conduct itself abroad in the future. First, it must distinguish realistically and explicitly among its essential, secondary, tertiary (and beyond) international interests and allocate political and material resources accordingly. High rhetoric and a crusading impulse that together could justify intervention anywhere in the world must also be eschewed. "There must be less posing," Kennan declared, "less striking of attitudes, less claims to altruism and virtue, less taking of sides in other people's disputes; more reservation of judgment, more readiness to let others work out their problems in their own way, a greater willingness to study and accept the lessons of our past failures, a greater readiness to recognize our own limitations."[48] As for the postwar future of international relations in Southeast Asia, he recommended in 1977 that the United States observe a policy of total disinterest. Nothing was to be gained by the promoting of economic and diplomatic relations with the victorious communist regimes. And if the Soviets and Chinese wanted to bicker for influence in the area, so be it; like the Americans they stood to gain nothing valuable from their meddling.[49]

Even more forceful than the quickening of Kennan's disquiet over the general course of US foreign policy, the Vietnam era pushed his conservatism violently into public view. What little had existed of dignity, decorum, continuity, and respect for authority in the United States seemed to disintegrate for him in a spasm of anger as the distinct generations and different races regarded their opposites in a spirit of mutual incomprehension and distrust. And, meanwhile, the country seemed to wallow in sleazy commercialism and dissipation. In Kennan, one had the lugubrious complaint of an older, solitary man who along with W. B. Yeats would have preferred "a house where all's accustomed, ceremonious."[50] Instead, an unpopular war had precipitated discord and mutiny:

> No more than anyone else can I forget the monumental error of Vietnam; the sudden disaffection and in part demoralization of American youth; the widespread watering down and undermining of educational standards; the deterioration in the underlying relationship between blacks and whites . . . the unmistakable signs of decadence in cultural life dominated by violence, pornography, and morbidity of all sorts; the [decay] of America's great cities . . . and finally the slightly retarded but still not halted deterioration of the natural environment under the onslaughts of a commercially-motivated industrial system.[51]

Worst of all, to Kennan, the nation's elected officials had abdicated their moral leadership and were unable to recognize, let alone counter, the decline in American civilization. Even when the tawdry political system did occasionally allow someone of vision and integrity to assume an important office, the built-in apparatus of checks and controls prevented him from realizing enlightened policies: "American policy remains the work not just of dilettantes but rather of great masses of them, milling around, debating and disputing within the framework of a bureaucracy too confused for thought and too ponderous for action."[52] As for the country's professions of being a democracy, the United States was altogether too big and varied to function as a proper (small-scale and socially homogeneous) democratic polity. According to Kennan, Americans should recognize that the fragmentation of power in the US, the elephantine clumsiness of the bureaucratic state, and the generally low level of intellectual competence in higher governmental circles placed immense constraints on the type of international role the United States should play. Because of these institutions and habits and because only a relatively small number of issues really mattered to the United States from an international standpoint, the country should concentrate its energies on them and reduce all extraneous, diverting enterprises overseas. By the end of Vietnam, Kennan considered himself a version of modified, neo-isolationist: "The dreams of glory that commanded American opinion around the turn of the century, and again in 1919, and still again in 1945, have worn themselves out. In the years and decades that lie immediately ahead, dreams of this nature are nothing for us; and if the day ever comes when we can indulge ourselves in anything like them, let us hope that it will be a different sort of glory to which we will aspire: one flowing from the achievements of our national life—one that will shine through us and be there for others to discover, not for us to proclaim."[53] As for existing international problems, the US should limit its involvement to those which were manageable and directly related to American interests; above all else the United States should seek to improve relations with Russia and find ways of containing the dangers inherent in the interminable nuclear arms race.

13

Detente and the Nuclear Arms Race

The dismal history of Soviet-US postwar relations, in which periods of mutual distrust and danger alternated with those of attenuated cooperation, struck some observers in the early 1970s as having exhausted itself. In its place there seemed emergent "a stable structure of peace" (the administration's rhetoric) that would insure for future generations of Soviets, Americans, Chinese, Europeans, and Japanese a secure international political order. Even if the center of this new order was not to be dominated by a traditional great power *condominium,* it would have to rely upon a greatly improved Soviet-US relationship. And superficially, at least, this object was achieved by Richard Nixon's and Leonid Brezhnev's signing in 1972 of the Basic Principles Agreement, wherein both sides affirmed the necessity of avoiding confrontation and the imperative of mutual restraint. They also rejected as unsound all attempts to exploit global problems to gain unilateral advantage, renounced claims of special influence in the world, and declared their willingness to coexist harmoniously and build a firm, long-term relationship. In effect, both sides formally repudiated military solutions to international problems and agreed to cooperate in settling all foreign issues of mutual concern. A year later, Nixon and Brezhnev signed the SALT I agreement and by that autumn negotiations had begun aimed at producing a SALT II. Talks were also undertaken to reduce the level of Soviet and US military forces in Europe and both countries agreed to increase by several fold their commercial, technological, scientific, and cultural exchanges. The Cold War and all of its hazards thus seemed at last to be making way for a belated, much needed era of detente.

Kennan was a cautious supporter of the Nixon-Kissinger effort to improve relations with the USSR; and, even as enthusiasm in the United States for detente waned from the mid-1970s onward and then was repudiated by the Reagan government, he clung—and does today—to the idea that Soviet-American relations need not remain a permanent hostage to Cold War suspicions. At the same time, he became most outspoken publicly, as he had always been privately, in opposing further improvements in nuclear weaponry and has advocated sweeping measures by which the United States might stop the arms race. While his numerous warnings and recommendations, and to a degree his own person, have been lauded by anti-nuclear partisans in North America and Western Europe, he has been strongly challenged by a broad range of critics worried that his advice, coming as it has from a recognized authority on Soviet-US relations, might help undermine Western resolve against the USSR.[1] From morally didactic Alexander Solzhenitsyn, to thoughtful Paul Nitze, to narrowly partisan William Buckley, Kennan has been excoriated for urging policies allegedly disastrous to Western security.

As he has usually been with umbrella terms, Kennan was impatient with the word detente and criticized it as too misleading and imprecise a label for the American effort at balanced policy toward the Soviet Union. He also blamed the US news media with its superficial coverage and comprehension of events and a plainly self-serving Soviet government for having raised unrealistically high expectations in the West: detente was misportrayed as marking the start of a new epoch of Soviet-US friendship when, in fact, no such prospect ever existed. Yet Kennan had no qualms about endorsing the main substance of Nixon-Kissinger diplomacy and believed that the middle ground it tried to attain between Cold War bellicosity and illusory Soviet-US intimacy was correct. During the peak period of detente, in 1972, Kennan remarked: "So far as the Soviet Union itself is concerned, I do not see a great deal that the Nixon administration could do that it is not now doing." And he had particular regard for Kissinger, whom he credited with intellectual imagination and political understanding.[2]

Implicit in John Gaddis's *Strategies of Containment* is the view that Kennan approved of the Kissinger (and Nixon) policy because it essentially conformed to the practical policy and theory about international power distribution that he had produced in the late 1940s. In large measure, Gaddis is right and he illustrates well the conceptual similarity between Kissinger's pentagonal international power schema and that posited by Kennan two and a half decades earlier. Like Kennan, Kissinger was determined that none of the non-Soviet centers of economic con-centration and military potential—Japan, China, Western Europe in the 1970s—should fall under Soviet sway or be otherwise lost to a properly functioning global balance of power, itself the best guarantee of US safety. Gaddis further explains that Kissinger shares with Kennan a multidimensional understanding of national power; while secretary of state, Kissinger did not subsume all else to military strength. Moreover, both men prize international stability far more than reforming the world in America's image and believe that Soviet behavior in the world can be favorably influenced by a mix of positive inducements and American steadfastness. Finally, Gaddis makes important comparisons between Kissinger's and Kennan's practice of distinguishing Soviet Russia from international communism and their insistence on insulating diplomacy and the foreign policy elite from Congress and the public.[3] In stressing the "strategic logic" and underlying assumptions common to Kennan and Kissinger, however, Gaddis overstates Kennan's certainty in the late 1940s about what constituted major US interests abroad. As we have seen (Chapter 6), Kennan was faltering in his attempts to identify a hierarchy of international power centers in

1947–1949; and, though he was eager to be clear, he did not always succeed in distinguishing between vital and peripheral US interests abroad. Lippmann also played a role here and certainly Kennan's practical advice about policy toward Europe, Asia, and the Middle East did not always correspond to the kind of tidy strategic framework attributed by Gaddis to Kennan. For example, although Greece and Turkey (1947) and Korea (1950) were not important as power centers to Kennan, he urged the Truman government to aid them, lest the global balance of power be adversely affected. More important for our present purposes, Gaddis passes too lightly over Kennan's understanding of the evolving USSR and the fearfulness inherent in the nuclear arms race as *basic* to his support in the early 1970s of improved East-West relations. Indeed, at the core of Kennan's support for Kissinger's and Nixon's Soviet policy was revulsion for the gargantuan Soviet and American arsenals containing weapons of mass destruction, and anguish that the two powers might not act in a timely fashion to contain their rivalry and avert nuclear holocaust.

Detente and Soviet-US Relations

In the 1970s, Kennan was diligent in interviews and his writings to emphasize those post-Stalinist changes in world communism and in the Soviet Union that were conducive to global stability. He repeatedly told his audiences that, unlike the period immediately following World War II, when Moscow enjoyed wide prestige and was still the capital of a coherent international movement, it was no longer perceived by all communists as the repository of Marxist-Leninist wisdom, but was increasingly defied by Chinese comrades and Eurocommunists alike. In the meantime, the Kremlin leadership had become anxious about retaining its geopolitical advantage in Eastern Europe and was not likely to take an offensive against the rest of the continent as such an exertion would jeopardize all past and present Soviet achievements. Kennan did concede that the Soviets were perfectly willing to play traditional great power politics with the United States around the world, wanted to outflank the West where possible, and hoped (vainly, as it usually has turned out) to secure for themselves various tactical advantages in the Third World. But, he reminded his readers and listeners, the US assiduously played the same game—a chess game of sorts as ancient as international politics itself. Come what may, the Soviets would never wish to push the West to the point where either the United States or its allies would feel compelled to wage a general war. In other words, the status quo was fundamentally acceptable to Brezhnev and "world revolution" mattered not at all. Were it not for the nuclear arms race, driven by forces—inertia, military-industrial combinations, pathological insecurity—not directly related to the actual substance of Soviet-US affairs, the United States and Russia would have little more to fear from one another than they did in 1910.[4]

Kennan also thought it significant that the Soviet government under Brezhnev had not revoked the new dispensation promulgated by Khrushchev: the regime of total police terror and the *universe concentrationnaire* were finished. Notwithstanding that many of its features were still distasteful to Western sensibility, the uninspired, geriatric leadership of the 1970s resembled traditional pre-Bolshevik Russian authoritarianism more than Stalinism. And even if the Soviet Union had not exactly softened, *pace* the "X article," the regime certainly did not constitute an affront to every concept of legality and justice—with such a regime one could more easily conduct business.

Although Kennan derived some reassurance that the Soviet Union was basically a satiated state and had gone far to repudiate its totalitarian past, he was adamant in the period of detente that Americans not deceive themselves into thinking that they could achieve anything more than correct relations and modest cooperation with the USSR. This is an important point and one usually lost upon Kennan's more conservative critics. In fact, while a type of euphoria swept the United States for detente and things Russian, Kennan warned that as no international relationship consists of total antagonism, so none is based on a perfect identity of interests. In 1972 he stated:

> The United States would do well not to indulge in unreal hopes for intimacy with either the Soviet regime or the Soviet population. There are deeply rooted traits in Soviet psychology—some of old Russian origin, some of more recent Soviet provenance—that would rule this out. Chief among these . . . are the congenital disregard of the truth, the addiction to propagandistic exaggeration, distortion and falsehood, the habitual foulness of mouth in official utterance. So pernicious has been the effect of fifty years of cynicism about the role of objective truth in political statement that one begins to wonder whether these Soviet leaders have not destroyed in themselves the power to distinguish truth from falsehood. The very vocabulary in which they have taught themselves to speak, politically, with its constant references to the American "imperialists" and "monopolists," is confusing and offensive and constitutes in itself a barrier to better international understanding. Add to this the hysterical preoccupation with espionage, and the role that the continued fear of foreigners and the effort to isolate the Soviet population is allowed to play in the conduct of Soviet diplomacy, and one is obliged to recognize that it is simply unrealistic for Americans to look for any great intimacy or even normalcy, as we understand it, of relations with the Soviet Union.[5]

Instead of expecting to witness the ushering in of an unprecedented era of Soviet-US friendship, Americans should content themselves with following a balance of power approach to the USSR while cooperating where feasible to solve common problems. Kennan did believe that the two states might find tentative or partial solutions to the arms race and conflict in the Middle East. Surely, they could work together on matters related to outer space and the global environment and for this reason Kennan endorsed Nixon's and Kissinger's promotion of commercial and cultural exchanges. In short, US relations with Russia could be somewhat more pleasant than hitherto, safer, and could serve limited, joint interests. To expect anything more, however, was to entertain a dangerous fantasy about the nature of international relations.

Despite the ratification of SALT I and progress on SALT II, despite the success of the Apollo-Soyuz mission and other less sensational instances of Soviet-US cooperation, detente and the high expectations surrounding it came undone in the mid-1970s. Passage of the Jackson-Vanik amendment, tying credits and MFN status for the Soviet Union to its emigration policy, damaged bilateral economic relations from early on and the anticipated increased levels of trade never materialized. Along with other expressions of concern for the human rights situation in Russia—here the plights of Andrei Sakharov and Solzhenitsyn figured prominently with that of Soviet Jewry—the Jackson-Vanik legislation demonstrated to Kremlin leaders that the US was, contrary to Nixon's and Kissinger's pledges, still prone to embarrass their country and was uninhibited in trying to meddle in Soviet internal affairs. Also annoying from a Soviet standpoint, under the "smokescreen" of detente the Americans had frozen the USSR out of most Middle Eastern diplomacy, helped destroy a Marxist regime in Chile, and were devious in playing the so-called China card. In the United States, meanwhile, popular and congressional support for detente began to erode in autumn 1973 as the Soviets were accused of numerous misdeeds during the Yom Kippur War. Soviet sponsorship of Cubans in Angola and maneuvering for advantage elsewhere in Africa (Somalia, Ethiopia), Brezhnev's failure to restrain North Vietnam in 1975 as it smashed the south, charges of cheating and bad faith over SALT, and the undeniable reality of Soviet strategic power and a modernizing Red Navy further contributed to widespread American disillusionment.[6]

As the pendulum of popular feeling in the United States swung from a practically breathless interest in detente toward its customary suspicion of the Soviet Union, Kennan continued to argue (and work through the American Committee on East-West Accord, which he co-chaired) for a policy of moderation that sought, as its ultimate aim, a constructive relationship with the USSR. At the same time, he did not exclude the possibility that the Soviets had betrayed the "spirit of detente" by their actions in Africa and the Middle East.[7] And he reiterated that the Soviets would continue some odious practices: persecuting dissidents, cultivating a needlessly large army (in the traditional Russian manner), increasing the potency of their strategic weapons, and drawing a curtain of secrecy around all of these activities in a way as to invite further fear on the Western side. Kennan was equally critical of what he called "formidable interests" in both the US and Soviet Union that prospered so long as a state of military tension existed. For the United States Kennan meant the servicemen and civilians who directed the physical expansion and distorting political influence of the "military-industrial complex." He also decried those American pundits, politicians, and associations (such as the Committee on the Present Danger, founded in 1976 by Eugene Rostow and Paul Nitze) that were too comfortable in using Cold War slogans, building greater quantities of arms, and trying to reform Soviet domestic practices. Could the likes of Henry Jackson, Patrick Moynihan, and Ronald Reagan not muster the statesmanship to resist exploiting the USSR as a target for rhetorical demonstrations of their vigilance against communism? Could the news media not respect the need for American diplomacy to operate in private when dealing with Soviet leaders and be less simplistic and histrionic in portraying emotional issues—such as Soviet misdeeds in the human rights area—to the public?

Kennan publicly objected to the Jackson-Vanik legislation. He adopted the Nixon administration's thesis that quiet diplomacy, not punitive legislation, would help Soviet Jewry and that Jackson-Vanik would undoubtedly injure the cause of

Soviet-US peace. He also publicly scored the military competition as extravagant and unrelated to the traditional reasons for which countries prepare for war against each other: irredentist grievances, rival border claims, previous defeats. Moreover, he persisted, the Soviets were acutely aware of the risks involved in nuclear competition and, at all costs, wanted to avoid war with the United States. "Along with all of its exaggerated military efforts," he said in 1976, the USSR "does not want, and will not want, a world war. It has a keen realization of the suicidal nature of any nuclear war; and it has too many internal problems to allow it to wish to assume inordinate risks."[8]

Regarding Western Europe, Kennan restated his conviction that the Soviets had no desire to occupy or conquer any part of the area by military means. After all, he reasoned, even a conventional Soviet military campaign against West Germany, France, Holland, Great Britain, and so forth would inflict extensive damage on their industries and agriculture. The Soviets would gain nothing by inheriting a ruined Europe and they would deprive their economy of the manifold benefits flowing from a Western Europe whose industrial plant was intact and able to supply the products of an advanced technology and science. In addition, the Soviets obviously lacked the administrative technique to govern Eastern Europe well; they would find it still harder to organize culturally superior nations in the West in the aftermath of war. Furthermore, the various communist parties of Western Europe no longer promised to be reliable Soviet instruments for administration and would probably continue to intensify their independent proclivities. In view of these and similar considerations, Kennan hoped the West Europeans would overcome their image of Russians as "ten feet tall," accept a greater share of NATO responsibilities commensurate with their vitality and affluence, and cease worrying about an imaginary Soviet blackmail of the West. Irrespective of their subjective views, the West Europeans had every reason to be confident vis-à-vis the Soviet bloc.[9] And for this reason Kennan hoped that they would support Jimmy Carter on SALT II in the late 1970s and urge the superpowers to explore the possibility of a reciprocal moratorium on all nuclear weapons testing.

By the end of Carter's tenure, hopes of a calm, sensible American approach to the Soviet Union had been smothered by a landslide of events: turmoil in Poland, the Soviet invasion of Afghanistan, wheat embargo, MX, and Olympics boycott. And the Americans elected a man as president who for years had attacked detente as a misconceived policy from which the Soviets acquired massive unilateral political and military benefits.

In this period—when bilateral cultural, trade, and arms agreements were under growing pressure—Kennan came under attack as an unregenerate apologist for a bankrupt detente. Hugh Seton-Watson (University of London), for example, charged that Kennan was grievously mistaken to deemphasize the imminent menace posed by Soviet imperialism and strength: Soviet rulers already possessed enormous military power and assigned first priority to increasing every type of armed force; they were driven by self-righteousness, lust for power, and a compulsive desire to extend their form of tyranny as widely as possible. Richard Pipes (Harvard University) similarly related Soviet military prowess to external aims and faulted Kennan for too easily dismissing any discussion of the East-West strategic balance. Michael

Novak (syndicated columnist and Syracuse University) adopted a harsh personal tone; he accused Kennan of manifesting those symptoms of weariness and timidity supposedly afflicting American political elites in the post-Vietnam era. The British journalist Henry Fairlie inexcusably accused an elderly Kennan of mental debilitation, while the *New Republic* published an article with the unfortunate subtitle "The Great Container Springs a Leak." And in 1980, William Buckley sniffily proclaimed: "Kennan in late years has had a vision concerning the vector of Soviet leadership, and if he turns out to be correct, I would give him the Nobel Prize, make him emperor of Siam, turn over the keys to Fort Knox, and—perhaps the greatest gift of all—resign my profession as a political commentator."[10]

Kennan's most illustrious critic was the prophetic moralist and historian Solzhenitsyn, who expressed impatience with Kennan's calls for pragmatic diplomacy, dismissed his views about SALT, and erroneously equated them with recommendations for unilateral disarmament. Yet despite immense differences between their respective intellectual traditions as well as their policy recommendations, the two men have held strikingly similar views about the condition of material, ethical, and spiritual life in the West. To Solzhenitsyn, the United States in the 1970s was awash with greedy commercialism, vice, civic cowardice, and every form of cheap self-gratification. He once caricatured American attitudes toward international and domestic problems this way: "Just let us live in peace and quiet. Just let us drive our big cars on our splendid highways; just let us play tennis and golf, in peace and quiet; just let us mix our cocktails in peace and quiet as we are accustomed to doing; just let us see the beautiful toothy smile with a glass on every advertisement page of our magazines."[11] In articles, interviews, and speeches, including a controversial commencement address at Harvard in 1978, he preached that the West must subdue its complacent self and be brave against Soviet "granite" and tanks. The United States should renounce the blunder of detente and bolster its declining military establishment.[12]

Kennan, of course, as we have seen, could also be astringent in judging the West and, like Solzhenitsyn, was revolted by what he identified as the social illnesses attendant with modernity. To the publisher of *Der Zeit*, Kennan wrote in 1976: "Poor old West: succumbing feebly, day by day, to its own decadence, sliding into debility on the slime of its own self-indulgent permissiveness; its drugs, its crime, its pornography, its pampering of the youth, its addiction to its bodily comforts, its rampant materialism and consumerism."[13] In an interview that same year with writer George Urban, Kennan allowed that an imaginary scene of energetic Soviet infantry set upon a swarm of promiscuous, drug-dazed "hippies" had something to recommend it. These, and similar withering comments he made in the 1970s, caused some of Kennan's critics to conclude that he loathed the West and so was disinclined to warn it against the East. He never went that far, in fact, but he did assert that unless the United States and its European allies reordered their moral life, there would be nothing really worth defending in the West. In any case, the dangers presented by a ravaged social existence were more distressing than anything Moscow could devise against the United States. "Show me an America," he told Urban, "which has successfully coped with the problems of crime, drugs, deteriorating educational standards, urban decay, pornography, and decadence of one sort or another—show me an America that has pulled itself together and is what it ought to be, then I will tell you how we are going to defend ourselves from the Russians."[14]

Whereas Solzhenitsyn perceived detente as a symptom of Western decline, Kennan hoped detente would afford the United States an opportunity to break its fixation on the Soviet Union and begin the multifaceted task of self-renewal. Consequently, he waged throughout the remainder of the 1970s and into the 1980s a vigorous counter-offensive against his critics. His arguments were never *ad hominem*, though they became repetitive and followed along the lines already mentioned: historical and psychological-ideological obstacles would always prevent a perfect normalization of Soviet-US relations and they would be plagued by elements of competition; but the conservative Soviet leadership wanted to remedy the economic problems in their empire, not weaken it further by costly external expansion; obstructionist groups in the United States must not be allowed to thwart a superpower *modus vivendi*.[15] As for the Soviet invasion of Afghanistan, Kennan wondered initially whether it was the inspiration of younger militarists in the Kremlin and represented their triumph over the more stolid Brezhnev. (Apart from his physical maladies and impaired mental alertness, Brezhnev was certainly politically vulnerable because of his inability by 1979 to produce tangible benefits from detente.) As it was, Kennan denounced the Carter administration's response to Afghanistan as strident and thoughtless. He puzzled over the president's public utterances on the subject, for they failed to appreciate the defensive-preemptive character of Soviet intervention: to buttress a wobbly Marxist regime in a border state and to check the spread of Afghan-Islamic revival, which might otherwise infect ethnically related co-religionists in the USSR. Kennan thought Carter particularly foolish in portraying the Soviet action to the American public as a first step toward Soviet aggression further afield—in the directions of the Persian Gulf and Pakistan. Still worse, in Kennan's assessment, the official American reaction—instantly offering aid to Pakistan (rudely rebuffed by the government in Islamabad), noisily creating a rapid deployment force, offering security guarantees to all and sundry (including Iran), and incessantly talking about forceful action—was unbalanced and provocative. "An unsuspecting stranger, plunged into [Washington's] midst," Kennan declared in 1980, "could only conclude that the last hope of peaceful, nonmilitary solutions had been exhausted—that from now on only weapons, however used, could count [in Soviet-US affairs]."[16] Could the administration not marshal some restraint and prudence?

Kennan hoped that China and the United States would refrain from taking actions *in* Afghanistan, thereby denying the Soviets any excuse to prolong their stay. He expected that Afghan civil resistance and guerrilla warfare would prove sufficiently fierce for the Soviets to realize the mistakenness of intervention and then withdraw. In the meantime, the United States might quietly, but very deliberately, build up its naval strength in the Arabian Sea and Persian Gulf to remind the Soviets that the West also possessed vital interests in the neighborhood: specifically, Hormuz. In turn, the world public should be informed that the United States was taking this action solely as a precaution and expected that fighting in Afghanistan would not escalate and could be resolved diplomatically. If in the long-term the Soviets succeeded over all obstacles of resistance and terrain and then converted Afghanistan into a strategic base for operations against nearby states, Kennan allowed that the United States should take strong counter-measures by making life uncomfortable for Moscow in a zone where it was vulnerable: thought might be given to placing a naval blockade around Cuba.[17]

Running parallel to his critique of Carter's policy on Afghanistan was Kennan's response to Reagan's use of economic sanctions against Poland after General Wojciech Jaruzelski imposed martial law. He admitted that the sanctions were useful as they documented where American sympathies lay, but was skeptical that economic measures of any sort applied against any country effected favorable results. He wished, too, that the administration had reserved its judgment and had not acted so precipitately before trying to influence a fluid, complicated situation in Eastern Europe. Poland, after all, had long been in the grip of staggering economic problems and political disorder; Jaruzelski's actions, though repellent to democrats, were not the worst that could have occurred (a Soviet occupation of Poland). Perhaps over time and with Western encouragement and patience, the government in Warsaw could evolve economic, political, and diplomatic policies tailored to fit its unenviable geographic location *and* satisfy justifiable popular yearnings. In the meantime, the US sanctions did nothing to alleviate Poland's economic crisis and, complained Kennan, were negative as they failed to suggest what measures the Soviets and Poles might adopt to cause their removal. He suggested that the United States officially recognize the extent of Soviet interests in Eastern Europe and at a more propitious moment enter into comprehensive negotiations—à la his 1957 Reith proposal—aimed at reducing Moscow's hold on East Germany and Poland.[18]

Kennan never expected the Reagan administration to take any bold policy initiatives in Europe. On the contrary, Reagan's Soviet policy in the early 1980s impressed him as being the most sterile and shortsighted of any administration's since before 1933; its inflated rhetoric about an "evil empire" left Kennan disconsolate. On the fiftieth anniversary of the establishment of formal relations between Washington and Moscow, Kennan declared that Russia and the United States were on a collision course. He even admitted to missing Franklin Roosevelt and guessed that were he alive, he would set about doggedly to improve matters between the superpowers. At the very least, Kennan suggested, the two governments must cool their rhetoric and investigate the possibilities of resuming limited cooperation as in the early 1970s.[19]

Later, Kennan hoped that the consolidation of "imaginative and energetic" leadership in the USSR under Mikhail Gorbachev would lead to a fruitful search for an accommodation between the two countries, but neither the official nor the popular mood in the United States seemed receptive.[20] As always, Kennan was quick to blame the news and entertainment media for playing a pernicious part in misrepresenting the Soviet Union. The broadcasting by ABC of "Amerika" (winter 1987), for example, depicting a fictionalized United States governed by the Soviet army, drew Kennan's scorn. Indifferent to first amendment issues, he pronounced that only irresponsible producers, sponsors, and network officials could countenance a program that, whatever its entertainment value, would encourage fear and misunderstanding in the viewing public—better not to have aired the drama at all than to implicate the Soviet leadership with intentions and capabilities beyond its ken.[21]

Against Kennan's more recent warnings and recommendation, hardline critics have sustained their end of the battle. To continue their attack became an especially important task for them in the mid-1980s as he was by then a talisman of sorts for the self-proclaimed peace and anti-nuclear movements. In 1985 Norman Podhoretz (*Commentary*) accused a "Kennan II" of having forgotten the wisdom of "Kennan I"; unlike the virtuous Kennan, the recent incarnation has provided endless mis-assessments of Soviet ambitions and of the overwhelming threat posed by Soviet armaments. Paul Hollander has criticized him for allegedly apportioning more blame to US than to Soviet leaders in locating the sources of great power discord and has wondered whether Kennan's critique of "the decadent West" meant a corresponding, if unconscious, preference for Soviet authoritarianism. Paul Seabury has thought Kennan curiously passive and fatalistic in the face of Soviet tyranny. To the essayist Max Lerner, Kennan's hypothesis that the USSR desires the establishment of approximate international equilibrium rests on fragile premises.[22] But, in fact, Kennan's premises have not been fragile so much as absolutely irreconcilable with those of his critics. They and he have agreed about the obvious: the Soviet Union of the 1980s is a great military power, far more capable of inflicting physical destruction on the West than in the time of Stalin. Where they have parted company is on the question of Soviet intentions. Kennan certainly has never attributed benign qualities to Soviet leaders, but has held that their perceptions of Soviet national interest dictate a moderate policy toward the West. To his critics, however, the line between intentions and capabilities is not so emphatic: as Soviet military capabilities have expanded so, too, have their aims—witness Angola, Ethiopia, Nicaragua. If the balance of power should change (or *appear* to change) to Soviet advantage, then America's diplomatic posture in the world will become increasingly defensive. In this regard, Kennan's oft-repeated charge that his critics believe the Soviet Union is bent on war has been unfair. Even so unapologetic a hawk as Richard Pipes has stated that the Soviets are no more eager for World War III than anyone else. But he and the others have insisted that political aims and political consequences have flowed, and will continue to flow, from Soviet power: "An overwhelmingly powerful military establishment will make it possible for [the Soviets] to achieve their aims without war. I see their entire design as offensive and not defensive."[23]

Despite his personal respect for many of his antagonists and acknowledgments of their sincerity, Kennan's confidence in his arguments on behalf of improved superpower relations has not diminished. That power rivalry, jingoism, and militarism as expressed in the existence of expanding Soviet and US nuclear arsenals might one day, regardless of the wishes and calculations of national leaders, result in the calamity of nuclear war has caused Kennan no end of despair and has justified for him the need of the United States to hazard a better relationship with a difficult, alien Soviet regime. This preoccupation of Kennan's with averting the apocalypse has been nowhere more eloquently expressed than in his recent scholarship on the origins of World War I. As in turn-of-the-century international relations, the military and diplomatic situation of the great powers in the late 1970s and 1980s has exhibited drift and political paralysis to Kennan. He ended his second volume (published 1984) about the deeper origins of the First World War with this warning:

> If, today, governments are still unable to recognize that modern nationalism and modern militarism are, in combination, self-destructive forces, and totally so; if they are incapable of looking clearly at those forces, discerning their true nature, and bringing them under some sort of control; if they continue, whether for reasons of fear or of ambition, to cultivate those forces and to try to use them as instruments for self-serving competitive purposes—if they do these things, they will be preparing, this time, a catastrophe from which there can be no recovery and no return.[24]

Not only would another world war, like the first one, destroy the established social-political, cultural, and intellectual order of the major belligerents, it would—inevitably in Kennan's view—entail the use of nuclear weapons and lead to the extinction of civilization and human life.

The Arms Race

It is notable that ever since the advent of atomic weapons, Kennan's views have been evolving in one direction: from reluctant acceptance of them as another sad fact of international life, to skepticism about their political utility, to outright opposition to them and calls for their abolition. Underlying this trend has been a philosophical objection, fully articulated as early as 1950, to weapons of mass destruction and to that hallmark of twentieth-century warfare: the saturation bombing and destroying of civilian life.[25]

Shortly after two American atomic bombs obliterated most of Hiroshima and Nagasaki, Kennan advised the State Department against any impulse to share its knowledge of atomic physics with the USSR; such a gesture of American goodwill, as sometimes contemplated by James Byrnes and Henry Stimson, would constitute a frivolous disregard of US security interests. Should Stalin and his colleagues ever come to possess atomic weaponry, they would not hesitate to brandish it to advance Soviet goals against the West. This did not mean for Kennan that the Soviets would necessarily use these weapons in anger, but they would not hesitate to apply them in ways compatible with *strictly* Soviet aims.[26] Rather than trying to build a fund of goodwill with Stalin's regime through scientific and atomic collaboration, he thought the United States should dispense with grand illusions and concentrate on determining Russia's rate of progress in developing atomic power.

Except for this admonition to Washington, issued at a time when Kennan was avid to dispel any conception that the Grand Alliance might last into the postwar world, he appears not to have paid much attention in 1945–1948 to the atomic bomb issue. The subject was not mentioned in his "Long Telegram" of February 1946 or in his "X article" and seldom appeared in other documents he composed. According to his memoirs and various later statements, he actually discounted the impact of atomic weapons upon diplomacy and relations with Soviet Russia.[27] These recollections are not entirely accurate, however, and their implications are somewhat misleading. That the Soviets lacked atomic devices suited Kennan and for this reason he was unsympathetic to the Acheson-Lilienthal and Bernard Baruch plans that, had they been accepted by the Soviets, would have surrendered a singular American advantage. Kennan also believed that the United States enjoyed some diplomatic and military edge due to its atomic monopoly. Even if not necessary in war, US maintenance of atomic bombs served the additional purpose of preserving peace. "It is important," he noted in September 1946, "that this country be *prepared* to use them if need be, for the mere fact of such preparedness may prove to be the only powerful deterrent to Russian aggressive action and in this sense the only sure guaranty of peace." And in case of real emergency, Kennan did not rule out the possibility that the United States would have to use these weapons against Soviet targets.[28] At the same time, he clearly hoped that competent military and political authorities would not overestimate the importance of the atomic bomb. As with any other military weapon, it could not decide the outcome of the Cold War that, despite the periodic threat of open warfare, would basically remain a political and diplomatic contest.

When Kennan became director of Policy Planning, the American stockpile of atomic bombs was small and did not number more than thirteen by July 1947.[29] In any case, nothing occurred during the first two years of Kennan's directorship to alter substantially his original views about atomic issues. He did conclude in August 1947 that the United States should continue that set of negotiations in the United Nations Atomic Energy Commission begun by Baruch and Andrei Gromyko, as the United States was certain to receive some propaganda benefits if it appeared to be striving for an international atomic energy regime; but Kennan recognized, and took comfort from the fact, that conflicting Soviet and American proposals were unlikely to be harmonized.[30]

The fundamental problem after fourteen months of Soviet-US negotiating in the UN was that the American side was unwilling to relinquish its monopoly on atomic energy in the absence of a powerful international control agency that would supervise all crucial operations related to the production of such energy. Until an appropriate agency was established, the United States was determined to retain its atomic weapons and resisted outlawry of them. The Soviets, by contrast, insisted on the immediate destruction of all atomic weapons—of which the Americans were the sole possessors at the time—but refused any future regulatory authority the right to inspect Soviet sites, as that would be inconsistent with national sovereignty. This deadlock was never broken—in retrospect, it is clear both sides were disingenuous in their proposals. By autumn 1947 the PPS, with the rest of the government, formally abandoned any notion that international arrangements for controlling atomic energy in the circumstances of Cold War were obtainable or desirable. For the remainder of 1947–1948 and much of 1949, Kennan's thinking about atomic matters was confined to ironing out problems among the Americans, British, and Canadians over the allocation of technical information and raw materials such as uranium. The difficulties encountered here were complex and raised delicate questions about trust and cooperation among the English-speaking allies. Kennan's diplomatic skill and personal tact were put to a bruising test, but the issues did not strike at the heart of Soviet-US rivalry or international stability.[31]

In the meantime, US defense policy was being adapted to the atomic age. After the Czech coup and against the background of the Berlin blockade, the NSC affirmed that atomic weapons would continue to occupy a privileged position in the national arsenal and, at the chief executive's determination, could be used in time of war. Indeed, the accepted political and military wisdom was that, should war occur with Russia, the United States would unhesitatingly use its atomic bombs. Kennan was not directly involved in the formulation of these plans, but he did express apprehension to Marshall and Forrestal that the US might fall into the trap of diverting too many human and material resources from European recovery to defense programs, thereby jeopardizing the best hope for genuine world security. Long before NSC 68 was even conceived, he was worried that the United States was spending an exorbitant amount of money on armaments and might soon enter into an unrestricted arms race with the USSR.[32] His anxiety about this matter was heightened by his belief that before long the Soviet Union would produce an atom bomb of its own.

Kennan did not think that Soviet acquisition of atomic weaponry would inspire Moscow toward greater international assertiveness. He reasoned the Soviet leadership would recognize that the USSR was perilously behind in atomic science and applied military technology and that crowded Soviet cities and concentrated industry could not be defended against US bombers. Kennan concluded that only in the extreme case of a similar attack against their territory would the Soviets be inclined to use atomic weapons. When the USSR exploded its first atomic bomb (August 1949), Kennan urged the administration to determine the *political* implications of the event and act to soothe fears among the American public and European allies. And he emphasized, once more, that the Soviets were not about to embark on the uncertain adventure of another war as a result of possessing atomic energy.[33]

The Truman government as a whole did not greet the Soviet detonation of an atomic bomb with Kennan's comparative equanimity. Rather, coinciding as it did with Mao's victory in China, this event called forth a drastic reappraisal by the administration of US security policy. After a period of debate within the government, NSC 68 was adopted and in late January 1950 Truman made the decision that the United States should go forward in developing a weapon more powerful than the fission bomb. Spearheaded by a number of prominent scientists such as Edward Teller and Ernest Lawrence, and by Lewis Strauss of the Atomic Energy Commission (AEC), the campaign for creating the "super"—or hydrogen bomb—was also enthusiastically supported by Senator Brien McMahon, Defense Secretary Louis Johnson, and the Joint Chiefs of Staff. After slight hesitation, Secretary Acheson also threw his influence behind the "superbomb" project. There was individual variation, but as a group advocates of the "super" believed that if the United States failed to develop this more destructive instrument—no less than a thousand times more powerful than the fission bomb—the Americans would lose their nuclear advantage to the Soviets. And they would without flinching manufacture such a weapon as soon as Soviet science allowed. If on that day the United States was not similarly equipped, the entire security system of the West would be irreparably compromised. At a minimum, the balance of power would be lost to Soviet favor, and the United States would be relegated permanently to second-class power status.

Teller wrote to Truman that the United States had to be as well armed as any potential adversary or risk catastrophe. And for Senator McMahon, "a failure to press ahead with the hydrogen bomb might well mean unconditional surrender in advance—by the United States to . . . forces of evil." An even more alarmist view was expressed by Admiral Sidney Souers of the NSC staff: "It's either we make [the hydrogen bomb] or wait until the Russians drop one on us without warning."[34] Alternatively, American production of the hydrogen bomb during the time when the Soviets still lacked one would constitute a "quantum jump" (Strauss's expression) in Western security, help compensate for the conventional forces imbalance, and restore the confidence of European allies in the deterrent power of the United States.

Opponents of the hydrogen bomb included such distinguished scientists and public servants as Enrico Fermi, I. I. Rabi, David Lilienthal (chairman of the Atomic Energy Commission), Hans Bethe, and James Conant, as well as Oppenheimer. As a group, they were skeptical about the technical aspects of making such a weapon and delivering it to a target. Virtually all of them objected to the hydrogen bomb for ethical reasons and feared that its coming into the world would place human existence "in a situation both measureless and laden with doom."[35] Oppenheimer, for one, who accepted the necessity for "nominal-sized" atomic bombs, argued that the "super" would be too murderous to achieve any positive goals and would not add to US security anyway. To his colleagues Fermi and Rabi, the proposed hydrogen bomb was something so fiendish and terrible that it did not belong to the category of military weapon, but was more akin to a great natural cataclysm. If the United States should construct such a thing then its moral standing among nations would plummet as the practical effect of the weapon's use would be genocidal. No political cause could possibly justify discharging the superbomb on an enemy target.[36]

Kennan's part in the fateful debate about the "super" was limited and its major significance does not lie in the impact his views had on top policymakers. His influence on the entire range of discussions and the final decision was, in fact, negligible. Still, it is worth reviewing the positions he took about the efficacy and ethicality of the "superbomb," as they have constituted the foundation of his attitude toward the nuclear arms race ever since.

As with Oppenheimer, upon whom he depended for much of his knowledge about nuclear weapons, Kennan was startled by the proposed "super" and held that nothing good could follow from it. In autumn 1949, he testified against the hydrogen bomb to the similarly inclined members of the AEC's General Advisory Committee (GAC), chaired by Oppenheimer. Kennan echoed the chairman's own sentiments in stating that, as a device causing indiscriminate mass slaughter, the "superbomb" could not possibly achieve any rational military or political objectives. Kennan also shared Oppenheimer's conviction that the current supply of atomic weapons was adequate to deter any theoretical aggressor. And he predicted that US development of the hydrogen bomb would oblige the Soviets to do the same; from there, the nuclear arms race would enter into an accelerated and unpredictable phase.[37] By and large, these views were favorably received by the GAC and were incorporated into their recommendations against the superbomb project.

Through November and December of 1949, Kennan also worked feverishly on a long memorandum (eighty pages) about questions related to the hydrogen bomb. In his view of many years later, this document was possibly the single most important one he ever wrote while in government service.[38] Certainly, for both perceptiveness and, at times, literary verve, it was much superior to the better-known "X article." Because the memorandum argued in a direction contrary to the views of Nitze and the PPS, Kennan submitted (January 20, 1950) his paper to Acheson as a strictly private one.[39]

Kennan's most far-reaching conclusion was that the hydrogen bomb should not be developed before all attempts had been made to establish a multilateral control of atomic energy through the UN or some other instrumentality. Here then was the quintessential traditional diplomat, comfortable with bilateral negotiations and precise agreements, wary of international organizations, and on record as having opposed previous ambitious programs for regulating atomic energy, asserting that a system of imperfect international control was better than any conceivable alternative. Also the hydrogen bomb, or its prospect, revolutionized Kennan's thinking in another respect: the United States must forswear first use of any nuclear weapon in time of war.

As Kennan framed them for Acheson, the primary questions were whether the United States should place its future reliance on numberless weapons of mass destruction, cultivate them as a major component of military strength, and use them without pause in event of war against the USSR? Or should the United States retain a small number of such devices as a deterrent to the use of atomic weapons against the West and as a means of retaliation if they were used first by the Soviets? His answer, which would remain the same for decades, was that the US should keep only the minimum necessary for deterrent-retaliatory purposes: constructing thermonuclear weapons and inventing means of their delivery were not only incalculably expensive, but redundant to a ludicrous degree.

Unlike Churchill and many others, Kennan did not believe that America's sole possession of the atomic bomb in 1945–1949 had prevented the USSR from attacking Western Europe: that country had no desire to undertake so reckless a policy. In any event, Kennan held in 1950 that since the atomic monopoly had been destroyed, it was imperative that the United States guarantee a conventional balance of forces in Europe and not allow itself to get locked into a nuclear arms race. The Soviets must understand in the future that the West possessed sufficient soldiers and nonnuclear armaments to doom any invasion of the Atlantic area from the start. Consequently, in the absence of serious efforts to coax the Soviets into leaving central Europe, the Americans would have to strengthen their existing land and air forces on the continent. From this it followed that the US and its allies could confidently adopt a policy of "no first use" of nuclear weapons in Europe and declare publicly "that we have no intention of initiating their use against anyone."[40]

In his memorandum to Acheson, Kennan also touched upon his long-held concern about the peculiar dilemmas facing the American democracy as it struggled to wage a successful Cold War. He argued that nuclear weapons, especially the more powerful ones, were disorienting and caused perceptible intellectual havoc in US foreign policy. Specifically, an accelerated nuclear arms race would distract American minds from the possibility that methods short of war could prove adequate in coping with the USSR, and policymakers would be less inclined than ever to seek diplomatic solutions: "The maxim 'to preserve the peace, prepare for war' seems to find the limits of its usefulness in the combination of the weapons of mass destruction and the gold-fish-bowl transparency of democratic public life. . . . The democratic society, which is really never at home in the medium of force, is naturally less subtle and sophisticated than the authoritarian regime in relating the maintenance and employment of force to national policy. It is thus handicapped in exploiting military potential for the purpose of *not* having a war."[41] In case of general war, Kennan feared that the American democracy, naturally viewing itself as the innocent victim of aggression and congenitally committed to justifying its cause in the loftiest terms, would be more apt than the USSR to use the most destructive available weapons. In contrast, the Soviets self-consciously connected ulterior political goals (control of additional economic resources, acquisition of buffer territories and new subjects) to their wartime military operations and, therefore, were predisposed against the wholesale extermination of any opponent.[42] Thus the nature of its war aims—namely, the ultimate triumph of good over evil rather than the prosaic goal of changing the status quo—suggested to Kennan the most baleful conduct of future American wars.

Rather than developing further their morbid fascination with the arms race, rather than devising a wicked and more powerful bomb, rather than concentrating on military solutions to international problems, Kennan hoped his compatriots would reaffirm peaceful goals and diplomatic means. A purely military policy against the USSR would, in the most fundamental sense, fail: "For such positive purposes as we wish to pursue, we must look to other things than war: above all, to bearing, to example, to persuasion, and to the judicious exploitation of our strength as a deterrent to world conflict. . . . I fear that the atomic bomb, with its vague and highly dangerous promise of 'decisive' results . . . of easy solutions to profound human problems, will impede understanding of the things that are important to a clean, clear policy and will carry us toward the misuse and dissipation of our national strength."[43] As for the general problem of war, Kennan reminded Acheson that conventional forms of it had often served recognizable political ends in the past, but the thermonuclear weapon stood opposed to politics and to life itself. In perfect, if unacknowledged, compliance with Clausewitz's injunction against making war into "something pointless and devoid of sense," Kennan wrote: "Warfare should be a means to an end other than warfare, an end connected with the beliefs and the feelings and the attitudes of people, an end marked by submission to a new political will and perhaps to a new regime of life, but an end which at least [does] not negate the principle of life itself."[44] In view of these considerations, Kennan implored Acheson to investigate with Soviet officials every possibility of organizing an international control over nuclear weapons before creating more terrifying ones, entirely without practical political merit.

The overwhelming majority of influential opinion in the State Department opposed Kennan's advice. R. Gordon Arneson, a special assistant on atomic energy policy, charged that it was impossible to reach any meaningful accord about atomic weapons with the Soviet Union as its government and ideology were fundamentally resistant to international cooperation for the maintenance of world peace. Deputy

Undersecretary of State Dean Rusk characterized Kennan's proposal for some form of international control as "the kind of proposition on which we could easily go wrong."[45] And John Hickerson, then assistant secretary of state for UN affairs, was incensed by the tone, as well as the content, of Kennan's memorandum. At times, it seemed to him, Kennan came close to accepting the Soviet position that the United States had not to date negotiated in good faith about the internationalization of atomic energy. Hickerson was also dumbfounded by any plan that required even a small measure of Soviet sincerity. The reasonable course of action was obvious: the US must maintain "a wide superiority in atomic weapons over the Soviet Union" for an indefinite period. Nitze voiced reservations about Kennan's recommendations, too, and was among those people most active in urging Acheson and Truman to authorize the AEC to begin in earnest its examination of the superbomb's feasibility. Moreover, he fully agreed with JCS chief Omar Bradley's estimation that nuclear bombs would constitute America's principal weapon in any future war.[46]

Despite his earlier work with David Lilienthal in the opposite direction, Secretary Acheson was persuaded by 1949 that efforts at the international control of atomic energy were futile and that, if the Soviets succeeded (or were widely perceived to have succeeded) in closing the nuclear gap and then surpassing the United States, Western physical security and psychological fortitude would never recover. It seemed to the secretary that Kennan was out of touch with the power realities of the mid-twentieth century, and he reviled him as a misguided pacifist: "I told Kennan if that was his view he ought to resign from the Foreign Service and go out and preach his Quaker gospel but not push it within the Department. He had no right being in the Service if he was not willing to face the questions as an issue to be decided in the interests of the American people under a sense of responsibility."[47] How astonishing it was to Acheson that Kennan failed to understand that ideologically minded dictators of the Hitler and Stalin variety never wasted an opportunity to damage the Western democracies and had a jaundiced regard for international agreements. The evidence strongly suggests that Acheson deliberately suppressed Kennan's memorandum and made sure that Truman did not see it—a pointless subterfuge, as the president had determined, even before Acheson, to support the "superbomb" project.[48]

Despite his defeat over a major policy issue and being prevented by Acheson from exercising potential influence with Truman, Kennan continued through the short remainder of his governmental career to campaign for a check on the arms race. He repeatedly warned in 1950 that the United States was becoming absurdly dependent in its war plans on nuclear weapons. And he argued that it would be wiser to establish a condition of "semi-mobilization" involving forms of compulsory military service (for millions of men), which would then allow the US to dispense with atomic weaponry as a major component of Western security.[49]

After leaving the Foreign Service, Kennan continued to inveigh through the 1950s against what he termed "the flat and inflexible thinking of the Pentagon, in which the false mathematics of relative effectiveness [of nuclear weapons] was given a sort of absolute value and all other possible factors dismissed from the equation as of no demonstrable importance."[50] The simple fact was that if ten or as few as five Soviet nuclear bombs struck their targets in the United States, the country would have endured a national loss too great to be offset by any of the emoluments of so-called victory. As for conducting a technically successful bombing against the USSR, Kennan told Arnold Wolfers (Yale University) that responsibility for the death and suffering of literally millions of Soviet citizens would place an unbearable moral burden upon the United States.[51] Consequently, on a number of occasions during the Eisenhower era, he called for the United States to forswear "first use" of nuclear weapons and urged NATO to concentrate its energies and resources on nonnuclear types of deterrence.[52] This logic led not only to Kennan's periodic calls for increasing the size of NATO's conventional forces, but also (as we have seen in Chapter 10) to his 1957 recommendation in the Reith Lectures for a type of militias defense of Western Europe. Though proffered in good faith, this last advice could not be seriously reviewed by Western leaders: its importance lies mainly as additional testimony to the depth of Kennan's determination that Americans and their allies find an escape from the nuclear dilemma.

It should be stressed that Kennan has never doubted the morality of defensive war. He has always believed that citizens can properly act in an immediate sense to protect the territorial integrity and national life of their own country. Still, he became most insistent in the 1950s that the traditional laws of war must not be violated again on the scale of 1939–1945, that every care must be taken to observe proportionality and to distinguish combatants from noncombatants. In other words, strategic bombing and the use of nuclear weapons would always be morally unsound, no matter how noble the political cause.[53] And, therefore, Sydney Hook's austere principle expressed at the time that "no world is better than some worlds" constituted for Kennan a most egocentric view for any single generation of people to adopt. Admittedly, he conceded, a given generation might collectively prefer "no world" for itself, but by what right, he wondered, could such a generation choose the same for its children or its children's children. A Soviet-US thermonuclear war would end all human possibilities, Kennan protested (to a round table discussion sponsored by the Congress for Cultural Freedom), including the possibility that future generations of communist-dominated peoples might emerge from a totalitarian dark age and inaugurate a new renaissance. Should the choice ever be so starkly placed before the West of choosing capitulation to Soviet communism or suicidal nuclear war, Kennan had no doubt about the desirable course:

> Bearing in mind the purely political limits to imperialism; bearing in mind the tendency of aggressors to be conquered culturally, in the end, by the victims of their own conquests; bearing in mind, the threadbare quality of the Marxist-Leninist ideology as a force in the intellectual life of the West and the unlikelihood that the Russian tail could really wag for very long the dog of western civilization, even if Russia's military power were unopposed; bearing in mind, finally, the irreversible effects that may be produced on the possibilities for the continuation of the human experience if these atomic bombs come to be used in anger, . . . bearing all these factors in mind, I begin to wonder whether there is any more hopeful or more dignified posture left to western man than the one which Gandhi once conceived and which he endeavored so valiantly to incorporate in his own person.[54]

As suggestive and passionate as this statement is, Kennan has never urged the Western powers to disarm unilaterally. His major point was simply that some fates that can befall the human race are worse than the most ferocious despotism and the loss of freedoms and comforts taken for granted in the West. These latter, he hastened to point out in typical fashion, had anyway been misused in the West and were effecting spiritual malaise and physical sloth.[55]

Kennan recognized that the dichotomy of Hook's "red or dead" formulation might have a certain rhetorical appeal, but it was a false choice, unrelated to real policy options, and mischievous in diverting popular and official attention from the primary issues of the East-West contest: "Let the West look sharply to the dangers and the evils of its own civilization . . . [and its inhabitants] make it their first concern to assure that they really have, and will continue to have in the future, something [worth preserving]." Indeed, it would be a tragedy of the first magnitude if the United States were deflected from its course of self-realization and improvement by the demands of nuclear competition with the Soviet regime.[56]

Through the 1960s and 1970s, Kennan continued to address the nuclear issue and sounded the same themes as before. To them, he also added a newer concern about nuclear proliferation and urged, even more affirmatively than before, the desirability of a US-Soviet comprehensive test ban treaty. He was incidentally not greatly bothered about possible Soviet violations of such a treaty as it was in Moscow's interest to do everything that might curb the arms race. It represented for the USSR a mammoth drain on resources that would be better employed on behalf of a battered domestic economy. The United States, in the meantime, should make every effort to wean itself away from reliance on nuclear weapons and acknowledge them for what they were: politically sterile, militarily useless things.[57] When the first round of SALT I negotiations began, Kennan wrote: "No one could be happier than I would be over any success they might achieve."[58] At the same time he thought that reciprocal unilateral acts of renunciation by the nuclear powers were more likely to produce positive results than "tortured efforts" to achieve detailed, formal agreements. Might both sides begin by reducing their nuclear armaments by 10 percent and agree to an immediate moratorium on all nuclear testing? Even then, both countries would retain enough nuclear explosives to destroy the other many times over.[59]

Kennan's public protests against nuclear weaponry became vehement in the late 1970s and 1980s as detente, and with it the hope that Soviet-US relations might be based on something resembling diplomatic correctness, were swept away. Along with McGeorge Bundy, Robert McNamara, and Gerard Smith, Kennan again called (1982)—in the pages of *Foreign Affairs*—for a formal American declaration of "no first use" of nuclear weapons in Europe. As had Kennan three decades earlier, this "gang of four" (so-named by the press) was at pains to make clear to readers that by their recommendation, the United States would not relinquish its nuclear weapons in Europe or fail to use them in retaliation for a Soviet nuclear attack. On the other hand, NATO must strive to improve the quantity and quality of its conventional forces while taking steps to guarantee the effectiveness of a survivable second-strike nuclear capability.[60]

Considerable support existed in the early 1980s (and still does) on both ends of the Atlantic for enhancing NATO's conventional forces, but the notion of renouncing the first-strike option seemed reckless to most influential opinion. Secretary of

State Alexander Haig, Paul Nitze, Hans Apel (West German Defense Minister), Chancellor Helmut Schmidt, General David Jones (Chairman of the JCS), Walter Mondale, and other civilian and military leaders argued that at the conventional level NATO was no match for the numerically superior Warsaw Pact and that it would be difficult and expensive to redraw Western security plans in conformance with a "no first use" doctrine. Haig estimated that a largely conventional defense posture in Europe would require the United States to triple its armed forces and place the entire economy on a wartime footing. On balance, concluded many of the critics, the "gang of four's" proposal was a notable tribute to the success of the North American and European anti-nuclear movements, but should it ever come to form the basis of NATO policy then the security, economy, and political life of the West would be jeopardized.[61]

It was disappointing to Kennan (and his co-authors in *Foreign Affairs*) to witness once more how Western leaders exaggerated the strength of Warsaw forces over those of NATO, imputed the most reckless motives to Moscow, and dismissed any concept of a workable conventional deterrent. As to the undoubted greater financial cost of improving NATO's conventional capabilities, Kennan contended that the price was perfectly justified if the nuclear threshold was ultimately raised. A few years earlier, he had written heatedly that the Western democracies must overcome their habits of misplaced economy:

> [NATO's conventional security] might cost more; it might require a bit higher sacrifice from the respective peoples. Why not? Is the minor convenience that might be derived from escaping these burdens sufficient to overbalance a danger to all the populations of the northern hemisphere, indeed to Western civilization itself, greater than any ever before known? Are the comforts of this particular generation so sacred, do they have such weight in the great span of Western civilization of which we are only a small and fleeting part, that the entire progress and survival of that civilization has to be jeopardized to assure them? What egotism![62]

Kennan's most dramatic advice concerning the arms race occurred on the occasion of his accepting the Albert Einstein Peace Prize in 1981. At the time, the condition of Soviet-US relations was horrifyingly bad, and the State Department had just declared that the United States was not legally bound by SALT I or II: the five-year limit of the former had expired; the latter was still unratified by the Senate. Against this backdrop, Kennan restated that Soviet Russia and the United States were likely to be consumed by war and nuclear disaster unless they took emergency corrective measures. Given the inadequacy of SALT and similar negotiations (e.g., those related to limiting medium-range nuclear weapons in Europe) and the present danger, he proposed that the Soviet and US governments agree to "an immediate across-the-boards reduction by fifty percent of the nuclear arsenals" held by the two countries.[63] This reduction would affect in equal number all of the strategic, intermediate, and tactical forms of nuclear weapons and their systems of delivery. Insistence on on-site inspection, that nemesis of arms control agreements, would also be dropped, and both countries would rely on their existing national means of verification. Eventually, a second operation should be undertaken to eliminate two thirds of the remaining Soviet and US nuclear weapons and, thereafter, additional reductions might be made.[64]

This proposal of Kennan's elicited a fair degree of ridicule from government officials and their apologists, who countered that America's defensive system was immensely complicated and its various components were closely integrated and interdependent. To cut the nuclear pieces of it by half would effectively dismantle US security. For the most part, however, Kennan was ignored and neither Reagan nor members of the White House staff dignified Kennan's suggestion by answering questions about it. The only administration official to take public notice was Eugene Rostow (then the designated head of the Arms Control and Disarmament Agency and a friend of Kennan's from earlier years), who offered platitudinously that the arms race was a miserable problem and Kennan's proposal deserved study.

Leon Sigal (political science, Wesleyan University) likened Kennan's 50-percent cut to earlier proposals made by the superpowers in which nobly phrased offers were made for total disarmament. And he correctly pointed out that, while these had made for passably good propaganda, they had not advanced the cause of real arms control. Still, some observers—such as Tom Wicker of the *New York Times,* Don Oberdorfer of the *Washington Post,* and Roscoe Drummond of the *Christian Science Monitor*—appreciated Kennan's ideas as they served to enliven public debate and move it in the direction of accepting some type of arms control beyond SALT II.[65] For the most part, however, Kennan's version of instant and deep cuts in Soviet and US nuclear stockpiles commended itself to few people outside the ranks of the West's populist anti-nuclear cause. Ironically, and this supports Sigal's thesis, the Reagan administration during its second term rhetorically committed itself—without, to be sure, invoking Kennan's name—to a somewhat altered draft of his solution: namely, verifiable 50-percent reductions in all Soviet and US long range nuclear weapons. Kennan's basic formula was thus coopted for public relations purposes by an administration suspicious of his international approach and whose record on arms control and reduction—notwithstanding apparent success of the relatively minor intermediate-range nuclear forces accord—has been disappointing to him.

Despite discouragement over his inability to find a receptive hearing in the higher echelons of government, Kennan has continued in the past few years to warn against the nuclear danger; has strenuously advocated the denuclearization of northern and central Europe, test ban treaty, "no first use," and freeze on further arms development; and has attacked Reagan's Strategic Defense Initiative (SDI) as unrealistic and dangerous in its implications. He has also spoken some uncharacteristically kind words about a spontaneous, popularly based movement: "This movement against nuclear armaments and nuclear war may be ragged and confused and disorganized; but at the heart of it lie some very fundamental, reasonable and powerful motivations: among them a growing appreciation by many people for the true horrors of a nuclear war."[66] Finally, Kennan has been unabashed in the past several years about giving rein to his own feelings of Christian conviction and duty in objecting to the arms race: the weapons of mass destruction are not only unusable for practical political purposes, but they go beyond anything acceptable to a Christian ethic. They challenge God's laws and dominion. As early as 1959, in regard to America's earlier testing of hydrogen bombs, Kennan demanded at the Princeton University Chapel: "My friends, what sort of a world is this in which we are living? Whoever gave us the right, as Christians, to take one innocent human life, much less one hundred and two or a hundred and two thousand? I recall no quantitative stipulation on the Sixth Commandment."[67] And, Kennan asked, might the Americans one day suffer a ghastly retribution for having used atomic bombs against noncombatants in Hiroshima and Nagasaki?[68]

More recently, he has reminded audiences that the intended victims of America's nuclear weapons matter as much in the sight of God as anyone living in the West. That many self-professed Christians living in NATO countries have lost sight of this fact has been further testimony to the corruption inflicted by nuclear weapons on Western morality and intellect.[69] How can anyone, Kennan has argued, who accepts the authority of Christ's teaching and example also accept the slightest responsibility for policies that might lead to nuclear war? And anyone, Christian or no, who recognizes a divine order and will must recoil at the prospect of exterminating God's creation on earth in the name of a presumed just cause. Surely, man in the late twentieth century can check his hubris before destroying the continuity of all human generations and ending world history, which originated in God's ultimate purposes. In 1982, Kennan exclaimed against what he saw as the moral deformity inherent in American strategic doctrine.

> I cannot help it. I hope I am not being unjust or uncharitable. But to me . . . the readiness to use nuclear weapons against other human beings—against people whom we do not know, whom we have never seen, and whose guilt or innocence it is not for us to establish—and, in doing so, to place in jeopardy the natural structure upon which all civilization rests, as though the safety and the perceived interests of our own generation were more important than everything that has ever taken place or could take place in civilization: this is nothing less than a presumption, . . . an indignity—an indignity of monstrous dimensions—offered to God![70]

*   *   *   *

The power of Kennan's assessment of contemporary Soviet-US relations and his critique of the nuclear arms race derives from the merging of three distinct conceptual frameworks, each of which is formidable in its own right. First, there is his appreciation for the unfolding of Soviet history and a recognition that the current regime, despite its multiple defects, is far more than an ossification of Stalinism. Soviet leaders from Khrushchev onward belong to another category of political kind and do not follow as in an apostolic succession from Stalin, that prototype of twentieth-century totalitarians. This appreciation of Kennan's stands in favorable contrast with that of many American hardliners who still think and argue as if no substantive changes have occurred in the USSR since 1953. The point is that the United States and its allies can, and have, more profitably treat with Stalin's successors. Kennan's contention that Moscow's international aims are unexceptional for a great power and not fatal for the West is also rooted in an historical understanding of Soviet intentions, themselves tempered by the experiences of traumatic warfare (1941–1945) and the vexations of administering a shaky empire in central and Eastern Europe. It is not out of sympathy for the West, then, or on the basis of dubious pledges of mutual trust and cooperation with the United States (i.e., the Basic Principles Agreement of 1972) that the current Soviet leaders are moderate. Rather, they have determined, as did Stalin earlier, that nothing positive can be achieved through aggressive war against the technological-industrial giants of Europe, North America, and Japan.

Second, there is Kennan's sober understanding of the peculiar problems that afflict any relationship between great powers and of the necessity, therefore, that diplomacy be primary, efficacious, and constant. This appreciation has consistently distinguished him from some liberals who hold the naive belief that if Americans and Russians can only recognize each other as human beings and strive to empathize with each other's feelings and experience, then peace will break out. Instead, not even during the halcyon period of detente did Kennan discount the obstacles in America's trying to improve relations with the Soviet Union. And in more recent years he has, as always before, advocated an official US approach to the Soviet Union premised on principles of reciprocity and regard for each other's vital interests. Diplomacy in such a context can help to manage problems between the superpowers, and can blunt their worst effects, but it cannot serve as a midwife to the millenium.

As for the nuclear arms race—born of Soviet-US rivalry, but surpassing it in gravity—Kennan has melded an appreciation of Clausewitz's teaching on war and national policy with the Christian stricture that commands human obedience to a divinely authored universe: nuclear war or even its possibility is devoid of political meaning (Clausewitz) and repugnant to the Judeo-Christian view that only God can transcend history and politics and pass verdict upon them. Hence Kennan has charged that the use of nuclear weapons would be the ultimate blasphemy as well as an act of political nihilism.

As one whose scholarly career is rooted in academic history, whose philosophical and religious orientation is traditional, and whose public service has been concerned with the ameliorationist tasks of diplomacy, Kennan has never had difficulty in accepting that the political life of nations, like individuals, is necessarily characterized by elements of insecurity. But, as he has witnessed with melancholy humor, the greatest national insecurity has flowed from the quest for total security in the nuclear age. Whether debating the hydrogen bomb in 1949–1950 or SDI today, Kennan's caveat to the United States has remained the same: "If you haven't got the courage and the strength of purpose to deal with the probabilities in this life, and if you're determined to hold out for the extremisms of an absolute certainty, it is your own security that you are undermining."[71] With full awareness of the possible risks, say, to the military balance in Europe or the perception of slackening American will, Kennan has not hesitated to urge that the United States renounce "first use" and, along with the Soviets, slash standing nuclear stockpiles and secure other arrangements that might lower the floodtide of nuclear and international dangers. Certainly, Kennan's proposal in 1950 that the United States explore with Russia some form of international control over atomic energy and, in effect, relinquish what was still widely held to be an American asset (advanced knowledge of nuclear physics) indicates, too, that he has long been willing to contemplate innovative types of solutions to national security problems.

In the end, Kennan's ideas concerning nuclear weapons have never persuaded the American government or those of its NATO allies. This has been so because his discourse on the subject has not only eschewed the arcane language of strategic-nuclear theory and is removed from its technical conundrums, but it contains a dose of moralism and as such belongs, at least partly, to the genre exemplified by the American Catholic bishops and Jonathan Schell's *The Fate of the Earth* (1982). This literature and the sentiments it expresses is of marginal interest to most people charged with devising workable, specific defense policy. Recall Acheson's blast to Kennan: preach elsewhere and resign from the government if you are unwilling to grapple with concrete security policy and choices. In addition, Kennan's views have failed because they are incompatible with the prevailing wisdom in all NATO capitals that America's nuclear defense policy has succeeded over decades in maintaining peace and deterring Soviet aggression. Tampering with a policy that has worked well is to court countless troubles; in a sense, Kennan's own absolutist position about nuclear issues has placed him outside of the established framework of official discussion. To these objections Kennan might respond that never more than in the nuclear age do Abraham Lincoln's words deserve closer attention by national leaders: "The dogmas of the quiet past are inadequate to the stormy present. The occasion is piled high with difficulty, and we must rise with the occasion. As our case is new, so we must think anew, and act anew. We must disenthrall ourselves, and then we shall save our country."[72]

14

Diplomacy and the
Politics of Amelioration

To this point, we have examined Kennan's explicit ideas about the diverse issues with which he has dealt as diplomat, policymaker, and critic. Yet over the course of his long career, he has also evolved a set of underlying concepts and assumptions that in their totality suggest a theory of politics and international relations—his impatience with academic social science and his skepticism about most formal philosophy notwithstanding.[1] In evaluating what might be construed as Kennan's theory, or what we can at least label as his philosophical precepts, we can also draw some broad conclusions about his overall contribution to US foreign policy.

Albeit not deliberately constructed by him or even acknowledged, Kennan's "theory" has informed his recommendations about every political and diplomatic dilemma that he has confronted: nuclear weaponry; the USSR; US involvement in Europe, Asia and elsewhere in the Third World; and his thinking about America's social and domestic political problems. In turn, his personal experience with these matters has, quite naturally, further influenced his general views. Too scholarly to be a bland functionary, Kennan's advice as a government official was suffused with historical interpretations and ethical judgments. Too worldly to be only donnish or abstract, Kennan's notions about international policy are strikingly devoid of the scientism and abstruseness that have spoiled so much of international relations theory in recent decades. His own contributions to theory are not without flaw, but on the whole they are instructive about the nature of world politics and helpful as a guide to US action abroad.

In a certain sense, Kennan's ideas about politics and external affairs have the effect—despite his stated preference for other, particularly European, intellectual *milieux*—of placing him in a recognizable American tradition. His pronouncements about politics reverberate with echoes of American strains stretching from John Winthrop to Reinhold Niebuhr and Walter Lippmann, and including Roger Williams, Alexander Hamilton, John Quincy Adams, and some of the more notable mugwumps.

As in Winthrop's instruction to the New England Calvinists that, to build a "Citty vpon a Hill," they must labor and suffer together as one body, so Kennan has enjoined his countrymen to greater discipline, collective effort, and purposefulness. In keeping with Roger Williams, who bore witness to the failure of Massachusetts as a model of Christian community and a willing victim of the "common Trinity" (profit, preferment, pleasure), Kennan has condemned America's straying from the gold of Puritan ascetic idealism and pursuing the dross of modern comforts. Like Hamilton, Kennan is by instinct and intellect a Federalist and has attributed many modern evils to the alleged excesses of democracy. Indeed, if any one person out of the American tradition can be singled out for his political commonality with Kennan, it must be Hamilton. They have both recommended national salvation in the form of increased governmental centralization and *dirigisme* to prevent the "raucous egalitarian republic" (Kennan's words) from spinning apart. Together they would insist on the executive branch as the sole legitimate center of gravity in handling all exceptional matters—foreign policy, as well as war. Although sharing with Thomas Jefferson a distrust of urban commercial culture and a predilection to wax eloquent on the virtues of nature and rural life, Kennan has been as likely as not to dismiss as "Jeffersonian heresy" any proposal that would further advance the influence of public opinion beyond presently established institutional arrangements.

In addition to invoking John Quincy Adams as authority during testimony (about Vietnam) before the Senate, Kennan has regularly affirmed with him that the United States must set a modest international agenda for itself and resist the temptation of intervening on behalf of various putatively humane causes abroad, as recklessness in this regard leads to ruinous wars and the corruption of political life at home. In company with the mugwumps, Kennan has not been drawn to any party or partisans operating in American politics and has yearned for the day when the United States might cultivate deeper tone and seriousness in its cultural and civic life. His displeasure, in fact his resentment, at the influx to American shores of millions of immigrants representing civilizations that share no affinity with his own recalls some of the typical mugwump ferocity on the subject (for example, that of E. L. Godkin). Similar to Lippmann, Kennan has exhibited the paradox of many modern pedagogues in combining a disdain for the popular mind and pessimism about its potential for growth with a vestigial Enlightenment optimism about education. Hence Lippmann's and Kennan's voluminous writings and lectures intended to tutor the public about political affairs. Finally, as to Niebuhr, whom Kennan has credited with exercising a greater intellectual influence on him than anyone else, the two of them—while differing in important ways, especially in their assessment of American democracy—have held out for an intellectual elite that would take upon itself the political and spiritual improvement of their nation. Whereas Niebuhr looked to what he termed a "prophetic minority," Kennan, at least once explicitly and many times implicitly, has called for a "protest minority" that would solemnly promote a level of aesthetics and ethics more deeply attuned to life's verities than that produced by an overindustrialized, overarmed, overpolluting American society.[2]

Probably there is no adequate single label under which could be grouped those Americans with whom Kennan might be usefully compared. Still, the line of thought that connects these seventeenth-century New Englanders and later mandarins is decidedly conservative in the conventional European, if not mainstream American, sense. At its most politically influential, this tradition—really a merging of Calvin and Burke—thrived in the 1790s under the guidance of Hamilton, but since his era has become increasingly weak and diluted until in late twentieth-century America it has nearly completely disappeared. As there is no European-style social democratic party or conscience in the United States, neither is there a genuinely conservative one along (pre-Thatcher) British Tory or continental lines. Rather, as Kennan has ruefully noted, there is in a doctrinal sense only one sect of consensus—the two so-called parties being "ideologically undistinguishable, their pronouncements form[ing] one integral body of banality and platitude." In such a political setting, a conservative of Kennan's taste is fated for political isolation and continuous frustration: thus his repeated remarks that he is not a citizen of this epoch.[3]

Despite Kennan's feelings of political marginality, he has had some reason to feel intermittently, at least, at home in post-1945 America. As one who has been closely identified with the realist tradition in international relations, Kennan has been part of that school of thought that has dominated political science circles— through the person of Hans Morgenthau and his disciples—and has played a role in practical affairs, exemplified by the career of Henry Kissinger. Kennan himself expressed what might pass for the realist credo, as well as anyone else could have, when he impressed upon students at the National War College in 1950 "the necessity of distinguishing constantly between that which is really important to us in this world in terms of potential power and that which is not. In doing that, I hope you will put aside such things as emotional judgment and moral indignation and require yourselves to look at our world environment absolutely coldly and realistically, with the clinical detachment of the surgeon or the research scholar, making a particular effort to understand precisely those things which are annoying and displeasing and irritating because they are the ones which are the most important to understand rather than to get mad about."[4] Undoubtedly, few people could remain faithful to this stern injunction; Kennan's own diplomatic and intellectual career is no exception. His version of realism blends principles of power politics with elements of conservatism (sometimes romantic) and an ethic of duty based on orthodox moral and religious precepts.

A Realist Perspective

The core of Kennan's realism and conservatism is rooted, like that of his Scottish Calvinist ancestors, in a view of human life and human nature that stresses tragedy and fallenness. Of the former and in reference to the individual self, Kennan has never lost sight of the ephemeralness of human experience, the chance phenomenon of injustice, the liabilities of the physical body, the loneliness of bereavement, and—taken from Freud—the endless conflict that arises in civilization between the emotional needs and physical instincts of the individual and society's requirements of order and restraint. These phenomena are built into every human life and impart to it, in Kennan's vivid phrase, an "ineradicable tragic dimension that nothing can change." Nor has Kennan doubted the partiality of human knowledge and understanding or the essential corruption embedded in human personality. Having witnessed at close quarters the ill effects produced in individuals by poverty, war, and purges, he has come to gloomy conclusions about people's capacity for weakness and cruelty: "Panicky, violent, chaotic behavior is always closer to the surface of man's nature than many of us suppose."[5]

Like Niebuhr, Kennan holds that man's self-will and vanity limit all human enterprises without exception—no matter how selflessly phrased or altruistically conceived they might appear to their authors. The fact is that human vision and judgment are circumscribed from the outset by the overwhelming power of self-love. And it takes multiple perverse forms in political life, often in ways more subtle than just the familiar shapes of self-glory and self-vindication. In a 1969 article for the *Princeton Seminary Bulletin,* Kennan wrote with the experience of himself and former colleagues no doubt in mind: "The mere experience of participation in government is an unsettling thing. . . . It arouses and stimulates a whole series of human qualities that have nothing to do with Christian purposes: ambition . . . greed, envy, competitiveness, the love of public attention, the appetite for flattery. These motivations enter at a thousand points into the final product of any political effort."[6] In view of this consideration and in view of the imperfections of human life, Kennan has repeatedly suggested that governments and citizens would be well served by being self-consciously skeptical, even humble, about their most morally ambitious projects. Certainly, he believes that no scientific breakthrough— such as SDI—or application of a clever philosophical-political formula—such as Marxism—will assure security or happiness or eliminate the tragic element from life.

For Kennan, as for virtually all traditional conservatives, civilization is fragile, and it cannot sustain violent shocks as caused by modern war or swift change. Vigorous diplomacy must preempt large-scale international violence; social and technological changes must come gradually. Like Burke, Kennan has consistently warned that abruptness and a super-velocity of change can shred the vital fabric of society and of people's lives and cause vastly more harm than anyone ever intended. All utopian projects—the history of Russian Marxism being, for Kennan, a powerful example—provide persuasive evidence that not only are people unable to create paradise on earth, but their energetic and enthusiastic efforts to do so invariably cause boundless mischief. (Similarly, in Kennan's mind, the accomplishments of American science and technology, and the conveniences they have produced, cannot compensate for the myriad of difficulties they have inflicted on the environment or on human understanding about man's relationship with the natural order.) He connects the failure of political utopian schemes not only to the fact that they are impossible of achievement, but to the blindness of their sponsors to recognize that methods—witness the Bolsheviks' war communism or Stalin's later brutalities— will determine the practical, palpable outcome. Worthy results cannot follow from unworthy means; rather, the means determine, and often become, the end. The politically responsible person for Kennan, as for Morgenthau, therefore recognizes that all choice exists along a spectrum of evil; one must distinguish gradations and choose the least imperfect policy from various unhappy possibilities. Kennan has given this rationale for his reliance on an ethics of the lesser evil: "In a less than perfect world, where the ideal so obviously lies beyond human reach, it is natural that the avoidance of the worst should be a more practical undertaking than the achievement of the best, and that some of the strongest imperatives of moral conduct should be ones of a negative rather than a positive nature. The strictures of the Ten Commandments are perhaps the best illustration of this state of affairs."[7]

Ever since his Walgreen Lectures at the University of Chicago in 1951, Kennan has also taught that utopianism in international life will lead to confusion and often disaster. As with most realists his portrayal of international relations is basically Thomas Hobbes's state of nature writ large: a conflict of all against all. In such a severe situation, in which the conventions of diplomacy and an etiolated species of law and international organization do not substitute for the continuing absence of a universally accepted moral or political authority, Americans cannot expect that a regime of order, justice, and peace will be allowed by sovereign, competitive states to prevail. And, alas, the record of American participation in attempts to outlaw war (the Kellogg-Briand pact), to establish an embryonic world government, or to rescue foreigners from themselves (Vietnam) is a discouraging one. Kennan has expressed the hope that one day his countrymen will, as a mark of their own political maturity, come to accept the inherent limits of foreign policy: "We are *not* going to change the nature of man, nor to solve the dilemmas of political society. We are *not* going to find means to overcome the great irrational, emotional currents that sweep through nations and races and entire world areas. . . . We are *not* going to be understood, as a nation. In many instances, we are *not* going to understand." All that Americans should do, apart from trying to make their own country a more satisfying place in which to live, is to follow the precepts of moderation and tolerance in foreign policy.[8]

Kennan's understanding of these principles has led him to object to the fighting of total wars and the aim of unconditional surrender, to protest the demonization of US adversaries and the idealization of its associates, and to urge the primacy of diplomacy over force. And his interpretation of these principles accounts for his long-sustained campaign against American political-moral evangelism. Since the early 1950s, when Father Edmund Walsh took Kennan to task for his statement at Chicago that the United States ought not make itself into a slave of international law and morality, various critics have charged him with believing that there is no place for concepts of right and wrong in judging the actions of independent states— except in making Machiavellian determinations about expediency. Walsh warned that such an ethic was appropriate only for the jungle and inadvertently helped lead to the exoneration of totalitarian aggression and inhumanity. Was Stalin not subject to the moral laws of the human race?[9] In recent years, critics have faulted Kennan for not more forcefully condemning South African apartheid or Soviet persecution of Jews and dissidents. His response, really a discourse conducted for over three and a half decades about the role of morality in foreign affairs, has been coherent and reflects a Niebuhrian anxiety about the willfulness of national pride oblivious to the dangers of hegemonial purpose and conceit.

In keeping with Niebuhr, Morgenthau, and other realists, Kennan has been eager to maintain the distinction between the moral obligation and ethical code of the individual person living in organized society and that of states existing in an anarchical system. Individuals in civil society can rightly be held to a fairly rigorous standard of personal ethical conduct, which in the case of martyrs or saints might even entail self-sacrifice. A government, however, operating in the foreign field, is charged with protecting its subjects' lives and property and beyond that is not properly concerned with anything else. Arthur Schlesinger, Jr. has described this position succinctly: "Saints can be pure, but statesmen must be responsible. As trustees for others, they must defend interests and compromise principles. In consequence politics is a field where practical and prudential judgment must have priority over simple moral verdicts."[10] Still, as Kennan once tried to assure James Shotwell (a proponent of the League of Nations and other forms of internationalism during the interwar period), an ethic of responsibility should be no more confused with an effort to promote cynicism in foreign policy than an ethic of ultimate ends. Kennan also told Shotwell that he had long despised the hypocrisy and the exploitation of moral sentiment by diverse American political leaders to gain domestic political advantage or to curry favor with one ethnic group or another. Besides, as he once wrote for another audience: "Morality is such a thing which, like dignity of character generally, loses its meaning and ceases to exist the moment one claims it or refers to it one's self."[11] True as this observation is in application to the individual, it is even more so in Kennan's view (taken from Niebuhr) in the case of nations: a people's self-perception is primitive, usually complacent and overdrawn, and the demon of collective self is almost impossible to subdue. Finally, as Kennan has often observed, the moral issue in any given international conflict is not always plain to see—even for a community based on shared values—and ascriptions of blame or praise are frequently meaningless. He would have us consider, for example, the Arab-Israeli dispute, in which neither side is wholly pure nor evil. This being so, the United States should seek solutions in a dispassionate manner and with the aim of containing the worst types of violence. In other words, nothing like a perfect solution is likely to exist for any international situation and Americans hamper their cause and that of others by incessantly invoking allegedly universalistic principles.[12]

Too often, then, the American propensity to moralize has appeared to Kennan as a substitute for real decency and intelligence in diplomacy; only constant reference to its own national interest can safely guide the United States as it tries to steer through the maze of conflicts between itself and others and between third parties.

Unlike Morgenthau, the national interest for Kennan does not possess anything so majestic as its own "moral dignity"; neither can it be defined concisely "in terms of power." Rather, he is relaxed about precise definitions of national interest. (Eugene Rostow was thus inspired to remark that his mind does not move along mathematical lines, but is like that of an impressionist painter or a poet.)[13] To Kennan, the US government, like that of every country, must use foreign policy to foster conditions conducive to national security and prosperity. Americans might enjoy talking about a high-sounding national purpose that manifests itself in foreign policy, but this is a delusion. Like people everywhere, they are mainly involved in the struggle for economic well-being and living without undue hindrance from the outside. These purposes are not reprehensible in themselves, but neither do they constitute an elevated morality. They are fundamentally neutral from a moral stand-point and represent a necessity handed down by an inexorable historical process that has culminated in an international system still dominated by rival nation-states. Kennan has agreed that Americans naturally do and should let their moral values play a dominant role in domestic matters, and it would be folly for the United States to adopt internal policies that represent a degradation of national tradition—for example the 1947 Loyalty Order and boards of interrogation. Regarding other nations, however, Americans should judge not lest they themselves be judged. In 1957, he wrote:

> I do not profess to know—I prefer, in fact, to ignore—what is moral and virtuous for the sovereign state of Libya or Viet Nam. And while I should always be interested, as a matter of practical politics, to learn their views on the actions and diplomatic methods of my own country, I should be reluctant to accept instruction from the inhabitants of these states on what is right or what is wrong in the conduct of foreign policy. I should resent, in fact, the suggestion that their traditional concepts ought to be relevant to our problems.[14]

So, too, the United States should exercise a comparable measure of restraint and admit that it has not been appointed guardian of the world's virtue: let Americans practice their version of morality at home and by their adherence to it impress the world with their steadfastness and seriousness of purpose. At the same time, Ameri-cans must be made to understand that nothing is more dangerous than moral feeling divorced from responsibility. Kennan has recorded: "In the eyes of many Ameri-cans it is enough for us to indicate the changes that ought, as we see it, to be made. We assume, of course, that the consequences will be benign and happy ones. But this is not always assured." The offending government and peoples must live with the consequences, not those Americans who enjoy measuring the moral deficiences of others against the presumed superiority of their own qualities.[15]

The fact that Kennan has not discerned any unique genius or special excellence in the US political system reinforces his objection to the impulse of American moral universalism. It is obvious to him that a country that is wasteful of its natural resources, is spiritually and physically weakened by bad living habits, and confuses the incidental longevity of its constitution and governmental institutions with wis-dom has little—except by negative example—to teach others. And yet, at exactly this point, Kennan the *American* diplomat would interpose: regardless of the inju-ries it inflicts upon itself, regardless of its political defects, the United States can without apology expect that other states will, on the basis of reciprocity, respect US interests abroad. Whatever failings they embody, Americans are not a warlike or aggressive people, and there is no reason, according to Kennan, that other countries cannot gracefully accommodate the United States on the basis of mutually tolerable arrangements.[16] To obtain these ends, the United States must unsparingly encour-age its professional diplomacy.

Kennan has periodically likened the conduct of a state's diplomacy to that of good manners in personal life. In each case, the principal obligation is to one's self. And as dignity of behavior has its origins in the needs of the person who practices it—rather than in "external compulsion"—so do such qualities as integrity and courtesy in international life stem from the inner dynamics of a country. Not only do these qualities enable a state to coexist with others, they, more importantly, allow a nation to live with itself. The United States, for example, must preserve and nourish a certain image, on which is dependent self-respect and, ultimately, the continuation of successful national life. Therefore, Kennan has reminded varied audiences over the years, the United States has always been well served in practicing honesty, decency, and helpfulness in small things. On the other hand, pettiness and a gross insensitivity to others have hindered the advancement of US foreign interests.[17] As for the actual vocation of diplomacy, it demands in Kennan's opinion persistence, composure, and personal equanimity. To be effective, the diplomat and negotiator must also renounce self-righteousness and realize that, as the perfect and best are unobtainable, one must concentrate on the acceptable. This implies that mechanical devices of multilateral treaty, international law, and so forth are inferior in assuring peace to diplomatically inclined governments. Certainly, Kennan's preference has always been for the traditional flexibility and freedom to act unimpeded by mass domestic constituencies that characterized eighteenth- and nineteenth-century European diplomacy. Although he has readily acknowledged that such techniques and arts as practiced in previous centuries cannot be resurrected, he has, as we have seen elsewhere, urged his government not to move too rapidly away from them.[18]

Two of the important implications of Kennan's views on diplomacy are that the United States is not obliged to restrain violence between third parties or to practice charity on a large scale (for example, in trying to "develop" the Third World). Though it may sometimes be in the US interest to perform one or both of these tasks, neither should be automatic. Just as the United States cannot serve as the international conscience, so, too, it should reject the Rooseveltian urge to police the world. Except in those instances that infringe upon the security or economic interests of the United States and its major allies, the undertakings or predicaments of great masses of people abroad should not be a cause to American diplomacy for moral or military excitement. The serious task of US diplomacy is to find modalities and strike compromises with other states that will allow them all to continue as national entities and to develop, however they can, their particular talents.

To insure their international success, the Americans must not only deploy a skillful diplomacy, but they must attend to the power of example and the conditions of social health in their polity. On this subject, perhaps on more than any other, Kennan has been adamant for decades. Sensitive to the point of personal anguish about his country's real (and imagined) shortcomings, Kennan has routinely pummeled it for lacking a sense of history, high culture, and refinement. The automobile has invaded and destroyed neighborhoods; rootlessness and an ethos of the peripatetic have killed any sense of community. These problems, combined with the country's low intellectual level of politics, have meant for Kennan, at times, that the United States is fundamentally lacking in texture, is boring. While he has discovered solace in a sort of personal antiquarianism, his Norwegian summer home, sailing, and other private pursuits, he has periodically recommended a "dramatic stiffening of public authority" for the United States. On the eve of the two-hundredth anniversary of the American Constitution, he ventured to suggest—

again—that it should be examined by a body of distinguished people to determine its suitability as a basis for government in the late twentieth century. As he has admitted on other occasions, his desire for a more disciplinary regime cannot be realized until a new philosophy (Kennan is vague here) has gained popular approval. In any case, however idiosyncratic he sometimes is on the subject, Kennan clearly belongs to that American political tradition that defines national greatness largely in terms of domestic behavior and cohesion. In 1985, at the National War College, he told an audience that the primary task of the United States for the foreseeable future was one of *self-containment*: it must master its fantastically high budgetary and trade deficits, cure its addiction to exorbitant defense spending, cease further violations against the environment, and carefully regulate the immigration of masses of people from alien political traditions. If the United States continues to live beyond its means and ignores its formidable domestic problems, it should not hope to play a constructive future role in world affairs.[19]

Nostalgia and Custodianship

As the preceding discussion suggests, Kennan partakes deeply of the realist canon. Similar to Morgenthau, he has crusaded against the crusading and moralistic spirit of American foreign policy, has insisted on some version of the national interest as primary, and has uncompromisingly affirmed the superiority of diplomacy over the rigidity of military thinking on the one hand and naive internationalism on the other. With Niebuhr, Kennan has warned against national self-righteousness and has shared with him and Kissinger the conviction that the United States has been handicapped in its understanding of politics because, unlike the Europeans and their searing experience, the ebullient Americans are essentially nescient of life's darker side. And, like the British realist E. H. Carr (also a diplomat-turned-scholar), Kennan has repeatedly asserted that the ultimate success of the West in the Cold War—and by extension America's own international standing—ultimately depends on the resolution of issues related to internal resilience and coping with the dilemmas of mass civilization.[20]

At the same time, Kennan's general thinking about international relations, foreign policy, and the United States has been permeated with some qualities that seem more distinctively his own or are, minimally, less germane to political realism as conventionally understood. For one thing, his version of conservatism—quite apart from its classically Burkean pessimism about human progress—has been anchored in an incurably romantic attachment for the past. In this respect, his realism suffers as it is oddly balanced by a kind of conservative utopianism in which the past possessed all manner of superior habits and institutions. By this standard of judgment, the United States reached its apogee in the age before televisions, automobiles, and great industrial conglomerations. In Kennan's imagination the "America of the barefoot boy and the whitewashed board fence, the America of the Webster cartoon . . . was a wonderful old America." In a similar nostalgic vein, he has expressed regret for the passing away of a quainter Department of State as it existed around 1900, when it was furnished with black leather rocking chairs and brass cuspidors, exuded quiet dignity and old fashioned simplicity, and was peopled by truly cosmopolitan gentlemen. As for Europe, he has found particular merit in the multinational, Christian empires, exemplified by the Holy Roman empire, and—as we have discussed elsewhere—has expressed a marked preference for the world of pre-1789.[21]

The consequences of this romantic idealization of the past are attractive in Kennan himself. It is related to his appreciation for traditions ceremonious, his personal courtliness, and his love and practice of a high literary style. This last trait, incidentally, apparently worried Acheson as he feared he might become beguiled by Kennan's use of language into adopting ill-considered policies.[22] On the more serious side, Kennan's dreamy view of the past has caused him to exaggerate the defects of the modern world and to trivialize some of the past's more unpleasant aspects. His indulgent view of European imperialism in Asia and Africa, for example, has helped blunt his sensibility to Third World dilemmas and grievances and has caused him to adopt a defensive tone about them. Combined with the fact that he has not enjoyed good physical health while in tropical climes and has been given to some racial and ethnic stereotyping, Kennan's reservations about Western collaboration with and assistance to Third World states are imbued with more than a standard realist's concern about national interest, technical feasibility, and overinvolvement.[23] Moreover, Kennan's preference for a mythical golden age of diplomacy when an aristocratic few masterfully sorted through international conflicts of power has misled him to the point where he finds almost nothing of value in modern summitry and not much more in international law, international public organizations, and multilateral negotiations. Now this is *not* to say that Kennan has been wrong in attacking the "stubborn illusion" of much American statesmanship that has regarded legal arrangements alone as adequate to absorb the strains and changes in strength of various countries. Indeed, à la Kennan, there is no substitute for sustained diplomacy in the nuclear age and for steady statesmanship. But, as he was forced to admit in 1950 when the US government debated whether to build the hydrogen bomb and as he has recognized throughout the 1980s, unless clear-eyed diplomacy receives some additional boost in the form of new concepts and creativity, then the perils of the nuclear era will linger indefinitely.[24] In addition, contrary to Kennan, Americans need not be wary of conferences between their leaders and those of the Soviet Union. They can be useful so long as both sides meet in good faith, do not posture or raise high expectations, and view such exercises as the symbolic ratification of negotiations successfully completed. As for multilateral meetings, they are indeed cumbersome and prone to propagandistic abuse, but it is also certain, as never before in history, that some international problems—including those important to Kennan: nuclear proliferation, global pollution, population explosion—cannot be managed on bilateral or *ad hoc* bases.

Kennan's fancy that the pre-1789 world enjoyed a social coherence, intellectual balance, and basic reasonableness all notably absent in contemporary life has inclined him to embrace a dubious, anti-democratic viewpoint in politics and diplomacy. Staunchly opposed to egalitarianism in political and other walks of life, he has never doubted that sophisticated foreign policy can only be conducted by trained, dedicated individuals not forced to consult continuously with an emotional

Congress and uninformed public.[25] As illustrated by his 1942 plans for a Foreign Service academy, he has even thought it possible to produce a quality of statesmanship from which venality, indiscipline, and other forms of human frailty have been bred out. Kennan's problem here, however, again derives from his version of conservative utopianism as it fails to deal adequately with the potential abuse of power or failure of leadership by political and diplomatic officers not subject to public accountability. Even the "best" people, irrespective of their background and capacity, are subject to misjudgment, temptations, and all the other failings of mortal men and women—as Kennan the Calvinist and student of Niebuhr should have more readily acknowledged. As Niebuhr might have protested, it was, for example, a combination of unbridled pride of power and pride of knowledge that led the "best and brightest" of one generation to commit the United States to a hopeless war in Southeast Asia. In other words, given the absence of angels and philosopher kings in government, and given the contingent character of all human purposes—including the formulation and execution of US foreign policy—democratic constraints have a useful role to play in diplomacy. From a purely theoretical standpoint, *per* Plato's *Republic,* this is not a perfect situation. But, in view of the actual condition of human material, it is not so bad as the worst case: policy by autocrats. Finally, contrary to Kennan's presumption, the broad citizenry in a representative democracy is not necessarily more intemperate or unreasonable than its government. From his perspective, it must have struck Kennan as ironic when a December 1981 Gallup poll indicated that 75 percent of American adults supported his proposal for a one-half reduction of all Soviet and US nuclear weapons, while the government and its battery of experts on diplomacy and armaments either ignored or denounced the idea.[26]

While Kennan's conservative disposition and interpretation of history are the source of his complaint against various expressions of modernity, they have also served positive ends: in particular, they have been a source of insight and have helped sustain his eloquent pleas—both in government and since—for diplomacy and the avoidance of large-scale interstate violence. Central to Kennan's thinking, especially in recent decades, is the concept of custodianship. Constant in expressing appreciation for natural beauty, the sturdiness of Christian faith, and the aesthetic and intellectual achievements of great civilizations, Kennan has derived from these a sense of the obligation to be discharged by the present generation: to pass the planet on to succeeding generations in a condition no poorer or less able to support "the wonder of life" than that in which they received it. This duty also stretches backward in time and entails a responsibility to history and its progression through the ages of man and nature. In the words of Kennan the Christian moralist:

> We of this generation are only the custodians, not the owners, of the earth on which we live. There were others who lived here before, and we hope there will be others who are going to live here afterwards. . . . We have an obligation to both of them, to past generations and to future ones, no less than our obligations to ourselves. I fail to see that we are in any way justified in making, for the safety or convenience of our own generation, alterations in our natural environment which may importantly change the conditions of life for those who come afterward. The moral laws which we acknowledge predicated the existence of a certain sort of world—a

certain sort of natural environment—in which the human predicament had its setting. This presumably reflected God's purpose. We didn't create it; we do not have the right to destroy it. . . . When we permit this environment to be altered quite basically by things we do today, and altered in ways the effects of which we cannot even predict, we are taking upon ourselves a responsibility for which I find no authority in Christian faith.[27]

From these considerations have sprung Kennan's refrains against further testing of nuclear weapons and nuclear stockpiling and his insistence on serious diplomacy as a means of averting catastrophic Soviet-US war. He has also advised Americans to tailor their foreign policy so that it does not run against the complex, organic processes of international life; the great forces of nationalism, rapid social change, technological progress, and the rest cannot be decisively affected by American will or power. Rather, for Kennan the United States must approach international issues with the patience of the gardener and work to influence the world environment in a direction that will contain or prevent fatal explosions.[28] This sensibility, in turn, requires Americans to understand that one's adversaries do not have a monopoly on evil, but have an ordained role to play within a greater scheme of history and purpose, that surpasses human understanding.[29]

*   *   *   *

In its essence, Kennan's intellectual career represents the submerged European conservative tradition in American political thought. Its strengths and its penetration, its weaknesses and its embarrassments, are equally Kennan's. This strain of thinking has never really commended itself to the jaunty American outlook, based on optimism, materialistic success, and the legend of the rugged individual who triumphs over all odds. And, certainly, the familiar themes of Kennan's and earlier conservatism are not in keeping with the irrepressible temper of twentieth-century (pre-Vietnam) Americans, be they conventional liberals or Republican-type conservatives.[30]

To begin with, Kennan's religiosity, occasional tart remarks about "sickly secularism," and his unabashed conviction that all reliable ethics reside in religious beliefs run counter to the prevailing liberal consensus, which rests on a wide tolerance of competing viewpoints and ways of living. And to those Republicans of the Reagan stripe who still dominate their party, Kennan must be a source of incomprehension when he says that evil is not an external problem located in America's adversaries—be they global communism, the Soviet Union, or Iran. Against this simplemindedness, he has brought to bear the devastating insight of those seventeenth century New England divines who were not deceived about the pervasiveness and ingeniousness of evil; its stain attaches equally to American and non-American alike. Speaking of anti-communism in 1964, Kennan declared:

I must reject it . . . and not just as a matter of critical logic, but rather out of a sense of Christian duty, because it implies a certain externalization of evil—a tendency to look for evil only outside ourselves—which is wholly incompatible with Christian teaching. Evil is an omnipresent substance of human life: around us and within us as well as without us. . . . When we struggle against it we must always regard that struggle as in part an overcoming of self. We cannot, for this reason, identify ourselves self-righteously with all that is good and clothe whatever opposes us in the colors of unmitigated evil.[31]

Kennan also recognized in assuming the roles of a diplomat and policymaker that he (as Max Weber taught) had of necessity to contract with "diabolical forces." This realization could account for his willingness to live only on the "fringes of power." Except for one inhibition or another, Kennan might have pursued personal power beyond the rank of counselor of state or ambassador. Elements within the Democratic party were prepared to support his running for Congress or the Senate, but he declined. Greater taciturnity and a willingness to go along with the prevailing line might have won him a more secure position within Acheson's State Department, saved his career under Dulles's regime, preserved his standing with Stevenson, and won him something more significant than envoy to Belgrade during Kennedy's administration. But he was clearly ambivalent about governmental work and often on the verge of official resignation from it. The administration of executive power even within so limited a setting as an embassy or the Policy Planning Staff did not come naturally to him, and he was apparently an ineffective bureaucratic operator. Did the prospect of exercising greater power in a larger arena so unsettle him that he *chose* not to seek it? From a purely philosophical standpoint, he certainly did not fully share Niebuhr's hope (and expectation) that justice could really be implicated in the manipulation of US power abroad.

And yet any case to be made about Kennan's reluctance to accept increased political responsibilities must take into account his earlier personal ambitions and vanity. As a young diplomat posted in Moscow, he could be snobbish toward fellow Foreign Service officers who lacked his training in and understanding of Russian history, language, and politics. As an instructor at the National War College, he was proud that his lectures were often attended by cabinet officers, generals, and senators. And he was careful at that delicate time in his career (1946–1947), when he was acquiring both reputation and position, not to let his interpretations alienate the affections of people who could advance his career. This concern was evident when he trimmed his memorandum—later the "X article"—for Forrestal. Similarly, when George Elsey sent Kennan in 1946 a draft of the Clifford-Elsey report, which went further in recommending military measures against the Soviets than he thought advisable, he muted his stronger objections and offered only minor suggestions for improvement.[32] He might also have pushed harder than he did in 1947–1948 to let Lippmann know that the two men were in substantial agreement about Soviet aims and US policy despite misimpressions caused by the "X article." But then, would such clarification by the director of Policy Planning have complicated his relations with Forrestal and further irritated Marshall, at the time already miffed by what he considered to be Kennan's indiscretion in *Foreign Affairs*? None of this speculation is meant to suggest that Kennan was a dissembler, but like most people, he was trying to get by without giving undue offense to individuals who could be professionally helpful. Still, the ambivalence remained strong in Kennan. While he wanted to be appreciated in the late 1940s by the government as a resident intellectual and to be deferred to in matters of large interpretation, he hesitated or became annoyed when powerful people invoked his concepts (e.g., containment), but put them into practice in ways that made him uneasy.

Irrespective of the complications that surrounded Kennan's attitude about exercising power and increased responsibility, his career possibilities in government were doubtless restricted by his aversion both to practical politics and America's mass democracy. While PPS director, he was too impatient and otherwise engaged to bother much with rallying support—either in the government apparatus or in the larger public—for policies that he thought were obviously worthwhile. Very likely, had he ever come to occupy a major political position, say, secretary of state, he would have failed even more than Acheson to retain public support for foreign policy. Later, as a private citizen, had he been able to overlook some of the less appealing aspects of the anti-Vietnam protestors, he could have helped improve their diplomatic-political education. And their popular movement might have served him well as a vehicle by which to spread his thoughtful objections against the war—beyond the Fulbright committee—to the nation at large. As we have seen, only recently and in a qualified way, has Kennan permitted his name to be associated with a mass movement—that against nuclear testing and arms buildup.

It is really as a diagnostician of American and international problems and as a prescriber of remedies, rather than as an implementer, that Kennan must finally be evaluated. And here, on balance, the record is very strong. However near he might have come to it, Kennan in the end has not completely despaired of the United States. As a consequence, he once entertained hopes for a third political party (oriented toward environmental issues), has tried teaching his compatriots to distinguish between the appearance of morality and its real substance in foreign policy, and has reminded them that ultimate international success for a wealthy, diverse, continental-sized state will be decided in the domestic sphere. This last point is especially important for Americans in general, whose understanding—witness the Reagan government—of national power and prestige tends to be depressingly narrow. Military might, after all, is only one feature of a country's strength; by emphasizing it and neglecting other aspects of power, the United States threatens to damage its overall security and world standing. Although Kennan might not phrase it this way, it is consistent with his viewpoint that continued neglect of social programs will eventually leave the United States less well nourished, less well tutored, and more divided than it can afford. Unless a comprehensive campaign against poverty, urban blight, and environmental destruction is aggressively fought, then the United States as a power in the conventional sense and an exemplar of enlightened wealth and orderly liberty will fade, just as Kennan has warned. As for the weaknesses in his assessment of the United States, the chief one—apart from a stunning myopia about immigrants and related ethnic issues—has been his inability to grant that representative democracy and its institutions have virtues that should recommend them to a conservative mind. Admittedly, American political institutions are not especially efficient and are often not run by high-minded people. But they are more responsive and appropriate as a corrective to a national leadership's misjudgment or moral waywardness than any realistic application of Kennan's elite principle.

Respecting foreign policy, Kennan's brand of conservatism holds little that can be very helpful in the management of relations between the Third World and the

West. The existing structural problems of the international economic order are lost on him, as is a strong sense of the need to alleviate harsh conditions in the Third World in order to promote stability in a global system that, for good or ill, is increasingly interdependent. Yet Kennan's other contributions to an understanding of US foreign policy have been astute. In the past, he has wisely counseled that to be effective the United States must recognize the limits of its power, acknowledge some hierarchy of interests abroad, play national differences in the communist world against each other, and pursue moderate balance of power policies in Europe and the Far East. As for the promotion of human rights, Kennan has recognized that the US government is more often effective when it uses discreet and diplomatic means than when it publicly bludgeons another regime—for example, the USSR and the Jackson-Vanik legislation. Kennan's most significant lesson for Americans is to be patient with history and historical processes. This is particularly important advice for a nation which traditionally has assigned a positive value to historical forgetfulness. While it might make sense—for purposes of integrating and forming a society from people of diverse cultural and racial backgrounds—that Americans not dwell on their respective heritages, their eagerness to assimilate has come at psychological costs to the American collectivity as well as for the individual. One of them is to place a low premium on history. Kennan has rightly insisted that international problems can be understood only when viewed in historical context and that successful diplomacy requires taking the long view of both problems and solutions. Certainly, his emphasis on patience and on allowing the forces of reform adequate time to begin operating in Soviet internal and foreign policies seems vindicated as Gorbachev's innovations—as those of Khrushchev's before—represent that very mellowing of Soviet paranoia and police power for which Kennan (in the late 1940s) hoped.

To study Kennan is far more than an examination of American foreign affairs; it is studying diplomacy as an art and international relations in a universal context. He himself would undoubtedly agree that the character of world politics is irreconcilable with "progressivist theory" and that international history is foremost a story of evanescent success and of tragedy. In certain measure, Kennan would also accept the severe truth of Thucydides's Athenian at Melos that in international affairs, "they that have odds of power exact as much as they can, and the weak yield to such conditions as they can get."[33] And yet, even while he has warned against extravagent forms of internationalism that promise more than they can deliver, Kennan has not given up on a world in which diplomacy and national self-restraint still exist. The following statement of his is really a testament of faith in diplomacy and the politics of amelioration:

> The best humanity can hope for . . . is an even and undramatic muddling along on its mysterious and unknowable paths, avoiding all that is abrupt, avoiding the great orgies of violence that acquire their own momentum and get out of hand—continuing, to be sure, to live by competition between political entities, but being sophisticated and wise about the relationships of power: recognizing and discounting superiority of strength . . . rather than putting it suicidally to the test of the sword—

imagining the great battles rather than fighting them; seeing to it that armies, if they must be employed at all, are exercised . . . "by temperate and indecisive contests;" remembering at all times that civilization has become a fragile thing that must be kept right-side up and will not stand too much jolting and abuse. In this sort of world, there is no margin for that form of self-indulgence which is called moral indignation, unless it be indignation with ourselves for failing to be what we know we could and should have been.[34]

At the core of Kennan's conception of diplomacy is a preoccupation with the continuity and intrinsic value of human cultures and history. As the West's supreme object must be the preservation of its civilization, and as the overriding challenge to Soviet and US leaders is to avoid nuclear war, this understanding of Kennan's will have to prevail.

NOTES

Preface

1. Henry Kissinger, *White House Years* (Boston: Little, Brown and Company, 1979), p. 135.

2. Barton Gellman, *Contending with Kennan* (New York: Praeger Publishers, 1984), p. xv.

3. Gellman's *Contending* and John Gaddis's *Strategies of Containment* (New York: Oxford University Press, 1982) are the two books that most deal in a sustained, in-depth way with important aspects of Kennan's career and thought. Also see the sections concerning Kennan in Walter Isaacson's and Evan Thomas's *The Wise Men: Six Friends and the World They Made* (New York: Simon and Schuster, 1986) and Michael Joseph Smith's original and excellent *Realist Thought from Weber to Kissinger* (Baton Rouge: Louisiana State University Press, 1986).

Introduction

1. Louis Halle, *The Cold War as History* (New York: Harper and Row, 1967), p. 116; John Paton Davies, *Dragon by the Tail* (New York: Norton, 1972), p. 390; Stanley Hoffmann, "After the Creation or the Watch and the Arrow," *International Journal,* Spring 1973; Stanley Hoffmann, *Duties Beyond Borders* (Syracuse: Syracuse University Press, 1981), pp. 102–103; Henry Fairlie, "The Special Senility of the Diplomat: Mr. X²," *The New Republic,* December 24, 1977; William Buckley, "George Kennan's Bomb," *National Review,* April 4, 1980; Paul Hollander, "The Two Faces of George Kennan," *Policy Review,* Summer 1985; Paul Seabury, "George Kennan Vs. Mr. X," *The New Republic,* December 16, 1981. In March 1988, just as this book was going to press, the Physicians for Social Responsibility also honored Kennan for his commitment to the prevention of nuclear war.

2. Robert Goldwin and Harry Clor (eds.), *Readings in American Foreign Policy* (New York: Oxford University Press, 1971), p. 6; Kennan's "Philosophy and Strategy in America's Postwar Policy," May 11, 1965, File "1-C-141-1V" in Box 21, Kennan Papers.

3. Reinhold Niebuhr, "The Social Myths in the Cold War" in John Farrell and Asa Smith (eds.), *Image and Reality in World Politics* (New York: Columbia University Press, 1967), p. 55.

4. Rossiter, Clinton (ed.), *The Federalist Papers* (New York: New American Library, 1961), Hamilton No. 6, p. 54.

5. Richard Fox, *Reinhold Niebuhr: A Biography* (New York: Pantheon Books, 1985), p. 238.

6. Dorothy Price and Dean Walley (eds.), *Never Give In! The Words of Winston Churchill* (New York: Hallmark, 1967), p. 21.

7. George Kennan, "A Modest Proposal," *The New York Review of Books,* July 16, 1981, p. 14.

8. George Kennan, "Certain World Problems in Christian Perspective," pp. 26–27, January 27, 1959, File "1-B-78" in Box 7, Kennan Papers.

9. Kenneth Thompson, *Political Realism and the Crisis of World Politics,* (Princeton: Princeton University Press, 1960), p. 7.

10. Kennan, "Certain World Problems in Christian Perspective," p. 23.

Chapter 1. Early Influences and Development

1. George Kennan, *Memoirs: 1925–1950* (Boston: Little, Brown and Company, 1967), p. 8.

2. Kennan's letter "My dear children," February 1942, p. 2, File "1942" in Box 28, Kennan Papers.

3. *Ibid.,* p. 3.

4. *Ibid.*

5. *Ibid.,* p. 4. Kennan to Mr. Checkland, February 2, 1965, File "2-B 1965" in Box 31, Kennan Papers.

6. Kennan's letter "My dear children," April 15, 1961, p. 14, File "1-C-109" in Box 20, Kennan Papers.

7. Kennan's letter "My dear children," February 1942, p. 4.

8. *Ibid.,* p. 1.

9. C. Ben Wright's interview with Jeanette (Kennan) Hotchkiss, p. 1, September 26, 1970, File "16" in Box 8, Wright Papers.

10. Michael Lesy, *Wisconsin Death Trip* (New York: Pantheon Books, 1973).

11. Kennan, "My dear children," February 1942, p. 2.

12. Kennan, "My dear children," April 15, 1961, p. 11.

13. *Ibid.*

14. Wright's interview with Jeanette (Kennan) Hotchkiss, p. 2. Kossuth Kennan did permit his son (by his third wife) Kent Wheeler to take music lessons. He became an accomplished musician. George Kennan in later years did learn to play the guitar with reasonable proficiency.

15. See La Vern Rippley, *The Immigrant Experience in Wisconsin* (Boston: Twayne Publishers, 1985), Chapters 5–8.

16. See Sinclair Lewis, *Babbitt* (New York: Harcourt, Brace and World, 1922).

17. *The Washington Post,* September 6, 1953.

18. Hugh De Santis, *The Diplomacy of Silence* (Chicago: University of Chicago Press, 1980) , p. 93.

19. John Stoessinger, *Nations in Darkness* (New York: Random House, 1978), p. 114.

20. C. Ben Wright's interview with Loy Henderson, p. 1, October 3, 1970, File "14" in Box 8, Wright Papers.

21. *Kennan, Memoirs: 1925–1950,* p. 9.

22. George Kennan, "Address to St. John's Military Academy," p. 1, June 4, 1960, File "1-B-100" in Box 9, Kennan Papers.

23. C. Ben Wright, *George F. Kennan, Scholar-Diplomat: 1926–1946* (PhD thesis, University of Wisconsin, 1972), p. 4.

24. Kennan, "Address to St. John's Military Academy," p. 28.

25. *The Milwaukee Journal,* April 7, 1957.

26. Kennan, *Memoirs: 1925–1950*, p. 9.

27. F. Scott Fitzgerald, *This Side of Paradise* (New York: Charles Scribner's, 1920), p. 53.

28. Kennan, *Memoirs: 1925–1950*, pp. 9–10.

29. Daniel Yergin, *Shattered Peace* (Boston: Houghton Mifflin Company, 1977), p. 168. Also see Wright's *George F. Kennan*, pp. 8–9.

30. George Kennan, "Commencement Speech at Dartmouth College," June 11, 1950, File "1-C-8" in Box 18, Kennan Papers.

31. Kennan, *Memoirs: 1925–1950*, p. 14.

32. Helpful analyses of the Foreign Service and the reforms to which it was subject are found in W. F. Ilchman's *Professional Diplomacy in the United States, 1779–1939* (Chicago: The University of Chicago Press, 1961); De Santis, *The Diplomacy of Silence*, Chapter 1.

33. George Kennan, "Problems of the Foreign Service," pp. 2–3, August 1, 1947, File "1947: June to December" in Box 17, Kennan Papers.

34. See Wright's *George F. Kennan*, p. 26.

35. Kennan's *Memoirs: 1925–1950*, p. 21.

36. George Kennan, Manuscript— Part I, p. 2, File "1933–1938" in Box 25, Kennan Papers. This particular manuscript was part of an autobiographical work by Kennan written in the late 1930s. It was never published, but some of its contents were integrated into his later, mature memoirs that appeared in 1967 and 1972.

37. See Daniel Yergin's *Shattered Peace*, Chapters 1 and 2; Daniel Harrington, "Kennan, Bohlen, and the Riga Axioms," *Diplomatic History*, Fall 1978; Arthur Schlesinger, Jr., *The Cycles of American History* (Boston: Houghton Mifflin Company, 1986), pp. 202–206.

38. Kennan's *Memoirs: 1925–1950*, pp. 31–49.

39. Good accounts of informal Soviet-US relations in the 1920s and early 1930s, of the question of recognition in 1933, and Soviet-US relations from 1933 to 1941 can be found in the following books: Robert Browder, *The Origins of Soviet-American Diplomacy* (Princeton: Princeton University Press, 1953); De Santis, *The Diplomacy of Silence;* Beatrice Farnsworth, *William C. Bullitt and the Soviet Union* (Bloomington: Indiana University Press, 1967); John Gaddis, *Russia, the Soviet Union and the United States* (New York: John Wiley and Sons, 1978); Thomas Maddux, *Years of Estrangement: American Relations with the Soviet Union, 1933–1941* (Tallahassee: University Presses of Florida, 1980); Donald Bishop, *The Roosevelt-Litvinov Agreements* (Syracuse: Syracuse University Press, 1965); Edward Bennett, *Recognition of Russia* (Waltham, Mass.: Ginn and Co., 1970); Joan Hoff Wilson, *Ideology and Economics: US Relations with the Soviet Union, 1918–1933* (Columbia: University of Missouri Press, 1974).

40. Kennan's Manuscript—Part I, p. 1.

41. *Ibid.*

42. De Santis, *The Diplomacy of Silence*, p. 30. Kennan once wrote of Bohlen: "Chip is among the circle of very few people whose friendship I know represents the maximum of what I am ever destined to have and what anyone could expect to have in the way of relationships." Kennan to Charles Thayer, July 3, 1947, File "1947" in Box 28, Kennan Papers.

43. Kennan's *Memoirs: 1925–1950*, p. 12.

44. Kennan's "Problems of the Foreign Service," p. 6.

45. Douglas Brinkley, "Kennan-Acheson: The Disengagement Debate," *The Atlantic Community Quarterly*, Winter 1987–1988, pp. 423–424.

46. Wright interview with Loy Henderson, p. 1.

47. For colorful details of Kennan's early years see Walter Isaacson and Evan Thomas, *The Wise Men* (New York: Simon and Schuster, 1986), pp. 72–80, Chapter 5.

Chapter 2. First Tour in the Soviet Union

1. Consult C. Ben Wright's *George F. Kennan, Scholar-Diplomat: 1926–1946* (PhD dissertation, University of Wisconsin, 1972), Chapter 3, for a straightforward cataloguing of Kennan's activities and memoranda in the Soviet Union during the 1930s.

2. Kennan's Manuscript—Part I, p. 5, File "1933–1938" in Box 25, Kennan Papers.

3. *Ibid.*, p. 9.

4. George Kennan, "Record Kept of Official Activities During the period in 1934 Prior to the Arrival of the Official Embassy Staff," File "1934" in Box 23, Kennan Papers.

5. Kennan's Manuscript—Part I, pp. 8–9.

6. *Ibid.*, p. 10. For more about Bohlen and his early impressions of the Soviet Union see T. Michael Ruddy, *The Cautious Diplomat: Charles E. Bohlen and the Soviet Union, 1929–1969* (Kent, Ohio: Kent State University Press, 1986), Chapter 1.

7. George Kennan, *Memoirs: 1950–1963* (New York: Little, Brown and Company, 1972), p. 130.

8. Kennan's Manuscript—Part I, pp. 46–47, 38. For corroboration of Kennan's assessment of the Soviet fine arts see Peter Kenez's excellent treatment of the Soviet cinema in his *The Birth of the Propaganda State: Soviet Methods of Mobilization, 1917–1929* (Cambridge: Cambridge University Press, 1985), Chapter 9.

9. Kennan's Manuscript—Part I, pp. 42–43.

10. *Ibid.*, pp. 25–26.

11. George Kennan, *Memoirs: 1925–1950* (New York: Little, Brown and Company, 1967), pp. 61–63, and Charles Bohlen, *Witness to History, 1929–1969* (New York: Norton, 1973), p. 17.

12. Kennan's Manuscript—Part I, p. 24.

13. *Ibid.*, p. 7.

14. *Ibid.*, p. 14.

15. *Ibid.*, p. 52.

16. See Sidney Webb and Beatrice Webb, *Soviet Communism: A New Civilization* (London: Victor Gollancz, 1937), and Paul Hollander, *Political Pilgrims: Travels of Western Intellectuals to the Soviet Union, China, and Cuba 1928–1978* (New York: Oxford University Press, 1981), Chapter 4.

17. Kennan's Manuscript—Part I, p. 53.

18. *Ibid.*, pp. 53–54.

19. See pp. 78–79, for example, of Arthur Koestler's *Darkness at Noon* (New York: Bantam Books, 1941).

20. US Department of State, *Foreign Relations of the United States, 1933–1939* (Washington, DC: Government Printing Office, 1952–1986; hereafter cited as *FRUS*), "The Soviet Union 1933–1939," p. 367.

21. Kennan's Manuscript—Part I, p. 58.

22. Adam Ulam, *Expansion and Coexistence* (New York: Praeger Press, 1974), pp. 214–215.

23. Kennan's Manuscript—Part I, pp. 13–14.

24. *Ibid.*, p. 14.

25. *Ibid.*, pp. 14–15.

26 *Ibid.*, p. 16.

27. Radek and Bukharin had been popular guests at the ambassador's residence. Distinguished intellectuals, they had engaged the US diplomats in intense but friendly debates over the virtues and flaws of socialism, capitalism, the proletariat, and state planning. Steiger was on extremely friendly terms with members of the American delegation; he was later executed by a firing squad.

28. *FRUS,* "The Soviet Union, 1933–1939," pp. 398–400, pp. 657–660.

29. Kennan's Manuscript—Part I, p. 71.

30. See Orville Bullitt (ed.), *For the President: Correspondence Between Franklin D. Roosevelt and William C. Bullitt* (Boston: Houghton Mifflin Company, 1972); Charles Thayer, *Diplomat* (New York: Harper and Brothers, 1959), p. 56; William Bullitt, *The Great Globe Itself* (New York: Charles Scribner's, 1946).

31. George Kennan, "Some Fundamentals of Russian-American Relations," pp. 1–2, File "1938" in Box 16, Kennan Papers. Also see Kennan's "The War Problem of the Soviet Union," File "1935" in Box 1, Kennan Papers, and "Russia," File "1938" in Box 16, Kennan Papers. In both essays Kennan made points similar to those in "Fundamentals."

32. Kennan's "Fundamentals," pp. 4–5.

33. See Alec Nove, *An Economic History of the USSR* (Middlesex, England: Penguin Books, 1975).

34. Kennan's "Fundamentals," p. 6.

35. *Ibid.,* p. 8.

36. *Ibid.,* p. 9.

37. *Ibid.,* p. 10.

38. *Ibid.,* p. 11.

39. See George Kennan's "The Sources of Soviet Conduct" in *Foreign Affairs,* July 1947 and his "Telegraphic Message from Moscow" in *Memoirs 1925–1950.*

40. Fine reviews of the subject can be found in Peter Filene's *American Views of Soviet Russia* (Homewood, Ill.: The Dorsey Press, 1968) and in Paul Hollander's *Political Pilgrims.*

41. Kennan's Manuscript—Part I, pp. 19–20.

42. Kennan to Charles Thayer, May 22, 1935, Thayer Papers.

43. Bohlen, *Witness to History,* p. 44.

44. *Ibid.,* p. 56.

45. Joseph E. Davies, *Mission to Moscow* (New York: Simon and Schuster, 1941), p. 280.

46. Daniel Yergin is one of the few commentators to champion Davies and does so cautiously. See his *Shattered Peace.* Robert Conquest, a prominent authority on the Great Purges, is astonished by the degree to which Davies was duped by Soviet propagandists. See Conquest's *The Great Terror* (New York: Collier Books, 1973).

47. Kennan's Manuscript—Part I, p. 5.

48. *Ibid.,* p. 8.

49. Kennan was pleased by the appointment of Laurence Steinhardt as the successor to Davies. Steinhardt was, in Kennan's estimate, competent and appropriately experienced.

50. Kennan's Manuscript—Part I, pp. 11–12.

Chapter 3. Criticisms and Recommendations

1. Thomas Jefferson, who knew France and loved its culture, understood better than most Americans how they might, as travelers abroad, develop intellectual sympathies and political affinities for different European countries. He warned one friend that an extensive stay in Europe would mean that, upon his return to America, he would regard his home as a "place of exile and condemnation." See Van Wyck Brooks, *The World of Washington Irving* (Kingsport: E. P. Dutton and Company, 1944), pp. 114–115. John Quincy Adams insisted that US diplomats should take leave home every few years in order "to be renovated by the wholesome republican atmosphere of their own country."

2. George Kennan, Manuscript—Part II, p. 16, File "1938" in Box 25—year written not indicated; possibly 1940—Kennan Papers. Once, during an earlier leave home in 1936, Kennan had visited his grandfather's old farm in Wisconsin, then in the hands of someone

else. He recalled: "I bicycled out there . . . and visited the farmer. The new farm house was made from the timbers of Grandfather's old house which had stood across the road. I lay there through the summer night, in the guest bedroom, listening to the chirping of crickets in the grass outside, and breathing the smell of hot, warm hay and manure from the barn; and I felt closer to home than I have ever felt before or since in my wandering life." Cited in Kennan's letter "My dear children," February 1942, p. 2, File "1942" in Box 28, Kennan Papers.

3. Kennan's Manuscript—Part II, pp. 18–19.

4. *Ibid.*, p. 18. C. Ben Wright interview with Loy Henderson, p. 3, October 3, 1970, File "14" in Box 8, Wright Papers.

5. James MacGregor Burns, *Roosevelt: The Lion and the Fox* (New York: Harcourt, Brace and World, 1956), p. 336.

6. Kennan's Manuscript Part II, pp. 29–30.

7. Kennan's Manuscript—Part I, pp. 32–33.

8. George Kennan, "The Prerequisites: Notes on Problems of the United States in 1938," p. 15, File "1938" in Box 25, Kennan Papers.

9. *Ibid.*, p. 20.

10. *Ibid.*, p. 16.

11. In 1930 Kennan read Charles Beard's *The Rise of American Civilization* (1927) and was intrigued to find that the framers of the Constitution were not intent upon establishing a mass democracy. He could not resist asking the following question: "if [the Founding Fathers] disapproved of democracy, for a population predominantly white, Protestant and British, faced with relatively simple problems, would they not turn over in their graves at the mere thought of the democratic principle being applied to a population containing over ten million Negroes, and many more millions of southern Europeans, to whom the democratic principle is completely strange and incomprehensible?" Consult C. Ben Wright's *George F. Kennan, Scholar-Diplomat: 1926–1946,* (PhD dissertation, University of Wisconsin, 1972), p. 24.

12. Kennan, "The Prerequisites," p. 17.

13. James McPherson, *Ordeal by Fire: The Civil War and Reconstruction* (New York: Alfred Knopf, 1982), p. 84.

14. Kennan, "The Prerequisites," pp. 18–19.

15. *Ibid.*, p. 19.

16. *Ibid.*, pp. 3–4.

17. *Ibid.*, p. 5.

18. *Ibid.*, p. 6.

19. *Ibid.*, p. 11.

20. In a personal communication (November 3, 1982), Kennan made the point that "The Prerequisites" stands in relation to his later ideas as an *esquisse* does to an artist's final painting. It was to be modified, polished, pushed in other directions. This is a fair assessment and especially true in relation to his ideas about the Foreign Service.

21. H. L. Mencken, *Notes on Democracy* (New York: Alfred Knopf, 1926), p. 180.

22. See Richard Hofstadter's portrait of Theodore Roosevelt in *The American Political Tradition* (New York: Vintage Books, 1948); Walter Lippmann's *A Preface to Politics* (New York: Mitchell Kennerley, 1913), *Drift and Mastery: An Attempt to Diagnose the Current Unrest* (New York: Mitchell Kennerly, 1914), *Public Opinion* (New York: Harcourt and Brace, 1922), *The Method of Freedom* (New York: Macmillan, 1934), *An Inquiry into the Principles of Good Society* (Boston: Atlantic-Little, Brown, 1937); Page Smith's Chapter 52 in *America Enters the World* (New York: McGraw-Hill, 1985); D. Steven Blum's *Walter Lippmann: Cosmopolitanism in the Century of Total War* (New York: Cornell University Press, 1984).

23. George Kennan, *Memoirs: 1925–1950* (New York: Little, Brown and Company, 1967), p. 493.

24. *Ibid.*, p. 139. Through the trying months of German detention, Kennan played an important role under the leadership of Leland Morris, the chargé d'affaires, in organizing the arrangements and comfort of the American delegation (and numerous journalists) both in Bad Nauheim and during transit to and from internment. The long weeks of physical discomfort caused by cold, crowding, and reduced nourishment took a toll on everyone, especially those men responsible for group morale and health. Kennan's general observations about the effects of living under house arrest and armed guard applied no less to himself than to others.

> Worst of all . . . was the mental strain arising from the sheer fact of confinement, coupled with the uncertainty as to when and how it would end. Being guarded night and day, listening night after night to the footsteps of the guards in the snow under your windows, being continually driven back into the little world of a few rooms and a few faces, does something to you, however you steel yourself to it. And as the weeks and months dragged on with no definite information about plans for release, people could not help wondering how much longer they could continue to take this.

The American group, despite its hardships and the claustrophobic quarters, demonstrated a fair degree of resilience and displayed some initiative and imagination. Many witnesses testified later that the group's survival and success owed much to the steadiness and competence of Morris and especially Kennan. The former established and directed an administrative office, or Group Secretariat, which was charged with responsibility for the internal organization of Bad Nauheim and which conducted copious correspondence with the Swiss legation in Berlin. Kennan for a brief period exercised immediate supervision of the Secretariat, but for the most part acted as liaison between the embassy personnel and German officials. In this capacity, he had no end of troubles, particularly from his compatriots: "Their cares, their quarrels, their jealousies, their complaints filled every moment of my waking days." Apart from the Secretariat, numerous other offices were established, including the Room Committee whose responsibility was to allot sleeping space. Kennan later quipped, "Any steamship purser can tell you that there is no more sensitive or irrational side of human nature than that which has to do with the living quarters of the individual; and Heaven help the dictator who has to apportion apartments among his followers, particularly those of the weaker sex." The Room Committee's first sessions were stormy, and Kennan was delighted to relinquish command to an army officer.

In general, lapses in forbearance were few, and the American diplomatic personnel, like their German counterparts held in White Sulphur Springs, were treated respectfully, were not subjected to unnecessary suffering, and were satisfactorily accommodated, at least within the limits of wartime economy and hospitality. The Americans in Bad Nauheim were restricted to Jeschke's Grand Hotel, which prior to hostilities in 1939 had been an attractive retreat. Even in 1942 the rooms were clean, agreeably modern, and well furnished. Furthermore, the Americans were left alone to establish their own laundry and ironing room services, to create a lending library, to operate a medical service, and to play sports—baseball in the spring—and take other forms of exercise.

Journalists in the party organized a newspaper, the "Bad Nauheim Pudding"; and an enterprising reporter named P. W. Whitcomb, who previously had been based in Paris, was the "founder" and principal mover behind "Badheim University." It soon possessed an array of invented traditions, pageantry, and legendary fathers: "Guiding spirit of the place was the mythical Professor Wurlitzer, whose motto was the preservation of 'education of the ignorant by the ignorant', and who was said to have remarked that he knew of no educational institution which excels Badheim in the watchful protection it gives its students against the outer world during the formative years of their training." Despite its self-mockery, the "university" did in fact offer a choice of fifteen lecture series and language instruction. It was probably the single most important factor in keeping people creatively employed and stiffening their resistance to boredom and stagnation. Kennan presented a number of lectures on Russian history ranging over such subjects as the Russian aristocracy in the eighteenth century, aspects of pre-Petrine Muscovite society, and Russia in the age of Napoleon.

Although they grumbled about the myriad of inconveniences they faced—a shortage of fuel coal and unpalatable food—the embassy staff and journalists were spared the direct brutality of war. They kept their wits and humor, and only in a few cases did people indulge in morbid introspection and refuse to cooperate in group efforts. Yet the more or less constant stress of living at close quarters with too many people and under armed guard made itself deeply felt on the nerves and thoughts of practically everyone. Kennan occasionally wondered whether or not he would leave Germany alive or see his two young daughters and his Norwegian-born wife, Annelise. Still, by the standards of most wartime hardship, and certainly in comparison to what the Germans did to millions of their captives, the inmates of Bad Nauheim got off extremely well. Nowhere in his memoirs or anywhere else does Kennan acknowledge this crucial point. For more on Bad Nauheim, see George Kennan, "Draft of Internment Story," File "1942" in Box 25, Kennan Papers. Although submitted for publication, this version of Kennan's tale of internment was never published. Another version, originally intended for the records of the State Department, appeared in *The American Foreign Service Journal* in two parts, August and September 1942. Also see Kennan's *Memoirs: 1925–1950*, pp. 134–141, and Charles Burdick's extremely good *An American Island in Hitler's Reich: The Bad Nauheim Internment* (Menlo Park, Calif.: Markgraf, 1987).

25. *FRUS 1949*, Vol. I, p. 404.

26. George Kennan, "The Organization for the Executive Branch of the Government for the Conduct of Foreign Affairs," pp. 224–225, September 26, 1951, File "1-B-19" in Box 2, Kennan Papers.

27. George Kennan, "History and Diplomacy as Viewed by a Diplomatist," *The Review of Politics*, April 1956, pp. 175–176.

28. George Kennan, "Background of the Present World Situation," pp. 1–3, Haverford College, April 19, 1955, File "1-C-50" in Box 19, Kennan Papers.

29. George Kennan, "Remarks at Stevenson-for-President Committee," p. 6, April 30, 1956, File "1-C-56" in Box 19, Kennan Papers.

30. Kennan to Dr. Marion Grafin Donhoff, March 15, 1965, File "2-B, 1965" in Box 31, Kennan Papers.

31. "George Kennan" in *Current Biography*, October 1947.

32. George Kennan's memorandum, "Adaptation of Foreign Service Training to Post-War Needs," p. 6, May 5, 1942, File "1942" in Box 32, Kennan Papers.

33. *Ibid.*, p. 8.

34. *Ibid.*, p. 16.

35. *Ibid.*, p. 9.

36. George Kennan, "Remarks to the Officer Staff of the Legation at Lisbon," p. 8, June 1944, File "1944" in Box 16, Kennan Papers.

37. *Ibid.*, pp. 8–10.

38. George Kennan, material for Reith Lecture, pp. 5 and 12, November 17, 1957, File "1-E-12" in Box 26, Kennan Papers.

39. Gufler and Kennan had been friends since their undergraduate years at Princeton. Later, they were posted to Riga, and in 1938 they shared an office in the State Department. Apparently, they spent much of their time together engaging in philosophical and political

discussions. Gufler served briefly in Kennan's Policy Planning Staff (1948). He was ambassador to Ceylon (1951–1954) and to Finland (1961–1963). Gufler died in September 1973.

40. See C. Ben Wright's interviews with Charles Bohlen, September 29, 1970; Carleton Savage, September 30, 1970; Llewelyn Thompson, October 2, 1970. These interviews are in Box 8 of the Wright Papers.

41. George Kennan, *Democracy and the Student Left* (Boston: Little, Brown and Company, 1968), p. 17.

42. George Kennan, *The Cloud of Danger* (Boston: Little, Brown and Company, 1977), pp. 224–227.

Chapter 4. Nazi Germany and the Future of Europe

1. George Kennan, Manuscript—Part II, p. 30, File "1938" in Box 25, Kennan Papers.

2. *Ibid.*, p. 33.

3. Winston Churchill, *The Gathering Storm* (New York: Houghton Mifflin Company, 1948), p. 282.

4. Although their interpretations are ultimately incompatible the following two books are useful in understanding Soviet policy in the late 1930s and in particular with reference to Munich and Czechoslovakia: Jonathan Haslam, *The Soviet Union and the Struggle for Collective Security in Europe, 1933–1939* (New York: St. Martin's Press, 1984), and Jiri Hochman, *The Soviet Union and the Failure of Collective Security, 1934–1938* (Ithaca: Cornell University Press, 1984).

5. Two excellent accounts of Czechoslovakia's dismemberment and surrender are Vojtech Mastny's *The Czechs under Nazi Rule* (New York: Columbia University Press, 1971) and Kennan's *From Prague after Munich* (Princeton: Princeton University Press, 1968). Probably the best analysis of the Munich Conference is Telford Taylor's *Munich* (Garden City, N.Y.: Doubleday, 1979). Arnold Wolfers's *Britain and France Between Two Wars: Conflicting Strategies of Peace from Versailles to World War II* (New York: Norton, 1968) provides a fine scholarly, contemporary treatment of Anglo-French interwar policies that led to Munich. Also see the 1939 edition of E. H. Carr's *Twenty Years' Crisis, 1919–1939* (London: Macmillan) in which he attempts to justify the Anglo-French appeasement policy. The American attitude toward Czechoslovakia and Munich is well summarized in both Robert Dallek's *Franklin D. Roosevelt and American Foreign Policy, 1932–1945* (New York: Oxford University Press, 1979) and Arnold Offner's *American Appeasement: United States Foreign Policy and Germany, 1933–1938* (New York: Norton, 1969).

6. Kennan, Manuscript—Part II, p. 44.

7. *Ibid.*, p. 67.

8. *Ibid.*, p. 68.

9. Kennan, *From Prague after Munich*, p. 224.

10. Kennan, Manuscript—Part II, p. 68.

11. George Kennan, *Memoirs: 1925–1950* (Boston, Little, Brown and Company, 1967), p. 94.

12. Kennan, Manuscript—Part II, p. 73.

13. *Ibid.*, p. 70.

14. See the following: remarks by Frederick Heymann in Kennan, *From Prague after Munich*, pp. 241–253; Maurice Hindus, *We Shall Live Again* (London: Collins, 1939); J. W. Bruegel, *Czechoslovakia Before Munich* (Cambridge: Cambridge University Press, 1973); V.S. Mametey and R. Luza (eds.), *A History of the Czechoslovakia Republic, 1918–1948* (Princeton: Princeton University Press, 1973); Joseph Rothschild, *East Central Europe Between the Two World Wars* (Seattle: University of Washington Press, 1974).

15. Kennan, *From Prague after Munich*, p. 104.

16. *Ibid.*, p. 239.

17. Kennan, *Memoirs: 1925–1950*, p. 102.

18. Kennan, *From Prague after Munich*, p. 171.

19. George Kennan, "The Technique of German Imperialism in Europe," April 1941, p. 24, File "1941" in Box 23, Kennan Papers. For a detailed discussion of German imperial rule in Norway see Kennan's "The Appointment of the New State Council in Norway," File "1940" in Box 23, Kennan Papers.

20. Kennan, "The Technique," p. 37.

21. Kennan to James Riddleberger, Chief of the Division of Central European Affairs, Department of State, November 20, 1941, File "1941" in Box 28, Kennan Papers.

22. Kennan, "Technique," p. 34.

23. Kennan to Riddleberger.

24. George Kennan, "Comments on the Treatment of Germany," p. 3, File "1945 January to April" in Box 23, Kennan Papers.

25. George Kennan, "On German Nationalism," February 1940, File "1940" in Box 1, Kennan Papers.

26. The literature on Nazi Germany and the sources of Hitler's support are vast. Helpful books include Karl Bracher, *The German Dictatorship* (New York: Praeger Publishers, 1973); F. L. Carsten, *The Rise of Fascism* (Berkeley: University of California Press, 1971); Nathanael Greene (ed.), *Fascism: An Anthology* (New York: Crowell Company, 1968); David Schoenbaum, *Hitler's Social Revolution* (New York: Anchor Books, 1967); Ernst Nolte, *Three Faces of Fascism* (New York: Holt, Rinehart and Winston, 1966); Alan Bullock, *Hitler: A Study in Tyranny* (New York: Harper and Row, 1964); Richard Hamilton, *Who Voted for Hitler?* (Princeton: Princeton University Press, 1982); Thomas Childers, *The Nazi Voter* (Chapel Hill: University of North Carolina Press, 1983); Theodore Abel, *Why Hitler Came into Power* (Cambridge: Harvard University Press, 1986); Peter Merkl, *Political Violence under the Swastika* (Princeton: Princeton University Press, 1975).

27. Ralf Dahrendorf, *Society and Democracy in Germany* (New York: Anchor Books, 1969), pp. 381–382.

28. Kennan, "On German Nationalism."

29. Again, the scholarly study of totalitarianism is immense. Good books on the subject include Hannah Arendt, *The Origins of Totalitarianism* (New York: World Publishing, 1951); Betty Burch (ed.), *Dictatorship and Totalitarianism* (Princeton: Von Nostrand Company, 1964); William Ebenstein, *Totalitarianism: New Perspectives* (New York: Holt, Rinehart and Winston, 1962); Carl Friedrich and Zbigniew Brzezinski, *Totalitarian Dictatorship and Autocracy* (Cambridge: Harvard University Press, 1965); Karl Popper, *The Open Society and Its Enemies* (London: Routledge and Kegan Paul, 1945); William Kornhauser, *The Politics of Mass Society* (Glencoe, Ill.: The Free Press, 1959); Paul Mason (ed.), *Totalitarianism: Temporary Madness or Permanent Danger?* (Boston: Heath and Company, 1967).

30. Kennan to Riddleberger.

31. *Ibid.*

32. *Ibid.*

33. *Ibid.*

34. Kennan, *Memoirs: 1925–1950*, pp. 108–109.

35. Manuscript—Part II, p. 45.

36. Kennan, *Memoirs: 1925–1950*, p. 123.

37. Kennan to Mr. G. van Roon, March 12, 1962, File "2–B 1962" in Box 31, Kennan Papers.

38. Hans Rothfels, *The German Opposition to Hitler* (London: Oswald Wolff, 1978), p. 112.

39. Kennan to Mr. G. van Roon.

40. See Kennan, *From Prague after Munich*, pp. 85–86, and *Memoirs: 1925–1950*, pp. 98–99.

41. See Ronald Steel, "Man Without a Country," *The New York Review of Books*, January 4, 1968; Wilson McWilliams, "George Kennan—the Myth Contained," *Commonweal*, March 22, 1968; George Kateb, "George F. Kennan: The Heart of a Diplomat," *Commentary*, January 1968; C. Ben Wright's Chapter 5 in *George F. Kennan, Scholar-Diplomat: 1926–1946* (PhD dissertation, University of Wisconsin, 1972).

42. Richard Barnet, *The Alliance* (New York: Simon and Schuster, 1983), p. 118.

43. Kennan's "Remarks to the Officer Staff of the Legation at Lisbon," June 1944, p. 5, File "1944" in Box 16, Kennan Papers.

44. Kennan, *Memoirs: 1925–1950*, p. 118.

45. Kennan, "On German Nationalism," p. 7.

46. *Ibid.*, p. 8.

47. *Ibid.*

48. *FRUS 1944*, Vol. I, p. 12.

49. See Bernard Bellush, *He Walked Alone: A Biography of John Gilbert Winant* (The Hague: Mouton, 1968).

50. Kennan, "Lisbon," p. 2.

51. Kennan to "Mr. Ambassador," March 1944, File "1944 March to mid-December" in Box 23, Kennan Papers.

52. Kennan, *Memoirs: 1925–1950*, pp. 260–261.

53. Kennan to "Mr. Ambassador."

54. *Ibid.*

55. Kennan's "Comments on the Treatment of Germany," probably written in February 1945, File "1945 January to April" in Box 23, Kennan Papers.

56. Kennan was not privately opposed to the Portuguese regime, and, based on his experiences in Lisbon (late summer 1942 to the end of November 1943) as counselor to the legation, formed an overall favorable impression of its authoritarian leader: "I am convinced that in that country Salazar, operating on a set of principles which are quite different from our own principles of democracy, has created and maintained conditions of life far more credible and acceptable to the psychology of the people than the conditions which prevailed there under a theoretically democratic and republican form of government prior to his advent to power." Kennan to "Mr. Ambassador," December 11, 1944, File "1944 March to mid-December" in Box 23, Kennan Papers.

57. Kennan, "Lisbon," p. 5.

58. Kennan to "Mr. Ambassador."

59. Kennan to Charles Bohlen, January 26, 1945, Box 3, Bohlen Papers.

60. Kennan to "Mr. Ambassador."

61. Barnet, *The Alliance*, pp. 28–29, 65.

62. Hajo Holborn, *A History of Modern Germany: 1840–1945* (New York: Alfred Knopf, 1969), p. 815.

63. Adam Ulam, *Stalin* (New York: The Viking Press, 1973), pp. 591–592.

64. Kennan, *Memoirs: 1925–1950*, p. 130.

Chapter 5. Soviet War Aims and the Grand Alliance

1. George Kennan, "Remarks to the Officer Staff of the Legation at Lisbon," p. 6, June 1944, File "1944" in Box 16, Kennan Papers.

2. Barton Bernstein (ed.), *Politics and Policies in the Truman Administration* (Chicago: Quadrangle Books, 1970), p. 23.

3. Abba Eban, *The New Diplomacy* (New York: Random House, 1983), p. 90.

4. In his *Franklin D. Roosevelt and American Foreign Policy, 1932–1945* (New York: Oxford University Press, 1979), Robert Dallek writes: " 'Russia's entry at as early a date as possible consistent with her ability to engage in offensive operations,' the Joint Chiefs had advised FDR in January 1945, 'is necessary to provide maximum assistance to our Pacific operations.' The defeat of Japanese forces in Manchuria, air attacks on Japanese forces in Siberia, and disruption of Japanese shipping between Japan and the Asian mainland were the gains American planners saw from Russian participation in the war. More important, the effective execution of these tasks seemed calculated to save many American lives in the Far East" (pp. 516–517).

This last point about the number of Anglo-US casualties is a source of continuing and extreme controversy in regard to the US decision to use the atomic bomb in August 1945. On the one hand, Churchill wrote: "To quell the Japanese resistance man by man and conquer the country yard by yard might well require the loss of a million American lives and half that number of British." See his *Triumph and Tragedy* (Boston: Houghton Mifflin Company, 1953), p. 545. On the other hand, see Rufus Miles's "Hiroshima: The Strange Myth of a Half a Million American Lives Saved," *International Security*, Fall 1985. There Truman is cited; he recalled Marshall guessing at one time that as many as a million American causalties might be incurred in an invasion of Japan. Other American military planners made similar high estimates. Marshall and all of the rest were speculating and their speculations varied over time and ranged greatly from 250,000 to roughly 1,000,000. Marshall's biographer Forrest Pogue has concluded that he saw the atomic weapon as a means "to wind up the war swiftly and thus effect enormous reduction in casualties. . . . There is no evidence that at any time his thinking or plans were influenced by any political effect use of the bomb might have on the Russians. Testing and planning proceeded almost automatically from the moment a decision was made that the bomb be used to end the war." Pogue's *George C. Marshall: Statesman 1945–1959* (New York: Viking, 1987), pp. 24–25.

5. "Russia—Seven Years Later," September 1944, reprinted in Kennan's *Memoirs: 1925–1950* (Boston: Little, Brown and Company, 1967), p. 504.

6. George Kennan, "The War Problem in the Soviet Union," p. 1, March 1935, File "1935" in Box 1, Kennan Papers.

7. *Ibid.*, pp. 1–2.

8. Hugh De Santis, *The Diplomacy of Silence* (Chicago: University of Chicago Press, 1980), p. 34.

9. Kennan, "The War Problem in the Soviet Union," p. 4.

10. Kennan, *Memoirs: 1925–1950*, pp. 133–134.

11. George Kennan, "Russia and the Post-War Settlement," p. 3, summer 1942, File "1942" in Box 25, Kennan Papers. Joseph Davies, *Mission to Moscow* (New York: Simon and Schuster, 1941), p. 357.

12. Walter Lippmann, *New York Herald Tribune*, June 6, 1942.

13. Kennan, "Russia and the Post-War Settlement," p. 6.

14. *Ibid.*, pp. 7–11.

15. *Ibid.*, p. 13.

16. George Kennan, "Report on Soviet Policy," p. 1, September 18, 1944, File "1-E" in Box 25, Kennan Papers. It was at Harriman's insistence that Kennan was assigned to Moscow in 1944, in effect rescued from the minor and numbing deliberations of the EAC. See Averell Harriman and Elie Abel, *Special Envoy to Churchill and Stalin, 1941–1946* (New York: Random House, 1975), pp. ix–x.

17. Kennan, "Russia—Seven Years Later," *Memoirs: 1925–1950*, p. 521.

18. Kennan, "Report on Soviet Policy," p. 1.

19. *Ibid.*, p. 2.

20. Kennan to Ambassador Harriman, September 18, 1944, File "1944" in Box 28, Kennan Papers.

21. Kennan to Charles Bohlen, p. 2, January 26, 1945, Box 3, Bohlen Papers.

22. *Ibid.*, p. 2.

23. *Ibid.*, p. 4.

24. *Ibid.*, p. 5.

25. *Ibid.*, p. 6.

26. *Ibid.*, pp. 7–8.

27. Charles Bohlen, *Witness to History, 1929–1969* (New York: Norton, 1973), p. 176.

28. *Ibid.*, p. 177. In 1970 Bohlen said that at the time of Yalta "there were something like six or seven million Poles in this country, to say nothing of the Czechs (Chicago is the second biggest Czech city in the world) and these things don't cover up. If you've done it in a sphere of interest, you would've seen into all of that minority . . . complaint and yell from home." See C. Ben Wright's interview with Bohlen, File "10" in Box 8, Wright Papers, and T. Michael Ruddy, *The Cautious Diplomat: Charles E. Bohlen and the Soviet Union, 1929–1969* (Kent, Ohio: Kent State University Press, 1986), pp. 35–51.

29. Kennan, "Comments On the Results of the Crimea Conference as Set Forth in The Published Communique," February 14, 1945, File "1945 Jan. to April," Box 23, Kennan Papers.

30. *Ibid.*

31. Kennan to H. Freeman Mathews, August 21, 1945, Record Group (hereafter RG) 59, National Archives (hereafter NA).

32. Kennan to Elbridge Durbrow, Chief of East European Division, January 21, 1946, File "1946" in Box 28, Kennan Papers.

33. Harriman to Secretary of State, April 4, 1945, Vol. 2, Box 1, Forrestal Diaries.

34. Lloyd Gardner, *Architects of Illusion* (Chicago: Quadrangle Books, 1970), p. 270.

35. Kennan's *Memoirs: 1925–1950*, p. 293.

36. *FRUS 1946*, Vol. VI, p. 700.

37. *Ibid.*, p. 705.

38. *Ibid.*, p. 708. For more about the "Long Telegram" see Hugh Thomas, *Armed Truce* (New York: Atheneum, 1987), pp. 486–489.

39. Kennan to John Osborn, July 31, 1962, File "2-B, 1962" in Box 31, Kennan Papers.

40. Daniel Yergin, *Shattered Peace* (Boston: Houghton Mifflin Company, 1977), pp. 169–170. Although I disagree with Yergin's assessment of Kennan's views in 1946, it is entirely serious and worth reviewing. In addition to seeing Yergin's fine work, readers would be well advised to see John Gaddis, *The United States and the Origins of the Cold War, 1941–1947* (New York: Columbia University Press, 1972); Louis Halle, *The Cold War as History* (New York: Harper and Row, 1967); Walter LaFeber, *America, Russia, and the Cold War* (New York: John Wiley and Sons, 1976).

41. "Russia's International Position at the Close of the War with Germany," May 1945, reprinted in Kennan's *Memoirs: 1925–1950*, p. 541.

42. Many scholars still claim that the USSR is importantly motivated by ideological considerations today and was so in 1945–1946. William Taubman for one argues that Stalin's foreign policy, and that of his successors, was dualistic and embraced ideology and *realpolitik*. See his *Stalin's American Policy* (New York: Norton, 1982), pp. 131–133. Stephen Cohen's assessment of official Soviet ideology is closer to my views. See Cohen's discussion in his *Rethinking the Soviet Experience: Politics and History Since 1917* (New York: Oxford University Press, 1985).

43. Kennan's *Memoirs: 1925–1950*, p. 219.

44. Benson Lee Grayson (ed.), *The American Image of Russia, 1917–1977* (New York: Frederick Ungar, 1978), p. 152.

45. Kennan's *Memoirs: 1925–1950,* p. 295.

Chapter 6. Containment and the Primacy of Diplomacy

1. Because of Kennan's importance in Cold War historiography and the notoriety of the "X article," an impressive amount of scholarly energy has been invested to discover, analyze, and criticize his views about Russia and Soviet-US rivalry in the late 1940s. The following should be consulted: John Gaddis, "Containment: A Reassessment" in *Foreign Affairs,* July 1977, and *Strategies of Containment* (New York: Oxford University Press, 1982); Eduard Mark, "The Question of Containment: A Reply to John Lewis Gaddis" in *Foreign Affairs,* January 1978; C. Ben Wright, "Mr. 'X' and Containment," *Slavic Review,* March 1976; Richard Pells, *The Liberal Mind in a Conservative Age* (New York: Harper and Row, 1985), pp. 100–105; Barton Gellman, *Contending with Kennan* (New York: Praeger Publishers, 1984); Louis Halle, *The Cold War as History* (New York: Harper and Row, 1967). Virtually every student of the Cold War who has written for publication has in one way or another addressed the interpretative problems raised by Kennan's formulation of containment and the "X article." An exhaustive list of authors and titles on these subjects would go on for pages.

2. George Kennan, *Memoirs: 1925–1950* (Boston: Little, Brown and Company, 1967), p. 303. Kennan declared to audiences in summer 1946:

> If we can keep them [the Soviets] maneuvered into a position where it is always hard and unprofitable for them to take action [contrary to US interests] and where there is always an open door to collaboration; if we can maintain that situation, keeping cool nerves, and maintaining it consistently, not in a provocative way but in a polite way, a calm way, preserving at all times our own strength and our firmness, but never blustering or threatening, always keeping the door open for when they finally do decide to come in—I personally am quite convinced that they will not be able to withstand . . . that sooner or later the logic of it will penetrate their government and will force changes there.

3. Kennan's report to Mr. Russell, p. 2, August 23, 1946, File "1946: Jan-mid Sept" in Box 16, Kennan Papers.

4. *Ibid.,* p. 6.

5. Kennan to Waldemar Gallman, March 14, 1947, File "1947" in Box 28, Kennan Papers.

6. *Ibid.*

7. *Ibid.*

8. Edward Willett, "Dialectical Materialism and Russian Objectives" January 14, 1946, p. 28, File "Russian Study" in Box 17, Forrestal Papers.

9. Kennan's memorandum for Admiral Hill, October 7, 1946, File "K" in Box 70, Forrestal Papers.

10. *Ibid.,* p. 5.

11. *Ibid.*

12. *Ibid.,* p. 4.

13. X, "The Sources of Soviet Conduct," in *Foreign Affairs,* July 1947, p. 574. Also see George Kennan, "The Soviet Way of Thought and Its Effect on Foreign Policy," January 24, 1947, Box 16, Kennan Papers.

14. "The Sources of Soviet Conduct," p. 578.

15. Kennan wrote: "Surely, there was never a fairer test of national quality . . . the thoughtful observer of Russian-American relations will find no cause for complaint in the

Kremlin's challenge to American society. He will rather experience a certain gratitude to a Providence which, by providing the American people with this implacable challenge, has made their entire security as a nation dependent on their pulling themselves together and accepting the responsibilities of moral and political leadership that history plainly intended them to bear." *Ibid.*, p. 582.

16. "Digest of Discussion," Council on Foreign Relations, January 7, 1947, p. 4, File "1947" in Box 16, Kennan Papers.

17. *Ibid.*, pp. 5–6.

18. *Ibid.*, p. 9.

19. H. F. Armstrong to Kennan, May 15, 1947, File "1947" in Box 28, Kennan Papers.

20. Kennan to H. F. Armstrong, May 20, 1947, File "1947" in Box 28, Kennan Papers.

21. Although the Council on Foreign Relations has traditionally had informal links to the foreign policy establishment in Washington, the former cannot possibly be viewed as a mere extension of the latter. The Council's *Foreign Affairs* in 1947 and since has deliberately sought to publish a range of authors and ideas while taking no particular responsibility for any of them. See Robert Schulzinger, *The Wise Men of Foreign Affairs: The History of the Council on Foreign Relations* (New York: Columbia University Press, 1984). Appearing in the same volume of *Foreign Affairs* as the "X article" were essays by such varied people as E. Varga, director of the Institute of World Economics and Politics in Moscow; W. W. Kulski, former minister plenipotentiary of the Polish embassy in London; and an assortment of French, British, and US academics, and a member of the British Parliament.

22. Walter Lippmann, *The Cold War: A Study in US Foreign Policy* (New York: Harper and Brothers, 1947), p. 9.

23. Arthur Krock, "Impressions of the Secretary," October 23, 1961, Box 31, Krock Papers.

24. Lippmann, *The Cold War,* pp. 30–31.

25. *Ibid.*, pp. 13–14, 18.

26. *Ibid.*, pp. 44–45, 50.

27. Kennan to H. F. Armstrong, November 7, 1947, File "1947" in Box 28, Kennan Papers.

28. For a more detailed analysis of the Truman Doctrine and its impact on US debate about foreign policy, see "Epilogue" in my *Cracking the Monolith: US Policy Against the Sino-Soviet Alliance, 1949–1955* (Baton Rouge: Louisiana State University Press, 1986). Also see Richard Freeland, *The Truman Doctrine and the Origins of McCarthyism* (New York: Schocken Books, 1974).

29. Kennan to Lippmann, April 6, 1948, File "Jan to April 1948" in Box 17, Kennan Papers.

30. *Ibid.*

31. *Ibid.*

32. *Ibid.*

33. *Ibid.*

34. *Ibid.*

35. *Ibid.*

36. *Ibid.*

37. Office Memorandum, April 7, 1948, File "Jan to April 1948" in Box 17, Kennan Papers.

38. See, for example, Ronald Steel's *Walter Lippmann and the American Century* (Boston: Little, Brown and Company, 1980), p. 445. Also consult "Containment: 40 Years Later," *Foreign Affairs,* July 1987, pp. 827–830.

39. George Kennan, "Concept in Foreign Policy" in *Harvard Today,* Autumn 1967, p. 14.

40. Kennan's remarks in "Organization Meeting on Russia," June 12, 1946, File "1946" in Box 16, Kennan Papers.

41. Kennan's "National Security Problem," March 14, 1947, File "1947 Jan to March" in Box 16, Kennan Papers.

42. See Kennan's *Memoirs: 1925–1950,* p. 360.

43. Kennan's "Comments on the General Trend of US Foreign Policy," August 20, 1948, File "1948" in Box 23, Kennan Papers.

44. Kennan's "US Foreign Policy," October 11, 1948, p. 1, File "1-C" in Box 17, Kennan Papers.

45. *Ibid.*, pp. 21–22.

46. *Ibid.*, p. 10.

47. Kennan's "Preparedness as Part of Foreign Relations," p. 7, January 8, 1948, File "Jan to April 1948" in Box 17, Kennan Papers.

48. Kennan's "What Is Policy?" December 18, 1947, pp. 18–19, Box 17, Kennan Papers.

49. Kennan's "Measures Short of War," p. 19, September 16, 1946, File "1946" in Box 16, Kennan Papers.

50. Kennan's "Preparedness," p. 7.

51. Kennan's "Measures Short of War," p. 19–20.

52. *Ibid.*, p. 20.

53. *Ibid.*

54. During World War II, Kennan thought that L. P. Beria and G. M. Malenkov determined Soviet policy as much as Stalin. See excerpts from Kennan's letter (1945) in the *Slavic Review,* September 1968.

55. Kennan's "The United States and Russia," Winter 1946, File "1946" in Box 23, Kennan Papers.

56. Kennan's "Structure of Internal Power in the USSR," Appendix, p. 4, October 10, 1946, File "1946" in Box 16, Kennan Papers.

57. Kennan's "Measures Short of War," p. 12.

58. *Ibid.*, p. 17.

59. *Ibid.*, p. 19.

60. Kennan's "Trust as a Factor in International Relations," October 1, 1946, Box 33, Armstrong Papers.

61. Kennan to Norman Graebner, February 26, 1960, File "2-B1960" in Box 31, Kennan Papers.

62. Kennan's letter in the *New York Times,* October 18, 1959.

63. Also see Dean Acheson's portrait of Marshall in Acheson's *Sketches from Life* (New York: Harper and Brothers, 1961), pp. 147–166, and Forrest Pogue, *George C. Marshall: Statesman 1945–1959* (New York: Viking, 1987), p. 521.

64. Kennan's "Forward" in Anna Nelson (ed.), *The State Department Policy Planning Staff Papers, 1947–1949* (New York: Garland Publishing, 1983; hereafter cited as *SDPPSP*) *1947,* p. vii.

65. *Executive Sessions of the Senate Foreign Relations Committee* (Washington, DC: Government Printing Office, 1976), Vol. I, p. 4; Pogue, *Marshall,* pp. 87, 154.

66. Kennan to Emile Despres, June 12, 1947, Box 8, Policy Planning Staff (hereafter PPS) Papers, RG 59, NA.

67. Kennan to James Baxter, June 11, 1947, Box 8, PPS Papers, RG 59, NA.

68. James Baxter to Kennan, June 16, 1947, Box 8, PPS Papers, RG 59, NA.

69. Kennan's memorandum to Acheson, January 22, 1952, p. 6, File "1-D-19" in Box 24, Kennan Papers.

70. Kennan to Dean Acheson, January 3, 1949, Box 64, Acheson Papers.

71. Kennan's "Measures Short of War," p. 21.

Chapter 7. Cold War in Europe

1. Kennan to Mr. Lyon, October 13, 1947, PPS Papers, RG 59, NA.

2. Kennan's *Memoirs: 1925–1950* (Boston: Little, Brown, and Company, 1967), p. 328.

3. Kennan's "Planning of Foreign Policy," p. 3, June 18, 1947, Bland Papers.

4. Interviews with Ware Adams, September 30, 1970, and Carleton Savage, September 30, 1970, both in Box 8, Wright Papers.

5. *FRUS 1950,* Vol. I, p. 240.

6. For a detailed account of the Greek and Turkish problems as perceived by political leaders in Washington see Joseph Jones, *The Fifteen Weeks* (New York: Viking Press, 1955). A more critical assessment is found in Richard Freeland's *The Truman Doctrine and the Origins of McCarthyism* (New York: Schocken Books, 1974).

7. Kennan's "Comments on the National Security Problem," p. 12, March 28, 1947, Box 17, Kennan Papers.

8. *Ibid.*, p. 17.

9. The House vote was 287 to 107; the Senate vote 67 to 23.

10. Jones, *The Fifteen Weeks*, pp. 177–179.

11. Kennan to Bohlen, March 20, 1947, File "1947" in Box 28, Kennan Papers.

12. Dean Acheson, *Present at the Creation* (New York: Norton, 1969), p. 375.

13. Henry Steele Commager (ed.), *Documents of American History,* Vol. II (New York: Appleton-Century-Crofts, 1968), "The Truman Doctrine," pp. 524–526.

14. In another attempt (*SDPPSP* 1947, Policy Planning Staff [PPS] 1, May 23, 1947, p. 11) to check the more extreme aspects of the Truman Doctrine, Kennan wrote:

> That the Truman Doctrine is [not] a blank check to give economic and military aid to any area in the world where the communists show signs of being successful. It must be made clear that the extension of American aid is essentially a question of political economy in the literal sense of that term and that such aid will be considered only in cases where the prospective results bear a satisfactory relationship to the expenditure of American resources and effort. It must be made clear that in the case of Greece and Turkey we are dealing with a critical area where the failure to take action would have had particularly serious consequences, where a successful action would promise particularly far-reaching results, and where the overall cost was relatively small; and that in other areas we should have to apply similar criteria.

15. Acheson, *Present at the Creation*, pp. 224–225.

16. Kennan's *Memoirs: 1925–1950*, pp. 322–324.

17. *SDPPSP* 1947, PPS 8, September 18, 1947, pp. 91–101.

18. *SDPPSP* 1948, PPS 18, January 10, 1948, pp. 1–4.

19. Alastair Buchan, *The End of the Postwar Era* (London: Weidenfeld and Nicolson, 1974), pp. 72, 183; Louis Halle, *The Cold War as History* (New York: Harper and Row, 1967), p. 144; Walter LaFeber, *America, Russia, and the Cold War, 1945–1975* (New York: John Wiley and Sons, 1976), p. 61; Franz Schurmann, *The Logic of World Power* (New York: Pantheon Books, 1974), pp. 117–123; B. Ponomaryov, A. Gromyko, V. Khvostov, *History of Soviet Foreign Policy, 1945–1970* (Moscow: Progress Publishers, 1974), pp. 160–167.

20. See Abba Eban, *The New Diplomacy* (New York: Random House, 1983), pp. 6, 136, 140.

21. The literature on the Marshall Plan is large. Among the many useful works are Harry Price, *The Marshall Plan and Its Meaning* (Ithaca: Cornell University Press, 1955); Forrest

Pogue, *George C. Marshall: Statesman 1945–1959* (New York: Viking, 1987); Jones, *The Fifteen Weeks*; John Gimbel, *The Origins of the Marshall Plan* (Stanford: Stanford University Press, 1976); Hadley Arkes, *Bureaucracy, the Marshall Plan, and the National Interest* (Princeton: Princeton University Press, 1972); Rostow, *The Division of Europe after World War II: 1946* (Austin: University of Texas Press, 1981); Charles Mee, Jr., *The Marshall Plan* (New York: Simon and Schuster, 1984); Barton Bernstein (ed.), *Politics and Policies of the Truman Administration* (Chicago: Quadrangle Books, 1970); Dean Acheson, *Present at the Creation;* Wilson Douglas Miscamble, *George F. Kennan, the Policy Planning Staff and American Foreign Policy, 1947–1950* (PhD dissertation, University of Notre Dame, 1980); Robert Wood, *From Marshall Plan to Debt Crisis: Foreign Aid and Development Choices in the World Economy* (Berkeley: University of California Press, 1986). See also John Gaddis, *The Long Peace* (New York: Oxford University Press, 1987), pp. 48–71.

22. Clark Clifford, "American Relations with the Soviet Union," September 24, 1946, p. 79, Elsey Papers.

23. Acheson, *Present at the Creation*, pp. 227–230.

24. *SDPPSP* 1947, PPS 1, May 23, 1947, p. 8.

25. T. Michael Ruddy, *The Cautious Diplomat: Charles E. Bohlen and the Soviet Union, 1929–1969* (Kent, Ohio: Kent State University Press, 1986), p. 75.

26. Commager, *Documents of American History,* Vol. II, "The Marshall Plan," pp. 531–532.

27. See *SDPPSP* 1947, PPS 4, July 23, 1947, pp. 26–68. It is the single longest and most thoughtful paper by Kennan about European recovery and the US role. Also see *ibid*. PPS 6, August 14, 1947, pp. 71–75.

28. Mee, *The Marshall Plan*, p. 125.

29. *Ibid.*, p. 189.

30. *FRUS 1947*, Vol. III, p. 398.

31. *Ibid.*, pp. 401–402.

32. For a good discussion see Michael Wala, "Selling the Marshall Plan at Home: The Committee for the Marshall Plan to Aid European Recovery" in *Diplomatic History,* Summer 1986, pp. 247–265.

33. Mee, *The Marshall Plan*, pp. 217–218; *SDPPSP* 1947, PPS 17, November 26, 1947, p. 175.

34. Kennan's *Memoirs: 1925–1950*, p. 405.

35. Kennan's talk, February 17, 1948, p. 19, Folder 7 in Box 7, C. Wright Papers.

36. *Ibid.*, p. 20. Also see Kennan's "Background to the Marshall Plan," File "1-C" in Box 17, Kennan Papers.

37. Kennan's "Notes on the Marshall Plan," December 15, 1947, File "1947" in Box 23, Kennan Papers.

38. See *SDPPSP* 1948, PPS 23, February 24, 1948, p. 108.

39. Freeland, *The Truman Doctrine and the Origins of McCarthyism*, p. 281; *Memoirs: 1925–1950*, p. 400.

40. Kennan's remarks in "Princeton: 1956: The Revolution in American Foreign Policy," p. 22, April 21, 1956, File "1-C-55" in Box 19, Kennan Papers.

41. *SDPPSP* 1947, PPS 13, November 6, 1947, pp. 130–131, 133–134; *SDPPSP* 1948, PPS 23, February 24, 1948, pp. 106, 110–114.

42. *SDPPSP* 1948, PPS 37, August 12, 1948, pp. 325–326.

43. *Ibid.*, p. 326.

44. Kennan, *Memoirs: 1925–1950*, pp. 429, 432.

45. *SDPPSP,* August 1948, PPS 37, 1948, August 1948, p. 332.

46. Miscamble, *George Kennan*, p. 121.

47. See *SDPPSP* 1948, PPS 37/1, November 15, 1948, pp. 335–371.

48. Miscamble, *George Kennan,* pp. 129–133; *FRUS 1948,* Vol. II, pp. 1287–1288; Walter Millis (ed.), *The Forrestal Diaries* (New York: Viking Press, 1951), pp. 506–507.

49. Miscamble, *George Kennan,* pp. 155–160; Kennan's *Memoirs: 1925–1950,* p. 444.

50. Miscamble's treatment of Kennan's views about Germany is excellent. In addition to the relevant sections of that work, the following provide a general assessment of Germany's division and status as an occupied country: John Gimbel, *The American Occupation of Germany* (Stanford: Stanford University Press, 1968); Lucius Clay, *Decision in Germany* (New York: Doubleday, 1950); Robert Murphy, *Diplomat Among Warriors* (New York: Doubleday, 1964); Konrad Adenauer, *Memoirs: 1943–1953* (London: Weidenfeld and Nicholson, 1966); Bruce Kuklick, *American Policy and the Division of Germany* (Ithaca: Cornell University Press, 1972); Roger Morgan, *The United States and West Germany, 1945–1973* (London: Oxford University Press, 1974); Eugene Davidson, *The Death and Life of Germany: An Account of the American Occupation* (New York: Alfred Knopf, 1959).

51. Marshall to Count Richard Coudenhove-Kalergi, March 22, 1948, Memorandum to the President, 1947–1948, Box 1, Lott File 488, RG 59, NA.

52. See PPS meetings for June 8, 1949; June 13, 1949; June 14, 1949. All are in PPS Papers, RG 59, NA. Also see Kennan's *Memoirs: 1925–1950,* p. 451. The consultants included Hans Morgenthau, General Walter Bedell Smith, John McCloy (US high commissioner for Germany), Robert Woodruff (Coca Cola), and J. Robert Oppenheimer.

53. *SDPPSP* 1949, PPS 55, July 7, 1949, p. 85.

54. *Ibid.,* p. 99.

55. Kennan to Bohlen, October 12, 1949, p. 7,PPS Papers, RG 59, NA.

56. *Ibid.,* p. 4.

57. Bohlen to Kennan, October 6, 1949, p. 4, *ibid.*

58. Bohlen to Kennan, October 29, 1949, p. 3, *ibid.*

59. Kennan to Adam Watson, December 7, 1967, File "2–B 1967" in Box 28, Kennan Papers.

60. Some of the better literature about postwar European integration includes Alastair Buchan, *Europe's Future, Europe's Choices* (New York: Columbia University Press, 1969); Miriam Camps, *European Unification in the Sixties* (New York: McGraw Hill, 1966); Ernst Haas, *The Uniting of Europe* (Stanford: Stanford University Press, 1958); Karl Deutsch, *Political Community and the North Atlantic Area* (Princeton: Princeton University Press, 1957).

61. *SDPPSP* 1947, PPS 9, September 24, 1947, pp. 106–107; *ibid.,* PPS 14, November 11, 1947, p. 138; *FRUS 1948,* Vol III, p. 849; *SDPPSP* 1948, PPS 23, February 24, 1948, pp. 115–116; *SDPPSP* 1949, PPS 52, June 23, 1949, p. 62.

62. *SDPPSP* 1948, PPS 22, February 19, 1948, PPS 22/1, March 11, 1948, pp. 88–102; *SDPPSP* 1949, PPS 54, June 28, 1949, pp. 75–81; NSC 10/2, June 18, 1948, pp. 125–128 in Thomas Etzold and John Gaddis (eds.), *Containment: Documents on American Policy and Strategy, 1945–1950* (New York: Columbia University Press, 1978). Kennan to "Mr. Secretary," September 29, 1947, PPS Papers, RG 59, NA.

63. Kennan's *Memoirs: 1950–1963,* p. 203. Kennan to Robert Lovett, June 8, 1948, PPS Papers, RG 59, NA; John Prados, *Presidents' Secret Wars: CIA and Pentagon Covert Operations Since World War II* (New York: William Morrow Company, 1986), p. 80.

64. Kennan's interview on "Walter Cronkite at Large," CBS News, March 31, 1987.

65. Alan Bullock, *Ernest Bevin: Foreign Secretary, 1945–1951* (London: Heinemann, 1983), p. 645.

66. *FRUS 1948,* Vol. III, pp. 3–6.

67. George Gallup (ed.), *The Gallup Poll: Public Opinion, 1935–1971,* Vol. I (New

York: Random House, 1972), pp. 735, 750. By early May 1948, 65% favored an alliance, 21% opposed. In mid-July, 73% were in favor, 16% against.

68. *SDPPSP* 1948, PPS 43, November 24, 1948, p. 491.

69. *Ibid.*, p. 492.

70. *Ibid.*, p. 494.

71. *Ibid.*, p. 495.

72. Nicholas Henderson, *The Birth of NATO* (London: Weidenfeld and Nicolson, 1982), p. 9.

73. *SDPPSP* 1948, PPS 27, March 23, 1948, pp. 161–164.

74. Miscamble, *George Kennan,* pp. 81–82.

75. Kennan to W.W. Rostow, May 15, 1962, File "2-B 1962" in Box 28, Kennan Papers; Kennan to Norman Graebner, May 16, 1959, File "2-B 1959" in Box 28, Kennan Papers; Kennan to Robert Matteson, December 16, 1958, File "2–B 1958" in Box 28, Kennan Papers.

76. *SDPPSP* 1948, PPS 38, August 18, 1948, pp. 372–411; Etzold and Gaddis, *Containment, p. 173; FRUS 1949,* Vol. I, pp. 271–284.

77. *SDPPSP* 1947, PPS 13, November 6, 1947, p. 132.

78. Established at Stalin's behest in September 1947, the ostensible mission of the Cominform (Communist Information Bureau) was to coordinate and exchange information among the communist parties of Russia, Bulgaria, Czechoslovakia, France, Hungary, Italy, Poland, Rumania, and Yugoslavia. The Cominform's chief propaganda publication was the awkwardly named *For a Lasting Peace, For a People's Democracy.* Except for expelling Yugoslavia from its membership, the Cominform accomplished little and was dissolved by the USSR in 1956.

79. Kennan's "The Communist States of Eastern Europe," p. 12, January 3, 1964, File "1-C-133" in Box 21, Kennan Papers; *SDPPSP* 1948, PPS 38, August 18, 1948, p. 386.

80. For more about the Belgrade-Moscow rift see Royal Institute of International Affairs, *The Soviet-Yugoslav Dispute* (London: Oxford University Press, 1948); Adam Ulam, *Titoism and the Cominform* (Cambridge: Harvard University Press, 1952); Milovan Djilas, *Conversations with Stalin* (New York: Harcourt, Brace and World, 1962); George Hoffmann and F. W. Neal, *Yugoslavia and the New Communism* (New York: Twentieth Century Fund, 1962); Ross Johnson, *The Transformation of Communist Ideology: The Yugoslav Case, 1945–1953* (Cambridge: MIT Press, 1972).

81. *FRUS 1948,* Vol. IV, p. 1077.

82. *Ibid.*, p. 1079, footnote 1.

83. *SDPPSP* 1948, PPS 35, June 30, 1948, p. 318.

84. A number of British officials suspected that the Soviet-Yugoslav dispute was "planned" in order that Belgrade might become eligible for US financial assistance. General Eisenhower wondered, as late as 1949, whether the intracommunist squabble was "an extremely subtle trick." See Henry Brands, "Redefining the Cold War: American Policy Toward Yugoslavia, 1948–1960" in *Diplomatic History,* Winter 1987, pp. 41–53; Lorraine Lees, "The American Decision to Assist Tito, 1948–1949" in *Diplomatic History,* Fall 1978, pp. 407–422; *FRUS 1948,* Vol. IV, pp. 1083, 1088, 1098. Also see Gaddis's *Long Peace,* pp. 147–194.

85. *SDPPSP* 1949, PPS 49, February 10, 1949, pp. 14–24.

86. *Ibid.*, PPS 60, September 10, 1949, pp. 139–149.

87. Barton Bernstein, "Walter Lippmann and the Early Cold War" in Thomas Paterson (ed.), *Cold War Critics: Alternatives to American Foreign Policy in the Truman Years* (Chicago: Quadrangle Books, 1971), pp. 30, 45; Gabriel Kolko, *The Politics of War* (New York: Random House, 1968), p. 338. *FRUS 1949,* Vol. V, p. 21.

88. *SDPPSP* 1948, PPS 38, August 18, 1948, pp. 386–387.

89. *SDPPSP* 1949, PPS 49, February 10, 1949, p. 18; *FRUS 1949,* Vol. V, pp. 9–10.

90. *FRUS 1949,* Vol. V, pp. 21–26, 42–54.

91. Kennan to Count Albrecht von Kessel, December 11, 1963, File "2-B 1963" in Box 28, Kennan Papers.

92. Kennan's "Unfinished Paper," September 1951, File "1-D-18" in Box 28, Kennan Papers.

93. *Ibid.*

94. David McLellan makes similar points in his excellent *Dean Acheson: The State Department Years* (New York: Dodd, Mead and Company, 1976), p. 172.

95. Kennan to Norman Graebner, May 15, 1959, File "2-B 1959" in Box 28, Kennan Papers.

96. *Ibid.* and McLellan, *Dean Acheson,* p. 174.

Chapter 8. Far Eastern Dilemmas

1. Kennan's "Problems of Far Eastern Policy," January 14, 1948, Box 17, Kennan Papers.

2. Kennan's "Japanese Peace Treaty," September 1949, Bland Papers.

3. George Kennan, *Memoirs: 1925–1950* (Boston: Little, Brown, and Company, 1967), p. 393.

4. Vorin Whan (ed.), *A Soldier Speaks: Public Papers and Speeches of General of the Army Douglas MacArthur* (New York: Praeger Publishers, 1965), pp. 182–183.

5. *FRUS 1947,* Vol. VI, pp. 485–487.

6. Michael Schaller, *The American Occupation of Japan* (New York: Oxford University Press, 1985), p. 82.

7. *SDPPSP* 1947, PPS 10, October 14, 1947, p. 112.

8. *Ibid.,* p. 113.

9. *Ibid.,* p. 243, and Kennan to Dean Acheson, May 26, 1951, Acheson Papers.

10. Kennan suggests in his *Memoirs: 1925–1950* (pp. 384–385) that MacArthur was impressed by him because of a lecture he delivered to senior SCAP officers about postwar developments in the Soviet Union.

11. Kennan's "Memorandum of Conversation" with Marshall, February 19, 1948, Box 33, PPS Papers, RG 59, NA.

12. *FRUS 1948,* Vol. VI, pp. 697–699.

13. *Ibid.,* pp. 699–706.

14. *Ibid.,* pp. 712–713.

15. Schaller, *Occupation,* p. 125.

16. *FRUS 1948,* Vol. VI, p. 689; Schaller, *Occupation,* p. 137.

17. *SDPPSP* 1948, "Observations," May 25, 1948, p. 241.

18. *FRUS 1948,* Vol. VI, pp. 691–696, PPS 28, March 25, 1948 and *SDPPSP* 1948, pp. 203–243.

19. *FRUS 1949,* Vol. VI, pp. 730–736, NSC 13/3, May 6, 1949.

20. *Ibid.,* pp. 752–754.

21. *Ibid.,* p. 780.

22. Kennan's "Draft Paper," June 28, 1949, p. 3, PPS Papers, RG 59, NA.

23. *SDPPSP* 1949, p. 184.

24. Yamamoto Mitsuru, "The Cold War and US-Japan Cooperation" in Yonosuke Nagai and Akira Iriye (eds.), *The Origins of the Cold War in Asia* (New York: Columbia University Press, 1977), pp. 412–413.

25. Richard Barnet, *The Alliance* (New York: Simon and Schuster, 1983), p. 81.

26. Kennan to Acheson, August 23, 1950, p. 5, Acheson Papers.

27. Dean Acheson, *Present at the Creation* (New York: Norton, 1969), p. 445.

28. J. A. S. Grenville (ed.), *The Major International Treaties 1914–1973* (London: Methuen, 1974), pp. 286–287. Any reader interested in further and more detailed study of the US occupation in Japan, the purges, and peace treaty should consult, at least, the following: Schaller, *The American Occupation of Japan;* Thomas Bisson, *Zaibatsu Dissolution in Japan* (Berkeley: University of California Press, 1954); William Borden, *The Pacific Alliance: United States Foreign Economic Policy and Japanese Trade Recovery, 1947–1955* (Madison: University of Wisconsin Press, 1984); Frederick Dunn, *Peacemaking and the Settlement with Japan* (Princeton: Princeton University Press, 1973); Yoshida Shigeru, *The Yoshida Memoirs* (Cambridge: Harvard University Press, 1961).

29. Kennan's "Unfinished Paper," September 1951, File "1-D-18" in Box 24, Kennan Papers.

30. According to Warren Cohen, Davies's analyses of the Chinese mind resembled the traditional European port mentality. See Cohen's "Acheson, His Advisers, and China, 1949–1950" in D. Borg's and W. Heinrichs (eds.), *Uncertain Years: Chinese-American Relations, 1947–1950* (New York: Columbia University Press, 1980). For the sake of simplicity and of conformity with US government documents from the late 1940s, I shall use the pre-1978 Romanization of Chinese proper nouns.

31. While in Moscow, Kennan and Davies established a reciprocal intellectual attachment, whereby the one advanced the education of the other. To a significant extent each came to accept as his own the other's opinions, interpretations, and prejudices about his area of expertise. Davies, for example, uncritically received Kennan's unlikely version of why in 1937 Roosevelt's administration had seen fit to merge the Department of State's Division of East European Affairs into the Division of European Affairs, banish the former's chief (Robert Kelly) to Turkey, order the destruction of East Europe's special files, and surrender its books to the Library of Congress: the weight of Soviet influence, or pro-Soviet influence in Washington, caused the dismantling of the one State Department unit best able to monitor and evaluate Stalin's purges. In fact, the elimination of East European Affairs was perfectly innocent and part of an attempt to streamline the State Department and make it more efficient.

Davies's job in America's Moscow embassy had been to analyze Soviet activities in East Asia and their possible consequences for US foreign policy. For this task he required some tutoring about the Soviet Union and later offered the following tribute to Kennan, his chief instructor: "It was a delight to watch him probe some sphinxlike announcement in *Pravda* for what might lie within or behind it, recalling some obscure incident in Bolshevik history or a personality conflict within the Party, quoting a passage from Dostoevsky on Russian character, or citing a parallel in Tsarist foreign policy. His subtle intellect swept the range of possibilities like a radar attuned to the unseen." In 1945 Davies was in strong sympathy with Kennan as he "suffered agonies" for being unable to influence Roosevelt toward a stronger stance against Russia. See Kennan's *Memoirs: 1925–1950,* pp. 84–85; Davies's *Dragon by the Tail* (New York: Norton, 1972), p. 390.

32. Kennan, *Memoirs: 1925–1950,* p. 239.

33. Compare Kennan's *Memoirs: 1950–1963,* pp. 56–57 with Davies's *Foreign and Other Affairs* (New York: Norton, 1964), pp. 206–208.

34. Kennan, *Memoirs: 1925–1950,* p. 239.

35. *The China White Paper* (Stanford: Stanford University Press, 1967), Vol. II, p. 565.

36. John Davies, *Dragon,* pp. 134–142.

37. *China White Paper,* Vol. II, p. 567.

38. Kennan's memorandum for Robert Lovett, June 23, 1947, File 7 in Box 6, C. Ben Wright Papers.

39. *SDPPSP* 1947, p. 135, PPS 13, November 6, 1947.

40. Kennan's "Unfinished Paper," September 1951, File "1-C-5" in Box 24, Kennan Papers.

41. John Sullivan's diary entry, January 11, 1948, File 6 in Box 8, Wright Papers.

42. Kennan's letter and "The Political-Strategic Background of US Aid Programs" to Bohlen, January 30, 1948, Box 6, Records of Charles Bohlen, RG 59, NA.

43. *SDPPSP* 1948, PPS 39, September 7, 1948, pp. 415–416.

44. *Ibid.*, p. 427.

45. *Ibid.*, p. 430.

46. *Ibid.*, p. 422.

47. *Ibid.*, p. 424.

48. *SDPPSP* 1949, PPS 39/2, February 25, 1949, p. 28.

49. *Ibid.*, PPS 53, July 6, 1949, p. 65.

50. *Ibid.*, PPS 53 Annex A, June 23, 1949, p. 73.

51. *Ibid.*, p. 74.

52. *Ibid.*, PPS 53, p. 65.

53. *Executive Sessions of the Senate Foreign Relations Committee: 1947–1948* (Historical Series), (Washington DC: US Government Printing Office, 1976), Vol. I, p. 4.

54. Marshall's memorandum for Kennan, September 18, 1948, File 7 in Box 6, Wright Papers.

55. See Chapter 3 of my *Cracking the Monolith: US Policy Against the Sino-Soviet Alliance, 1949–1955* (Baton Rouge: Louisiana Sate University Press, 1986). Other accounts of Sino-Soviet-US relations in the late 1940s, early 1950s include Robert Blum, *Drawing the Line: The Origin of the American Containment Policy in East Asia* (New York: Norton, 1982); Lewis Purifoy, *Harry Truman's China Policy* (New York: New Viewpoints, 1976); Tang Tsou, *America's Failure in China* (Chicago: University of Chicago Press, 1963); Nancy Tucker, *Patterns in the Dust: Chinese-American Relations and the Recognition Controversy, 1949–1950* (New York: Columbia University Press, 1983). Of related interest is Paul Gordon Lauren (ed.), *The China Hands' Legacy: Ethics and Diplomacy* (Boulder, Colo.: Westview Press, 1987).

56. *FRUS 1950,* Vol. VI, p. 313.

57. NSC 6, March 1948, NSC File, Modern Military Branch, NA.

58. *SDPPSP* 1948, PPS 39/1, November 24, 1948, p. 447.

59. *FRUS 1949,* Vol. IX, pp. 460–461.

60. Kennan, *Memoirs: 1925–1950,* p. 493.

61. George Kennan's "Suggested Course of Action in East and South Asia," July 8, 1949, p. 1, PPS Papers, RG 59, NA.

62. See Chapter 3 of Mayers, *Cracking the Monolith.*

63. *SDPPSP* 1948, PPS 23, February 24, 1948, p. 122.

64. *FRUS 1950,* Vol. VI, p. 396.

65. Kennan, *Memoirs: 1925–1950,* pp. 486–487.

66. *Ibid.*, pp. 484–485. Also Kennan, personal communication, January 15, 1986.

67. John Gaddis, "Korea in American Politics, Strategy, and Diplomacy, 1945–1950" in Nagai and Iriye (eds.), *The Origins of the Cold War in Asia,* p. 287.

68. See Robert Simmons, *The Strained Alliance* (New York: The Free Press, 1975). For other aspects of the Korean War see John Spanier, *The Truman-MacArthur Controversy and the Korean War* (New York: Norton, 1965); Allen Whiting, *China Crosses the Yalu* (Stanford: Stanford University Press, 1960); Bruce Cummings, *The Origins of the Korean War: Liberation and the Emergence of Separate Regimes* (Princeton: Princeton University Press, 1981) and Cummings (ed.), *Child of Conflict: The Korean-American Relationship, 1943–1953* (Seattle: University of Washington Press, 1983).

69. *FRUS 1947,* Vol. VI, p. 814; *FRUS 1951,* Vol. VII, p. 417.

70. Kennan, *Memoirs: 1925–1950*, p. 490.

71. *FRUS 1950*, Vol. VII, pp. 1335–1336.

72. Kennan's "Possible Further Communist Initiatives in the Light of the Korean Situation," June 26, 1950, File "1-D-12" in Box 24, Kennan Papers.

73. *Ibid.*

74. Kennan's "Possible Further Danger Points in Light of the Korean Situation," June 30, 1950, File "1-D-12" in Box 24, Kennan Papers.

75. Kennan to Mr. Secretary, August 8, 1950, p. 3, PPS Papers, Box 8, RG 59, NA.

76. *Ibid.*, p. 5.

77. *FRUS 1950*, Vol. VII, pp. 574–576.

78. Kennan to Acheson, August 23, 1950, p. 3, Acheson Papers.

79. *Ibid.*, p. 4.

80. *Ibid.*

81. Acheson, *Present at the Creation*, p. 446.

82. M. J. McDermott to Kennan, November 13, 1950; Kennan to McDermott, November 10, 1950; Kennan's "Memo for the files," November 30, 1950, File "1-D-15" in Box 24, Kennan Papers.

83. Kennan's "Possible Further Danger Points in Light of the Korean Situation," June 30, 1950.

84. *Ibid.*

85. Kennan to Mr. Secretary, August 8, 1950, pp. 4–5.

86. Kennan to Mr. Secretary, November 24, 1950, Acheson Papers.

87. Quoted in Acheson, *Present at the Creation*, p. 476.

88. *FRUS 1950*, Vol. VII, p. 1384.

89. Acheson, *Present at the Creation*, p. 477.

90. See, for example, Kennan's "Draft for Statement by Secretary of State on Public Reaction to Korean Situation," December 14, 1950, File "1-D-16" in Box 24, Kennan Papers.

91. Kennan, *Memoirs: 1950–1963*, p. 35.

92. *FRUS 1951*, Vol. VII, p. 242.

93. *Ibid.*, pp. 242–243.

94. *Ibid.*, pp. 406–407.

95. *Ibid.*, pp. 507–511.

96. *Ibid.*, pp. 509–511.

97. Acheson, *Present at the Creation*, p. 533.

98. Kennan, *Memoirs: 1950–1963*, p. 38.

99. See Kennan's *The Cloud of Danger* (Boston: Little, Brown and Company, 1977), pp. 107–111, and his "Japanese Security and American Policy," *Foreign Affairs*, October 1964, pp. 14–28.

100. Kennan's "Transcript of Remarks" to the Research and Analysis Division of the State Department, p. 14, January 22, 1953, File "1-D-28" in Box 24, Kennan Papers.

101. Acheson, *Present at the Creation*, p. 446.

102. Kennan's "Unfinished Paper," September 1951.

103. Kennan, *Memoirs: 1950–1963*, p. 30.

104. Wilson Miscamble, *George Kennan, the Policy Planning Staff and American Foreign Policy, 1947–1950* (PhD dissertation, University of Notre Dame, 1980), p. 181.

105. Kennan to Dean Acheson, November 24, 1950, Acheson Papers.

Chapter 9. Two Ambassadorships

1. The following books are useful for anyone interested in Stalin's Russia, 1946–1953: Werner Hahn, *Postwar Soviet Politics: The Fall of Zhdanov and the Defeat of Moderation,*

1946–1953 (Ithaca: Cornell University Press, 1982); Leonard Schapiro, *The Communist Party of the Soviet Union* (New York: Vintage Books, 1971); Marshall Shulman, *Stalin's Foreign Policy Reappraised* (New York: Atheneum, 1965); Adam Ulam, *Stalin: The Man and His Era* (New York: Viking Press, 1973).

2. See Carl Friedrich and Zbigniew Brzezinski, *Totalitarian Dictatorship and Autocracy* (Cambridge: Harvard University Press, 1957), p. 22, and William Kornhauser, *The Politics of Mass Society* (Glencoe, Ill.: The Free Press, 1959), p. 123. For an excellent antidote to prevailing literature about Soviet "totalitarianism" see Stephen Cohen's *Rethinking the Soviet Experience: Politics and History Since 1917* (New York: Oxford University Press, 1985).

3. Isaac Deutscher, *Stalin* (New York: Oxford University Press, 1966), p. 575.

4. *Ibid.*, p. 580. Also see Joseph Brodsky, "In a Room and a Half" in *The New York Review of Books*, February 27, 1986, p. 40–48.

5. Edward Crankshaw (ed.), *Khrushchev Remembers* (Boston: Little, Brown, and Company, 1970), pp. 234–235.

6. Kennan Transcript of Remarks" to the Research and Analysis Division of the State Department, January 22, 1953, File "1-D-28" in Box 24, Kennan Papers.

7. Kennan's letter to H. Freeman Mathews, July 15, 1952, p. 2, File "1-D-2" in Box 24, Kennan Papers.

8. *Ibid.*, p. 4.

9. *Ibid.*, p. 11. In connection with Kennan's comments also see Vera Dunham, *In Stalin's Time: Middleclass Values in Soviet Fiction* (Cambridge: Cambridge University Press, 1976).

10. Kennan to H. Freeman Mathews, July 15, 1952.

11. *Ibid.*, p. 9.

12. Kennan's "Address to State Department Personnel," late November 1952, p. 7, File "1-D-26" in Box 24, Kennan Papers.

13. See Nikita Khrushchev's "Special Report to the 20th Congress of the Communist Party of the Soviet Union," in "The Crimes of the Stalin Era" in *The New Leader* (New York: 1962).

14. Something of the isolation that surrounded such gifted figures as Boris Pasternak and Anna Akhmatova is captured in Isaiah Berlin's recounting of his meeting with them in 1956: "I told . . . the assembled company all that I could of English, American, French writing: it was like speaking to the victims of shipwreck on a desert island, cut off for decades from civilization—all they heard, they received as new, exciting and delightful." Cited in Isaiah Berlin's *Personal Impressions* (New York: Viking Press, 1981), p. 187.

15. Kennan to H. Freeman Mathews, July 15, 1952, p. 10.

16. Kennan's "Transcript of Remarks," January 22, 1953, p. 11.

17. Kennan to H. Freeman Mathews, July 15, 1952, pp. 7–8.

18. *Ibid.*, p. 14.

19. Arnold Toynbee's "The Wisdom of Experience," File "1952" in Box 29, Kennan Papers.

20. Kennan to Hugh Cummings, December 31, 1951, File "1951" in Box 29, Kennan Papers.

21. Transcript of Kennan's Press Conference, April 1, 1952, File "1-C-28" in Box 18, Kennan Papers.

22. Kennan's *Memoirs: 1950–1963* (New York: Pantheon Books, 1972), p. 122.

23. Kennan's "Draft of Line to be Taken with Soviet Leaders," May 1952, File "1-D-20" in Box 24, Kennan Papers.

24. Kennan to H. Freeman Mathews, May 16, 1952, File "1952" in Box 29, Kennan Papers.

25. Kennan's *Memoirs: 1950–1963*, p. 136.

26. Kennan's "Outline of Advice," December 1952, File "1-D-27" in Box 24, Kennan Papers.

27. Kennan to Walworth Barbour, Director of the Office of East European Affairs, August 1, 1952, File "1952" in Box 29, Kennan Papers.

28. Kennan to H. Freeman Mathews, August 8, 1952, File "1952" in Box 29, Kennan Papers.

29. Kennan to Lewis Douglas, August 12, 1952, File "1952" in Box 29, Kennan Papers.

30. Kennan to H. Freeman Mathews, June 6, 1952, File "1-D-21" in Box 24, Kennan Papers.

31. Kennan's telegram, October 20, 1952, File "1-D-25" in Box 24, Kennan Papers.

32. Kennan to H. Freeman Mathews, June 6, 1952.

33. Kennan to Truman, August 11, 1952, File "1952" in Box 29, Kennan Papers.

34. Kennan's "Transcript of Remarks," January 22, 1953, p. 3.

35. Kennan to Bernard Gufler, August 12, 1953, File "1952" in Box 29, Kennan Papers.

36. Kennan to Charles Bohlen, August 21, 1952, File "1952" in Box 29, Kennan Papers; Frank Rounds, Jr., interview September 21, 1962, Oral History Project, Columbia University.

37. Kennan to Bohlen, August 21, 1952.

38. Kennan to Acheson, July 1952, File "1952" in Box 29, Kennan Papers. This letter was actually unsent but remains a valid indication of Kennan's thinking, intentions, and other statements at the time.

39. *Ibid.*

40. Kennan, personal communication, October 8, 1985.

41. "Slanderer in Guise of Diplomat," by Observer in *Pravda,* September 26, 1952.

42. Charles Bohlen's letter and memorandum to L. Merchant, August 23, 1955, Box 36, Bohlen Papers.

43. *Ibid.*

44. Kennan, *Memoirs: 1950–1963*, p. 166 and Dean Acheson, *Present at the Creation* (New York: Norton, 1969), p. 697.

45. Kennan's "Transcript of Remarks to the Research and Analysis Division of the State Department," January 22, 1953, File "1-D-28 in Box 24, Kennan Papers.

46. Kennan's "Address to State Department Personnel," late November 1952, File "1-D-26" in Box 24, Kennan Papers.

47. *Ibid.*

48. Acheson's *Present at the Creation*, p. 697.

49. Kennan to Acheson, January 1, 1953, File "1953" in Box 29, Kennan Papers.

50. *Ibid.*

51. Kennan to C. C. Burlington, March 25, 1953, File "1953" in Box 29, Kennan Papers.

52. Kennan to Charles Thayer, September 4, 1953, Kennan File, Thayer Papers.

53. Kennan's "Address to State Department Personnel," late November 1952, File "1-D-26" in Box 24, Kennan Papers.

54. While serving in Prague just before the start of World War II Kennan met John Kennedy for the first time. Kennedy was on a fact-finding tour for his father, at the time US ambassador to Great Britain.

55. Louis Fischer interview with Kennan, March 23, 1965, p. 7, Oral Histories, John Kennedy Library.

56. *Ibid.*, p. 19.

57. Kennan to Kennedy, August 17, 1960, appended to Fischer interview.

58. *Ibid.*

59. "Administration of National Security," Senate Subcommittee on National Security Staffing and Operations (Washington, DC: US Government Printing Office, 1964), pp. 358, 362.

60. *Ibid.*, p. 362.

61. Kennan to Max Beloff, October 2, 1961, File "2-B 1961" in Box 31, Kennan Papers.

62. Kennan's "Briefing for National War College Group," April 5, 1962, File "1-C-114" in Box 20, Kennan Papers.

63. Fischer interview, p. 56.

64. Kennan's *Memoirs: 1950–1963,* pp. 292–293.

65. Kennan's "Briefing to Newspaper Editors," August 15, 1961, File "1-C-110" in Box 20, Kennan Papers.

66. Fischer interview, p. 70.

67. Kennan to H. F. Armstrong, November 2, 1961, File "2-B 1961" in Box 31, Kennan Papers.

68. Kennan's "Draft Notes," December 23, 1961, File "2-B 1961" in Box 31, Kennan Papers.

69. Kennan's "Briefing to Newspaper Editors," August 15, 1961, File "1-C-110" in Box 20, Kennan Papers.

70. Kennan to Walter Lippmann, February 8, 1963, File "2-B 1963" in Box 31, Kennan papers.

71. *Ibid.*

72. Kennan's Memorandum of a Conversation with Veljko Micunovic, June 22, 1961, File "2-B 1962" in Box 31, Kennan Papers.

73. Kennan's "Briefing to Newspaper Editors," August 15, 1961.

74. Fischer interview, p. 59.

75. Kennan to Paul Findley, September 14, 1964, File "1-C-136" in Box 21, Kennan Papers.

76. Fischer interview, p. 100. Also see C. Ben Wright's interviews with Charles Bohlen, p. 15, September 29, 1970 in File "10" in Box 8, Wright Papers.

77. In 1985 a US magistrate ordered Artukovic's extradition to Yugoslavia to stand trial for crimes alleged against him; he was returned to Belgrade in February 1986.

78. Fischer interview, pp. 71–72.

79. Kennan to Harold Hochschild, October 6, 1964, File "2-B 1964" in Box 31, Kennan Papers.

80. "Administration of National Security," p. 363.

81. "And above everything, do not allow yourself to become excited about your work." See Harold Nicolson's *Diplomacy* (London: Oxford University Press, 3rd ed., 1980), p. 62.

82. Kennan's "Address to State Department Personnel," late November 1952.

83. See Gordon Craig and Felix Gilbert (eds.), *The Diplomats* (Princeton: Princeton University Press, 1953), pp. 3–11. Useful studies of diplomacy also include Martin Mayer, *The Diplomats* (Garden City: Doubleday, 1983); John Harr, *The Professional Diplomat* (Princeton: Princeton University Press, 1969); Martin Weil, *A Pretty Good Club: The Founding Fathers of the US Foreign Service* (New York: Norton, 1978).

84. Kenneth Thompson (ed.), *The Virginia Papers on the Presidency* (Lanham, Md.: University Press of America, 1979), pp. 98–99. The Kennedy administration employed two distinguished academics as ambassadors, each one of whom ably represented US interests abroad. John Kenneth Galbraith was sent to India, Edwin O. Reischauer to Japan.

85. See Laurence Silberman's provocative "Toward Presidential Control of the State

Department" in *Foreign Affairs*, Spring 1979, pp. 872–893. Kennan's retort to Silberman is in *The Virginia Papers on the Presidency*, pp. 95–106. Papers.

Chapter 10. Cold War Critic

1. See Kennan's *Soviet-American Relations, 1917–1920*, Vol. I: *Russia Leaves the War* (Princeton: Princeton University Press, 1956) and Vol. II: *The Decision to Intervene* (Princeton: Princeton University Press, 1958).

2. See Kennan's *Realities of American Foreign Policy* (Princeton: Princeton University Press, 1954), *Russia, the Atom and the West* (New York: Harper and Brothers, 1957), *Russia and the West under Lenin and Stalin* (Boston: Little, Brown and Company, 1960), and *Soviet Foreign Policy, 1917–1941* (Princeton: D. Van Nostrand Company, 1960).

3. See Kennan's *On Dealing with the Communist World* (New York: Harper and Row, 1964), *Memoirs: 1925–1950* (Boston: Little, Brown and Company, 1967), *Democracy and the Student Left* (Boston: Little Brown and Company, 1968), *Memoirs: 1950–1963* (Boston: Little, Brown and Company, 1972), *The Cloud of Danger* (Boston: Little, Brown and Company, 1977), *The Decline of Bismarck's European Order* (Princeton: Princeton University Press, 1979), *The Nuclear Delusion* (New York: Pantheon, 1983), and *The Fateful Alliance* (New York: Pantheon, 1984).

4. William Appleman Williams, "The Convenience of History" in *The Nation*, September 15, 1956, pp. 222–224; Christopher Lasch, "The Historian as Diplomat," in *The Nation*, November 24, 1962, pp. 348–353; Paul Seabury and Patrick Glynn, "Kennan: The Historian as Fatalist," in *The National Interest*, Winter 1985–1986, pp. 97–111.

5. Kennan, *The Decision to Intervene*, pp. 471–472.

6. *Ibid.*, p. 472.

7. Kennan to Anna Kallin, January 29, 1957, File "2–B 1957" in Box 28, Kennan Papers.

8. The following books are representative of the scholarly revision of the standard line, which from the 1950s through most of the 1960s portrayed Eisenhower as an ineffective, unimaginative President who let a moralistic and priggish Dulles run foreign policy: Robert Divine, *Eisenhower and the Cold War* (New York: Oxford University Press, 1981); Fred Greenstein, *The Hidden-Hand Presidency: Eisenhower as Leader* (New York: Basic Books, 1982); Richard Melanson and David Mayers (eds.), *Reevaluating Eisenhower: American Foreign Policy in the Fifties* (Chicago: University of Illinois Press, 1987); Herbert Parmet, *Eisenhower and the American Crusades* (New York: Macmillan, 1972); Peter Lyon, *Eisenhower: Portrait of the Hero* (Boston: Little, Brown and Company, 1974).

9. Louis Fischer's interview of Kennan, March 23, 1965, pp. 140–141, Oral Histories, John Kennedy Library. Also see Kenneth Thompson, "The Strengths and Weaknesses of Eisenhower's Leadership" in Melanson and Mayers, *Reevaluating Eisenhower*, p. 22.

10. See the following: Richard Rovere, "Eisenhower Revisited: A Political Genius? A Brilliant Man," *The New York Times Magazine*, February 7, 1971, pp. 14, 59–61; Emmet J. Hughes, *The Living Presidency: The Resources and Dilemmas of the American Presidential Office* (New York: Coward, McCann, and Geohegan, 1972); Arthur Schlesinger, Jr., *The Imperial Presidency* (Boston: Houghton Mifflin Company, 1973); Kennan, *Memoirs: 1950–1963*, pp. 186–187, 227.

11. Kennan, *Memoirs: 1950–1963*, pp. 182–183.

12. Interview of Kennan, March 1967, p. 39, John Foster Dulles History Project, Dulles Papers.

13. *Ibid.*, p. 49. Charles Bohlen, who also had his share of difficulties with Dulles, gave a slightly better account of the secretary than did Kennan. See Bohlen's *Witness to History, 1929–1969* (New York: Norton, 1973) in which he concluded: "I am not sure how history

will evaluate John Foster Dulles. He was a strong Secretary of State; whether he was a wise one is doubtful" (pp. 456–457).

14. Interview of Kennan, March 3, 1967, p. 13.

15. Senators Knowland, Bridges, and McCarthy raised questions about Bohlen's fitness to serve as ambassador to Moscow. They wondered about his political loyalty and sexual proclivities. Despite Dulles's stunning lack of public support for an ambassadorial nomination made by the President, Bohlen won Senate confirmation by a vote of 74 to 13. See Walter Isaacson and Evan Thomas, *The Wise Men* (New York: Simon and Schuster, 1986), pp. 566–570.

16. Emmet Hughes to Sherman Adams, July 2, 1953, Hughes Papers; Townsend Hoopes, *The Devil and John Foster Dulles* (Boston: Little, Brown and Company, 1973), p. 156.

17. Interview of Kennan, March 1967, p. 47; Kennan to Loy Henderson, January 24, 1955, and June 1, 1955; Henderson to Kennan, June 18, 1955, all in File "K" in Box 2, Henderson Papers.

18. Kennan to Louis Halle, April 20, 1966, File "2-B 1966" in Box 28, Kennan Papers.

19. Kennan to Allen Dulles, April 25, 1953, PPS Papers, RG 59, NA; Kennan's *Memoirs: 1950–1963*, p. 180.

20. For more about Austria and its role in the early Cold War see Audrey Kurth Cronin's *Great Power Politics and the Struggle over Austria, 1945–1955* (Ithaca: Cornell University Press, 1986).

21. *FRUS 1952–1954*, Vol. II, pp. 325–326; Kennan's *Memoirs: 1950–1963*, p. 182.

22. "Summary of Points made in Discussion Following Presentation by Task Forces," July 16, 1953, p. 51, "Solarium Project," Freedom of Information Act request by author.

23. *Ibid.*, pp. 49–50.

24. *FRUS 1952–1954*, Vol. II, pp. 397, 434.

25. *Ibid.*, pp. 513–514.

26. Joseph Alsop's interview with Kennan, "The Soviet Union Will Never Recover," *The Saturday Evening Post*, November 24, 1956, pp. 117–118.

27. Kennan to Brainard Cheney, October 29, 1956, File "2-B 1956" in Box 28, Kennan Papers.

28. Interview of Kennan, March 1967, pp. 49–50.

29. Kennan's "Overdue Changes in Our Foreign Policy," *Harper's Magazine*, August 1956, p. 29.

30. John Bartlow's two-volume study stands as the most useful biography of Stevenson. See his *Adlai Stevenson of Illinois* (Garden City: Doubleday, 1976) and *Adlai Stevenson and the World* (Garden City: Doubleday, 1977).

31. Archibald MacLeish's address to the UN General Assembly, July 19, 1965, p. 3, Box 899, Stevenson Papers.

32. *Newsweek*, August 27, 1956.

33. See Kennan's "Remarks at Stevenson-for-President Committee," April 30, 1956, p. 9, File "1-C-56" in Box 19, Kennan Papers.

34. For more about the Finletter Group and Thomas Finletter see Bartlow, *Adlai Stevenson and the World*, pp. 82–89 and John Kenneth Galbraith, *A Life in Our Times* (Boston: Houghton Mifflin Company, 1981), pp. 313–315.

35. Stevenson to Kennan, March 31, 1956, Box 434, Stevenson Papers; Kennan to Stevenson, January 26, 1954, Box 401, Stevenson Papers.

36. See, for example, Kennan to Stevenson, September 9, 1954, and Stevenson to Kennan, September 11, 1954, both in Box 401, Stevenson Papers; *The Papers of Adlai E. Stevenson*, Vol. VI (Boston: Little, Brown and Company, 1976), pp. 85–87.

37. Kennan to Stevenson, March 28, 1956, p. 3, Box 434, Stevenson Papers.

38. Kennan to Thomas Finletter, April 12, 1956, Box 434, Stevenson Papers.

39. *Ibid.*

40. Bartlow, *Adlai Stevenson and the World,* pp. 297–298.

41. Thaddeus Machrowicz to Stevenson, May 10, 1956, Box 434, Stevenson Papers.

42. See Kennan to "Tom" Finletter, April 12, 1956, Box 434, Stevenson Papers.

43. Stevenson to Machrowicz, May 23, 1956 and Kennan to Lewis Stevens, October 8, 1956, both in Box 434, Stevenson Papers.

44. Kennan's memorandum, August 24, 1956; Lewis Stevens to Kennan, October 4, 1956; Kennan to Stevens, October 8, 1956—all in Box 434, Stevenson Papers. Also see Kennan to Stanley Norcum, November 1, 1956, File "2-B 1956" in Box 28, Kennan Papers.

45. Stevenson to Kennan, February 11, 1958, Box 750 Stevenson Papers; Kennan to Stevenson, January 31, 1960, Box 789, Stevenson Papers. In 1969, during the height of the Vietnam War and protests, and on the occasion of the unveiling of a bust of Stevenson's likeness in Princeton, Kennan offered this tribute: "The image of the man that we are here to honor needs no idealization. I can think, in fact, of no one out of the whole register of American political life during my own time whom I would rather have back with us again today, just as he was, with all his faults and human limitations—no one who would be a better antidote to all the hysteria and illnesses of our own day." See Kennan's remarks, November 9, 1969, File "1-B-167" in Box 14, Kennan Papers.

46. BBC Symposium, December 20, 1957, p. 1, File "1-B-63" in Box 7, Kennan Papers. Also see *FRUS 1955–1957,* Vol. IV, p. 227.

47. Walter Lippmann, "Mr. Kennan and Reappraisal in Europe," *The Atlantic,* April 1958, p. 33.

48. Kennan, *Russia, the Atom and the West,* pp. 14–15.

49. *Ibid.,* p. 54.

50. *Ibid.,* pp. 58–59.

51. *Ibid.,* p. 63.

52. *Ibid.,* pp. 64–65.

53. Oppenheimer to Kennan, December 19, 1957, Box 43, Oppenheimer Papers; Kennan's *Memoirs: 1950–1963,* pp. 267–268; Stevenson to Kennan, February 11, 1957, Box 750, Stevenson Papers.

54. Kennan, *Memoirs: 1950–1963,* p. 250. Also see Acheson's "The Illusion of Disengagement," *Foreign Affairs,* April 1958, pp. 371–382.

55. Raymond Aron, *On War* (New York: Norton, 1968), p. 133. Aron's *On War* is a classic and its "Postscript" is devoted to rebutting many of Kennan's ideas in the Reith talks. Also see Acheson's *Power and Diplomacy* (Cambridge: Harvard University Press, 1958), wherein he attacks "the illusion of German neutrality" and defends NATO's placing nuclear weapons in Europe.

56. BBC Symposium, December 20, 1957, p. 7, File "1-B-63" in Box 7, Kennan Papers.

57. Kennan "The Dialectics of Disengagement" (unused), Spring 1958, pp. 1–2, File "1-E-16" in Box 26, Kennan Papers.

58. *Ibid.,* pp. 2–3; BBC Symposium, December 20, 1957; Kennan's "Alternate Strategic Concepts and Policies for the U.S.," November 26, 1958, pp. 9–11, National War College Library; Kennan's "Disengagement Revisited," *Foreign Affairs,* January 1959; Kennan to Joseph Wheelan, July 3, 1959, File "2-B 1959" in Box 28, Kennan Papers; Kennan's "Russia, the Atom, and the West, 1959" in *The Listener,* October 29, 1959; Kennan's "Peaceful Coexistence: A Western View," *Foreign Affairs,* January 1960, pp. 180, 183; Kennan to W. W. Rostow, May 15, 1962, File "2-B 1962"; Kennan to Gerhard

Wetting, January 24, 1966, File "2-B 1966"; Kennan to Louis Halle, April 20, 1966, File "2-B-1966"; Kennan to Louis Halle, May 2, 1966 in File "2-B 1966"; Kennan to Hans Morgenthau, December 6, 1966 in File "2-B 1966," all in Box 28, Kennan Papers; Kennan's "A New Philosophy of Defense," *The New York Review of Books,* February 13, 1986, pp. 3–6 and his "Forward" to Gene Sharp's *Making Europe Unconquerable* (Cambridge: Ballinger, 1986).

59. For more about NATO and Warsaw see the following: D. M. O. Miller et al., *The Balance of Power: An Illustrated Assessment Comparing the Weapons and Capabilities of NATO and the Warsaw Pact* (New York: St. Martin's Press, 1981); Jacquelyn Davis et al., *Soviet Theater Strategy: Implications for NATO* (Washington, DC: United States Strategic Institute, 1978); NATO Information Service, *The Atlantic Alliance and the Warsaw-Pact: A Comparative Study* (Brussels: NATO Information Service, 1970); George Quester, *Defense over Offense in Central Europe* (Palo Alto, Calif.: Aspen Institute for Humanistic Studies, 1978); United States Congressional Budget Office, *Assessing the NATO/Warsaw Pact Military Balance* (Washington, DC: Government Printing Office, 1977).

60. In a letter (January 27, 1987) to the author, Kennan continued his argument on behalf of the militias concept. He wrote:

> You cite, as an argument against the civil resistance concept I had put together in the fourth of the Reith lectures, the fact that during World War II such resistance 'contributed little to the defeat of German arms. . . .' I would like to point out that in none of the respective occupied countries had there been anything resembling a systemic preparation for such resistance before the occupation was established. I had personally been in most of these countries while they were under German occupation, and I was struck by the fact that their resistance, such as it was, would have been far more effective had it been properly organized and prepared in advance than it could possibly be when it had to be mounted under the eyes and the guns of the Germans. It was in fact precisely the first-hand observation of the relative failure of these efforts, and the great and unnecessary sacrifices they involved, that led me to the thoughts I attempted, so unwisely and in so incomplete a manner, to convey to the BBC's listeners.

61. Kennan, *Russia, the Atom and the West,* p. 14.

62. Kennan's "Speech to the Pennsylvania State Bar Association," July 16, 1953, Box 383, Stevenson Papers.

63. There is a very large literature about McCarthyism. Some of the better works on the subject include Ellen Schrecker, *No Ivory Tower: McCarthyism and the Universities* (New York: Oxford University Press, 1986); Richard Freeland, *The Truman Doctrine and the Origins of McCarthyism* (New York: Schocken Books, 1974); Walter Goodman, *The Committee: The Extraordinary Career of The House Committee on Un-American Activities* (New York: Farrar, Straus and Giroux, 1968); Richard Rovere, *Senator Joe McCarthy* (New York: Meridian Books, 1960).

64. Kennan, *Memoirs: 1950–1963,* pp. 190–228 and Kennan to Charles Thayer, April 20, 1959, Thayer Papers.

65. Kennan to Thayer, April 20, 1959.

66. Robert Oppenheimer to Kennan, December 19, 1957, Box 43, Oppenheimer Papers.

67. Kennan to Oppenheimer, date not indicated, Box 43, Oppenheimer Papers.

68. Kennan to Oppenheimer, June 26, 1966, Box 43, Oppenheimer Papers.

69. See *In the Matter of J. Robert Oppenheimer: Transcript of Hearing Before Personnel Security Board* (Washington, DC: US Government Printing Office, 1954), pp. 350–372.

70. Kennan, *Memoirs: 1950–1963,* p. 20. Also see Joseph Alsop and Stewart Alsop "We Accuse" in *Harper's,* October 1954, pp. 25–45.

71. See Kennan's "Remarks at Stevenson-for-President Committee," April 30, 1956, File "1-C-56" in Box 19, Kennan Papers; Kennan to *Time,* December 4, 1952, File "1-

B-20" in Box 2, Kennan Papers; Kennan to *National Review,* April 11, 1960, File "1-E-21" in Box 27, Kennan Papers; Kennan's "The Illusion of Security" in *The Atlantic,* August 1954; Kennan to Loy Henderson, January 24, 1955, File "K" in Box 2, Henderson Papers; Kennan's "Where Do You Stand on Communism?" *The New York Times Magazine,* May 27, 1951.

72. Kennan's "Where Do You Stand on Communism?" p. 55.

73. Kennan's "The Illusion of Security," p. 32.

74. *Ibid.,* p. 34.

75. Kennan, *Memoirs: 1950–1963,* p. 223.

76. *In the Matter of J. Robert Oppenheimer,* pp. 354–355; Yeats, "The Second Coming" in *The Collected Poems of W. B. Yeats* (New York: MacMillan, 1970), p. 185; Kennan's *Memoirs: 1950–1963,* p. 228.

77. Kennan's "Overdue Charges in Our Foreign Policy," *Harper's Magazine,* August 1956.

78. Kennan to Thomas Finletter, April 12, 1956.

Chapter 11. America and the Third World

1. George Kennan, *Realities of American Foreign Policy* (Princeton: Princeton University Press, 1954), p. 56.

2. Kennan to J. Tinbergen, March 10, 1955, File "2-B 1955" in Box 31, Kennan Papers.

3. *Ibid.*

4. George Kennan, *The Cloud of Danger* (New York: Little, Brown and Company, 1977), p. 32.

5. *Ibid.,* p. 33.

6. George Kennan, *Russia, the Atom and the West* (New York: Harper and Brothers, 1957), p. 112.

7. Kennan, *Realities,* p. 53.

8. Kennan, *Russia, the Atom and the West,* pp. 74–75.

9. Kennan to Carlos Romulo, November 14, 1956, File "2-B 1956" in Box 31, Kennan Papers.

10. Kennan to Norman Graebner, February 26, 1960, File "2-B 1960" in Box 31, Kennan Papers.

11. Kennan, *Russia, the Atom and the West,* pp. 71–73.

12. *SDPPSP* 1948, PPS 19, January 19, 1948, p. 37.

13. *Ibid.,* p. 41.

14. *Ibid.,* p. 42.

15. *Ibid.,* PPS 19/1 January 29, 1948, p. 68.

16. *Ibid.,* PPS 21 February 11, 1948, p. 87.

17. NSC 47, May 17, 1949, NSC File, Modern Military Branch, NA.

18. See NSC 47/1, September 1, 1949, and NSC 47/2, October 17, 1949, NSC File, Modern Military Branch, NA. Also see Steven Spiegel, *The Other Arab-Israeli Conflict* (Chicago: University of Chicago Press, 1985), Chapter 2; Robert Donovan, *Conflict and Crisis* (New York: Norton, 1977), Chapter 34.

19. Kennan's Memorandum to Acheson, January 22, 1952, File "1-D-19" in Box 24, Kennan Papers.

20. *Ibid.*

21. *Ibid.*

22. Berry's Memorandum, February 23, 1952, File "1-D-19" in Box 24, Kennan Papers.

23. Kennan's Memorandum to Bohlen, April 3, 1952, File "1-D-19" in Box 24, Kennan Papers.

24. Kennan's letter to the *Washington Post,* November 3, 1956.

25. Kennan's "Certain Long Term Implications of Suez," October 17, 1956, File "1-C-60" in Box 19, Kennan Papers. This piece was actually delivered as a speech at Johns Hopkins University and, by Kennan's later admission, was one of the most important statements he ever made about the West and the Third World.

26. *Ibid.*

27. *Ibid.*

28. *Ibid.*

29. *Ibid.*

30. *Ibid.*

31. *Ibid.*

32. *Ibid.*

33. See the following for analyses of the US position regarding Suez: Herman Finer, *Dulles over Suez: The Theory and Practice of His Diplomacy* (Chicago: Quadrangle Books, 1964); Donald Neff, *Warriors at Suez* (New York: Linden Press, 1981); C. L. Cooper, *The Lion's Last Roar: Suez 1956* (New York: Harper and Row, 1978); Spiegel, *The Other Arab-Israeli Conflict,* Chapter 3.

34. Kennan to Charles Thayer, July 17, 1958, Thayer Papers.

35. Kennan, *The Cloud of Danger,* pp. 80–91.

36. Walter LaFeber, *Inevitable Revolutions: The United States in Central America* (New York: Norton, 1984), pp. 107–110.

37. *SDPPSP* 1948, PPS 24, March 15, 1948; PPS 47, December 10, 1948, pp. 135–141, 523–526.

38. *Ibid.*, PPS 26, March 22, 1948, pp. 150–160.

39. *Ibid.*, PPS 63, September 20, 1949, pp. 168–182.

40. George Kennan, *Memoirs: 1925–1950* (Boston: Little Brown and Company, 1967), pp. 476–484.

41. Kennan's "Report of South American Trip," March 29, 1950, p. 5, File "1-C-5" in Box 18, Kennan Papers. Kennan's report also appears in *FRUS 1950,* Vol. II, pp. 598–624.

42. *Ibid.*, pp. 29–32.

43. *Ibid.*, pp. 26–27.

44. Kennan's "Report to Secretary of State," April 1950, File "1-D-2" in Box 24, Kennan Papers.

45. The single best account of Eisenhower's policy in Guatemala is Richard Immerman, *The CIA in Guatemala: The Foreign Policy of Intervention* (Austin: University of Texas Press, 1982).

46. Kennan to Edmund Walsh, March 24, 1964, File "2-B 1964" in Box 31, Kennan Papers.

47. Kennan, *The Cloud of Danger*, p. 67.

48. *SDPPSP* 1948, PPS 25, March 22, 1948; PPS 30, June 4, 1948, pp. 142–149; 246–254.

49. Kennan's talk to US-South Africa Leader Exchange Program, November 1, 1967, File "1-C-156" in Box 22, Kennan Papers.

50. Kennan to Waldamar Nielsen, October 19, 1967, File "2-B 1967" in Box 31, Kennan Papers.

51. *Ibid.*

52. *Ibid.*

53. *Ibid*. Also see Kennan's "Hazardous Courses in Southern Africa," *Foreign Affairs*, January 1971, pp. 218–236.

54. Kennan's talk to US-South Africa Leader Exchange Program, November 1, 1967, File "1-C-156" in Box 22, Kennan Papers.

55. Mark Orkin, "Black Attitudes to Disinvestment: The Real Story." This essay prepared (September 1985) for the Community Agency for Social Enquiry in Johannesburg and the Institute for Black Research at the University of Natal showed that 73 percent of South Africa's blacks supported some form of disinvestment as a means of ending apartheid. Half preferred "conditional" disinvestment and 24 percent urged "total" disinvestment.

56. Kennan, *The Cloud of Danger*, p. 78.

57. See Sanford Ungar and Peter Vale, "Why Constructive Engagement Failed" in *Foreign Affairs*, Winter 1985–1986, pp. 234–258.

58. Kennan, *The Cloud of Danger*, pp. 70, 73, 75.

59. Kennan, *Memoirs: 1925–1950*, p. 184.

60. Kennan's Official Notes, March 29, 1950, File "1-C-5" in Box 18, Kennan Papers.

61. Kennan's "Unfinished Paper," September 1951, File "1-D-18" in Box 24, Kennan Papers.

62. Kennan, *The Cloud of Danger*, pp. 38–39.

63. Gordon Merriam's "The Jewish Minority in the United States," May 27, 1949, pp. 7, 12, PPS Papers, RG 59, NA. Also see Michael Hunt, *Ideology and US Foreign Policy* (New Haven: Yale University Press, 1987); Robert Beisner, *Twelve Against Empire* (New York: McGraw-Hill, 1968).

64. Robert Tucker believes that Western policies aimed at satisfying Third World grievances will not lead to greater justice and equality, but will increase international political disorder. See his *The Inequality of Nations* (New York: Basic Books, 1977); Gaddis Smith, *Morality, Reason and Power: American Diplomacy in the Carter Years* (New York: Hill and Wang, 1986.

65. Kennan's address to Congress for Cultural Freedom, Milan, September 18, 1955, File "1-B-43" in Box 5, Kennan Papers.

66. "Report of South American Trip," March 29, 1950, p. 25.

Chapter 12. War and Protest

1. See *SDPPSP* 1949, PPS 51, March 29, 1949, pp. 32–58; Michael Schaller, *The American Occupation of Japan*, (New York: Norton, 1984), pp. 158–163; New York Times, *The Pentagon Papers* (New York: Bantam Books, 1971), pp. 1–7; Stanley Karnow, *Vietnam* (New York: Penguin Books, 1984), pp. 128–205.

2. Kennan's "America's Day Speech," August 24, 1968, File "1-C-162" in Box 22, Kennan Papers.

3. Kennan to Sir Llewellyn Woodward, March 4, 1965, File "2-B 1965" in Box 31, Kennan Papers.

4. Kennan's "A Policy for the Far East," April 1965, File "1-B-134" in Box 11, Kennan Papers.

5. Kennan to Reverend Sloan Coffin, August 27, 1965, File "2-B 1965" in Box 31, Kennan Papers.

6. Kennan's essay in *Outlook, Washington Post,* December 12, 1965.

7. "New Poll on Vietnam," *The New Republic*, March 26, 1966, p. 9.

8. "Kennan on Vietnam," *The New Republic*, February 26, 1966, p. 20.

9. *Ibid.*, p. 22.

10. *Ibid.*

11. Kennan to Klaus Knorr, May 3, 1966, File "2-B 1966" in Box 31, Kennan Papers.

12. Kennan to John Hughes, May 31, 1966, File "2-B 1966" in Box 31, Kennan Papers.

13. Kennan to John Crocker, undated, probably October 1967, File "2-B 1967" in Box 31, Kennan Papers.

14. In defense of Kennan's position one could counter that China deployed as many as 50,000 men in North Vietnam. These included mostly rail and road engineering units, but also three anti-aircraft divisions, all of which were subject to American bombing and suffered casualties. The Chinese also constructed a massive redoubt northwest of Hanoi that numbered 185 five buildings and a 5,000-foot long runway and it was protected by anti-aircraft artillery. One could thus conclude, as did Kennan, that Peking's support of and commitment to Hanoi was such that the Chinese would not have cut and run in the face of a US invasion; to have so acted in the 1960s when they had accepted battle under worse domestic circumstances in the 1950s was not credible.

I still believe, however, that the disruptive impact of the Cultural Revolution on Chinese society, the fact that the Vietnamese-China border is less important to Peking than the Korean-Manchurian border, and the general level of unpreparedness of the PLA in the 1960s versus the veteran, victorious PLA that prevailed in the Chinese civil war argue in favor of Chinese restraint had the Americans marched north toward Hanoi. In the end, of course, neither interpretation can be proven; mercifully, the United States did not launch such an invasion. (My thanks here to an anonymous reviewer.)

15. This and the preceding quotes are in Kennan to Arthur Schlesinger, Jr., October 17, 1967, File "2-B 1967" in Box 31, Kennan Papers.

16. Kennan to John Crocker; Kennan to Arthur Schlesinger, Jr.

17. George Kennan, *Memoirs: 1925–1950* (Boston: Little, Brown and Company, 1967), p. 437.

18. Kennan's remarks introducing Eugene McCarthy, February 29, 1968, File "1-B-158" in Box 14, Kennan Papers.

19. Kennan's "Negotiation Now," November 19, 1967, File "1-C-158" in Box 22, Kennan Papers; for one of the best accounts of just war theory see Michael Walzer's *Just and Unjust Wars* (New York: Basic Books, 1977).

20. See Telford Taylor, *Nuremberg and Vietnam: An American Tragedy* (New York: Bantam Books, 1971); Bertrand Russell, *War Crimes in Vietnam* (London: Allen and Unwin, 1967); Frank Browning and Dorothy Forman (eds.), *The Wasted Nations: Report of the International Commission of Enquiry into United States Crimes in Indochina* (New York: Harper Colophon Books, 1972); Virginia Held, Sidney Morgenbesser, Thomas Nagel (eds.), *Philosophy, Morality, and International Affairs* (New York: Oxford University Press, 1974).

21. Kennan's remarks introducing Eugene McCarthy.

22. George Kennan, *Democracy and the Student Left* (Boston: Little, Brown and Company, 1968), p. 19.

23. Kennan's "Education for What?" March 3, 1960, File "1-C-95" in Box 20, Kennan Papers.

24. Kennan, *Democracy*, p. 9.

25. *Ibid.*, p. 19.

26. Kennan's "America's Day Speech."

27. Kennan's "America after Vietnam," June 1, 1968 (Williamsburg, Va.: private printing, 1968), p. 10.

28. *Ibid.*, p. 8.

29. Kennan's "America's Day Speech."

30. Kennan to David Horowitz, January 17, 1966, File "2-B 1966" in Box 31, Kennan Papers.

31. Kennan to Gar Alperovitz, undated, File "2-B 1965" in Box 31, Kennan Papers.

32. Kennan to Theodore Sands, March 16, 1970, File "1-C-159" in Box 22, Kennan Papers.

33. *Ibid.*

34. Kennan to Paul Kattenburg, April 11, 1970, File "1-C-159" in Box 22, Kennan Papers.

35. Miscellaneous material on revisionist scholarship, File "1-C-159" in Box 22, Kennan Papers.

36. See Chapter 4 of Richard Melanson's *Writing History and Making Policy* (Lanham, Md.: University Press of America, 1983) and Part 6 of Jerald Combs's *American Diplomatic History: Two Centuries of Changing Interpretations* (Berkeley, University of California Press, 1983) for an excellent review of the debates involving Cold War revisionism and its critics. The following books constitute a fair sample of revisionist scholarship: Diane Clemens, *Yalta* (London: Oxford University Press, 1970); Lloyd Gardner, *Architects of Illusion* (Chicago: Quadrangle Books, 1970); Gar Alperovitz, *Atomic Diplomacy: Hiroshima and Potsdam* (New York: Vintage Books, 1967); Gabriel Kolko, *The Politics of War* (New York: Random House, 1968); Walter LaFeber, *America, Russia, and the Cold War* (New York: John Wiley and Sons, 1967). Maddox's campaign against the revisionists was joined by various scholars, including Robert W. Tucker and Charles Maier. See respectively *The Radical Left and American Foreign Policy* (Baltimore: Johns Hopkins University Press, 1971) and "Revisionism and the Interpretation of Cold War Origins" in R. Abrams and L. W. Levine (eds.), *The Shaping of Twentieth Century America: Interpretative Essays* (Cambridge: Harvard University Press, 1971).

37. Kennan's "America after Vietnam," pp. 9–10.

38. *Ibid.*, p. 12.

39. Kennan's "The US, Its Problems, Impact, and Image in the World," December 2, 1968, File "1-B-169" in Box 15, Kennan Papers.

40. George Kennan, et al., *Encounters with Kennan: The Great Debate* (London: Frank Cass and Company, Ltd., 1979), p. 4.

41. Kennan's unused material for *Memoirs*, "Norway," File "1-E-28 1970" in Box 27, Kennan Papers.

42. Kennan's "America after Vietnam," p. 12.

43. Kennan to Dean Frank, March 23, 1964, File "2-B 1964" in Box 31, Kennan Papers.

44. Kennan's "The US, Its Problems, Impact, And Image in the World."

45. Kennan et al., *Encounters with Kennan*, p. 28; also see Kennan's "Forward" in Norman Cousins, *The Pathology of Power* (New York: Norton, 1987).

46. Kennan et al., *Encounters with Kennan*, pp. 29–33. Also see Barton Gellman's very good Chapter 4 in his *Contending with Kennan* (New York: Praeger Publishers, 1984).

47. "Kennan on Vietnam," *The New Republic*, pp. 20–23; Kennan's unused material for *Memoirs*, "Epilogue," File "1-E-28 1970" in Box 27, Kennan Papers.

48. Kennan, "Epilogue."

49. George Kennan, *The Cloud of Danger* (Boston: Little, Brown and Company, 1977), pp. 95–96.

50. W. B. Yeats, "A Prayer for My Daughter" in *The Collected Poems of W. B. Yeats* (New York: Macmillan, 1970), p. 187.

51. Kennan's unused material for *Memoirs*, "Epilogue."

52. *Ibid.*

53. *Ibid.* Also see Kennan et al., *Encounters with Kennan*, p. 33. For a somewhat different assessment than mine of Kennan and Vietnam see Walter Hixson's thoughtful "Containment on the Perimeter: George F. Kennan and Vietnam," *Diplomatic History*, forthcoming.

Chapter 13. Detente and the Nuclear Arms Race

1. See, for example, Paul Hollander's "Et tu, George Kennan? The Old Cold Warrior Makes Anti-communism the Real Enemy," *Prospect*, September 1984, pp. 9–12.

2. Kennan's *Memoirs: 1950–1963* (New York: Pantheon Books, 1972), p. 326; *The Nuclear Delusion* (New York: Pantheon Books, 1983), pp. 41–42; "Is Detente Worth Saving?" in Robert Pranger (ed.), *Detente and Defense* (Washington, DC: American Enterprise Institute, 1977), p. 234; Robert Tucker and William Watts (eds.), *Beyond Containment: US Foreign Policy in Transition* (Washington, DC: Potomac Associates, 1973), pp. 15–16.

3. John Gaddis, *Strategies of Containment* (New York: Oxford University Press, 1982), pp. 280–281, 283, 291, 307–308.

4. Tucker and Watts, *Beyond Containment*, p. 6.

5. *Ibid.*, p. 9.

6. For an encyclopedic account of detente see Raymond Garthoff, *Detente and Confrontation: American-Soviet Relations from Nixon to Reagan* (Washington, DC: The Brookings Institution, 1985). Also see the following: Alexander George (ed.), *Managing US-Soviet Rivalry: Problems of Crisis Prevention* (Boulder, Colo.: Westview Press, 1983); Henry Kissinger, *White House Years* (Boston: Little, Brown and Company, 1979); Kissinger's *Years of Upheaval* (Boston: Little, Brown and Company, 1982); Richard Nixon, *Memoirs* (New York: Grosset and Dunlap, 1978).

7. Kennan, *The Nuclear Delusion*, p. 43.

8. *Ibid.*, p. 45. Also see the pertinent sections in Kennan's *The Cloud of Danger* (Boston: Little, Brown, and Company, 1977).

9. Martin Herz (ed.), *Decline of the West? George Kennan and His Critics* (Washington, DC: Ethics and Policy Center, Georgetown University, 1978), pp. 28–29.

10. *Ibid.*, pp. 47, 62–69, 72–74; Henry Fairlie, The Special Senility of the Diplomat: Mr. X²" in *The New Republic*, December 24, 1977, pp. 9–11; Paul Seabury, "George Kennan Vs. Mr. 'X': The Great Container Springs a Leak" in *The New Republic*, December 16, 1981, pp. 17–20; William Buckley, "George Kennan's Bomb" in *National Review*, April 4, 1980, p. 432.

11. Pranger, *Detente and Defense*, p. 248.

12. See the following of Solzhenitsyn's: *A World Split Apart* (New York: Harper and Row, 1978); *Detente* (New Brunswick, N.J.: Transaction Books, 1980); *Nobel Lecture* (New York: Farrar, Straus and Giroux, 1972).

13. Herz, *Decline of the West: George Kennan and His Critics*, p. 8.

14. *Ibid.*, pp. 14–15, 32–33, 40–48, 114–131.

15. The following are representative: Herz, *Decline of the West? Kennan and His Critics*, pp. 49–60; George Kennan's *The Nuclear Delusion*, pp. 127–147; "A Risky US Equation" in the *New York Times*, February 18, 1981; "Two Views of the Soviet Problem" in the *New Yorker*, November 2, 1981, pp. 54–58; "America's Unstable Soviet Policy" in the *Atlantic Monthly*, November 1982, pp. 71–80.

16. Kennan's "Was This Really Mature Statesmanship?" in the *New York Times*, February 1, 1980.

17. Kennan, *The Nuclear Delusion*, pp. 165–167; "The Kennan-Reagan Axis," *Wall Street Journal*, February 21, 1980.

18. Kennan, "Jaruselski's Course," *New York Times*, January 5, 1982; "The Polish Crisis Could Be a Watershed," *New York Times*, February 14, 1982.

19. "Regrets and Promises" in the *Washington Post*, November 16, 1983; Kennan's "Breaking the Spell" in the *New Yorker*, October 3, 1983, pp. 44–53. Kennan's "Reflections (Soviet-American Relations)" in the *New Yorker*, September 24, 1984, pp. 55–80.

20. Kennan's talk to the Kennan Institute for Advanced Russian Studies, November 13, 1986. Also see Kennan's "The Gorbachev Prospect" in *The New York Review of Books,* January 21, 1988, and "George Kennan and Josef Skvorecky: An Exchange on Gorbachev" in *The New York Review of Books,* March 17, 1988.

21. Kennan to the *New York Times,* January 5, 1987.

22. Norman Podhoretz, "The Rise and Fall of Containment: Informal Remarks" in Terry Deibel and John Gaddis (eds.), *Containment: Concept and Policy,* Vol. II (Washington, DC: National Defense University Press, 1986), p. 716; Paul Hollander, "Et tu, George Kennan?" pp. 9–12; Paul Seabury and Patrick Glynn, "Kennan: The Historian as Fatalist" in *The National Interest,* Winter 1985–1986, p. 111; Max Lerner, "Two Paradigms for Russia" in the *New Republic,* March 10, 1982, p. 11.

23. "Opposing Views: How Real Is the Soviet Threat" in *US News and World Report,* March 10, 1980, p. 33.

24. George Kennan, *The Fateful Alliance* (New York: Pantheon, 1984), p. 258. Other scholars in addition to Kennan were impressed during the early 1980s by similarities between their era and that of 1914. See, for example, two excellent volumes of *International Security,* Summer 1984 and Fall 1986.

25. George Kennan, *Memoirs: 1925–1950* (Boston: Little, Brown and Company, 1967), pp. 435–437.

26. *FRUS 1945,* Vol. V, p. 885.

27. Kennan's *Memoirs: 1925–1950* p. 296. Also see Wilson Miscamble, *George Kennan, the Foreign Policy Staff and American Foreign Policy, 1947–1950* (PhD dissertation, University of Notre Dame, 1980), p. 198; Gregg Herken, "The Great Foreign Policy Fight" in *American Heritage,* April–May 1986, p. 71.

28. Kennan's notes on Clark Clifford's "American Relations with the Soviet Union," September 16, 1946, p. 6, Elsey Papers. Also see Gregg Herken, *The Winning Weapon* (New York: Vintage Books, 1982), p. 264, and Barton Bernstein, "The Quest for Security: American Foreign Policy and International Control of Atomic Energy, 1942–1946" in the *Journal of American History,* March 1974, p. 1043.

29. Lawrence Freedman, "The First Two Generations of Nuclear Strategists" in Peter Paret (ed.), *Makers of Modern Strategy* (Princeton: Princeton University Press, 1986), p. 737.

30. *SDPPSP* 1947, PPS 7, April 21, 1947, pp. 76–90.

31. *Ibid.,* PPS 11, October 24, 1947, pp. 118–123; *FRUS 1949,* Vol. I, pp. 419–428; Richard Hewlett and Francis Duncan, *A History of the United States Atomic Energy Commission,* Vol. II (University Park: Pennsylvania State University Press, 1969), pp. 270–279, 300–306.

32. Thomas Etzold and John Gaddis (eds.), *Containment: Documents on American Policy and Strategy, 1945–1950* (New York: Columbia University Press, 1978), pp. 339–343; *SDPPSP* 1949 PPS 50, Annex A, March 22, 1949, pp. 30–31.

33. *SDPPSP* 1948, PPS 33, June 23, 1948, pp. 286–288; *SDPPSP* 1949, PPS 58, August 16, 1949, pp. 122–123; Kennan to Dean Acheson, December 14, 1949, PPS Papers, RG 59, NA.

34. Herbert York, *The Advisors: Oppenheimer Teller and the Superbomb* (San Francisco: W. H. Freeman and Company, 1975), pp. 58–60; Herken, *The Winning Weapon,* pp. 305–308.

35. Winston Churchill cited in McGeorge Bundy, "The Missed Chance to Stop the H-Bomb" in the *New York Review of Books,* May 13, 1982, p. 13.

36. York, *The Advisors,* pp. 158–159.

37. Kennan's notes, November 18, 1949, Box 43, Oppenheimer Papers.

38. Kennan, *Memoirs: 1925–1950*, p. 472.

39. *FRUS 1950*, Vol. I, pp. 22–44 has about half of Kennan's memorandum. Notes following refer to the fuller "Memorandum: International Control of Atomic Energy," January 20, 1950, in Folder 11, Box 7, Wright Papers.

40. *Ibid.*, pp. 43–44, 65.

41. *Ibid.*, pp. 37–38.

42. *Ibid.*, pp. 56–57.

43. *Ibid.*, pp. 67–68.

44. *Ibid.*, p. 70. Michael Carver, "Conventional Warfare in the Nuclear Age" in Paret, *Makers of Modern Strategy*, p. 814.

45. *FRUS 1950*, Vol. I, p. 9.

46. *Ibid.*, pp. 13–17.

47. David McLellan, *Dean Acheson* (New York: Dodd, Mead and Company, 1976), p. 176.

48. Herken, *The Winning Weapon*, p. 320.

49. *FRUS 1950*, Vol. I, p. 165; "Unfinished Paper," September 1951, File "1-D-18" in Box 24, Kennan Papers.

50. Kennan, *Memoirs: 1950–1963*, p. 111.

51. Kennan to Arnold Wolfers, January 26, 1954, Stevenson Papers.

52. See for example: Kennan's *Realities of American Foreign Policy* (Princeton: Princeton University Press, 1954), p. 84–85; "Seminar Paper on Industrial Society," September 20–26, 1959, File "1-E-19" in Box 26, Kennan Papers; "Alternate Strategic Concepts and Policies for US," November 26, 1958, File "1-C-84" in Box 20, Kennan Papers.

53. Kennan to Paul Ramsey, November 11, 1959, File "2-B.1959" in Box 28, Kennan Papers.

54. Kennan's "Comment on the Round Table Discussion of the Congress for Cultural Freedom," January 1958, File "1-B-64" in Box 7, Kennan Papers.

55. Kennan's "Seminar Paper on Industrial Society," September 20–26, 1959.

56. *Ibid.* For more on Hook and his debate with Bertrand Russell over "red versus dead" see Sidney Hook, *Political Power and Personal Freedom: Critical Studies in Democracy, Communism, and Civil Rights* (New York: Criterion books, 1959), pp. 421–445.

57. Kennan to General Earle Wheeler, November 16, 1965, File "2-B.1965 in Box 28, Kennan Papers; "dinner talk" at Woodrow Wilson School, November 5, 1966, File "1-C-152" in Box 22, Kennan Papers; Kennan to Louis Halle, April 20, 1966 in File "2-B.1966" in Box 28, Kennan Papers.

58. Kennan's unused "Epilogue," File "1-E-28" 1970, in Box 27, Kennan Papers.

59. Kennan, *The Cloud of Danger* (Boston: Little, Brown and Company, 1977), pp. 203–204.

60. McGeorge Bundy, George Kennan et al., "Nuclear Weapons and the Atlantic Alliance," *Foreign Affairs*, Spring 1982, pp. 753–766.

61. William Bundy (ed.), *The Nuclear Controversy* (New York: New American Library, 1985), pp. 67–76; Paul Nitze, "A-Arms and NATO," *New York Times*, April 3, 1982; Tom Wicker, "The Other Balance," *New York Times*, April 6, 1982.

62. Kennan, *The Cloud of Danger*, p. 206.

63. Kennan, "A Modest Proposal" in *The New York Review of Books*, July 16, 1981, pp. 14–16.

64. *Ibid.*

65. Leon Sigal, "Kennan's Cuts" in *Foreign Policy*, Fall 1981, pp. 70–81; Tom Wicker, "A Collision Course" in the *New York Times*, May 26, 1981; Don Oberdorfer, "George Kennan's 30-Year Nightmare of Our Final Folly" in the *Washington Post*, May 24, 1981;

Roscoe Drummond, "Kennan Stirs Things Up Usefully" in the *Christian Science Monitor*, June 19, 1981.

66. Kennan, "World Peace Through Law—Two Decades Later" in *Vital Speeches*, December 15, 1981, pp. 137–140. Also see "George Kennan: A Critical Voice," Blackwood Production Inc., 1982, p. 1 of script; Bundy, Kennan et al., "Back from the Brink" in *The Atlantic*, August 1986, pp. 35–41. Bundy, Kennan et al., "The President's Choice: Star Wars or Arms Control" in William Hyland (ed.), *The Reagan Foreign Policy* (New York: New American Library, 1987).

67. Kennan, "Certain World Problems in Christian Perspective," January 27, 1959, File "1-B-78" in Box 27, Kennan Papers.

68. Kennan to Eugene Rabinowitch, September 11, 1956, File "2-B 1956" in Box 28, Kennan Papers.

69. Kennan, *The Cloud of Danger*, p. 207.

70. Kennan, "A Christian's View of the Arms Race" in *Theology Today*, Summer 1982, p. 166. Also see Kennan, "Toward Peace on Two Fronts" in *Christianity and Crisis*, December 13, 1982, pp. 398–402.

71. "George Kennan: A Critical Voice," pp. 40–41.

72. Richard Current (ed.), *The Political Thought of Abraham Lincoln* (Indianapolis: Bobbs-Merrill, 1981), p. 234.

Chapter 14. Diplomacy and the Politics of Amelioration

1. Kennan to Professor Mead, 1950, File "2-A-1950" in Box 29, Kennan Papers; Kennan to Robert Lovett, August 22, 1947, PPS Papers, RG 59, NA; George Kennan et al., *Encounters with Kennan: The Great Debate* (London: Frank Cass and Company, Ltd., 1979), p. 82.

2. Kennan, "Statement for National Book Awards," March 6, 1968, File "1-C-161" in Box 22, Kennan Papers; Raymond Aron (ed.), *World Technology and Human Destiny* (Ann Arbor: University of Michigan Press, 1963), pp. 191–195; Kennan, "Sermon," March 17, 1963, File "1-C-120" in Box 20, Kennan Papers; Kennan, *American Diplomacy* (Chicago: University of Chicago Press, expanded edition 1984), pp. 3–20. Also see Richard Fox, *Reinhold Niebuhr* (New York: Pantheon Books, 1985), p. 238. Fox reports that while Kennan did not recall (1980) describing Niebuhr as "the father of us all," he had an abiding appreciation for the theologian's "philosophical perspective."

3. Aron, *World Technology*, p. 123; Terry Deibel and John Gaddis (eds.), *Containment: Concept and Policy* (Washington, DC: National Defense University Press, 1986), p. 31.

4. Kennan, "Internatonal Political Relations—Where We Are Today—Where Are We Going," August 29, 1950, Bland Papers.

5. Aron, *World Technology*, p. 191; Kennan's "talk" for Mount Kisco Conference, Summer 1963, File "1-C-129" in Box 21, Kennan Papers; Kennan, "Princeton Alumni Day Speech," February 21, 1953, File "1-B-22" in Box 2, Kennan Papers; Martin Herz (ed.), *Decline of the West? George Kennan and His Critics* (Washington, DC: Ethics and Public Policy Center, Georgetown University, 1978), p. 36.

6. Kennan, "The Relation of Religion to Government" in *The Princeton Seminary Bulletin*, Winter 1969, p. 43.

7. Kennan et al., *Encounters with Kennan*, p. 9; Kennan, "Sermon," March 17, 1963; Kennan, "Sermon," April 15, 1962, File "1-C-115" in Box 20, Kennan Papers; Kennan, "Christianity Reexamined," December 6, 1953, File "1-B-31" in Box 3, Kennan Papers; Kennan to Arnold Toynbee, April 7, 1952, File "1952" in Box 29, Kennan Papers; Michael Smith, *Realist Thought from Weber to Kissinger* (Baton Rouge: Louisiana State University Press, 1986), p. 139; Kennan, "Morality and Foreign Policy" in *Foreign Affairs*, Winter 1985/1986, p. 212.

8. Kennan, *American Diplomacy*, pp. 95–103; Kennan, "Princeton Alumni Speech," February 21, 1953; Kennan, "American Capitalist Democracy in a Collectivist Environment," May 2, 1947, p. 6, PPS Papers, RG 59, NA.

9. Kennan to the *New York Times*, August 11, 1952, File "1-E-3" in Box 26, Kennan Papers; Barry Rubin, *Secrets of State* (New York: Oxford University Press, 1987), p. 42.

10. Arthur Schlesinger, Jr., *The Cycles of American History* (Boston: Houghton Mifflin Company, 1986), p. 72.

11. Kennan to James Shotwell, January 11, 1957, File "2-B 1957" in Box 28, Kennan Papers; Kennan to George Kateb, December 15, 1967, File "2-B 1967" in Box 28, Kennan Papers.

12. Kennan to Senator Ralph Flanders, November 30, 1956, File "2-B 1956" in Box 28, Kennan Papers; Kennan, "Morality and Foreign Policy," 1957, File "1-E-14" in Box 26, Kennan Papers.

13. Herz, *Decline of the West?* p. 114.

14. Kennan to the *New York Times*, August 11, 1952; Kennan, "Morality and Foreign Policy," 1957.

15. Kennan, "Morality and Foreign Policy," Winter 1985/1986, p. 210.

16. Kennan, "Morality and Foreign Policy," 1957; Kennan, *Realities of American Foreign Policy* (Princeton: Princeton University Press, 1954), pp. 47–50.

17. Kennan to Louis Halle, January 3, 1956, File "2-B 1956" in Box 28, Kennan Papers.

18. Kennan, "Morality and Foreign Policy," 1957.

19. Kennan, "International Exchange in the Arts," *Congressional Record*, January 27, 1956; Kennan, "Commencement, 1955," *Social Research*, Summer 1955; Kennan to Dean Frank, March 23, 1964, File "2-B 1964" in Box 31, Kennan Papers; "unused material for memoirs," 1970, File "1-E-28 1970" in Box 27, Kennan Papers; Kennan, "The US, Its Problems, Impact and Image in the World," December 2, 1968, File "1-B-169" in Box 15, Kennan Papers; Kennan, "In the American Mirror," *The New York Review of Books*, November 6, 1986; Kennan's "talk" for Mount Kisco Conference, summer 1963; Stanley Hoffmann, *Gulliver's Troubles or the Setting of American Foreign Policy* (New York: McGraw-Hill, 1968), p. 479; Kennan, "Morality and Foreign Policy"; Kennan, "The Origins of Containment" in Deibel and Gaddis, *Containment: Concept and Policy*, p. 30.

20. Representative works by realists other than Kennan include: E. H. Carr, *The Twenty Years' Crisis, 1919–1939: An Introducton to the Study of International Relations* (London: Macmillan, 1946), *The Soviet Impact on the Western World* (London: Macmillan, 1947); Reinhold Niebuhr, *Moral Man and Immoral Society: A Study in Ethics and Politics* (New York: Charles Scribner's, 1932), *The Nature and Destiny of Man*, 2 vol. (New York: Charles Scribner's, 1943 and 1964), *The Irony of American History* (New York: Charles Scribner's, 1952), *The Structure of Nations and Empires* (New York: Charles Scribner's, 1958), *The Children of Light and the Children of Darkness* (New York: Charles Scribner's, 1945); Hans Morgenthau, *Scientific Man vs. Power Politics* (Chicago: University of Chicago Press, 1946), *Politics Among Nations* (New York: Alfred Knopf, 1985). Recent critical books about realism include: John Vasquez, *The Power of Power Politics: A Critique* (New Brunswick, N.J.: Rutgers University Press, 1983); J. E. Hare and Carey Joynt, *Ethics and International Affairs* (New York: St. Martin's Press, 1982); Smith, *Realist Thought from Weber to Kissinger.*

21. Kennan, *Realities of American Foreign Policy*, p. 109; Kennan, *American Diplomacy*, pp. 91–92; Kennan to R. E. Ward, November 26, 1952, File "2-A-1952" in Box 29, Kennan Papers.

22. Kennan, "Commencement Speech at Dartmouth College," June 11, 1950, File "1-C-8" in Box 18, Kennan Papers; Loy Henderson interview, October 3, 1970, File "14" in Box 8, Wright Papers.

23. Kennan to Bernard Gufler, April 12, 1952, File "2-A-1952" in Box 29, Kennan Papers.

24. Kennan to Erich Hula, February 13, 1957, File "2-A-1952" in Box 29, Kennan Papers; Kennan, *The Nuclear Delusion* (New York: Pantheon, 1983), pp. i. xxx.

25. Barton Gellman, *Contending with Kennan* (New York: Praeger Publishers, 1984), p. 100; Kennan, "Seminar Essay," File "1-E-19" in Box 26, Kennan Papers; Kennan, "Philosophy and Strategy in America's Postwar Policy," May 11, 1965, File "1-C-141-IV" in Box 21, Kennan Papers.

26. J. A. Nathan and J. K. Oliver, *Foreign Policy Making and the American Political System* (Boston: Little, Brown and Company, 1987), pp. 221, 227.

27. Kennan, "Certain World Problems in Christian Perspective," January 27, 1959, File "1-B-78" in Box 7, Kennan Papers.

28. *Ibid.*; Kennan, "Why Do I Hope?" February 13, 1966, File "1-B-143" in Box 12, Kennan Papers; Kennan's "talk" for Mount Kisco Conference, summer 1963; Kennan, "Education for What?" March 30, 1960, File "1-C-95" in Box 20, Kennan Papers; Kennan, "Remarks at Stevenson-for-President Committee," April 30, 1956, File "1-C-56" in Box 19, Kennan Papers; Kennan, *Realities of American Foreign Policy*, pp. 93–94; Aron, *World Technology and Human Destiny*, p. 183.

29. Kennan, "The Relation of Religion to Government," p. 47; Kennan, "Sermon," October 18, 1953, File "1-B-27" in Box 3, Kennan Papers; Kennan, "The Ethics of Anti-Communism," October 28, 1964, File "1-B-128" in Box 10, Kennan Papers.

30. See Clinton Rossiter's still timely and very good *Conservatism in America: The Thankless Persuasion* (New York: Vintage Books, 1962). Chapter 7 contains a useful comparison between European and US versions of conservative principles.

31. Kennan, *Democracy and the Student Left* (Boston: Little, Brown and Company, 1968), p. 189; Kennan, "Morality and Foreign Policy" in *Foreign Affairs*, p. 217; Kennan, "The Ethics of Anti-Communism," 1964.

32. The phrase "the fringes of power" is from the title of John Colville's published diaries, *The Fringes of Power: 10 Downing Street Diaries, 1939–1955* (New York: Norton, 1985); Kennan, *Memoirs: 1925–1950* (Boston: Little, Brown and Company, 1967), p. 306; Walter Isaacson and Evan Thomas, *The Wise Men* (New York: Simon and Schuster, 1986), p. 376; Hugh De Santis, *The Diplomacy of Silence* (Chicago: University of Chicago Press, 1980), pp. 15–16.

33. Anonymous Oxford University Press reviewer to Press, August 28, 1986, author's possession. Alastair Buchan, *Can International Relations Be Professed?* (Oxford: Clarendon Press, 1973), p. 12. Richard Schlatter (ed.), *Hobbes's Thucydides* (New Brunswick, N.J.: Rutgers University Press, 1975), p. 379.

34. Kennan to Arnold Toynbee, April 7, 1952.

BIBLIOGRAPHY

Archives and Manuscript Collections

Acheson, Dean. Papers. (Harry S Truman Library)

Armstrong, Hamilton Fish. Papers. (Seeley Mudd Library, Princeton University)

Bland, Larry. Papers. (private collection)*

Bohlen, Charles. Papers. (Library of Congress)

Bohlen, Charles. Records. Record Group 59 (Diplomatic Branch, National Archives)

Clayton, William. Papers. (Harry S Truman Library)

Clifford, Clark. Papers. (Harry S Truman Library)

Davies, Joseph. Papers. (Library of Congress)

Dulles, Allen. Papers. (Seeley Mudd Library, Princeton University)

Dulles, John Foster. Papers. (Dwight D. Eisenhower Library)

Dulles, John Foster. Papers. (Seeley Mudd Library, Princeton University)

Elsey, George. Papers. (Harry S Truman Library)

Feis, Herbert. Papers. (Library of Congress)

Forrestal, James. Diaries. (Seeley Mudd Library, Princeton University)

Forrestal, James. Papers. (Seeley Mudd Library, Princeton University)

Henderson, Loy. Papers. (Library of Congress)

Hughes, Emmet. Papers. (Dwight D. Eisenhower Library)

Jones, Joseph. Papers. (Harry S Truman Library)

Kennan, George Frost (senior). Papers. (Library of Congress)

Kennan, George Frost. Papers (Seeley Mudd Library, Princeton University)

Krock, Arthur. Papers. (Seeley Mudd Library, Princeton University)

Marshall, George. Papers. (George Marshall Library)

Oppenheimer, J. Robert. Papers. (Library of Congress)

Oral Histories (Columbia University)

Oral Histories (Harry S Truman Library)

Oral Histories (John F. Kennedy Library)

*I am grateful to Larry Bland for having allowed me to see his papers about Kennan. Bland and C. Ben Wright collaborated in a large study about Kennan.

Oral Histories (Seeley Mudd Library, Princeton University)

Smith, Alexander. Papers. (Seeley Mudd Library, Princeton University)

Steinhardt, Laurence. Papers. (Library of Congress)

Stevenson, Adlai. Papers. (Seeley Mudd Library, Princeton University)

Truman, Harry. Papers. (Harry S Truman Library)

Thayer, Charles. Papers. (Harry S Truman Library)

US Department of State. Records of the Policy Planning Staff and Decimal Files. Record Group 59 (Diplomatic Branch, National Archives)

US National Security Council. File of Declassified National Security Council Records. (Modern Military Records Branch, National Archives)

Wright, C. Ben. Papers. (George Marshall Library)**

Books by George Frost Kennan

American Diplomacy: 1900–1950 (Chicago: University of Chicago Press, 1951 and 1984). Walgreen Lectures.

Realities of American Foreign Policy (Princeton: Princeton University Press, 1954). Stafford Little Lectures.

Soviet-American Relations, 1917–1920, Vol. I: *Russia Leaves the War* (Princeton: Princeton University Press, 1956). Awarded Pulitzer Prize.

Russia, the Atom and the West (New York: Harper and Brothers, 1957). BBC Reith Lectures.

Soviet-American Relations, 1917–1920, Vol. II: *The Decision to Intervene* (Princeton: Princeton University Press, 1958).

Russia and the West under Lenin and Stalin (Boston: Little, Brown and Company, 1960). Chichele Lectures.

Soviet Foreign Policy, 1917–1941 (Princeton: D. Van Nostrand Company, 1960).

On Dealing with the Communist World (New York: Harper and Row, 1964). Elihu Root Lectures.

Memoirs: 1925–1950 (Boston: Little, Brown and Company, 1967). Awarded Pulitzer Prize.

Democracy and the Student Left (Boston: Little, Brown and Company, 1968).

From Prague after Munich: Diplomatic Papers 1938–1940 (Princeton: Princeton University Press, 1968).

The Marquis de Custine and His "Russia in 1839" (Princeton: Princeton University Press, 1971).

Memoirs: 1950–1963 (New York: Pantheon, 1983).

The Cloud of Danger: Current Realities of American Foreign Policy (Boston: Little, Brown and Company, 1977).

The Decline of Bismarck's European Order (Princeton: Princeton University Press, 1979).

et al. *Encounters with Kennan: The Great Debate* (London: Frank Cass and Company, 1979).

The Nuclear Delusion: Soviet-American Relations in the Atomic Age (New York: Pantheon, 1983).

The Fateful Alliance (New York: Pantheon, 1984).

Articles by George Frost Kennan

Note: Over the course of his career, Kennan has written numerous articles, book reviews, letters to the editor. Many interviews with him and congressional testimony that he has

---

**The Wright Papers are very extensive and drawn from many sources. Wright organized these materials in preparation for his biography (never published) of Kennan.

provided have also appeared in published form. Listed here are only those journal articles that should prove of major interest to the student of US foreign policy.

"University Education and the Public Service," *American Foreign Service Journal*, May 1947.

[X], "The Sources of Soviet Conduct," *Foreign Affairs*, July 1947.

"Current Problems in the Conduct of Foreign Policy," *The Department of State Bulletin*, May 15, 1950.

"Russia and the United States," *The New Republic*, June 26, 1950.

"Let Peace Not Die of Neglect," *The New York Times Magazine*, February 25, 1951.

"America and the Russian Future," *Foreign Affairs*, April 1951.

"Where Do You Stand on Communism?" *The New York Times Magazine*, May 27, 1951.

"Training for Statesmanship," *The Atlantic Monthly*, May 1953.

"The Nature of the Soviet Challenge," *The New Republic*, August 24, 1953.

"To Be or Not to Be a Christian," *Christianity and Crisis*, May 3, 1954.

"The Illusion of Security," *The Atlantic Monthly*, August 1954.

"For the Defense of Europe: A New Approach," *The New York Times Magazine*, September 12, 1954.

"Commencement 1955," *Social Research*, Summer 1955.

"The Future of Our Professional Diplomacy," *Foreign Affairs*, July 1955.

"The Challenge of Freedom," *The New Leader*, December 26, 1955.

"History and Diplomacy as Viewed by a Diplomatist," *The Review of Politics*, April 1956.

"Overdue Changes in Our Foreign Policy," *Harper's Magazine*, August 1956.

"America's Administrative Response to its World Problems," *Daedalus*, Spring 1958.

"American Troops in Russia," *The Atlantic Monthly*, January 1959.

"Disengagement Revisited," *Foreign Affairs*, January 1959.

"Foreign Policy and the Christian Conscience," *The Atlantic Monthly*, May 1959.

"Russia, the Atom, and the West, 1959," *The Listener*, October 29, 1959.

"A Proposal for Western Survival," *The New Leader*, November 16, 1959.

"Peaceful Coexistence: A Western View," *Foreign Affairs*, January 1960.

"That Candles May Be Brought," *Encounter*, February 1961.

"Diplomacy as a Profession," *Foreign Service Journal*, May 1961.

"Can We Deal With Moscow?" *The Saturday Evening Post*, October 5, 1963.

"Japanese Security and American Policy," *Foreign Affairs*, October 1964.

"The Price We Paid for War," *The Atlantic Monthly*, October 1964.

"A Fresh Look at Our China Policy," *The New York Times Magazine*, November 22, 1964.

"Kennan Reviews Foreign Policy in Light of Pacem," *National Catholic Reporter*, March 3, 1965.

"The Ethics of Anti-Communism," *University: A Princeton Quarterly*, Spring 1965.

"George F. Kennan's Testimony on Vietnam," *The New Republic*, February 26, 1966.

"Why Do I Hope?" *University: A Princeton Quarterly*, Summer 1966.

"The Russian Revolution—Fifty Years After. Its Nature and Consequences," *Foreign Affairs*, October 1967.

"Concept in Foreign Policy," *Harvard Today*, Autumn 1967.

"The Relation of Religion to Government," *The Princeton Seminary Bulletin*, Winter 1969.

"To Prevent a World Wasteland," *Foreign Affairs*, April 1970.

"Hazardous Courses in Southern Africa," *Foreign Affairs*, January 1971.

"After the Cold War: American Foreign Policy in the 1970s," *Foreign Affairs*, October 1972.

"Europe's Problems, Europe's Choices," *Foreign Policy,* Spring 1974.

"Is Detente Worth Saving?" *Saturday Review,* March 6, 1976.

"The United States and the Soviet Union, 1917–1976," *Foreign Affairs,* July 1976.

"Foreign Policy and the Professional Diplomat," *The Wilson Quarterly,* Winter 1977.

"America's Relations with the Soviet Union," *Bulletin of the Atomic Scientists,* June 1978.

"A Last Warning: Reply to My Critics," *Encounter,* July 1978.

"US-Soviet Relations: Turning from Catastrophe," *Christianity and Crisis,* May 26, 1980.

"A Modest Proposal," *The New York Review of Books,* July 16, 1981.

"Reflections: Two Views of the Soviet Union," *New Yorker,* November 2, 1981.

"On Nuclear War," *The New York Review of Books,* January 21, 1982.

et al., "Nuclear Weapons and the Atlantic Alliance," *Foreign Affairs,* Spring 1982.

"A Christian's View of the Arms Race," *Theology Today,* Summer 1982.

"America's Unstable Soviet Policy," *The Atlantic Monthly,* November 1982.

"Toward Peace on Two Fronts," *Christianity and Crisis,* December 13, 1982.

"Breaking the Spell," *New Yorker,* October 3, 1983.

"Reflections (Soviet-American Relations)," *New Yorker,* September 24, 1984.

et al., "The President's Choice: Star Wars or Arms Control," *Foreign Affairs,* Winter 1984.

"Morality and Foreign Policy," *Foreign Affairs,* Winter 1985/86.

"A New Philosophy of Defense," *The New York Review of Books,* February 13, 1986.

et al., "Back from the Brink," *The Atlantic Monthly,* August 1986.

"In the American Mirror," *The New York Review of Books,* November 16, 1986.

"The Gorbachev Prospect," *The New York Review of Books,* January 21, 1988.

"The Marshall Plan and the Future of Europe" in *Transatlantic Perspectives,* Winter 1988.

"George Kennan and Josef Skvorecky: An Exchange on Gorbachev" in *The New York Review of Books,* March 17, 1988.

Selected Books and Unpublished Manuscripts of Related Interest

Abrams, R., and Levine, L. W. (eds.). *The Shaping of Twentieth Century America: Interpretative Essays* (Cambridge: Harvard University Press, 1971).

Acheson, Dean. *Power and Diplomacy* (Cambridge: Harvard University Press, 1958).

Acheson, Dean. *Present at the Creation: My Years in the State Department* (New York: Norton, 1969).

Acheson, Dean. *Sketches from Life* (New York: Harper and Brothers, 1961).

Adams, Henry. *The Education of Henry Adams* (Boston: Houghton Mifflin Company, 1918, 1961).

Adenauer, Konrad. *Memoirs: 1943–1953* (London: Weidenfeld and Nicholson, 1966).

Alperovitz, Gar. *Atomic Diplomacy: Hiroshima and Potsdam* (New York: Vintage Books, 1967).

Ambrose, Stephen. *Eisenhower: The President* (New York: Simon and Schuster, 1984).

Ambrose, Stephen. *Rise to Globalism* (Baltimore: Penguin, 1984).

American Committee on East-West Accord (ed.). *Detente or Debacle: Common Sense in US-Soviet Relations* (New York: Norton, 1979).

Arendt, Hannah. *The Origins of Totalitarianism* (New York: World Publishing, 1951).

Arkes, Hadley. *Bureaucracy, the Marshall Plan, and the National Interest* (Princeton: Princeton University Press, 1972).

Aron, Raymond. *The Imperial Republic: The United States and the World, 1945–1963* (Englewood Cliffs: Prentice-Hall, 1974).

Aron, Raymond (ed.). *On War* (New York: Norton, Inc., 1968).

Aron, Raymond. *World Technology and Human Destiny* (Ann Arbor: University of Michigan Press, 1963).

Backer, John. *The Decision to Divide Germany: American Foreign Policy in Transition* (Durham, N.C.: Duke University Press, 1978).

Ball, George. *The Discipline of Power: Essentials of a Modern World Structure* (Boston: Little, Brown and Company, 1968).

Barber, Joseph (ed.). *The Containment of Soviet Expansion: A Report on the Views of Leading Citizens in Twenty-Four Cities* (New York: Council on Foreign Relations, 1951).

Barnet, Richard. *The Alliance: America-Europe-Japan Makers of the Postwar World* (New York: Simon and Schuster, 1983).

Barnet, Richard. *Real Security: Restoring American Power in a Dangerous Decade* (New York: Simon and Schuster, 1981).

Barnet, Richard. *Roots of War* (New York: Penguin Books, 1980 reprint).

Bartlow, John. *Adlai Stevenson and the World* (Garden City: Doubleday, 1977).

Bartlow, John. *Adlai Stevenson of Illinois* (Garden City: Doubleday, 1976).

Beard, Charles. *An Economic Interpretation of the Constitution of the United States* (New York: The Free Press, 1913, 1969).

Beisner, Robert. *Twelve Against Empire: The Anti-Imperialists, 1898–1900* (New York: McGraw-Hill, 1968).

Beitz, Charles. *Political Theory and International Relations* (Princeton: Princeton University Press, 1979).

Bellush, Bernard. *He Walked Alone: A Biography of John Gilbert Winant* (The Hague: Mouton, 1968).

Bemis, Samuel. *John Quincy Adams and the Foundations of American Foreign Policy* (New York: Norton, 1949).

Bennett, Edward. *Recognition of Russia* (Waltham, Mass.: Ginn and Co., 1970).

Berlin, Isaiah. *Personal Impressions* (New York: Viking Press, 1981).

Berman, Larry. *Planning a Tragedy: The Americanization of the War in Vietnam* (New York: Norton, 1982).

Bernstein, Barton (ed.). *Politics and Policies of the Truman Administration* (Chicago: Quadrangle Books, 1970).

Bernstein, Barton, and Matusow, Allen (eds.). *The Truman Administration: A Documentary History* (New York: Harper and Row, 1966).

Bialer, Seweryn. *The Soviet Paradox: External Expansion Internal Decline* (New York: Alfred Knopf, 1986).

Bishop, Donald. *The Roosevelt-Litvinov Agreements* (Syracuse: Syracuse University Press, 1965).

Bisson, Thomas. *Zaibatsu Dissolution in Japan* (Berkeley: University of California Press, 1954).

Blum, D. Steven. *Walter Lippmann: Cosmopolitanism in the Century of Total War* (Ithaca: Cornell University Press, 1984).

Blum, Robert. *Drawing the Line: The Origin of the American Containment Policy in East Asia* (New York: Norton, 1982).

Bohlen, Charles. *The Transformation of American Foreign Policy* (New York: Norton, Inc., 1969).

Bohlen, Charles. *Witness to History, 1929–1969* (New York: Norton, 1973).

Boorstin, Daniel (ed.). *An American Primer* (Chicago: University of Chicago Press, 1966).

Borden, William. *The Pacific Alliance: United States Foreign Economic Policy and*

Japanese Trade Recovery, 1947–1955 (Madison: University of Wisconsin Press, 1984).

Borg, Dorothy and Heinrichs, Waldo (eds.). *Uncertain Years: Chinese-American Relations, 1947–1950* (New York: Columbia University Press, 1980).

Bracher, Karl. *The German Dictatorship: The Origins, Structure, and Effects of National Socialism* (New York: Praeger Publishers, 1973).

Brodie Bernard. *War and Politics* (New York: Macmillan, 1973).

Browder, Robert. *The Origins of Soviet-American Diplomacy* (Princeton: Princeton University Press, 1953).

Browning, Frank, and Forman, Dorothy (eds.). *The Wasted Nations: Report of the International Commission of Enquiry into United States Crimes in Indochina* (New York: Harper Colophon Books, 1972).

Bruegel, J. W. *Czechoslovakia Before Munich* (Cambridge: Cambridge University Press, 1973).

Buchan, Alastair. *The End of the Postwar Era* (London: Weidenfeld and Nicolson, 1974).

Buchan, Alastair. *Europe's Future, Europe's Choices* (New York: Columbia University Press, 1969).

Bull, Hedley. *The Anarchical Society: A Study in World Politics* (New York: Columbia University Press, 1977).

Bullitt, Orville (ed.). *For the President: Correspondence Between Franklin D. Roosevelt and William C. Bullitt* (Boston: Houghton Mifflin Company 1972), with forward by George Kennan.

Bullitt, William. *The Great Globe Itself* (New York: Charles Scribner's, 1946).

Bullock, Alan. *Ernest Bevin: Foreign Secretary, 1945–1951* (London: Heinemann, 1983).

Bullock, Alan. *Hitler: A Study in Tyranny* (New York: Harper and Row, 1964).

Bundy, William (ed.). *The Nuclear Controversy: A Foreign Affairs Reader* (New York: New American Library, 1985).

Burdick, Charles. *An American Island in Hitler's Reich: The Bad Nauheim Internment* (Menlo Park, Calif.: Markgraf, 1987).

Burnham, James. *Containment or Liberation: An Inquiry into the Aims of United States Foreign Policy* (New York: John Day Company, 1952).

Burns, James McGregor. *Roosevelt: The Lion and the Fox, 1882–1940* (New York: Harcourt, Brace, and World, 1956).

Camps, Miriam. *European Unification in the Sixties: From the Veto to the Crisis* (New York: McGraw-Hill, 1966).

Carnesale, Albert, et al. *Living with Nuclear Weapons* (Tononto: Bantam Books, 1983).

Carr, E. H. *The Twenty Years' Crisis, 1919–1939: An Introduction to the Study of International Relations* (London: Macmillan, 1939, 1946).

Carsten, F. L. *The Rise of Fascism* (Berkeley: University of California Press, 1971).

Childs, Marquis, and Reston, James (eds.). *Walter Lippmann and His Times* (New York: Harcourt, Brace, and Company, 1959). Kennan chapter: "Walter Lippmann, 'The New Republic,' and the Russian Revolution."

Churchill, Winston. *The Gathering Storm* (Boston: Houghton Mifflin Company, 1948).

Churchill, Winston. *The Grand Alliance* (Boston: Houghton Mifflin Company, 1950).

Clark, Ian. *Reform and Resistance in the International Order* (Cambridge: Cambridge University Press, 1980).

Clay, Lucius. *Decision in Germany* (New York: Doubleday, 1950).

Clemens, Diane. *Yalta* (London: Oxford University Press, 1970).

Cochran, Bert. *Adlai Stevenson: Patrician Among the Politicians* (New York: Funk and Wagnalls, 1969).

Cohen, Stephen. *Rethinking the Soviet Experience: Politics and History Since 1917* (New York: Oxford University Press, 1985).

Cohen, Stephen. *Sovieticus: American Perceptions and Soviet Realities* (New York: Norton, 1985).

Colville, John. *The Fringes of Power: 10 Downing Street Diaries, 1939–1955* (New York: Norton, 1985).

Combs, Jerald. *American Diplomatic History: Two Centuries of Changing Interpretations* (Berkeley: University of California Press, 1983).

Commager, Henry (ed.). *Documents of American History Since 1898,* 2 vols. (New York: Appleton-Century-Crofts, 1968).

Conquest, Robert. *The Great Terror* (New York: Collier Books, 1973).

Cooper, C. L. *The Lion's Last Roar: Suez 1956* (New York: Harper and Row, 1978).

Cousins, Norman. *The Pathology of Power* (New York: Norton, 1987).

Crabb, Cecil. *The Doctrines of American Foreign Policy: Their Meaning, Role, and Future* (Baton Rouge: Louisiana State University Press, 1982).

Craig, Gordon, and Gilbert, Felix (eds.). *The Diplomats* (Princeton: Princeton University Press, 1953).

Cronin, Audrey. *Great Power Politics and the Struggle over Austria, 1945–1955* (Ithaca: Cornell University Press, 1986).

Cummings, Bruce (ed.). *Child of Conflict: The Korean-American Relationship, 1943–1953* (Seattle: University of Washington Press, 1983).

Cummings, Bruce. *The Origins of the Korean War: Liberation and the Emergence of Separate Regimes* (Princeton: Princeton University Press, 1981).

Current, Richard (ed.). *The Political Thought of Abraham Lincoln* (Indianapolis: Bobbs-Merrill, 1981).

Dahrendorf, Ralf. *Society and Democracy in Germany* (New York: Anchor Books, 1969).

Dallek, Robert. *Franklin D. Roosevelt and American Foreign Policy, 1932–1945* (New York: Oxford University Press, 1979).

Daniels, Robert (ed.). *A Documentary History of Communism*, 2 vols. (New York: Vintage Books, 1960).

Davidson, Eugene. *The Death and Life of Germany: An Account of the American Occupation* (New York: Alfred Knopf, 1959).

Davies, John. *Dragon by the Tail* (New York: Norton, 1972).

Davies, John. *Foreign and Other Affairs* (New York: Norton, 1964).

Davies, Joseph. *Mission to Moscow* (New York: Simon and Schuster, 1941).

Davis, Jacquelyn, et al. *Soviet Theater Strategy: Implications for NATO* (Washington, DC: United States Strategic Institute, 1978).

Davis, Lynn. *The Cold War Begins: Soviet-American Conflict over Eastern Europe* (Princeton: Princeton University Press, 1974).

Deane, John. *The Strange Alliance: The Story of Our Efforts at Wartime Cooperation with Russia* (New York: Viking Press, 1947).

Deibel, Terry, and Gaddis, John (eds.). *Containment: Concept and Policy*, 2 vols. (Washington, DC: National Defense University Press, 1986).

De Santis, Hugh. *The Diplomacy of Silence* (Chicago: University of Chicago Press, 1980).

DePorte, A. W. *Europe Between the Superpowers: The Enduring Balance* (New Haven: Yale University, 1979).

Deutsch, Karl. *Political Community and the North Atlantic Area* (Princeton: Princeton University Press, 1957).

Deutscher, Isaac. *Stalin: A Political Biography* (New York: Oxford University Press, 1966, second edition).

Divine, Robert. *A Second Chance: The Triumph of Internationalism in America During World War II* (New York: Atheneum, 1967).

Divine, Robert. *Eisenhower and the Cold War* (New York: Oxford University Press, 1981).

Djilas, Milovan. *Conversations with Stalin* (New York: Harcourt, Brace, and World, 1962).

Donovan, Robert. *Conflict and Crisis: The Presidency of Harry S Truman, 1945–1948* (New York: Norton, 1977).

Donovan, Robert. *Tumultuous Years: The Presidency of Harry S Truman* (New York: Norton, 1982).

Dunham, Vera. *In Stalin's Time: Middleclass Values in Soviet Fiction* (Cambridge: Cambridge University Press, 1976).

Dunn, Frederick. *Peacemaking and the Settlement with Japan* (Princeton: Princeton University Press, 1973).

Dyson, Freeman. *Weapons and Hope* (New York: Harper and Row, 1984).

Earle, Edward. *Makers of Modern Strategy: Military Thought from Machiavelli to Hitler* (Princeton: Princeton University Press, 1943).

Eban, Abba. *The New Diplomacy: International Affairs in the Modern Age* (New York: Random House, 1983).

Edmonds, Robin. *Soviet Foreign Policy: The Brezhnev Years* (Oxford: Oxford University Press, 1983).

Etzold, Thomas, and Gaddis, John (eds.). *Containment: Documents on American Policy and Strategy, 1945–1950* (New York: Columbia University Press, 1978).

Farnsworth, Beatrice. *William C. Bullitt and the Soviet Union* (Bloomington: Indiana University Press, 1967).

Farrell, John, and Smith, Asa (eds.). *Image and Reality in World Politics* (New York: Columbia University Press, 1967).

Feis, Herbert. *From Trust to Terror* (New York: Norton, 1970).

Filene, Peter. *American Views of Soviet Russia* (Homewood, Ill.: The Dorsey Press, 1968).

Finer, Herman. *Dulles over Suez: The Theory and Practice of his Diplomacy* (Chicago: Quadrangle Books, 1964).

Fischer, Louis. *The Road to Yalta: Soviet Foreign Relations* (New York: Harper and Row, 1972), with forward by George Kennan.

Fitzgerald, F. Scott. *This Side of Paradise* (New York: Charles Scribner's, 1920).

Fitzgerald, Frances. *Fire in the Lake: The Vietnamese and the Americans in Vietnam* (New York: Vintage Books, 1973).

Foot, Rosemary. *The Wrong War: American Policy and the Dimensions of the Korean Conflict, 1950–53* (Ithaca: Cornell University Press, 1985).

Fox, Richard. *Reinhold Niebuhr: A Biography* (New York: Pantheon Books, 1985).

Freeland, Richard. *The Truman Doctrine and the Origins of McCarthyism* (New York: Schocken Books, 1974).

Friedrich, Carl, and Brzezinski, Zbigniew. *Totalitarian Dictatorship and Autocracy* (Cambridge: Harvard University Press, 1957).

Gaddis, John. *The Long Peace: Inquiries into the History of the Cold War* (New York: Oxford University Press, 1987).

Gaddis, John. *Russia, the Soviet Union and the United States* (New York: John Wiley and Sons, 1978).

Gaddis, John. *Strategies of Containment: A Critical Appraisal of Postwar American National Security Policy* (New York: Oxford University Press, 1982).

Gaddis, John. *The United States and the Origins of the Cold War, 1941–1947* (New York: Columbia University Press, 1972).

Galbraith, John K. *A Life in Our Times* (Boston: Houghton Mifflin Company, 1981).

Galbraith, John K. *A View From the Stands* (Boston: Houghton Mifflin Company 1986).

Gallup, George (ed.). *The Gallup Poll: Public Opinion, 1935–1971*, Vol. 1 (New York: Random House, 1972).

Gardner, Lloyd. *Architects of Illusion: Men and Ideas in American Foreign Policy* (Chicago: Quadrangle Books, 1970).

Garthoff, Raymond. *Detente and Confrontation: American-Soviet Relations from Nixon to Reagan* (Washington, DC: The Brookings Institution, 1985).

Gelb, Leslie, and Betts, Richard. *The Irony of Vietnam: The System Worked* (Washington, DC: The Brookings Institution, 1979).

Gellman, Barton. *Contending with Kennan: Toward a Philosophy of American Power* (New York: Praeger Publishers, 1984).

George, Alexander (ed.). *Managing US-Soviet Rivalry: Problems of Crisis Prevention* (Boulder, Colo.: Westview Press, 1983).

Gilpin, Robert. *War and Change in World Politics* (Cambridge: Cambridge University Press, 1981).

Gimbel, John. *The American Occupation of Germany* (Stanford: Stanford University Press, 1968).

Gimbel, John. *The Origins of the Marshall Plan* (Stanford: Stanford University Press, 1976).

Goldwin, Robert, and Clor, Harry (eds.). *Readings in American Foreign Policy* (New York: Oxford University Press, 1971).

Goodman, Walter. *The Committee: The Extraordinary Career of the House Committee on Un-American Activities* (New York: Farrar, Straus and Giroux, 1968).

Gorbachev, Mikhail. *Perestroika: New Thinking for Our Country and the World* (New York: Harper and Row, 1987).

Graebner, Norman (ed.). *The National Security: Its Theory and Practice, 1945–1960* (New York: Oxford University Press, 1986).

Grayson, Benson L. (ed.). *The American Image of Russia, 1917–1977* (New York: Frederick Ungar, 1978).

Greene, Nathaneal (ed.). *Fascism: An Anthology* (New York: Crowell Company, 1968).

Greenstein, Fred. *The Hidden-Hand Presidency: Eisenhower as Leader* (New York: Basic Books, 1982).

Grenville, J. A .S. (ed.) *The Major International Treaties, 1914–1973: A History and Guide with Texts* (London: Methuen, 1974).

Griffith, Robert, and Theoharis, Athan (eds.). *The Specter: Original Essays on the Cold War and the Origins of McCarthyism* (New York: New Viewpoints, 1974).

Haas, Ernst. *The Uniting of Europe* (Stanford: Stanford University Press, 1958).

Hahn, Werner. *Postwar Soviet Politics: The Fall of Zhdanov and the Defeat of Moderation, 1946–1953* (Ithaca: Cornell University Press, 1982).

Halberstam, David. *The Best and the Brightest* (New York: Random House, 1969).

Halle, Louis. *The Cold War as History* (New York: Harper and Row, 1967).

Halloran, Bernard (ed.). *Essays on Arms Control and National Security* (Washington, DC: US Arms Control and Disarmament Agency, 1986).

Hammond, Thomas (ed.). *Witnesses to the Origins of the Cold War* (Seattle: University of Washington Press, 1982).

Hare, J. E. and Joynt, Carey. *Ethics and International Affairs* (New York: St. Martin's Press, 1982).

Harr, John. *The Professional Diplomat* (Princeton: Princeton University Press, 1969).

Harriman, W. Averell, and Abel, Elie. *Special Envoy to Churchill and Stalin, 1941–1946* (New York: Random House, 1975).

Haslam, Jonathan. *The Soviet Union and the Struggle for Collective Security in Europe, 1933–1939* (New York: St. Martin's Press, 1984).

Heinrichs, Waldo, Jr. *American Ambassador: Joseph C. Grew and the Development of the United States Diplomatic Tradition* (New York: Oxford University Press, 1986).

Held, Virginia, Morgenbesser, Sidney, and Nagel, Thomas (eds.). *Philosophy, Morality, and International Affairs* (New York: Oxford University Press, 1974).

Henderson, Nicholas. *The Birth of NATO* (London: Weidenfeld and Nicolson, 1982).

Herken, Gregg. *Counsels of War* (New York: Oxford University Press, 1987, expanded edition).

Herken, Gregg. *The Winning Weapon: The Atomic Bomb in the Cold War, 1945–1950* (New York: Vintage Books, 1982).

Herring, George. *America's Longest War: The United States and Vietnam* (New York: Knopf, 1986).

Herz, Martin (ed.). *Decline of the West? George Kennan and His Critics* (Washington, DC: Ethics and Public Policy Center, Georgetown University, 1978).

Hewlett, Richard and Duncan, Francis. *A History of the United States Atomic Energy Commission*, 2 vols. (University Park: Pennsylvania State University Press, 1969).

Hindus, Maurice. *We Shall Live Again* (London: Collins, 1939).

Hochman, Jiri. *The Soviet Union and the Failure of Collective Security, 1934–1938* (Ithaca: Cornell University Press, 1984).

Hoffmann, George, and Neal, F. W. *Yugoslavia and the New Communism* (New York: Twentieth Century Fun ! 1962).

Hoffmann, Stanley. *Dead Ends: American Foreign Policy in the New Cold War* (Cambridge: Ballinger Publishing Company, 1983).

Hoffmann, Stanley. *Duties Beyond Borders* (Syracuse: Syracuse University Press, 1981).

Hoffmann, Stanley. *Gulliver's Troubles or the Setting of American Foreign Policy* (New York: McGraw Hill, 1968).

Hoffmann, Stanley. *Janus and Minerva: Essays in the Theory and Practice of International Politics* (Boulder, Colo.: Westview Press, 1987).

Hoffmann, Stanley. *Primacy or World Order: American Foreign Policy Since the Cold War* (New York: McGraw-Hill, 1978).

Hofstadter, Richard. *The American Political Tradition* (New York: Vintage Books, 1948).

Hogan, Michael. *The Marshall Plan: America, Britain and the Reconstruction of Western Europe, 1947–1952* (Cambridge: Cambridge University Press, 1987).

Holborn, Hajo. *A History of Modern Germany: 1840–1945* (New York: Alfred Knopf, 1969).

Hollander, Paul. *Political Pilgrims: Travels of Western Intellectuals to the Soviet Union, China, and Cuba 1928–1978* (New York: Oxford University Press, 1981).

Holloway, David. *The Soviet Union and the Arms Race* (New Haven: Yale University Press, 1983).

Hood, Donald. *Lessons of the Vietnam War: Henry Kissinger, George F. Kennan, Richard Falk and the Debate over Containment, 1965–1980* (PhD dissertation, University of Washington, 1982).

Hook, Sidney. *Political Power and Personal Freedom: Critical Studies in Democracy, Communism, and Civil Rights* (New York: Criterion Books, 1959).

Hoopes, Townsend. *The Devil and John Foster Dulles* (Boston: Little, Brown and Company, 1973).

Hughes, Emmet J. *The Living Presidency: The Resources and Dilemmas of the American Presidential Office* (New York: Coward, McCann, and Geohegan, 1972).

Hunt, Michael. *Ideology and US Foreign Policy* (New Haven: Yale University Press, 1987).

Hyland, William (ed.). *The Reagan Foreign Policy* (New York: New American Library, 1987).

Ilchman, W. F. *Professional Diplomacy in the United States, 1779–1939* (Chicago: University of Chicago Press, 1961).

Immerman, Richard. *The CIA in Guatemala: The Foreign Policy of Intervention* (Austin: University of Texas Press, 1982).

Ireland, Timothy. *Creating the Entangling Alliance: The Origins of the North Atlantic Treaty Organization* (Westport, Conn.: Greenwood Press, 1981).

Isaacson, Walter and Thomas, Evan. *The Wise Men: Six Friends and the World They Made* (New York: Simon and Schuster, 1986).

Johnson, Ross. *The Transformation of Communist Ideology: The Yugoslav Case, 1945–1953* (Cambridge: MIT Press, 1972).

Jonas, Manfred. *Isolationism in America, 1935–1941* (Ithaca: Cornell University Press, 1966).

Jones, Joseph. *The Fifteen Weeks* (New York: Viking Press, 1955).

Kalicki, J. H. *The Pattern of Sino-American Crises* (Cambridge: Cambridge University Press, 1975).

Karnow, Stanley. *Vietnam: A History* (New York: Penguin Books, 1984).

Kegley, Charles, and Bretall, Robert (eds.). *Reinhold Niebuhr: His Religious, Social, and Political Thought* (New York: Macmillan, 1961).

Kenez, Peter. *The Birth of the Propaganda State: Soviet Methods of Mobilization, 1917–1929* (Cambridge: Cambridge University Press, 1985).

Kennan, George Frost (senior). *Siberia and the Exile System* (Chicago: University of Chicago Press, 1958), with an introduction by George Kennan (junior).

Kennedy, Edward. *Decisions for a Decade* (Garden City, N.Y.: Doubleday, 1968), with forward by George Kennan.

Kissinger, Henry. *American Foreign Policy* (New York: Norton, 1977 third edition).

Kissinger, Henry. *Nuclear Weapons and Foreign Policy* (Garden City, N.Y.: Doubleday, 1957).

Kissinger, Henry. *White House Years* (Boston: Little, Brown and Company, 1979).

Kissinger, Henry. *Years of Upheaval* (Boston: Little, Brown and Company, 1982).

Koestler, Arthur. *Darkness at Noon* (New York: Bantam Books, 1941).

Kolko, Gabriel. *The Politics of War: Allied Diplomacy and the World Crisis of 1943–1945* (New York: Random House, 1968).

Kolko, Joyce, and Kolko, Gabriel. *The Limits of Power: The World and United States Foreign Policy, 1945–1954* (New York: Harper and Row, 1972).

Kornhauser, William. *The Politics of Mass Society* (Glencoe, Ill.: The Free Press, 1959).

Kuklick, Bruce. *American Policy and the Division of Germany* (Ithaca: Cornell University Press, 1972).

Kuniholm, Bruce. *The Origins of the Cold War in the Near East: Great Power Conflict and Diplomacy in Iran, Turkey, and Greece* (Princeton: Princeton University Press, 1980).

LaFeber, Walter. *America, Russia, and the Cold War, 1945–1975* (New York: John Wiley and Sons, 1967).

LaFeber, Walter. *Inevitable Revolutions: The United States in Central America* (New York: Norton, 1984).

Larson, Deborah. *Origins of Containment: A Psychological Explanation* (Princeton: Princeton University Press, 1985).

Lauren, Paul (ed.). *The China Hands' Legacy: Ethics and Diplomacy* (Boulder, Colo.: Westview Press, 1987).

Lederer, Ivo (ed.). *Russian Foreign Policy: Essays in Historical Perspective* (New Haven: Yale University Press, 1962). Kennan chapter: "Contemorary Perspectives."

Lesy, Michael. *Wisconsin Death Trip* (New York: Pantheon Books, 1973).

Levering, Ralph. *American Opinion and the Russian Alliance* (Chapel Hill: University of North Carolina Press, 1976).

Lewis, Sinclair. *Babbitt* (New York: Harcourt, Brace and World, 1922).

Lilienthal, David. *Journals*, 5 vols. (New York: Harper and Row, 1965).

Lippmann, Walter. *The Cold War: A Study in US Foreign Policy* (New York: Harper and Brothers, 1947).

Lippmann, Walter. *Drift and Mastery: An Attempt to Diagnose the Current Unrest* (New York: Mitchell Kennerly, 1914).

Lippmann, Walter. *An Inquiry into the Principles of Good Society* (Boston: Atlantic-Little, Brown, 1937).

Lippmann, Walter, *The Method of Freedom* (New York: Macmillan, 1934).

Lippmann, Walter. *A Preface to Politics* (New York: Mitchell Kennerly, 1913).

Lippmann, Walter, *Public Opinion* (New York: Harcourt and Brace, 1922).

Lyon, Peter. *Eisenhower: Portrait of the Hero* (Boston: Little, Brown and Company, 1974).

McLellan, David. *Dean Acheson: The State Department Years* (New York: Dodd, Mead and Company, 1976).

McPherson, James. *Ordeal By Fire: The Civil War and Reconstruction* (New York: Alfred Knopf, 1982).

Maddux, Thomas. *Years of Estrangement: American Relations with the Soviet Union, 1933–1941* (Tallahassee: University Presses of Florida, 1980).

Mametey, V. S. and Luza, R. (eds.). *A History of the Czechoslovak Republic, 1918–1948* (Princeton: Princeton University Press, 1973).

Mastny, Vojtech. *The Czechs under Nazi Rule* (New York: Columbia University Press, 1971).

Matray, James. *The Reluctant Crusade: American Foreign Policy in Korea, 1941–1950* (Honolulu: University of Hawaii Press, 1985).

May, Ernest. *Lessons of the Past* (New York: Oxford University Press, 1973).

Mayer, Martin. *The Diplomats* (Garden City, N.Y.: Doubleday, 1983).

Mayers, David. *Cracking the Monolith: US Policy Against the Sino-Soviet Alliance, 1949–1955* (Baton Rouge: Louisiana State University Press, 1986).

Mee, Charles, Jr. *The Marshall Plan: The Launching of the Pax Americana* (New York: Simon and Schuster, 1984).

Melanson, Richard and Mayers, David (eds.). *Reevaluating Eisenhower: American Foreign Policy in the Fifties* (Chicago: University of Illinois Press, 1987).

Melanson, Richard. *Writing History and Making Policy: The Cold War, Vietnam, and Revisionism* (Lanham, Md.: University Press of America, 1983).

Mencken, H. L. *Notes on Democracy* (New York: Alfred Knopf, 1926).

Messer, Robert. *The End of an Alliance: James F. Byrnes, Roosevelt, Truman, and the Origins of the Cold War* (Chapel Hill: University of North Carolina Press, 1982).

Micunovic, Veljko. *Moscow Diary* (Garden City: Doubleday, 1980), with introduction by George Kennan.

Miller, D. M. O. et al. *The Balance of Power: An Illustrated Assessment Comparing the Weapons and Capabilities of NATO and the Warsaw Pact* (New York: St. Martin's Press, 1981).

Miller, James E. *The United States and Italy, 1940–1950: The Politics and Diplomacy of Stabilization* (Chapel Hill: University of North Carolina Press, 1986).

Millis, Walter (ed.). *The Forrestal Diaries* (New York: Viking Press, 1951).

Milward, Alan. *The Reconstruction of Western Europe, 1945–51* (London: Methuen, 1984).

Miscamble, Wilson. *George F. Kennan, the Policy Planning Staff and American Foreign Policy, 1947–1950* (PhD dissertation, University of Notre Dame, 1980).

Morgan, Roger. *The United States and West Germany, 1945–1973* (London: Oxford University Press, 1974).

Morgenthau, Hans. *In Defense of the National Interest: A Critical Examination of American Foreign Policy* (New York: Alfred Knopf, 1951).

Morgenthau, Hans. *Politics in the Twentieth Century* (Chicago: University of Chicago Press, 1962).

Morgenthau, Hans. *Scientific Man vs. Power Politics* (Chicago: University of Chicago Press, 1946).

Morgenthau, Hans. *Truth and Power* (New York: Praeger Publishers, 1970).

Morgenthau, Hans with Thompson, Kenneth. *Politics Among Nations: The Struggle for Power and Peace* (New York: Alfred Knopf, 1985, sixth edition).

Murphy, Robert. *Diplomat Among Warriors* (New York: Doubleday, 1964).

Nagai, Yonosuke, and Iriye, Akira (eds). *The Origins of the Cold War in Asia* (New York: Columbia University Press, 1977).

Nathan, James, and Oliver, James. *Foreign Policy Making and the American Political System* (Boston: Little, Brown and Company, 1987, second editon).

Neff, Donald. *Warriors at Suez* (New York: Linden Press, 1981).

Nelson, Anna (ed.). *The State Department Policy Planning Staff Papers, 1947–1949*, 3 vols. (New York: Garland Publishing, 1983), forward by George Kennan.

Neustadt, Richard, and May, Ernest. *Thinking in Time: The Uses of History for Decision-Makers* (New York: The Free Press, 1986).

New York Times. *The Pentagon Papers* (New York: Bantam Books, 1971).

Nicolson, Harold. *Diplomacy* (London: Oxford University Press, 1980, third edition).

Niebuhr, Reinhold. *Moral Man and Immoral Society: A Study in Ethics and Politics* (New York: Charles Scribner's, 1932).

Niebuhr, Reinhold. *The Children of Light and the Children of Darkness* (New York: Charles Scribner's, 1945).

Niebuhr, Reinhold. *The Irony of American History* (New York: Charles Scribner's, 1952).

Niebuhr, Reinhold. *The Nature and Destiny of Man* (New York: Charles Scribner's, 1943 and 1964).

Niebuhr, Reinhold. *The Structure of Nations and Empires* (New York: Charles Scribner's, 1958).

Nixon, Richard. *The Memoirs of Richard Nixon* (New York: Grosset and Dunlap, 1978).

Nolte, Ernest. *Three Faces of Fascism* (New York: Holt, Rinehart and Winston, 1966).

Nove, Alex. *An Economic History of the USSR* (Middlesex, England: Penguin Books, 1975).

Nye, Joseph. *The Making of America's Soviet Policy* (New Haven: Yale University Press, 1984).

Offner, Arnold. *American Appeasement: United States Foreign Policy and Germany, 1933–1938* (New York: Norton, 1969).

Osgood, Robert. *Ideals and Self-Interest in America's Foreign Relations* (Chicago: University of Chicago Press, 1953).

Paret, Peter (ed.). *Makers of Modern Strategy: From Machiavelli to the Nuclear Age* (Princeton: Princeton University Press, 1986).

Parmet, Herbert. *Eisenhower and the American Crusades* (New York: Macmillan, 1972).

Paterson, Thomas (ed.). *Cold War Critics: Alternatives to American Foreign Policy in the Truman Years* (Chicago: Quadrangle Books, 1971).

Paterson, Thomas (ed.). *Containment and the Cold War* (Reading, Mass.: Addison-Wesley Publishing Company, 1973).

Paterson, Thomas. *On Every Front: The Making of the Cold War* (New York: Norton, 1979).

Pells, Richard. *The Liberal Mind in a Conservative Age: American Intellectuals in the 1940s and 1950s* (New York: Harper and Row, 1985).

Pipes, Richard (ed.). *Soviet Strategy in Europe* (New York: Crane, Russak and Company, Inc., 1976).

Pogue, Forrest. *George C. Marshall: Statesman 1945–1959* (New York: Viking, 1987).

Pollard, Robert. *Economic Security and the Origins of the Cold War* (New York: Columbia University Press, 1985).

Ponomaryov, B., Gromyko, A., and Khvostov, V. *History of Soviet Foreign Policy, 1945–1970* (Moscow: Progress Publishers, 1974).

Popper, Karl. *The Open Society and Its Enemies* (London: Routledge and Kegan Paul, 1945).

Prados, John. *Presidents' Secret Wars: CIA and Pentagon Covert Operations Since World War II* (New York: William Morrow Company, 1986).

Pranger, Robert (ed.). *Detente and Defense* (Washington, DC: American Enterprise Institute, 1977).

Price, Dorothy, and Walley, Dean (eds.). *Never Give In! The Words of Winston Churchill* (New York: Hallmark, 1967).

Price, Harry. *The Marshall Plan and Its Meaning* (Ithaca: Cornell University Press, 1955).

Purifoy, Lewis. *Harry Truman's China Policy* (New York: New Viewpoints, 1976).

Quester, George. *Defense over Offense in Central Europe* (Palo Alto, Calif.: Aspen Institute for Humanistic Studies, 1978).

Ramsey, Paul. *War and the Christian Conscience* (Durham, N.C.: Duke University Press, 1961).

Rapoport, Anatol (ed.). *Clausewitz on War* (New York: Penguin Books, 1968).

Ricci, David. *The Tragedy of Political Science: Politics, Scholarship, and Democracy* (New Haven: Yale University Press, 1984).

Rippley, La Vern. *The Immigrant Experience in Wisconsin* (Boston: Twayne Publishers, 1985).

Rossiter, Clinton. *Conservatism in America: The Thankless Persuasion* (New York: Vintage Books, 1962).

Rossiter, Clinton (ed.). *The Federalist Papers* (New York: New American Library, 1961).

Rostow, W. W. *The Division of Europe after World War II: 1946* (Austin: University of Texas Press, 1981).

Rothfels, Hans. *The German Opposition to Hitler* (London: Oswald Wolff, 1978 reprint).

Rothschild, Joseph. *East Central Europe Between the Two World Wars* (Seattle: University of Washington Press, 1974).

Rovere, Richard. *Senator Joe McCarthy* (New York: Meridian Books, 1960).

Royal Institute of International Affairs. *The Soviet-Yugoslav Dispute* (London: Oxford University Press, 1948).

Rubin, Barry. *Secrets of State: The State Department and the Struggle over US Foreign Policy* (New York: Oxford University Press, 1987).

Ruddy, T. Michael. *The Cautious Diplomat: Charles E. Bohlen and the Soviet Union, 1929–1969* (Kent, Ohio: Kent State University Press, 1986).

Russell, Bertrand. *War Crimes in Vietnam* (London: Allen and Unwin, 1967).

Scammell, Michael. *Solzhenitsyn: A Biography* (New York: Norton, 1984).

Schaller, Michael. *The American Occupation of Japan* (New York: Oxford University Press, 1985).

Schandler, Herbert. *The Unmaking of a President: Lyndon Johnson and Vietnam* (Princeton: Princeton University Press, 1977).

Schapiro, Leonard. *The Communist Party of the Soviet Union* (New York: Vintage Books, 1971).

Schlatter, Richard (ed.). *Hobbes's Thucydides* (New Brunswick, N.J.: Rutgers University Press, 1975).

Schlesinger, Arthur, Jr. *The Cycles of American History* (Boston: Houghton Mifflin Company, 1986).

Schlesinger, Arthur, Jr. *The Imperial Presidency* (Boston: Houghton Mifflin Company, 1973).

Schoenbaum, David. *Hitler's Social Revolution: Class and Status in Nazi Germany, 1933–1939* (New York: Anchor Books, 1967).

Schrecker, Ellen. *No Ivory Tower: McCarthyism and the Universities* (New York: Oxford University Press, 1986).

Schulzinger, Robert. *The Wise Men of Foreign Affairs: The History of the Council on Foreign Relations* (New York: Columbia University Press, 1984).

Schurmann, Franz. *The Logic of World Power: An Inquiry into the Origins, Currents, and Contradictions of World Politics* (New York: Pantheon Books, 1974).

Sharp, Gene. *Making Europe Unconquerable* (Cambridge: Ballinger, 1986), forward by George Kennan.

Sherwin, Martin. *A World Destroyed: The Atomic Bomb and the Grand Alliance* (New York: Vintage Books, 1975).

Shigeru, Yoshida. *The Yoshida Memoirs* (Cambridge: Harvard University Press, 1961).

Shlaim, Avi. *The United States and the Berlin Blockade, 1948–1949: A Study in Crisis Decision-Making* (Berkeley: University of California Press, 1983).

Shulman, Marshall (ed.). *East-West Tensions in the Third World* (New York: Norton, 1986).

Shulman, Marshall. *Stalin's Foreign Policy Reappraised* (New York: Atheneum, 1965).

Simmons, Robert. *The Strained Alliance: Peking, P'yongyang, Moscow and the Politics of the Korean War* (New York: The Free Press, 1975).

Simpson, Christopher. *Blowback: America's Recruitment of Nazis and Its Effects on the Cold War* (New York: Wiedenfeld and Nicolson, 1988).

Smith, Gaddis. *Dean Acheson* (New York: Cooper Square, 1972).

Smith, Gaddis. *Morality, Reason and Power: American Diplomacy in the Carter Years* (New York: Hill and Wang, 1986).

Smith, Michael Joseph. *Realist Thought from Weber to Kissinger* (Baton Rouge: Louisiana State University Press, 1986).

Smith, Page. *America Enters the World* (New York: McGraw-Hill, 1985).

Smoke, Richard. *National Security and the Nuclear Dilemma: An Introduction to the American Experience* (New York: Random House, 1987 second edition).

Solzhenitsyn, Alexander. *Detente: Prospects for Democracy and Dictatorship* (New Brunswick, N.J.: Transaction Books, 1980).

Solzhenitsyn, Alexander. *Nobel Lecture* (New York: Farrar, Straus and Giroux, 1972).

Solzhenitsyn, Alexander. *A World Split Apart: Commencement Address Delivered at Harvard University* (New York: Harper and Row, 1978).

Spanier, John. *The Truman-MacArthur Controversy and the Korean War* (New York: Norton, 1965).

Spiegel, Steven. *The Other Arab-Israeli Conflict: Making America's Middle East Policy, from Truman to Reagan* (Chicago: University of Chicago Press, 1985).

Spykman, Nicholas. *America's Strategy in World Politics: The United States and the Balance of Power* (New York: Harcourt, Brace, 1942).

Spykman, Nicholas. *The Geography of Peace* (New York: Harcourt, Brace, 1944).

Stebbins, Richard. *The United States in World Affairs, 1949* (New York: Harper and Row, 1950), with an introduction by George Kennan.

Steel, Ronald. *Walter Lippmann and the American Century* (Boston: Little, Brown and Company, 1980).

Steinbruner, John, and Sigal, Leon (eds.). *Alliance Security: NATO and the No-First-Use Question* (Washington, DC: The Brookings Institution, 1983).

Stoessinger, John. *Crusaders and Pragmatists: Movers of Modern American Foreign Policy* (New York: Norton, 1979).

Stoessinger, John. *Nations in Darkness* (New York: Random House, 1978).

Talbott, Strobe (ed.). *Khrushchev Remembers* (Boston: Little, Brown and Company, 1970).

Talbott, Strobe. *The Russians and Reagan* (New York: Vintage Books, 1984).

Taubman, William. *Stalin's American Policy: From Entente to Detente to Cold War* (New York: Norton, 1982).

Taylor, Telford. *Munich* (Garden City, N.Y.: Doubleday, 1979).

Taylor, Telford. *Nuremberg and Vietnam: An American Tragedy* (New York: Bantam Books, 1971).

Thayer, Charles. *Diplomat* (New York: Harper and Brothers, 1959).

Thomas, Hugh. *Armed Truce: The Beginnings of the Cold War, 1945–1946* (New York: Atheneum, 1987).

Thompson, Kenneth. *Masters of International Thought* (Baton Rouge: Louisiana State University Press, 1980).

Thompson, Kenneth. *Political Realism and the Crisis of World Politics* (Princeton: Princeton University Press, 1960).

Thompson, Kenneth. *The Virginia Papers on the Presidency: The White Burkett Miller Center Forums, 1979* (Lanham, Md.: University Press of America, 1979).

Travis, Frederick. *George Kennan and Russia, 1865–1905* (PhD dissertation, Emory University, 1974).

Truman, Harry S. *Memoirs: Year of Decisions* (Garden City, N.Y.: Doubleday, 1955).

Truman, Harry S. *Memoirs: Years of Trial and Hope* (Garden City, N.Y.: Doubleday, 1956).

Tschebotarioff, Gregory. *Russia, My Native Land* (New York: McGraw-Hill, 1964), with forward by George Kennan.

Tsou, Tang. *America's Failure in China, 1941–1950* (Chicago: University of Chicago Press, 1963).

Tucker, Nancy. *Patterns in the Dust: Chinese-American Relations and the Recognition Controversy, 1949–1950* (New York: Columbia University Press, 1983).

Tucker, Robert. *The Inequality of Nations* (New York: Basic Books, 1977).

Tucker, Robert W. *The Radical Left and American Foreign Policy* (Baltimore: Johns Hopkins University Press, 1971).

Tucker, Robert, and Watts, William (eds.). *Beyond Containment: US Foreign Policy in Transition* (Washington, DC: Potomac Associates, 1973).

US Department of State. *Foreign Relations of the United States, 1933–1957* (Washington, DC: Government Printing Office, 1952–1986).

Ulam, Adam. *Dangerous Relations: The Soviet Union in World Politics, 1970–1982* (New York: Oxford University Press, 1983).

Ulam, Adam. *Expansion and Coexistence: Soviet Foreign Policy, 1917–1973* (New York: Praeger Press, 1974).

Ulam, Adam. *Stalin: The Man and His Era* (New York: Viking Press, 1973).

Ulam, Adam. *Titoism and the Cominform* (Cambridge: Harvard University Press, 1952).

Ungar, Sanford (ed.). *Estrangement: America and the World* (New York: Oxford University Press, 1985).

Van Slyke, Lyman (ed.). *The China White Paper*, 2 vols. (Stanford: Stanford University Press, 1949, 1967).

Vasquez, John. *The Power of Power Politics: A Critique* (New Brunswick, N.J.: Rutgers University Press, 1983).

Waltz, Kenneth. *Theory of International Politics* (Reading, Mass: Addison-Wesley Publishing Company, 1979).

Walzer, Michael. *Just and Unjust Wars: A Moral Argument with Historical Illustrations* (New York: Basic Books, 1977).

Ward, Patricia. *The Threat of Peace: James F. Byrnes and the Council of Foreign Ministers, 1945–1946* (Kent, Ohio: Kent State University Press, 1979).

Webb, Beatrice, and Webb, Sidney. *Soviet Communism: A New Civilization* (London: Victor Gollancz, 1937).

Weil, Martin. *A Pretty Good Club: The Founding Fathers of the US Foreign Service* (New York: Norton, 1978).

Whan, Vorin (ed.). *A Soldier Speaks: Public Papers and Speeches of General of the Army Douglas MacArthur* (New York: Praeger Publishers, 1965).

Whiting, Allen. *China Crosses the Yalu: The Decision to Enter the Korean War* (Stanford: Stanford University Press, 1960).

Williams, William A. *The Tragedy of American Diplomacy* (New York: Dell, 1962).

Wilson, Joan Hoff. *Ideology and Economics: US Relations with the Soviet Union, 1918–1933* (Columbia: University of Missouri Press, 1974).

Wolfe, Thomas. *Soviet Power and Europe, 1945–1970* (Baltimore: Johns Hopkins University Press, 1970).

Wolfers, Arnold. *Britain and France Between Two Wars: Conflicting Strategies of Peace from Versailles to World War II* (New York: Norton, 1968).

Wood, Robert. *From Marshall Plan to Debt Crisis: Foreign Aid and Development Choices in the World Economy* (Berkeley: University of California Press, 1986).

Wright, C. Ben. *George F. Kennan, Scholar-Diplomat: 1926–1946* (PhD dissertation, University of Wisconsin, 1972).

Yergin, David. *Shattered Peace: The Origins of the Cold War and the National Security State* (Boston: Houghton Mifflin Company, 1977).

York, Herbert. *Race to Oblivion: A Participant's View of the Arms Race* (New York: Simon and Schuster, 1970).

York, Herbert. *The Advisors: Oppenheimer, Teller and the Superbomb* (San Francisco: W. H. Freeman and Company, 1975).

Selected Articles of Related Interest

Acheson, Dean. "The Illusion of Disengagement," *Foreign Affairs*, April 1958.

Alsop, Joseph. "The Soviet Union Will Never Recover," *The Saturday Evening Post*, November 24, 1956.

Alsop, Joseph, and Alsop, Stewart. "We Accuse," *Harper's*, October 1954.

Ashley, Richard. "The Poverty of Neo-Realism," *International Organization*, Spring 1984.

Berger, Marilyn. "An Appeal for Thought," *The New York Times Magazine*, May 7, 1978.

Bernstein, Barton. "The Quest for Security: American Foreign Policy and International Control of Atomic Energy, 1942–1946," *Journal of American History*, March 1974.

Bernstein, Barton. "Roosevelt, Truman and the Atomic Bomb, 1941–1945: A Reinterpretation," *Political Science Quarterly*, Spring 1975.

Brands, Henry. "Redefining the Cold War: American Policy Toward Yugoslavia, 1948–1960," *Diplomatic History*, Winter 1987.

Brinkley, Douglas. "Kennan-Acheson: The Disengagement Debate," *The Atlantic Community Quarterly*, Winter 1987–1988.

Brodsky, Joseph. "In a Room and a Half," *The New York Review of Books*, February 27, 1986.

Buckley, William. "George Kennan's Bomb," *National Review*, April 4, 1980.

Bull, Hedley. "A View from Abroad: Consistency under Pressure," *Foreign Affairs* ("America and the World: 1978").

Bundy, McGeorge. "The Missed Chance to Stop the H-Bomb," *The New York Review of Books*, May 13, 1982.

Campbell, John. "An Interview with George F. Kennan," *Foreign Service Journal*, August 1970.

Draper, Theodore. "Appeasement and Detente," *Commentary*, February 1976.

Fairlie, Henry. "The Special Senility of the Diplomat: Mr. X²," *The New Republic*, December 24, 1977.

Gaddis, John. "Containment: A Reassessment," *Foreign Affairs*, July 1977.

Gaddis, John. "Was the Truman Doctrine a Real Turning Point?" *Foreign Affairs*, January 1974.

Gati, Charles. "What Containment Meant," *Foreign Policy*, Summer 1972.

Gilpin, Robert. "The Richness of the Tradition of Political Realism," *International Organization*, Spring 1984.

Halle, Louis. "George F. Kennan and the Common Mind," *Virginia Quarterly Review*, Winter 1969.

Harrington, Daniel. "Kennan, Bohlen, and the Riga Axioms," *Diplomatic History*, Fall 1978.

Herken, Gregg. "The Great Foreign Policy Fight," *American Heritage*, April-May 1986.

Hixson, Walter. "Containment on the Perimeter: George F. Kennan and Vietnam," *Diplomatic History*, forthcoming.

Hoffmann, Stanley. "After the Creation or the Watch and the Arrow," *International Journal*, Spring 1973.

Hoffmann, Stanley. "Weighing the Balance of Power," *Foreign Affairs*, July 1972.

Hogan, Michael. "American Marshall Planners and the Search for a European Neocapitalism," *American Historical Review*, February 1985.

Hogan, Michael. "The Search for a 'Creative Peace': The United States, European Unity, and the Origins of the Marshall Plan," *Diplomatic History*, Summer 1984.

Hollander, Paul. "Et tu, George Kennan? The Old Cold Warrior Makes Anti-communism the Real Enemy," *Prospect*, September 1984.

Hollander, Paul. "The Two Faces of George Kennan." *Policy Review*, Summer 1985.

Hyland, William. "With the Soviet Union," *Foreign Policy*, Winter 1982–83.

Kaplan, Fred. "Our Cold War Policy, Circa '50," *The New York Times Magazine*, May 18, 1980.

Kateb, George. "George F. Kennan: The Heart of a Diplomat," *Commentary*, January 1968.

Kissinger, Henry. "Domestic Structures and Foreign Policy," *Daedelus*, Spring 1966.

Knight, Jonathan.; "George Frost Kennan and the Study of American Foreign Policy: Some Critical Comments," *Western Political Quarterly*, March 1967.

Labedz, Leopold. "A Last Critique," *Encounter*, July 1978.

Labedz, Leopold. "The Two Minds of George Kennan: How to Un-Learn from Experience," *Encounter*, April 1978.

Lasch, Christopher. "The Historian as Diplomat," *The Nation*, November 24, 1962.

Lasky, Melvin. "A Conversation With Kennan," *Encounter*, March 1960.

Lees, Lorraine. "The American Decision to Assist Tito, 1948–1949," *Diplomatic History*, Fall 1978.

Leffler, Melvyn. "Adherence to Agreement: Yalta and the Experience of the Early Cold War," *International Security*, Summer 1986.

Leffler, Melvyn. "The American Conception of National Security and the Beginnings of the Cold War, 1945–48," *American Historical Review*, April 1984.

Lerner, Max. "Two Paradigms for Russia," *The New Republic*, March 10, 1982.

Lippmann, Walter, "Mr. Kennan and Reappraisal in Europe," *The Atlantic*, April 1958.

Luttwak, Edward. "The Strange Case of George F. Kennan: From Containment to Isolationism," *Commentary*, November 1977.

MacKinder, Halford. "The Geographical Pivot of History," *Geographical Journal*, April 1904.

MacKinder, Halford. "The Round World and the Winning of the Peace," *Foreign Affairs*, July 1943.

McWilliams, Wilson. "George Kennan—the Myth Contained," *Commonweal*, March 22, 1968.

Maddux, Thomas. "American Diplomats and the Soviet Experiment: The View from the Moscow Embassy, 1934–1939," *South Atlantic Quarterly*, Autumn 1975.

Mark, Eduard. "The Question of Containment: A Reply to John Lewis Gaddis," *Foreign Affairs*, January 1978.

Messer, Robert. "Paths Not Taken: The United States Department of State and Alternatives to Containment, 1945–1946," *Diplomatic History*, Fall 1977.

Morgenthau, Hans. "American Diplomacy: The Dangers of Righteousness," *The New Republic*, October 11, 1951.

Moskin, Robert. "Our Foreign Policy Is Paralyzed," *Look*, November 19, 1963.

Nitze, Paul. "The Development of NSC 68," *International Security*, Spring 1980.

Pearcy, G. Etzel. "Geopolitics and Foreign Relations," *Department of State Bulletin*, March 1964.

Popas, Frederic. "Creating a Hard Line Toward Russia: The Training of State Department Experts, 1927–1937," *Diplomatic History*, Summer 1984.

Rosenberg, David. "American Atomic Strategy and the Hydrogen Bomb Decision," *Journal of American History*, June 1979.

Rosenberg, David. "The Origins of Overkill: Nuclear Weapons and American Strategy, 1945–1960," *International Security*, Spring 1983.

Rosenberg, David. "US Nuclear Stockpile, 1945–1950," *Bulletin of the Atomic Scientists*, Winter 1983/84.

Rostow, Eugene. "Searching for Kennan's Grand Design," *The Yale Law Journal*, June 1978.

Rovere, Richard. "Eisenhower Revisited: A Political Genius? A Brilliant Man," *The New York Times Magazine*, February 7, 1971.

Seabury, Paul. "George Kennan Vs. Mr. 'X': The Great Container Springs a Leak," *The New Republic*, December 16, 1981.

Seabury, Paul, and Glynn, Patrick. "Kennan: The Historian as Fatalist," *The National Interest*, Winter 1985/1986.

Sigal, Leon. "Kennan's Cuts," *Foreign Policy*, Fall 1981.

Silberman, Laurence. "Toward Presidential Control of the State Department," *Foreign Affairs*, Spring 1979.

Steel, Ronald. "Man Without a Country," *The New York Review of Books*, January 4, 1968.

Steel, Ronald. "Russia, the West, and the Rest," *The New York Review of Books*, July 14, 1977.

Taft, John. "Grey Eminences, X: A Diplomat for the Eighties," *The New Republic*, March 17, 1979.

Thompson, Kenneth. "Beyond National Interest: A Critical Evaluation of Reinhold Niebuhr's Theory of International Politics," *Review of Politics*, April 1955.

Ullman, Richard. "The 'Realities' of George F. Kennan," *Foreign Policy*, Fall 1977.

Ungar, Sanford, and Vale, Peter. "Why Constructive Engagement Failed," *Foreign Affairs*, Winter 1985–1986.

Wala, Michael. "Selling the Marshall Plan at Home: The Committee for the Marshall Plan to Aid European Recovery," *Diplomatic History*, Summer 1986.

Weiss, Robert. "George F. Kennan Looks at US Foreign Policy," *The Daily Princetonian*, March 13, 1973.

Wells, Samuel, Jr. "Sounding the Tocsin: NSC 68 and the Soviet Threat," *International Security*, Fall 1979.

Williams, William Appleman. "The Convenience of History," *The Nation*, September 15, 1956.

Wright, C. Ben. "Mr. 'X' and Containment," *Slavic Review*, March 1976.

Index